W9-AAX-555

Pro Oracle Spatial

RAVI KOTHURI, ALBERT GODFRIND, and EURO BEINAT

Pro Oracle Spatial

Lead Editor: Tony Davis
Technical Reviewers: Carel-Jan Engel, John Herring, Jayant Sharma
Editorial Board: Steve Anglin, Dan Appleman, Ewan Buckingham, Gary Cornell, Tony Davis, Jason Gilmore, Chris Mills, Dominic Shakeshaft, Jim Sumser
Project Manager: Tracy Brown Collins
Copy Editor: Nicole LeClerc
Production Manager: Kari Brooks-Copony
Production Editor: Katie Stence
Compositor: Kinetic Publishing Services, LLC
Proofreader: Christy Wagner
Indexer: Valerie Perry
Cover Designer: Kurt Krames
Manufacturing Manager: Tom Debolski

Library of Congress Cataloging-in-Publication Data

Kothuri, Ravi.
Pro Oracle Spatial / Ravi Kothuri, Albert Godfrind, and Euro Beinat.
p. cm.
ISBN 1-59059-383-9
1. Oracle (Computer file) 2. Business—Data processing.
3. Geographical information systems. 4. Management information systems.
I. Godfrind, Albert. II. Beinat, Euro. III. Title.
HF5548.2.K645 2004
910'.285'57565—dc22 2004023323

Printed and bound in the United States of America 9 8 7 6 5 4 3 2 1

Distributed to the book trade in the United States by Springer-Verlag New York, Inc., 233 Spring Street, 6th Floor, New York, NY 10013, and outside the United States by Springer-Verlag GmbH & Co. KG, Tiergartenstr. 17, 69112 Heidelberg, Germany.

In the United States: phone 1-800-SPRINGER, fax 201-348-4505, e-mail `orders@springer-ny.com`, or visit `http://www.springer-ny.com`. Outside the United States: fax +49 6221 345229, e-mail `orders@springer.de`, or visit `http://www.springer.de`.

For information on translations, please contact Apress directly at 2560 Ninth Street, Suite 219, Berkeley, CA 94710. Phone 510-549-5930, fax 510-549-5939, e-mail `info@apress.com`, or visit `http://www.apress.com`.

The source code for this book is available to readers at `http://www.apress.com` in the Downloads section. You will need to answer questions pertaining to this book in order to successfully download the code.

Contents at a Glance

PART 4 ■■■ Advanced Spatial

Contents

PART 2 ■■■ Basic Spatial

CHAPTER 12 A Sample Application ... 479

PART 4 Advanced Spatial

CHAPTER 13 Case Studies ... 535

Foreword

In the past decade, *location analysis* has outgrown its traditional use in Geographic Information Systems (GIS) and has become a critical component in business applications. The vast majority of commercial franchises employ location-based analysis and services in their day-to-day activities. With this growing usage, scalable and manageable solutions for location-based analysis and management have become a necessity rather than an option.

Oracle Spatial is the principal component of Oracle that effectively addresses this need for location or spatial information management. This product has evolved from its simple beginnings in Oracle8*i* and prior releases to a full-fledged suite of products in Oracle10*g*. The suite supports efficient and scalable storage and retrieval of spatial data using native data types and indexes, and provides new functionality for analysis and visualization of spatial data. Consistent with Oracle's motto of enabling storage of "all" data inside an Oracle database, Oracle Spatial not only extends all the benefits of an Oracle database to spatial data, but also enhances this functionality by adding location-specific analysis and visualization.

In recent years, Oracle Spatial emerged as the de facto solution for storing and managing spatial data inside the database. This technology is the most advanced database solution for managing spatial information. A wide variety of Oracle partners and a growing list of customers support and use this technology on a daily basis in their applications. In short, it is essential to develop Oracle Spatial expertise to easily incorporate location intelligence in existing applications that run on top of Oracle.

Given the comprehensive set of features in the Oracle Spatial technology suite, this book—the first devoted exclusively to Oracle Spatial—will go a long way in enhancing your understanding of and expertise in Oracle Spatial technology. Authors, Ravi Kothuri, Albert Godfrind, and Euro Beinat do a remarkable job of explaining different features and components of Oracle Spatial. The presentation is lucid, illustrative, and punctuated with explicit hands-on code examples and expert advice. This book covers in its first three parts the essential components needed for enabling location analysis such as storage, indexing, analysis, and visualization of spatial data. In the fourth part, you'll find several real-world case studies that combine and illustrate different features of Oracle Spatial. In the appendixes, the authors give an overview of some advanced features of Oracle Spatial, such as GeoRaster and the Topology Data Model, that enable high-end GIS.

This book serves as an essential guide to anyone wanting to be an Oracle Spatial expert user. It includes all the ingredients, from detailed information on location-enabling business applications to expert advice in fine-tuning performance. As such, it is a "must have" for all consultants, DBAs, and developers that use or intend to use Oracle Spatial.

Charles Rozwat
Executive Vice President, Server Technologies
Oracle Corporation

About the Authors

RAVI KOTHURI holds a Ph.D. in computer science from the University of California, Santa Barbara, and has worked in spatial and multimedia research and development for the past 10 years. Currently, he serves as a principal member in the spatial development team of Oracle Corporation. He is responsible for several patented features in Oracle Spatial and has authored numerous articles for database conferences and journals. Ravi enjoys music, movies, and playing with his children in his spare time.

ALBERT GODFRIND has over 25 years of experience in designing, developing, and deploying IT applications. His interest and enthusiasm for spatial information and geographical information systems started at Oracle when he discovered the spatial extensions of the Oracle database in 1998. Ever since, Albert has been "evangelizing" the use of spatial information both to GIS and IT communities across Europe, consulting with partners and customers, speaking at conferences, and designing and delivering in-depth technical training. Prior to joining Oracle Corporation, Albert held several positions in database engineering at Digital Equipment Corporation (DEC), where he worked on the development of the Rdb database system.

EURO BEINAT holds a Ph.D. in economics and a master's degree in electronics and systems engineering. He has been involved in consultancy for over 10 years in evaluation and strategic advice in sectors ranging from IT, government, the oil industry, and large corporations. At present, he is the managing director of Geodan Mobile Solutions and holds a chair at the Vrije Universiteit of Amsterdam as director of the spatial information laboratory. His main skills combine geo-IT and the Internet, with an extensive competence in decision analysis and strategy.

About the Technical Reviewers

CAREL-JAN ENGEL is a member of the OakTable Network, lives in the Netherlands, and works as a freelancer. He has been working in IT since 1982, and he started to work with Oracle version 4 in 1985. Fastforms (Forms 1.3) didn't meet the requirements of the software project he was on, and he joined the team that was developing "better" programming tools and applications in C, based on the HLI, now known as the OCI. In 1992, he founded the Dutch software company Ease Automation, which he headed for almost 10 years. Some of his projects during this time related to airports, and had an important high-availability aspect to them, which inspired him to develop several techniques for standby databases, often pushing Oracle technology to its limits. In 1998, he won the Chamber of Commerce of Rotterdam's Entrepreneur of the Year award. In 2002, he decided to continue his career as a freelancer. He's been a regular author for several (Dutch) Oracle-related magazines since 1998.

DR. JOHN R. HERRING is a software architect at Oracle Corporation in New Hampshire. He has been working in geographic information since 1983, when he started to work for Intergraph Corporation. He was technical lead on the TIGRIS project and built a feature-based, topologically integrated, single-user GI system. This system was the first to be based on the MiniTopo data model, fully integrating geometry, topology, and attributes, and including a full implementation of the Egenhofer spatial operators within a complete spatial query system. In 1995, Dr. Herring decided that the major shortcoming of GIS systems was their failure to integrate with mainstream IT, and he moved to Oracle, where there was interest in solving this problem. He has worked on Oracle Spatial ever since.

Dr. Herring has had a long involvement with GI standards, having been involved in OGC since 1994. He was the first recipient of the Gardels Award in 1999, and he has been a member of the U.S. delegation to ISO/TC 211 since 1996. He is co-editor of the journal *GeoInformatica*.

DR. JAYANT SHARMA has over 15 years experience in spatial information systems and works for Oracle Corporation as technical director of Oracle Spatial. He is on the Program Committee of conferences on spatial reasoning, spatial databases, and spatial information theory. He is also a reviewer for academic journals on these topics and has delivered invited talks, tutorials, and research papers at various academic and industry conferences.

Dr. Sharma received a NSF/ESF Young Scholar's Fellowship for his doctoral research on spatial reasoning. He has represented Oracle at various OGC Technical Committees.

Acknowledgments

Many people contributed to this book in numerous and important ways while remaining in the background. Together they have made it possible for us to complete this project and hopefully publish a good book.

We would like to thank the team at Apress, and in particular Tony Davis for his role in initiating this project, and then for his patience with shifting schedules, flexible submission times, and above all for his willingness to consider at any moment improvements, changes, and adaptations that could make the book better. Tracy Brown Collins, Nicole LeClerc, and Katie Stence have been very helpful and accommodating in editing and proofreading the book.

We acknowledge the efforts of Daniel Abugov, Daniel Geringer, James Steiner, Jayant Sharma, Jay Banerjee, Siva Ravada, Steven Hagan, and Steven Serra at Oracle Corporation for their help in getting this book off the ground. Once we started writing the book, many other Oracle Spatial development team members, including John Herring, Bruce Blackwell, Jeffrey Xie, Jack Wang, Ning An, and Richard Pitts, contributed with reviews of the chapters that fell in their respective areas of expertise. The reviews of these multiple Oracle experts (in addition to those from Apress reviewers) had a tangible effect on the quality of the text, its structure, and its completeness. Among these reviewers, special thanks go to Daniel Abugov and Siva Ravada for their multiple reviews of a majority of the chapters. Dan's comprehensive reviews and valuable suggestions have greatly enhanced the professional quality of the content. Finally, this book would not have been a reality if it were not for the cooperation and flexibility in work schedules extended by the Oracle Spatial management team (Siva Ravada and Steven Serra).

Consultants and application developers at Geodan Mobile Solutions provided most of the material for the case studies and reviewed several sections of the book. We would like to thank Evert van Kootwijk, Valik Solorzano, Han van Veldhuizen, Marnix Tentij, and Victor van Katwijk for their contributions, in particular regarding implementations of Oracle Spatial, and for comments and input that are the result of extensive practical experience. We are also grateful for the contribution of Henk Scholten. As founder and president of Geodan, as well as a professor of spatial informatics, he combines academic and professional skills that have been of great value at various stages of the book's preparation.

The book has been reviewed by several independent external experts. We would like to thank in particular Carel-Jan Engel for his meticulous and sometimes very critical comments. We wished, occasionally, to be given an easier ride, but his comments have had a major impact on the book structure and content. They made a tangible and positive contribution to the overall quality of the book.

Several parties helped us to collect the material necessary to compile the case studies. We would like to thank all organizations involved for their willingness to share with us their experiences in some important Oracle Spatial implementations. We are grateful, in particular to

Transport for London (London Buses), the Center for Advanced Spatial Technologies at the University of Arkansas, the Dutch Ministry of the Interior and the ISC (ICT service association for the Dutch police, judicial authorities, and public safety), Hutchison 3G Limited in the UK, and the Netherlands Ministry of Housing, Spatial Planning and the Environment (VROM) and The National Institute of Public Health and the Environment (RIVM).

Finally, we are indebted to our families for their patience and encouragement during the book writing process. It is indeed difficult to understand why SQL, geometries, or long-distance conference calls have priority over holidays, birthdays, or weekends. Nonetheless, we also enjoyed some special events in this period, such as the birth of twins for Ravi, and the birth of a second child for Euro. We are grateful that our spouses managed to keep us on track while handling such diverse priorities.

Introduction

Organizations are discovering with increasing frequency that the vast majority of their information assets have a spatial component, for example, the location of customers, shipments, facilities, personnel, competitors, and so on. The ability to use this information properly is fundamental to reducing operational costs, optimizing production efficiency, and increasing the quality of service. Evidence of the benefits that can be achieved by exploiting spatial information is plentiful, and many organizations are looking at ways of harvesting these benefits.

We have been professionally involved in a variety of projects that introduced spatial information management into public and private organizations. The idea of writing this book came from these projects, and from discussing spatial information management with the software developers and architects involved in them. We noticed a clear gap between the knowledge and skills necessary for successful spatial information management projects and the common background of the technical personnel usually involved in large IT and database developments.

The vast majority of these staff members had backgrounds in such diverse areas as database technology, Java, C++, PL/SQL, data models, security, availability, and scalability. However, only a small number had some experience with spatial data—for most, working with spatial data was completely new. It was easy to discover that "spatial objects," "geocoding," and "map projections," for example, were foreign terms to most (and, of course, spatial information management is not about processing signals from space probes).

It appears that this is a common situation. Even within the extensive community of Oracle experts, Oracle Spatial skills are relatively new to many. For those of us who work at the interface between IT, spatial informatics, management, and the traditional world of geography and mapping, the realization of this gap was especially revealing, and it presents a clear barrier to the diffusion of spatial information management through private and government organizations, where the demand for spatial applications is steadily growing. Furthermore, while Geographical Information Systems (GIS) are extensively used to manage spatial data, often as stand-alone systems, the vast majority of spatial data resides in corporate databases. It is by adding spatial intelligence to these databases that we probably disclose one of the largest untapped reservoirs of added value to organizations.

Oracle Spatial has grown to be one of the most established solutions for providing spatial intelligence to databases. Besides the extensive installed base of Oracle databases, Oracle Spatial manages spatial data just like any other data type, making it in principle easy for experienced database developers and architects to extend their scope into spatial information management.

However, despite the plethora of available books on spatial information management and GIS, we still encounter a lack of suitable material for Oracle developers or architects that do not have any spatial background. This leads to simplistic uses of Oracle Spatial and suboptimal implementations that frequently ignore the extensive list of Oracle Spatial capabilities.

Besides the reference user guides, most knowledge about Oracle Spatial is scattered around in technical papers or—even worse—in the heads of those who have developed expertise and mastered the tool.

Our motivation for writing this book was to provide developers and architects with a reference source to master Oracle Spatial and take their skills to a professional level. This book does not replace the technical references. Instead, it presents concepts, examples, case studies, and tips to guide you toward a full understanding of the potential of Oracle Spatial and how to use it at an advanced level. We do not want to just familiarize you with Oracle Spatial; we want you to become an expert in Oracle Spatial.

What Does This Book Cover?

This book covers spatial information management in the Oracle database. In particular

- It introduces the main concepts of spatial information management and how they relate to database concepts and tools.
- It describes the tools provided by Oracle Spatial to store, retrieve, analyze, and visualize spatial information.
- It presents examples, applications, and case studies that will help you facilitate the incorporation of these concepts and tools into your applications.

While most conceptual discussions will be of general validity, this book is about Oracle Spatial 10g, the newest release of the Oracle database product.

The focus of the chapters in this book is the application of Oracle Spatial technology to general e-business applications. All of the features that are relevant to such applications are discussed in full detail, with working examples based on the sample data supplied with the book. In the appendixes, we cover the topics that are more relevant to highly specialized GIS applications. These provide a more general overview of each topic and reference the Oracle documentation for full details.

The following list contains a chapter-by-chapter breakdown summarizing the key topics covered:

- *Setting Up*: The next section of this book, after this introduction, describes how to set up Oracle Spatial and the example schema required to run the code examples in this book. It then describes the specific e-business application and related dataset that are used for most examples in this book. The data used includes mapping data (e.g., state boundaries, rivers, built-up areas), geocoding data (e.g., lists of addresses with their x, y coordinates), network data (e.g., road networks for computing travel distance and providing navigation instructions), and application-specific data (in this case, a set of tables with customers, stores/branches, and competitors). The data covers parts of the United States, such as the cities of Washington, D.C. and San Francisco, and uses typical U.S. terms and notations (e.g., counties, interstates, etc.). This does not imply any loss of generality—the same examples can be made for any other similar dataset.

- *Chapter 1: Spatial Information Management*: In this chapter, we describe how spatial information is used in different industry segments and cover the typical functionality required for managing spatial/location information. We use a site-location example to illustrate different aspects of spatial information management: representation and storage using appropriate types and analysis functionality for stored spatial data. We then discuss the systems that enable spatial information management, such as Geographic Information Systems (GIS), and their evolution. We finally look at the benefits of spatial information management using Oracle Spatial.

- *Chapter 2: Overview of Oracle Spatial*: The Oracle Spatial technology suite enables spatial information management inside Oracle. This chapter provides an overview of this suite, its architecture, and its functionality. The overview includes a concise description of the different features of Oracle Spatial, including storage using the `SDO_GEOMETRY`, analysis using spatial operators, and visualization using Oracle MapViewer. We also illustrate how this functionality is productized into the components that are shipped with different editions of Oracle. Finally, we explain what to expect during and in a typical Oracle Spatial installation.

- *Chapter 3: Location-Enabling Your Applications*: In this chapter, we consider how to augment existing application tables with location information. We introduce an e-business application for this purpose, which we use in examples throughout the rest of the book. We also describe several design choices to consider while storing geographic data in Oracle tables. Location-enabling an application requires populating appropriate metadata tables to enable spatial processing on spatial tables. In the last part of the chapter, we look at the details of populating such metadata.

- *Chapter 4: The SDO_GEOMETRY Data Type*: This chapter focuses on the storage and modeling of location information using the `SDO_GEOMETRY` data type in Oracle. The type can store a wide variety of spatial data, including points, line strings, polygons, and complex geometries. We take a detailed look at the structure of `SDO_GEOMETRY`, and at the different attributes and the values it can take to store different types of geometric data. We then show how to construct `SDO_GEOMETRY` objects for geometries such as points, lines, polygons, and more complex geometries.

- *Chapter 5: Loading, Transporting, and Validating Spatial Data*: In this chapter, we describe different ways to populate Oracle tables that contain `SDO_GEOMETRY` columns. These tables could be part of an e-business application or could be tables in CAD/CAM, GIS, GPS, wireless, or telematics applications. We explain how to import the data that comes with this book using the Oracle Import utility. We also describe other utilities and functions/procedures for transferring data between Oracle databases and/or external formats. Finally, we look at how to validate the loaded `SDO_GEOMETRY` objects and how to correct some invalid objects.

- *Chapter 6: Geocoding*: In this chapter, we cover the functionality of the geocoder in Oracle Spatial. We first introduce geocoding concepts and the geocoding process to provide an understanding of how the conversion from addresses to `SDO_GEOMETRY` objects takes place. We then discuss how to set up data/a catalog to enable geocoding in your application. This catalog is used to determine and extrapolate the location for a specified address. Finally, we describe how to add location columns to application data. We illustrate this using different functions/APIs of the geocoder in Oracle that serve this purpose.

- *Chapter 7: Manipulating SDO_GEOMETRY in Application Programs*: Advanced application developers often need to access and manipulate spatial objects in their applications. In this chapter, we look at how to manipulate `SDO_GEOMETRY` types in programming languages such as PL/SQL and Java. We also briefly cover C and Pro*C. We examine how to read, decode, construct, and write geometries, providing extensive code examples throughout.

- *Chapter 8: Spatial Indexes and Operators*: In this chapter and in the next chapter, we describe how to use spatial information to perform proximity analysis. In this chapter, we focus on spatial indexes and spatial operators. Spatial indexes ensure effective response times for queries that perform proximity analysis. The chapter introduces the concepts of spatial indices and their creation. We then describe different spatial operators that Oracle Spatial supports for performing spatial analysis for indexed tables. We give an overview of their syntax and semantics, and describe in detail various operators. We also suggest tips that can ensure a faster evaluation of spatial operators. In the final part of the chapter, we address some advanced spatial indexing features that are useful for large spatial repositories.

- *Chapter 9: Geometry Processing Functions*: In this chapter, we discuss geometry processing functions, simply referred to as spatial functions. In contrast to the spatial operators, these geometry processing functions do not require a spatial index, provide more detailed analyses than the spatial operators associated with a spatial index, and can appear in the `SELECT` list as well as in the `WHERE` clause of a SQL statement. We discuss each of the spatial functions in turn, including tips for their use.

- *Chapter 10: Network Modeling*: In this chapter, we introduce another way of modeling spatial data based on the concept of the network. A network is a useful way to model information when we need to compute, for instance, routes, travel distances, or proximity based on travel time. We describe the general concepts and terminology for setting up networks, and then we discuss the Oracle Network Data Model and its data structures. We then specify how to set up a network in Oracle and how to perform network analysis.

- *Chapter 11: Generating Maps Using MapViewer*: MapViewer is the tool available in Oracle to visualize spatial information stored in a spatial database. The tool is part of Oracle Application Server. In this chapter, we describe MapViewer and introduce the basic mapping concepts, such as themes, style rules, and user controls. We look at how to install, deploy, and configure MapViewer, as well as how to construct maps and store them in the database using the map definition (MapDef) tool. We then describe how to use MapViewer and the maps that defined with it in Spatial applications via the available XML and Java APIs. Finally, we illustrate how to manage and administer the MapViewer server.

- *Chapter 12: A Sample Application*: In this chapter, we use most of the techniques and tools illustrated so far in the book to create a simple application that integrates spatial analysis and visualization. This chapter presents and dissects such an application. The application includes map and data display, map functionality (zoom, pan, etc.), geocoding, spatial analysis, and routing. We look at how the application was designed and coded, and review some of the source code that implements the major features of the application. The complete source code is provided for download from the Downloads section of the Apress website (`www.apress.com`). (See the upcoming "Setting Up" section for more details.)

- *Chapter 13: Case Studies*: This chapter describes five case studies that illustrate the use of Oracle Spatial for storing, analyzing, visualizing, and integrating spatial data in business and government applications. The *BusNet* case study illustrates the use of Oracle Spatial for managing the bus network of the city of London. The *P-Info* case study describes a system to provide location-enabled information access to police officers operating in the field, in the Netherlands. The case study on the Dutch *Risk Repository for Hazardous Substances* shows the use of Oracle Spatial to spatially enable a repository for (bio)chemical risks and effects. The *GeoStor* case illustrates a spatial data warehouse based on Oracle Spatial that provides a single access point to spatial data for the state of Arkansas. The "3" UMTS services case study describes one of the first deployments of Oracle Spatial to power wireless location services for third-generation telecommunications.
- *Chapter 14: Tips, Common Mistakes, and Common Errors*: In this chapter, we describe some useful tips in location-enabling your application. We also discuss some of the mistakes most application developers make that can be easily avoided. Finally, we address some common errors that you may encounter in location-enabling your application and the actions to take to sort out these errors.
- *Appendix A: Additional Spatial Analysis Functions*: In this appendix, we describe analysis functions that are provided, in addition to those described in Chapters 8 and 9, to cater to specific business analysis needs. These functions enable tiling-based analysis, neighborhood analysis, and clustering analysis.
- *Appendix B: Linear Referencing*: Linear referencing is widely used in the transportation and utility industries. It uses one parameter (measure) to identify an object position along a linear feature with respect to some known point (such as its start point). This appendix introduces the concept of linear referencing and its most common operations. It then discusses the `SDO_LRS` package that contains all functions that manipulate linear-referenced geometries.
- *Appendix C: Topology Data Model in Oracle*: In some applications, such as land management, sharing and updating of boundaries between multiple spatial objects is common. This process may cause data inconsistency problems due to updates of underlying shared boundaries. In this appendix, we describe an alternate model, the Topology Data Model, for effective management of shared geometry features. We introduce topology modeling in Oracle Spatial and the functionality to operate on the Topology Data Model.
- *Appendix D: Storing Raster Data in Oracle*: In this appendix, we briefly discuss how to store raster objects in Oracle Spatial. This appendix introduces the `SDO_GEORASTER` data type and explores how raster data is stored in an Oracle database. The chapter also describes how to manipulate GeoRaster objects.

This book is not meant to repeat the content of user and installation guides. It is highly recommended that you have those guides available when reading this book, and especially when running the examples. In several cases, we refer you to the user or installation guide for details. The complete documentation for Oracle Database and Oracle Application Server is available online on the Oracle Technology Network website at `www.oracle.com/technology/documentation`. The manuals relevant to this book are as follows:

- *Oracle Spatial User's Guide and Reference* (part number B10826-01)
- *Oracle Application Server 10g, MapViewer User's Guide* (part number B10559-01)
- *Oracle Spatial Topology and Network Data Models* (part number B10828-01)
- *Oracle Spatial GeoRaster* (part number B10827-01)

Who Should Read This Book?

The primary audience for this book is application developers who are familiar with Oracle technologies and want to enhance their applications with spatial information. They typically know about database design, PL/SQL, Java, and so on, but they do not know much (if anything) about spatial data or geographical information systems.

The book will also have appeal to the more general technical user of Oracle who is interested in the advanced features of database technology. The book introduces the world of spatial information gradually, and guides the reader from the basic concepts to sophisticated analysis and case studies. It has a hands-on style, with extensive examples and practical information.

The book should open up new application domains to developers and prompt them to incorporate spatial aspects to existing applications. However, the book should also attract GIS programmers or users, if only because this is the first book that addresses Oracle Spatial in its entirety. In spite of its title, this book does in fact cover the full spectrum of geospatial technologies at Oracle—that is, the database (Oracle Spatial and Locator) and also Oracle Application Server (MapViewer and Router).

If you're brand new to PL/SQL and database technology, then we suggest taking some time to get familiar with the language and the main concepts of object-relational databases before reading this book. It's not intended for the total beginner. On the other hand, we do not assume any previous knowledge of spatial information management.

Once you're up and running, we're certain that you'll find our book an invaluable guide for creating robust spatially enhanced applications that perform well.

Copyrights and Disclaimer

Oracle is a registered trademark, and Oracle9*i*, 10*g*, Oracle iAS (Application Server), and Oracle Spatial are trademarks of Oracle Corporation.

All other company and product names mentioned in the book are used for identification purposes only and may be trademarks of their respective owners.

The data used in this book is provided exclusively to illustrate the concepts in this book and is not authorized for use in any other way. The datasets cannot be transferred, changed, or modified in full or in part without the written consent of the authors. In particular, we refer you to the End User License Agreement for the sample data provided by NAVTEQ and data publishers used in this book. This agreement is accessible at `www.navteq.com/oracle-download/end_user_terms.pdf`. By installing and using the data provided with this book, you implicitly agree to the terms of this agreement.

The authors, the publishers, and the companies that originally sourced code and data cannot be liable for any damages incurred by using the data shipped with this book. The authors and the publishers do not guarantee that the data is complete, up to date, or accurate.

Most of the figures in the book were generated using Oracle MapViewer based on data from NAVTEQ and DCW. The data is copyright of the respective owners.

Setting Up

To be able to work through all the content and examples of this book, you need to set up some software and download some data and code. Specifically

- You need to have Oracle Database 10*g* and Oracle Spatial installed and configured.
- You need to have Oracle MapViewer (a part of Oracle Application Server 10*g*) installed and configured. The instructions for installing and configuring MapViewer are in Chapter 11.
- You need to download data and scripts for this book from the Downloads section of the Apress website (`www.apress.com`).

The Oracle software (Database 10g, Application Server, and MapViewer) is available for download from the Oracle Technology Network website at `www.oracle.com/technology/products`. Note that any software you download from the Oracle Technology Network site is for evaluation purposes only.

Downloads

Data, code, and links to software are provided for this book in the Downloads section of the Apress web site (`www.apress.com`). Here you will find a compressed file that contains the following:

- An HTML file with a hierarchical folder structure that contain links to
  - The code and the examples shown in the book chapters
  - The datasets used for these examples and described briefly
  - The download areas of the software tools used in the book, such as OC4J
- The files containing the example code and the data files. You can access all files from the hyperlinks in the HTML file.
- A `readme.txt` file that contains all information needed to use this material.

Note Please read the `readme.txt` file. It contains the most relevant information regarding the code, data, and links provided in support of this book. This information is not provided in the book itself.

Setting Up Oracle Spatial and MapViewer

If you already have a recent version of an Oracle database up and running, you probably do not need to do anything specific to set up Oracle Spatial. Oracle Spatial technology is automatically installed with the Standard or Enterprise Edition of an Oracle database server. As long as you are using version 10.1.0.2 or higher, you should be able to work through the examples in the book.

Note that the Database Server license includes only a few of the functions described in the book (the so-called Locator feature). To be able to work through all examples and explore the entire functionality of Oracle Spatial, you need to obtain a separate product license for the Spatial option. Chapter 2 includes detailed information on how to set up Oracle Spatial for this book.

MapViewer serves to create mapping applications. You can deploy MapViewer either within a full Oracle Application Server environment or as a stand-alone installation of the Oracle Application Server Containers for J2EE (OC4J). Both MapViewer and OC4J are available for download from the Oracle Technology Network website (see the links in the support material for this book). The instructions to deploy MapViewer within Application Server are provided in Chapter 11, where we use MapViewer for the first time.

The Example Data

Once you have your Oracle 10*g* database up and running, to run the examples in this book you first need to do the following:

1. Create a user `spatial` with the password `spatial`.
2. Grant `resource`, `connect`, and `unlimited tablespace` privileges to the `spatial` user.
3. Create a tablespace called `users` and make it the default tablespace for the `spatial` schema. This tablespace should have at least 100MB of space.

For each chapter, you should re-create the `spatial` schema and import appropriate datasets listed at the beginning of the chapter using the Oracle Import utility. Starting from Chapter 2, every chapter that requires code or data to be downloaded from the Apress site will clearly specify this. You will find a checklist of all data, scripts, and code that you need to download to be able to run the examples in the chapter, as well as any particular operation that needs to be carried out to prepare for that.

We do not expect that you are using any specific tool for programming or for SQL, which means that you should be able to run all examples using your preferred tools.

The data used in the examples for this book comes from several sources. The detailed street-level data is derived from a sample made available by NAVTEQ to Oracle users. (The original sample is available for download at `www.navteq.com/oracle-download`.) This data includes detailed information on San Francisco and Washington, D.C. as separate files. For the purposes of this book, we merged the data and extracted a relevant subset.

The other sources of data are the U.S. Census Bureau and the GIS Data Depot. The GIS Data Depot (`http://data.geocomm.com`) is a central distribution point for free and public domain data.

As noted, we provide the example data as a set of Oracle dump files, which you can import into your database using the standard import (`imp`) tool. The following is a brief overview of what each dump file contains.

app_data.dmp

Source: NAVTEQ
Size: 640KB
Tables: BRANCHES, CUSTOMERS, and COMPETITORS
Description: This file contains the definitions of our "application" tables: branches, customers, and competitors.

app_data_with_loc.dmp

Source: NAVTEQ
Size: 640KB
Tables: BRANCHES, CUSTOMERS, and COMPETITORS
Description: This file is identical to the app_data.dmp file described earlier. The only difference is that all the tables (branches, customers, and competitors) have an additional column called location of type SDO_GEOMETRY to store the location of the corresponding entities.

map_large.dmp

Source: Digital Chart of the World
Size: 34.2MB
Tables: US_STATES, US_COUNTIES, US_CITIES, US_INTERSTATES, US_PARKS, US_RIVERS, WORLD_CONTINENTS, and WORLD_COUNTRIES
Description: This file contains the boundaries of states and counties in the United States, as well as the locations of major cities, national parks, rivers, and interstates. It also contains the boundaries of world continents and countries. In addition to the boundaries stored as SDO_GEOMETRY columns, some of the tables have demographic information such as population density or area.

map_detailed.dmp

Source: NAVTEQ
Size: 3.1MB
Tables: MAP_MAJOR_HIGHWAYS, MAP_SEC_HIGHWAYS, MAP_MAJOR_ROADS, MAP_STREETS, MAP_PARKFACILITY_POINTS, and US_RESTAURANTS
Description: This file contains the detailed definition of streets for San Francisco and Washington, D.C.

gc.dmp

Source: NAVTEQ
Size: 9.2MB
Tables: GC_COUNTRY_PROFILE, GC_PARSER_PROFILEAFS, GC_PARSER_PROFILES, GC_AREA_US, GC_INTERSECTION_US, GC_POI_US, GC_POSTAL_CODE_US, GC_ROAD_SEGMENT_US, and GC_ROAD_US
Description: This file contains the geocoding data for two cities in the United States: Washington, D.C. and San Francisco.

net.dmp

Source: NAVTEQ
Size: 5.2MB
Tables: `NET_LINKS_SF`, `NET_NODES_SF`, and `MY_NETWORK_METADATA`
Description: This file contains the description of the street network for San Francisco.

styles.dmp

Source: Oracle
Size: 400KB
Tables: `MY_MAPS`, `MY_THEMES`, and `MY_STYLES`
Description: This file contains a set of map, theme, and style definitions for use by MapViewer.

zip.dmp

Source: U.S. Census Bureau
Size: 24KB
Table: `ZIP5_DC`
Description: This file contains the boundaries of the zip codes areas in Washington, D.C. with some attributes (area, perimeter, and population).

PART 1

Overview

CHAPTER 1

Spatial Information Management

Location is an inherent part of business data: organizations maintain customer address lists, own property, ship goods from and to warehouses, manage transport flows among their workforce, and perform many other activities. A majority of these activities entail managing locations of different types of entities, including customers, property, goods, and employees. Those locations need not be static—in fact, they may continually change over time. For instance, goods are manufactured, packaged, and channeled to warehouses and retail/customer destinations. They may have different locations at various stages of the distribution network.

Let's consider an example of parcel services to illustrate how location is used. We have become increasingly accustomed to monitoring the status of parcel deliveries on the Web, by locating our shipment within the distribution channel of our chosen service supplier. The simplicity and usefulness of this service is the result of a very complex underlying information system. The system relies on the ability to locate the parcel as it moves across different stages of the distribution network. Many information systems share location information in this process, which can be used to estimate, for instance, transit or delivery times. Systems such as RFID[1] are used to automatically record the movements of parcels along the distribution chain. Aircraft, trains, container ships, or trucks that move goods between distribution hubs use systems such as Global Positioning System (GPS) to locate their position in real time. Even the "last mile"—that is, the delivery of an individual parcel to the end customer—is based on the geographical optimization of the delivery schedule as well as on the ability to locate, in real time, the truck drivers, to guide them to their destinations and to estimate delivery times.

All of this location information is stored, analyzed, and exchanged among multiple systems, and is the basis for making the entire operation cheaper, faster, and more reliable. Most of these systems are connected to each other through the Internet. The end user also uses the Internet to access the system and to query the current status of his parcel. By analyzing the system in its entirety, you can recognize that the added value is the result of the integration of various systems, of their interoperability, and of the pervasive role of spatial information across the entire process. Spatial information plays a crucial role in enabling the systems and processes to run smoothly and efficiently.

---

1. RFID stands for *Radio Frequency IDentification*, a technology to exchange data between tags and readers over a short range.

This example illustrates the pervasiveness of location or spatial information in day-to-day business. In fact, market research estimates that the majority of the data handled by organizations—perhaps as much as 80 percent of all data—has a spatial dimension.[2] The ability to properly manage the "where," or the spatial information, is key to the efficiency of organizations and could translate to substantial costs savings and commercial competitiveness. For instance, healthcare, telecommunications, and local government organizations depend on spatial information to run their daily business. Other organizations in the fields of retail, distribution, and marketing use spatial information for strategic decision-making—for example, choosing store locations, making investment decisions, examining market segmentation, and supporting clients.

At one point in time, the Internet seemed to have made location irrelevant. The Web emerged as a locationless cloud, where we could contact anybody around the world instantly and shop anywhere without the usual constraints of geography. It seemed that the worlds of transport, logistics, and location received a critical blow. Of course, that thinking was naive. The Internet has made geography ever more relevant and bound digital and physical worlds closer than ever. It is now possible to do business over much farther distances, and tracking the locations of different components of a business and analyzing them has become all the more important.

The emergence of wireless and location services promises to add location to every information item that we use or process. Technologies such as RFID have the potential to radically alter the retail and distribution worlds, making it possible to cheaply locate and track individual items, however small they are. With these new developments, the relevance of location has grown, and this is why it has become increasingly important to master the tools that handle spatial information.

Software tools for spatial information management have been traditionally known under the name of Geographical Information Systems (GIS). These systems are specialized applications for storing, processing, analyzing, and displaying spatial data. They have been used in a variety of applications, such as land-use planning, geomarketing, logistics, distribution, network and utility management, and transportation.[3] However, until recently GIS have employed specific spatial data models and proprietary development languages, which held them separate from the main corporate databases. This has represented a barrier for the full deployment of the added value of spatial data in organizations.

As the use of GIS in enterprises and in the public sector has grown in popularity, some of the limitations of GIS have become apparent. Organizations often have to deal with multiple and incompatible standards for storing spatial data, and they have to use different languages and interfaces to analyze the data. Furthermore, systems such as Customer Relationship Management (CRM), Enterprise Resource Planning (ERP), or the systems used in logistics increasingly rely on the integration of spatial information with all other types of information. This has often been an operational and technical challenge that in some cases was solved by manually extracting information from one system and loading it into another to perform the necessary spatial analysis.

---

2. See Daratech Inc.'s analysis titled "Geographical Information Systems: Markets and Opportunities" (`www.daratech.com/research/index.php`).
3. For an introduction to GIS and its applications, see Ian Heywood, Sarah Cornelius, and Steve Carver, *An Introduction to Geographical Information Systems, Second Edition* (Upper Saddle River, NJ: Prentice Hall, 2002).

Oracle Spatial has an important role in changing this situation. Once the spatial data is stored in an Oracle database, it can be processed, retrieved, and related to all the other data stored in the database: spatial information, or location, is just another attribute of a business object. This eliminates both the need for coordinating multiple data sources due to an application's dependence on special data structures and the use of different languages to query the data. Relevant features of Oracle Spatial are the ability to access spatial data through SQL statements, just like any other database content, and support for industry standards for spatial information (SQL and OpenGIS[4]). Above all, Oracle Spatial facilitates leveraging the full added value of spatial information, which becomes an integrated part of the information assets of organizations.

Given this overview of what location information is and how it can be used, in this chapter we will elaborate on the following topics:

- First, we describe how location information is used in different industry segments. Chances are that this will relate to your application and give you a head start putting spatial information to good use.
- Next, we describe different sources for spatial data. The data could be location information from different applications, or it could be geographical data representing, for instance, political boundaries.
- We then describe typical functionality required for managing spatial/location information. This functionality involves storing and analyzing the spatial data. We look at a specific example to illustrate the different components of such spatial processing.
- Finally, we discuss the systems that enable spatial information management, such as GIS, and their evolution. We consider an out-of-the-box approach to spatial information and the Oracle Spatial approach that integrates spatial data with other data in an Oracle database. We elaborate on this comparison and highlight the benefits of using Oracle Spatial.

Using Spatial Information in Various Industries

Let's now consider a simple business application example. The database for this application contains data about available products (a `Products` table), customers (a `Customers` table), suppliers (a `Suppliers` table), delivery sites (a `Delivery` table), and competitors (a `Competitors` table). The tables for customers, suppliers, delivery sites, and competitors contain information on the location of each item in the table. For instance, the `Customers` table contains the address of each customer and also the x, y coordinates of the address.

Notice that only the address is usually known, but for many spatial analyses, such as the calculation of the distance between customer's location and delivery sites, you need to know the x, y coordinates of this address. The conversion of address fields to x, y coordinates is one of the most fundamental spatial operations described in this book, called *geocoding*. It serves to translate a text string such as "Abbey Road, 3, London NW8" into something like "longitude = –0.1784; latitude = 51.5320," which is the information used to relate spatial information items to each other.

---

4. See `www.opengis.org`.

With this information available, we might want to conduct valuable business analyses that can help determine new marketing campaigns, opening of new stores, discontinuation of poorly located stores, as well as identify more efficient home-delivery schedules, changes in the stores' product portfolio, and so on. Consider the following options:

- Identify customers who are close to a competitor store (say less than 5 kilometers). To prevent them from switching stores, we could design a specific marketing campaign proposing special discounts for these customers.
- Optimize the distribution network. By counting the number of customers who are located within a certain distance from a distribution center, we can see if some centers are overloaded or underutilized. This may lead to a redesign of the distribution network.
- Identify routes from delivery sites to customer locations, and cluster goods in such a way that the same delivery can serve multiple customers and save money. Note that this analysis requires additional data, such as the road network.
- Superimpose the location of our stores on a population map, and check if the store locations are appropriate. If some areas are underserved, this will alert us to opportunities for new outlets. Note that additional demographic data is often useful for this analysis.
- Visualize table data and analysis results as maps (e.g., customer maps, delivery site maps, etc.) and produce rich visual material better suited for communication and decision–making.
- Integrate these maps with existing applications, such as a CRM system, so that location information and analysis can promote effective customer relations.

To perform these types of analyses, we need to store location information for customers, delivery sites, and competitors. In practice, this will mean augmenting the corresponding tables with additional columns for storing location information. We also need to store additional information, such as street networks, rivers, city and state boundaries, and so on, to use in visualization and analysis.

The preceding analyses are representative of a vast class of uses for spatial information. The following list summarizes some of the main uses of spatial data, analysis, and visualization in various industries.

- *Banking and finance*: These industries use location data for analysis of retail networks and for market intelligence. The customer database combined with demographics and wealth information helps banks define an optimal retail network and define the best product mix to offer at each branch.
- *Telecommunications*: Location analysis helps telecom operators and carriers improve their competitive position. Spatial data is used for network planning, site location, maintenance organization, call-center and customer support, marketing, and engineering.
- *Local and central government*: Spatial information is heavily used by all government agencies, since they manage a multitude of assets distributed over large territories. Uses include natural resource management or land-use planning, road maintenance, housing stock maintenance, emergency management, and social services.

- *Law enforcement*: Spatial information helps officers in operational duties, as well as in crime analysis and prevention. Location information is used by field officers to locate places and other resources in the field in real time. Investigators use spatial data for crime analysis. Spatial patterns of crime are used to better locate police resources and improve prevention.
- *Real estate and property management*: Geographic data and demographics are used to identify and assess locations for outlets, housing, or facilities. Land-use, transport, and utility networks are used to site industrial and production facilities.
- *Retail*: Location data serves as a basis for operational and strategic decisions. It can be used to identify the profile of the best customers and help reach similar prospects. Spatial data can increase the relevance and focus of marketing campaigns, and find the best layout of a distribution network for maximum profit.
- *Utilities*: Many different utility systems can be found under almost every street. Utility companies use spatial information to design these underground systems, plan and monitor groundwork, and maintain their cable and pipe networks.
- *Communications, media, and advertising*: Location data are frequently used for increasing the return of communications campaigns. Segmentation and location-based targeting help companies finesse the timing and appropriateness of marketing campaigns, thereby increasing their expectation of success.
- *Wireless data services*: Wireless data services increasingly use location data to enrich the user experience and provide valuable services. Uses include personal navigation systems, friend finders, roadside emergency, location-based yellow page searches, and the like. Wireless location services are necessary for fast returns on investment made on third-generation telecom networks.

Sources of Spatial Data

In the previous section we described the uses of spatial information in applications and in various industries, and introduced the distinction between application data and spatial data. The simplest example is that of address lists collected as text items and subsequently enhanced by associating geographical (longitude, latitude) coordinates to each address. This association makes it possible to analyze the address information from the spatial perspective, an otherwise impossible operation based on the original address list.

In general, the association between nonspatial objects and their corresponding geometry makes it possible to relate the objects based on spatial concepts (close, far, overlap, joined, and so on). Very often the tables derive their spatial dimension from some primarily spatial data sources. In the case of address geocoding, for instance, postal data provides the locations of individual addresses, in the form of a reference address list with the associated coordinates.

This is only one of the multitude of spatial datasets and sources used in practice. Some datasets, such as cadastral data, land-use data, road network data, administrative boundary data, rivers and lakes data, and so on, are almost always present in spatial analysis and visualization. This data is collected, updated, and distributed by public bodies or by companies (the latter is the case, for instance, for the road networks for car navigation). All these datasets are first of all spatial, as the geographic component of the data content defines the usefulness and relevance of the entire dataset, and they are often used as reference layers.

The vast majority of these datasets are dynamic, at least to some extent. However, there are several cases in which the reason for using spatial data is specifically because of their dynamics. For example, use of *real-time location* is increasingly common, thanks to the widespread use of GPS and the growing use of location systems such as Wi-Fi location or RFID tagging, to locate people or objects.

GPS receivers can be located with high accuracy and can feed a database with the real-time location of a moving person/object (a field engineer, a car, a truck, a container, and so on). Note that there are also many commercial GPS applications, such as car navigators, that use real-time location within closed applications that support a specific purpose (such as door-to-door navigation) without connection to corporate data infrastructures. However, in most cases, it is the ability to feed the enterprise databases with the location of the mobile users or assets of an organization that allows planning, scheduling, and logistics improvements.

This is increasingly becoming the case in the retail and distribution industries, where the use of RFID, instead of bar codes, makes it possible to track vast amounts of goods automatically, while they travel through the distribution chain from supplier to end user. RFID tagging can be implemented at the level of single items, products, or even documents. With RFID, goods can be followed precisely—for instance, within a warehouse—and this information can be used to minimize inventory, optimize supply schedules, and create a unique opportunity to link logistics with administrative, CRM, and ERP systems. It is likely that these areas, often referred to as *location-based* or *sensor-based* systems and services, will stimulate a rapid increase in the use of spatial information in the near future.

Managing and Analyzing Spatial Data

In this section, we will examine how to manage spatial data and what the typical analysis functions on spatial data are. Note that a variety of spatial processing systems such as GIS and spatial-enabled databases can provide this functionality using their own types and functions. We first describe spatial processing using generic terminology without referring to any specific solution (such as Oracle Spatial).

Spatial operations typically include, but are not limited to

- *Storage of spatial data*: In most cases, this involves the following.
    - Storing the data in an appropriate form in the database. For instance, the database system could have a *geometry* type to store spatial information as points, lines, polygons, and other types of vector representations. The system may also have a *network* type for modeling road networks.[5]
    - Inserting, deleting, and updating these types of spatial data in the database.
- *Analysis of vector spatial data*: This typically includes the following analysis functionality.
    - *Within-distance*: This operation identifies all spatial data within a specified distance of a query location.

5. Oracle Spatial includes an additional data type called *raster*, which is used for images and grid data. Raster data and the raster data model are covered in Appendix D.

- *Contains*: This operation identifies all spatial data that contain a specified query location (geometry). Functions to detect other types of relationships may also be defined.
- *Nearest-neighbor*: This operation identifies all spatial data closest to a query location.
- *Distance*: This operation computes the distance between two spatial objects.
- *Buffer*: This operation constructs buffer zones around spatial data.
- *Overlay*: This operation overlays different layers of spatial data.
- *Visualization*: This operation presents spatial data using maps.

- *Analysis of network data*: Typically, most spatial data, such as road networks, can also be represented as network data (in addition to vector data). We can perform the preceding analysis on such data using network proximity rather than spatial proximity.

The subjects of spatial analysis and management have filled dozens of books and hundreds of university courses. Our goal here is not to repeat all this—the references at the end of this chapter will provide you with a good background on these topics. Here, we will illustrate spatial analysis and management by describing how you can apply them to solve a common problem in the retail industry: site selection.

The consideration of location in Figure 1-1 streamlines the selection of candidate sites for a shopping mall. The process involves limiting the choice to those locations that are

- Included in areas where construction is allowed
- On sale and of a suitable size
- Not exposed to natural risks, such as floods
- Close to main roads to ensure good accessibility

For the selection of suitable sites, we are going to make use of spatial information and spatial analysis. To keep the example simple, however, we ignore demographic issues.

The main steps of the analysis are as follows:

1. From the land-use map (provided by a public organization), we first select areas for which we can obtain permits to build commercial sites. These areas are labeled as "commercial" and denote sites where new commercial activities can be located.
2. From a map that contains sites for sale (provided by a large real-estate agency), we restrict the choice to sites that are sufficiently large for a shopping mall.
3. On the basis of a risk map, which indicates safety buffer areas around rivers, we eliminate those sites that may be subject to floods.
4. Finally, of the remaining sites, only those close to main roads are deemed suitable for accessibility reasons.

Figure 1-1 shows the sequence of steps, the data used, and the spatial operations involved in this process. Note that the maps are numbered M1–M12 and the steps are numbered 1–8.

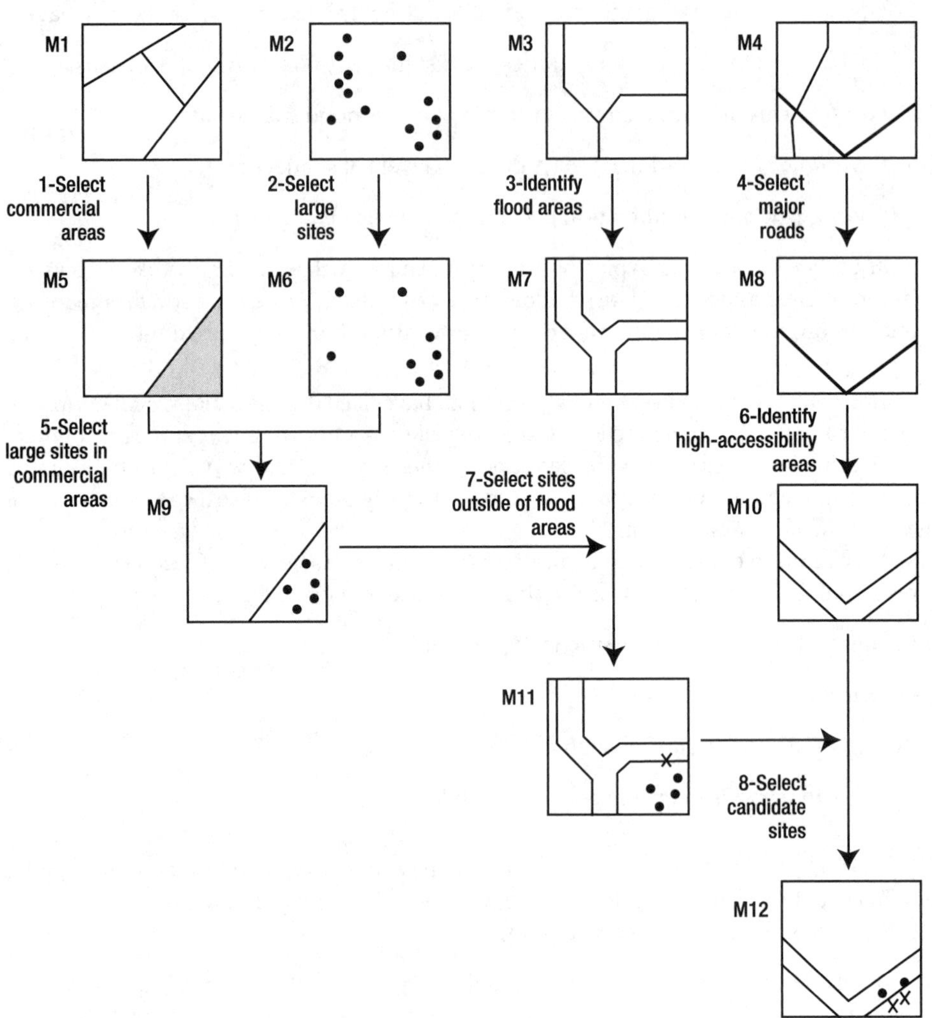

Figure 1-1. *Spatial data and spatial analysis for choosing a site for a shopping mall*

The combination of the first two steps leads to five candidate sites. One of them is excluded because of high flood risk, and two additional ones are excluded because they are located too far away from the main roads. This narrows the results to two suitable candidate sites.

Table 1-1 details the steps in this process. Note that the usual way of representing the data used in this example is through maps, as in Figure 1-1. Note also that the description can be easily translated into database and SQL terms. The various "maps" correspond to one or more database tables. The data objects (points, polygons, lines, grids, etc.) and their attributes are table records, while the analysis is performed with SQL statements. It is clear that some SQL extensions are needed to handle spatial and nonspatial objects simultaneously. The rest of this book will essentially deal with the models and tools available in Oracle Spatial for storing and processing this type of data for types of analysis like this one.

Table 1-1. *Steps, Data, and Analysis for Choosing a Site for a Shopping Mall*

Step	Data	Analysis	Result
1. Select commercial areas.	M1: Land use map. Collection of polygons, described by an attribute "land-use type."	Select polygons where the attribute is "commercial."	M5: Commercial areas. A set of polygons with the "commercial" attribute.
2. Select large sites.	M2: Sites for sale. Locations described by price, plot size, etc.	Select points where the size is larger than a certain value.	M6: Large sites. A selection of points corresponding to large sites for sale.
3. Identify flood areas.	M3: River map.	Create a buffer around the riverbed (e.g., 1 km) that is at risk of floods.	M7: Flood risk areas.
4. Select major roads.	M4: Road network map. Road segment attributes are "road type," "max speed," etc.	Select road segments where the attribute is "major roads."	M8: Major roads.
5. Select large sites in commercial areas.	M5 and M6.	Overlay M5 and M6. Select "large" points within "commercial" polygons.	M9: A selection of points corresponding to large sites within commercial areas.
6. Identify high-accessibility zones.	M8.	Create a buffer of 500 meters on each side of a major road.	M10: High accessibility zones.
7. Select sites outside of flood areas.	M9 and M7.	Overlay M9 and M7, and eliminate sites in the flood areas.	M11: Points corresponding to large sites within commercial areas not subject to flood risks.
8. Select candidate sites.	M10 and M11.	Select safe sites within high–accessibility zones.	M12: Large sites in commercial areas that are not subject to floods and are highly accessible.

For simplicity, in the example we have assumed that a new map is created at the end of every step. This is certainly a possibility, but it is not necessarily the best option. Later on, we will discuss data modeling and how to optimize the sequence of operations. In particular, Chapters 8 and 9 cover spatial operators and functions that make it possible to cluster some of the steps in the example into single queries, making the process much simpler and more efficient.

Storing Spatial Data in a Database

Looking at vector data, we usually distinguish between

- *Points* (e.g., the plots for sale in Figure 1-1), whose spatial description requires only x, y coordinates (or x, y, z if 3D is considered)
- *Lines* (e.g., roads), whose spatial description requires a start coordinate, an end coordinate, and a certain number of intermediate coordinates
- *Polygons* (e.g., a residential area), which are described by closed lines

Figure 1-2 shows an example containing point, line, and polygon data. The figure corresponds to a small portion of the area used in the previous site selection example. The vector representation, here simplified for convenience, shows a point (the stadium), three lines (the roads), and four polygons (the built-up areas, clipped at the picture borders, and the sports complex).

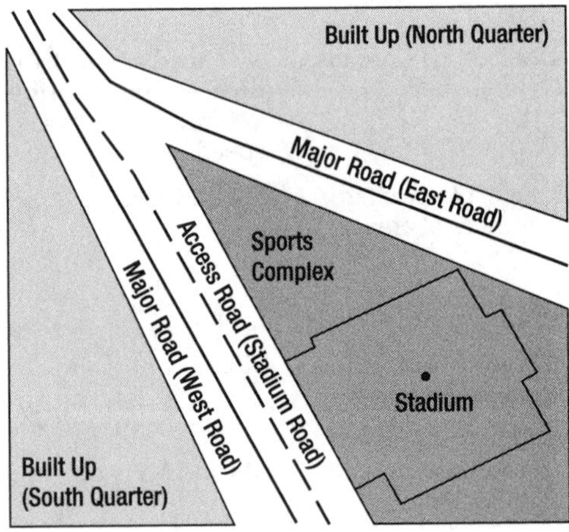

Figure 1-2. *Vector representation of the spatial objects in the picture*

The vector data in Figure 1-2 could be stored in one or multiple tables. The most natural way of looking at this data is to identify *data layers*—sets of data that share common attributes—which become data tables. Most spatial databases use a special data type to store spatial data in a database. Let's refer to this type as the *geometry*. Users can add columns of type *geometry* to a database table in order to store spatial objects.

In this case, the choice of tables would be rather simple with three main data layers present: "Road infrastructures," "Land use," and "Points of interest." These three layers contain objects that share common attributes, as shown in the three tables later in this section. The same objects could have been aggregated into different data layers, if desired. For instance, we could have stored major and minor roads in different tables, or we could have put roads and land use in the same table. The latter would make sense if the only attributes of relevance for roads and land-use areas were the same, for instance, the province name and the city name. It is also worth stressing that every *geometry* column can contain any mix of valid spatial object (points, lines, polygons), and also that every table can contain one or more *geometry* columns.

Structuring spatial data into tables and defining the right table structure are the first logical activities of any spatial analysis. Fortunately, in most cases there is an intuitive correspondence between the data and the table structure used to store them. However, in several cases you may find that the spatial database design can be a complex activity. Proper designs may facilitate analysis enormously, while poor data structures may make the analysis complex and slow. These issues are addressed in various places in the book, but in particular in Chapter 3.

Table 1-2 shows the road infrastructure table of Figure 1-2. This table contains three records corresponding to the east road, the west road, and the stadium road. All of them are represented as lines using the *geometry* type. Each road is described by three types of attributes: road type (one column containing either "major," "local," or "access" road), road name (a column containing the name of the road as used in postal addresses), and the area attributes (two columns containing the name of the province and city where the road is located).

Table 1-2. *Road Infrastructure Table*

ID	Province	City	Road Name	Road Type	Road Geometry
1	Province name	City name	West road	Major road	
2	Province name	City name	East road	Major road	
3	Province name	City name	Stadium road	Access road	

Table 1-3 shows the land use table. It contains three records corresponding to the north quarter, the south quarter, and the sports complex. In this case, all spatial objects are polygons. Each object has three types of attributes: the surface of the area (in square meters), the name of the area, and the area location (province and city names).

Table 1-3. *Land Use Table*

ID	Province	City	Area Name	Surface (Square Meters)	Area Geometry
1	Province name	City name	North quarter	10,000	
2	Province name	City name	South quarter	24,000	
3	Province name	City name	Sports complex	4,000	

Table 1-4 shows the points of interest (POI) in the area. It contains two records: a point (in this case, the center of the stadium complex) and a polygon (in this case, the contour of the stadium complex). Attributes include the type of POI from a classification list, the POI name, and the province and city where they are located.

Table 1-4. *Points of Interest Table*

ID	Province	City	POI Name	Type of POI	POI Geometry
1	Province name	City name	Olympic stadium	Sports location	●
2	Province name	City name	Olympic stadium	Sports infrastructure	

In Table 1-4, we use two records to describe the same object with two different geometries. Another option for storing the same information is presented in Table 1-5, where we use two columns of type *geometry* to store two different spatial features of the same object. The first *geometry* column stores the POI location, while the second stores the outline of the complex. Under the assumption that all other nonspatial attributes are the same, Table 1-5 is a more efficient use of table space than Table 1-4.

Table 1-5. *Points of Interest Table: Two* Geometry *Columns*

ID	Province	City	POI Name	Location (POI) Geometry	Infrastructure Geometry
1	Province name	City name	Olympic stadium	●	⬠

The objects in the preceding tables are represented with different line styles and fill patterns. This information is added for clarity, but in practice it is not stored in the *geometry* object. In Oracle Spatial, the *geometry* data are physically stored in a specific way (which we will describe in Chapters 3 and 4) that does not have a direct relationship to the visual representation of the data. Chapter 11, which describes the Oracle Application Server MapViewer, shows how symbology and styling rules are used for rendering *geometry* instances in Oracle.

Geometry models in the SQL/MM and OpenGIS (OGC) specifications describe in detail the technical features of *geometry* type and how points, lines, and polygons are modeled using this type.

Spatial Analysis

Once data is stored in the appropriate form in a database, spatial analysis makes it possible to derive meaningful information from it. Let's go back to the site selection example and look again at the three types of spatial operations that we used.

- *Select*, used in
  - Step 1 (to select areas where the attribute was a certain value)
  - Step 2 (to select large sites from the sites for sale)
  - Step 4 (to select major roads from the road network)
- *Overlay*, used in
  - Step 5 (large sites in commercial areas)
  - Step 7 (sites away from risk areas)
  - Step 8 (sites within highly accessible areas)
- *Buffer*, used in
  - Step 3 (areas subject to flood risk)
  - Step 6 (high accessibility areas)

Going back to our example, assuming we have the data stored in a database, we can use the following eight *pseudo*-SQL statements to perform the eight operations listed previously.

Please note that for the sake of the example, we have assumed certain table structures and column names. For instance, we have assumed that M1 contains the columns LAND_USE_TYPE, AREA_NAME, and AREA_GEOMETRY.

1. Use

   ```
   SELECT AREA_NAME, AREA_GEOMETRY
   FROM M1
   WHERE LAND_USE_TYPE='COMMERCIAL'
   ```

   to identify available plots of land for which a construction permit can be obtained for a shopping mall.

2. Use

   ```
   SELECT SITE_NAME, SITE_GEOMETRY
   FROM M2
   WHERE SITE_PLOT_AREA > <some value>
   ```

   to identify available sites whose size is larger than a certain value.

3. Use

   ```
   SELECT BUFFER(RIVER_GEOMETRY, 1,'unit=km')
   FROM M3
   WHERE RIVER_NAME= <river_in_question>
   ```

   to create a buffer of 1 kilometer around the named river.

4. Use

   ```
   SELECT ROAD_NAME, ROAD_GEOMETRY
   FROM M4
   WHERE ROAD_TYPE='MAJOR ROAD'
   ```

   to identify major roads.

5. Use the *contains* operator to identify the sites selected in step 2 that are within areas selected in step 1. We could also achieve this in one step starting directly from M1 and M2.

   ```
   SELECT SITE_NAME, SITE_GEOMETRY
   FROM M2 S, M1 L
   WHERE CONTAINS(L.AREA_GEOMETRY, S.SITE_GEOMETRY)='TRUE'
     AND L.LAND_USE_TYPE= 'COMMERCIAL'
     AND S.SITE_AREA > <some value>;.
   ```

6. As in step 3, use the *buffer* function to create a buffer of a certain size around the major roads.

7. Use *contains* to identify sites selected in step 5 that are outside the flood-prone areas identified in step 3.

8. Use *contains* to identify safe sites selected in step 7 that are within the zones of easy accessibility created in step 6.

Oracle Spatial contains a much wider spectrum of SQL operators and functions (see Chapters 8 and 9). As you might also suspect, the preceding list of steps and choice of operators is not optimal. By redesigning the query structures, changing operators, and nesting queries, it is possible to drastically reduce the number of intermediate tables and the queries. M11, for instance, could be created starting from M9 and M3 directly by using the *nearest-neighbor* and *distance* operations together. They would select the nearest neighbor and verify if the distance is larger than a certain value.

Benefits of Oracle Spatial

The functionality described in the previous section has been the main bread and butter for Geographic Information Systems (GIS) for decades. In the past 5 to 10 years, database vendors such as Oracle have also moved into this space. Specifically, Oracle introduced the *Oracle Spatial* suite of technology to support spatial processing inside an Oracle database.

Since GIS have been around for several years, you may wonder why Oracle is now introducing yet another tool for carrying out the same operations. After all, we can already do spatial analysis with existing tools.

The answer lies in the evolution of spatial information technology and in the role of spatial data in mainstream IT solutions. GIS have extensive capabilities for spatial analysis, but they have historically developed as stand-alone information systems. Most systems still employ some form of dual architecture, with some data storage dedicated to spatial objects (usually based on proprietary formats) and some for their attributes (usually a database). This choice was legitimate when mainstream databases were unable to efficiently handle the spatial data. However, it has resulted in the proliferation of proprietary data formats that are so common in the spatial information industry. Undesired consequences were the isolation of GIS from mainstream IT and the creation of automation islands dedicated to spatial processing, frequently disconnected from the central IT function of organizations. While the capabilities of GIS are now very impressive, spatial data may still be underutilized, inaccessible, or not shared.

Two main developments have changed this situation: the introduction of open standards for spatial data and the availability of Oracle Spatial. Two of the most relevant open standards are the OpenGIS Simple Feature Specification[6] and SQL/MM Part 3.[7] The purpose of these specifications is to define a standard SQL schema that supports storage, retrieval, query, and update of spatial data via an application programming interface (API). Through these mechanisms, any other OpenGIS-compliant or SQL/MM-compliant system can retrieve data from a database based on the specifications. Oracle Spatial provides an implementation for these standards[8] and offers a simple and effective way of storing and analyzing spatial data from within the same database used for any other data type.

---

6. See `www.opengis.org` for information on approved standards, for an overview of ongoing standardization initiatives for spatial information data and systems, and for an up-to-date list of compliant products.
7. See ISO/IEC 13249-3:2003, "Information technology – Database languages – SQL multimedia and application packages – Part 3: Spatial" (`www.iso.org/iso/en/CatalogueDetailPage.CatalogueDetail?CSNUMBER=31369`).
8. The Oracle Spatial relational model is conformant with the OGC Simple Feature Specification for Relational Model. The Oracle Spatial `SDO_GEOMETRY` model is equivalent to, but not conformant with, the OGC Simple Feature Specification for Object Model.

The combination of these two developments means that spatial data can be processed, retrieved, and related to all other data stored in corporate databases and across multiple sources. This removed the isolation of spatial data from the mainstream information processes of an organization. It is now easy to add location intelligence to applications, to relate location with other information, and to manage all information assets in the same way. This paradigm shift is summarized in Figures 1-3 and 1-4.

Figure 1-3 illustrates the industrywide shift from monolithic/proprietary GIS to open, universal, spatially enabled architectures.

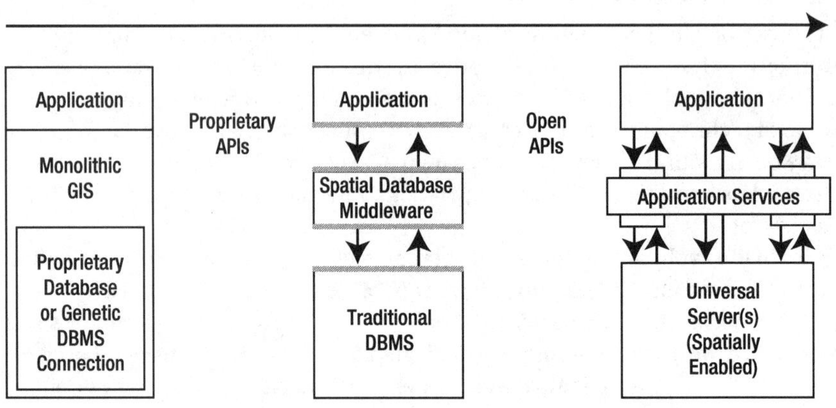

Source: UNIGIS-UNIPHORM project

Figure 1-3. *From monolithic/proprietary GIS to universal, spatially enabled servers*

Figure 1-4 emphasizes the shift from geo-centric processing to information-centric processing, where the added value is not in the sophistication of the spatial analysis but in the benefits that it delivers.

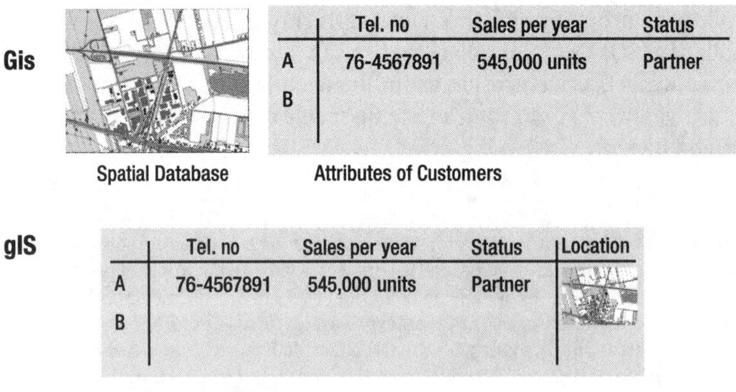

Figure 1-4. *From Gis to gIS*

The benefits of using Oracle Spatial can be summarized as follows:

- It eliminates the need for dual architectures, as all data can be stored in the same way. A unified data storage means that all types of data (text, maps, and multimedia) are stored together, instead of each type being stored separately.
- It uses SQL, a standard language for accessing relational databases, thus removing the need for specific languages to handle spatial data.
- It defines the `SDO_GEOMETRY` data type, which is essentially equivalent to the spatial types in the OGC and SQL/MM standards.
- It implements SQL/MM "well-known" formats for specifying spatial data. This implies that any solution that adheres to the SQL/MM specifications can easily store the data in Oracle Spatial and vice versa, without the need for third-party converters.
- It is the de-facto standard for storing/accessing data in Oracle and sharing data across applications by many vendors, including NAVTEQ, Tele Atlas, Autodesk, MapInfo, ESRI, Bentley, Intergraph, Radius, Skyline, and many others.[9]
- It provides scalability, integrity, security, recovery, and advanced user management features for handling spatial data that are the norm in Oracle databases but are not necessarily so in other spatial management tools.
- It removes the need for separate organizations to maintain a spatial data infrastructure (hardware, software, support, etc.), and it eliminates the need for specific tools and skills for operating spatial data.
- Through the application server, it allows almost any application to benefit from the availability of spatial information and intelligence, reducing the costs and complexity of spatial applications.
- With Oracle 10*g*, it introduces the benefits of grid computing to spatial databases. For large organizations that manage very large data assets, such as clearinghouses, cadastres, or utilities, the flexibility and scalability of the grid can mean substantial cost savings and easier maintenance of the database structures.
- With Oracle 10*g*, powerful visualization of spatial data is introduced, eliminating the need to rely on separate tools for many applications.

Summary

This first chapter provided an introduction to spatial information management, its importance in business applications, and how it can be implemented in practice. The example of situating a shopping mall illustrated the relationship between the logical operations necessary to make a proper choice, and the spatial data and analysis tools that can be used to support it.

---

9. For a list of partners, visit `http://otn.oracle.com/products/spatial/index.html` and click the Partners link (in the Quick Picks section).

After describing the example, we discussed how spatial functionality is enabled by database vendors such as Oracle. We enumerated the benefits of a database approach, specifically that of Oracle Spatial. We observed that the most basic and essential feature of Oracle Spatial is that of eliminating the separation between spatial and nonspatial information in a database. This separation was mainly the result of technology choices and technology limitations, but it does not have any conceptual ground or practical justification. On the contrary, all evidence points toward the need to integrate spatial and nonspatial information, to be able to use the spatial dimension in business operations and decision making.

We have also made the explicit choice of emphasizing the relevance of adding the spatial dimension to mainstream database technology, thereby introducing spatial information starting from the database. A GIS specialist, a geographer, or an urban planner would have probably described the same examples with a different emphasis—for instance, highlighting the features and specific nature of spatial data and analysis. This would have been a perfectly legitimate standpoint, and is one very common in literature and well served by the selected titles in the "References" section at the end of this chapter.

In the next chapter, we will give a brief overview of the functionality of Oracle Spatial. The subsequent chapters in the book present an in-depth tour of the different features and functionality of Oracle Spatial, and how you can implement them in applications.

References

Grimshaw, David J. *Bringing Geographical Information Systems into Business, Second Edition.* New York: John Wiley & Sons, 1999.

Haining, Robert. *Spatial Data Analysis: Theory and Practice.* Cambridge: Cambridge University Press, 2003.

Heywood, Ian, Sarah Cornelius, and Steve Carver. *An Introduction to Geographical Information Systems.* Upper Saddle River, NJ: Prentice Hall, 2002.

Korte, George B. *The GIS Book, 5th Edition.* Clifton Park, NY: OnWord Press, 2000.

Longley, Paul A., Michael F. Goodchild, David J. Maguire, and David W. Rhind, eds. *Geographical Information Systems: Principles, Techniques, Applications, and Management, Second Edition.* 2 vols. New York: John Wiley & Sons, 1999.

CHAPTER 2

Overview of Oracle Spatial

To run the examples in this chapter, you need to load three datasets in the spatial schema as follows. Please refer to the Introduction for instructions on creating the spatial schema and other setup details.

```
imp spatial/spatial file=gc.dmp ignore=y full=y
imp spatial/spatial file=map_large.dmp tables=us_interstates
imp spatial/spatial file=map_detailed.dmp tables=us_restaurants
```

In Chapter 1, we observed that spatial information can add value to a range of different applications. We examined the benefits of storing spatial information together with other data in the database.

The Spatial technology suite in Oracle enables storage of spatial data in the database and facilitates different types of analyses on spatial data. This chapter provides an overview of the Spatial technology suite and covers the following topics:

- An overview of the Oracle Spatial architecture and technology.
- An examination of the *functionality* of different components of this Spatial technology suite in Oracle. This includes a brief introduction to the data type that stores spatial data (SDO_GEOMETRY), the query predicates for performing spatial query and analysis, and additional functionality to perform visualization.
- A description of how this functionality is *packaged* into different products that are shipped with different editions of Oracle software. We will discuss the relative merits of each product in turn.
- What to expect in a typical install of Oracle Spatial. This knowledge should get you off to a smooth start in spatially enabling your application.

Technology and Architecture Overview

Oracle Spatial technology is spread across two tiers: the Database Server and the Application Server. Figure 2-1 depicts the various components that comprise Oracle's spatial technology stack and indicates the distribution of the components across the Database Server and Application Server tiers. Basic components that are provided as part of Oracle Database Server 10*g* include storage model, query and analysis tools, and location-enabling/loading utilities. The MapViewer component is provided in Oracle Application Server 10*g*.

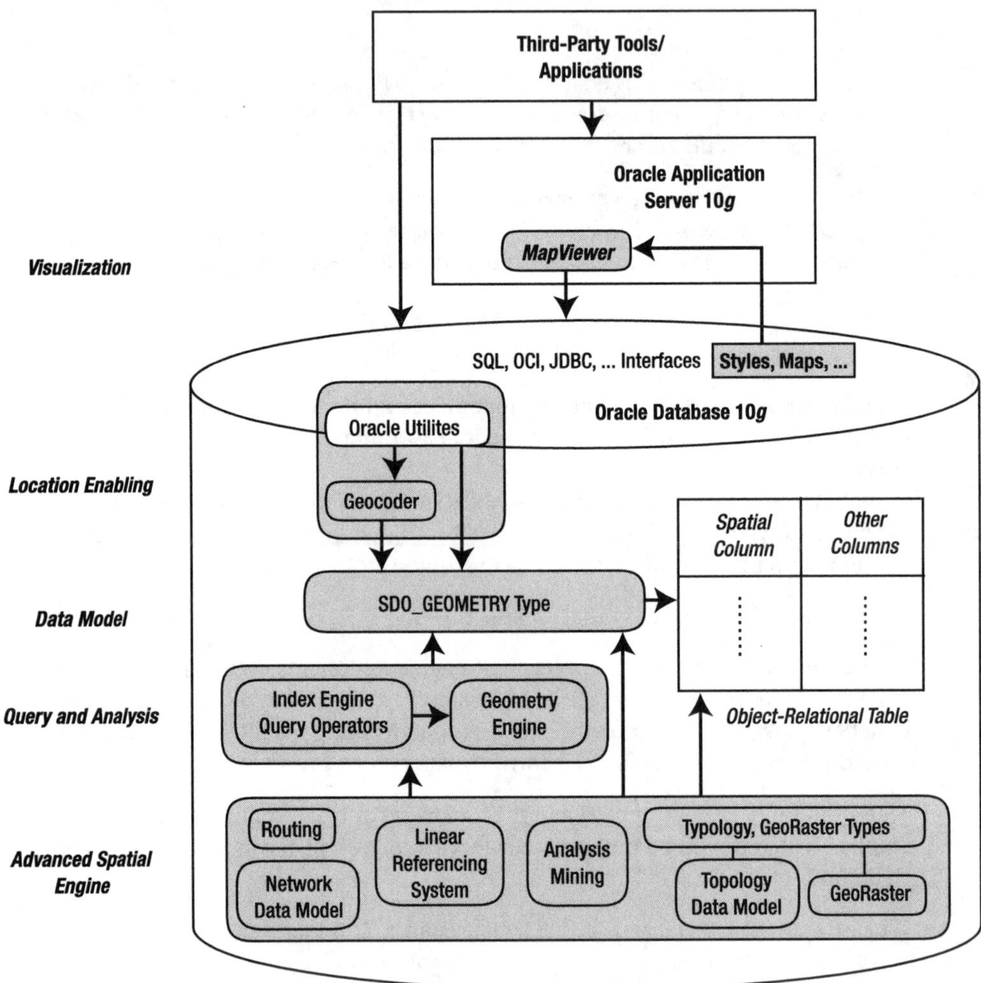

Figure 2-1. *Oracle Spatial technology components*

The basic components from Figure 2-1 can be described as follows:

- *Data model*: Oracle Spatial uses a SQL data type, SDO_GEOMETRY, to store spatial data inside an Oracle database. Users may define tables containing columns of type SDO_GEOMETRY to store the locations of customers, stores, restaurants, and so on, or the locations and spatial extents of geographic entities such as roads, interstates, parks, and land parcels. This data type is described in detail in Chapter 4.
- *Location enabling*: Users can add SDO_GEOMETRY columns to application tables. This process is described in detail in Chapter 3. Users can populate the tables with SDO_GEOMETRY data using standard Oracle utilities such as SQL*Loader, Import, and Export. This process is described in Chapter 5. Alternatively, users can convert implicit spatial information, such as street addresses, into SDO_GEOMETRY columns using the geocoder component of Oracle Spatial, as described in Chapter 6.
- *Spatial query and analysis*: Users can query and manipulate the SDO_GEOMETRY data using the query and analysis component, comprising the Index and Geometry Engines. Full details of this process are given in Chapters 8 and 9.
- *Advanced Spatial Engine*: This component comprises several components that cater to sophisticated spatial applications, such as GIS and bioinformatics. This includes, for example, the GeoRaster component that allows storage of spatial objects using images (groups of pixels) rather than points, lines, and vertices. These components are covered in Appendixes A through D.
- *Visualization*: The Application Server components of Oracle's spatial technology include the means to visualize spatial data via the MapViewer tool. MapViewer renders the spatial data that is stored in SDO_GEOMETRY columns of Oracle tables as displayable maps. This feature is described in detail in Chapter 11.

Note also in Figure 2-1 that third-party tools may access spatial data either through the Application Server or directly from the database using SQL, OCI, JDBC, or other appropriate interfaces. Programming with spatial data via these APIs is described in Chapter 7.

Note The core subset of this functionality (known as the *Locator* component) is included for free in all editions of the database (essentially, the SDO_GEOMETRY data type and the Index Engine). The rest of the components, along with the data type and the Index Engine, are packaged in a priced option of the Enterprise Edition of the database (known as the *Spatial* option). We discuss this in more detail later in this chapter.

In the following sections, we'll preview these components and introduce you to some (very basic) SQL to create a table that stores spatial data, to populate that data, and to perform simple proximity analysis. All of these topics are covered in full detail in subsequent chapters, as described previously, but this should serve as a useful introduction to the technology and help you to get started.

Getting Started with Oracle Spatial

Oracle Spatial technology is automatically installed with the Standard or Enterprise Edition of an Oracle database server. So, as long as you have one of these editions of version 10.1.0.2 or higher, you should be able to work through the simple examples in the coming sections. If you encounter any problems, you can refer to the "What to Expect in an Oracle Spatial Install" section at the end of this chapter. Note that the Database Server license includes only a few of the functions described in this section. To use the rest of the functionality, you should obtain a separate product license for the Spatial option.

Data Model: Storing Spatial Data

In Chapter 1, we briefly discussed the idea that spatial information is specified using two components: a *location* with respect to some origin and a geometric *shape.*

- *Location* specifies where the data is located with respect to a two-, three-, or four-dimensional coordinate space. For instance, the center of San Francisco is located at coordinates (–122.436, –37.719) in the two-dimensional "latitude, longitude" space.

- *Shape* specifies the geometric structure of the data. Point, line, and polygon are examples of possible shapes. For instance, the center of San Francisco is located at coordinates (–122.436, –37.719) in the two-dimensional "latitude, longitude" space and is a *point* shape. Note that point specifies both a location and a default shape. Alternately, shape could specify a *line* or a *polygon* connecting multiple points (specified by their locations). For instance, the city boundary of San Francisco could be a *polygon* connecting multiple *points.*

  In some applications, the shapes could be more complex and could have multiple polygons, and/or polygons containing holes. For instance, the state boundaries for Texas and California include multiple polygons and some with islands. In general, spatial information, occurring in GIS, CAD/CAM, or simple location-enabled applications, could be arbitrarily complex.

The SDO_GEOMETRY data type captures the *location* and *shape* information of data rows in a table. This data type is internally represented as an Oracle object data type. It can model different shapes such as points, lines, polygons, and appropriate combinations of each of these. In short, it can model spatial data occurring in most spatial applications and is conformant with the Open GIS Consortium (OGC) Geometry model.[1]

Chapter 4 provides details about what types of spatial data SDO_GEOMETRY can model and what it cannot, and it also covers the structure of SDO_GEOMETRY and the tools to construct, validate, and debug SDO_GEOMETRY objects. For now, it is sufficient to understand that we can create tables with SDO_GEOMETRY columns to store the locations of objects.

---

1. Open GIS Consortium, Inc., "OpenGIS Simple Features Specification for SQL, Revision 1.1," http://www.opengis.org/docs/99-049.pdf, May 5, 1999.

Location Enabling

We can create tables with the SDO_GEOMETRY columns to store locations. For instance, we can create the us_restaurants_new[2] table as shown in Listing 2-1.

Listing 2-1. *Creating the* us_restaurants_new *Table*

```
SQL> CREATE TABLE  us_restaurants_new
(
  id              NUMBER,
  poi_name        VARCHAR2(32),
  location        SDO_GEOMETRY     -- New column to store locations
);
```

Now that you know basically how to create tables to store locations, let's briefly examine the tools to populate such tables. Since SDO_GEOMETRY is an object type, just like any other object type, you can populate an SDO_GEOMETRY column using the corresponding object constructor. For example, you can insert a location of (–87, –78) for a Pizza Hut restaurant into the us_restaurants table as shown in Listing 2-2.

Listing 2-2. *Inserting a Value for the* SDO_GEOMETRY *Column in an Oracle Table*

```
SQL> INSERT INTO  us_restaurants_new  VALUES
(
  1,
  'PIZZA HUT',
  SDO_GEOMETRY
  (
    2001,  -- SDO_GTYPE attribute: "2" in 2001 specifies dimensionality is 2.
    NULL,    -- other fields are set to NULL.
    SDO_POINT_TYPE  -- Specifies the coordinates of the point
    (
      -87,  -- first ordinate, i.e., value in longitude dimension
      -78,  -- second ordinate, i.e., value in latitude dimension
      NULL  -- third ordinate, if any
    ),
    NULL,
    NULL
  )
);
```

2. Note that the us_restaurants table already exists. So we name this new table us_restaurants_new.

The SDO_GEOMETRY object is instantiated using the object constructor. In this constructor, the first argument, 2001, specifies that it is a two-dimensional point geometry (a line would be represented by 2002, a polygon by 2003, and a collection by 2004).

The fourth argument stores the location of this point in the SDO_POINT attribute using the SDO_POINT_TYPE constructor. Here, we store the geographic coordinates (–87, –78). In this example, the remaining arguments are set to NULL.

Note In Chapter 4, we examine the structure of the SDO_GEOMETRY type in detail and describe how to choose appropriate values for each field of the SDO_GEOMETRY type.

Note that the preceding example shows a single SQL INSERT statement. Data loading can also be performed in bulk using Oracle utilities such as SQL*Loader, Import/Export, or programmatic interfaces such as OCI, OCCI, and JDBC. These utilities and interfaces come in very handy when populating data from GIS vendors or data suppliers.

In some applications, spatial information is not explicitly available as coordinates. Instead, the address data of objects is usually the only spatial information available. You can convert such address data into an SDO_GEOMETRY object using the geocoder component (provided with the Spatial option). The geocoder takes a postal address, consults an internal country-wide database of addresses and locations, and computes the longitude, latitude coordinates for the specified address. This process is referred to as *geocoding* in spatial terminology. The address/location database is usually provided by third-party data vendors. For the United States, Canada, and Europe, NAVTEQ and Tele Atlas provide such data.

Listing 2-3 shows how to use the geocoder to obtain the coordinates in the form of an SDO_GEOMETRY object for the address '3746 CONNECTICUT AVE NW' in Washington, D.C.

Listing 2-3. *Converting Address Data (Implicit Spatial Information) to the* SDO_GEOMETRY *(Explicit Spatial Information) Object*

```
SQL> SELECT
SDO_GCDR.GEOCODE_AS_GEOMETRY
(
   'SPATIAL',                   -- Spatial schema storing the geocoder data
   SDO_KEYWORDARRAY             -- Object combining different address components
   (
     '3746  CONNECTICUT AVE NW',
     'WASHINGTON, DC 20008'
   ),
   'US'                         -- Name of the country
) geom
FROM DUAL ;
```

```
GEOM(SDO_GTYPE, SDO_SRID, SDO_POINT(X, Y, Z), SDO_ELEM_INFO, SDO_ORDINATES)
--------------------------------------------------------------------------
SDO_GEOMETRY
(
   2001,
   8307,
   SDO_POINT_TYPE(-77.060283, 38.9387083, NULL),
   NULL,
   NULL
)
```

This geocoding function, geocode_as_geometry, takes three arguments. The first argument is the schema. In this example, we use the 'spatial' schema. The second argument specifies an SDO_KEYWORDARRAY object, composed from different components of an address. In this example, SDO_KEYWORDARRAY is constructed out of the street component '3746 Connecticut Ave NW' and the city/zip code component 'Washington, DC 20008'. The third argument to the geocoding function specifies the 'US' dataset that is being used to geocode the specified street address. The function returns an SDO_GEOMETRY type with the longitude set to –77.060283 and the latitude set to 38.9387083.

The geocoder can also perform fuzzy matching (via tolerance parameters, which we'll cover in the next chapter). In the same way that search engines can search on related words as well as exact words, Oracle can perform fuzzy matching on the street names and so on. So, for example, suppose the address field in the preceding example was misspelled as 'CONNETICUT AVE'. The geocoder could perform approximate matching to match the misspelled fields with those in the database.

Note that the SDO_GEOMETRY data type is just like any other object type in the database. Users can view the data, and examine and modify the attributes. In contrast, several GIS data vendors and partners have their own proprietary binary formats for representing spatial information. These vendors usually provide tools for loading the data or converting the data into standard Oracle formats. Discussion of these tools, however, is beyond the scope of this book.

Query and Analysis

Now that you've seen how to define SDO_GEOMETRY for storage of spatial data in Oracle, and how to populate Spatial tables with data, the next thing to look at is how to query and analyze this SDO_GEOMETRY data.

The query and analysis component provides the core functionality for querying and analyzing spatial geometries. This component has two subcomponents: a Geometry Engine and an Index Engine. It is via these components that we perform our spatial queries and analysis, for example, to identify the five nearest restaurants along Interstate 795 or the five nearest hospitals to a construction site.

The Geometry Engine

The Geometry Engine provides functions to analyze, compare, and manipulate geometries. For instance, you could use the Geometry Engine functionality to identify the nearest five restaurants on I-795 in the greater Washington, D.C. area. This involves computing the distance between I-795 and all the restaurants in the us_restaurants table, sorting them in order of increasing distance, and returning the top five restaurants. The SQL in Listing 2-4 illustrates this operation.

Listing 2-4. *Finding the Five Nearest Restaurants on I-795*

```
SQL> SELECT poi_name
FROM
  (
    SELECT poi_name,
      SDO_GEOM.SDO_DISTANCE(P.location, I.geom, 0.5) distance
    FROM us_interstates  I, us_restaurants  P
    WHERE I.interstate = 'I795'
      ORDER BY distance
  )
WHERE ROWNUM <= 5;

POI_NAME
-----------------------------------
PIZZA BOLI'S
BLAIR MANSION INN DINNER THEATER
KFC
CHINA HUT
PIZZA HUT

5 rows selected.
```

Observe that the inner SELECT clause computes the distance between I-795 (which is not a major highway) and each "restaurant" row of the us_restaurants table using the Geometry Engine function SDO_GEOM.SDO_DISTANCE. Also, note that the ORDER BY clause sorts the results in ascending order of distance. The outer SELECT statement selects the first five rows, or the five nearest restaurants.

In the preceding query, the location of the I-795 highway is compared with every restaurant row of the table, irrespective of how far they are from I-795. This could mean considerable time is spent in processing rows for restaurants that are too far from the I-795 highway and hence are irrelevant to the query. To speed up query processing by minimizing the processing overhead, we need to create *indexes* on the location of the restaurants.

The Index Engine

Oracle Spatial provides the spatial Index Engine for this purpose. Listing 2-5 shows an example of how to create an index on the locations of restaurants.

Listing 2-5. *Creating an Index on Locations (*`SDO_GEOMETRY` *Column) of Restaurants*

```
SQL> DROP INDEX us_restaurants_sidx;
SQL> CREATE INDEX us_restaurants_sidx ON us_restaurants(location)
INDEXTYPE IS mdsys.spatial_index;
```

Listing 2-5 first drops the index that exists. In the second and third lines, it shows the SQL for creating the spatial index. Note that the clause `INDEXTYPE` tells the database to create a spatial index on the location (`SDO_GEOMETRY`) column of the `us_restaurants` table. This index is a specialized index to cater to the `SDO_GEOMETRY` data. Using such an index, the Index Engine in Oracle Spatial prunes far-away rows from query processing and thus speeds up the query for most applications. The Index Engine provides equivalent functions, referred to as *operators*, for identifying rows of the table that satisfy a specified proximity predicate such as closeness to I-795. You can rewrite the preceding query to find the five nearest restaurants to I-795 using such *index-based operators*. Listing 2-6 shows the resulting query.

Listing 2-6. *Finding the Five Nearest Restaurants on I-795 Using the Spatial Index*

```
SQL> SELECT  poi_name
FROM us_interstates  I,  us_restaurants  P
WHERE I.interstate = 'I795'
  AND SDO_NN(P.location, I.geom) ='TRUE'
  AND ROWNUM <= 5;
POI_NAME
-----------------------------------
PIZZA BOLI'S
BLAIR MANSION INN DINNER THEATER
KFC
CHINA HUT
PIZZA HUT

5 rows selected.
```

Note that this query returns the same five rows as Listing 2-4. However, this query has a simpler structure with no subqueries. It uses only a new index-based operator called `SDO_NN`, with `NN` being short for Nearest-Neighbor. This index-based operator returns rows of the `us_restaurants` table whenever the location column is close to the I-795 highway geometry. The `SDO_NN` operator returns these rows in order of proximity to the I-795 geometry. So, the row with closest location is returned first, the next closest next, and so on. The `ROWNUM` predicate determines how many close restaurants need to be returned in the query. The query uses a spatial index and examines only those rows that are likely to be close to the location of I-795. Consequently, it is likely to execute faster than the query in Listing 2-4.

As a variation on this, suppose that instead of having to find the five nearest restaurants on I-795, you wish to identify all restaurants within 50 kilometers of I-795. One way to accomplish this would be to construct a buffer around the I-795 highway and determine all businesses inside this buffer geometry. Figure 2-2 shows an example. I-795 is shown in black. The 50 km buffer is shown by the gray oval around it, and the restaurants inside this buffer are shown by *x* marks.

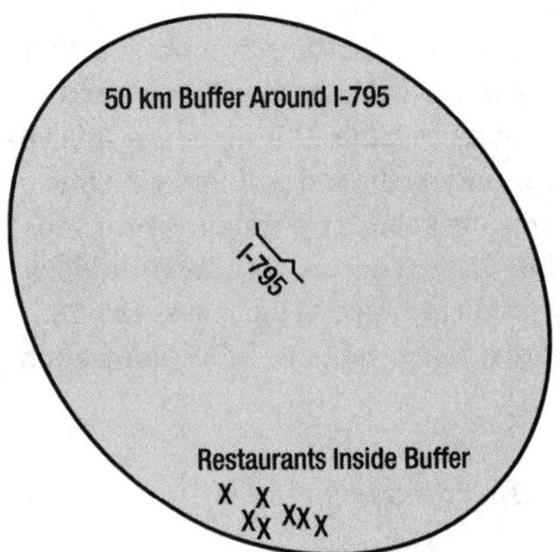

Figure 2-2. *Restaurants in the 50 km buffer around I-795*

Listing 2-7 shows the corresponding SQL query and the results.

Listing 2-7. *Identifying All Restaurants in a 50 km Radius Around I-795*

```
SQL> SELECT POI_NAME
FROM us_interstates I,  us_restaurants P
WHERE
  SDO_ANYINTERACT
  (
    P.location,
    SDO_GEOM.SDO_BUFFER(I.geom, 50, 0.5, 'UNIT=KM')
  ) ='TRUE'
  AND I.interstate='I795' ;
POI_NAME
-----------------------------------
SPICY DELIGHT
PHILLY'S STEAK EXPRESS
EL TAMARINDO
MCDONALD'S
PIZZA HUT
CHINA HUT
KFC
BLAIR MANSION INN DINNER THEATER
PIZZA BOLI'S

9 rows selected.
```

The function SDO_ANYINTERACT is an index-based operator just like the SDO_NN operator in Listing 2-6. This operator identifies all rows of us_restaurants where the locations intersect with the geometry passed in as the second parameter. The second parameter, in this case, is the result returned by an SDO_BUFFER function. The SDO_BUFFER function generates and returns a 50 km buffer around the I-795 geometry. This SDO_BUFFER function is part of the Geometry Engine, which also provides additional functions to facilitate more complex analysis and manipulation of spatial information.

Note that the number of restaurants returned in Listing 2-7 is nine, as opposed to five in Listings 2-4 and 2-6. This means that we may not know the cardinality of the result set when we use a query buffer. With an SDO_ANYINTERACT operator, we may get more answers than we expect, or fewer answers. The cardinality of the result set depends on distribution of the data (in other words, the restaurants). In general, when you know how far to search (for example, a 50 km radius, as in Listing 2-7), you may use the SDO_BUFFER and SDO_ANYINTERACT functions.[3] Alternatively, if you know how many results you wish to return, then you should use the SDO_NN function, as described in Listing 2-6. In Chapters 8 and 9, we will describe in greater detail the different operators and functions in the Index and Geometry Engines.

Visualizing Spatial Data

How do you visualize the results of spatial queries? Oracle technology includes the MapViewer component to facilitate generation of maps from spatial data. Each map is associated with a set of *themes*. Each theme denotes spatial data from a specific table and is associated with a *rendering style*. For instance, you can specify that the interstates theme (data from the INTERSTATES table) should be rendered as thick blue lines. Oracle Spatial provides appropriate dictionary views, USER_SDO_MAPS, USER_SDO_THEMES, and USER_SDO_STYLES, to define new maps, to associate them with themes, and to specify rendering styles for the themes inside the database, respectively.

In addition, MapViewer renders the map for a specified map name. Basically, a servlet consults the database views and retrieves the themes and associated styling rules for a specified map name. Using this information, the MapViewer servlet generates an image of the constructed map. Figure 2-3 shows an image of such a map constructed using MapViewer (constructed entirely using spatial technology and the data provided in this book). This map shows I-795 along with the larger interstates.

3. In Chapter 8, we will describe a better alternative using SDO_WITHIN_DISTANCE operator.

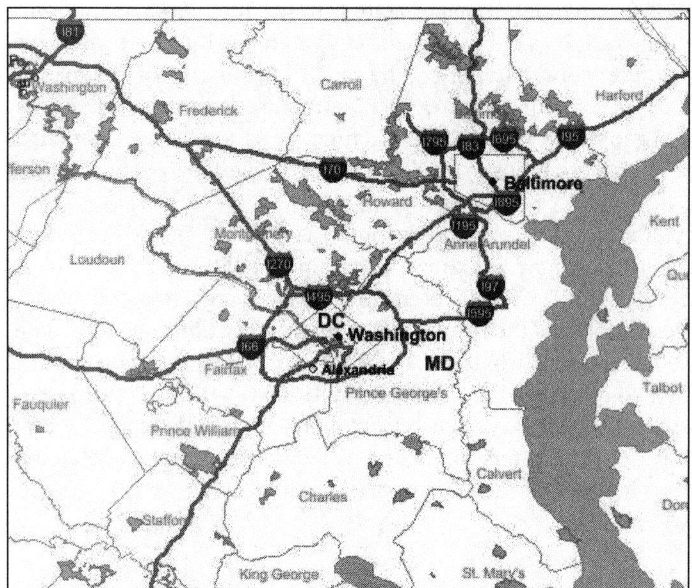

Figure 2-3. *Sample map with multiple themes generated using MapViewer*

The map consists of multiple themes: cities, county boundaries, rivers, interstates, and parks. The cities, D.C. and Baltimore, are rendered as points in black color. The counties, Howard, Fairfax, Charles, Frederick, etc., are shown as white polygons. The river in the right side of the map is shown in a dark grey color. The interstates, such as I-795, are rendered as *line strings* in black, and the parks are rendered as *polygons* in light gray.

Onto this map, we can also superimpose the locations of the five closest restaurants to I-795. In addition to rendering predefined themes/base maps, the MapViewer request can specify a predefined base-map (such as the map in Figure 2-3) and a *dynamic* theme, such as a SQL/JDBC query retrieving the locations of the five nearest restaurants. MapViewer will then generate a new map that contains the locations of the five restaurants superimposed on the predefined base map.

Note that the map in Figure 2-3 displays vector data stored as `SDO_GEOMETRY` columns in different (theme) tables. In addition to vector data, MapViewer can display spatial data stored in the raster (or image) format. Such data is stored in Oracle tables using the `SDO_GEORASTER` data type. Chapter 11 provides full details of how to construct maps and display the results of queries on such maps using MapViewer technology.

Advanced Spatial Engine

The Advanced Spatial Engine has several subcomponents that cater to the complex analysis and manipulation of spatial data that is required in traditional GIS applications.

■Note Our focus in this book is the applicability of Oracle Spatial to Oracle business applications, so we do not cover most of these advanced options, with the exception of the network data model, in great detail. However, we provide a good overview of these topics in the appendixes, with references for further details.

Internally, each of these additional components uses the underlying geometry data type and index and geometry engine functionality.

- The *Network Data Model* provides a data model for storing networks inside the Oracle database. Network elements (links and nodes) can be associated with costs and limits, for example, to model speed limits for road segments. Other functionality includes computation of the shortest path between two locations given a network of road segments, finding the *N* nearest nodes, and so on. The network data model is useful in routing applications. Typical routing applications include web services such as MapQuest and Yahoo! Maps, or navigation applications for roaming users using GPS technology. We cover more details about this component in Chapter 10.
- The *Linear Referencing System* (LRS) facilitates the translation of mile-markers on a highway (or any other linear feature) to geographic coordinate space and vice versa. This component allows users to address different segments of a linear geometry, such as a highway, without actually referring to the coordinates of the segment. This functionality is useful in transportation and utility applications, such as gas pipeline management.
- The *Spatial Analysis and Mining Engine* provides basic functionality for combining demographic and spatial analysis. This functionality is useful in identifying prospective sites for starting new stores based on customer density and income. These tools can also be used to materialize the influence of the neighborhood, which in turn can be used in improving the efficacy and predictive power of the Oracle Data Mining Engine.
- *GeoRaster* facilitates the storage and retrieval of georeferenced images using their spatial footprints and the associated metadata. GeoRaster defines a new data type for storing raster images of geographically referenced objects. This functionality is useful in the management of satellite imagery.
- The *Topology Data Model* supports detailed analysis and manipulation of spatial geometry data using finer topological elements such as nodes and edges. In some land-management applications, geometries share boundaries, as in the case of a property boundary and the road on which the property is situated. Oracle Spatial defines a new data type to represent topological elements (such as the shared "road segment") that can be shared between different spatial objects. Updates to shared elements implicitly define updates to the sharing geometry objects. In general, this component allows for the editing and manipulation of nodes and edges without disturbing the topological semantics of the application.

Oracle Spatial Technology Products

In the previous sections, we briefly described the functionality that Oracle Spatial provides to support the following operations on spatial data:

- Storage data model using the SDO_GEOMETRY data type
- Query and analysis using the Index Engine and Geometry Engine
- Location enabling using the geocoder by conversion of address data into SDO_GEOMETRY data
- Visualization using MapViewer
- Advanced Spatial Engine functionality such as network analysis

Let's next look at how this functionality is productized or licensed in Oracle Database 10g, version 10.1.0.2, and Oracle Application Server 10g, version 9.0.4. Note, though, that this packaging may change with later versions of Oracle.

MapViewer, the visualization tool of Spatial, is included as part of the Oracle Application Server. You can also deploy MapViewer by just installing the Oracle Containers for Java (OC4J) without installing the entire Application Server. We will look at these details in Chapter 11. The remainder of the Spatial functionality is included, sometimes optionally, with the Database Server. Let's look at these details next.

In the Lite edition of Oracle Database Server, none of the spatial functionality is included. As mentioned in an earlier Note, in the Personal, Standard,[4] and Enterprise editions, a *subset* of the spatial functionality is included for free with the database. This subset is referred to as the *Locator*. In the Personal and the Enterprise Editions, the full functionality of spatial technology is available as a *priced* option, called *Spatial*. Let's look at each of these versions of Oracle Spatial and what you can do with them.

Locator

Locator provides a *core* subset of spatial functionality to cater to specific applications. Specifically, it includes the following functionality:

- *The data model for storing spatial data using the* SDO_GEOMETRY *data type*: This includes storing all types of geometries (points, lines, polygons, and so on).
- *Query and analysis using the Index Engine*: This includes creating spatial indexes and querying using associated spatial operators like SDO_NN.
- *The* SDO_GEOM.SDO_DISTANCE *and the* SDO_GEOM.VALIDATE_GEOMETRY_XXX *functions*: These functions are also part of Locator.

Figure 2-4 shows the functionality provided in Locator. The Locator components are highlighted in black. The non-Locator components of Spatial technology are shown in solid gray.

4. "Standard" implies both Standard Edition One and Standard Edition.

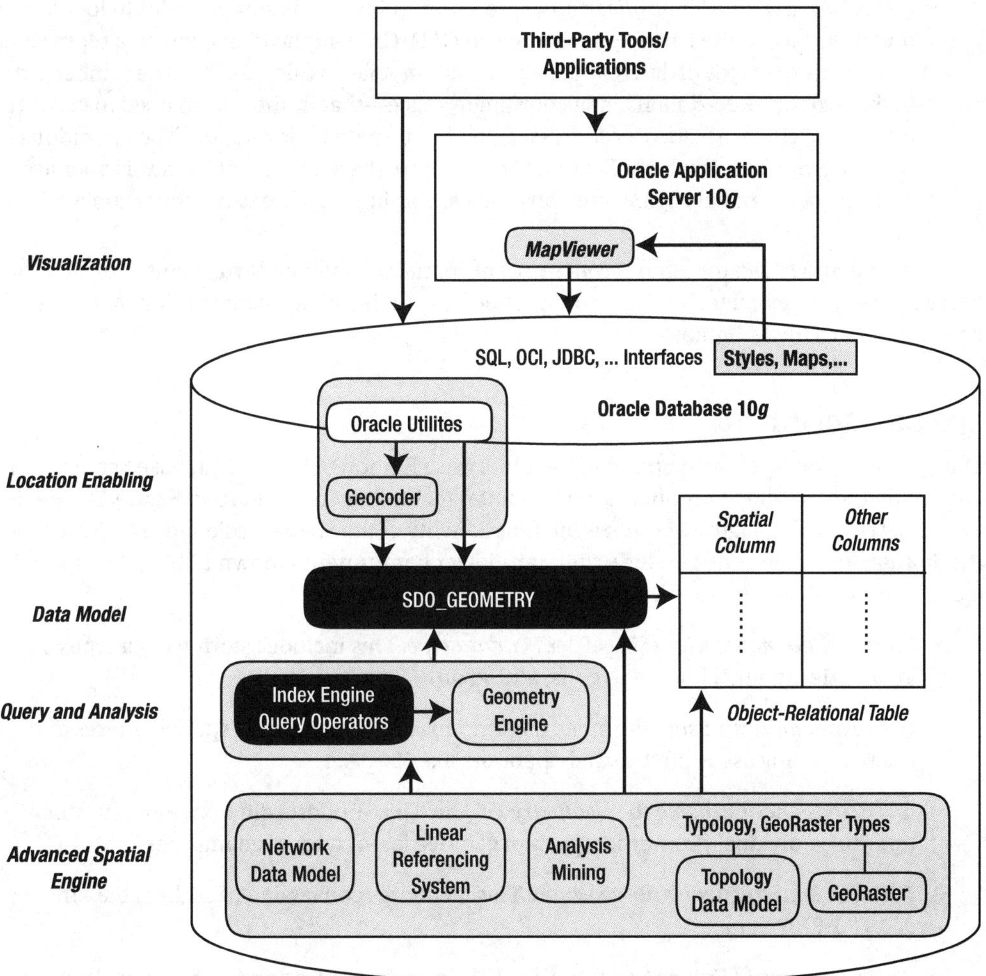

Figure 2-4. *The functionality of Locator, the free part of Spatial technology, is shown in black ovals.*

Applications that use Locator may need to use third-party geocoding services to convert addresses in application tables. After storing the spatial locations as `SDO_GEOMETRY` columns, Locator enables a variety of spatial queries, such as identification of customers within a specified sales territory or the nearest ATM to a specific location. Locator is typically used in the following applications:

- *Simple GIS applications*, which may just work with geographic data such as state, city, or property boundaries and index-based query using associated spatial operators. Typically, though, most GIS applications may need the Geometry Engine functionality (which is not supported in Locator).

- *Simple business applications*, where the spatial data is obtained from third-party vendors. As you will see in Chapter 8, the index-based operators supported in Locator can perform a great deal of analysis in business applications.

- *CAD/CAM and similar applications*, where the spatial data does not refer to locations on the surface of the Earth. For instance, in CAD/CAM applications, the data represents the structure/shapes of different parts of an automobile. In this case, the data is inherently in the two- or three-dimensional coordinate space—that is, there is no need to convert nonspatial columns (such as addresses) to obtain spatial information. The operations that are needed for such applications are the index-based proximity analysis operators. The advanced spatial engine functions such as routing are of no use in these applications.

To summarize, Locator offers a *core subset* of spatial technology. If you want to exploit the full feature-set of spatial technology, you will need to purchase the Spatial option in the Enterprise Edition of Oracle Database.

Spatial Option

The Spatial option is a priced option of the Enterprise Edition of Oracle Database Server. This option includes all the components of the spatial technology referred to in Figure 2-4 and is a superset of Locator. Figure 2-5 shows the functionality of the Spatial option in gray. Note that the Spatial option does not include the MapViewer component (shown in black) of spatial technology. The Spatial option consists of

- *Storage data model using* `SDO_GEOMETRY` *data type*: This includes storing of all types of geometries (points, lines, polygons, and so on).
- *Query and analysis using the Index Engine*: This includes creating spatial indexes and querying using associated spatial operators like `SDO_NN`.
- *Query and analysis using the Geometry Engine*: This supports different analysis functions for individual geometries, pairs of geometries, or a set of geometries.
- *Location enabling using the geocoder*: This facilitates conversion of address data into `SDO_GEOMETRY` data.
- *Advanced Spatial Engine functionality*: This includes routing and network analysis.

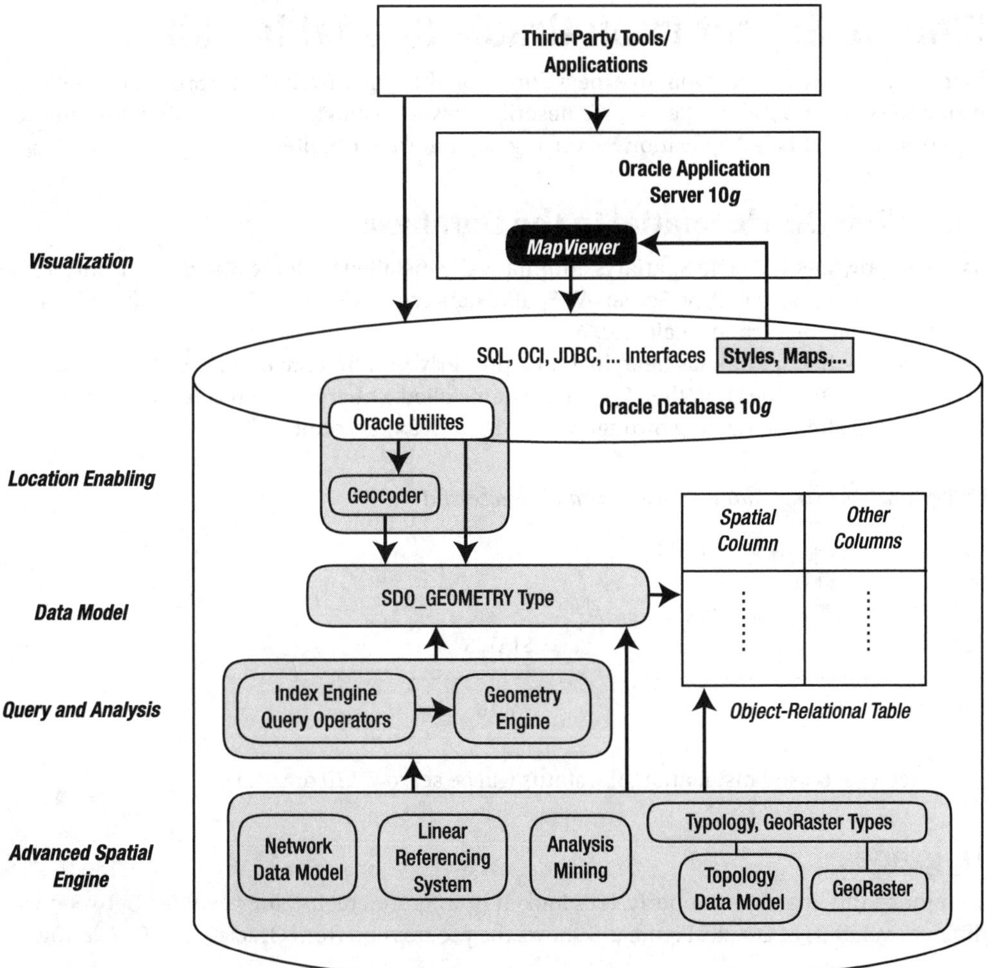

Figure 2-5. *The functionality of the Spatial option is shown in gray.*

A wide variety of applications can use the full set of functionality provided in the Spatial option.

By now, you should have a good idea of how Oracle Spatial functionality is packaged. This understanding is helpful in determining whether or not your application needs to license the full set of spatial functionality using the Spatial option. For the remainder of this book, we will not differentiate or explicitly refer to Locator and Spatial option products. Instead, we will refer to the entire set of functionality as "Oracle Spatial technology" or simply as "Oracle Spatial."

What to Expect in an Oracle Spatial Install

In this section, we discuss what to expect during or after you install Oracle Spatial technology inside the Oracle Database Server. We describe how to install the MapViewer component, which is part of Oracle Application Server 10g, separately in Chapter 11.

Installing Oracle Spatial in the Database

As noted previously, Oracle Spatial is automatically installed with the Standard or Enterprise Edition of an Oracle Database Server. All Spatial data types, views, packages, and functions are installed as part of a schema called `MDSYS`.

To verify that Spatial has been installed properly, you first have to check that the `MDSYS` account exists. If it does not, then Spatial is not installed. Otherwise, you can execute the SQL in Listing 2-8 after connecting through your `SYS (SYSDBA)` account.

Listing 2-8. *Verifying That a Spatial Install Is Successful*

```
SQL> SELECT COMP_NAME, STATUS
FROM DBA_REGISTRY
WHERE COMP_NAME = 'Spatial';
COMP_NAME                              STATUS
-----------------------------          -----------
Spatial                                VALID
```

After a successful installation, the status will be set to `VALID` or `LOADED`.

Upgrades

To understand upgrades properly, let's look at how Spatial technology evolved between different versions of Oracle. Figure 2-6 shows the progression from Oracle 7.2 to Oracle 10g.

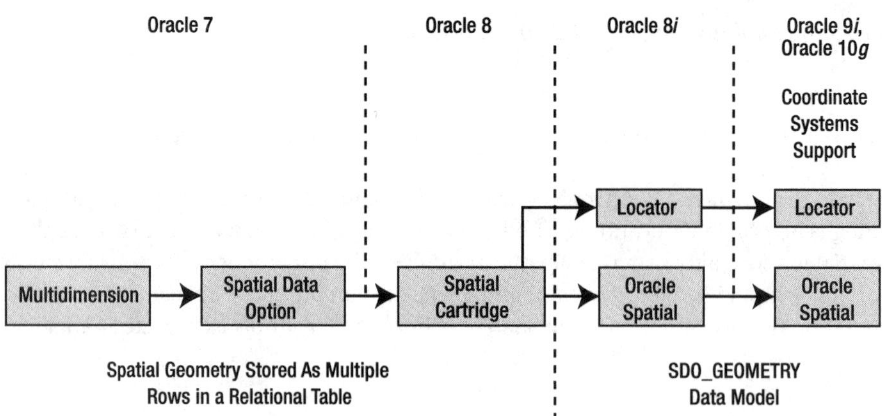

Figure 2-6. *Evolution of Spatial technology in Oracle*

Spatial technology was first introduced in Oracle 7.2 under the name *Oracle MultiDimension* (MD). Later, the product name was changed to *Oracle Spatial Data Option* (or SDO) and to *Spatial Data Cartridge* in Oracle 8. Since objects were not supported in these releases, the coordinates of a geometry were stored as multiple rows in an associated table. Managing spatial (geometry) data in these prior versions was inefficient and cumbersome.

Starting with Oracle8*i*, the `SDO_GEOMETRY` data type was introduced to store spatial data. Even in Oracle 10*g*, the same `SDO_GEOMETRY` model is used to store spatial data in Oracle. In Oracle9*i* (and Oracle 10*g*), the geometry data also included support for coordinate systems information specified using the `SRID` attribute in the `SDO_GEOMETRY` data type. In Oracle 10*g*, additional functionality (that exists in the Advanced Spatial Engine) such as the Network Data Model is introduced in the Spatial option of Oracle.

Since the prior versions are named MultiDimension (MD) and Spatial Data Option (SDO), you will see the prefixes `MD` and `SDO` for the files and schemas that install Spatial technology. The name of the spatial install schema is `MDSYS` in all versions of Oracle.

In spite of the evolution of Spatial technology with each release, upgrading to the latest version, Oracle 10*g*, is not difficult. *Spatial technology is automatically upgraded with the upgrade of Oracle Database Server.* The upgrade may not need your intervention at all.[5] However, if you are upgrading from pre-8*i* releases, you need to additionally migrate your geometry data from the pre-8*i* format to the `SDO_GEOMETRY` data model. Oracle Spatial provides the `SDO_MIGRATE` package to migrate the data from pre-8*i* models to the current `SDO_GEOMETRY` data model. We discuss this migration package's functionality in Chapter 5.

Understanding a Spatial Install

In this section, we cover where to find appropriate spatial files and how to perform some preliminary investigation when an installation or upgrade fails.

To view all the spatial files, you can go to the `$ORACLE_HOME/md/admin` directory. In this directory, you will find all files relevant to Oracle Spatial. You will observe that a majority of the files have a prefix of either `SDO` or `PRVT`. In other words, the files are of the form `sdoxxxx.sql` or `prvtxxxx.plb`. The `SDO` files, in most cases, contain package definitions for different components of Spatial technology. The `PRVT` files, on the other hand, are binary files and define the package bodies and so on.[6] You should not tamper with these `SDO` and `PRVT` files at any time.

During the creation of the database,[7] the `MDSYS` account is created with appropriate privileges (see scripts `mdinst.sql` and `mdprivs.sql` for more details) and the `catmd.sql` file is loaded into the `MDSYS` schema. This file loads all the `SDO` and `PRVT` files in an appropriate order that resolves all dependencies between all the Spatial packages. In the case of Locator, `catmdloc.sql` (instead of `catmd.sql`) is loaded. Likewise, appropriate files in this directory such as `sdodbmig.sql` or `sdopatch.sql` are loaded/executed at the time of upgrades, downgrades, and patches.

---

5. Note that some spatial components such as GeoRaster have dependencies on other Oracle components such as interMedia and XML. You need to ensure that these components are also upgraded properly or installed if they do not exist in a custom install.
6. Most functions in these package bodies are linked to C/Java libraries that are included with the Oracle kernel.
7. The database can be created either at install time or using a variety of Oracle tools such as DBCA.

During some installations or upgrades, you may find that several package dependencies are unresolved and hence invalid. You may check for such invalid packages or other objects in your Spatial installation by running the SQL in Listing 2-9.

Listing 2-9. *Checking for Invalid Objects in a Spatial Installation*

```
SQL> SELECT OBJECT_NAME, OBJECT_TYPE, STATUS
FROM ALL_OBJECTS
WHERE OWNER='MDSYS'  AND STATUS <> 'VALID'
ORDER BY OBJECT_NAME;
```

If Listing 2-9 returns any rows, you should contact Oracle Support for troubleshooting help.

Summary

This chapter provided a brief overview of the various components of Oracle Spatial technology. First, we examined the functionality provided in Oracle Spatial. This functionality included a SQL-level data type for storing spatial data, new operators and functions to perform spatial query and analysis, a MapViewer tool for visualizing spatial data, and advanced components to perform more sophisticated analysis such as routing or network analysis. We then described how this functionality is packaged in the Database and Application Servers. Finally, we described what to expect in a typical Spatial installation and where to find appropriate Spatial files.

Starting with the next chapter, we will look at Oracle Spatial functionality in more detail. Specifically in Chapter 3, we describe how to location-enable your application.

CHAPTER 3

Location-Enabling Your Applications

To run the examples in this chapter, you need to import a dataset in the `spatial` schema as follows. Please refer to the Introduction for instructions on creating the `spatial` schema and other setup details.

```
imp spatial/spatial file=gc.dmp ignore=y full=y
```

Consider a business application that stores information about its branches (or stores), customers, competitors, suppliers, and so on. If we location-enable such a business application, we can perform the following types of analysis:

- *Spatial query and analysis*: Identify the number of customers in different sales territories of a branch of this business or a competitor.
- *Network/routing analysis*: Compute the route between a branch and the nearest customer or the supplier.
- *Visualization*: Display the results of spatial query or network analysis on a map and integrate this map in other components of the business application.

In order to exploit the benefits of the above types of analysis in a business application, you will first need to location-enable your application. In this chapter, we describe how to augment existing application tables with location information. This location information is usually derived from the address components in application tables such as customers, branches, and competitors, and is stored as point locations in these tables. Such location-enabling of the application tables allows simple spatial analysis. Such analysis is described in Chapter 8.

You can further this analysis, as described in Chapters 8 and 9, by combining the application data with geographic data such as street networks, city boundaries, etc. The street networks and city boundaries are more complex than the location information in application tables. Such street networks and city boundaries (i.e., the geographic data) need to be stored as lines, polygons, and other complex geometry types. We describe several design choices to consider while storing such geographic data in Oracle tables. This geographic data will aid in a more comprehensive analysis for a business application.

After setting up the application and geographic data tables, we need to insert spatial-specific metadata to location-enable these tables for subsequent analysis. In the last section of this chapter, we discuss how to populate this metadata into appropriate dictionary views for each table that contains spatial data.

Adding Location Information to Tables

Most application data can be categorized into two sets of tables:

- *Application-specific tables*: These contain information that is specific to the application (product and customer information, and so on). Application tables will use standard normalization techniques to arrive at an appropriate set of tables to store the data. These tables might not contain explicit spatial data. However, these tables may have implicit spatial information in the form of addresses.
- *Geographic tables*: Geographic data is independent of the application and contain columns to store explicit spatial information for street networks, city boundaries, and so on. This data may be used as a value-add in the application.

Figure 3-1 shows an example of these two sets of tables for a sample business application. We will use this application along with the associated tables to illustrate all the concepts in this book. Appendix D has appropriate instructions for loading these data.

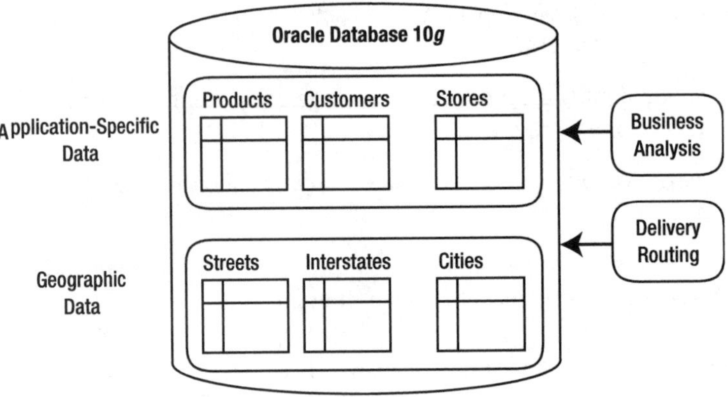

Figure 3-1. *Data for the sample application*

Application-Specific Data

As discussed earlier, for application-specific data, standard normalization rules may be employed to design a set of application tables best suited to the needs of the application. Let's assume that, via this design process, we arrive at the following set of tables for the application layer:

- A `products` table to hold information about all available products
- A `customers` table to hold information about customers
- A `suppliers` table to hold information about suppliers

- A branches table to hold information about different branch locations of a business franchise (corresponding to the business application)
- A competitors table to hold information about competitors of the business franchise

These tables can be created with appropriate attributes. Listing 3-1 shows the sample SQL for creating the customers table. Other tables such as branches, competitors, and products may likewise be created. Note that the customers table does not, at this stage, have an explicit column that stores spatial information. The same may apply to other tables in the application that store application-specific data.

Listing 3-1. *Creating the* customers *Table*

```
SQL> CREATE TABLE customers
(
  id                                NUMBER,
  datasrc_id                        NUMBER,
  name                              VARCHAR2(35),
  category                          VARCHAR2(30),
  street_number                     VARCHAR2(5),
  street_name                       VARCHAR2(60),
  city                              VARCHAR2(32),
  postal_code                       VARCHAR2(16),
  state                             VARCHAR2(32),
  phone_number                      VARCHAR2(15),
  customer_grade                    VARCHAR2(15)
);
```

These tables may be populated using SQL INSERT statements or other loading tools such as SQL*Loader. Listing 3-2 shows an example.

Listing 3-2. *Populating the* customers *Table*

```
SQL> INSERT INTO customers VALUES
(
  1,                                -- id
  1,                                -- datasrc_id
  'Pizza Hut' ,                     -- name
  'Restaurant',                     -- restaurant
  '134',                            -- street_number
  '12TH STREET',                     -- street_name
  'WASHINGTON',                     -- city
  '20003',                          -- postal_code
  'DC',                             -- state
  NULL,                             -- phone_number
  'GOLD'                            -- customer_grade
);
```

At a fundamental level, to location-enable this business application, we need to store location information for customers, branches, competitors, and so on. This means we need to augment the corresponding tables with an additional column for storing location. This basic location information is stored as a point, using the SDO_GEOMETRY type.

For example, to add location information to the customers table, we simply alter it as shown in Listing 3-3.

Listing 3-3. *Adding a* location *Column to the* customers *Table*

```
SQL> ALTER TABLE customers  ADD (location SDO_GEOMETRY);
```

This, by itself, does not populate the location column. If you select the location column in the table, you will observe that it contains only null values.

The most common way to populate the location columns in the application tables is by *geocoding* the appropriate address columns. Figure 3-2 illustrates the geocoding process. A variety of tools from different vendors support this geocoding.

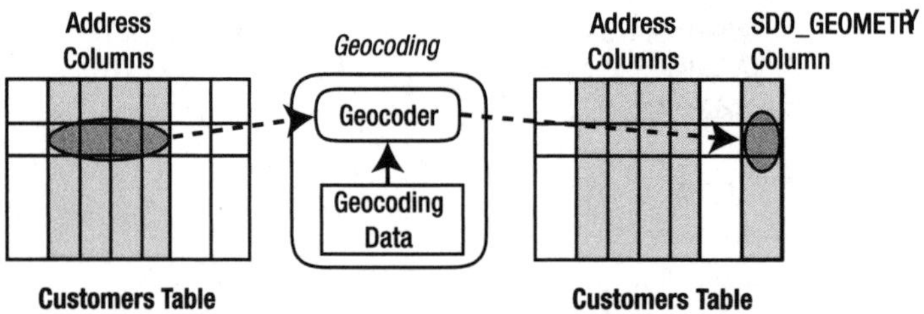

Figure 3-2. *Geocoding application data to populate* SDO_GEOMETRY *columns*

As shown in Figure 3-2, these tools consult an internal database to determine the longitude and latitude values for a specified address. These <longitude, latitude> pairs can then be stored as a point geometry using the SDO_GEOMETRY data type. Oracle Spatial provides a built-in geocoding tool for translating addresses (implicit spatial information) into SDO_GEOMETRY objects.

For instance, let's say the customers, suppliers, branches, and competitors tables do store address information. This address is typically stored using the following attributes: street_number (or Apt#), street_name, city, and postal_code, all of the VARCHAR2 data type. Listing 3-4 shows the address information from the customers table for a specific customer.

Listing 3-4. *Sample Address for a Specific Customer in the* customers *Table*

```
SQL> SELECT street_number, street_name, city, state, postal_code
FROM customers
WHERE id = 1;
134   12TH ST SE   WASHINGTON  DC  20003
```

Oracle Spatial allows you to convert this address (street_number, street_name, city, and postal_code) into a two-dimensional point location on the surface of the Earth. The specific function that you need is called sdo_gcdr.geocode_as_geometry. This function takes the schema name and the geocoding dataset name as the first and the last arguments. The second argument is an sdo_keywordarray object constructed out of the address components street_number, street_name, city, and postal_code. You will learn more about the details of this function in Chapter 6. For now, it is sufficient to note that the simple SQL statement in Listing 3-5 will do the trick.

Listing 3-5. *Geocoding Addresses to Obtain Explicit Spatial Information*

```
SQL> UPDATE customers
  SET location =
  SDO_GCDR.GEOCODE_AS_GEOMETRY
  (
    'SPATIAL',
    SDO_KEYWORDARRAY
    (
      street_number || ` ` || street_name,
      city  || `, ` || state || ` `  || postal_code
    ),
    'US'
  ) ;
```

We can now examine what the location information looks like. We will simply select the location column from the customers table. Listing 3-6 shows the SQL to do this.

Listing 3-6. *Geocoded* location *Column in the* customers *Table*

```
SQL> SELECT location
FROM customers
WHERE id=1;

LOCATION(SDO_GTYPE, SDO_SRID, SDO_POINT(X, Y, Z), SDO_ELEM_INFO, SDO_ORDINATES)
--------------------------------------------------------------------
SDO_GEOMETRY(2001, 8307, SDO_POINT_TYPE(-76.99022, 38.888654,  NULL), NULL, NULL)
```

Notice that the specified address (street_number='134', street_name='12th ST SE', city='WASHINGTON', and postal_code='20003') translates to an SDO_GEOMETRY object with longitude and latitude values of –76.99 and 38.889 in the sdo_point attribute (instantiated using the SDO_POINT_TYPE object). The sdo_gtype value of 2001 indicates that the location is a *two*-dimensional (*2* in 2001) *point* (*1* in 200*1*) location. We will look at other attributes of the location column in the next chapter.

■ Caution Coordinate positions are commonly referred to as "latitude/longitude." However, in Oracle Spatial, the coordinates are stored as longitude followed by latitude.

Once an SDO_GEOMETRY object is constructed, we can insert it, update it, and query it just like any other column in an Oracle table. For instance, we can update the location column directly by constructing a geometry object using an SDO_GEOMETRY constructor, as shown in Listing 3-7.

Listing 3-7. *Updating a* location *Column Using an* SDO_GEOMETRY *Constructor*

```
SQL> UPDATE customers
SET location =
  SDO_GEOMETRY
  (
    2001,                                  -- Specify that location is a point
    8307,                                  -- Specify coordinate system id
    SDO_POINT_TYPE(-77.06, 38.94, NULL),   -- Specify coordinates here
    NULL,
    NULL
  )
WHERE id=1;
```

Once we have basic location data for the application tables, such as customers, branches, and suppliers, we can perform some basic proximity analysis (using SQL-level queries on SDO_GEOMETRY columns; this is covered in Chapters 8 and 9). For instance, we can identify the following:

- Customers close to (for example, within a quarter-mile of) a competitor store. For all such customers, we can do some promotion to wean them from our competitor or retain them.

- How many customers are within a quarter-mile of each store or delivery site. Some store sites may be overloaded, and we need to start new store sites at appropriate places.

Design Considerations for Application-Specific Data

As noted, the organization of application-specific data into appropriate tables will be application dependent and will probably involve standard design techniques such as normalization, entity-relationship (ER) diagram-based modeling, and so on. Oracle Spatial does not have any specific recommendations or restrictions for how the application data is to be organized.

One point we can emphasize here, though, is that you should strongly consider table partitioning when table data runs into millions of rows. Consider, for example, the customers data for an entire country. These customers share the same attributes. As a result, normalization and other modeling techniques may recommend storing all customers in a single table. However, for spatial applications, the number of customers may be high, running into tens of millions or billions.

In such cases, where the access patterns for the table in question can be tied to a nonspatial attribute (such as city or postal_code), then partitioning the customers table based on the city or postal_code attribute can ensure good performance and at the same time present a single table on which to operate.

Note Table partitioning in Oracle is an option in the Enterprise Edition of Oracle (it is not available in the Standard Edition).

Partitioning may help in effective and efficient management of large tables. In addition, it may also improve the efficiency of spatial analysis operations, by using partition pruning whenever the partition key is specified in the SQL query. We will look at such analysis examples with partitioned tables in Chapter 8.

Geographic Data

To perform more sophisticated analysis such as routing between two locations or visualization using regional maps, we need to store more than just locations of customers and branches. We may need geographic data such as street networks, city boundaries, and so on. For example, to identify routes from delivery sites to customer locations, we need to store additional information that describes the street network. Likewise, if we want to be able to accurately visualize the locations stored in application tables on a *map*, then we need to display the boundaries of not just streets and cities, but also rivers, national parks, and so on.

Such geographic data is usually available from a variety of sources, including commercial GIS vendors and national mapping agencies. NAVTEQ and Tele Atlas are two such vendors, and both sell geographic data for the United States and Europe. The Ordnance Survey is the national mapping agency for Great Britain: it supplies a highly detailed coverage of Great Britain called MapsterMap. The U.S. Census Bureau is a similar organization serving the United States. Appendix D has details to load different components of this geographic data to enable network analysis, geocoding, and map-based visualization. In the following sections, we describe the general guidelines for storing and modeling the geographic data inside the database.

To enable effective integration and analysis, the geographic data, just like the application-specific data, needs to be stored inside the database. This means that we need to be able to store a range of different types of data. For example, a street network might be represented by a set of lines connecting different two-dimensional points. Likewise, a city boundary might be represented by a polygon connected by lines. We can represent these types of spatial data using the same SDO_GEOMETRY data type that is also used to represent the customer locations (point data) in the application-specific tables. Use of a single data type to store all sorts of spatial data ensures a seamless integration and analysis of spatial data in business applications.

Design Considerations for Geographic Data

The next question that arises is how to best store the geographic data. We will illustrate the concepts using typical geographic data (the actual tables used in the book will be directly loaded by importing the appropriate dmp files as discussed in the Introduction). Each type of geographic data may have the following attributes:

- *States*: Attributes may include the state name, the abbreviation of the state name, the population of the state, average household income, and the boundary of the state (the latter of these being stored in an SDO_GEOMETRY object).
- *Counties*: Attributes may include the county name, the state name in which the county belongs, the land area, the population per square mile, and an SDO_GEOMETRY object to store the boundary of the county.

- *Interstates*: Attributes may include the name and an SDO_GEOMETRY object to store the linear shape of the interstate.
- *Streets*: Attributes may include the name, the city, the state, and an SDO_GEOMETRY object to store the linear shape of the street.

Storage of streets, interstates, counties, and states in a single table is likely to be inefficient (it may slow down subsequent analysis) and should be avoided. You should store this data in different tables, based on the following general criteria:

1. *Separate spatial data that does not share the same attributes*: This is similar to normalization techniques used for regular data. For instance, the `states` will have different attributes from the `counties`, `streets`, or `interstates` data.
2. *Separate coarser data from finer data*: Streets and interstates both represent linear shapes. Sometimes, they may even share the same set of attributes. But interstates tend to go across multiple states, whereas streets tend to be localized to a specific city or region. Since the number of streets is likely to be much larger than the number of interstates, storing streets and interstates in the same table may cause performance problems when you wish to access just the interstate data. Conversely, the large size of the interstates may pose performance problems when you query for the street data.
3. *Separate based on the shape of the geometry*: If you separate out spatial data based on the geometric shape—in other words, based on whether it is a point, a line, or a polygon—then you can use the type-checking mechanisms provided by Oracle Spatial indexes at insertion time. For example, if you created a spatial index and specified that a table had only points, the index would raise an error if it encountered nonpoint geometry in the table. Spatial indexes can perform better if they know what type of geometry to expect in a table. We will discuss these features of spatial indexes in Chapter 5.
4. *Partition localized data*: Consider the street data for an entire country. The streets share the same attributes and are also at the same resolution level. Based on the previous three criteria, we might store all the streets in the same table. However, due the large number of the rows in this table, the application may benefit from partitioning this table. We will discuss the actual benefits in Chapter 8.

Based on the preceding criteria, we can divide the geographic data, discussed at the beginning of this section, into multiple tables. First, since states have different attributes from other geometries (criterion 1), we create a separate `us_states` table as shown in Listing 3-8.

Listing 3-8. *Creating the* `us_states` *Table*

```
SQL> CREATE TABLE us_states
(
  state                         VARCHAR2(26),
  state_abrv                    VARCHAR2(2),
  totpop                        NUMBER,
  landsqmi                      NUMBER,
  poppssqmi                     NUMBER,
```

```
  medage                            NUMBER,
  medhhinc                          NUMBER,
  avghhinc                          NUMBER,
  geom                              SDO_GEOMETRY
);
```

Likewise, we can separate out the county data from the rest, as shown in Listing 3-9.

Listing 3-9. *Creating the* `us_counties` *Table*

```
SQL> CREATE TABLE us_counties
(
  id                                NUMBER NOT NULL,
  county                            VARCHAR2(31),
  state                             VARCHAR2(30),
  state_abrv                        VARCHAR2(2),
  landsqmia                         NUMBER,
  totpop                            NUMBER,
  poppsqmi                          NUMBER,
  geom                              SDO_GEOMETRY
);
```

Now we have the streets and the interstates, both of which have the same attributes. However, based on criterion 2, we store them as separate tables, as shown in Listing 3-10.

Listing 3-10. *Creating the* `us_interstates` *Table*

```
SQL> CREATE TABLE us_interstates
(
  id                                NUMBER,
  interstate                        VARCHAR2(35),
  geom                              SDO_GEOMETRY
);
SQL> CREATE TABLE us_streets
(
  id                                NUMBER,
  street_name                       VARCHAR2(35),
  city                              VARCHAR2(32),
  state                             VARCHAR2(32),
  geom                              SDO_GEOMETRY
);
```

Until now, we have described how to location-enable the application-specific tables. We have also discussed how to set up geographic data as regular Oracle tables. This involved creating appropriate tables with a column of the `SDO_GEOMETRY` type to store associated spatial information. We can populate these tables by either geocoding address data, as we will discuss in Chapter 6, or by using appropriate loading tools, as we will discuss in Chapter 5.

In addition to separating the application-specific data and geographic data into appropriate tables, we also need to specify additional information called *metadata* to location-enable the application. This metadata is used in a variety of spatial functions, such as validation, indexing, and querying of spatial data (as you will see in subsequent chapters).

Metadata for Spatial Tables

Spatial treats all the objects in a single SDO_GEOMETRY column of a table as a *spatial layer*. For instance, the geometry objects stored in the location column of the customers table are treated as a spatial layer.

To perform validation, index creation, and querying with respect to each spatial layer (in other words, all the geometry objects in a specific SDO_GEOMETRY column of a table), you need to specify the appropriate metadata for each layer. This will include the following information:

- The number of dimensions
- The bounds for each dimension
- The tolerance for each dimension (which will be explained later)
- The coordinate system (which will also be explained later)

This information for each spatial layer is populated in the USER_SDO_GEOM_METADATA dictionary view.

Dictionary View for Spatial Metadata

Oracle Spatial provides the USER_SDO_GEOM_METADATA dictionary view to store metadata for spatial layers. This metadata view has the structure shown in Listing 3-11.

Listing 3-11. *The* USER_SDO_GEOM_METADATA *View*

```
SQL> DESCRIBE USER_SDO_GEOM_METADATA;
Name                                      Null?      Type
 -------------------------------------   ---------- ------------------
TABLE_NAME                                NOT NULL   VARCHAR2(32)
COLUMN_NAME                               NOT NULL   VARCHAR2(1024)
DIMINFO                                              MDSYS.SDO_DIM_ARRAY
SRID                                                 NUMBER
```

Together, the TABLE_NAME and COLUMN_NAME columns uniquely identify each spatial layer. For the identified layer, the metadata stores information about the individual dimensions for the layer in the DIMINFO attribute. The information about the coordinate system of the geometry data is stored in the SRID attribute. We will discuss how to choose the SRID attribute in more detail in Chapter 4, but we will briefly describe it here before moving on to examine the DIMINFO attribute.

Note The TABLE_NAME and the COLUMN_NAME values are always converted to uppercase when you insert them into the USER_SDO_GEOM_METADATA view.

SRID Attribute

This attribute specifies the *coordinate system* in which the data in the spatial layer is stored. The coordinate system could be one of the following:

- *Geodetic:* Angular coordinates, expressed in terms of longitude, latitude with respect to the Earth's surface.
- *Projected:* Cartesian coordinates that result from performing a mathematical mapping from an area on the Earth's surface to a plane.
- *Local*: Cartesian coordinate systems with no link to the Earth's surface and sometimes specific to an application. These are used in CAD/CAM and other applications where the spatial data does not pertain to locations on the Earth.

Different geodetic and projected coordinate systems are devised to maximize the accuracy (of distances and other spatial relationship calculations) for different parts/regions of the world. We will describe coordinate systems in detail in Chapter 4.

In the case of geodetic coordinate systems, you can consult the MDSYS.CS_SRS table for possible values by selecting rows where the WKTEXT column[1] starts with a prefix of 'GEOGCS'. Listing 3-12 shows the SQL.

Listing 3-12. *Selecting* SRIDs *of Geodetic Coordinate Systems*

```
SQL> SELECT SRID
FROM MDSYS.CS_SRS
WHERE WKTEXT LIKE 'GEOGCS%';
```

As shown in Listing 3-13, you can select the SRIDs for the projected coordinate system from the MDSYS.CS_SRS table by searching for rows where the WKTEXT column starts with 'PROJCS'. Analogously, the SRIDs for local coordinate systems can be found by searching for the prefix 'LOCAL_CS' in the WKTEXT column of the MDSYS.CS_SRS table.

Listing 3-13. *Selecting* SRIDs *of Projected Coordinate Systems*

```
SQL> SELECT SRID
FROM MDSYS.CS_SRS
WHERE WKTEXT LIKE 'PROJCS%';
```

In most cases, you don't have to choose the coordinate system. Instead, you obtain the geometry data from a third-party vendor, and the SRID is already populated in these geometries.

1. The wktext column stores the "well-known text" for a coordinate system. This is explained in detail in Chapter 4.

■ **Caution** If the coordinate system is geodetic (i.e., the SRID corresponds to one of the values in the MDSYS.GEODETIC_SRIDS table), then the dimensions in the DIMINFO attribute are always longitude and latitude. The first element in the DIMINFO attribute should always specify the dimension information for the longitude column, and the second element should always specify the information for the latitude dimension.

DIMINFO Attribute

Spatial data is multidimensional in nature. For example, the location column in the customers table of our business application has two dimensions: longitude and latitude (see Listing 3-3). The DIMINFO attribute in USER_SDO_GEOM_METADATA specifies information about each dimension of the specified layer. The DIMINFO attribute is of type MDSYS.SDO_DIM_ARRAY. Listing 3-14 shows this structure.

Listing 3-14. *The* SDO_DIM_ARRAY *Structure*

```
SQL> DESCRIBE SDO_DIM_ARRAY;
 SDO_DIM_ARRAY VARRAY(4) OF MDSYS.SDO_DIM_ELEMENT
 Name                          Null?         Type
 ----------------------- ----------- --------------
SDO_DIMNAME                                 VARCHAR2(64)
SDO_LB                                      NUMBER
SDO_UB                                      NUMBER
SDO_TOLERANCE                               NUMBER
```

Note that SDO_DIM_ARRAY is a variable-length array (VARRAY) of type SDO_DIM_ELEMENT. Each SDO_DIM_ARRAY is sized according to the number of dimensions (so for a two-dimensional geometry, the DIMINFO attribute will contain two SDO_DIM_ELEMENT types, and so on).

Each SDO_DIM_ELEMENT type stores information for a specific dimension and consists of the following fields:

- SDO_DIMNAME: This field stores the name of dimension. For instance, we can set it to 'Longitude' or 'Latitude' to indicate that the dimension represents the longitude or the latitude dimension. The name that we specify here is not interpreted by Spatial. You can specify 'X' for the longitude dimension and 'Y' for the latitude dimension.

- SDO_LB and SDO_UB: These two numbers define the lower bound and the upper bound limits for the values in a specific dimension. For instance, values in the longitude dimension range from –180 to 180. So, we can set SDO_LB to –180 and SDO_UB to 180. Likewise, for the latitude dimension, SDO_LB and SDO_UB will be set to –90 and 90, respectively. Note that these bounds are application specific. For instance, in a CAD/CAM application, the values in a specific dimension may range from 0 to 100 and the bounds will be set accordingly.

- SDO_TOLERANCE: An SDO_TOLERANCE value, or simply a *tolerance* value, is used to specify a degree of precision for spatial data. It essentially specifies the distance that two values must be apart to be considered different. For example, if the tolerance is specified as 0.5, and the distance between two points A and B is less than 0.5, then points A and B are considered to be at the same location.

  By default, the tolerance value is in the same units as the SDO_LB and SDO_UB values (in other words, in the same units as the ordinates in a dimension). However, in geodetic coordinate systems, the tolerance value is always in meters (whereas the SDO_LB, SDO_UB bounds are in degrees). Oracle additionally requires that the tolerance be the same value in all dimensions (i.e., in all SDO_DIM_ELEMENTs).

In the following sections, we will describe the tolerance field in more detail and examine its potential impact on different spatial functions and how to set the tolerance appropriately in an application.

Understanding Tolerance

As discussed, tolerance is specified as a field of the DIMINFO attribute in the USER_SDO_GEOM_METADATA view. The spatial indexes and other spatial layer-level operations use the DIMINFO attribute and the associated tolerance from this view.

A second usage of tolerance is in spatial functions described in Chapters 5, 8, and 9. The majority of these spatial functions do not read the USER_SDO_GEOM_METADATA view and instead expect the tolerance to be passed in as an input parameter. We will see such uses of tolerance in spatial validation or analysis functions that are described in Chapters 5, 8, and 9. In this subsection, we will first discuss what tolerance is and then how to set it properly for your application.

Setting incorrect tolerance values can cause incorrect and unexpected results in a variety of functions. Let's illustrate this with an example, as shown in Figure 3-3.

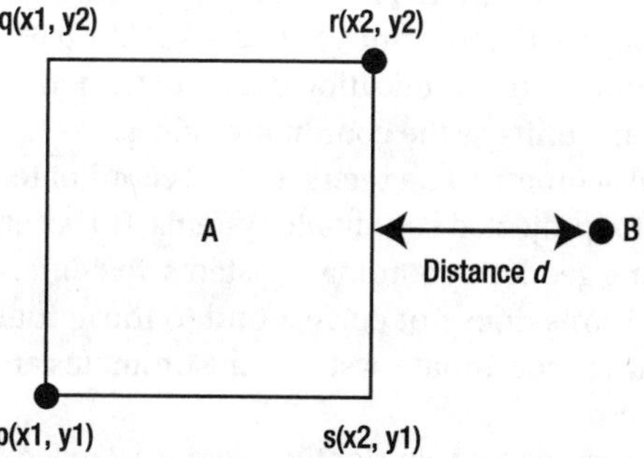

Figure 3-3. *Tolerance and its impact on the validity and relationship of two objects, A and B*

Figure 3-3 shows two objects, A and B. Object A is a rectangle with four vertices: *p*, *q*, *r*, and *s*. The lower-left vertex *p* is at coordinates (x1, y1), and the upper-right vertex *r* is at coordinates (x2, y2). The distance between objects A and B is *d*. The spatial relationship between objects A and B, and whether object A is considered a valid or invalid geometry, will vary depending on depend on how you set the tolerance value.

- *Relationship between A and B*: If the distance *d* < tolerance, then B is considered to be on the outer boundary of A. In other words, object A is considered to be intersecting object B.

  If the distance *d* >= tolerance, then A and B are considered to be disjoint or, in other words, nonintersecting.

- *Validation check for object A*: If the distance between *p* and *s* is less than the tolerance value—that is, (x2 – x1) < tolerance—then *p* and *s* are considered duplicate points/vertices. Likewise, *q* and *r* will be considered duplicate vertices. Oracle Spatial does not allow duplicate points in the specification of a geometry, so geometry object A would be considered invalid. The same holds true if the distance (y2 – y1) between *p* and *q* or *r* and *s* is less than the tolerance.

  If the preceding distances are greater than or equal to the tolerance, then the vertices are considered distinct and geometry object A is considered a valid Oracle Spatial geometry.

From this example, you can understand that tolerance plays an important role in your application. Setting it appropriately is an important step in location-enabling your application.

Choosing the Tolerance Value

As a general rule, the *tolerance value should be set to the smallest distinguishable distance in your application*. In most applications, this distance corresponds to half the difference between two individual coordinate values. For example, if the closest points in your application have the values 0.1 and 0.2 in a specific dimension, you may set the tolerance to (0.2 – 0.1)/2 = 0.05. This will ensure that the two points (and all other points in the application data) are treated as distinct. Note that the tolerance is specified in the same units as the coordinate values.

This technique can be applied directly when the geometry data refers to local coordinate systems (as in CAD/CAM and other applications), or for projected coordinate systems. However, for locations on the surface of the Earth modeled using geodetic coordinate systems, the difference in the longitude or latitude values of two locations does not correspond to the actual distance between them. In these cases (i.e., in a geodetic coordinate system), the ordinates are interpreted to be in *degrees* and the tolerance in *meters*.

From this discussion, it is clear that specifying an appropriate value for the tolerance depends on the coordinate system (i.e., the `SRID` attribute that specifies the coordinate system). In Table 3-1, we describe some recommendations for different coordinate systems.

Table 3-1. *Suggested Values for Tolerance Based on* SRID *for Applications*

Coordinate System	SRID Values	Tolerance	Units
Geodetic coordinate system	Select SRID from MDSYS.CS_SRS, where WKTEXT is like 'GEOGCS%' (e.g., 8265, 8307).	0.5 (should not be less than 0.05)	Meters for tolerance; degrees for longitude, latitude dimensions.
Projected coordinate system	Select SRID from MDSYS.CS_SRS, where WKTEXT is like 'PROJCS%' (e.g., 32774).	Half of the smallest difference between any two values in a dimension	Units for tolerance are the same as the units for the ordinates in the dimensions.
Local coordinate system	Select SRID from MDSYS.CS_SRS, where WKTEXT is like 'LOCAL_CS%'.	Half of the smallest difference between any two values in a dimension	Units for tolerance are the same as the units for the ordinates in the dimensions.
No specific coordinate system	NULL	Half of the smallest difference between any two values in a dimension	Units for tolerance are the same as the units for the ordinates in the dimensions.

Populating Spatial Metadata for Your Application

Given this background on the different attributes in the USER_SDO_GEOM_METADATA view, we can now populate the tables in our sample application with metadata.

Since we are dealing with locations on the Earth and mostly for the continental United States, we choose the SRID of 8307. This SRID is used in a majority of mobile navigation systems (GPS). The tolerance value for this geodetic coordinate system can be set to 0.5 meters. Using this value, we insert a row in the USER_SDO_GEOM_METADATA view for the spatial layer corresponding to the location column of the customers table. Listing 3-15 shows the corresponding SQL.

Listing 3-15. *Inserting Metadata for the Spatial Layer Corresponding to the* location *Column of the* customers *Table*

```
SQL> INSERT INTO  USER_SDO_GEOM_METADATA  VALUES
(
  'CUSTOMERS',       -- TABLE_NAME
  'LOCATION',        -- COLUMN_NAME
  SDO_DIM_ARRAY      -- DIMINFO attribute for storing dimension bounds, tolerance
  (
    SDO_DIM_ELEMENT
    (
      'LONGITUDE',    -- DIMENSION NAME for first dimension
      -180,           -- SDO_LB for the dimension
      180,            -- SDO_UB for the dimension
      0.5             -- Tolerance of 0.5 meters
    ),
```

```
    SDO_DIM_ELEMENT
    (
      'LATITUDE',     -- DIMENSION NAME for second dimension
      -90,            -- SDO_LB for the dimension
      90,             -- SDO_UB for the dimension
      0.5             -- Tolerance of 0.5 meters
    )
  ),
  8307                -- SRID value for specifying a geodetic coordinate system
);
```

Note that the SRID of 8307 specifies that the data in the corresponding spatial layer are in a geodetic coordinate system. There are specific restrictions when specifying the metadata for geodetic coordinate systems:

- The first dimension in SDO_DIM_ARRAY should correspond to the longitude dimension. The bounds should always be set to –180 and 180.
- The second dimension in SDO_DIM_ARRAY should correspond to the latitude dimension. The bounds should always be set to –90 and 90.
- The tolerance for the dimensions must always be specified in meters. Meters are the "units" of distance in all geodetic coordinate systems in Oracle.

Inserting incorrect metadata that does not conform to the preceding guidelines for geodetic coordinate systems is one of the most common mistakes that Oracle developers make. To ensure accurate distance calculations, you are advised to memorize the preceding three rules, because in most applications you will use a geodetic coordinate system (specified by your data vendor).

In the earlier example, we constructed the metadata for the spatial layer corresponding to location column of customers table and inserted it into the USER_SDO_GEOM_METADATA view. Likewise, you have to insert rows into USER_SDO_GEOM_METADATA for other spatial layers such as the location column in the branches table and the geom column in the us_interstates table.

Additional Information for Visualization and Network Analysis

In the preceding subsections, we discussed how to insert metadata for a spatial layer. This metadata will enable validation, spatial indexing, and spatial query and analysis operations, which are discussed in Chapters 5, 8, and 9.

In addition to such spatial analysis, you may want to enable your application with additional functionality such as map-based visualization and network/routing analysis. To enable these types of functionality, you will need to specify additional information in appropriate dictionary views. We will discuss the details of this process in Chapters 10 and 11.

Summary

In this chapter, we covered the main steps required to location-enable your business applications, namely

- Designing and creating tables to store application-specific data
- Designing and creating tables to store geographic data
- Defining metadata for each spatial layer both in the application-specific and the geographic tables

Both the spatial application data and the geographic data are stored using an SDO_GEOMETRY object. It is time to move on and discuss this object in detail.

PART 2

■■■

Basic Spatial

CHAPTER 4

The SDO_GEOMETRY Data Type

In the previous chapter, we discussed how to location-enable application data and how to organize geographic data into multiple tables, each containing SDO_GEOMETRY columns. In this chapter, we focus on storing and modeling different types of location information using the SDO_GEOMETRY data type in Oracle. The SDO_GEOMETRY type can store a wide variety of spatial data, including the following:

- A *point*, which can be used to store the coordinate location of, for example, a customer site, a store location, a delivery address, and so on
- A *line string*, which can be used to store the location and shape of a road segment
- A *polygon*, which can be used to store city boundaries, business regions, and so on
- *Complex geometries*, such as multiple polygons, which can be used to store boundaries for states such as Texas, Hawaii, and California

First, we take a detailed look at the structure of SDO_GEOMETRY: the different attributes and the values it can take to store the different types of geometric data listed.

After this, we cover how to actually construct SDO_GEOMETRY objects for simple geometries such as points, lines, and polygons (as an application developer, you'll mostly be working with such simple geometries).

Finally, we show how to construct more-complex geometries, such as multipolygons. This knowledge is useful in defining spatial regions of interest on the fly. In Chapters 8 and 9, you'll see how to use such constructed geometries to perform spatial analysis in an application. Throughout this chapter, we illustrate potential uses for these different SDO_GEOMETRY data objects with examples applicable to a typical business application.

The SDO_GEOMETRY examples that are constructed in this chapter are stored in the geometry_examples table. This table can be created as shown in Listing 4-1.

Listing 4-1. *Creating a Table to Store All Geometry Examples*

```
SQL> CREATE TABLE geometry_examples
(
  name            VARCHAR2(100),
  description     VARCHAR2(100),
  geom            SDO_GEOMETRY
);
```

The geometry_examples table contains a description of the name and a description of the geometry and the corresponding SDO_GEOMETRY object. You can use this table as a quick reference to construct geometries of appropriate types on the fly. For simple types, you may just have to modify the ordinates in the geom column.

Types of Spatial Geometries in Oracle

Let's take a closer look at the types of spatial data that an SDO_GEOMETRY can store. Figure 4-1 illustrates some of these types.

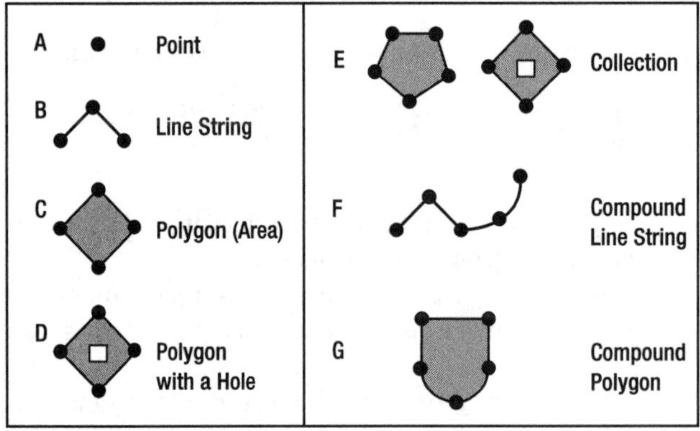

Figure 4-1. *Examples of spatial data that an* SDO_GEOMETRY *can represent*

In the sections that follow, we'll take a closer look at the geometry types in Figure 4-1.

Points

The simplest geometry is a *point*, which we have used in previous chapters. A *point* may represent the location of a customer, a delivery site, or a competitor store. Object A in Figure 4-1 is an example of a point geometry.

Line Strings

A *line string* connects multiple points (or vertices as they are sometimes referred). In general, roads, transportation networks, utility lines, and pipelines are represented as a line string type of SDO_GEOMETRY. If the line string is closed, then it is a *ring*. Otherwise, it is just a *line*. A line string connects two or more points by

- *Straight lines.* We refer to this simply as a *straight-line* line string or as a *line string* when there is no ambiguity. Object B in Figure 4-1 is an example of straight-line line string.
- *Circular arcs.* We refer to this as an *arc string.*[1]
- *A combination* of straight lines and circular arcs. We refer to this as a *compound* line string (curve). Object F in Figure 4-1 is an example of such a compound line string.

Polygons

A Polygon is specified by one or more rings (closed line strings) and is associated with an area. Object C in Figure 4-1 is a polygonal area bounded by straight lines connecting four points (area shown shaded in Figure 4-1). In this example, object C is shaped like a diamond, but in general a *polygon* can have any arbitrary shape. A polygon could represent a city boundary, a zip code area, or a buffer zone around a store site. A polygon has the following properties:

- The boundary of a polygon is made up of one or more rings (a closed line string). Special cases for the polygon boundary that can be specified easily in SDO_GEOMETRY include rectangles and circles.
- A polygon, unlike a line string, is associated with an area enclosed by the boundary. The area has to be *contiguous*—that is, the edges of the polygon cannot cross. This means the digit 8 cannot be a valid polygon. (However, the digit 8 can be modeled as a multi-polygon or collection geometry, as described later.) Object C in Figure 4-1 is an example of a (valid) polygon.
- The ring specifying the boundary or collection of a polygon can be composed of straight lines, arcs, or a combination of arcs and lines. If it is a combination of arcs and lines, we refer to the polygon as a *compound* polygon. Object G in Figure 4-1 is an example of such a compound polygon, as its boundary is connected by straight lines and arcs.
- The area covered by a polygon can be expressed using one *outer* ring and any number (zero or more) of *inner* rings. The inner rings are referred to as *holes* or *voids* as they void out (subtract) the area covered by the outer ring. Object D in Figure 4-1 shows a polygon with one outer ring and one inner ring (void). The inner ring in this example is a rectangle. The area covered by this polygon is the shaded region between the two rings.

---

1. Oracle supports only *circular arcs*. From now on, we refer to *circular arcs* simply as *arcs*.

Collections

A *collection* has multiple geometry elements. A collection could be *heterogeneous*—that is, it could be any combination of points, lines, and polygons. Alternatively, a collection could be *homogeneous*—that is, it could consist of elements of a single type. Specific types of such homogeneous collections are multipoint, multiline, or multipolygon collections.

Object E in Figure 4-1 has two polygons, a pentagon-shaped polygon and a polygon with a void, and is an example of a multipolygon collection. The shaded regions in the figure show the area covered by this geometry. The boundaries for some states, such as Texas and California, are represented as collections of polygons, where noncontiguous elements (islands) are stored as separate polygons. Likewise, the digit 8 can also be stored as a collection geometry with two polygons.

Logical Implementation of SDO_GEOMETRY

In general, the shape of spatial objects can be quite complex, requiring a large number of connected points (or *vertices*). For instance, the Amazon River may have thousands of vertices. State boundaries, which are modeled as polygons, could also have a large number of vertices. Any data type that models spatial data should be able to represent the wide variety of shapes—from complex road-segments to an arbitrarily-shaped city and property boundaries.

To represent such complex geometric shapes, the SDO_GEOMETRY type is logically implemented using an array of elements as shown in Figure 4-2.

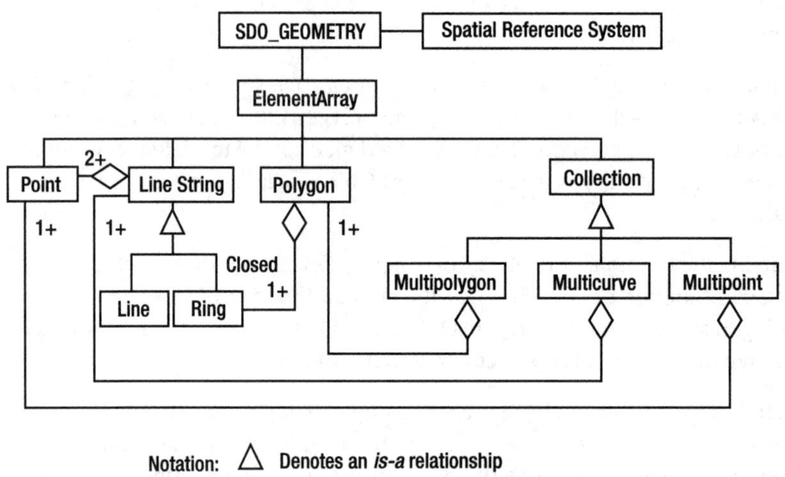

Figure 4-2. *Conceptual class diagram of the* SDO_GEOMETRY *data type*

The SDO_GEOMETRY data type has two logical components: the *spatial reference system* (also called the *coordinate system*) of the geometry and the ElementArray.

■Note The coordinate system specifies the reference frame in which the coordinates of the geometry are represented. Different coordinate systems exist to model the surface of the Earth. Alternatively, a coordinate system may refer to a non-Earth surface. You will learn more about different coordinate systems in the next section.

The `ElementArray`, or the array of elements, describes the shape and location of the `SDO_GEOMETRY` (with reference to the specified coordinate system). This array of elements constitutes (or makes up) the `SDO_GEOMETRY` object. The array of elements represents any of the different types of spatial data represented in Figure 4-1: point, line string, polygon, or collection type geometry. This is depicted in Figure 4-2 by the *is-a* relationship, illustrated by the triangle symbol between these types and the `ElementArray`. Note that the diamond symbol shows a *many-to-one* relationship between different types. For instance, a diamond between a point and a line string indicates that "many" points make up "one" line string. Note that the "2+" next to the diamond symbol indicates the minimum number. For example, at least two or more points make up a line string. Likewise, observe that one or more rings constitute a polygon, and one or more polygons constitute a multipolygon.

Spatial Data in SQL/MM and OGC

SQL/MM is the ISO/IEC international standard for "Text, Spatial, Still Images, and Data Mining." SQL/MM Part 3[2] specifically deals with spatial user-defined types and associated routines to store, manage, and retrieve spatial data. This standard specifies the `ST_Geometry` type to store spatial data. This type has subtypes such as `ST_Point`, `ST_LineString`, and `ST_Polygon` to model different types of spatial geometries. This standard also specifies a well-known text format for specifying geometries. For instance, the string `'POINT( 1 1)'` indicates a point geometry with coordinates at (1, 1).

The Open GIS Consortium (OGC for short) has the Simple Features Specification[3] for storage, retrieval, query, and update of simple geospatial features. This specification defines a `Geometry` type with appropriate subtypes to model points, line strings, polygons, and so on. The types represented are a subset of those defined by SQL/MM.

The `SDO_GEOMETRY` data type in Oracle models a majority of the types described in these standards/specifications. It models all the types and subtypes described in OGC Simple Features Specification and a subset of those in SQL/MM Part 3. In addition, Oracle Spatial provides constructors for converting data between the `SDO_GEOMETRY` data type and the well-known text (`WKT`) and well-known binary (`WKB`) notations of SQL/MM. We describe these converters at appropriate places in this chapter and in Chapter 5.

---

2. ISO/IEC 13249-3:2003, "Information technology – Database languages – SQL multimedia and application packages – Part 3: Spatial," `http://www.iso.org/iso/en/CatalogueDetailPage.CatalogueDetail?CSNUMBER=31369`.
3. Open GIS Consortium, "OpenGIS Simple Features Specification for SQL Revision 1.1," `http://www.opengis.org/docs/99-049.pdf`, May 5, 1999.

In the next section, we take a closer look at the SDO_GEOMETRY data type. In the subsequent sections, we describe how to construct SDO_GEOMETRY objects to store different types of spatial data.

SDO_GEOMETRY Type, Attributes, and Values

Now that you know what an SDO_GEOMETRY can represent and how it is internally constituted, let's examine its structure in Oracle. Listing 4-2 describes the SDO_GEOMETRY data type.

Listing 4-2. SDO_GEOMETRY *Data Type in Oracle*

```
SQL> DESCRIBE SDO_GEOMETRY
 Name                           Null?    Type
 ------------------------------ -------- --------------------
 SDO_GTYPE                               NUMBER
 SDO_SRID                                NUMBER
 SDO_POINT                               SDO_POINT_TYPE
 SDO_ELEM_INFO                           SDO_ELEM_INFO_ARRAY
 SDO_ORDINATES                           SDO_ORDINATE_ARRAY
```

Let's look at the purpose served by each attribute of the SDO_GEOMETRY.

- The SDO_GTYPE attribute specifies which type of shape (point, line, polygon, collection, multipoint, multiline, or multipolygon) that the geometry actually represents. Although the SDO_GTYPE attribute captures what type of geometry is being represented, it does not specify the actual coordinates.
- The SDO_SRID attribute specifies the ID of the spatial reference system (coordinate system) in which the location/shape of the geometry is specified.

In Figure 4-2, we noted that a geometry is made up of an element array (i.e., one or more elements make up a geometry). How do you specify the coordinates of the elements? You can do it in one of the following ways:

- If the geometry is a point (e.g., the location of customers), then you can store the coordinates in the SDO_POINT attribute of the SDO_GEOMETRY.
- If the geometry is an arbitrary shape (e.g., a street network or city boundaries), then you can store the coordinates using the SDO_ORDINATES and SDO_ELEM_INFO array attributes.
    - The SDO_ORDINATES attribute stores the coordinates of all elements of the geometry.
    - The SDO_ELEM_INFO attribute specifies where in the SDO_ORDINATES array a new element starts, how it is connected (by straight lines or arcs), and whether it is a point (although we recommend you use the SDO_POINT for storage and performance reasons listed later in the chapter), a line, or a polygon.

Let's look at each of these attributes in more detail.

SDO_GTYPE Attribute

This attribute describes the type of geometric shape modeled in the object. It reflects roughly the top levels in the class hierarchy of Figure 4-2. Specifically, it has a distinct value to indicate whether the geometry is a point, a line string, a polygon, a multipoint, a multipolygon, a multiline, or an arbitrary collection. You can think of this attribute as a high-level description of the geometry object. The geometry object may itself be a combination of multiple elements, each of a different shape. But this attribute specifies the general type for the *entire object* (with all elements it is composed of).

The SDO_GTYPE attribute is a four-digit number structured as follows: D00T. The first and the last digits take different values based on dimensionality and shape of the geometry, as described in Table 4-1. The second and third digits are set to 0.

Table 4-1. *Values for D, T in the* D00T *Format of the* SDO_GTYPE *Attribute of* SDO_GEOMETRY

Digit	Values
D (dimension of the geometry)	2 = Two-dimensional 3 = Three-dimensional 4 = Four-dimensional
T (shape/type of the geometry)	0 = Uninterpreted type 1 = Point 5 = Multipoint 2 = Line 6 = Multiline 3 = Polygon 7 = Multipolygon 4 = Collection

The *D* in the D00T representation of the SDO_GTYPE is used to store the dimensionality of (each vertex in the shape of) the geometry object. Spatial can work with two- to four-dimensional geometries. If the geometry is two-dimensional, then it has two ordinates for each vertex in the geometric shape. If the geometry is three-dimensional, then each vertex has three ordinates, and so on. These ordinates for vertices of the geometry are stored in the SDO_ORDINATES (or SDO_POINT) attribute, which we discuss later.

The *T* in the SDO_GTYPE specifies the type/shape of the geometry. Let's go over the values. For simple types, such as points, lines, and polygons, *T* is in the range of 1 to 3. For multiple-item geometries, *T* is simple_type + 4. For instance, *T* for a point is 1, and for a multipoint it is 1 + 4 = 5. Likewise, *T* for a line is 2, and for multiline string it is 2 + 4 = 6, and so on.

The value of *T* (in SDO_GTYPE) is 1 if the geometry consists of a single point, and it is 5 if the geometry has multiple points. For example, for object A in Figure 4-1, the value of *T* is 1 and the SDO_GTYPE value is 2001. Listing 4-3 shows the SDO_GTYPE for a point geometry from the customers table. Note that to retrieve the SDO_GTYPE attribute of the location column, you need a table alias.

Listing 4-3. *Example of the* SDO_GTYPE *in the* location *Column of the* customers *Table*

```
SQL> SELECT a.location.sdo_gtype FROM customers a WHERE id=1;
SDO_GTYPE
------------------
2001
```

The value of *T* is 2 if the geometry represents a line string. This line could be a simple line connecting any number of points by straight lines or arcs. Alternatively, this line could be a combination of multiple parts specifying straight-line segments and arc segments. Note that the line is still contiguous. If the geometry consists of multiple line segments that are not connected, then the type is 6 (multiline). For objects B and F in Figure 4-1, the value of *T* is 2 and the SDO_GTYPE is 2002. Listing 4-4 shows an example.

Listing 4-4. *Example of the* SDO_GTYPE *in the* geom *Column of the* us_interstates *Table*

```
SQL> SELECT a.geom.sdo_gtype FROM us_interstates a WHERE rownum=1;
SDO_GTYPE
------------------
2002
```

The type *T* is 3 if the geometry represents an area bounded by a closed line string (also referred to as *ring*) of edges. Listing 4-5 shows an example. The boundary may be connected by lines, arcs, or a combination of both. The polygon can contain one or more inner rings called *voids*. In such cases, the area of the polygon is computed by subtracting the areas of the voids. The area covered by a geometry that has *T* equal to 3 should be contiguous. Objects C, D, and G are examples. Note that object D has one outer and one inner ring (rectangle), but there is still only one single "contiguous" area shown by the shaded region. So, this is considered a single polygon with type *T* set to 3.

Listing 4-5. *Example of the* SDO_GTYPE *in the* location *Column of the* us_states *Table*

```
SQL> SELECT a.location.sdo_gtype FROM us_states a WHERE state_abrv='NH';
SDO_GTYPE
------------------
2003
```

If there is more than one (nonvoid) polygon in the geometry (i.e., if the area of the geometry is not contiguous), then it is a multipolygon geometry and the type is 7. Object E in Figure 4-1 is an example of this.

If the geometry is a collection of points, lines, and/or polygons, the geometry is a collection geometry. The value of *T* for this geometry is 4. For object E, which has two polygons (one with a void), you can set the type to 7, a multipolygon. Alternatively, you can set it to the more generic description of a collection. The type *T* in this case will be 4. Listing 4-6 shows an example when *T* is 7.

Listing 4-6. *Example of the* SDO_GTYPE *in the* location *Column of the* us_states *Table*

```
SQL> SELECT a.location.sdo_gtype FROM us_cities a WHERE state_abrv='TX';
SDO_GTYPE
------------------
2007
```

Note that most of the shapes represent only two-dimensional geometries. In nearly all cases, Oracle Spatial does not interpret third- and fourth-dimension values even if they are specified. How do you specify three (or four)-dimensional geometries? Just set the *D* in D00T for the SDO_GTYPE to 3 (or 4). Oracle Spatial then allows you to store three (or four) ordinates for each vertex of the geometry. So, if you have two points (1, 1, 4) and (2, 2, 5), and you specify the SDO_GTYPE to be 3002 (line), then Oracle Spatial treats the geometry as a line connecting points (1, 1) and (2, 2). This allows you to use the third and fourth dimensions to hold additional information that can be stored with each vertex of the geometry. For example, the third dimension could model the height of each vertex point in the geometry. In transportation applications, the third ordinate for each vertex in a road segment is used to store the mile marker.

Tip Since the geometry has a provision to store four-dimensional ordinates (as specified by *D* in the SDO_GTYPE), even if you model a two-dimensional geometry, such as a road, you can store additional information such as the elevation, mile markers, timestamps, or speed limits as third and fourth dimensions.

So, Oracle Spatial does not interpret the third and fourth dimensions by default. Oracle Spatial does provide some functions to operate on these third and fourth dimensions for specific applications. You will learn about such applications in Appendix B. In addition, Oracle Spatial can support explicit processing on specific three- and four-dimensional objects. These include the following types of geometries (you can easily generalize these types to four-dimensional objects):

- *Point, multipoint geometry*: For three-dimensional point geometry, the type *T* is 1 for point and 5 for multipoint.
- *Cuboid polygon, multicuboid polygons*: The type *T* is again 3 for a single cuboid and 7 for multiple ones.

SDO_SRID Attribute

This attribute specifies the spatial reference system, or coordinate system, for the geometry. To understand what a coordinate system is, consider the example in Figure 4-3. Recall that we briefly discussed coordinate systems in Chapter 3. Here, we continue that discussion in more detail.

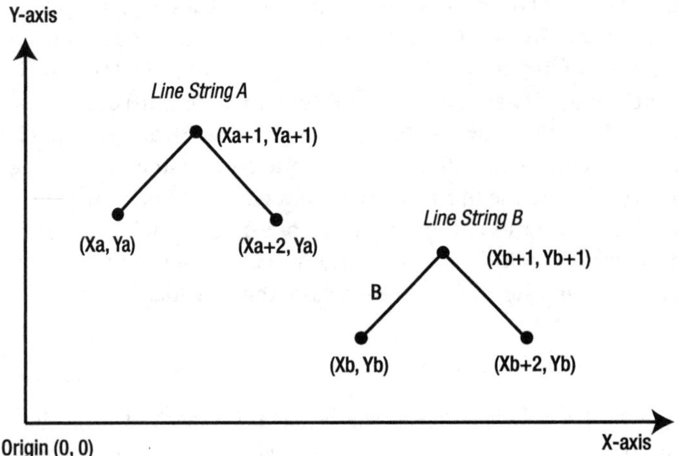

Figure 4-3. *Coordinate systems example*

Note that in Figure 4-3, the locations of two line string objects, A and B, are specified with respect to the origin and using the coordinates in the orthogonal x- and y-axes. Note that both A and B have the same shape; however, their positioning (i.e., location) with respect to the origin is different. If you change the origin, the absolute locations (coordinates) of the two line string objects change. Such a frame of reference using the x- and y-axes is termed as the *Cartesian system*. This system is popular in representing two-dimensional data in CAD/CAM applications. But how good is it for representing customer locations and delivery sites on the surface of the Earth?

To answer this question, let's examine the surface of the Earth. The Earth is approximately ellipsoidal in shape. Location has traditionally been specified using the longitude and latitude lines on the Earth. Flattening the surface of the Earth to a two-dimensional plane loses *spatial proximity* and distorts the shape. Figure 4-4 shows a map of the countries of the world. In Figure 4-4, by dividing the surface of the Earth at the dateline meridian, California and Japan appear to be farther apart than they actually are. Also, countries at the North and South Poles, such as Antarctica and Greenland, are distorted in shape.

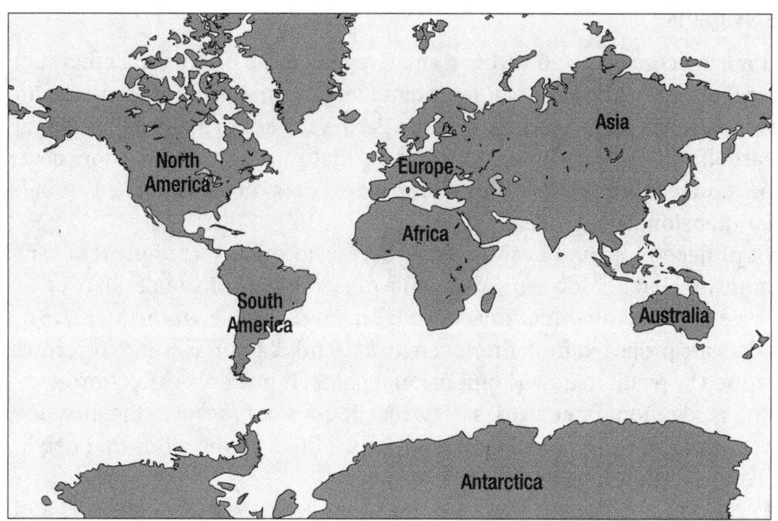

Figure 4-4. *Example map of the world, with countries and distances distorted*

How do we represent locations on the surface of the Earth without inaccuracies and distortions? This has been a challenge to many geographers, mathematicians, and inventors for centuries. Several books have dealt with this topic in great detail.[4] There are two general techniques to model the data on Earth's surface. The first is to model the Earth using three-dimensional ellipsoidal surfaces. The second is to project the data into a two-dimensional plane. Let's look at each of these in turn. Note that in most cases, an application developer may not need to know much about different coordinate systems. All that is required is to choose an appropriate coordinate system as described in the subsection "Choosing an Appropriate Coordinate System." The casual reader may skip the discussion in the next three subsections.

Geodetic Coordinate Systems

If you model the surface of the Earth as a regular three-dimensional ellipsoid, you can measure distance relationships between objects by computing the distances of the locations on the corresponding ellipsoid. Unfortunately, the Earth is not a perfect ellipsoid, and therefore a single ellipsoid cannot accurately model the Earth in all areas. This led geographers to define multiple ellipsoids to suit their needs. Oracle Spatial supplies commonly used reference ellipsoids in the `MDSYS.SDO_ELLIPSOIDS` table.

Sometimes in your model, you will need to shift the center of the Earth and rotate the axes to better suit the curvature at the local region. For this, you can create models referred to as *datums* by shifting and rotating specific ellipsoids to better suit the Earth's curvature at different regions. You can examine the different three-dimensional models by looking at the datums in the `MDSYS.SDO_DATUMS` table. Positioning data on the surface of the Earth by referring to the coordinates (longitude and latitude) on a specific datum is known as a *geodetic coordinate system* (or *geodetic spatial reference system*).

---

4. For example, refer to John P. Snyder's *Flattening the Earth: Two Thousand Years of Map Projections* (The University of Chicago Press, 1997).

Projected Coordinate Systems

In most applications, data are concentrated within a small region of the Earth. Projecting such data to a two-dimensional plane may be a simpler representation and may also be more accurate for the application needs. How do you project data on the Earth's surface to a two-dimensional flat plane? First, you start off with a three-dimensional model (datum) of the Earth. Then, using one of a variety of projection techniques, the three-dimensional data on the reference model is transformed to two-dimensional data on a flat plane.

Why have different projection techniques? Because there is no single technique that can project from three-dimensional to two-dimensional while preserving the distances between objects, the areas of large objects, the directions, and so on. For example, in the Mercator cylindrical projection, data are projected from the sphere to a cylindrical surface, and the cylindrical surface is unwrapped to result in a two-dimensional plane. It preserves direction and has been used in marine navigation for centuries. However, it does not preserve the area of objects. So the Mercator cylindrical projection would not be useful in applications that need to compute land area (spatial object area, in other words).

Alternate types of projections include *conic* projections (projecting to a conic surface) and *azimuthal* projections (projecting from the center of a region to a tangential plane). Examples of these projections include Lambert Azimuthal Equal-Area, Azimuthal Equidistant, Albers Equal-Area Conic, and Equidistant Conic projections.

The equal-area projections preserve areas of the objects (unlike the Mercator) but distort direction and distance. The equidistant projections are good for measuring the distance from the center of the projection area (say, New York City) to distant locations, such as San Diego, California, and Seattle, Washington. However, such a projection cannot be used to compute distances between San Diego and Seattle, two locations that are far off from the center of the projection. In short, the specific projection that is to be used depends on which of the following parameters are to be preserved: direction, distance, and area. We can examine the different projections that can be applied to a specific datum by looking at the table `MDSYS.SDO_PROJECTIONS`.

To summarize, by choosing a projection and a three-dimensional reference datum, locations on the surface of the Earth can be represented in a two-dimensional plane. Such referencing using a specific datum and an appropriate projection is referred to as a *projected coordinate system* or a *projected spatial reference system*.

Georeferenced, Local Coordinate Systems

Coordinate systems pertaining to locations on the Earth (i.e., projected and geodetic coordinate systems) are called *georeferenced*. All other coordinate systems, such as those in CAD/CAM, are referred to as *local* or *nongeoreferenced*.

Choosing an Appropriate Coordinate System

You choose the coordinate system by setting an appropriate value for the `SDO_SRID` attribute. Next, we will describe how to determine the appropriate values for projected, geodetic, and local coordinate systems.

If the geometry does not refer to a location on the Earth's surface, but instead refers to layout in CAD/CAM or other applications, then you can set it either to `NULL` or to a value specified by your data vendor.

Otherwise, if the geometry refers to a location on the Earth's surface, you can set the `SDO_SRID` to a value corresponding to either a *projected* coordinate system or a *geodetic* coordinate system. Projected coordinate systems are used whenever all the data are located in a small region of the Earth. Projected coordinate systems are useful to suit application needs such as preserving the distances between locations, shapes, or areas of geometry objects (such as city boundaries) and other appropriate geometric properties. Geodetic coordinate systems are useful if the data are located in a much larger portion on the surface of the Earth, and slight inaccuracies in some geometric properties such as distances, areas, and so on can be tolerated. For example, when dealing with data fully concentrated in southern Texas, you can use a state-plane projection appropriate for southern Texas. However, when dealing with the United States as a whole, you can use a geodetic coordinate system. You can look up the SDO_SRIDs for the geodetic or projected coordinate systems in the MDSYS.CS_SRS table. Listing 4-7 shows the columns in this table.

Listing 4-7. MDSYS.CS_SRS *Table*

```
SQL> DESCRIBE MDSYS.CS_SRS

 Name                                      Null?      Type
 ----------------------------------------- --------   ---------------
 CS_NAME                                              VARCHAR2(68)
 SRID                                      NOT NULL   NUMBER(38)
 AUTH_SRID                                            NUMBER(38)
 AUTH_NAME                                            VARCHAR2(256)
 WKTEXT                                               VARCHAR2(2046)
 CS_BOUNDS                                            SDO_GEOMETRY
```

The MDSYS.CS_SRS table has the following columns:

- CS_NAME: This specifies the name of the coordinate system.
- SRID: This is short for *spatial reference system ID*. This is a unique ID for the spatial reference or coordinate system.
- AUTH_SRID and AUTH_NAME: These refer to the values assigned by the originator of this coordinate system.
- WKTEXT: This is short for *well-known text*. This field provides a detailed description of the coordinate system. For geodetic coordinate systems, the WKTEXT field starts with a prefix of 'GEOGCS'. For projected systems, it starts with 'PROJCS'. You can use this information to search for an appropriate coordinate system for your application's needs.
- CS_BOUNDS: This specifies a geometry where the coordinate system is valid. Storing data beyond the bounds may lead to inaccurate results. Currently, set to NULL.

As an application developer, chances are you will only be interested in how to choose the coordinate system (you are not likely to have to populate these rows in the MDSYS.CS_SRS table). You might be able to do this by examining the coordinate system description in the WKTEXT field. For example, to identify a projected coordinate system for southern Texas, you can execute the SQL in Listing 4-8. Note that the ROWNUM=1 predicate displays only one out of three rows for southern Texas.

Listing 4-8. *Selecting an* `SRID` *for the Southern Texas Region from the* `MDSYS.CS_SRS` *Table*

```
SQL> SELECT cs_name, srid, wktext
FROM  MDSYS.CS_SRS
WHERE WKTEXT LIKE 'PROJCS%'
  AND CS_NAME LIKE '%Texas%'
    AND CS_NAME LIKE '%Southern%'
    AND ROWNUM=1;

CS_NAME
-------------------------------
Texas 4205, Southern Zone (1927)

SRID
-----
41155

WKTEXT
--------------------------------------------
PROJCS
  [
    "Texas 4205, Southern Zone (1927)",
  GEOGCS
  [
    "NAD 27 (Continental US)",
    DATUM
    [
      "NAD 27 (Continental US)",
      SPHEROID ["Clarke 1866", 6378206.4, 294.9786982]
    ] ,
    PRIMEM [ "Greenwich", 0.000000 ],
    UNIT ["Decimal Degree", 0.01745329251994330]
  ],
  PROJECTION ["Lambert Conformal Conic"],
  PARAMETER ["Standard_Parallel_1", 26.166667],
  PARAMETER ["Standard_Parallel_2", 27.833333],
  PARAMETER ["Central_Meridian", -98.500000],
  PARAMETER ["Latitude_Of_Origin", 25.666667],
  PARAMETER ["False_Easting",   2000000.0000],
  UNIT ["U.S. Foot", 0.3048006096012]
]
```

The query returns a projected coordinate system for southern Texas. This coordinate system is formed using the Lambert Conformal Conic projection technique on a datum formed using the NAD 27 (continental United States) reference ellipsoid. You can use the corresponding `SRID` of 41155 to specify a geometry in this coordinate system.

For most business applications that have location data spread over the entire United States, you can choose one of the widely used geodetic systems for North America, such as WGS84 (SRID=8307) or NAD83 (SRID=8265). For applications in other countries, you can choose either an appropriate geodetic system or a projected system depending on how widely distributed the location data are. Note that Oracle supports approximately 1000 coordinate systems that cover almost all countries/regions of the world. These coordinate systems are all described in the MDSYS.CS_SRS table. All you have to do is choose one of them (the SRID field) by searching for the region/country in the WKTEXT field.

■ **Note** All geometries in a specific column of a table (e.g., `location` column of `customers` table) should have the same SDO_SRID value.

SDO_POINT Attribute

Now that we have finished discussing the SDO_SRID attribute of the SDO_GEOMETRY, let's move on to the next attribute: the SDO_POINT. This attribute is used to specify the location of a point geometry, such as the location of a customer. Notice that this attribute is of type SDO_POINT_TYPE, which is another object type. Listing 4-9 shows the structure of this type.

Listing 4-9. SDO_POINT_TYPE *Data Type*

```
SQL> DESCRIBE SDO_POINT_TYPE
 Name                         Null?    Type
 ---------------------------- -------- -----
 X                                     NUMBER
 Y                                     NUMBER
 Z                                     NUMBER
```

The SDO_GTYPE for a point geometry is set to D001. Consider point A in Figure 4-5, identified by coordinates X_A and Y_A representing a customer location.

A ●

(X_A, Y_A)

Figure 4-5. *Example of a point at coordinates X_A, Y_A*

Listing 4-10 shows how to populate the SDO_GEOMETRY object in the geometry_examples table to represent point A (substitute (-79, 37) with actual coordinates).

Listing 4-10. *Point Data in* geometry_examples

```
SQL> INSERT INTO geometry_examples (name, description, geom) VALUES
(
  'POINT',
  '2-dimensional Point at coordinates (-79,37)  with srid set to 8307',
  SDO_GEOMETRY
  (
    2001,    -- SDO_GTYPE format: DOOT. Set to 2001 for a 2-dimensional point
    8307,    -- SDO_SRID (geodetic)
    SDO_POINT_TYPE
    (
      -79,   -- ordinate value for Longitude
      37,    -- ordinate value Latitude
      NULL   -- no third dimension (only 2 dimensions)
    ),
    NULL,
    NULL
  )
);
```

Caution Oracle Spatial requires that the longitude ordinates be entered as the first dimension and that the latitude ordinates be entered as the second dimension.

The notation for specifying the geometry column may seem obscure, but it is logical. Objects in Oracle are instantiated using the corresponding object constructors. The geom column is an object of type SDO_GEOMETRY and is instantiated as shown. The fields of this object are populated as follows:

- SDO_GTYPE: The format is D00T, where *D* is 2 and *T* is 1 for 2-dimensional POINT.
- SDO_SRID: Set to 8307.
- SDO_POINT: This sets the x- and y-coordinates in SDO_POINT_TYPE to (–79, 37) in the example. The z-coordinate is set to NULL.
- SDO_ELEM_INFO: Not used; is set to NULL.
- SDO_ORDINATES: Not used; is set to NULL.

An alternate mechanism to construct a point geometry is by using the *well-known text* (WKT) description of the point geometry as referenced in SQL/MM Part 3. Oracle Spatial provides an SDO_GEOMETRY constructor that takes the WKT and an SRID as arguments to construct an SDO_GEOMETRY object. Listing 4-11 shows an example.

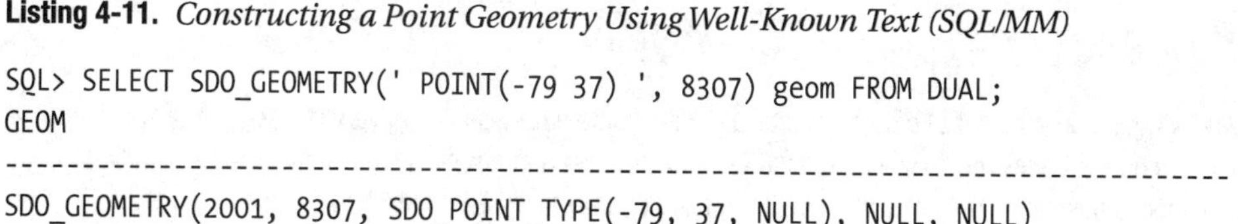

Listing 4-11. *Constructing a Point Geometry Using Well-Known Text (SQL/MM)*

```
SQL> SELECT SDO_GEOMETRY(' POINT(-79 37) ', 8307) geom FROM DUAL;
GEOM
--------------------------------------------------------------------------------
SDO_GEOMETRY(2001, 8307, SDO_POINT_TYPE(-79, 37, NULL), NULL, NULL)
```

■ **Caution** The ordinates of a vertex are separated by a "space" rather than by a "comma" in a WKT. Commas separate multiple vertices, if any, in the WKT. Refer to ISO IEC 12349 (http://www.iso.org/iso/en/CatalogueDetailPage.CatalogueDetail?CSNUMBER=31369) for details on how to construct the well-known text for different types of geometries.

The constructed SDO_GEOMETRY object can be passed in anywhere an SDO_GEOMETRY object can be used—to insert into the geom column of geometry_examples as in Listing 4-10, to update the geom column value, or in spatial query operators and functions (you will see examples of these in later chapters).

Note that the SDO_POINT can store only three ordinates (x, y, and z). This representation is suitable if your data have three or fewer dimensions. For four-dimensional points, you have to use the SDO_ELEM_INFO and SDO_ORDINATES attributes.

SDO_ELEM_INFO and SDO_ORDINATES Attributes

In the previous example, you saw how to store a point element in the SDO_GEOMETRY using the SDO_POINT attribute. Obviously, you may want to store elements more complex than points; you may also want to store lines and polygons, which may need a large number of vertices. To store such complex elements, you will use the other two structures in the SDO_GEOMETRY type, the SDO_ORDINATES and SDO_ELEM_INFO attributes. Together these attributes allow you to specify different *elements* that compose a geometry: the SDO_ORDINATES stores the coordinates of the vertices in all elements of a geometry, and the SDO_ELEM_INFO specifies the type of elements and where they start in the SDO_ORDINATES.

First, you should understand how to represent elements using the SDO_ELEM_INFO and SDO_ORDINATES attributes. You will learn about the different *element-types* that are supported in Oracle in subsequent subsections.

SDO_ORDINATES Attribute

We'll start with the SDO_ORDINATES attribute. This attribute stores the ordinates in all dimensions of all elements of a geometry. The SDO_ORDINATES attribute is of type SDO_ORDINATE_ARRAY, which, as you can see in the following snippet, is a collection of type VARRAY (variable-length array) of numbers. The VARRAY is useful for storing the points that describe a geometric shape in the proper order, so that no explicit processing is needed when fetching that shape. If the data dimensionality is *D*, then every consecutive *D* numbers in the SDO_ORDINATES specify the coordinates of a vertex. For example, if you want to model a line connecting point A that has coordinates (Xa, Ya) with point B that has coordinates (Xb, Yb), then the SDO_ORDINATES will

VARRAYS

A VARRAY is an ordered set of data elements, all of the same data type. It can vary in size up to a specified maximum number of elements. Each element in the array has an *index*, which is a number corresponding to the element's position in the array and can be fetched directly using the index. The index starts at 1.

A VARRAY requires only the exact[5] storage space needed to store the required number of elements, and it can be expanded to accommodate new elements at the end of array. Note that VARRAYs can be made of complex types (i.e., object types), which themselves can contain other VARRAYs. This is a powerful mechanism that enables you to construct complex structures.

contain the numbers Xa, Ya, Xb, and Yb, in that order. The size of this array attribute is set to 1048576. This large size limit provides enough room to store the vertices of large and complex geometries.

```
SQL> DESCRIBE SDO_ORDINATE_ARRAY
 SDO_ORDINATE_ARRAY VARRAY(1048576) OF NUMBER
```

If the SDO_ORDINATES attribute specifies the ordinates (in all dimensions) of all elements of a geometry object, how are these ordinates interpreted and separated out to represent different elements that make up the geometry? The information that is needed to interpret and separate out the ordinates into elements is specified in the SDO_ELEM_INFO attribute. We will look at that next.

SDO_ELEM_INFO Attribute

The SDO_ELEM_INFO attribute is of type SDO_ELEM_INFO_ARRAY, which is also a VARRAY of numbers with a maximum size of 1,048,576 numbers. Every three consecutive numbers in the SDO_ELEM_INFO are grouped into a *descriptor triplet*, describing an element or a part of an element. So, logically, the SDO_ELEM_INFO attribute is an array of triplets (three numbers). This means the size of this array attribute is always a multiple of 3.

Each descriptor triplet is associated with an element of the geometry. The triplet is of the form <*offset, element-type, interpretation*>. The *offset* specifies the *starting index* in the SDO_ORDINATES array where the ordinates of the element are stored. The other two numbers, *element-type* (*etype* for short) and *interpretation*, take different values depending on whether the associated element represents a point, a line, or a polygon, and whether the boundaries are connected by straight lines, arcs, or both.

Let's first look at SDO_ELEM_INFO values for the data that application developers are most likely to construct. For instance, in our business application, the geometries that we construct could be

5. This is excluding the additional overhead to store information such as the size of the VARRAY.

- Points representing location of customers, competitors, and so on
- Line strings representing streets and highways
- Polygons representing city boundaries

In most cases, these geometries have *at most one element descriptor triplet and represent at most one element of a point, line string, or polygon type*. We refer to such elements and geometries as *simple* elements and *simple* geometries. In those cases, the descriptor triplet has the following values:

- *Offset*: This is always set to 1, as there is only one element in the SDO_ORDINATES field.
- *Element-type*: This has a direct correspondence with the type *T* value in the SDO_GTYPE for the geometry.
  - For points, the *element-type* is 1 (the *T* value in SDO_GTYPE is 1).
  - For lines, the *element-type* is 2 (the *T* value in SDO_GTYPE is also 2).
  - For polygons, the *element-type* is 1003 (the *T* value in SDO_GTYPE is 3).
- *Interpretation*: This is the only subtle information an element contains.
  - For a point, *interpretation* is 1.
  - For line strings and polygons, the *interpretation* is 1 if the connectivity is by straight lines, and the *interpretation* is 2 if the connectivity is by arcs. For instance, a line string connected by straight lines has the SDO_ELEM_INFO set to (1, 2, 1) (i.e., a starting *offset* of 1, an *element-type* of 2, and an *interpretation* of 1).
  - For polygons, you could have *interpretation* set to 3 to indicate that the polygon is a rectangle.
  - Likewise, for polygons you could have *interpretation* set to 4 to indicate that the polygon is a circle.

Table 4-2 summarizes the possible values for the SDO_ELEM_INFO array (and the SDO_ORDINATES array) based on the type of the element. Using these values, you can construct an SDO_GEOMETRY by additionally populating the SDO_GTYPE and SDO_SRID fields appropriately. In the next section, we present detailed examples for such *simple* geometries. In the subsequent section, we describe more complex geometries with more than one element descriptor triplet. Examples of such data would be a street that has both straight lines and arcs. Such geometries are referred to as *complex* geometries.

Table 4-2. *Values for* SDO_ELEM_INFO *(and* SDO_ORDINATES*) for Simple Geometries*

Name	Element-Type (Etype)	Interpretation	SDO_ELEM_INFO: (1, Etype, Interpretation)	SDO_ORDINATES	Illustration
Point (e.g., customer location)	1	*N*, where *N* is the number of points. 1 is for a single point.	(1, 1, 1)	(Xa, Ya)	A (XA, YA)
Line string (e.g., streets, highways)	2	1 = Connected by straight lines 2 = Connected by arcs	(1, 2, 1) (1, 2, 2)	(Xa, Ya, Xb, Yb, Xc, Yc) (Xa, Ya, Xb, Yb, Xc, Yc)	B (Xb, Yb) A (Xa, Ya) C (Xc, Yc)
Polygon (e.g., city boundary, buffer zone)	1003	1 = Polygon boundary connected by straight lines	(1,1003, 1)	(Xa, Ya, Xb,Yb, Xc, Yc, Xd, Yd, Xa, Ya)	D (Xd, Yd) C (Xc, Yc) A (Xa, Ya) B (Xb, Yb)
		3 = Rectangle polygon (only specify lower-left and upper-right corners)	(1, 1003, 3)	(Xa, Ya, Xc, Yc)	D (Xd, Yd) C (Xc, Yc) (Xa, Ya) A (Xb, Yb) B
		4 = Circle polygon (specify three points on boundary of circle)	(1, 1003, 4)	(Xa, Ya, Xb, Yb, Xc, Yc)	C (Xc, Yc) (Xb, Yb) B A (Xa, Ya)

Simple Geometry Examples

A simple geometry consists of only *one element descriptor triplet and represents a point, line string, or polygon.* The ordinates for the geometry are always stored at a starting offset of 1 (as there is only one element). This means the SDO_ELEM_INFO is always of the form (1, x, y). Let's look at each simple geometry type next.

Point

In Listing 4-11, you saw how to represent a two-dimensional point using the SDO_POINT attribute of the SDO_GEOMETRY. An alternate (but not recommended) mechanism is to store the point coordinates in the SDO_ORDINATES array. Listing 4-12 shows the example.

Listing 4-12. *Storing the Point Coordinates in the* SDO_ORDINATES *Array Instead of* SDO_POINT

```
SQL> INSERT INTO geometry_examples VALUES
(
  '2-D POINT stored in SDO_ORDINATES',
  '2-dimensional Point at coordinates (-79, 37) with srid set to 8307',
```

```
  SDO_GEOMETRY
  (
    2001,  -- SDO_GTYPE format: DOOT. Set to 2001 for as a 2-dimensional point
    8307,  -- SDO_SRID
    NULL,  -- SDO_POINT attribute set to NULL
    SDO_ELEM_INFO_ARRAY  -- SDO_ELEM_INFO attribute (see Table 4-2 for values)
    (
      1,   -- Offset is 1
      1,   -- Element-type is 1 for a point
      1    -- Interpretation specifies # of points. In this case 1.
    ),
   SDO_ORDINATE_ARRAY   -- SDO_ORDINATES attribute
   (
      -79, -- Ordinate value for Longitude
      37   -- Ordinate value for Latitude
    )
  )
);
```

In Listing 4-12, note that the SDO_GEOMETRY object is instantiated using the object constructor with all the appropriate attributes for this type. Likewise, the SDO_ORDINATES and SDO_ELEM_INFO attributes are VARRAYs, and they are instantiated using the corresponding types, SDO_ELEM_INFO_ARRAY and SDO_ORDINATE_ARRAY, respectively.

■Tip Never store the coordinates of a two- or three-dimensional point in the SDO_ORDINATES attribute (as in Listing 4-12). Always store them in the SDO_POINT attribute (as in Listing 4-11). The latter representation is storage efficient as well as better performing during fetches.

Since SDO_POINT can store only three numbers, this attribute cannot store four-dimensional points. Examples of such points include locations that store temperature and height. For such four-dimensional points, you need to use the SDO_ELEM_INFO and SDO_ORDINATES attributes of the SDO_GEOMETRY. Let (Xa, Ya, Za, La) be the ordinates of the four-dimensional point. The SDO_GEOMETRY is populated as shown in Listing 4-13. Note that the only change in the geom column, as compared to Listing 4-13, is that the SDO_ORDINATES attribute has four numbers (corresponding to the four dimensions), as opposed to two in Listing 4-12.

Listing 4-13. *Four-Dimensional Point Example*

```
INSERT INTO geometry_examples VALUES
(
  '4-D POINT',
  '4-dimensional Point at (Xa=>2, Ya=>2, Za=>2, La=>2) with srid set to NULL',
  SDO_GEOMETRY
  (
```

```
    4001, -- SDO_GTYPE: DOOT. Set to 4001 as it is a 4-dimensional point
    NULL, -- SDO_SRID
    NULL, -- SDO_POINT_TYPE is null
    SDO_ELEM_INFO_ARRAY(1,1,1),  -- Indicates a point element
    SDO_ORDINATE_ARRAY(2,2,2,2)  -- Store the four ordinates here
  )
);
```

Line String: Connected by Straight Lines

Let's go back to two-dimensional data again and look at line geometries that could represent streets and highways. Consider the three points A, B, and C shown in Figure 4-6. How do you represent a line connecting these three points? Will the connection be using straight lines or arcs? First, let's consider straight lines.

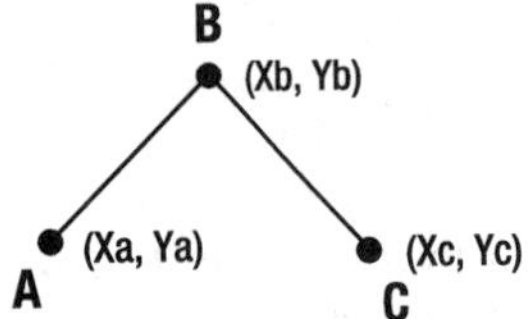

Figure 4-6. *Example of a line string connected by straight lines*

The SDO_GEOMETRY object can be populated as shown in Listing 4-14.

Listing 4-14. *Two-Dimensional Line String Example*

```
SQL> INSERT INTO geometry_examples VALUES
(
  'LINE STRING',
  '2-D line string connecting A(Xa=>1,Ya=>1),B(Xb=>2, Yb=>2), C(Xc=>2,Yc=>1)',
  SDO_GEOMETRY
  (
    2002,   -- SDO_GTYPE: DOOT. Set to 2002 as it is a 2-dimensional line string
    32774,  -- SDO_SRID
    NULL,   -- SDO_POINT_TYPE is null
    SDO_ELEM_INFO_ARRAY  -- SDO_ELEM_INFO attribute (see Table 4-2 for values)
    (
      1,    -- Offset is 1
      2,    -- Element-type is 2 for a LINE STRING
      1     -- Interpretation is 1 if line string is connected by straight lines.
    ),
    SDO_ORDINATE_ARRAY   -- SDO_ORDINATES attribute
    (
```

```
      1,1,  -- Xa, Ya values
      2,2,  -- Xb, Yb values
      2,1   -- Xc, Yc values
    )
  )
);
```

Since the geometry is a line string connected by straight lines, the SDO_ELEM_INFO attribute is set to the triplet (1, 2, 1), as described in Table 4-2. The SDO_ORDINATES attribute is then populated with the ordinates of each of the three vertices A, B, and C in the order they appear in the line string.

Observe that all the line segments are contiguous (i.e., they share vertices). If you want to store lines that do not share vertices, you can model them using multiline string geometries. We discuss these later in the chapter.

What happens if there are not just three points, but *N* points with coordinates (X1, Y1) . . . (XN, YN), and all of them need to be connected by straight lines in the order (X1, Y1), (X2, Y2), . . . , (XN, YN)? All you have to do is store these vertices in the SDO_ORDINATES attribute (in the order in which they need to be connected). Nothing else needs to change. The geometry constructor looks as follows:

```
SDO_GEOMETRY
(
  2002, 32774, NULL,
  SDO_ELEM_INFO_ARRAY(1,2,1),
  SDO_ORDINATE_ARRAY(X1, Y1, X2, Y2, ...., XN, YN)
)
```

■Note All lines joining successive vertices in a simple (i.e., noncompound) element use the *same interpretation*—that is, they are connected by straight lines (or by arcs).

Line String: Connected by Arcs

The example in Figure 4-7 stores a line string composed of three points. However, those same three points could actually represent a very different shape: a circular arc that passes through those three points.

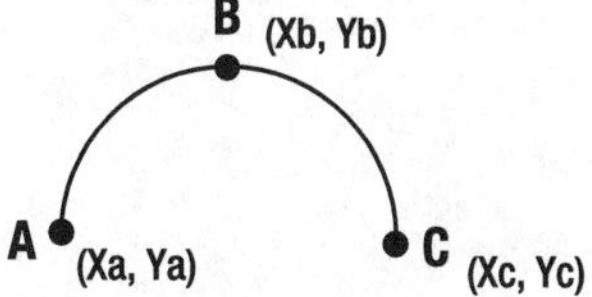

Figure 4-7. *Example of a line string connected by arcs*

How do you do that? Simply change the *interpretation* in the SDO_ELEM_INFO to 2 (ARC). The SDO_ELEM_INFO then changes from (1, 2, 1) to (1, 2, 2), as shown in Listing 4-15.

Listing 4-15. *Two-Dimensional Line String Connected by Arcs*

```
SQL> INSERT INTO geometry_examples VALUES
(
  'ARCSTRING',
  '2-D arc connecting A(Xa=>1,Ya=>1),B(Xb=>2, Yb=>2), C(Xc=>2,Yc=>1)',
  SDO_GEOMETRY
  (
    2002,  --  SDO_GTYPE: DOOT. Set to 2002 as it is a 2-dimensional line string
    32774, -- SDO_SRID
    NULL,  -- SDO_POINT_TYPE is null
    SDO_ELEM_INFO_ARRAY  -- SDO_ELEM_INFO attribute (see Table 4-2 for values)
    (
      1,    -- Offset is 1
      2,    -- Element-type is 2 for a LINE STRING
      2     -- Interpretation is 2 if line string is connected by ARCs.
    ),
    SDO_ORDINATE_ARRAY  -- SDO_ORDINATES attribute
    (
      1,1, -- Xa, Ya values
      2,2, -- Xb, Yb values
      2,1  -- Xc, Yc values
      )
    )
);
```

If you compare this representation with that of the example in Listing 4-14, you will notice that the only difference is the *interpretation* (the third argument in SDO_ELEM_INFO_ARRAY), which is now set to 2. The result is a line circular arc instead of a straight line.

Again, what if the line string has more than three points? Since an arc is defined by three points at a time, the line string should have an odd number of vertices. An arc is constructed with the three points starting at every *odd* vertex (except the last vertex). So, if there are five points A, B, C, D, and E, there will be two arcs: arc ABC at vertex A and arc CDE at vertex C, as shown in Figure 4-8.

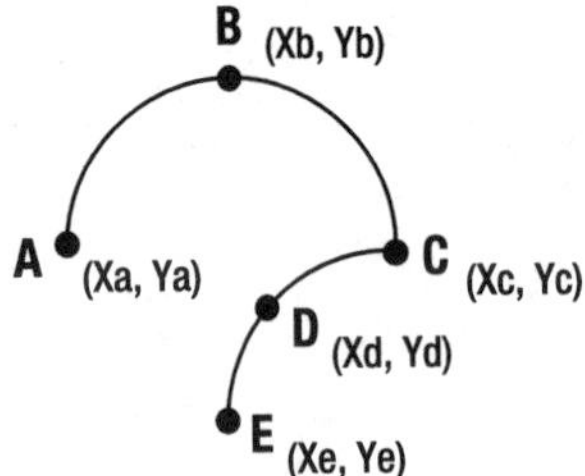

Figure 4-8. *Example of a line string with multiple arcs*

The constructor for this geometry is

```
SDO_GEOMETRY
(
  2002, 32774, null,
  SDO_ELEM_INFO_ARRAY(1,2,2),
  SDO_ORDINATE_ARRAY(Xa, Ya, Xb, Yb, Xc, Yc, Xd, Yd, Xe, Ye)
)
```

■ **Note** In Oracle Spatial, every arc is specified by three points: a starting vertex, any distinct middle vertex, and an ending vertex (e.g., A, B, C). As a consequence, an arc-based line string (arc string) should always have an odd number of vertices. The individual arcs are always contiguous and always start at the odd-numbered vertices.

If you want to model arcs that are not contiguous, these are considered multiline/curve geometries. We describe them later.

What happens if the line string ends at the starting vertex? This causes a loop or a ring. Can it be considered a polygon? The answer is no. To be considered a polygon, the *element-type* in the SDO_ELEM_INFO attribute needs to be 1003 (or 2003).

Polygon: Ring (Boundary) Connected by Straight Lines

Next let's look at another type of geometry: the polygon. The polygon boundary (ring) can be connected by lines, connected by arcs, or specified as a rectangle or as a circle. Let's look at examples for each of these in turn.

In this section, we will consider simple geometries. We will consider more complex polygons (those with voids and so on) later in the "Complex Geometry Examples" section. Figure 4-9 shows an example polygon where the boundary is connected by lines.

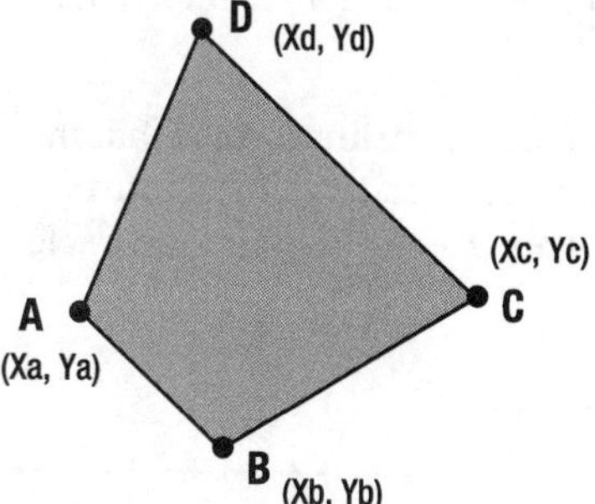

Figure 4-9. *Example of a polygon boundary connected by lines*

Listing 4-16 shows how to insert the polygon into the geometry_examples table.

Listing 4-16. *Example of a Simple Polygon Connected by Lines*

```
SQL> INSERT INTO geometry_examples VALUES
(
  'POLYGON',
  '2-D polygon connecting  A(Xa, Ya), B(Xb, Yb),  C(Xc, Yc), D(Xd, Yd)',
  SDO_GEOMETRY
  (
    2003,    -- SDO_GTYPE: D00T. Set to 2003 as it is a 2-dimensional polygon
    32774,   -- SDO_SRID
    NULL,    -- SDO_POINT_TYPE is null
    SDO_ELEM_INFO_ARRAY  -- SDO_ELEM_INFO attribute (see Table 4-2 for values)
    (
      1,     -- Offset is 1
      1003,  -- Element-type is 1003 for an outer POLYGON element
      1      -- Interpretation is 1 if boundary is connected by straight lines.
    ),
    SDO_ORDINATE_ARRAY   -- SDO_ORDINATES attribute
    (
      1,1,   -- Xa, Ya values
      2,-1,  -- Xb, Yb values
      3,1,   -- Xc, Yc values
      2,2,   -- Xd, Yd values
      1,1    -- Xa, Ya values : Repeat first vertex to close the ring
      )
  )
);
```

Compared to the previous examples, the main points to note in this example are as follows:

- The SDO_GTYPE is set to 2003 (two-dimensional polygon).
- The *element-type* in the SDO_ELEM_INFO attribute is set to 1003 to indicate it is an outer polygon, and the *interpretation* is set to 1 to indicate a polygon element connected by straight lines (see Table 4-2 for reference).
- The ordinates of the polygon are stored in the SDO_ORDINATES attribute. Note that the first vertex (Xa, Ya) is repeated as the last vertex (to close the boundary). Also note that the vertices are specified in counterclockwise order. This is a requirement in Oracle Spatial.

Caution The vertices in an outer ring of a polygon need to be specified in counterclockwise order. The vertices for the inner rings, if any, are specified in clockwise order. This is a convention of Oracle Spatial.

Polygon: Ring (Boundary) Connected by Arcs

The previous example can be easily modified to model a polygon where every three consecutive vertices are connected by an arc by simply changing the *interpretation* in the `SDO_ELEM_INFO` attribute to 2. For this to be valid, you need an odd number of vertices. However, such circular polygons are rarely used in representing spatial data.

Rectangle Polygon

Another popular shape to consider is the rectangle. A rectangle can be modeled as a polygon with four vertices connected by straight lines as in the previous example. However, a simplified representation is possible by specifying 3 instead of 1 for the *interpretation* in `SDO_ELEM_INFO`. Figure 4-10 shows an example rectangle.

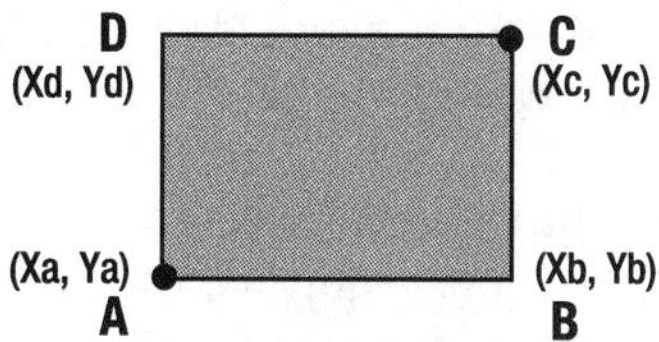

Figure 4-10. *Example of a rectangular polygon*

How is this rectangle different from the polygon in Figure 4-9? The rectangle needs only two vertices to be specified instead of all four (i.e., a much more compact representation): Oracle Spatial uses the lower-left and the upper-right corner vertices (i.e., specify only the corresponding ordinates).

- The *lower-left* corner vertex has the minimum values for the ordinates in x- and y-dimensions. In Figure 4-10, A is the lower-left corner vertex.
- The *upper-right* corner vertex has the maximum values for the ordinates in x- and y-dimensions. In Figure 4-10, C is the upper-right corner vertex.

Listing 4-17 shows how to insert the rectangular polygon into the `geometry_examples` table using the lower-left and upper-right vertices.

Listing 4-17. *Rectangular Polygon Example*

```
SQL> INSERT INTO geometry_examples VALUES
(
  'RECTANGLE POLYGON',
  '2-D rectangle polygon with corner points A(Xa, Ya),  C (Xc, Yc)',
  SDO_GEOMETRY
  (
    2003,    -- SDO_GTYPE: DOOT. Set to 2003 as it is a 2-dimensional polygon
    32774,   -- SDO_SRID
    null,    -- SDO_POINT_TYPE is null
```

```
    SDO_ELEM_INFO_ARRAY  -- SDO_ELEM_INFO attribute (see Table 4-2 for values)
    (
      1,     -- Offset is 1
      1003,  -- Element-type is 1003 for (an outer) POLYGON
      3      -- Interpretation is 3 if polygon is a RECTANGLE
    ),
    SDO_ORDINATE_ARRAY   -- SDO_ORDINATES attribute
    (
      1,1,   -- Xa, Ya values
      2,2    -- Xc, Yc values
    )
  )
);
```

Once again, note that the *interpretation* is set to 3 in the SDO_ELEM_INFO attribute. Listing 4-17 specifies only two corner vertices in the SDO_ORDINATES attribute. You can appropriately modify these ordinates to store your own rectangle.

What is a rectangle in three dimensions? A cuboid. Can the same values for SDO_ELEM_INFO be used to represent a three-dimensional cuboid (or its four-dimensional equivalent)? Yes. If you have a cuboid with the lower-left corner vertex at (Xa, Ya, Za) (the minimum value ordinates in x-, y-, and z-dimensions) and the upper-right corner vertex (the maximum value ordinates in x-, y-, and z-dimensions) at (Xc, Yc, Zc), then the geometry looks like the following. Note the SDO_GTYPE has changed to 3003 from 2003. The changes from the two-dimensional rectangle are bolded. You can construct the SDO_GEOMETRY for the rectangle equivalent in four dimensions analogously.

```
SDO_GEOMETRY
(
  3003,         -- SDO_GTYPE set 3003 to indicate 3-dimensional Polygon.
  32774,
  NULL,
  SDO_ELEM_INFO_ARRAY(1, 1003,3),
  SDO_ORDINATE_ARRAY(Xa, Ya, Za, Xc, Yc, Zc)
)
```

Circle Polygon

Next, let's look at another regular structure: the circle. Figure 4-11 shows an example. Just like rectangles, circles are different from linear polygons/arc polygons only in the *interpretation* in the SDO_ELEM_INFO attribute and the number of ordinates in the SDO_ORDINATES array. The *interpretation* is set to 4, and the ordinate array stores any three distinct points on the circumference of the circle.

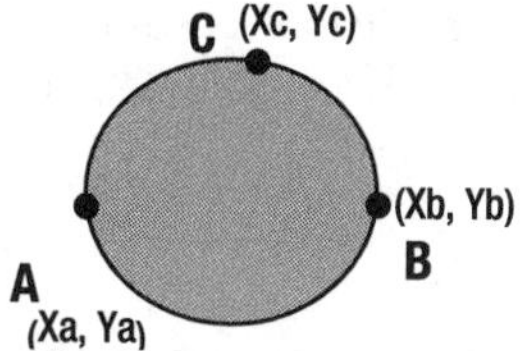

Figure 4-11. *Example of a circular polygon*

Listing 4-18 shows how to insert the circular polygon into the `geometry_examples` table.

Listing 4-18. *Circular Polygon Example*

```
SQL> INSERT INTO geometry_examples VALUES
(
  'CIRCLE POLYGON',
  '2-D circle polygon with 3 boundary points A(Xa,Ya), B(Xb,Yb), C(Xc,Yc)',
  SDO_GEOMETRY
  (
    2003,     -- SDO_GTYPE: DOOT. Set to 2003 as it is a 2-dimensional polygon
    32774,    -- SDO_SRID
    NULL,     -- SDO_POINT_TYPE is null
    SDO_ELEM_INFO_ARRAY  -- SDO_ELEM_INFO attribute (see Table 4-2 for values)
    (
      1,      -- Offset is 1
      1003,   -- Element-type is 1003 for (an outer) POLYGON
      4       -- Interpretation is 4 if polygon is a CIRCLE
    ),
    SDO_ORDINATE_ARRAY  -- SDO_ORDINATES attribute
    (
      1,1,    -- Xa, Ya values
      3,1,    -- Xb, Yb values
      2,2     -- Xc, Yc values
    )
  )
);
```

Caution You cannot specify circles and arcs if the `SRID` corresponds to a geodetic coordinate system. Circles and arcs are valid only in projected and local coordinate systems. In geodetic coordinate systems, "densify" the circumference of the circle with many points and represent the points a linear polygon using the `sdo_util.arc_densify` function.

Can you specify a circle by its center and radius? Yes. In Chapter 7, we will look at some functions that take the x and y ordinates of the center and a radius, and return an SDO_GEOMETRY.

Complex Geometry Examples

So far, we have described how to represent simple geometries. These geometries are composed of a *simple* element—an element with just one descriptor triplet. In contrast, *complex* geometries have more than one element descriptor triplet for an element. A complex geometry can be

- *A compound line string or a compound polygon*: In such a geometry, the boundary is connected by both straight lines and circular arcs. For instance, streets that have both straight line segments and arcs (to denote connecting roads) can be stored as a compound line string geometry. Objects F and G in Figure 4-1 are examples of such a compound line string element and a compound polygon geometry, respectively.
- *A voided polygon*: This geometry has an outer ring and one or more inner rings. The outer and inner ring polygon elements are specified as *simple* polygon elements. Object D in Figure 4-1 is an example of a voided polygon geometry. Lakes and other bodies of water that have islands can be stored as voided polygons. Note that the area of the interior rings is not considered part of these geometries.
- *A collection*: This geometry is a collection of multiple elements such as points, lines, and/or polygons. Object E in Figure 4-1 is an example of such a collection. The state boundaries for Texas and California have one or more islands and can be stored as collection geometries.

Guidelines for Constructing Complex Geometries

How do you construct complex geometries? Here are the general guidelines:

- The SDO_ELEM_INFO triplets of the simple elements constituting the complex geometry are concatenated in the appropriate order.
- The SDO_ORDINATES values are also concatenated. (Duplication of any shared vertices in contiguous elements is removed.)
- As a result of the concatenation of the SDO_ORDINATES, the offsets in the SDO_ELEM_INFO attribute for each simple element are adjusted to reflect the correct start of the element in the SDO_ORDINATES array.
- For *compound* (line string or polygon) elements, additional triplets are added to SDO_ELEM_INFO to specify the combination of subsequent simple elements. Table 4-3 presents the possible values for the *element-type* for these additional triplets.
- The SDO_GTYPE is set to reflect the resulting geometry.

Let's examine the *compound* geometries and *voided-polygon* geometries. We will consider *collection* geometries in the last part of the section. First, we will illustrate how to construct the SDO_ELEM_INFO attributes (i.e., the corresponding element descriptor triplets) for these geometries. Table 4-3 shows the SDO_ELEM_INFO values for the compound geometries and the voided-polygon geometries.

Table 4-3. *V[illegible] [illegible]lement Descriptor Triplet for Compound[illegible]*

Name	[illegible]	[illegible]nterpretation
Voided polygon	1[illegible] 2003 = Interior polygon (hole)	1 = Polygon boundary connected by straight lines. 2 = Polygon boundary connected by circular arcs. 3 = Rectangle polygon. The `lower_left` and `upper_right` corner vertices of the rectangle are specified in the `SDO_ORDINATES` array. 4 = Circular polygon. Any three vertices on the boundary of the circle are specified in the `SDO_ORDINATES` array.
Compound line string	4	*N* = Specifies the number of subelements that constitute the compound line string. The *N* triplets for these *N* subelements follow the current (header) triplet.
Compound polygon	1005 = Outer polygon 2005 = Interior polygon	*N* = Specifies the number of straight-line and circular-arc subelements that constitute the polygon boundary. The *N* triplets for these *N* subelements follow this triplet.

SDO_ELEM_INFO for Compound Elements

If the compound element has *N* subelements, then there will be *N* + 1 descriptor triplets: one *header* triplet specifying that it is a compound element, followed by *N* triplets, one for each subelement. The *N* subelements have to be simple elements, and their descriptor triplets will be constructed as specified previously for simple elements. The header triplet has the following form:

- The *offset* specifies the starting offset for the compound element in the `SDO_ORDINATES` array.
- The *element-type* specifies one of the following:
  - A compound line string (*element-type* = 4).
  - A compound polygon (*element-type* = 1005 or 2005). The *element-type* will be 1005 if the compound element is used an outer polygon ring, and it will be 2005 if it is used an inner ring (void).
- The *interpretation* for the header triplet specifies the number of subelements that make up this compound element.

For example, for the compound line string object F in Figure 4-1, the *element-type* for the header triplet will be 4 and *interpretation* will be 2 since it has two subelements. The next two triplets in the SDO_ELEM_INFO array will have the description for these subelements. Both elements are lines and have an *element-type* of 2 but one subelement will have an *interpretation* of 1, indicating straight-line connectivity, and another element will have an *interpretation* of 2, indicating arc-based connectivity.[6] The SDO_ELEM_INFO will have the triplets in the following order:

- (1, 4, 2) for the header triplet specifying the compound line string
- (1, 2, 1) for the first subelement triplet connected by straight lines
- (5, 2, 2) for the next subelement triplet representing the arc

SDO_ELEM_INFO for Voided Polygon Element

If the voided polygon has *N* void (inner ring) subelements and one outer ring subelement, then there will be at least *N* + 1 descriptor triplets. The first triplet will specify the descriptor triplet for the outer ring. This will be followed by descriptor triplets for each of the *N* void subelements. If all of the subelements are simple elements, then there will be exactly *N* + 1 descriptor triplets. Otherwise, the size will reflect the descriptors for any compound subelements.

For example, the voided-polygon object D in Figure 4-1 has two descriptor triplets. The first triplet represents the outer polygon ring and has an *element-type* of 1003. The second triplet represents the rectangular void and has an *element-type* of 2003.

Next let's look at some examples of such complex shapes and how to represent them using the SDO_GEOMETRY data type in Oracle.

Compound Line String Example

Most road segments are connected by straight lines. However, there are some segments where the road takes a sharp circular turn. How do you model roads that have a combination of straight-line segments and circular segments? Figure 4-12 shows an example.

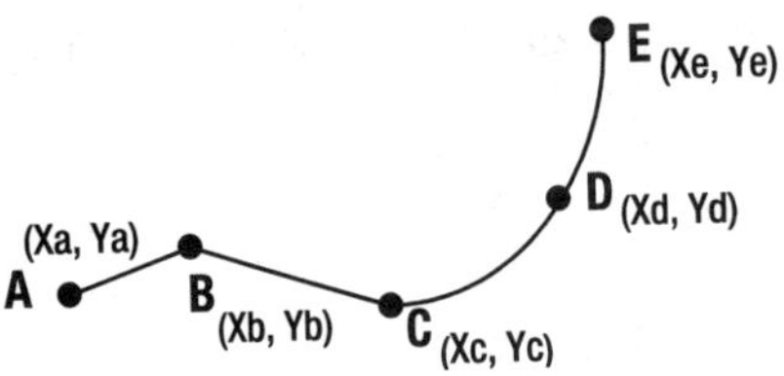

Figure 4-12. *Example of a compound line string connected by lines and arcs*

Line segment ABC is connected by straight lines, and CDE is connected by arcs. How do you represent this compound line? The answer is to construct a compound element by specifying a header triplet followed by simple element triplets for the SDO_ELEM_INFO attribute as described in Table 4-3.

6. Recall that Oracle supports only circular arcs. "Arcs" in this chapter always refers to circular arcs.

- *Header triplet*: The number of subelements is 2 and the starting offset is 1, so the header triplet is (1, 4, 2). The 4 specifies that it is a header triplet for a compound line string, and the 2 specifies that the number of simple elements is two.
- *The triplet for line ABC*: Since this is the first simple element in the compound, the offset in SDO_ORDINATES will still be 1. The *element-type* is set to 2 (line string) and the *interpretation* is set to 1 to indicate straight-line connectivity. This triplet is thus (1, 2, 1). The six ordinates for this element are the first to be stored in SDO_ORDINATES array.
- *The triplet for arc CDE*: Also, this element shares the vertex C with the previous element ABC, so the ordinates for vertex C need not be repeated. Since this element (CDE) starts at vertex C, which is stored at offset 5, the starting offset is set to 5. The *element-type* is set to 2 (line string) and the *interpretation* is set to 2 to indicate arc-based connectivity. The triplet therefore is (5, 2, 2).

Since the geometry has only two-dimensional lines, the SDO_GTYPE is set to 2002. This representation is described using the SDO_GEOMETRY elements in Figure 4-13.

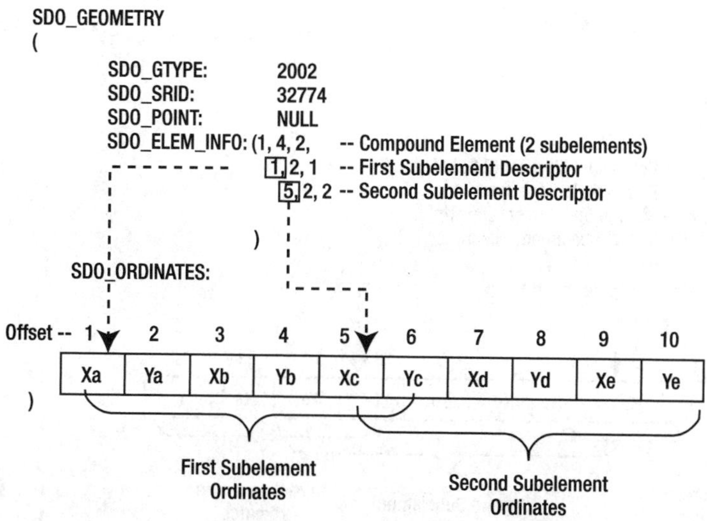

Figure 4-13. *Storing a compound line string as an* SDO_GEOMETRY

■ Note Compound line strings should be contiguous (i.e., they should share a vertex). In Figure 4-13, the vertex (Xc, Yc) is shared by both the first and second elements. Also note that a compound line string (or elements with the *element-type* set to 4) can have only line string subelements (i.e., subelements of *element-type* = 2).

Compound Polygon Example

If you connect vertex E back to vertex A in Figure 4-13, it becomes a closed line as shown in Figure 4-14.

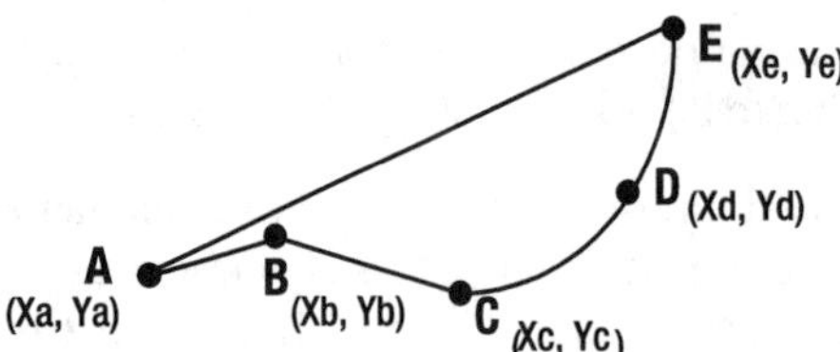

Figure 4-14. *Example of a "closed" compound line string connected by lines and arcs*

You can use this closed compound line string to be the boundary of a polygon by appropriately modifying the SDO_GTYPE (and the *element-types*). Figure 4-15 shows the elements for the SDO_GEOMETRY.

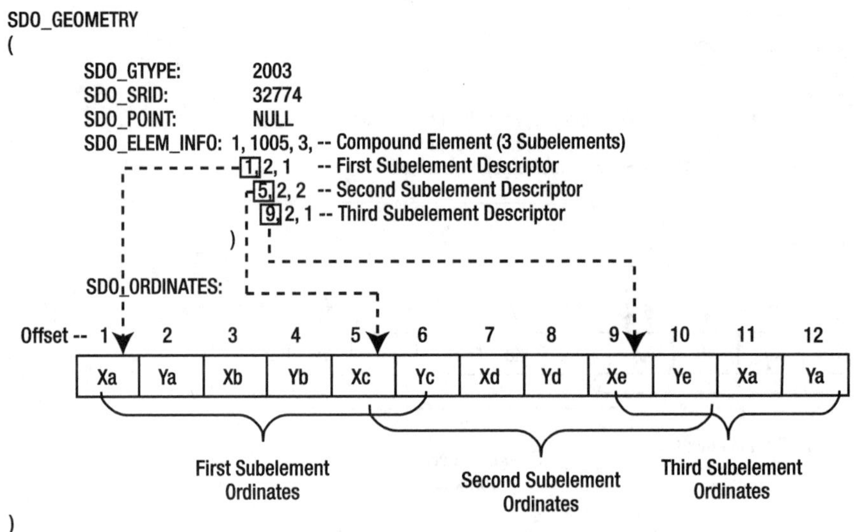

Figure 4-15. *Storing a compound polygon as an* SDO_GEOMETRY

Here we note the following changes:

- The SDO_GTYPE is set to 2003.
- For the compound element header triplet, the *element-type* is set to 1005 (compound polygon) instead of 4, and the number of subelements changes to three from two.

- A new subelement represents the straight line connecting E to A. This subelement has SDO_ELEM_INFO set to (9, 2, 1) where 9 represents the starting offset for the ordinates of E, 2 indicates it is a line, and 1 indicates connectivity by straight line.
- The ordinates of vertex A are repeated at the end in the SDO_ORDINATES array.

Remember that except for the header triplet, all other subelement triplets still have an *element-type* of 2 (line), as these elements are only representing lines. The header triplet that signifies the compound has an *element-type* of 1005.

Caution A compound polygon (or elements of *element-type* = 5) can only be made up of line string subelements (i.e., subelements of *element-type* = 2).

Polygon with a Void

What about oceans that have islands? How do you represent the area occupied such large bodies of water? Polygons with voids will help here. Figure 4-16 shows a diamond-shaped polygon with vertices A, B, C, and D. Inside this polygon is a rectangle polygon with corners at E and F. This rectangle polygon serves as a *void*—that is, an area not covered by the outer ABCD polygon. How do you represent this polygon with the void?

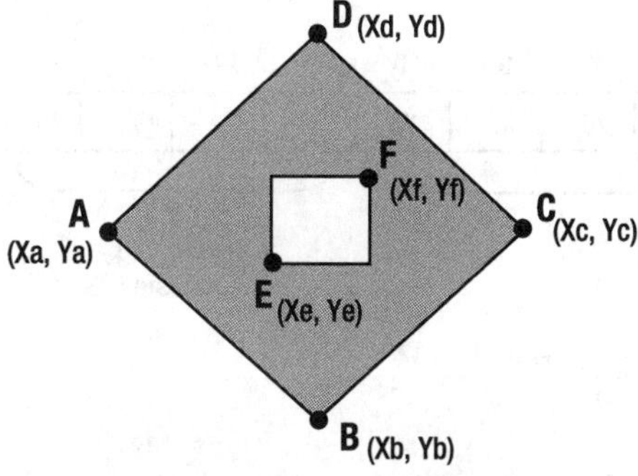

Figure 4-16. *Example of a polygon with a void*

First let's examine the constructors for the two polygons in Figure 4-16 separately. Polygon ABCD (without the void) is a simple polygon whose boundary is connected by straight lines. The constructor looks like this:

```
SDO_GEOMETRY
(
  2003, 32774, NULL,
  SDO_ELEM_INFO(1, 1003,1),
  SDO_ORDINATE_ARRAY(Xa, Ya, Xb, Yb, Xc, Yc, Xd, Yd, Xa, Ya)
)
```

Assuming that the rectangular polygon EF is not inside ABCD, the constructor looks as follows:

```
SDO_GEOMETRY
(
  2003, 32774, NULL,
  SDO_ELEM_INFO(1, 1003, 3),
  SDO_ORDINATE_ARRAY(Xe, Ye, Xf, Yf)
)
```

Using these two constructors, you can combine the two polygons to represent a polygon with a void as shown in Figure 4-17. In this figure, the outer element descriptor describes the outer polygon, and the inner element descriptor describes the inner polygon.

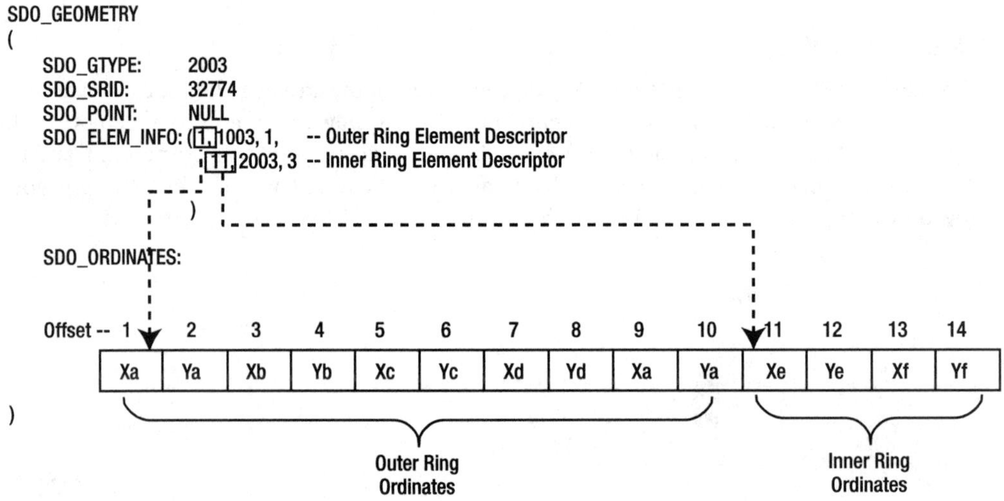

Figure 4-17. *Storing a polygon with a void as an* SDO_GEOMETRY

In this example, the combined polygon has two elements: an outer polygon and an inner polygon. You need to specify these elements as follows.

- The element triplets for the outer polygon are specified first, followed by that for the inner polygon (i.e., the void). The outer polygon ring should have the *element-type* set to 1003 and inner polygon ring should have the *element-type* set to 2003. (If there is more than one inner polygon, these are specified in any order after the outer polygon is specified.)
- Likewise, the ordinates of the outer polygon are specified first, followed by those of the inner polygon.
- The starting offset for the ordinates of inner polygon are adjusted from 1 to 11 (as they are preceded by the ordinates of the outer polygon).

■ **Note** Unlike in a compound (line or polygon) geometry (see Figures 4-13 and 4-15), there is no header triplet for constructing a polygon with a void. All inner elements (i.e., triplets with an *element-type* of 2003 or 2005) that follow an outer element (i.e., triplets with an *element-type* of 1003 or 1005) are considered to be voids of (i.e., inside) the outer element.

Can you have a polygon inside the void (i.e., inside the inner ring)? Yes, but that will be treated as a multipolygon geometry (the SDO_GTYPE is 7). The reason is that the area represented by the resulting polygon is not *contiguous*.

Collections

Next, we come to the last geometry type: the collection. Collections can be *homogeneous*, as in a multipoint, multiline, multipolygon collection. Or they can be *heterogeneous*, containing a combination of point, line, and/or polygon geometries. In Table 4-1 you saw that multipoint, multiline, multipolygon, and heterogeneous collections each have a different SDO_GTYPE. Now you will see how to represent these geometries using the SDO_GEOEMTRY data type. At the end of this section, you will learn about a function that appends two geometries. A collection of N geometries can be constructed simply by calling this function $N-1$ times.

Note that collections are created in much the same way as other "complex" geometries. See "Guidelines for Constructing Complex Geometries" in this section.

Multipoint Collection Example

Earlier in the chapter, you learned how to model a single point using the SDO_POINT attribute in the SDO_GEOMETRY type. Here we will model multiple points as a *single* collection geometry—that is, we will store all three points A, B, and C in Figure 4-18 as subelements of a single multipoint geometry.

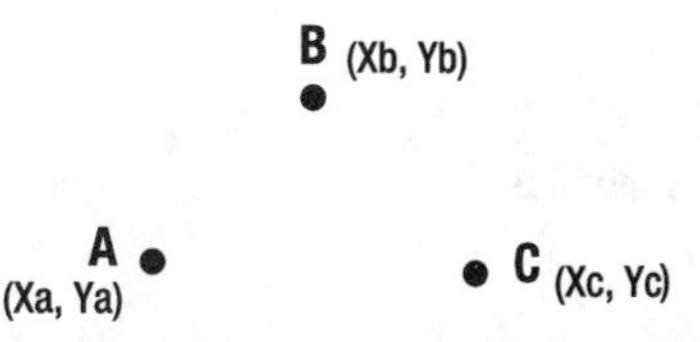

Figure 4-18. *Example of a multipoint collection*

How do you store this geometry? You first construct SDO_GEOMETRY objects for the individual points and combine them using the guidelines described in the beginning of this section.

1. Set the SDO_GTYPE to 5 (multipoint).

2. Combine the SDO_ORDINATES attributes of the three point SDO_GEOMETRY objects.

3. Combine the corresponding SDO_ELEM_INFO attributes of the three point objects. The offset in the resulting SDO_ELEM_INFO is adjusted to reflect the offset in the SDO_ORDINATES attribute for each point.

The resulting SDO_GEOMETRY will look like this:

```
SDO_GEOMETRY
(
  2005, 32774, NULL,
  SDO_ELEM_INFO_ARRAY  -- SDO_ELEM_INFO: multiple elements each with 1 pt
  (
    1,1,1,             -- triplet for first "point" element
    3,1,1,             -- triplet for second "point" element
    5,1,1              -- triplet for third "point" element
  ),
  SDO_ORDINATE_ARRAY
  (
    Xa, Ya,            -- coordinates of first point
    Xb, Yb,            -- coordinates of second point
    Xc, Yc             -- coordinates of third point
  )
)
```

In this example, the three points are represented as three elements. Oracle, however, has a much simpler representation: you can represent the three points as a *single* element (and store all the ordinates in the SDO_ORDINATES attribute). The element will have a descriptor triplet of the form (1, 1, *N*) where *N* represents the number of points (if *N* = 1, then the element has just one point). The corresponding constructor is as follows, and the changes are bolded.

```
SDO_GEOMETRY
(
  2005, 32774, NULL,
  SDO_ELEM_INFO_ARRAY  -- SDO_ELEM_INFO attribute
  (
    1, 1, 3            -- "Point cluster" element with 3 points
  ),
  SDO_ORDINATE_ARRAY
  (
    Xa, Ya,            -- coordinates of first point
    Xb, Yb,            -- coordinates of second point
    Xc, Yc             -- coordinates of third point
  )
)
```

We recommend the usage of a single element of *N* points instead of an array of point elements. This representation is more storage efficient and helps in performance.

Multiline String

Multiline string geometry consists of multiple line strings. Figure 4-19 shows an example. The triplets in SDO_ELEM_INFO are used to denote and demarcate each line segment.

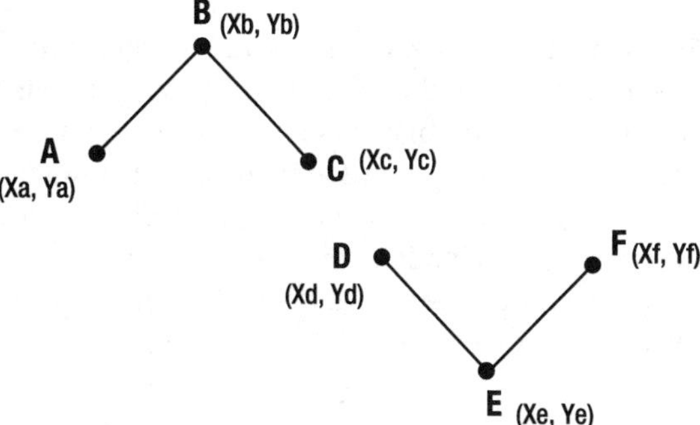

Figure 4-19. *Example of a multiline string*

We will use one triplet in the SDO_ELEM_INFO array to represent each of the elements in our geometry. The offset in each triplet points to the first element in the SDO_ORDINATES array where the first point of the geometric primitive starts. Figure 4-20 shows the resulting SDO_GEOMETRY constructor for a multiline string.

- The first line string (ABC) starts at offset 1 and ends at offset 6 (i.e., there are two ordinates for each of the three points).
- The second line string (DEF) starts at offset 7 and ends at offset 12 (i.e., there are two ordinates for each of the three points).

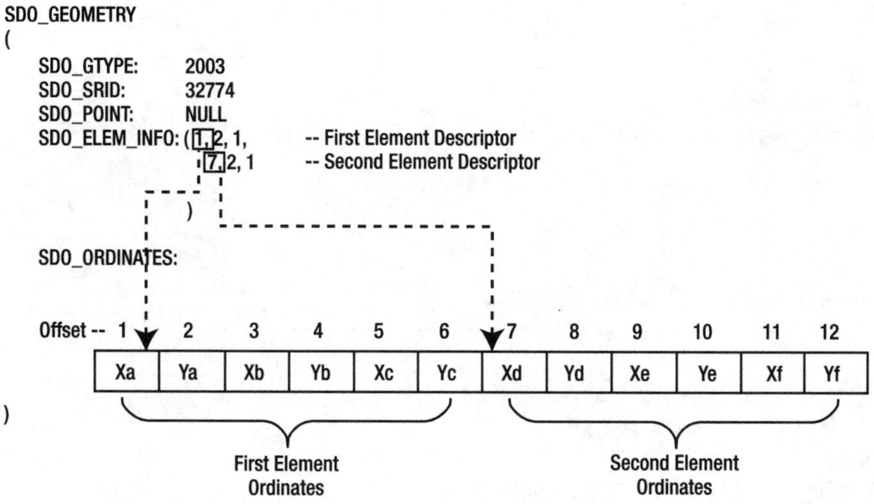

Figure 4-20. *Storing a multiline string in* SDO_GEOMETRY

Note that the two geometry elements could have different *interpretations*: one could be a straight line, and the other could be a circular arc. Note also that if the geometry was three-dimensional, the offsets (other than the first) would be different.

Multipolygon and Heterogeneous Collections

Just as in the case of multipoint and multiline string geometry collections, the triplets in the SDO_ELEM_INFO structure are used to describe each element of the collection. The SDO_GTYPE is set to the appropriate value for the collection. The ordinates of each collection element are stored in the SDO_ORDINATES array, and the starting offsets are recorded in the corresponding SDO_ELEM_INFO triplet for each collection element. We leave it as an exercise to the reader to come up with examples of multipolygon and heterogeneous collections by consulting Tables 4-2 and 4-3 and previous examples. You can compare your answers with the collections created using an alternate mechanism. This mechanism is described next.

Creating Collections: The Easy Way

The function SDO_UTIL.APPEND takes in two nonoverlapping geometries and returns an appended geometry. For example, if you invoke APPEND using two polygons, you get a multipolygon geometry as the result. Note that if the input geometries overlap, this function may return an invalid geometry.

```
SQL> SELECT SDO_UTIL.APPEND
(
  SDO_GEOMETRY
  (
    2003, 32774, null,
    SDO_ELEM_INFO_ARRAY(1,1003, 3),
    SDO_ORDINATE_ARRAY(1,1, 2,2)
  ),
  SDO_GEOMETRY
  (
    2003, 32774, NULL,
    SDO_ELEM_INFO_ARRAY(1, 1003, 3),
    SDO_ORDINATE_ARRAY(2,3, 4,5)
  )
)
FROM dual;

SDO_UTIL.APPEND(SDO_GEOMETRY(2003,32774,NULL,...
------------------------------------------------------------------
SDO_GEOMETRY
(
  2007,  -- SDO_GTYPE=  Multi-polygon
  32774, NULL,
  SDO_ELEM_INFO_ARRAY(1, 1003, 3, 5, 1003, 3),
  SDO_ORDINATE_ARRAY(1, 1, 2, 2, 2, 3, 4, 5)
)
```

If you pass in a line and a polygon, you get a heterogeneous collection (SDO_GTYPE =2007) geometry, as in the following example:

```
SQL> SELECT SDO_UTIL.APPEND
(
  SDO_GEOMETRY
  (
    2003, 32774, null,
    SDO_ELEM_INFO_ARRAY(1,1003, 3),
    SDO_ORDINATE_ARRAY(1,1, 2,2)
  ),
  SDO_GEOMETRY
  (
    2002, 32774, NULL,
    SDO_ELEM_INFO_ARRAY(1, 2, 2),
    SDO_ORDINATE_ARRAY(2,3, 3,3,4,2)
  )
)
FROM dual;

SDO_UTIL.APPEND(SDO_GEOMETRY(2003,32774,NULL,...
-------------------------------------------------------------------------------
SDO_GEOMETRY
(
  2004,  -- SDO_GTYPE =(Heterogenous) Collection
  32774, NULL,
  SDO_ELEM_INFO_ARRAY(1, 1003, 3, 5, 2, 2),
  SDO_ORDINATE_ARRAY(1, 1, 2, 2, 2, 3, 3, 3, 4, 2)
)
```

Summary

You can model locations of customers, delivery sites, and competitors as two-dimensional points. You can model locations and the shapes of streets and highways as line strings, and you can model the shapes of city boundaries as polygons. You can store all this location data using SDO_GEOMETRY columns in Oracle.

This chapter demonstrated that the SDO_GEOMETRY data type is a powerful structure in Oracle. You can use this data type to store point, line, or polygon geometries, and collections of such geometries. The SDO_GTYPE attribute of SDO_GEOMETRY specifies the type (shape) and the SDO_ELEM_INFO and SDO_ORDINATES attributes together specify the ordinate information and connectivity for the shape object. The SDO_POINT attribute stores the location for two- or three-dimensional points.

Having looked at how to construct SDO_GEOMETRY objects for different types of spatial data, in the next chapter we will look at how to insert and load such objects into an Oracle table.

CHAPTER 5

■ ■ ■

Loading, Transporting, and Validating Spatial Data

To run the examples in this chapter, you need to import a dataset as shown in the following spatial schema. Please refer to the Introduction for instructions on creating the spatial schema and other setup details.

```
imp spatial/spatial FILE=app_with_loc.dmp FULL=Y INDEXES=N
```

In the previous chapter, we introduced a new data type called SDO_GEOMETRY to store spatial data. This data type can store a variety of spatial objects: points (including those obtained by geocoding address strings), line strings, polygons, or more complex shapes. Points primarily represent the locations of application-specific entities such as businesses, customers, or suppliers. Line strings and polygons, on the other hand, represent the boundaries of geographical entities such as roads, cities, or states. In CAD/CAM-type applications, line strings and polygons can represent different entities such as the layouts of buildings, printed circuit boards, or shapes of different parts of an automobile.

In Chapter 3, we described how to add SDO_GEOMETRY columns to existing (application-specific) tables such as customers. We also described how to create tables with SDO_GEOMETRY columns to store geographic data such as states, counties, and interstates. These tables could be part of an e-business application or a variety of other spatial applications such as CAD/CAM, GIS, GPS, wireless, or telematics.

In this chapter, we work with our example business application, the tables for which we created in Chapter 3, and we move on to describe how to populate these tables with data and how to ensure that the data are valid and free of bugs. Specifically, we cover the following topics:

- *Inserting into a table with* SDO_GEOMETRY *columns*. We look at how to insert a single geometry into a table with SDO_GEOMETRY. This may not be the right approach to populate the application-specific and geographic tables because inserting geometries one by one may be time consuming and error prone. A better approach is to bulk load the data.

- *Loading and publishing spatial data to and from Oracle databases*. We describe how to use Oracle utilities to bulk load spatial data into Oracle tables from operating system files or Oracle Import/Export (.dmp) files. We also describe a utility to convert third-party formats such as Environmental Systems Research Institute's (ESRI's) shapefiles to SQL*Loader files and load the resulting files into Oracle.

- *Validating spatial data.* We describe functions available to check whether or not the loaded spatial data are in a valid Oracle Spatial format.
- *Debugging spatial data.* We explain how to identify and correct any invalid spatial data in a table.

The functions that we describe in this chapter are part of two packages: SDO_GEOM and SDO_UTIL. The SDO_GEOM functions that we use in this chapter are part of the Locator product (shipped for free with Oracle Database Server). The SDO_UTIL package and the associated functions, however, are included only in the priced option of Spatial.

Inserting Data into an SDO_GEOMETRY Column

Let's create a table to model the sales regions of a business franchise. Listing 5-1 shows the SQL.

Listing 5-1. *Creating the* sales_regions *Table*

```
SQL> CREATE TABLE sales_regions
(
  id         NUMBER,
  geom       SDO_GEOMETRY
);
```

We can insert polygons representing sales regions into the geom column of this table. Listing 5-2 shows an example.

Listing 5-2. *Inserting a Polygon Geometry into the* sales_regions *Table*

```
SQL> INSERT INTO  sales_regions  VALUES
(
  10000,   -- SALES_REGIONS ID
  SDO_GEOMETRY  --  use  the SDO_GEOMETRY constructor
  (
    2003,  -- A two-dimensional Polygon
    8307,  -- SRID is GEODETIC
    NULL,  -- SDO_POINT_TYPE is null as it is not a point
    SDO_ELEM_INFO_ARRAY (1, 1003,  1),  -- A polygon with just one ring
    SDO_ORDINATE_ARRAY  -- SDO_ORDINATES field
    (
      -77.04487, 38.9043742,   -- coordinates of first vertex
      -77.046645, 38.9040983, -- other vertices
      -77.04815, 38.9033127, -77.049155, 38.9021368,
      -77.049508, 38.9007499, -77.049155, 38.899363, -77.048149, 38.8981873,
      -77.046645, 38.8974017, -77.04487, 38.8971258, -77.043095, 38.8974017,
      -77.041591, 38.8981873, -77.040585, 38.899363, -77.040232, 38.9007499,
      -77.040585, 38.9021368, -77.04159, 38.9033127, -77.043095, 38.9040983,
      -77.04487, 38.9043742   -- coordinates of last vertex same as first vertex
    )
  )
);
```

Note that the second argument is the SDO_GEOMETRY constructor presented in the previous chapter. We can insert any type of geometry into this column, be it a point, a line, a polygon, and so on. In this example, the geometry is a two-dimensional polygon geometry. The vertices of this polygon are stored in the SDO_ORDINATES attribute instantiated using the SDO_ORDINATE_ARRAY type. In Chapter 4, we noted that for a polygon the first and last vertex coordinates should be same. Accordingly, in Listing 5-2, the coordinates for the first and last vertices (shown in the first and the last lines of the SDO_ORDINATE_ARRAY object) are identical.

■ **Caution** INSERT statements with an SDO_GEOMETRY constructor cannot take more than 1,000 numbers in the SDO_ORDINATES array. One alternative is to create an SDO_GEOMETRY object in PL/SQL and bind this object in the INSERT statement (refer to Chapter 14 for details).

Populating tables by inserting the data rows one by one (as in Listing 5-2) is very time-consuming. In this chapter, we discuss how to load the data in bulk and how to check that the populated data are in the required Oracle Spatial format.

Loading and Publishing Spatial Data

Spatial data can be loaded from different formats, including text files, Oracle export formats, or third-party proprietary formats. In this section, we describe each of these formats in sequence.

Loading from Text Files Using SQL*Loader

SQL*Loader is an Oracle utility to load data from files into Oracle tables. This utility performs *bulk loading*—that is, it can load more than one row into a table in one attempt.

■ **Tip** Always drop any associated spatial indexes before bulk loading into a table. Otherwise, spatial indexes may slow down the loading process.

SQL*Loader takes a control file that specifies how to break the file data into Oracle rows and how to separate these records into individual columns. We do not discuss all the details of SQL*Loader here. Instead, we highlight the object-specific issues that come into play when loading SDO_GEOMETRY columns.

Loading Point Data

First, let's look at how to insert data into the `sales_regions` table. Say the sales regions are point data. We can directly insert the regions into the x, y components of the `geom` column (`SDO_GEOMETRY` object) as described in the control file in Listing 5-3.

Listing 5-3. *Control File for Loading "Point"* `sales_regions` *Data*

```
LOAD DATA
INFILE *
INTO TABLE sales_regions
FIELDS TERMINATED BY '|'
TRAILING NULLCOLS
(
  id NULLIF ID = BLANKS,
  geom COLUMN OBJECT
  (
    SDO_GTYPE       INTEGER EXTERNAL,
    SDO_POINT       COLUMN OBJECT
    (
      X             FLOAT EXTERNAL,
      Y             FLOAT EXTERNAL
    )
  )
)
BEGINDATA
1|2001|-76.99022|38.888654|
2|2001|-77.41575|38.924753|
```

Notice that there is no need to specify the `SDO_SRID`, the `SDO_ELEM_INFO_ARRAY`, and the `SDO_ORDINATE_ARRAY` components. These are automatically set to `NULL`. The control file in Listing 5-3 has two records, one with an ID of 1 and another with an ID of 2. Both records have the x, y components specified as the last two fields. Just as in other SQL*Loader control files, the fields in each record are terminated by the pipe symbol, | (because we specified fields terminated by |). We will use this "control" file to load the `sales_regions` data as shown in Listing 5-4. A log of the operation that records which rows are loaded and which are rejected is available in `sales_regions.log`.

Listing 5-4. *Using SQL*Loader to Load Data into the* `sales_regions` *Table*

```
SQLLDR spatial/spatial CONTROL=sales_regions.ctl
```

Note that the format for the data is specified in the initial part of the control file. The data are specified in the same control file right after the `BEGINDATA` keyword. Instead of specifying the data in the control file, we can store the data in a separate file, say `sales_regions.dat`. We can then specify the data file at the command line, as shown in Listing 5-5.

Listing 5-5. *Using SQL*Loader with a Data File*

```
SQLLDR spatial/spatial CONTROL=sales_regions.ctl DATA=sales_regions.dat
```

Alternatively, we can specify the data file name in the control file (and load the data, as in Listing 5-5). In the control file, we have to modify `INFILE *` to `INFILE sales_regions.dat`. The modified control file is shown in Listing 5-6, and the corresponding data file is shown in Listing 5-7. You can run the SQL*Loader command as in Listing 5-4 to load the data.

Listing 5-6. `sales_regions.ctl` *File*

```
LOAD DATA
INFILE  sales_regions.dat
INTO TABLE sales_regions
FIELDS TERMINATED BY '|'
TRAILING NULLCOLS
(
  id NULLIF ID = BLANKS,
  geom COLUMN OBJECT
  (
    SDO_GTYPE       INTEGER EXTERNAL,
    SDO_POINT       COLUMN OBJECT
    (
      X             FLOAT EXTERNAL,
      Y             FLOAT EXTERNAL
    )
  )
)
```

Listing 5-7. `sales_regions.dat` *File*

```
1|2001|-76.99022|38.888654|
2|2001|-77.41575|38.924753|
```

Loading Nonpoint Data

What if the data you want to load contains nonpoint data? In that case, you need to populate the `SDO_ELEM_INFO` and `SDO_ORDINATES` fields of the `SDO_GEOMETRY` column. The control file in Listing 5-8 shows an example of how to do this for the `sales_regions` table, where most of the `sales_regions` are nonpoint geometries.

Listing 5-8. *Control File for Loading Nonpoint* `SDO_GEOMETRY` *Data*

```
LOAD DATA
INFILE *
CONTINUEIF NEXT(1:1)='#'
INTO TABLE sales_regions
FIELDS TERMINATED BY '|'
TRAILING NULLCOLS
(
  id CHAR(6),
  geom COLUMN OBJECT
```

```
  (
    SDO_GTYPE INTEGER EXTERNAL,
    SDO_SRID INTEGER EXTERNAL,
    SDO_ELEM_INFO VARRAY terminated by '/'   (E FLOAT EXTERNAL),
    SDO_ORDINATES VARRAY terminated by '/' (O FLOAT EXTERNAL)
  )
)
BEGINDATA
 10000| 2003| 8307|
#1| 1003| 1|/
#-77.04487| 38.9043742| -77.046645| 38.9040983| -77.04815| 38.9033127|-77.049155|
#38.9021368| -77.049508| 38.9007499| -77.049155| 38.899363| -77.048149|
#38.8981873| -77.046645| 38.8974017| -77.04487| 38.8971258| -77.043095|
#38.8974017| -77.041591| 38.8981873| -77.040585| 38.899363| -77.040232|
#38.9007499| -77.040585| 38.9021368| -77.04159| 38.9033127| -77.043095|
#38.9040983| -77.04487| 38.9043742| -77.04487| 38.9043742|/
```

Note that SQL*Loader cannot process records that are more than 64KB in size if the data are included the control file (as in Listing 5-3). (If the data are in a separate data file, the default limit for a record is 1MB, which can be increased up to 20MB by overriding the default using the `READSIZE` parameter.) To work around this restriction, the record is split into multiple lines. The line `CONTINUEIF NEXT(1:1)='#'` specifies that the record is continued if a hash mark (#) is the first character of each line. Note that the `SDO_ORDINATES` field could contain up to 1 million numbers. This means SQL*Loader will need to concatenate multiple records of a size less than 64KB to create one `SDO_ORDINATE_ARRAY` containing up to 1 million numbers.

Caution In direct path mode for SQL*Loader, spatial indexes that are associated with the tables being loaded are not maintained. You need to rebuild or drop and re-create such spatial indexes (see Chapter 8 for details on rebuilding/re-creating spatial indexes).

Transporting Spatial Data Between Oracle Databases

In this section, we discuss how to exchange spatial data between different Oracle databases. Oracle provides a variety of ways to perform such exchanges. These include the Import/Export utilities and the transportable tablespace mechanisms. In addition, Oracle Spatial provides a mechanism to migrate some of the pre-10*g* spatial formats to current formats using the `SDO_MIGRATE` function.

Import/Export Utilities

The easiest method to load data is through the use of Oracle's platform-independent `.dmp` files. These files are used by Oracle's Import/Export utilities. For instance, we can export the `customers` table from the `spatial` schema as shown in Listing 5-9.

Listing 5-9. *Exporting the* `customers` *Table into the* `customers.dmp` *File*

```
EXP spatial/spatial FILE=customers.dmp TABLES=customers
```

We can later import this data (i.e., the `.dmp` file) into another schema, say the `scott` schema, using Oracle's Import utility. Listing 5-10 shows an example.

Listing 5-10. *Importing the* `customers` *Table into the* `scott` *Schema*

```
IMP scott/tiger  FILE=customers.dmp  IGNORE=Y INDEXES=N
```

`ignore=y` ignores any warnings if objects already exist in the schema. If we do not specify any command-line arguments, the Import utility will prompt us to specify the import file name and the tables that we want to import. We can then choose only a subset of the tables in `sample_data.dmp` to be imported.

Note that if the `location` column in the `customers` table had a spatial index before it was exported, then after the import, the spatial index will be automatically created on this table. The user `scott` in Listing 5-10 does not have to do anything specific in this instance to create the index. In addition, the spatial index will also populate the spatial metadata for the corresponding spatial layer (i.e., the `location` column in the `customers` table) in the `USER_SDO_GEOM_METADATA` view. It uses the metadata from the exported database.

We can also import data into the `scott` schema using the `fromuser` and `touser` command-line arguments. The import command is run as a system account (`system/manager`). Listing 5-11 shows an example.

Listing 5-11. *Importing Using the* `fromuser` *and* `touser` *Arguments*

```
IMP SYSTEM/MANAGER FROMUSER=spatial TOUSER=scott FILE=customers.dmp
```

If the `customers` table has a spatial index, this will be re-created on import (as in Listing 5-10). Note that to re-create the index when we import with the `touser` argument, `scott` needs to have the `CREATE TABLE` and `CREATE SEQUENCE` privileges. We can use the following SQL to grant these privileges to `scott`:

```
SQL> CONNECT SYSTEM/MANAGER
SQL> GRANT create table to SCOTT;
SQL> GRANT create sequence to SCOTT;
```

You want to import just the table data without any indexes. You can then import the data by specifying `indexes=n` on the command line.

The Oracle Data Pump component provides alternate and more efficient mechanisms for transferring data between databases. It provides the `EXPDP` and `IMPDP` utilities, which are equivalent to the Export (`EXP`) and Import (`IMP`) utilities of Oracle.

Transportable Tablespaces

An alternate mechanism to transfer data between different Oracle databases is the use of transportable tablespaces. In this case, you can transport an entire tablespace (along with its contents) between two Oracle databases (10*g* or higher). For instance, if the `customers` table is part of a tablespace, `TBS`, then we can transport this tablespace. To ensure that any spatial indexes existing on the `customers` table are also transported, we need to perform the following steps:

1. Execute `SDO_UTIL.PREPARE_FOR_TTS('TBS')` before transporting the tablespace `TBS`.

2. Execute `SDO_UTIL.INITIALIZE_INDEXES_FOR_TTS` after transporting the tablespace `TBS`.

Listing 5-12 shows how to create the `.dmp` file for transporting the tablespace `TBS` from a source database.

Listing 5-12. *Transporting the Tablespace* `TBS` *from a Source Database*

```
SQLPLUS spatial/spatial
EXECUTE SDO_UTIL.PREPARE_FOR_TTS('TBS');
CONNECT SYSTEM/MANAGER AS SYSDBA
EXECUTE DBMS_TTS.TRANSPORT_SET_CHECK('TBS', TRUE);
ALTER TABLESPACE TBS READ ONLY;
EXIT;

EXP USERID = "'SYSTEM/MANAGER AS SYSDBA'"  TRANSPORT_TABLESPACE=Y TABLESPACES=TBS
FILE=trans_ts.dmp
```

This will create the tablespace metadata in the file `trans_ts.dmp`. Copy this file and `sdo_tts.dbf` (the data file for the tablespace) to the target database system. We should create the `spatial` schema into which this data needs to be populated and then import the contents of `trans_ts.dmp` as shown in Listing 5-13.

Listing 5-13. *Creating the Transported Tablespace in the Target Database*

```
<copy the file to new system with user spatial created>
IMP USERID = "'SYSTEM/MANAGER AS SYSDBA'"  TRANSPORT_TABLESPACE=Y FILE=trans_ts.dmp
DATAFILES='sdo_tts.dbf' TABLESPACES=tbs
```

This will create the tablespace and populate the contents in the target database. Note that the tablespace should not already exist in the target database. This restricts the import operation to being performed only once (as it creates the tablespace) in the target database.

After importing, we should alter the tablespace `TBS` to allow read/write operations and execute the `SDO_UTIL.INITIALIZE_INDEXES_FOR_TTS` procedure to enable spatial indexes. Listing 5-14 shows the corresponding SQL.

Listing 5-14. *Enabling Spatial Indexes for the Tables in the Transported Tablespace*

```
SQLPLUS SYSTEM/MANAGER AS SYSDBA
ALTER TABLESPACE TBS READ WRITE;
CONNECT spatial/spatial;
EXEC SDO_UTIL.INITIALIZE_INDEXES_FOR_TTS;
```

Spatial-Specific Restriction

The INITIALIZE_INDEXES_FOR_TTS function re-enables the spatial indexes that exist on the tables in the transported tablespace. *Spatial indexes, however, will work only if the endian format of the source and the target databases remains the same.* If the endian format is different, then the spatial indexes need to be rebuilt using the ALTER INDEX REBUILD command. Listing 5-15 shows an example for the customers_sidx index on the location column of the customers table. (Chapter 8 provides details on creating and rebuilding indexes.)

Listing 5-15. *Rebuilding a Spatial Index After Transporting Across Endian Platforms*

```
SQL> ALTER INDEX customers_sidx REBUILD;
```

Migrating from Prior Versions of Oracle Spatial

The SDO_GEOMETRY data type has evolved significantly over past releases of Oracle (see Chapter 2 for details), and it may continue to change in future releases. The SDO_MIGRATE package has functions, such as TO_CURRENT, to migrate spatial data from prior versions to the "current" version, whatever that is. Listing 5-16 shows an example to migrate the geometry data in the location column data of the customers table to Oracle10*g* (format). Note the third parameter specifies the commit interval as 100, which tells the database to commit after migration of every 100 rows of the customers table.

Listing 5-16. *Migrating* location *Column Data in the* customers *Table to the Current Format (10g)*

```
SQL> EXECUTE SDO_MIGRATE.TO_CURRENT('customers', 'location', 100);
```

This function has other signatures to accommodate migration of a single geometry instead of a set of geometries in a table. You can refer to the *Oracle Spatial User's Guide* for more details on this package. These migration functions work in only one direction—that is, they migrate data from older versions to the current version.

Loading from External Formats

Several GIS vendors have their own formats to store spatial data. The ESRI shapefile format is one such example. Oracle Spatial does not understand these formats. A variety of third-party converters are available to perform conversion between other formats and the Oracle Spatial format. A full discussion of these formats and the converters is beyond the scope of this book; however, to illustrate the concept, we will use the free but unsupported Oracle utility called SHP2SDO, which reads ESRI shapefiles and outputs SQL*Loader control and data files (see Listing 5-17). These files can then be used to populate the SDO_GEOMETRY column in an Oracle table.

Listing 5-17. *Using* shp2sdo *to Convert from ESRI Shapefiles*

```
SHP2SDO customers -g location  -x(-180,180) -y(-90,90) -s 8307 -t 0.5
```

Note that the command-line argument customers in Listing 5-17 indicates three different files as input: customers.shp, customers.shx, and customers.dbf. These three files contain different components of an ESRI shapefile named customers. The -x and -y arguments specify the extent of the data in x- and y-dimensions. The -t argument specifies the tolerance for the dimensions. The -s argument specifies the SRID (coordinate system) for the data.

The SHP2SDO utility outputs three files:

- customers.sql: This file creates the customers table and loads spatial metadata for the customers table (associated spatial layers). Listing 5-18 shows an example.
- customers.ctl: This file is the control file for SQL*Loader.
- customers.dat: This file contains the data for loading using SQL*Loader.

Listing 5-18. customers.sql *File*

```
CREATE TABLE customers
(
  id                          NUMBER,
  datasrc_id                  NUMBER,
  name                        VARCHAR2(35),
  category                    VARCHAR2(30),
  street_number               VARCHAR2(5),
  street_name                 VARCHAR2(60),
  city                        VARCHAR2(32),
  postal_code                 VARCHAR2(16),
  state                       VARCHAR2(32),
  phone_number                VARCHAR2(15),
  customer_grade              VARCHAR2(15)
);
INSERT INTO USER_SDO_GEOM_METADATA VALUES
(
  'CUSTOMERS',                   -- Table_name
  'LOCATION',                    -- Column name
  MDSYS.SDO_DIM_INFO_ARRAY       -- Diminfo
  (
    MDSYS.SDO_DIM_ELEMENT('Longitude', -180, 180, 0.5), --Longitude dimension
    MDSYS.SDO_DIM_ELEMENT('Latitude', -90, 90, 0.5)     --Latitude dimension
  ),
  8307                           -- Geodetic SRID
);
```

■ **Note** See Chapter 3 for more information on different values in the SQL `INSERT` statement in Listing 5-18.

The `customers.ctl` and `customers.dat` files will be similar to those shown in Listings 5-6 and 5-7, respectively.

We can then load the data into the `customers` table in Oracle using SQL*Loader, as shown in Listing 5-19. This will create the table in Oracle and load the data into the table.

Listing 5-19. *Executing the Output Files from* `SHP2SDO` *to Load Data into Oracle*

```
SQLPLUS spatial/spatial @customers.sql
SQLLDR spatial/spatial CONTROL=customers.ctl
```

For more details on this utility, you can run `SHP2SDO -h`.

Conversion Between SDO_GEOMETRY and WKT/WKB

SQL/MM is the ISO/IEC international standard for "Text, Spatial, Still Images, and Data Mining." SQL/MM specifies the well-known text (`WKT`) and the well-known binary (`WKB`) formats for specifying geometries (see Chapter 4 for details). You can convert these formats to an `SDO_GEOMETRY` (and store the data in Oracle Spatial) and vice versa. For instance, Listing 4-11 shows how to convert `WKT` to an `SDO_GEOMETRY` by taking the `WKT` and an `SRID` as parameters (you can also pass `WKB` and `SRID` as parameters in that example). Listing 5-20 shows how to do the reverse—that is, how to convert an `SDO_GEOMETRY` object to `WKT` format. This example uses the `GET_WKT` *method* of the `SDO_GEOMETRY` data type and returns the well-known text as a character large object (CLOB).

Listing 5-20. *Converting from an* `SDO_GEOMETRY` *to* `WKT` *Format*

```
SQL> SELECT a.location.GET_WKT() wkt FROM customers a WHERE id=1;
WKT
----------------------------------
POINT (-76.9773898 38.8886508)
```

Analogously, the `GET_WKB` method of the `SDO_GEOMETRY` data type converts an `SDO_GEOMETRY` object to `WKB` format. This method returns the result as a binary large object (BLOB).

Since `WKT` and `WKB` are standard formats for spatial data supported by many external spatial vendors, the preceding conversion methods enable the easy exchange of spatial data between Oracle Spatial (`SDO_GEOMETRY`) format and other external formats.

Publishing SDO_GEOMETRY Data in GML

Geographic Markup Language (GML) is an XML-based encoding standard for spatial information. Oracle Spatial currently does not provide any SQL functions to load from GML formats. However, it does provide functions to publish SDO_GEOMETRY data to GML format.

SDO_UTIL.TO_GMLGEOMETRY takes a single argument of type SDO_GEOMETRY and returns a GML-encoded document fragment in the form of a CLOB. This returned object contains information about the type of the geometry, the SRID, and the coordinates specified using appropriate GML tags.

Listing 5-21 shows an example of converting a customer location into a GML document fragment. The geometry information is specified between <gml> and </gml> tags. The type is specified as a POINT, and coordinates are included between the <gml:coordinates> and </gml:coordinates> tags. Note that although we use the point locations in the customers table for illustration, this function can work with arbitrary types of geometries (e.g., polygons in the sales_regions or us_states table).

Listing 5-21. *Publishing an* SDO_GEOMETRY *to a GML Document*

```
SQL> SELECT  TO_CHAR(SDO_UTIL.TO_GMLGEOMETRY(location)) gml_location
FROM customers
WHERE id=1;
GML_LOCATION
----------------
<gml:Point  srsName="SDO:8307"  xmlns:gml="http://www.opengis.net/gml">
     <gml:coordinates decimal="." cs="," ts=" ">
          -76.99022,38.888654
      </gml:coordinates>
</gml:Point>
```

The preceding function publishes each SDO_GEOMETRY as a GML geometry. You can encode multiple geometries in a GML document using the XMLFOREST function and other SQLX functions. Listing 5-22 shows an example using the XMLFOREST function. We refer interested readers to the *Oracle XML Database Developer's Guide* or the *Oracle XML API Reference Guide* for details on these functions.

Listing 5-22. *Publishing Multiple Geometries to a GML Document Fragment*

```
SQL> SELECT xmlelement("State", xmlattributes(
    'http://www.opengis.net/gml' as "xmlns:gml"),
     xmlforest(state as "Name", totpop as "Population",
               xmltype(sdo_gml.to_gmlgeometry(geom)) as
              "gml:geometryProperty"))
        AS theXMLElements
FROM spatial.us_states
WHERE state_abrv in ('DE', 'UT');
THEXMLELEMENTS
------------------------------------------
<State xmlns:gml="http://www.opengis.net/gml">
 <Name>Delaware</Name> <Population>666168</Population>
```

```
<gml:geometryProperty><gml:Polygon srsName="SDO:8307"
xmlns:gml="http://www.opengis.net/gml">
 <gml:outerBoundaryIs> <gml:LinearRing>
     <gml:coordinates decimal="." cs="," ts=" ">
       -75.788704,39.721699 ...
```

Validating Spatial Data

Once the data are in Oracle tables, you need to check if the SDO_GEOMETRY data are in valid Spatial format. Otherwise, you may get the wrong results, errors, or failures. Oracle Spatial provides two functions, VALIDATE_GEOMETRY_WITH_CONTEXT and VALIDATE_LAYER_WITH_CONTEXT, for this validation. These functions check for the following common errors:

- If the geometry contains a self-crossing (e.g., eight-shaped) polygon element.
- If any two polygonal elements of a geometry overlap.
- If a line element has fewer than two vertices.
- If there are duplicate points in any element.
- If any polygonal ring is oriented incorrectly. Oracle Spatial expects exterior rings to be counterclockwise and interior rings to be clockwise.
- If a polygon with holes (voids) has a hole that touches the boundary of the polygon at more than a single point. That is, a hole cannot share a line segment with the outer polygon's boundary.

All validation and debugging functions use a user-specified numeric value called tolerance to determine whether or not a geometry is valid. In Chapter 3, we described the significance of this parameter and how to set it. As explained there, this tolerance parameter is also stored in the DIMINFO column of the USER_SDO_GEOM_METADATA view.

VALIDATE_GEOMETRY_WITH_CONTEXT

This function is part of the SDO_GEOM package. It checks that a single specified geometry is in valid (Oracle Spatial) format. It has the two signatures shown in Listing 5-23, both of which return a VARCHAR2 string.

Listing 5-23. *Signatures of the* VALIDATE_GEOMETRY_WITH_CONTEXT *Function*

```
SDO_GEOM.VALIDATE_GEOMETRY_WITH_CONTEXT
(
  geometry          IN SDO_GEOMETRY,
  tolerance         IN NUMBER
) RETURN VARCHAR2;
```

```
SDO_GEOM.VALIDATE_GEOMETRY_WITH_CONTEXT
(
  geometry          IN SDO_GEOMETRY,
  diminfo           IN SDO_DIM_ARRAY
) RETURN VARCHAR2;
```

The arguments are as follows:

- `geometry`: This specifies the input `SDO_GEOMETRY` object that needs to be validated.
- `tolerance`: This specifies the tolerance to use to validate the geometry (see Chapter 3 for details on tolerance).
- `diminfo`: This specifies dimension (bounds) information and tolerance information.

The function returns the string `'TRUE'` if the geometry is valid. If it is invalid, it returns the Oracle error number if it is known; otherwise, it returns `'FALSE'`.

For instance, we can run a validation check on the geometry loaded into the `sales_regions` table. This geometry has an ID of 10000. Listing 5-24 shows the SQL.

Listing 5-24. *Validation Check on a Geometry from the* `sales_regions` *Table*

```
SQL> SELECT SDO_GEOM.VALIDATE_GEOMETRY_WITH_CONTEXT(a.geom, 0.5)
is_valid
FROM sales_regions a
WHERE a.id=10000;

IS_VALID
--------------------------------------------------------------------------------
13356 [Element <1>] [Coordinate <17>][Ring <1>]
```

Error 13356 signals that the geometry corresponding to `id=10000` has duplicate vertices. The duplicate vertex is the seventeenth one in the first element of the geometry. Note that it also specifies the element number, which will be quite helpful in debugging specific elements.

You can also run this function on more complex geometries. Listing 5-25 validates the self-crossing (eight-shaped) geometry shown in Figure 5-1.

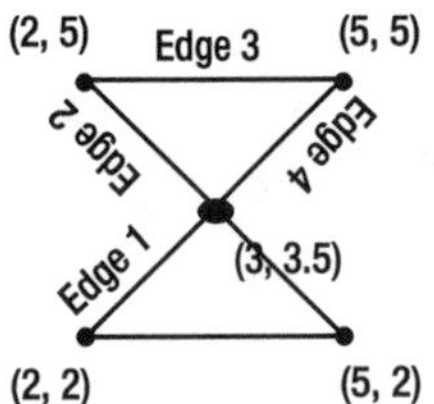

Figure 5-1. *A self-crossing (eight-shaped) polygon. This is not a valid polygon in Oracle Spatial.*

Listing 5-25. *Validation on a Self-Crossing Geometry*

```
SQL> SELECT SDO_GEOM.VALIDATE_GEOMETRY_WITH_CONTEXT
(
   SDO_GEOMETRY
   (
      2003,
      NULL,
      NULL,
      SDO_ELEM_INFO_ARRAY
      (
         1, 1003,1  -- Polygonal ring connected by lines
      )
     SDO_ORDINATE_ARRAY
      (
         2,2,        -- first vertex
         3,3.5,      -- second vertex. Edge 1 is between previous and this vertex.
         2,5,
         5,5,
         3,3.5,      -- fifth vertex. Edge 4 is between previous and this vertex.
         5,2,
         2,2
      )
      0.000005
)
FROM dual;

SDO_GEOM.VALIDATE_GEOMETRY_WITH_CONTEXT(MDSYS.SDO_GEOMETRY(200
3,NULL,NULL,MDSYS.
--------------------------------------------------------------------------------
13349 [Element <1>] [Ring <1>][Edge <1>][Edge <4>]
```

The result indicates that element 1 is invalid. For this element, edge 1 connecting (2, 2) with (3, 3.5) and edge 4 connecting (5, 5) and (3, 3.5) are self-crossing (in other words, the polygon boundary crosses itself).

Note that the second signature to this function specifies `diminfo` instead of `tolerance` as a second parameter. This signature/usage has an advantage: in addition to basic validation, the function checks whether all the coordinates are within the bounds specified in the `diminfo` attribute. For example, consider the point geometry with `longitude=-80` and `latitude=20`. If the `diminfo` is set to (0, 50) for both dimensions, then the point will be invalid, as shown in Listing 5-26. The SQL returns the ORA-13011 error. This error implies that the longitude value of `-80` is out of range (0 to 50) for that dimension.

Listing 5-26. *Using the* diminfo *Parameter in the* VALIDATE_GEOMETRY_WITH_CONTEXT *Function*

```
SQL> SELECT SDO_GEOM.VALIDATE_GEOMETRY_WITH_CONTEXT
(
  SDO_GEOMETRY     -- first argument to validate is geometry
  (
    2001,          -- point type
    NULL,
    SDO_POINT_TYPE(-80,20,NULL), -- point is <80,20> and is out of range.
    NULL,
    NULL
  ),
  SDO_DIM_ARRAY    -- second argument is diminfo (of type SDO_DIM_ARRAY)
  (

    SDO_DIM_ELEMENT('X', 0, 50, 0.5),  -- lower, upper bound range is 0 to 50
    SDO_DIM_ELEMENT('Y', 0, 50, 0.5)   -- lower, upper bound range is 0 to 50
  )
) is_valid FROM DUAL;
IS_VALID
-------------------------------------------------------------------------------
13011 -- Coordinate value out of dimension range
```

VALIDATE_LAYER_WITH_CONTEXT

Instead of validating geometries one by one, you can validate the geometries in an entire table using the VALIDATE_LAYER_WITH_CONTEXT procedure. This procedure is also part of the SDO_GEOM package and has the signature in Listing 5-27.

Listing 5-27. *Signature of the* VALIDATE_LAYER_WITH_CONTEXT *Procedure*

```
SDO_GEOM.VALIDATE_LAYER_WITH_CONTEXT
(
  table_name       IN VARCHAR2,
  column_name      IN VARCHAR2,
  result_table     IN VARCHAR2
  [,
  commit_interval  IN NUMBER
  ]
)
```

The arguments are as follows:

- table_name and column_name: These specify the names of the table and column storing the SDO_GEOMETRY data.
- result_table: This specifies the table where the validation results, specifically the ROWIDs of invalid geometries, will be stored. This table should have been created with the following

fields prior to execution of this function. The SDO_ROWID field stores the ROWID, and STATUS stores either a specific validation error or the string 'FALSE' (to indicate that the row is invalid).

```
SDO_ROWID          ROWID
STATUS             VARCHAR2(2000)
```

- commit_interval: This optional argument specifies the frequency at which the updates to the results table are to be committed. If this argument is set to 100, then the validation results are committed to result_table after validating every 100 geometries.

To illustrate the usage with an example, run this procedure on the sales_regions table. Listing 5-28 shows the corresponding SQL.

Listing 5-28. *Using the* VALIDATE_LAYER_WITH_CONTEXT *Procedure*

```
SQL> CREATE TABLE validate_results(sdo_rowid ROWID, status VARCHAR2(2000));

Table created.

SQL>
BEGIN
  SDO_GEOM.VALIDATE_LAYER_WITH_CONTEXT
  (
    'SALES_REGIONS',
    'GEOM',
    'VALIDATE_RESULTS'
  );
END;
/

SQL> SELECT * FROM validate_results;
SDO_ROWID                     STATUS
--------------------          ----------------------------------------------
AAALctAADAAATRvAAA            13356 [Element <1>] [Coordinate <17>][Ring <1>]
```

Note that this returns the ROWID of the geometry with ID=10000, which is invalid. The reason is the same as that in the VALIDATE_GEOMETRY_WITH_CONTEXT example in Listing 5-24: coordinate 17 and the subsequent one are duplicates.

Debugging Spatial Data

How do you remove the duplicate vertices? Oracle Spatial provides a number of functions to debug and clean data loaded into an SDO_GEOMETRY column. In this section, we describe these functions, as they will be useful in cleaning spatial data. These functions are part of the SDO_UTIL package.

REMOVE_DUPLICATE_VERTICES

This function removes duplicate vertices from an SDO_GEOMETRY object. It takes in an SDO_GEOMETRY and a tolerance value as input, and returns a new SDO_GEOMETRY that does not have duplicate vertices. The SQL in Listing 5-29 shows its usage.

Listing 5-29. *Example of Removing Duplicate Vertices in a Geometry*

```
SQL> SELECT geom, SDO_UTIL.REMOVE_DUPLICATE_VERTICES(a.geom,0.5) nodup_geom
FROM sales_regions a
WHERE id=1000;

GEOM
------------
SDO_GEOMETRY
(
  2003, 8307, NULL, SDO_ELEM_INFO_ARRAY(1, 1003, 1),
  SDO_ORDINATE_ARRAY
  (
    -77.04487, 38.9043742, -77.046645, 38.9040983, -77.04815, 38.9033127,
    -77.049155, 38.9021368, -77.049508, 38.9007499, -77.049155, 38.899363,
    -77.048149, 38.8981873, -77.046645, 38.8974017, -77.04487, 38.8971258,
    -77.043095, 38.8974017, -77.041591, 38.8981873, -77.040585, 38.899363,
    -77.040232, 38.9007499, -77.040585, 38.9021368, -77.04159, 38.9033127,
    -77.043095, 38.9040983, -77.04487, 38.9043742, -77.04487, 38.9043742
  )
)
NODUP_GEOM
----------------------
SDO_GEOMETRY
(
  2003, 8307, NULL, SDO_ELEM_INFO_ARRAY(1, 1003, 1),
  SDO_ORDINATE_ARRAY
  (
    -77.04487, 38.9043742, -77.046645, 38.9040983, -77.04815, 38.9033127,
    -77.049155,38.9021368, -77.049508, 38.9007499, -77.049155, 38.899363,
    -77.048149, 38.8981873,-77.046645, 38.8974017, -77.04487, 38.8971258,
    -77.043095, 38.8974017, -77.041591,38.8981873, -77.040585, 38.899363,
    -77.040232, 38.9007499, -77.040585, 38.9021368, -77.04159, 38.9033127,
    -77.043095, 38.9040983, -77.04487, 38.9043742
  )
)
```

Notice that the last two vertices (look at the bold four numbers) of the original geometry are the same. After invoking the REMOVE_DUPLICATE_VERTICES function, the duplicate vertex (which is the eighteenth in this case) is removed (both ordinates of this vertex are removed) from the geometry. If we rerun the VALIDATE_GEOMETRY_WITH_CONTEXT function on this result geometry as shown in Listing 5-30, it returns the string 'TRUE'. Since the geometry is a polygon (sdo_gtype=2003), observe that the first point (at –77.04487, 38.9043742) and the last point (at –77.04487, 38.9043742) are the same.

Listing 5-30. *Validating After Removing the Duplicate Vertices*

```
SQL> SELECT  SDO_GEOM.VALIDATE_GEOMETRY_WITH_CONTEXT
(
  SDO_UTIL.REMOVE_DUPLICATE_VERTICES(a.geom, 0.5)
  0.5
) is_valid
FROM sales_regions a
WHERE id=10000;

IS_VALID
--------------------------------------------------------------------------------
TRUE
```

EXTRACT

This function extracts a specific element from an SDO_GEOMETRY object. It comes in handy while debugging multielement geometries such as multipolygons. This function takes as arguments an SDO_GEOMETRY, an element number and, optionally, a ring number (within the element). It returns the extracted element as an SDO_GEOMETRY object.

Listing 5-31 shows an example of how to extract the second element of a multipolygon geometry. Note that the second argument, 2, in the EXTRACT function specifies that the second element is to be fetched. Looking at SDO_ELEM_INFO_ARRAY (1,1003,3, 5, 1003,1), we have two element descriptor triplets (1,1003,3) for the first element, and (5, 1003,1) for the second element. This means that the second element starts at ordinate 5 (i.e., the third vertex). This is the element that will be extracted.

Listing 5-31. *Extracting the Second Element from a Geometry*

```
SQL> SELECT SDO_UTIL.EXTRACT
(
  SDO_GEOMETRY
  (
    2007,  -- multipolygon collection type geometry
    NULL,
    NULL,
    SDO_ELEM_INFO_ARRAY
    (
      1,1003,3,     -- first element descriptor triplet: mbr
      5, 1003, 1    -- second element descriptor triplet:
                    -- starting offset 5 means it starts at  the 5th ordinate
    ),
```

```
    SDO_ORDINATE_ARRAY
    (
      1,1,2,2,                           -- first element ordinates (four for mbr)
      3,3, 4, 3, 4,4, 3,4, 3,4,3,3 -- second element starting at 5th ordinate:
                                         -- this second element is returned
    )
  ), -- End of the Geometry
  2  -- specifies the element number to extract
) second_elem
FROM dual;
SECOND_ELEM(SDO_GTYPE, SDO_SRID, SDO_POINT(X, Y, Z), SDO_ELEM_INFO,
SDO_ORDINATE
------------------------------------------------------------------------------
SDO_GEOMETRY
(
  2003,
  NULL,
  NULL,
  SDO_ELEM_INFO_ARRAY(1, 1003, 1),
  SDO_ORDINATE_AR RAY
  (
    3, 3,     -- first vertex coordinates
    4, 3,     -- second vertex coordinates
    4, 4,     -- third vertex coordinates
    3, 4,     -- fourth vertex coordinates
    3, 4,     -- fifth vertex coordinates
    3, 3      -- sixth vertex coordinates (same as first for polygon)
  )
)
```

After extracting the appropriate element, we can perform validation on the specific element to identify what is wrong with it. Listing 5-32 shows an example.

Listing 5-32. *Validation of an Extracted Geometry*

```
SQL> SELECT  SDO_GEOM.VALIDATE_GEOMETRY_WITH_CONTEXT
(
  SDO_UTIL.EXTRACT
  (
    SDO_GEOMETRY
    (
      2007, null, null,
      SDO_ELEM_INFO_ARRAY(1,1003,3, 5, 1003, 1),
      SDO_ORDINATE_ARRAY
```

```
      (
        1,1,2,2,                        -- first element of  multipolygon geometry
        3,3, 4, 3, 4,4, 3,4, 3,4,3,3    -- second element of multipolygon geometry
      )
    ),
    2                                   -- element number to extract
  ),
  0.00005
)
FROM dual;
```

Note that the highlighted (bolded) portion of the SQL in Listing 5-32 is the same as the SQL in Listing 5-31. That means Listing 5-32 is equivalent to performing the validation check on the result of Listing 5-31. Listing 5-33 shows the SQL rewritten using the result of Listing 5-31.

Listing 5-33. *Validation on the Result of* SDO_UTIL.EXTRACT

```
SQL> SELECT SDO_GEOM.VALIDATE_GEOMETRY_WITH_CONTEXT
(
  SDO_GEOMETRY
  (
    2003, NULL, NULL,
    SDO_ELEM_INFO_ARRAY(1, 1003, 1),
    SDO_ORDINATE_ARRAY
    (
      3, 3,      -- first vertex coordinates
      4, 3,      -- second vertex coordinates
      4, 4,      -- third vertex coordinates
      3, 4,      -- fourth vertex coordinates
      3, 4,      -- fifth vertex coordinates
      3, 3       -- sixth vertex coordinates (same as first for polygon)
    )
  )
  0.00005        -- tolerance
) FROM dual;

SDO_GEOM.VALIDATE_GEOMETRY_WITH_CONTEXT(SDO_UTIL.EXTRACT(SDO_GE
OMETRY(2007,NULL,
------------------------------------------------------------------------------
13356 [Element <1>] [Coordinate <4>][Ring <1>]
```

The result of 13356 <Coordinate 4> indicates a duplicate vertex at the fourth (and fifth) vertex *coordinates* of the SDO_ORDINATE_ARRAY5-. The ordinate array is (3, 3, 4, 3, 4, 4, 3, 4, 3, 4, 3, 3), and the fourth and fifth vertexes (coordinates) are at (3, 4) and (3, 4), which are duplicates. We can remove this duplicate coordinate using the REMOVE_DUPLICATE_VERTICES function, as shown in Listing 5-34. This function removes the duplicate vertex from the geometry.

Listing 5-34. *Removing Duplicate Vertices*

```
SQL> SELECT SDO_UTIL.REMOVE_DUPLICATE_VERTICES
(
  SDO_UTIL.EXTRACT
  (
    SDO_GEOMETRY
    (
      2007, NULL, NULL,
      SDO_ELEM_INFO_ARRAY(1,1003,3, 5, 1003, 1),
      SDO_ORDINATE_ARRAY
      (
        1,1,2,2,
        3,3, 4, 3, 4,4, 3,4, 3,4,3,3
      )
    ),
    2
  ),
  0.00005
)
FROM  dual;

SDO_UTIL.REMOVE_DUPLICATE_VERTICES(SDO_UTIL.EXTRACT(SDO_GEOMETRY(
2007,NULL,NULL,
--------------------------------------------------------------------------------
  SDO_GEOMETRY
  (
    2003,
    NULL,
    NULL,
    SDO_ELEM_INFO_ARRAY(1, 1003, 1),
    SDO_ORDINATE_ARRAY
    (
      3, 3,    -- first vertex coordinates
      4, 3,    -- second vertex coordinates
      4, 4,    -- third vertex coordinates
      3, 4,    -- fourth vertex coordinates (duplicate (3,4) at fifth removed)
      3, 3     -- fifth vertex coordinates (same as first for polygon)
    )
  )
```

Tip You can directly run REMOVE_DUPLICATE_VERTICES on the collection geometry, and that will remove the duplicate vertex. Listing 5-34 uses SDO_UTIL.EXTRACT mainly for illustration.

APPEND

How do you recombine the new element after removing the duplicate with element 1? The `SDO_UTIL.APPEND` function combines multiple geometries as long as they do not intersect. This function takes two geometries and a tolerance, and appends them into a single geometry. Listing 5-35 shows an example.

Listing 5-35. *Example of* `SDO_UTIL.APPEND`

```
SQL> SELECT
SDO_UTIL.APPEND
(
  SDO_UTIL.EXTRACT
  (
    SDO_GEOMETRY
    (
      2007, NULL, NULL,
      SDO_ELEM_INFO_ARRAY(1,1003,3, 5, 1003, 1),
      SDO_ORDINATE_ARRAY(1,1,2,2,
      3,3, 4, 3, 4,4, 3,4, 3,4,3,3)
    ),
    1
  ),
  SDO_UTIL.REMOVE_DUPLICATE_VERTICES
  (
    SDO_GEOMETRY
    (
      2007, NULL, NULL,
      SDO_ELEM_INFO_ARRAY(1,1003,3, 5, 1003, 1),
      SDO_ORDINATE_ARRAY
      (
        1,1,2,2,
        3,3, 4, 3, 4,4, 3,4, 3,4,3,3
      )
    ),
   0.00005
  )
) combined_geom
FROM  dual;

COMBINED_GEOM(SDO_GTYPE, SDO_SRID, SDO_POINT(X, Y, Z), SDO_ELEM_INFO,
SDO_ORDINATES)
--------------------------------------------------------------------------------
SDO_GEOMETRY
(
  2007, NULL, NULL,
  SDO_ELEM_INFO_ARRAY(1, 1003, 1, 11, 1003, 1),
  SDO_ORDINATE_ARRAY
  (1, 1, 2, 1, 2, 2, 1, 2, 1, 1, 3, 3, 4, 3, 4, 4, 3, 4, 3, 3)
)
```

GETNUMELEM, GETNUMVERTICES, and GETVERTICES

These functions allow you to inspect the number of elements or vertices, or to get the set of vertices in an SDO_GEOMETRY object. These functions are also part of the SDO_UTIL package. The SQL in Listing 5-36 shows an example of the usage of the first two functions.

Listing 5-36. *Finding the Number of Elements in a Geometry*

```
SQL> SELECT SDO_UTIL.GETNUMELEM(geom) nelem
FROM  sales_regions
WHERE id=10000;
NELEM
----------
1
SQL> SELECT  SDO_UTIL.GETNUMVERTICES(geom) nverts
FROM sales_regions
WHERE id=10000;
NVERTS
----------
18
```

Miscellaneous Functions

The SDO_UTIL package has a number of other functions to manipulate SDO_GEOMETRY objects. The following is a list of functions that may aid in debugging or cleaning up spatial data. We will discuss other functions at appropriate times throughout the book.

- SDO_CONCAT_LINES: This function concatenates two line string geometries. The line strings are expected to be nonintersecting. Because of this assumption, this function executes much faster than the SDO_UNION function, which we will discuss in Chapter 9.
- SDO_REVERSE_LINESTRING: This function reverses the order of vertices in a line string. Such functions may be useful in routing and other navigation applications.
- SDO_POLYGONTOLINE: This function converts a polygon to a line string geometry.

In short, the SDO_UTIL and SDO_GEOM packages provide a rich set of functions to validate and debug SDO_GEOMETRY data.

Summary

In this chapter, we described how to load data into and out of SDO_GEOMETRY columns. We discussed how to load from text files using SQL*Loader, and how to load using the Oracle utilities such as Import/Export and transportable tablespaces. We also described how to publish SDO_GEOMETRY data as GML documents.

Once data are loaded into SDO_GEOMETRY columns, the data need to be validated. We described how to perform validation to check for conformity with Oracle Spatial formats. In case of invalid data, we described a set of functions that are helpful in debugging such geometries and correcting the inaccuracies.

We also explained how to import data into the example application described in Chapter 3. In the next chapter, we will describe how to derive the SDO_GEOMETRY data from the address columns of an application's table. We can use this alternate method to populate the columns in application-specific tables such as branches and customers. Once the spatial data is populated in the tables, we will describe how to perform analysis and visualization in Chapters 8 to 11.

CHAPTER 6

Geocoding

To run the examples in this chapter, you need to import the following dataset. For complete details on creating this user and loading the data, refer to the Introduction.

```
imp spatial/spatial file=gc.dmp ignore=y full=y
```

In preceding chapters, we discussed how to perform spatial searches and analysis. In each example, the entities manipulated (customers, ATMs, stores, etc.) were spatially located. They all included an SDO_GEOMETRY column containing their spatial location, using geographical coordinates (longitude and latitude).

But how did this happen? Where did this information come from? Certainly, you cannot ask your customers to give their geographical coordinates when they register with you or when they place an order! We used a process called *geocoding*—we geocoded addresses and stored the resulting locations as SDO_GEOMETRY objects.

By "geocoding," we mean a process that converts an address (for example, "3746 Connecticut Avenue NW, Washington, D.C. 20008, United States") to geographical coordinates (longitude = –77.060283, latitude = 38.9387083). In addition, geocoding may also *normalize* and *correct* the input address (HouseNumber=3746; StreetName=Connecticut Avenue NW; City=Washington; State=D.C.; Zip=20008; Country=US).

In this chapter, we describe the functionality of the geocoder in Oracle Spatial and how to use it to location-enable a business application. We start with a brief overview of the geocoding process. This will give you an understanding of how the conversion from addresses to SDO_GEOMETRY objects happens.

Next, we discuss how to set up the reference data used by the geocoder. This reference data is used to determine/extrapolate the location for a specified address. You can obtain this data from a data provider such as NAVTEQ.

Then we describe different geocoding functions that use the reference data. We provide generic examples to illustrate their functionality.

Finally, we describe how to add SDO_GEOMETRY columns to application data and how to populate them using the Oracle geocoder. We illustrate this using different functions/APIs of the geocoder.

What Is Geocoding?

Geocoding serves two purposes. The main purpose is to associate geographical coordinates with an address. Listing 6-1 shows an example of how to get the coordinates from an address using the simple GEOCODE_AS_GEOMETRY function that returns a point SDO_GEOMETRY object. That object contains the geographical coordinates that the geocoder associated with this address.

Listing 6-1. *Geocoding an Address*

```
SQL> SELECT SDO_GCDR.GEOCODE_AS_GEOMETRY
(
  'SPATIAL',
  SDO_KEYWORDARRAY
  (
    '3746  CONNECTICUT AVE NW',
    'WASHINGTON, DC 20008'
  ),
  'US'
) geom
FROM DUAL;

GEOM(SDO_GTYPE, SDO_SRID, SDO_POINT(X, Y, Z), SDO_ELEM_INFO, SDO_ORDINATES)
--------------------------------------------------------------------------------
SDO_GEOMETRY(2001, 8307, SDO_POINT_TYPE(-77.060283, 38.9387083, NULL), NULL, NULL)
```

What would happen if the address was misspelled? This brings us to the second purpose of geocoding, which is to correct various errors in addresses. This process is often called *normalization*, and it involves structuring and cleaning the input address.

Normalization is important: it corrects mistakes and ensures that all address information is complete, well structured, and clean. A set of clean and normalized addresses is necessary to derive meaningful location information and to remove duplicates.

It is very common, for instance, to find variations of the same customer address in a customer database. The information may be provided by the same customer at different occasions in slightly different ways, and without normalization it would lead to semantic duplicates that are treated as separate entries in the customer database.

Listing 6-2 shows how to obtain corrections for a misspelled address using the GEOCODE function. “Connecticut” is spelled “Connectict” here, and the postal code is incorrect.

Listing 6-2. *Geocoding and Normalizing an Address*

```
SQL> SELECT SDO_GCDR.GEOCODE
(
    'SPATIAL',
    SDO_KEYWORDARRAY
    (
      '3746  CONNECTICT AVE NW',
      'WASHINGTON, DC 20023'
    ),
```

```
    'US',
    'DEFAULT'
  ) geom
FROM DUAL;

GEOM(ID, ADDRESSLINES, PLACENAME, STREETNAME, INTERSECTSTREET, SECUNIT,
SETTLEM
--------------------------------------------------------------------------------
SDO_GEO_ADDR
(0, SDO_KEYWORDARRAY(NULL), NULL, 'CONNECTICUT AVE NW', NULL, NULL,
 'WASHINGTON', NULL, 'DC', 'US', '20008', NULL, '20008', NULL, '3746', 'CONNECT
ICUT', 'AVE', 'F', 'F', NULL, 'NW', 'L', .944444444, 18571166, '????#E?UT?B281C
??', 10, 'DEFAULT', -77.060283, 38.9387083)
```

The result of this function is a fairly complex structure of type SDO_GEO_ADDR. For now, we merely note that the structure contains the correct street name and the correct postal code. Later in this chapter, we take an in-depth look at the structure, and you will see how to format it in a readable way.

Architecture of the Oracle Geocoder

How is geocoding done? Figure 6-1 illustrates this process. First, the geocoder requires reference data—a list of addresses with known coordinates such as roads and streets, but also towns, postal codes, and so on, with their geographical locations and shapes.

With this reference data, the geocoder performs the following three steps:

1. Parse the input address.
2. Search for an address with a matching name.
3. Compute a location (spatial coordinates) for the address that was found.

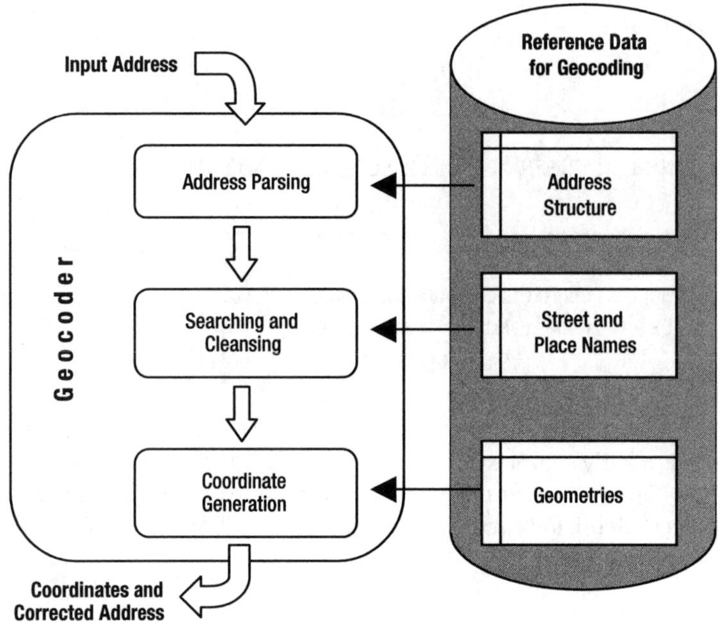

Figure 6-1. *Oracle geocoder architecture*

Let's examine these three steps in detail.

Parsing the Input Address

The geocoder first recognizes the parts of a street address and separates them into recognizable elements such as street name, street type (street, avenue, boulevard, etc.), house number, postal code, and city.

This process can be tricky—there are many ways to write the same address, especially in different countries, cultures, and languages. For example, the street type can precede (e.g., Rue de la Paix), follow (e.g., Elm Square), or be attached to the street name (e.g., Bahnoffstraße).

The Oracle geocoder recognizes a variety of address formats in various countries and languages. The formats are defined in one table, `GC_PARSER_PROFILEAFS`, in the reference data. Table 6-1 illustrates the effect of parsing some common international addresses.

Table 6-1. *Parsing International Addresses*

Address Element	United States	Germany	France
Full address	3746 Connecticut Avenue NW Washington, D.C. 20008	Arabellastraße 6 D-81925 München	12, Avenue Robert Soleau 06600 Antibes
House number	3746	6	12
Street base name	Connecticut	Arabella	Robert Soleau
Street type	Avenue	Strasse	Avenue

Address Element	United States	Germany	France
Street suffix	NW		
City	Washington	München	Antibes
Postal code	20008	81925	06600
Region	D.C.		

Note Postal organizations have defined an official way to format addresses. The Universal Postal Union (`http://www.upu.int`) compiles and publishes this information.

Searching for the Address

Once the address has been parsed into recognizable elements, the geocoder can search the list of street names for the one that most closely matches the given address.

This search is *fuzzy*, meaning it finds a match even if the input address is misspelled (e.g., "avenue" spelled as "avnue" or "Van Ness" spelled as "Van Neus") or represented differently from the stored addresses (e.g., "street" entered as "st." or "straße" entered as "strasse").

The various keywords used in an address, with their multiple spellings (including common spelling errors), are stored in the `GC_PARSER_PROFILES` table in the reference data. For example, `JUNCTION` can be spelled `JCT`, `JCTN`, `JUNCTN`, or even `JCTION` or `JUNCTON`.

The search may also be "approximate"—that is, if the exact street cannot be found, then the geocoder will fall back to the postal code or city name. The user is able to specify whether or not this is acceptable by passing a *matching mode* parameter. We will look at the various possible modes later in the chapter.

In some cases, there may be multiple matches. For example, the chosen street name "Warren Street" may not exist, but "Warren Place" and "Warren Avenue" might. In such a case, both results will be returned. It is up to the calling application to decide which result to choose or, more likely, to let the user of the application choose.

One important result of the address search is a cleaned-up address, with the correct formatting and spelling of the street name, complete with elements that were missing from the input address, such as the postal code.

Computing the Spatial Coordinates

Once the proper street has been located, the geocoder needs to convert it into a geographical point. Let's examine this final step of the geocoding process.

The geocoding reference data used by the Oracle geocoder holds the house numbers at each end of a street segment, on each side of that street. When the input address contains a house number, the geocoder computes the geographical position of the house number by *interpolation*.

This process is illustrated in Figure 6-2.The figure shows a section of Elm Street. Only the numbers of houses at each end are known: numbers 10 and 11 are at one end, and numbers 18 and 19 are at the other end. Where, then, is "13 Elm St"? The Oracle geocoder assumes that houses are regularly spaced along the linear geometry that represents the street segment, and positions (i.e., interpolates) house number 13 accordingly.

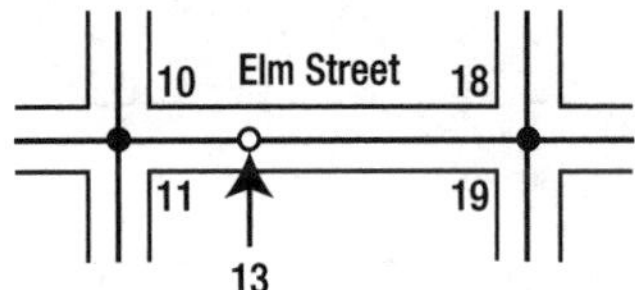

Figure 6-2. *Interpolation example*

When there is a good correlation between the house numbers and the distance along the road, the result will be quite precise. Otherwise, it will be approximate and may be erroneous. Even in the latter case, the margin of error is generally small.

■ **Note** Streets are modeled as line strings, the "centerline" of the actual street. The Oracle geocoder actually positions houses on the centerline—that is, the actual coordinates are in the middle of the street!

Note that the input address may be incomplete. This is what happens when the input address has missing components.

- When no house number is given in the address, the geocoder returns the midpoint of the street. The reference data of the Oracle geocoder stores the precomputed location of the house number at the midpoint.
- When no street is given in the input address, or when the street is not found, the geocoder falls back to the postal code or city (built-up area, settlement, or municipality). In those cases, it returns a geographical point that corresponds to the "center" of the postal code or city.

Note that the required precision of a geographical location for a given address varies with the application.

- For an application that returns the current weather at a chosen location, geocoding at the postal code or city level is quite sufficient.
- For an application that compares customer locations with branch (business) locations or sales territories, geocoding at the street level is generally sufficient.
- For a pizza delivery or taxi pickup application, geocoding at the house level is nice, but just knowing the street segment (i.e., the city block) and the side of the street is generally sufficient.

■Note The coordinates returned by the geocoder are always in the coordinate system used in the reference data. For most data providers (as is the case for NAVTEQ) this will be longitude, latitude (WGS84).

In the next section, we discuss how to set up the reference data for the geocoder. We then illustrate the previously discussed geocoding process with appropriate examples.

Setting Up the Reference Data for the Geocoder

The reference data used by the Oracle geocoder is a set of tables with a specific structure. All the tables start with the `GC_` prefix. There are two kinds of tables:

- *Parameter tables* control the operation of the geocoder.
- *Data tables* contain the place names and their geographical coordinates.

The way you load those tables depends on the way your data supplier provides them. At the time of this writing, only NAVTEQ supplies the reference data for the geocoder, in Oracle export (`.dmp`) files or transportable tablespaces. Other suppliers may choose other mechanisms, such as SQL*Loader and SQL scripts, to provide their data.

For the examples in this book, we use the sample data that NAVTEQ provides, which covers San Francisco, California, and Washington, D.C. For ease of use, the data is provided to you as a single Oracle export file.

Loading this reference data for the Oracle geocoder is as easy as running the following import command. This will create all tables (parameter as well as data) and populate them.

```
imp spatial/spatial file=gc.dmp full=y ignore=y
```

For real geocoder reference data, you will most likely need to perform multiple such imports, as the data for each country is provided as one or more dump files. Note that you can load the data for different countries in the same Oracle schema or in different schemas. The data for each country uses different tables. See the "Data Tables" section of this chapter for details.

The rest of this section describes the overall structure and purpose of all tables in the reference data. You do *not* need to understand the details of the tables to use the geocoder.

Parameter Tables

Three tables contain information about the structuring of addresses in each country supported by the Oracle geocoder. You should not change the content of these tables.

GC_COUNTRY_PROFILE

This table contains general information about each country known to the Oracle geocoder, such as the definition of administrative levels for that country. One important piece of information is the suffix of the data tables for that country (more on this later).

GC_PARSER_PROFILEAFS

This table describes the structuring of the addresses for each country supported by the Oracle geocoder. There is one row per country, with the address structure defined in an XML notation.

GC_PARSER_PROFILES

The Oracle geocoder uses this table to recognize some address elements. It defines address elements with their synonyms, including possible misspellings. For example, it defines that `AV`, `AVE`, `AVEN`, `AVENU`, `AVN`, and `AVNUE` are all possible spellings for `AVENUE`. It also defines `1ST` and `FIRST` as synonyms.

Data Tables

The data tables have names with a country-specific suffix (defined in the `GC_COUNTRY_PROFILE` table). For example, the reference data for France is in tables with the `FR` suffix, while the data for the United States is in tables with the `US` suffix. The `xx` in the following descriptions represents this suffix.

GC_AREA_xx

This table stores information on all administrative areas. The Oracle geocoder defines three levels of administrative areas: `REGION`, `MUNICIPALITY`, and `SETTLEMENT`. The way administrative areas are mapped to those levels varies from country to country.

For the United States, the administrative areas correspond to states, counties, and cities. For the United Kingdom, they correspond to counties, postal towns, and localities.

Note that the same area can appear multiple times—this is the case when an area has multiple names, in different languages.

GC_POSTAL_CODE_xx

This table describes all postal codes, and it also contains the coordinates of the *center point* for each postal code. The center point is the point returned by the geocoder when the street name in the input address is invalid (or the input address contains no street name).

GC_POI_xx

This table contains a selection of points of interest (hospitals, airports, hotels, restaurants, parking garages, ATMs, etc.). The number of points of interest (POIs) and their classification varies among data suppliers.

GC_ROAD_xx

This is the main table used for address searches. It contains one row per road per settlement and postal code. If a road crosses multiple postal codes, then it will appear multiple times in this table.

GC_ROAD_SEGMENT_xx

This table provides the information needed to compute the coordinates of an address by interpolation. It contains one row for each segment of a road with the geometric shape of that road segment (an SDO_GEOMETRY type), as well as the house numbers on each side, at each end of the segment.

GC_INTERSECTION_xx

When multiple road segments meet, they form an intersection. This table defines one row for each couple of such road segments.

Using Geocoder Functions

The geocoding API is very simple: it is composed of a PL/SQL package (SDO_GCDR) with only three functions. All three accept an address as input and return geographical coordinate information as the geocoded result. The difference between the functions is in the amount of information they return. Table 6-2 summarizes the functions and their behaviors.

Table 6-2. *Comparing the Geocoding Functions*

Function	Address Conversion	Address Correction	Description
GEOCODE_AS_GEOMETRY	Yes	No	Returns a geometric point (with the geographical coordinates) for the address. It returns no indication as to the precision or quality of the result. This is best used when the addresses are known to be valid.
GEOCODE	Yes	Yes	Returns the geographical coordinates and a corrected address with detailed indications of the quality of the result.
GEOCODE_ALL	Yes	Yes	Like GEOCODE, but can return multiple matches if the input address is ambiguous. This is best used for interactive applications, when the end user chooses which of the matches is correct.

In the rest of this section, we examine each function in detail with examples.

■ **Note** The first call to a geocoding function in a session requires more time (is longer) than the subsequent calls. This is because the function needs to load and parse the profile tables.

GEOCODE_AS_GEOMETRY

This is the simplest function to use. You just pass it the address to geocode, and it returns an SDO_GEOMETRY object with the corresponding geographical location for that address. Recall that we used this function to illustrate geocoding in Chapters 2 and 3.

Here is the syntax of the function:

```
SDO_GCDR.GEOCODE_AS_GEOMETRY (
       username          IN VARCHAR2,
       addr_lines        IN SDO_KEYWORDARRAY,
       country           IN VARCHAR2
) RETURN SDO_GEOMETRY;
```

Function Parameters

The following sections outline the parameters for the GEOCODE_AS_GEOMETRY function.

username

This is the name of the Oracle schema that contains the geocoding tables for the specified country. It is a required argument. If the data is in the same schema as the one that calls the function, then you can also use the SQL built-in USER.

addr_lines

The type SDO_KEYWORDARRAY is a simple array (VARRAY) of character strings that is used to pass address lines to the geocoding functions. Fill each array entry with one line of the street address to geocode as illustrated in the list that follows.

The lines of the address must be passed according to the structure described in GC_PARSER_PROFILEAFS. They should be in the order defined and formatted properly. This formatting varies from country to country. If an address is incorrectly formatted, then the geocoder will reject it (i.e., it will return NULL).

There is, however, a certain degree of flexibility in the formatting. For example, all of the following are valid ways to format the same U.S. address, "1250 Clay Street, San Francisco, CA 94108":

- The state and postal code are on separate lines:

```
SDO_KEYWORDARRAY (
  '1250 Clay St',
  'San Francisco',
  'CA',
  '94108'
)
```

- The state and postal code are together on a separate line:

```
SDO_KEYWORDARRAY (
  '1250 Clay St',
  'San Francisco',
  'CA 94108'
)
```

- The city, state, and postal code are on the same line:

```
SDO_KEYWORDARRAY (
  '1250 Clay St',
  'San Francisco CA 94108'
)
```

The following, however, is incorrect:

- The address is on one line:

```
SDO_KEYWORDARRAY (
  '1250 Clay St, San Francisco CA 94108'
)
```

country

This is the two-letter ISO code for the county the address to be geocoded belongs to. It also corresponds to the suffix of the reference data tables read by the geocoder.

Function Result: SDO_GEOMETRY

The result of the function is a simple SDO_GEOMETRY object that contains a point geometry.

If the function is unable to parse the input address (because it is incorrectly formatted), or if it is unable to geocode the address (because it could not find any street with that name), then it returns a NULL geometry.

Let's look at a few examples.

Examples

Listing 6-3 shows how to geocode a street address in San Francisco.

Listing 6-3. *Using the* GEOCODE_AS_GEOMETRY *Function*

```
SQL> SELECT SDO_GCDR.GEOCODE_AS_GEOMETRY
(
  'SPATIAL',
  SDO_KEYWORDARRAY('1250 Clay Street', 'San Francisco, CA'),
```

```
  'US'
  )
FROM DUAL;
SDO_GEOMETRY(2001, 8307, SDO_POINT_TYPE -122.41356, 37.7932878, NULL), NULL, NULL)
```

The result is a simple point geometry object that contains the geographical coordinates for that address. The coordinates may not point exactly to number 1250 on Clay Street; they are computed by interpolation between known house numbers.

If the house number does not exist, such as in the example in Listing 6-4 (the highest house number on Clay Street is 3999), you still get a valid geometry pointing to a house on the street, but you have no indication of the exact house on which the geocoder positioned the coordinates.

Listing 6-4. *Using the* `GEOCODE_AS_GEOMETRY` *Function with an Invalid House Number*

```
SQL> SELECT SDO_GCDR.GEOCODE_AS_GEOMETRY
(
  'SPATIAL',
  SDO_KEYWORDARRAY('4500 Clay Street', 'San Francisco, CA'),
  'US'
)
FROM DUAL;
SDO_GEOMETRY(2001, 8307, SDO_POINT_TYPE(-122.41437, 37.79318, NULL), NULL, NULL)
```

If the street does not exist at all, then you get a `NULL` geometry back. This is illustrated in Listing 6-5.

Listing 6-5. *Using the* `GEOCODE_AS_GEOMETRY` *Function with an Invalid Street Name*

```
SQL> SELECT SDO_GCDR.GEOCODE_AS_GEOMETRY
(
  'SPATIAL',
  SDO_KEYWORDARRAY('Cloy Street', 'San Francisco, CA'),
  'US'
)
FROM DUAL;
NULL
```

The drawback of this function is that you have no indication of the quality of the result—the address you passed may contain a house number that does not exist. In this case, the address may have been matched to the house halfway down the street, but you have no way of knowing that. Or the street may not exist, and the address is then positioned in the middle of the postal code area or city. You also have no way to tell the geocoder what precision level (match mode) to use; it always uses the `DEFAULT` mode.

Therefore, you will mostly use the GEOCODE_AS_GEOMETRY function on addresses that you know are valid, such as the existing shipping addresses of your customers.

On the other hand, there are times when you cannot be sure that the input address is valid, for example, when you register a new customer in your database in your order-entry system. Or when a user types an address to find the nearest store to that address. In those cases, you will use the GEOCODE or GEOCODE_ALL function, which we describe next.

GEOCODE

GEOCODE is the main geocoding function. Contrary to the GEOCODE_AS_GEOMETRY function, which returns only coordinates, the GEOCODE function also returns a fully formatted address and codes that tell you precisely how the address matched.

This is the syntax of the GEOCODE function:

```
SDO_GCDR.GEOCODE
(
  username       IN VARCHAR2,
  addr_lines     IN SDO_KEYWORDARRAY,
  country        IN VARCHAR2
  match_mode     IN VARCHAR2
) RETURN SDO_GEO_ADDR;
```

Function Parameters

The following sections outline the parameters for the GEOCODE function. They are the same as those of the GEOCODE_AS_GEOMETRY function, except for the additional MATCH_MODE parameter.

username

This is the same as for the GEOCODE_AS_GEOMETRY function.

addr_lines

This is the same as for the GEOCODE_AS_GEOMETRY function.

country

This is the same as for the GEOCODE_AS_GEOMETRY function.

match_mode

The match mode lets you decide how closely the elements of an input address must match the data in the geocoding catalog. Note that you do not specify this parameter for the GEOCODE_AS_GEOMETRY function—it always uses the DEFAULT mode.

The match mode can be specified as shown in Table 6-3.

Table 6-3. *Match Modes and Their Meanings*

Match Mode	Meaning
EXACT	All fields provided must match exactly.
RELAX_STREET_TYPE	The street type can be different from the official street type.
RELAX_POI_NAME	The POI name does not have to match exactly.
RELAX_HOUSE_NUMBER	The house number and street type do not have to match.
RELAX_BASE_NAME	The street (base) name, house number, and street type do not have to match.
RELAX_POSTAL_CODE	The postal code (if provided), street (base) name, house number, and street type do not have to match.
RELAX_BUILTUP_AREA	This mode searches the address outside the city specified, but within the same county, and includes RELAX_POSTAL_CODE.
RELAX_ALL	Same as RELAX_BUILTUP_AREA.
DEFAULT	Same as RELAX_BASE_NAME.

You will see the effect of the various modes in the upcoming examples.

Function Result: SDO_GEO_ADDR

This structure contains the detailed results of a geocoding operation. See Table 6-4 for the exact content of the structure.

As you can see, this structure is quite rich and contains many pieces of information. They can be summarized as follows:

- LONGITUDE and LATITUDE: The coordinates of the address.
- MATCHCODE and ERRORMESSAGE: Together, they indicate how close the match is. The possible values are detailed later.
- SIDE: The side of the street on which this address lies (L for left; R for right).
- PERCENT: The relative position of the address on the road segment when traveling from lower to higher numbered addresses. This is expressed as a percentage. A setting of 50 percent indicates that the address is halfway down the road segment.
- EDGE_ID: The ID of the road segment this address is located on.

The other attributes hold the cleansed and completed address, broken down into individual components. This includes settlement, municipality, and region names; postal code; and street base name, suffix, prefix, and so on.

Table 6-4. SDO_GEO_ADDR *Object Structure*

Column Name	Data Type
ID	NUMBER
ADDRESSLINES	SDO_KEYWORDARRAY
PLACENAME	VARCHAR2(9000)
STREETNAME	VARCHAR2(9000)
INTERSECTSTREET	VARCHAR2(9000)
SECUNIT	VARCHAR2(9000)
SETTLEMENT	VARCHAR2(9000)
MUNICIPALITY	VARCHAR2(9000)
REGION	VARCHAR2(9000)
COUNTRY	VARCHAR2(9000)
POSTALCODE	VARCHAR2(9000)
POSTALADDONCODE	VARCHAR2(9000)
FULLPOSTALCODE	VARCHAR2(9000)
POBOX	VARCHAR2(9000)
HOUSENUMBER	VARCHAR2(9000)
BASENAME	VARCHAR2(9000)
STREETTYPE	VARCHAR2(9000)
STREETTYPEBEFORE	VARCHAR2(1)
STREETTYPEATTACHED	VARCHAR2(1)
STREETPREFIX	VARCHAR2(9000)
STREETSUFFIX	VARCHAR2(9000)
SIDE	VARCHAR2(1)
PERCENT	NUMBER
EDGEID	NUMBER
ERRORMESSAGE	VARCHAR2(9000)
MATCHCODE	NUMBER
MATCHMODE	VARCHAR2(30)
LONGITUDE	NUMBER
LATITUDE	NUMBER

Interpreting the Results of a Geocode Operation

The results of the GEOCODE function indicate the way the input address was matched with the list of addresses from the reference data. All that was returned from the GEOCODE_AS_GEOMETRY function was a geographical point. The GEOCODE function allows you to find out if there were any mistakes in the input address. Two attributes of the SDO_GEO_ADDR structure give you this information: MATCHCODE and ERRORMESSAGE.

MATCHCODE

The `MATCHCODE` attribute indicates the general "quality" of the match and is described in Table 6-5.

Table 6-5. *Match Codes and Their Meanings*

Match Code	Meaning
1	Exact match. The city name, postal code, street base name, street type/suffix/prefix, and house number are all matched.
2	The city name, postal code, street base name, and house number are matched, but the street type and suffix or prefix is not matched.
3	The city name, postal code, and street base name are matched, but the house number is not matched.
4	The postal code and city name are matched, but the street address is not matched.
10	The city name is matched, but the postal code is not matched.
11	The postal code is matched, but the city name is not matched.

Note that the code specifies how close the match is with only those address elements that are specified in the input address. It does not consider the ones that are not passed. For example, an address such as "Clay St, San Francisco, CA" receives a match code of 1, even though no house number or postal code was specified. On the other hand, an address such as "9650 Clay St, San Francisco, CA 92306" receives a match code of 10, which indicates that neither the postal code nor the house number matched.

ERRORMESSAGE

The `ERRORMESSAGE` attribute further details the quality and precision of the match by telling you how each individual address element matched.

The error message is a character string in which each character specifies how each address element was matched. When the address element is not matched, then its corresponding character position contains a question mark (?). Table 6-6 shows the meaning of each position in the `ERRORMESSAGE` string.

Table 6-6. *Detailed* `ERRORMESSAGE` *Structure*

Position	Meaning	Value When Matched
5	House or building number	#
6	Street prefix	E
7	Street base name	N
8	Street suffix	U
9	Street type	T
10	Secondary unit	S
11	Built-up area or city	B
14	Region	1
15	Country	C
16	Postal code	P
17	Postal add-on code	A

Used together, the MATCHCODE and ERRORMESSAGE attributes let your application decide whether to accept the results of a geocode operation or reject the results and flag the containing record for later resolution by a human. Common reasons for rejecting a geocode are as follows:

- The geocoder was unable to correct errors in the address (such as an invalid house number).
- The application wants all addresses to be geocoded at the street level at a minimum, but the address was geocoded at the postal code or city level.

Examples

Let's look at a various examples. We start with valid addresses, and then we move on to see what happens when addresses contain various errors.

A Street Address Without a House Number

Listing 6-6 shows the geocoding of a street address in San Francisco. The address specifies the street name and town, but no postal code.

Listing 6-6. *Example of Calling the* GEOCODE *Function*

```
SQL> SELECT SDO_GCDR.GEOCODE
(
  'SPATIAL',
  SDO_KEYWORDARRAY('Clay Street', 'San Francisco, CA'),
  'US',
  'DEFAULT'
)
FROM DUAL;
SDO_GEO_ADDR(0, SDO_KEYWORDARRAY(NULL), NULL, 'CLAY ST', NULL, NULL, 'SAN
FRANCISCO',
NULL, 'CA', 'US', '94108', NULL, '94108', NULL, '978', 'CLAY', 'ST', 'F',
 'F', NULL,
NULL, 'L', 0, 1, 23600689, 'nul?#ENUT?B281CP?', 1, 'DEFAULT', -122.40904, 37.79385)
```

The result is hard to read, so we will write a PL/SQL stored procedure that will format and display the result in a more readable way. Procedure FORMAT_GEO_ADDR takes an SDO_GEO_ADDR object as input and formats it using the DBMS_OUTPUT package. Listing 6-7 details the procedure.

Listing 6-7. FORMAT_GEO_ADDR *Procedure*

```
SQL>
CREATE OR REPLACE PROCEDURE format_geo_addr
(
  address SDO_GEO_ADDR
)
AS
```

```
BEGIN
  dbms_output.put_line ('- ID                       ' || address.ID);
  dbms_output.put_line ('- ADDRESSLINES');
  if address.addresslines.count() > 0 then
    for i in 1..address.addresslines.count() loop
      dbms_output.put_line ('- ADDRESSLINES['||i||']        ' ||
          address.ADDRESSLINES(i));
    end loop;
  end if;
  dbms_output.put_line ('- PLACENAME                ' || address.PLACENAME);
  dbms_output.put_line ('- STREETNAME               ' || address.STREETNAME);
  dbms_output.put_line ('- INTERSECTSTREET          ' || address.INTERSECTSTREET);
  dbms_output.put_line ('- SECUNIT                  ' || address.SECUNIT);
  dbms_output.put_line ('- SETTLEMENT               ' || address.SETTLEMENT);
  dbms_output.put_line ('- MUNICIPALITY             ' || address.MUNICIPALITY);
  dbms_output.put_line ('- REGION                   ' || address.REGION);
  dbms_output.put_line ('- COUNTRY                  ' || address.COUNTRY);
  dbms_output.put_line ('- POSTALCODE               ' || address.POSTALCODE);
  dbms_output.put_line ('- POSTALADDONCODE          ' || address.POSTALADDONCODE);
  dbms_output.put_line ('- FULLPOSTALCODE           ' || address.FULLPOSTALCODE);
  dbms_output.put_line ('- POBOX                    ' || address.POBOX);
  dbms_output.put_line ('- HOUSENUMBER              ' || address.HOUSENUMBER);
  dbms_output.put_line ('- BASENAME                 ' || address.BASENAME);
  dbms_output.put_line ('- STREETTYPE               ' || address.STREETTYPE);
  dbms_output.put_line ('- STREETTYPEBEFORE         ' || address.STREETTYPEBEFORE);
  dbms_output.put_line ('- STREETTYPEATTACHED       ' || address.STREETTYPEATTACHED);
  dbms_output.put_line ('- STREETPREFIX             ' || address.STREETPREFIX);
  dbms_output.put_line ('- STREETSUFFIX             ' || address.STREETSUFFIX);
  dbms_output.put_line ('- SIDE                     ' || address.SIDE);
  dbms_output.put_line ('- PERCENT                  ' || address.PERCENT);
  dbms_output.put_line ('- EDGEID                   ' || address.EDGEID);
  dbms_output.put_line ('- ERRORMESSAGE             ' || address.ERRORMESSAGE);
  if address.errormessage is not null and address.errormessage <> 'Not found' then
    if substr (address.errormessage,5,1)  <> '?' then
      dbms_output.put_line ('-   # House or building number');
    end if;
    if substr (address.errormessage,6,1)  <> '?' then
      dbms_output.put_line ('-   E Street prefix');
    end if;
    if substr (address.errormessage,7,1)  <> '?' then
      dbms_output.put_line ('-   N Street base name');
    end if;
    if substr (address.errormessage,8,1)  <> '?' then
      dbms_output.put_line ('-   U Street suffix');
    end if;
    if substr (address.errormessage,9,1)  <> '?' then
      dbms_output.put_line ('-   T Street type');
    end if;
```

```
    if substr (address.errormessage,10,1) <> '?' then
      dbms_output.put_line ('-    S Secondary unit');
    end if;
    if substr (address.errormessage,11,1) <> '?' then
      dbms_output.put_line ('-    B Built-up area or city');
    end if;
    if substr (address.errormessage,14,1) <> '?' then
      dbms_output.put_line ('-    1 Region');
    end if;
    if substr (address.errormessage,15,1) <> '?' then
      dbms_output.put_line ('-    C Country');
    end if;
    if substr (address.errormessage,16,1) <> '?' then
      dbms_output.put_line ('-    P Postal code');
    end if;
    if substr (address.errormessage,17,1) <> '?' then
      dbms_output.put_line ('-    A Postal add-on code');
    end if;
  end if;
  dbms_output.put_line ('- MATCHCODE                  ' ||
    address.MATCHCODE || ' = ' ||
    case address.MATCHCODE
      when  1 then 'Exact match'
      when  2 then 'Match on city, postal code, street base name and number'
      when  3 then 'Match on city, postal code and street base name'
      when  4 then 'Match on city and postal code'
      when 10 then 'Match on city but not postal code'
      when 11 then 'Match on postal but not on city'
    end
  );
  dbms_output.put_line ('- MATCHMODE          ' || address.MATCHMODE);
  dbms_output.put_line ('- LONGITUDE          ' || address.LONGITUDE);
  dbms_output.put_line ('- LATITUDE           ' || address.LATITUDE);
END;
/
show errors
```

Listing 6-8 shows how to use the procedure with our previous example.

Listing 6-8. *Example of Using the* FORMAT_GEO_ADDR *Procedure*

```
SQL> SET SERVEROUTPUT ON
SQL> BEGIN
       FORMAT_GEO_ADDR (
         SDO_GCDR.GEOCODE (
           'SPATIAL',
           SDO_KEYWORDARRAY('Clay Street', 'San Francisco, CA'),
           'US',
```

```
            'DEFAULT'
        )
      );
    END;
    /
- ID                   0
- ADDRESSLINES
- PLACENAME
- STREETNAME           CLAY ST
- INTERSECTSTREET
- SECUNIT
- SETTLEMENT           SAN FRANCISCO
- MUNICIPALITY
- REGION               CA
- COUNTRY              US
- POSTALCODE           94108
- POSTALADDONCODE
- FULLPOSTALCODE       94108
- POBOX
- HOUSENUMBER          978
- BASENAME             CLAY
- STREETTYPE           ST
- STREETTYPEBEFORE     F
- STREETTYPEATTACHED F
- STREETPREFIX
- STREETSUFFIX
- SIDE                 L
- PERCENT              0
- EDGEID               23600689
- ERRORMESSAGE         ????#ENUT?B281CP?
-   # House or building number
-   E Street prefix
-   N Street base name
-   U Street suffix
-   T Street type
-   B Built-up area or city
-   1 Region
-   C Country
-   P Postal code
- MATCHCODE            1 = Exact match
- MATCHMODE            DEFAULT
- LONGITUDE            -122.40904
- LATITUDE             37.79385
```

We receive a geographical point that lies on Clay Street. We also receive a corrected address with the street name as CLAY ST, and a zip code, 94108. The house number returned (978) corresponds to the middle point of the part of Clay Street that lies in zip code 94108 (Clay Street actually spreads over five postal codes, as shown in Listing 6-9).

The MATCHCODE returned is 1, indicating that we had a full match, including street type. The ERRORMESSAGE is ????#ENUT?B281CP?, which indicates a successful match on the elements shown in Table 6-7.

Table 6-7. *Matching Elements in the* ERRORMESSAGE

Code	Match On
#	House or building number
E	Street prefix
N	Street base name
U	Street suffix
T	Street type
B	Built-up area or city
1	Region
C	Country
P	Postal code

Notice the letter T in the error message code. It indicates a match on the street type, even though the input address used "Street" and the actual type is "St".

However, the ERRORMESSAGE also contains the characters # and P, which indicate matches on the house number and postal code, despite the fact that the input address contained no house number or postal code.

■ **Caution** The indication of a positive match for an address element in ERRORMESSAGE does *not* necessarily mean that the corresponding address element actually matched—the address element may simply be missing from the input address.

Dissecting Clay Street

For the following examples, it is useful to know more about the house numbers on Clay Street. This will help you understand the preceding example as well as those that follow. Listing 6-9 shows how to find out the house numbers for a street.

Listing 6-9. *Getting Street Details from the Geocode Reference Data*

```
SQL> SELECT road_id, name, postal_code, start_hn, center_hn, end_hn
FROM gc_road_us
WHERE name = 'CLAY ST' AND postal_code like '94%'
ORDER BY start_hn;
```

```
  ROAD_ID NAME                      POSTAL   START_HN  CENTER_HN     END_HN
---------- -------------------- ------ ---------- ---------- ----------
       767 CLAY ST                  94111           1        398        699
       427 CLAY ST                  94108         700        978       1299
       505 CLAY ST                  94109        1300       1698       1999
      1213 CLAY ST                  94115        2200       2798       3299
      1446 CLAY ST                  94118        3300       3698       3999
```

The results show the house numbers on Clay Street for each postal code: the first house number, the last house number, and the number of the house halfway down the street.

Since our address did not include any explicit postal code, the geocoder picked the one with the smallest number (94108) and then the center house number (978).

A Street Address with a House Number

The example in Listing 6-10 includes a house number but does not specify the street type. Note that we use the FORMAT_GEO_ADDR procedure to make the results clearer.

Listing 6-10. *Using the* GEOCODE *Function with a Valid House Number*

```
SQL> SET SERVEROUTPUT ON
SQL> BEGIN
       FORMAT_GEO_ADDR (
         SDO_GCDR.GEOCODE (
           'SPATIAL',
           SDO_KEYWORDARRAY('1350 Clay', 'San Francisco, CA'),
           'US',
           'DEFAULT'
         )
       );
     END;
     /
- ID                    0
- ADDRESSLINES
- PLACENAME
- STREETNAME            CLAY ST
- INTERSECTSTREET
- SECUNIT
- SETTLEMENT            SAN FRANCISCO
- MUNICIPALITY
- REGION                CA
- COUNTRY               US
- POSTALCODE            94109
- POSTALADDONCODE
- FULLPOSTALCODE        94109
- POBOX
- HOUSENUMBER           1350
- BASENAME              CLAY
```

```
- STREETTYPE          ST
- STREETTYPEBEFORE    F
- STREETTYPEATTACHED F
- STREETPREFIX
- STREETSUFFIX
- SIDE                L
- PERCENT             .49
- EDGEID              23600696
- ERRORMESSAGE        ????#ENU??B281CP?
-   # House or building number
-   E Street prefix
-   N Street base name
-   U Street suffix
-   B Built-up area or city
-   1 Region
-   C Country
-   P Postal code
- MATCHCODE           2 = Match on city, postal code, street base name and number
- MATCHMODE           DEFAULT
- LONGITUDE           -122.4152166
- LATITUDE            37.7930729
```

This time, the `MATCHCODE` returned is 2. This is because we did not match on the street type (we specified only the street base name). The letter `T` no longer appears in the error message code.

Notice also that we received the correct postal code (94109) that corresponds to the house number we specified. Number 1350 is in the range of houses from 1300 to 1999, in postal code 94109.

Correcting Invalid Addresses

If the house number does not exist on this street, we still get a successful match, as shown in Listing 6-11.

Listing 6-11. *Using the* `GEOCODE` *Function with an Invalid House Number*

```
SQL> SET SERVEROUTPUT ON
SQL> BEGIN
       FORMAT_GEO_ADDR (
         SDO_GCDR.GEOCODE (
           'SPATIAL',
           SDO_KEYWORDARRAY('4500 Clay Street', 'San Francisco, CA'),
           'US',
           'DEFAULT'
         )
       );
     END;
     /
- ID                  0
- ADDRESSLINES
```

```
- PLACENAME
- STREETNAME          CLAY ST
- INTERSECTSTREET
- SECUNIT
- SETTLEMENT          SAN FRANCISCO
- MUNICIPALITY
- REGION              CA
- COUNTRY             US
- POSTALCODE          94108
- POSTALADDONCODE
- FULLPOSTALCODE      94108
- POBOX
- HOUSENUMBER         1299
- BASENAME            CLAY
- STREETTYPE          ST
- STREETTYPEBEFORE    F
- STREETTYPEATTACHED F
- STREETPREFIX
- STREETSUFFIX
- SIDE                R
- PERCENT             0
- EDGEID              23600695
- ERRORMESSAGE        ?????ENUT?B281CP?
-   E Street prefix
-   N Street base name
-   U Street suffix
-   T Street type
-   B Built-up area or city
-   1 Region
-   C Country
-   P Postal code
- MATCHCODE           3 = Match on city, postal code and street base name
- MATCHMODE           DEFAULT
- LONGITUDE           -122.41437
- LATITUDE            37.79318
```

This time, the MATCHCODE returned is 3, confirming that the house number did not match. The coordinates returned are positioned on the highest house number in the first segment of the street (i.e., the postal code with the smallest number): house 1299 in postal code 94108.

Contrast this with the "naïve" use of the GEOCODE_AS_GEOMETRY function in Listing 6-4, where we received coordinates but had no way of knowing that the house number was actually invalid and that the coordinates were pointing elsewhere. The GEOCODE function gives us this indication, allowing our application to reject the address or flag it as requiring human correction.

Let's see what happens if the postal code in the address is invalid. As illustrated in Listing 6-12, we still get the right answer, including a corrected postal code.

Listing 6-12. *Using the* GEOCODE *Function with an Invalid Postal Code*

```
SQL> SET SERVEROUTPUT ON
SQL> BEGIN
       FORMAT_GEO_ADDR (
         SDO_GCDR.GEOCODE (
           'SPATIAL',
           SDO_KEYWORDARRAY('1350 Clay St', 'San Francisco, CA 99130'),
           'US',
           'DEFAULT'
         )
       );
     END;
     /
- ID                   0
- ADDRESSLINES
- PLACENAME
- STREETNAME           CLAY ST
- INTERSECTSTREET
- SECUNIT
- SETTLEMENT           SAN FRANCISCO
- MUNICIPALITY
- REGION               CA
- COUNTRY              US
- POSTALCODE           94109
- POSTALADDONCODE
- FULLPOSTALCODE       94109
- POBOX
- HOUSENUMBER          1350
- BASENAME             CLAY
- STREETTYPE           ST
- STREETTYPEBEFORE     F
- STREETTYPEATTACHED F
- STREETPREFIX
- STREETSUFFIX
- SIDE                 L
- PERCENT              .49
- EDGEID               23600696
- ERRORMESSAGE         ????#ENUT?B281C??
-   # House or building number
-   E Street prefix
-   N Street base name
-   U Street suffix
-   T Street type
-   B Built-up area or city
-   1 Region
-   C Country
```

```
- MATCHCODE           10 = Match on city but not postal code
- MATCHMODE           DEFAULT
- LONGITUDE           -122.4152166
- LATITUDE            37.7930729
```

The resulting MATCHCODE is 10, indicating that the postal code was not matched. However the coordinates are correctly positioned on number 1350 Clay Street, and the correct postal code (94109) is given back to us.

Using the EXACT Match Mode

All the previous examples use the default match mode, RELAX_BASE_NAME. However, if we repeat the last geocode using a stricter match mode such as EXACT, then the operation fails, as shown in Listing 6-13.

Listing 6-13. *Using the* GEOCODE *Function with an Invalid Postal Code (in* EXACT *Mode)*

```
SQL> SET SERVEROUTPUT ON
SQL> BEGIN
       FORMAT_GEO_ADDR (
         SDO_GCDR.GEOCODE (
           'SPATIAL',
           SDO_KEYWORDARRAY('1350 Clay St', 'San Francisco, CA 99130'),
           'US',
           'EXACT'
         )
       );
     END;
     /
- ID                    0
- ADDRESSLINES
- PLACENAME
- STREETNAME
- INTERSECTSTREET
- SECUNIT
- SETTLEMENT
- MUNICIPALITY
- REGION
- COUNTRY
- POSTALCODE
- POSTALADDONCODE
- FULLPOSTALCODE
- POBOX
- HOUSENUMBER
- BASENAME
- STREETTYPE
- STREETTYPEBEFORE    F
- STREETTYPEATTACHED F
```

```
- STREETPREFIX
- STREETSUFFIX
- SIDE
- PERCENT               0
- EDGEID                0
- ERRORMESSAGE          Not found
- MATCHCODE             0 =
- MATCHMODE             DEFAULT
- LONGITUDE             0
- LATITUDE              0
```

Here the MATCHCODE is 0 and the ERRORMESSAGE is Not found.

Geocoding on Business Name

This final example demonstrates a very powerful technique: instead of specifying an address, we specify the name of a POI. This allows us to find POIs by just specifying their name, for example, "City Hall," "Central Station," or "General Hospital." The result will be not only the coordinates of the POI, but also its full address.

Listing 6-14 shows how to find the location and address of the Transamerica Pyramid in San Francisco.

Listing 6-14. *Using the* GEOCODE *Function to Find a POI*

```
SQL> SET SERVEROUTPUT ON
SQL> BEGIN
       FORMAT_GEO_ADDR (
         SDO_GCDR.GEOCODE (
          'SPATIAL',
          SDO_KEYWORDARRAY('Transamerica Pyramid', 'San Francisco, CA'),
          'US',
          'DEFAULT'
         )
       );
     END;
     /
- ID                      0
- ADDRESSLINES
- PLACENAME               TRANSAMERICA PYRAMID
- STREETNAME              MONTGOMERY ST
- INTERSECTSTREET
- SECUNIT
- SETTLEMENT              SAN FRANCISCO
- MUNICIPALITY
- REGION                  CA
- COUNTRY                 US
- POSTALCODE              94111
- POSTALADDONCODE
```

```
- FULLPOSTALCODE        94111
- POBOX
- HOUSENUMBER           600
- BASENAME
- STREETTYPE
- STREETTYPEBEFORE      F
- STREETTYPEATTACHED    F
- STREETPREFIX
- STREETSUFFIX
- SIDE                  R
- PERCENT               0
- EDGEID                23611721
- ERRORMESSAGE          ????#ENUT?B281CP?
-   # House or building number
-   E Street prefix
-   N Street base name
-   U Street suffix
-   T Street type
-   B Built-up area or city
-   1 Region
-   C Country
-   P Postal code
- MATCHCODE             1 = Exact match
- MATCHMODE             DEFAULT
- LONGITUDE             -122.40305
- LATITUDE              37.79509
```

The response contains the exact address of the Transamerica Pyramid: 600 Montgomery Street, San Francisco, CA 94111, as well as its geographical position (longitude and latitude).

The GEOCODE function is powerful, but it has a limitation: it returns only one match. When the input address results in multiple matches, the GEOCODE function returns only the first one. The GEOCODE_ALL function returns *all* matches.

GEOCODE_ALL

Some addresses may be ambiguous and result in multiple matches. For example, the address "12 Presidio, San Francisco, CA" is ambiguous—there are several matching streets. Is "12 Presidio Avenue" intended or "12 Presidio Boulevard"? Perhaps "12 Presidio Terrace"? The GEOCODE function returns only one of them. To see them all, use the GEOCODE_ALL function.

Another cause for ambiguity is when a street extends into multiple postal codes, and no house number or postal code is passed to refine the match. Finally, when geocoding to a POI, the name of that POI may be that of the brand or a chain with multiple branches (such as "Bank of America" or "Hertz").

The GEOCODE_ALL function is very similar to the GEOCODE function; it takes the same input arguments. However, instead of returning a single match in an SDO_GEO_ADDR object, it returns an array of SDO_GEO_ADDR objects as an object of type SDO_ADDR_ARRAY.

The syntax of the GEOCODE_ALL function is as follows:

```
SDO_GCDR.GEOCODE_ALL (
      username          IN VARCHAR2,
      addr_lines        IN SDO_KEYWORDARRAY,
      country           IN VARCHAR2
      match_mode        IN VARCHAR2
) RETURN SDO_ADDR_ARRAY;
```

Function Parameters

The following sections outline the parameters for the GEOCODE_ALL function. They are the same as those of the GEOCODE function.

username

This is the same as for the GEOCODE function.

addr_lines

This is the same as for the GEOCODE function.

country

This is the same as for the GEOCODE function.

match_mode

This is the same as for the GEOCODE function.

Function Result: SDO_ADDR_ARRAY

This is a VARRAY of up to 1,000 SDO_GEO_ADDR objects. Each SDO_GEO_ADDR object contains the details about one matching address. The structure of each SDO_GEO_ADDR is the same as the one returned by the GEOCODE function.

Examples

Before running the actual examples, we create a stored procedure that will help in decoding the results of a call to the GEOCODE_ALL function. That procedure calls the procedure FORMAT_GEO_ADDR that we created previously, and it is shown in Listing 6-15.

Listing 6-15. FORMAT_ADDR_ARRAY *Procedure*

```
CREATE OR REPLACE PROCEDURE format_addr_array
(
  address_list SDO_ADDR_ARRAY
)
AS
BEGIN
```

```
  IF address_list.count() > 0 THEN
    FOR i in 1..address_list.count() LOOP
      dbms_output.put_line ('ADDRESS['||i||']');
      format_geo_addr (address_list(i));
    END LOOP;
  END IF;
END;
/
show errors
```

Our first example is to geocode the ambiguous address "12 Presidio." Listing 6-16 shows this operation.

Listing 6-16. *Using* GEOCODE_ALL *over an Ambiguous Address*

```
SQL> SET SERVEROUTPUT ON
SQL> BEGIN
       FORMAT_ADDR_ARRAY (
         SDO_GCDR.GEOCODE_ALL (
           'SPATIAL',
           SDO_KEYWORDARRAY('12 Presidio', 'San Francisco, CA'),
           'US',
           'DEFAULT'
         )
       );
     END;
     /
ADDRESS[1]
- ID                 1
- ADDRESSLINES
- PLACENAME
- STREETNAME         PRESIDIO AVE
- INTERSECTSTREET
- SECUNIT
- SETTLEMENT         SAN FRANCISCO
- MUNICIPALITY
- REGION             CA
- COUNTRY            US
- POSTALCODE         94115
- POSTALADDONCODE
- FULLPOSTALCODE     94115
- POBOX
- HOUSENUMBER        12
- BASENAME           PRESIDIO
- STREETTYPE         AVE
- STREETTYPEBEFORE   F
- STREETTYPEATTACHED F
```

```
- STREETPREFIX
- STREETSUFFIX
- SIDE              R
- PERCENT           .8877551020408163
- EDGEID            23614728
- ERRORMESSAGE      ????#ENU??B281CP?
-   # House or building number
-   E Street prefix
-   N Street base name
-   U Street suffix
-   B Built-up area or city
-   1 Region
-   C Country
-   P Postal code
- MATCHCODE         2 = Match on city, postal code, street base name and number
- MATCHMODE         DEFAULT
- LONGITUDE         -122.44757091836735
- LATITUDE          37.7915968367347
ADDRESS[2]
- ID                1
- ADDRESSLINES
- PLACENAME
- STREETNAME        PRESIDIO TER
- INTERSECTSTREET
- SECUNIT
- SETTLEMENT        SAN FRANCISCO
- MUNICIPALITY
- REGION            CA
- COUNTRY           US
- POSTALCODE        94118
- POSTALADDONCODE
- FULLPOSTALCODE    94118
- POBOX
- HOUSENUMBER       12
- BASENAME          PRESIDIO
- STREETTYPE        TER
- STREETTYPEBEFORE  F
- STREETTYPEATTACHED F
- STREETPREFIX
- STREETSUFFIX
- SIDE              R
- PERCENT           .6428571428571429
- EDGEID            28488847
- ERRORMESSAGE      ????#ENU??B281CP?
-   # House or building number
-   E Street prefix
-   N Street base name
```

```
-    U Street suffix
-    B Built-up area or city
-    1 Region
-    C Country
-    P Postal code
- MATCHCODE           2 = Match on city, postal code, street base name and number
- MATCHMODE           DEFAULT
- LONGITUDE           -122.46105691438208
- LATITUDE            37.788768523050976
ADDRESS[3]
- ID                  1
- ADDRESSLINES
- PLACENAME
- STREETNAME          PRESIDIO BLVD
- INTERSECTSTREET
- SECUNIT
- SETTLEMENT          SAN FRANCISCO
- MUNICIPALITY
- REGION              CA
- COUNTRY             US
- POSTALCODE          94129
- POSTALADDONCODE
- FULLPOSTALCODE      94129
- POBOX
- HOUSENUMBER         12
- BASENAME            PRESIDIO
- STREETTYPE          BLVD
- STREETTYPEBEFORE    F
- STREETTYPEATTACHED F
- STREETPREFIX
- STREETSUFFIX
- SIDE                L
- PERCENT             .7931034482758621
- EDGEID              23622533
- ERRORMESSAGE        ????#ENU??B281CP?
-    # House or building number
-    E Street prefix
-    N Street base name
-    U Street suffix
-    B Built-up area or city
-    1 Region
-    C Country
-    P Postal code
- MATCHCODE           2 = Match on city, postal code, street base name and number
- MATCHMODE           DEFAULT
- LONGITUDE           -122.45612528011925
- LATITUDE            37.798262171909265
```

The result of the function is an array of three SDO_GEO_ADDR objects, each describing one match, complete with normalized address and geographical location.

So what do we do with this result? Which of the matches is the right one for the address passed as input? There is no way for a program to decide that. The proper approach is to ask the end user. If the geocoding request is done in an interactive application (web or client/server), then the application can display the list of matches and allow the user to pick the right one. This would be the case for a call-center application where the operator asks the caller to clarify his or her address.

If the geocoding request is done in batch mode (i.e., without direct user interaction), then the application program should just flag the record for later manual investigation, or write it out to a "rejected addresses" table or report.

Our second example is to geocode a POI whose name appears multiple times in the geocoding reference data, such as a chain brand name (hotel, car rental company, etc.) or a common name. The geocoder then returns a list of those POIs that match the given name.

The example in Listing 6-17 (still using the FORMAT_ADDR_ARRAY function) shows how to get the full address and geographical location of the two YMCAs in San Francisco.

Listing 6-17. *Using* GEOCODE_ALL *over an Ambiguous Address*

```
SQL> SET SERVEROUTPUT ON
SQL> BEGIN
       FORMAT_ADDR_ARRAY (
         SDO_GCDR.GEOCODE_ALL (
           'SPATIAL',
           SDO_KEYWORDARRAY('YMCA', 'San Francisco, CA'),
           'US',
           'DEFAULT'
         )
       );
     END;
     /

ADDRESS[1]
- ID                        1
- ADDRESSLINES
- PLACENAME                 YMCA
- STREETNAME                GOLDEN GATE AVE
- INTERSECTSTREET
- SECUNIT
- SETTLEMENT                SAN FRANCISCO
- MUNICIPALITY
- REGION                    CA
- COUNTRY                   US
- POSTALCODE                94102
- POSTALADDONCODE
- FULLPOSTALCODE            94102
- POBOX
- HOUSENUMBER               220
```

```
- BASENAME
- STREETTYPE
- STREETTYPEBEFORE        F
- STREETTYPEATTACHED      F
- STREETPREFIX
- STREETSUFFIX
- SIDE                    L
- PERCENT                 0
- EDGEID                  23605184
- ERRORMESSAGE            ????#ENUT?B281CP?
-   # House or building number
-   E Street prefix
-   N Street base name
-   U Street suffix
-   T Street type
-   B Built-up area or city
-   1 Region
-   C Country
-   P Postal code
- MATCHCODE               1 = Exact match
- MATCHMODE               DEFAULT
- LONGITUDE               -122.41412
- LATITUDE                37.78184
ADDRESS[2]
- ID                      1
- ADDRESSLINES
- PLACENAME               YMCA
- STREETNAME              SACRAMENTO ST
- INTERSECTSTREET
- SECUNIT
- SETTLEMENT              SAN FRANCISCO
- MUNICIPALITY
- REGION                  CA
- COUNTRY                 US
- POSTALCODE              94108
- POSTALADDONCODE
- FULLPOSTALCODE          94108
- POBOX
- HOUSENUMBER             855
- BASENAME
- STREETTYPE
- STREETTYPEBEFORE        F
- STREETTYPEATTACHED      F
- STREETPREFIX
- STREETSUFFIX
- SIDE                    R
- PERCENT                 0
- EDGEID                  23615793
```

```
- ERRORMESSAGE              ????#ENUT?B281CP?
-   # House or building number
-   E Street prefix
-   N Street base name
-   U Street suffix
-   T Street type
-   B Built-up area or city
-   1 Region
-   C Country
-   P Postal code
- MATCHCODE                 1 = Exact match
- MATCHMODE                 DEFAULT
- LONGITUDE                 -122.40685
- LATITUDE                  37.7932
```

The response contains two matches (i.e., two SDO_GEO_ADDR objects): one for the YMCA at 220 Golden Gate Avenue and the other for the YMCA at 855 Sacramento Street (with, of course, their geographical coordinates).

■ **Caution** Do not use the GEOCODE_ALL function as a way to search for businesses in a city. The proper way is to perform proximity searches ("within distance" or "nearest neighbor") on POI tables, using the techniques described in Chapter 8.

Geocoding Business Data

Now that you know how to use the geocoder, how can you use it to location-enable business data—that is, the customers, branches, and competitors tables?

Adding the Spatial Column

The first step is to add a spatial column (type SDO_GEOMETRY) to the tables. This is easily done using an ALTER statement, as shown in Listing 6-18. We previously explained the process in Chapter 3.

Listing 6-18. *Adding a Spatial Column*

```
SQL> ALTER TABLE customers ADD (location SDO_GEOMETRY);
SQL> ALTER TABLE branches ADD (location SDO_GEOMETRY);
SQL> ALTER TABLE competitors ADD (location SDO_GEOMETRY)
```

Geocoding the Addresses: The "Naïve" Approach

As you have seen, geocoding an address is really quite simple when you are certain that the address is valid. Just use the result of the GEOCODE_AS_GEOMETRY function to update the location column you just added, as shown in Listing 6-19 for the branches table. The process is identical for the other tables (they all have the same structure).

Listing 6-19. *Populating the* location *Column of the* branches *Table*

```
SQL> UPDATE branches
SET location = SDO_GCDR.GEOCODE_AS_GEOMETRY
(
  'SPATIAL',
  SDO_KEYWORDARRAY
  ( street_number || ' ' || street_name, city  || ' ' || state || ' '
    || postal_code),
  'US'
  );
SQL> COMMIT;
```

The GEOCODE_AS_GEOMETRY function expects the input address to be passed as a series of formatted lines. However, the branches table already contains a structured address (i.e., it has address elements in multiple columns):

```
STREET_NUMBER                                  VARCHAR2(5)
STREET_NAME                                    VARCHAR2(60)
CITY                                           VARCHAR2(32)
POSTAL_CODE                                    VARCHAR2(16)
STATE                                          VARCHAR2(32)
```

All you need is to construct a multiline address using this information. You can do this simply by concatenating the address elements:

- *First address line*: street_number || ' ' || street_name
- *Second address line*: city || ' ' || state || ' ' || postal_code

Then, just pass each resulting string as one element to the SDO_KEYWORDARRAY object constructor.

We assume that all addresses are U.S. addresses, but this may not be the case. Addresses in different countries must be formatted according to the formatting rules of addresses in those countries before being passed to the geocoder.

For example, if you were geocoding German addresses, Listing 6-20 shows what the previous code becomes.

Listing 6-20. *Populating the* location *Column of the* branches *Table for German Addresses*

```
SQL> UPDATE branches
SET location = SDO_GCDR.GEOCODE_AS_GEOMETRY
(
  'SPATIAL',
  SDO_KEYWORDARRAY
```

```
  ( street_name || ' ' || street_number  || postal_code || ' ' || city),
  'DE'
);
SQL> COMMIT;
```

The address lines are now formatted according to the German rules: the house number follows the street name, and the postal code precedes the city. There is no state. The country code (DE) passed indicates that this is a German address. Note that we assume that the geocoding reference data tables (GC_ROAD_DE and so on) are in the database schema called SPATIAL.

■ **Note** For U.S. addresses, the state is optional if the address contains a postal code.

Address Verification and Correction

The preceding approach is simple to use, but it has limitations:

- You cannot be sure of the quality of the geocoding result (i.e., there may be errors in the input addresses). Failed or ambiguous addresses should be flagged for later manual correction, but status information is not returned from the GEOCODE_AS_GEOMETRY function.
- If an address contains errors (e.g., an invalid postal code), you should be able to update it with the corrected information.
- For large data sets, it is not practical to do the update as a single transaction. You may need to perform intermediate commits.

To overcome these limitations, we need to use PL/SQL. The procedure in Listing 6-21 geocodes the addresses in the customers table.

Listing 6-21. *Address Geocoding and Correction*

```
SET SERVEROUTPUT ON SIZE 32000
DECLARE
  type match_counts_t is table of number;

  geo_addresses     sdo_addr_array;      -- Array of matching geocoded addresses
  geo_address       sdo_geo_addr;        -- Matching address
  geo_location      sdo_geometry;        -- Geographical location

  address_count     number;              -- Addresses processed
  geocoded_count    number;              -- Addresses successfully geocoded
  corrected_count   number;              -- Addresses geocoded and corrected
  ambiguous_count   number;              -- Ambiguous addresses (multiple matches)
  error_count       number;              -- Addresses rejected
```

```
  match_counts      match_counts_t        -- Counts per matchcode
    := match_counts_t();

  update_address    boolean;              -- Should update address ?

BEGIN

  -- Clear counters
  address_count := 0;
  geocoded_count := 0;
  error_count := 0;
  corrected_count := 0;
  ambiguous_count := 0;
  match_counts.extend(20);
  for i in 1..match_counts.count loop
    match_counts(i) := 0;
  end loop;

  -- Range over the customers
  for b in
    (select * from customers)
  loop

    -- Geocode the address
    geo_addresses := sdo_gcdr.geocode_all (
      'SPATIAL',
      SDO_KEYWORDARRAY (
        b.street_number || ' ' || b.street_name,
        b.city  || ' ' || b.postal_code),
      'US',
      'DEFAULT'
    );

    -- Check results
    address_count := address_count + 1;

    if geo_addresses.count() > 1 then

      -- Address is ambiguous: reject
      geo_location := NULL;
      ambiguous_count := ambiguous_count + 1;

    else
      -- Extract first or only match
      geo_address := geo_addresses(1);
```

```
      -- Keep counts of matchcodes seen
      match_counts(geo_address.matchcode) :=
        match_counts(geo_address.matchcode) + 1;

      -- The following matchcodes are accepted:
      --    1 = exact match
      --    2 = only street type or suffix/prefix is incorrect
      --   10 = only postal code is incorrect
      if geo_address.matchcode in (1,2,10) then
        -- Geocoding succeeded: construct geometric point
        geo_location := sdo_geometry (2001, 8307, sdo_point_type (
          geo_address.longitude, geo_address.latitude, null),
          null, null);
        geocoded_count := geocoded_count + 1;

        -- If wrong street type or postal code (matchcodes 2 or 10)
        -- accept the geocode and correct the address in the database
        if geo_address.matchcode <> 1 then
          update_address := true;
          corrected_count := corrected_count + 1;
        end if;

      else
        -- For all other matchcodes, reject the geocode
        error_count := error_count + 1;
        geo_location := NULL;
      end if;

    end if;

    -- Update location and corrected address in database
    if update_address then
      update customers
      set location = geo_location,
          street_name = geo_address.streetname,
          postal_code = geo_address.postalcode
      where id = b.id;
    else
      update customers
      set location = geo_location
      where id = b.id;
    end if;

  end loop;
```

```
  -- Display counts of records processed
  dbms_output.put_line ('Geocoding completed');
  dbms_output.put_line (address_count || ' Addresses processed');
  dbms_output.put_line (geocoded_count || ' Addresses successfully geocoded');
  dbms_output.put_line (corrected_count || ' Addresses corrected');
  dbms_output.put_line (ambiguous_count || ' ambiguous addresses rejected');
  dbms_output.put_line (error_count || ' addresses with errors');

  for i in 1..match_counts.count loop
    if match_counts(i) > 0 then
      dbms_output.put_line ('Match code '|| i || ': ' || match_counts(i));
    end if;
  end loop;

END;
/
```

Let's now look at some of the important parts of that procedure.

The following is where we do the actual geocoding of each address. The address is formatted in two lines and passed to the `GEOCODE_ALL` function, which returns a list of matches. Notice that we do not pass the state name in the address. This is not needed because we know that all addresses contain a postal code.

```
-- Geocode the address
geo_addresses := sdo_gcdr.geocode_all (
  'SPATIAL',
  SDO_KEYWORDARRAY (
    b.street_number || ' ' || b.street_name,
    b.city  || ' ' || b.postal_code),
  'US',
  'DEFAULT'
);
```

If the function returned multiple results in the `SDO_ADDR_ARRAY`, that means the address is *ambiguous* and we reject it.

```
if geo_addresses.count() > 1 then
  -- Address is ambiguous: reject
  geo_location := NULL;
  ambiguous_count := ambiguous_count + 1;
else
...
```

If the function returned one result, we can find out the quality of the result by looking at the `MATCHCODE` for that result. Match codes 1, 2, and 10 are accepted. Match code 1 indicates an exact match—the address was found and a geographical location was returned.

Match code 2 indicates that the street type, prefix, or suffix is in error. This is a common mistake. For example, the address is stored as "1250 Clay Avenue," when it should really be "1250 Clay *Street*."

Match code 10 indicates that the postal code is incorrect. This is also an easy mistake to make, especially for streets that span multiple postal codes. For example, for the address "1250 Clay Street, San Francisco, CA 94109" the correct postal code is 94108.

In both cases, we choose to accept the corrected information returned by the geocoder, and we use it to update the address in the table.

We also construct an SDO_GEOMETRY object using the coordinates returned. Notice that the coordinate system is set to 8307 (longitude/latitude, WGS84), which we know is the coordinate system used for the geocoding reference data.[1]

Finally, if the match code is anything else, we reject the result.

```
if geo_address.matchcode in (1,2,10) then
    -- Geocoding succeeded: construct geometric point
    geo_location := sdo_geometry (2001, 8307, sdo_point_type (
      geo_address.longitude, geo_address.latitude, null),
      null, null);
    geocoded_count := geocoded_count + 1;

    -- If wrong street type or postal code (matchcodes 2 or 10)
    -- accept the geocode and correct the address in the database
    if geo_address.matchcode <> 1 then
      update_address := true;
      corrected_count := corrected_count + 1;
    end if;
  else
    -- For all other matchcodes, reject the geocode
    error_count := error_count + 1;
    geo_location := NULL;
  end if;

end if;
```

We can now update the table row inside the database. If the address error (if any) can be corrected, we do so. We replace the street_name and postal_code columns with the values returned by the geocoder.

In all cases, we update the location column with the geographical point object that contains the coordinates of the address. If the address was ambiguous, or if the geocoder indicated a problem that we chose not to correct automatically, then the location column is set to NULL to indicate failure.

```
-- Update location and corrected address in database
if update_address then
  update customers
  set location = geo_location,
      street_name = geo_address.streetname,
      postal_code = geo_address.postalcode
```

1. We know this because NAVTEQ, the supplier of the geocoder reference data, uses this coordinate system.

```
    where id = b.id;
  else
    update customers
    set location = geo_location
    where id = b.id;
  end if;
```

When all addresses have been processed, we print out some statistics. Those numbers are useful to measure the quality of the input addresses. A *hit rate* can be computed as the ratio of successfully geocoded addresses to the total addresses to process.

```
-- Display counts of records processed
dbms_output.put_line ('Geocoding completed');
dbms_output.put_line (address_count || ' Addresses processed');
dbms_output.put_line (geocoded_count || ' Addresses successfully geocoded');
dbms_output.put_line (corrected_count || ' Addresses corrected');
dbms_output.put_line (ambiguous_count || ' ambiguous addresses rejected');
dbms_output.put_line (error_count || ' addresses with errors');
```

Running the preceding code produces results like the following:

```
SQL> @geocode_customers.sql
Geocoding completed
3173 Addresses processed
3146 Addresses successfully geocoded
6 Addresses corrected
10 ambiguous addresses rejected
17 addresses with errors
Match code 1: 3140
Match code 2: 6
Match code 4: 9
Match code 11: 8
PL/SQL procedure successfully completed.
```

The hit rate for this run is 99.1 percent. Out of 3,173 addresses, 3,146 were successfully geocoded, among which 6 had minor errors that were corrected. Twenty-seven addresses were rejected; 10 addresses are ambiguous; and 17 addresses have various errors, for example, street name errors (match code 4) or city name errors (match code 11).

The next step is for someone to look at those failed addresses and correct them manually. Finding them is easy; we need only look at those rows where the `location` column is `NULL`. Once those addresses are corrected, we can rerun the process, possibly on only the new addresses.

Further Refinements

You can build upon and improve the preceding code in several ways:

- Turn it into a stored procedure that takes a `table_name` column as input. Use dynamic SQL to make the procedure work with any table.
- Perform periodic commits.
- Only geocode those addresses that have the `location` column set to `NULL`. This allows you to use the same process after correcting the rejected addresses. It also enables you to restart the process should it fail for any reason. It will skip those addresses that were already geocoded.
- Add a `match_code` column to the data tables and populate it with the match codes returned by the geocoder. This can help the user who later on corrects the addresses to better understand the nature of each error.

Automatic Geocoding

The geocoder is invoked using simple function calls. Those function calls can be used from anywhere, including from triggers. This is a powerful mechanism—it allows addresses to be geocoded automatically whenever an address is changed. Listing 6-22 shows a simple trigger that automatically geocodes addresses in the `branches` table.

Listing 6-22. *Automatic Geocoding of the* `branches` *Table Using a Simple Trigger*

```
CREATE OR REPLACE TRIGGER branches_geocode
  BEFORE INSERT OR UPDATE OF street_name, street_number, postal_code, city
  ON branches
  FOR EACH ROW
DECLARE
  geo_location SDO_GEOMETRY;
BEGIN
  geo_location := SDO_GCDR.GEOCODE_AS_GEOMETRY (
    'SPATIAL',
    SDO_KEYWORDARRAY (
      :new.street_number || ' ' || :new.street_name,
      :new.city  || ' ' || :new.postal_code),
    'US'
  );
  :new.location := geo_location;
END;
/
```

This trigger uses the "naïve" approach: the new location is accepted no matter what errors exist in the new address. Consider the following example, in which the address of one of our branches is changed. The branch is currently at 1 Van Ness Avenue.

```
SQL> SELECT name, street_number, street_name, city, postal_code, location
     FROM branches
     WHERE id =
77;

NAME                 STREE STREET_NAME         CITY          POSTAL_CODE
-------------------- ----- ------------------- ------------- -------------------
LOCATION(SDO_GTYPE, SDO_SRID, SDO_POINT(X, Y, Z), SDO_ELEM_INFO, SDO_ORDINATES)
--------------------------------------------------------------------------------
BANK OF AMERICA      1     S VAN NESS AVE      SAN FRANCISCO 94103
SDO_GEOMETRY(2001, 8307, SDO_POINT_TYPE(-122.41915, 37.7751038, NULL), NULL, NULL)
```

The branch relocates to 1500 Clay Street:

```
SQL> UPDATE branches
     SET street_name = 'Clay Street', street_number = 1500
     WHERE id = 77;
1 row updated.
```

This is the result:

```
SQL> SELECT name, street_number, street_name, city, postal_code, location
     FROM branches
     WHERE id = 77;

NAME                 STREE STREET_NAME         CITY          POSTAL_CODE
-------------------- ----- ------------------- ------------- -------------------
LOCATION(SDO_GTYPE, SDO_SRID, SDO_POINT(X, Y, Z), SDO_ELEM_INFO,
SDO_ORDINATES)
-------------------- ----- ------------------- ------------- -------------------
BANK OF AMERICA      1500  Clay Street         SAN FRANCISCO 94103
SDO_GEOMETRY(2001, 8307, SDO_POINT_TYPE(-122.41768, 37.7927675, NULL), NULL, NULL)
```

The branch now has the new address, and the geographic coordinates point to the new address. However, the address has the wrong postal code—we forgot to change it!

A better approach is to proceed as in the previous example—that is, use the `GEOCODE_ALL` procedure and use the result to automatically correct the address in addition to simply geocoding it. The trigger in Listing 6-23 illustrates this technique.

Listing 6-23. *Automatic Geocoding with Address Correction*

```
CREATE OR REPLACE TRIGGER branches_geocode
  BEFORE INSERT OR UPDATE OF street_name, street_number, postal_code, city ON
branches
  FOR EACH ROW
```

```
DECLARE
  geo_location SDO_GEOMETRY;
  geo_addresses SDO_ADDR_ARRAY;
  geo_address SDO_GEO_ADDR;
  update_address BOOLEAN;

BEGIN
  -- Geocode the address
  geo_addresses := sdo_gcdr.geocode_all (
    'SPATIAL',
    SDO_KEYWORDARRAY (
      :new.street_number || ' ' || :new.street_name,
      :new.city  || ' ' || :new.postal_code),
    'US',
    'DEFAULT'
  );

  -- Check results
  if geo_addresses.count() > 1 then
    -- Address is ambiguous: reject
    geo_location := NULL;
  else
    -- Extract first or only match
    geo_address := geo_addresses(1);
    -- The following matchcodes are accepted:
    --   1 = exact match
    --   2 = only street type or suffix/prefix is incorrect
    --  10 = only postal code is incorrect
    if geo_address.matchcode in (1,2,10) then
      -- Geocoding succeeded: construct geometric point
      geo_location := sdo_geometry (2001, 8307, sdo_point_type (
        geo_address.longitude, geo_address.latitude, null),
        null, null);
      -- If wrong street type or postal code (matchcodes 2 or 10)
      -- accept the geocode and correct the address in the database
      if geo_address.matchcode <> 1 then
        update_address := true;
      end if;
    else
      -- For all other matchcoded, reject the geocode
      geo_location := NULL;
    end if;
  end if;

  -- Update location
  :new.location := geo_location;
  -- If needed, correct address
```

```
  :new.street_name := geo_address.streetname;
  :new.postal_code := geo_address.postalcode;

END;
/
```

Once this trigger is created, let's see what happens if we perform the same address change of branch 77 from 1 Van Ness Avenue to 1500 Clay Street:

```
SQL> UPDATE branches
     SET street_name = 'Clay Street', street_number = 1500
     WHERE id = 77;
1 row updated.
```

This is the result:

```
SQL> SELECT name, street_number, street_name, city, postal_code, location
FROM branches WHERE id = 77;

NAME                 STREE STREET_NAME          CITY          POSTAL_CODE
-------------------- ----- -------------------- ------------- --------------------
LOCATION(SDO_GTYPE, SDO_SRID, SDO_POINT(X, Y, Z), SDO_ELEM_INFO,
SDO_ORDINATES)
----------------------------------------------------------------------------------
BANK OF AMERICA      1500  CLAY ST              SAN FRANCISCO  94109
SDO_GEOMETRY(2001, 8307, SDO_POINT_TYPE(-122.41768, 37.7927675, NULL), NULL, NULL)
```

The geographical location is the same as computed previously, but notice that the street name was corrected to match the name in the reference data and, more important, the postal code is now the right one for that location.

Let's say the branch moves again, this time to 1200 Montgomery Street:

```
SQL> UPDATE branches SET street_name = 'Montgommery street', street_number = 1200
WHERE id = 77;
```

Notice that again we did not specify any postal code, but we also made a typing mistake: *Montgommery* instead of *Montgomery*. The result of the update is as follows:

```
SQL> SELECT name, street_number, street_name, city, postal_code, location
     FROM branches
     WHERE id = 77;

NAME                 STREE STREET_NAME          CITY          POSTAL_CODE
-------------------- ----- -------------------- ------------- --------------------
LOCATION(SDO_GTYPE, SDO_SRID, SDO_POINT(X, Y, Z), SDO_ELEM_INFO,
SDO_ORDINATES)
----------------------------------------------------------------------------------
BANK OF AMERICA      1200  MONTGOMERY ST        SAN FRANCISCO  94133
SDO_GEOMETRY(2001, 8307, SDO_POINT_TYPE(-122.40405, 37.8001438, NULL), NULL, NULL)
```

The street name was automatically corrected, and the postal code is also now correct for that section of Montgomery Street.

If the address given cannot be corrected or is ambiguous, then the `location` column is automatically set to `NULL`.

The major benefit of this approach is that it allows addresses to be automatically geocoded and corrected without needing any changes to the existing applications.

Summary

In this chapter, you learned how to location-enable your data by converting street addresses into geographical locations that you can then use for spatial searches and various analyses. This is the first step in adding spatial intelligence to your applications.

You also learned that the geocoder can do much more than just generate geographical coordinates: it can also correct and clean errors in the input addresses.

The next step is to use the geocoded locations for spatial analysis. In the next few chapters, we describe spatial operators and functions to perform this spatial analysis.

CHAPTER 7

Manipulating SDO_GEOMETRY in Application Programs

So far, you have seen how to define and load spatial objects using the SDO_GEOMETRY type. You have also seen how to read spatial objects from SQL using SQL*Plus. In this chapter, we look at how to manipulate SDO_GEOMETRY types in the PL/SQL and Java programming languages. We also briefly cover C and Pro*C.

Note that there are actually few occasions when you need to write explicit code to manipulate SDO_GEOMETRY types in your application. In most cases, you can directly examine the contents of an SDO_GEOMETRY in SQL. For instance, you can obtain the geographical coordinates from an SDO_GEOMETRY object as shown in Listing 7-1.

Listing 7-1. *Extracting Coordinates*

```
SQL> SELECT b.name,
b.location.sdo_point.x b_long,
b.location.sdo_point.y b_lat
FROM branches b
WHERE b.id=42 ;

NAME                                    B_LONG      B_LAT
----------------------------------- ---------- ----------
BANK OF AMERICA                      -122.4783 37.7803596
```

This example illustrates a simple, yet powerful technique for extracting information from objects: *dot notation*. You can use this technique to extract any scalar value from geometry objects—in other words, the geometry type (SDO_GTYPE); spatial reference system ID (SDO_SRID); and the X, Y, and Z attributes of the point structure (SDO_POINT.X, .Y, and .Z).

This technique is generic; it applies to all object types, not just the SDO_GEOMETRY type. The advantage of this technique is that the result set produced does not include any object types—only native types—so it can be processed using any application tool, without the need to manipulate objects.

■ **Caution** To use this technique, you *must* use a table alias (b in Listing 7-1). If you forget, your query will fail with the "ORA-00904: invalid identifier" error.

In most application scenarios, you will be either extracting information from SDO_GEOMETRY as in Listing 7-1 or selecting data based on spatial relationships using spatial operators and functions (as discussed in Chapters 8 and 9). Listing 7-2 shows the selection of customers within a quarter-mile distance of a specific branch. All you need for such spatial selection is a spatial operator, called SDO_WITHIN_DISTANCE, in the WHERE clause of the SQL statement.

Listing 7-2. *Simple Spatial Query*

```
SELECT c.name, c.phone_number
  FROM branches b, customers c
 WHERE b.id=42
   AND SDO_WITHIN_DISTANCE (c.location,b.location,'distance=0.25 unit=mile')
       = 'TRUE';

NAME                                 PHONE_NUMBER
------------------------------------ ---------------
GLOWA GARAGE                         415-7526677
PUERTOLAS PERFORMANCE                415-7511701
TOPAZ HOTEL SERVICE                  415-9744400
CLEMENT STREET GARAGE                415-2218868
ST MONICA ELEMENTARY SCHOOL          NULL
```

Including SQL statements such as the ones in Listing 7-1 or Listing 7-2 in your application is no different from including any regular query. They may include spatial predicates (operators or functions, as discussed in Chapters 8 and 9) but return regular data types. They can be submitted and processed from any programming language.

Nonetheless, there are cases in which you need to deploy specific functionalities. In these cases, it may be necessary to develop specific code to read or write SDO_GEOMETRY types. This is typically an advanced use of Oracle Spatial, but one that makes the difference in practice.

Typical cases in which you may need to manipulate SDO_GEOMETRY data are as follows:

- *Advanced location analysis*: You may want to create geometries for new branch locations, for appropriate sales regions, or to track the route of a delivery truck inside a business application. In addition to creating geometries, you may need to know how to update existing geometries. You may want to create new functions for such creation/manipulation.

- *Data conversion*: You may need to load data that comes in a format for which no standard converter exists. Many commercial tools provide format-translation facilities, but there are still numerous cases in which legacy databases store spatial and/or attribute data in specific proprietary formats. This is also a relatively frequent issue when importing CAD/CAM diagrams in Oracle Spatial. In all these cases, you need to create interfaces between the external format and the Oracle Spatial objects.

- *Visualization analysis*: You may decide to write your own graphical map renderer and not use a standard component for this, such as Oracle MapViewer. This may not be a frequent need, but be aware that there are many specific viewing tools that fetch objects from Oracle Spatial for display on computer, handheld, and phone displays. The companies that create these tools need to develop software that has in-depth access to the spatial objects in the SDO_GEOMETRY column to perform efficient visualizations.

These tasks may require more than issuing SQL statements from application programs—you may need to know how to manipulate Oracle objects (as SDO_GEOMETRY is an object type) in the programming language in which the application is coded. In the rest of this chapter, we examine how to manipulate SDO_GEOMETRY data in detail in PL/SQL and then Java, after which we take a quick look at C and Pro*C. The types of manipulations that we describe include the following:

- Mapping the object into corresponding data structures for that language
- Reading/writing SDO_GEOMETRY objects into an application program
- Extracting information from SDO_GEOMETRY objects
- Creating new SDO_GEOMETRY objects in the program
- Modifying existing SDO_GEOMETRY objects (PL/SQL)

Whenever possible, we illustrate these types of manipulations using typical tasks in a business application, such as creating a new branch location, creating a new sales region, updating delivery routes, and so on. However, such manipulation can be used for a variety of other different purposes in different applications, as described earlier.

Manipulating Geometries Using PL/SQL

Listing 7-3 shows a sample application using SDO_GEOMETRY objects in PL/SQL. This PL/SQL code creates a new branch location, computes a rectangular sales region, creates a delivery route for its business, and extends the delivery route as the delivery truck moves on.

Listing 7-3. *Sample Application in PL/SQL*

```
SQL>
DECLARE
  b_long            NUMBER;
  b_lat             NUMBER;
  new_long          NUMBER;
  new_lat           NUMBER;
  new_branch_loc    SDO_GEOMETRY;
  sales_region      SDO_GEOMETRY;
  route             SDO_GEOMETRY;
```

```
BEGIN
  -- Obtain old location for branch id=1
  SELECT br.location.sdo_point.x, br.location.sdo_point.y
  INTO b_long, b_lat
  FROM branches br
  WHERE id=1;

  -- Compute new coordinates: say the location is displaced by 0.0025 degrees
  new_long := b_long+ 0.0025;
  new_lat := b_lat + 0.0025;

  -- Create new branch location using old location
  new_branch_loc :=
    point
    (
      X=>    new_long,
      Y=>    new_lat,
      SRID=> 8307
     ) ;

  -- Compute sales region for this branch
  sales_region :=
    rectangle
    (
      CTR_X=> new_long,
      CTR_Y=> new_lat,
      EXP_X=> 0.005,
      EXP_Y=> 0.0025,
      SRID=>  8307
    ) ;

  -- Create Delivery Route
  route :=
    line
    (
      FIRST_X=> -122.4804,
      FIRST_Y=> 37.7805222,
      NEXT_X=> -123,
      NEXT_Y=> 38,
      SRID=>  8307
    ) ;

  -- Update Delivery Route by adding new point
  route :=
    add_to_line
    (
      GEOM=> route,
```

```
      POINT => POINT(-124, 39, 8307)
    ) ;

  -- Perform additional analysis such as length of route
  -- or # of customers in sales region (we give examples in Chapters 8 and 9)
  -- ...
  -- Update geometry in branches table
  UPDATE branches SET LOCATION = new_branch_loc WHERE id=1;

END;
/
```

First, note that all SQL types can be directly used in PL/SQL, so no explicit mapping needs to be done to use an SDO_GEOMETRY in PL/SQL. As you can observe in Listing 7-3, you use the SDO_GEOMETRY type in your code in exactly the same way as you use native types (NUMBER, VARCHAR, and so on). In general, you can

- Declare variables of type SDO_GEOMETRY to hold geometry objects. For instance, we have declared three variables, new_branch_loc, sales_region, and route in Listing 7-3, each of type SDO_GEOMETRY.

- Use regular PL/SQL operations to extract information from these geometry objects or to modify their structure. Listing 7-3 shows an example of how to extract the x and y coordinates of an SDO_GEOMETRY object.

- Use SDO_GEOMETRY objects as bind (or result) variables in static or dynamic SQL statements. This allows SDO_GEOMETRY objects to be read from and written to database tables. Listing 7-3 shows how to pass an SDO_GEOMETRY object to a SQL statement that updates the location of a branch.

- Create stored functions that may take SDO_GEOMETRY type arguments and/or return SDO_GEOMETRY objects. For instance, in Listing 7-3, the point function is a stored function that takes scalar (numeric) arguments and returns an SDO_GEOMETRY object. The add_to_line function has an SDO_GEOMETRY as the first argument and returns an SDO_GEOMETRY.

Next we will fill the gaps in Listing 7-3 and describe how to code some of the stored functions in Listing 7-3. The code for the point, rectangle, and line stored functions illustrates how to create new geometries in PL/SQL, and the code for the add_to_line function shows how to modify existing geometries.

Since an SDO_GEOMETRY object contains two VARRAY structures, SDO_ELEM_INFO and SDO_ORDINATES (as described in Chapter 4), it would be wise for us to take a detour here and present a primer on manipulating VARRAYs. These VARRAY structures are primarily used to store polygons and line strings, such as the sales region of a branch or the route of the delivery truck in our application. If you are already familiar with how to manipulate VARRAYs in PL/SQL, you can skip to the section titled "Reading and Writing SDO_GEOMETRY Objects."

VARRAY Manipulation Primer

VARRAYs (short for *varying arrays*) behave pretty much like arrays in any programming language: they hold a *fixed* number of elements, but they can be extended and shrunk. They also have a *maximum capacity* beyond which you cannot extend them. They use sequential numbers as subscripts, starting from 1. They also have a number of methods that allow you to manipulate the entries in the array. Methods are called by appending them to the name of the VARRAY variable.

VARRAYs (as well as NESTED TABLES, another collections form) are not really new; they have been available in the Oracle database since version 8.0. They are a fundamental part of the object/relational aspects of Oracle. They make it possible to define multivalued attributes, and so to overcome a fundamental characteristic (some would say limitation) of the relational model: an attribute (e.g., a column) can hold only one value per row.

What makes VARRAYs especially powerful is that their elements can themselves be object types. And those objects can themselves contain other VARRAYs. This makes it possible to construct very complex structures such as collections or matrices, and so represent complex objects. The SDO_GEOMETRY type, however, does not use such complex structures. It contains only two VARRAYs of NUMBERs.

Another important property of VARRAYs is that they are *ordered*. This is especially useful for geometric primitives, since the order in which points are defined is very important—a shape defined by points A, B, C, and D is obviously not the same as one defined by A, C, B, and D.

The code in Listing 7-4 illustrates various array manipulations.

Listing 7-4. *Manipulating* VARRAY*s*

```
SET SERVEROUTPUT ON
DECLARE

  -- Declare a type for the VARRAY
  TYPE MY_ARRAY_TYPE IS VARRAY(10) OF NUMBER;

  -- Declare a VARRAY variable
  V               MY_ARRAY_TYPE;

  -- Other variables
  I               NUMBER;
  K               NUMBER;
  L               NUMBER;
  ARRAY_CAPACITY  NUMBER;
  N_ENTRIES       NUMBER;

BEGIN
  -- Initialize the array
  V := MY_ARRAY_TYPE (1,2,3,4);

  -- Get the value of a specific entry
  DBMS_OUTPUT.PUT_LINE('* Values for specific array entries');
  K := V(3);
  DBMS_OUTPUT.PUT_LINE('V(3)='|| V(3));
  I := 2;
  L := V(I+1);
```

```
DBMS_OUTPUT.PUT_LINE('I=' || I);
DBMS_OUTPUT.PUT_LINE('V(I+1)=' || V(I+1));

-- Find the capacity of a VARRAY:
DBMS_OUTPUT.PUT_LINE('* Array capacity');
ARRAY_CAPACITY := V.LIMIT();
DBMS_OUTPUT.PUT_LINE('Array Capacity: V.LIMIT()='||V.LIMIT());
N_ENTRIES := V.COUNT();
DBMS_OUTPUT.PUT_LINE('Current Array Size: V.COUNT()='||V.COUNT());

-- Range over all values in a VARRAY
DBMS_OUTPUT.PUT_LINE('* Array Content');
FOR I IN 1..V.COUNT() LOOP
  DBMS_OUTPUT.PUT_LINE('V('||I||')=' || V(I));
END LOOP;

FOR I IN V.FIRST()..V.LAST() LOOP
 DBMS_OUTPUT.PUT_LINE('V('||I||')=' || V(I));
END LOOP;

I := V.COUNT();
WHILE I IS NOT NULL LOOP
  DBMS_OUTPUT.PUT_LINE('V('||I||')=' || V(I));
  I := V.PRIOR(I);
END LOOP;

-- Extend the VARRAY
DBMS_OUTPUT.PUT_LINE('* Extend the array');
I := V.LAST();
V.EXTEND(2);
V(I+1) := 5;
V(I+2) := 6;

DBMS_OUTPUT.PUT_LINE('Array Capacity: V.LIMIT()='||V.LIMIT());
DBMS_OUTPUT.PUT_LINE('Current Array Size: V.COUNT()='||V.COUNT());
FOR I IN 1..V.COUNT() LOOP
  DBMS_OUTPUT.PUT_LINE('V('||I||')='|| V(I));
END LOOP;

-- Shrink the VARRAY
DBMS_OUTPUT.PUT_LINE('* Trim the array');
V.TRIM();

DBMS_OUTPUT.PUT_LINE('Array Capacity: V.LIMIT()='||V.LIMIT());
DBMS_OUTPUT.PUT_LINE('Current Array Size: V.COUNT()='||V.COUNT());
FOR I IN 1..V.COUNT() LOOP
  DBMS_OUTPUT.PUT_LINE('V('||I||')='|| V(I));
END LOOP;
```

```
  -- Delete all entries from the VARRAY
  DBMS_OUTPUT.PUT_LINE('* Empty the array');
  V.DELETE();

  DBMS_OUTPUT.PUT_LINE('Array Capacity: V.LIMIT()='||V.LIMIT());
  DBMS_OUTPUT.PUT_LINE('Current Array Size: V.COUNT()='||V.COUNT());
  FOR I IN 1..V.COUNT() LOOP
    DBMS_OUTPUT.PUT_LINE('V('||I||')='|| V(I));
  END LOOP;
END;
/
```

Let's look at this code in detail next.

Declaring and Initializing VARRAY Variables

You cannot declare a VARRAY variable directly. You must first declare a type that includes the maximum capacity of the array.

```
TYPE MY_ARRAY_TYPE IS VARRAY(10) OF NUMBER;
```

You can then declare your VARRAY variable using this type:

```
V   MY_ARRAY_TYPE;
```

Before you can do anything with the array, it must be initialized. You can do this at the same time as you declare it, or you can initialize it later by assigning it a value. The following shows the simultaneous declaration and initialization of an array:

```
V   MY_ARRAY_TYPE := MY_ARRAY_TYPE ();
```

Getting the Value of a Specific Entry

Just use the number of the entry as a subscript. The subscript can be any expression that returns an integer equal to or less than the number of entries in the array, for example:

```
K := V(3);
I := 2;
L := V(I+1);
```

Finding the Capacity of a VARRAY

Use the COUNT() method on the VARRAY variable. Note that you do not have to specify the parentheses, since this method takes no arguments.

```
N_ENTRIES := V.COUNT();
```

This tells you the number of entries currently in use in the array. A VARRAY also has a maximum capacity that was specified when the type was declared. You can find out that capacity using the LIMIT() method:

```
ARRAY_CAPACITY := V.LIMIT;
```

Ranging Over All Values in a VARRAY

You can use several techniques. The simplest is to use a FOR loop:

```
FOR I IN 1..V.COUNT() LOOP
   DBMS_OUTPUT.PUT_LINE('V('||I||')='  || V(I));
END LOOP;
```

You can also use the FIRST() and LAST() methods. FIRST() returns the subscript of the first entry in the array (which is always 1), and LAST() returns the subscript of the last entry in the array (which is always the same as COUNT).

```
FOR I IN V.FIRST()..V.LAST() LOOP
   DBMS_OUTPUT.PUT_LINE('V('||I||')='  || V(I));
END LOOP;
```

You could also use the PRIOR(n) and NEXT(n) methods, which return the subscript of the entry that precedes or follows a given entry, respectively. For example, use this to range backward over the array:

```
I := V.COUNT();
WHILE I IS NOT NULL LOOP
  DBMS_OUTPUT.PUT_LINE('V('||I||')='  || V(I));
  I := V.PRIOR(I);
END LOOP;
```

PRIOR(n) is really the same as n-1, and NEXT(n) is the same as n+1, but PRIOR(1) and NEXT(V.COUNT()) return NULL.

Extending a VARRAY

Use the EXTEND(k) method. This method adds k new entries at the end of the VARRAY. When k is not specified, the array is extended by a single entry. The new entries have no value yet (they are set to NULL), but they can now be initialized. The COUNT() and LAST() methods now reflect the new capacity of the VARRAY. The following adds two entries to the array and initializes them:

```
I := V.LAST();
V.EXTEND(2);
V(I+1) := 5;
V(I+2) := 6;
```

Note that you cannot extend a VARRAY beyond its maximum capacity (returned by the LIMIT() method). Note also that the VARRAY must be instantiated before you can extend it. The following does *not* work:

```
VT MY_ARRAY_TYPE;
VT.EXTEND(5);
```

But the following does work:

```
VT MY_ARRAY_TYPE;
VT := MY_ARRAY_TYPE();
VT.EXTEND(5);
```

Shrinking a VARRAY

Use the TRIM(k) method. This method removes the last k entries from the end of the VARRAY. When k is not specified, the last entry of the array is removed. The values of the removed entries are lost. COUNT() and LAST() reflect the new capacity. The following removes the last entry from the VARRAY:

```
V.TRIM;
```

You can trim all entries from the array, like this:

```
V.TRIM(V.COUNT());
```

Or you can use the DELETE() method, which has the same effect. It removes all entries from the array and sets its capacity to zero (i.e., V.COUNT() now returns 0).

```
V.DELETE;
```

Now that you know how to manipulate VARRAYs, let's apply those techniques to the SDO_GEOMETRY type. We will start by covering the techniques to extract information from an SDO_GEOMETRY object, and then we will present an example of how to update an SDO_GEOMETRY object.

Next, we will revert to our original discussion on how to read/write SDO_GEOMETRY data, how to create new geometries, how to extract information from existing ones, and how to modify existing geometries. We cover each of these topics in a separate subsection.

Reading and Writing SDO_GEOMETRY Objects

Reading and writing SDO_GEOMETRY data in a PL/SQL program is easy. You define new variables of SDO_GEOMETRY and read INTO or write USING these variables while executing a SQL statement. Listing 7-3 shows an example of both reading the x,y components of a branch location and updating the new location in the branches table.

Creating New Geometries

In this section, we illustrate how to create new geometries using stored functions, as described in Listing 7-3. These functions simplify the writing of some SQL statements and hide some of the complexities in dealing with geometries. You can use these constructors to populate new branch locations or to create new sales regions, for example.

Point Constructor

Inserting point geometries using the SDO_GEOMETRY constructor may seem unduly complicated. Listing 7-5 shows a simple stored function that makes this operation easier by hiding some of the complexity of spatial objects from developers and/or end users.

Listing 7-5. *Point Constructor Function*

```
CREATE OR REPLACE FUNCTION point (
  x NUMBER, y NUMBER, srid NUMBER DEFAULT 8307)
DETERMINISTIC
RETURN SDO_GEOMETRY
IS
BEGIN
  RETURN SDO_GEOMETRY (
           2001, srid, SDO_POINT_TYPE (x,y,NULL), NULL, NULL);
END;
/
```

As you can see, we just declare the function to return an SDO_GEOMETRY type. It is then a simple matter to use the standard constructor of SDO_GEOMETRY to generate a proper point object using the arguments provided (X, Y, and an optional spatial reference system).

We can then use this new constructor to simplify our SQL statements. For example, here is how to update the geographical location of a new branch using the constructor in Listing 7-5:

```
UPDATE branches
    SET location = point (-122.48049, 37.7805222, 8307)
WHERE id = 1;
```

■ **Tip** Always use the DETERMINISTIC keyword when the result of the function depends only on the input arguments (and not on the database state). This will help you to reuse cached evaluations of the function when the same arguments are passed in, and it also results in better overall performance.

Rectangle Constructor

In Listing 7-3, we used the rectangle function to create a new geometry to represent a sales region around a branch location. We can code this function to define a region around the branch location by expanding from the location by a specified amount in each of the two dimensions. The following listing shows the corresponding SQL. Note that rectangles are used extensively in visualization; many interactions that select objects to include on a map use rectangles to define the area of interest. As for the point constructor, our goal here is to simplify the writing of SQL statements that need to use rectangles.

Listing 7-6 shows how to define a rectangular shape. The function takes the coordinates of the center of the rectangle, the distances from the center to each side, and optionally a spatial reference system ID. As shown in Listing 7-6, the SDO_ORDINATES attribute in the SDO_GEOMETRY constructor stores the lower-left and upper-right points. Note that all we do here is create a new object using the SDO_GEOMETRY constructor, populate it with the appropriate information, and return the object as the function result.

Listing 7-6. *Rectangle Constructor*

```
CREATE OR REPLACE FUNCTION rectangle (
  ctr_x NUMBER, ctr_y NUMBER, exp_x NUMBER, exp_y NUMBER, srid NUMBER)
RETURN SDO_GEOMETRY
DETERMINISTIC
IS
  r SDO_GEOMETRY;
BEGIN
  r := SDO_GEOMETRY (
    2003, srid, NULL,
    SDO_ELEM_INFO_ARRAY (1, 1003, 3),
    SDO_ORDINATE_ARRAY (
      ctr_x - exp_x, ctr_y - exp_y,
      ctr_x + exp_x, ctr_y + exp_y));
  RETURN r;
END;
/
```

We can use this function anywhere in our SQL statements. For example, the following code counts the number of customers inside a rectangular window, grouped by grade. Without the rectangle function, we would have to use the more complex generic SDO_GEOMETRY constructor.

```
SELECT count(*), customer_grade
  FROM customers WHERE SDO_INSIDE (location,
         rectangle (-122.47,37.79,  0.01, 0.01, 8307)) = 'TRUE'
GROUP BY customer_grade;

  COUNT(*) CUSTOMER_GRADE
---------- ---------------
       307 GOLD
         4 PLATINUM
       457 SILVER
```

Line Constructor

In Listing 7-3, we used the line function to create a new line geometry with a start point and an end point. Listing 7-7 shows how to write such a function.

Listing 7-7. *Line Constructor*

```
CREATE OR REPLACE FUNCTION line (
  first_x NUMBER, first_y NUMBER, next_x NUMBER, next_y NUMBER, srid NUMBER)
RETURN SDO_GEOMETRY
DETERMINISTIC
IS
  l SDO_GEOMETRY;
```

```
BEGIN
  l := SDO_GEOMETRY (
    2002, srid, NULL,
    SDO_ELEM_INFO_ARRAY (1, 2, 1),
    SDO_ORDINATE_ARRAY (
      first_x, first_y,
      next_x, next_y));
  RETURN l;
END;
/
```

Extracting Information from Geometries

In this section, we illustrate the manipulation of geometries with two examples. The first is very simple and demonstrates how to find out the number of points in a geometry. The second is a slightly more complex example in which we write a function to extract a specific point from a line geometry.

The functions we present here are intended primarily to illustrate the techniques you can use to manipulate geometry objects in PL/SQL.

Counting the Number of Points in a Geometry

The `get_num_points` function in Listing 7-8 computes the number of points in a geometry by dividing the count of elements in the `SDO_ORDINATES` array (i.e., the total number of ordinates) by the dimensionality of the geometry (i.e., the number of ordinates per point).

Listing 7-8. *Counting the Number of Points in a Geometry*

```
CREATE OR REPLACE FUNCTION get_num_points (
  g SDO_GEOMETRY)
RETURN NUMBER
IS
BEGIN
  RETURN g.SDO_ORDINATES.COUNT() / SUBSTR(g.SDO_GTYPE,1,1);
END;
/
```

You can use the function as follows to find out the number of points in a geometry:

```
SELECT get_num_points(geom) FROM us_states WHERE state = 'California';
GET_NUM_POINTS(GEOM)
--------------------
                1146
```

Extracting a Point from a Line

Let's assume our application keeps track of the route followed by a delivery truck. When the truck is moving, it reports its position every minute. Those points are stringed together to form a line geometry that represents the route followed by the truck so far. (This operation is described later in this chapter.)

Listing 7-9 shows a function that extracts a selected point from a geometry. The function takes two input arguments: a geometry object and the number of the point in that geometry. The first point in the geometry is point number 1. It then returns a new geometry object that contains only the selected point.

Listing 7-9. *Function to Extract a Point from a Geometry*

```
CREATE OR REPLACE FUNCTION get_point (
  geom SDO_GEOMETRY, point_number NUMBER DEFAULT 1
) RETURN SDO_GEOMETRY
IS
  g MDSYS.SDO_GEOMETRY; -- Updated Geometry
  d NUMBER;             -- Number of dimensions in geometry
  p NUMBER;             -- Index into ordinates array
  px NUMBER;            -- X of extracted point
  py NUMBER;            -- Y of extracted point

BEGIN
  -- Get the number of dimensions from the gtype
  d := SUBSTR (geom.SDO_GTYPE, 1, 1);

  -- Verify that the point exists
  IF point_number < 1
  OR point_number > geom.SDO_ORDINATES.COUNT()/d THEN
    RETURN NULL;
  END IF;

  -- Get index in ordinates array
  p := (point_number-1) * d + 1;

  -- Extract the X and Y coordinates of the desired point
  px := geom.SDO_ORDINATES(p);
  py := geom.SDO_ORDINATES(p+1);

  -- Construct and return the point
  RETURN
    MDSYS.SDO_GEOMETRY (
      2001,
      geom.SDO_SRID,
      SDO_POINT_TYPE (px, py, NULL),
      NULL, NULL);
END;
/
```

In this function, we perform some error checking. If the number of the point is larger than the number of points in the object, then we return a NULL object. If the point number is not specified, then we just return the first point of the geometry. Notice that the extracted point is always returned as a two-dimensional point (even if the geometry is three- or four-dimensional). The returned point is always in the same coordinate system as the input geometry.

Further refinements to the function could be to make it throw an exception if the point number is incorrect or if the geometry is not a line.

Listing 7-10 shows some examples of how to use this function to get the first, middle, and last points of a line string (the line that represents Interstate 95).

Listing 7-10. *Getting the First, Middle, and Last Points of a Line String*

```
-- Getting the first point of a line string
SELECT get_point(geom) p
FROM us_interstates
WHERE interstate='I95';
P(SDO_GTYPE, SDO_SRID, SDO_POINT(X, Y, Z), SDO_ELEM_INFO, SDO_ORDINATES)
-----------------------------------------------------------------------
SDO_GEOMETRY(2001, 8307, SDO_POINT_TYPE(-80.211761, 25.74876, NULL), NULL, NULL)

-- Getting the last point of a line string
SELECT get_point(geom, get_num_points(geom)) p
FROM us_interstates
WHERE interstate='I95';
P(SDO_GTYPE, SDO_SRID, SDO_POINT(X, Y, Z), SDO_ELEM_INFO, SDO_ORDINATES)
-----------------------------------------------------------------------
SDO_GEOMETRY(2001, 8307, SDO_POINT_TYPE(-74.118584, 40.754608, NULL), NULL, NULL)

-- Getting the middle point of a line string
SELECT get_point(geom, ROUND(get_num_points(geom)/2)) p
FROM us_interstates
WHERE interstate='I95';
P(SDO_GTYPE, SDO_SRID, SDO_POINT(X, Y, Z), SDO_ELEM_INFO, SDO_ORDINATES)
-----------------------------------------------------------------------
SDO_GEOMETRY(2001, 8307, SDO_POINT_TYPE(-68.118683, 46.120701, NULL), NULL, NULL)
```

Modifying Existing Geometries

Array manipulation techniques are most useful when updating geometries. In this section, we present a few examples. They are all stored functions that take an SDO_GEOMETRY object as input and return a new SDO_GEOMETRY object.

Removing a Point from a Line

A common editing operation on geometries is to add and remove points from a geometry, which is what this and the next stored function do. First we look at the removal of a point using the remove_point function in Listing 7-11.

Listing 7-11. remove_point *Function*

```
CREATE OR REPLACE FUNCTION remove_point (
  geom SDO_GEOMETRY, point_number NUMBER
) RETURN SDO_GEOMETRY
IS
  g MDSYS.SDO_GEOMETRY; -- Updated Geometry
  d NUMBER;             -- Number of dimensions in geometry
  p NUMBER;             -- Index into ordinates array
  i NUMBER;             -- Index into ordinates array
BEGIN
  -- Get the number of dimensions from the gtype
  d := SUBSTR (geom.SDO_GTYPE, 1, 1);

  -- Get index in ordinates array
  -- If 0 then we want the last point
  IF point_number = 0 THEN
    p :=  geom.SDO_ORDINATES.COUNT() - d + 1;
  ELSE
    p := (point_number-1) * d + 1;
  END IF;

  -- Verify that the point exists
  IF p > geom.SDO_ORDINATES.COUNT() THEN
    RETURN NULL;
  END IF;

  -- Initialize output line with input line
  g := geom;

  -- Step 1: Shift the ordinates "up"
  FOR i IN p..g.SDO_ORDINATES.COUNT()-d LOOP
    g.SDO_ORDINATES(i) := g.SDO_ORDINATES(i+d);
  END LOOP;

  -- Step 2: Trim the ordinates array
  g.SDO_ORDINATES.TRIM (d);

  -- Return the updated geometry
  RETURN g;
END;
/
```

Just like in the get_point() function, we begin by converting the number of the point to remove into the index of the SDO_ORDINATE element where the ordinates of the point start (p).

The subsequent process is illustrated in Figure 7-1. We first remove the point by shifting the ordinates "up." Assume we want to remove the third point (point C) from the line string. Its index in the ordinate array is 5. The ordinates for points D, E, and F are then shifted up from elements 7–12 into elements 5–10. This is step 1 in the figure.

Then, we trim the array by removing the last elements we no longer need. This is step 2 in the figure.

	Original Ordinates		Step 1		Step 2
1	Xa	1	Xa	1	Xa
2	Ya	2	Ya	2	Ya
3	Xb	3	Xb	3	Xb
4	Yb	4	Yb	4	Yb
5	Xc	5	Xd	5	Xc
6	Yc	6	Yd	6	Yc
7	Xd	7	Xe	7	Xd
8	Yd	8	Ye	8	Yd
9	Xe	9	Xf	9	Xe
10	Ye	10	Yf	10	Ye
11	Xf	11	Xf		
12	Yf	12	Yf		

Figure 7-1. *Removing a point from a line*

We can use this function, for example, to remove the last point from I-95:

```
UPDATE US_INTERSTATES
   SET GEOM = REMOVE_POINT (GEOM, 0)
 WHERE INTERSTATE = 'I95';
```

Adding a Point to a Line

This is the reverse of the previous operation: we now insert a new point into a line string. The function needs the geometry to update, the geometry of the point to insert, and an indication of where to insert the new point in the line. This is done by passing the number of the point *before* which the new point should be inserted.

To insert the point at the start of the line, pass the value 1. To append it at the end of the line, pass the value 0. Listing 7-12 shows the SQL.

Listing 7-12. *Adding a Point in a Line String* (add_to_line *in Listing 7-3)*

```
CREATE OR REPLACE FUNCTION add_to_line (
  geom         SDO_GEOMETRY,
  point        SDO_GEOMETRY,
  point_number NUMBER DEFAULT 0
) RETURN SDO_GEOMETRY
IS
  g   SDO_GEOMETRY;          -- Updated geometry
  d   NUMBER;                -- Number of dimensions in line geometry
  t   NUMBER;                -- Geometry type
  p   NUMBER;                -- Insertion point into ordinates array
  i   NUMBER;
BEGIN
  -- Get the number of dimensions from the gtype
  d := SUBSTR (geom.SDO_GTYPE, 1, 1);

  -- Get index in ordinates array
  -- If 0, then we want the last point
  IF point_number = 0 THEN
    p :=  geom.SDO_ORDINATES.COUNT() + 1;
  ELSE
    p := (point_number-1) * d + 1;
  END IF;

  -- Verify that the insertion point exists
  IF point_number <> 0 THEN
    IF p > geom.SDO_ORDINATES.LAST()
    OR p < geom.SDO_ORDINATES.FIRST() THEN
      RAISE_APPLICATION_ERROR (-20000, 'Invalid insertion point');
    END IF;
  END IF;

  -- Initialize output line with input line
  g := geom;

  -- Step 1: Extend the ordinates array
  g.SDO_ORDINATES.EXTEND(d);

  -- Step 2: Shift the ordinates "down".
  FOR i IN REVERSE p..g.SDO_ORDINATES.COUNT()-d LOOP
    g.SDO_ORDINATES(i+d) := g.SDO_ORDINATES(i);
  END LOOP;

  -- Step 3: Store the new point
  g.SDO_ORDINATES(p) := point.SDO_POINT.X;
  g.SDO_ORDINATES(p+1) := point.SDO_POINT.Y;
```

```
  IF d = 3 THEN
    g.SDO_ORDINATES(p+2) := point.SDO_POINT.Z;
  END IF;

  -- Return the new line string
  RETURN g;
END
/
```

Again, we begin by converting the place to insert the new point into the index of the first SDO_ORDINATE element of the point before we want to insert the new point.

The process for inserting the point is illustrated in Figure 7-2. We begin, in step 1, by extending the SDO_ORDINATE array by the number of elements needed to represent a point, according to the dimensionality (two-, three-, or four-dimensional) of the line string. Then in step 2, we make room for the new point by shifting the ordinates "down." Assume we want to insert a new point (point G) before point D (the fourth point). The index of point D in the ordinate array is 7. The ordinates for points D, E, and F are then shifted down from elements 7–12 into elements 9–14. Finally, in step 3 we fill elements 7 and 8 with the x and y of the new point G.

	Original Ordinates		Step 1		Step 2		Step 3
1	Xa	1	Xa	1	Xa	1	Xa
2	Ya	2	Ya	2	Ya	2	Ya
3	Xb	3	Xb	3	Xb	3	Xb
4	Yb	4	Yb	4	Yb	4	Yb
5	Xc	5	Xc	5	Xc	5	Xc
6	Yc	6	Yc	6	Yc	6	Yc
7	Xd	7	Xd	7	Xd	7	Xg
8	Yd	8	Yd	8	Yd	8	Yg
9	Xe	9	Xe	9	Xd	9	Xd
10	Ye	10	Ye	10	Yd	10	Yd
11	Xf	11	Xf	11	Xe	11	Xe
12	Yf	12	Yf	12	Ye	12	Ye
		13		13	Xf	13	Xf
		14		14	Yf	14	Yf

Figure 7-2. *Inserting a point into a line*

Manipulating Geometries in Java

As you have seen, spatial objects are stored in database tables as `SDO_GEOMETRY` types. To process them in Java, you must first read them from the database using JDBC, and then you need to map them to Java classes.

Mapping an `SDO_GEOMETRY` type into a Java class is easy, thanks to the API provided with Oracle Spatial. The API itself is simple: it contains one package (`oracle.spatial.geometry`), which contains one main class (`JGeometry`).

The Java API for Oracle Spatial is distributed as a JAR file located in the Oracle installation (at `$ORACLE_HOME/md/lib/sdoapi.jar`). To use the API in your applications, be sure to include `sdoapi.jar` into your classpath. The documentation (Javadoc) is available in your Oracle installation as well, in the file `$ORACLE_HOME/md/doc/sdoapi.zip`.

We will study the basics of manipulating geometry types in Java using two complete examples. The first example is a Java program that can read any spatial table and dissects the geometries it finds. You can use it to examine the geometries in any of the example tables populated in the preceding examples. It illustrates how to read geometries and how to extract information from those geometries.

The second example reads a specially formatted text file and uses it to load polygon shapes into the `sales_regions` table. It illustrates how to construct new geometries and write them to the database.

Mapping SDO_GEOMETRY to JGeometry

When you read an object type (such as the `SDO_GEOMETRY` type) using a SQL `SELECT` statement, JDBC returns a Java structure—more precisely, an `oracle.sql.STRUCT` object. To write an object type (using an `INSERT` or `UPDATE` statement), you are also expected to pass an `oracle.sql.STRUCT` object. Decoding and constructing `STRUCT`s is rather complex, and the main goal of the Oracle Spatial Java API (the `JGeometry` class) is to make that task easy.

The `JGeometry` class provides two methods to convert a `STRUCT` into a `JGeometry` object:

- The `load()` method reads the `STRUCT` and returns a `JGeometry`. Use it when you convert the geometries returned by a `SELECT` statement.
- The `store()` method performs the reverse conversion to the `load()` method. It converts a `JGeometry` object into a `STRUCT` that you can then write back to the database using an `INSERT` or `UPDATE` statement.

This conversion process is illustrated in Figure 7-3.

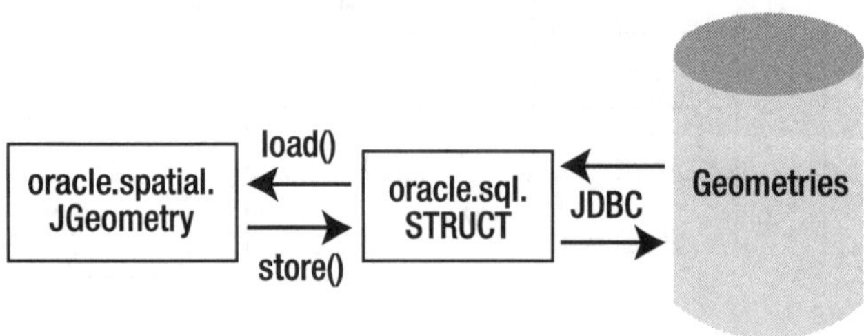

Figure 7-3. *Reading and writing geometries in Java*

Reading Geometries

To read geometries in Java, you must first construct and execute a SELECT statement that fetches columns of type SDO_GEOMETRY. The SDO_GEOMETRY objects are passed to your Java program as STRUCT objects. The static method JGeometry.load() converts the STRUCT into a JGeometry object. You can then use a number of the methods of JGeometry to extract information from the object.

Listing 7-13 illustrates this process in a Java program that lets you print the details of any SDO_GEOMETRY column from any table.

Listing 7-13. SdoPrint *Class*

```
/*
 * @(#)SdoPrint.java 1.0 12-Jul-2003
 *
 * This program uses the Java API for Oracle Spatial supplied with
 * version 10.1 of the Oracle Server (class JGeometry)
 *
 * It illustrates the use of JGeometry to extract and process geometry
 * objects stored in tables inside the Oracle database using the
 * SDO_GEOMETRY object type.
 *
 * The program lets you specify connection parameters to a database, as
 * well as the name of a table and the name of a geometry column to
 * process. You can optionally specify a predicate (a WHERE clause) to select
 * the rows to fetch.
 *
 * Finally, you can choose the way the geometries will be formatted:
 *
 *  0 = no output.
 *  1 = format as an SDO_GEOMETRY constructor (similar to SQL*Plus output)
 *  2 = display the results from each getXxx() and isXxx() method of the
 *      Geometry objects
 * You can combine the settings. For example, 3 shows everything.
 *
 * The program also times the individual steps needed to process a geometry,
 * and displays the total time elapsed for each step:
 *
 * - Getting object = time needed to perform the getObject() method, which
 *   extracts the object from the result set and returns an oracle.sql.STRUCT.
 * - Converting geometry = time to convert the STRUCT into a Geometry object.
 * - Extracting information = time to extract information from the Geometry
 *   object into regular Java variables.
 */

import java.io.*;
import java.sql.*;
import java.util.*;
import java.awt.geom.*;
```

```
import java.awt.Shape;
import oracle.jdbc.driver.*;
import oracle.sql.*;
import oracle.spatial.geometry.*;

public final class SdoPrint
{
  public static void main(String args[]) throws Exception
  {
    System.out.println ("SdoPrint - Oracle Spatial (SDO) read");

    // Check and process command-line arguments
    if (args.length != 7) {
      System.out.println ("Parameters:");
      System.out.println ("<Connection>:  JDBC connection string");
      System.out.println ("               e.g: jdbc:oracle:thin:@server:port:sid");
      System.out.println ("<User>:        User name");
      System.out.println ("<Password>:    User password");
      System.out.println ("<Table name>:  Table to unload");
      System.out.println ("<Geo column>:  Name of geometry column,");
      System.out.println ("<Predicate>:   WHERE clause");
      System.out.println ("<Print Style>: 0=none, 1=raw, 2=format");
      return;
    }

    String connectionString  = args[0];
    String userName          = args[1];
    String userPassword      = args[2];
    String tableName         = args[3];
    String geoColumn         = args[4];
    String predicate         = args[5];
    int    printStyle        = Integer.parseInt(args[6]);

    // Register the Oracle JDBC driver
    DriverManager.registerDriver(new oracle.jdbc.driver.OracleDriver());

    // Get a connection to the database
    System.out.println ("Connecting to database '"+connectionString+"'");
    Connection dbConnection = DriverManager.getConnection(connectionString,
      userName, userPassword);
    System.out.println ("Got a connection: "+dbConnection.getClass().getName());

    // Perform the database query
    printGeometries(dbConnection, tableName, geoColumn, predicate, printStyle);

    // Close database connection
    dbConnection.close();
  }
```

```
static void printGeometries(Connection dbConnection, String tableName,
  String geoColumn, String predicate,int printStyle)
  throws Exception
{
  long totalPoints = 0;
  long totalSize = 0;
  JGeometry geom;

  // Construct SQL query
  String sqlQuery = "SELECT " + geoColumn + " FROM " + tableName + " "
    + predicate;
  System.out.println ("Executing query: '"+sqlQuery+"'");

  // Execute query
  Statement stmt = dbConnection.createStatement();
  OracleResultSet ors = (OracleResultSet) stmt.executeQuery(sqlQuery);

  // Process results
  int rowNumber = 0;
  while (ors.next())
  {
    ++rowNumber;

    // Extract JDBC object from record into structure
    STRUCT dbObject = (STRUCT) ors.getObject(1);

    // Import from structure into Geometry object
    geom = JGeometry.load(dbObject);

    // extract details from JGeometry object
    int gType =                 geom.getType();
    int gSRID =                 geom.getSRID();
    int gDimensions =           geom.getDimensions();
    long gNumPoints =           geom.getNumPoints();
    long gSize =                geom.getSize();
    boolean isPoint =           geom.isPoint();
    boolean isCircle =          geom.isCircle();
    boolean hasCircularArcs =   geom.hasCircularArcs();
    boolean isGeodeticMBR =     geom.isGeodeticMBR();
    boolean isLRSGeometry =     geom.isLRSGeometry();
    boolean isMultiPoint =      geom.isMultiPoint();
    boolean isRectangle =       geom.isRectangle();

    // point
    double gPoint[]  =          geom.getPoint();
    // element info array
    int gElemInfo[] =           geom.getElemInfo();
    int gNumElements =          (gElemInfo == null ? 0 : gElemInfo.length / 3);
```

```
// ordinates array
double gOrdinates[] =     geom.getOrdinatesArray();

// other information
double[] gFirstPoint =    geom.getFirstPoint();
double[] gLastPoint =     geom.getLastPoint();
Point2D gLabelPoint =     geom.getLabelPoint();
Point2D gJavaPoint =      geom.getJavaPoint();
Point2D[] gJavaPoints =   (isMultiPoint ? geom.getJavaPoints():null);
double[] gMBR =           geom.getMBR();
Shape gShape =            geom.createShape();

totalSize += gSize;
totalPoints += gNumPoints;

if (printStyle > 0)
  System.out.println ("Geometry # " + rowNumber + ":");

// Print out geometry in SDO_GEOMETRY format
if ((printStyle & 1) == 1 )
  System.out.println (printGeom(geom));

// Print out formatted geometry
if ((printStyle & 2) == 2) {
  System.out.println (" Type:             " + gType);
  System.out.println (" SRID:             " + gSRID);
  System.out.println (" Dimensions:       " + gDimensions);
  System.out.println (" NumPoints:        " + gNumPoints);
  System.out.println (" Size:             " + gSize);
  System.out.println (" isPoint:          " + isPoint);
  System.out.println (" isCircle:         " + isCircle);
  System.out.println (" hasCircularArcs: " + hasCircularArcs);
  System.out.println (" isGeodeticMBR:    " + isGeodeticMBR);
  System.out.println (" isLRSGeometry:    " + isLRSGeometry);
  System.out.println (" isMultiPoint:     " + isMultiPoint);
  System.out.println (" isRectangle:      " + isRectangle);
  System.out.println (" MBR:              ("
      + gMBR[0] + " " + gMBR[1] + ") (" + gMBR[2] + " " + gMBR[3] + ") ");
  System.out.println (" First Point:      " + printPoint(gFirstPoint));
  System.out.println (" Last Point:       " + printPoint(gLastPoint));
  System.out.println (" Label Point:      " + printPoint(gLabelPoint));
  System.out.println (" Point:            " + printPoint(gPoint));
  System.out.println (" Java Point:       " + printPoint(gJavaPoint));
  System.out.println (" Java Points List: " +
    (gJavaPoints==null ? "NULL": "["+gJavaPoints.length+"]"));
  if (gJavaPoints != null)
    for (int i=0; i<gJavaPoints.length; i++)
      System.out.println ("    ["+(i+1)+"] (" +
```

```
          gJavaPoints[i].getX() + ", " +
          gJavaPoints[i].getY() +")");

      System.out.println (" Elements:        [" + gNumElements + " elements]" );
      if (gElemInfo != null)
        for (int i=0; i<gNumElements; i++)
          System.out.println ("   ["+(i+1)+"] (" +
            gElemInfo[i*3] + ", " +
            gElemInfo[i*3+1] + ", " +
            gElemInfo[i*3+2] + ")");

      System.out.println (" Points List:     [" + gNumPoints + " points]" );
      if (gOrdinates != null)
        for (int i=0; i<gNumPoints; i++) {
          System.out.print ("   ["+(i+1)+"] (");
          for (int j=0; j<gDimensions; j++) {
            System.out.print (gOrdinates[i*gDimensions+j]);
            if (j<gDimensions-1)
              System.out.print (", ");
          }
          System.out.println (")");
        }
    }
  }
  stmt.close();
  System.out.println("");
  System.out.println("Done - "+rowNumber+" geometries extracted");
  System.out.println(" " + totalPoints + " points");
  System.out.println(" " + totalSize + " bytes");
}

static String printPoint(double[] point)
{
  String formattedPoint;
  if (point == null)
    formattedPoint = "NULL";
  else {
    formattedPoint = "["+point.length + "] (";
    for (int i=0; i<point.length; i++) {
      formattedPoint += point[i];
      if (i < point.length-1)
        formattedPoint += ", ";
    }
    formattedPoint += ")";
  }
  return (formattedPoint);
}
```

```
  static String printPoint(Point2D point)
  {
    String formattedPoint;
    if (point == null)
      formattedPoint = "NULL";
    else
      formattedPoint = "[2] (" + point.getX() + ", " + point.getY() + ")";
    return (formattedPoint);
  }

 static String printGeom (JGeometry geom)
  {
    String fg;

    // extract details from JGeometry object
    int gType =                 geom.getType();
    int gSRID =                 geom.getSRID();
    int gDimensions =           geom.getDimensions();
    boolean isPoint =           geom.isPoint();
    // point
    double gPoint[]  =          geom.getPoint();
    // element info array
    int gElemInfo[] =           geom.getElemInfo();
    // ordinates array
    double gOrdinates[] =       geom.getOrdinatesArray();

    // Format JGeometry in SDO_GEOMETRY format
    int sdo_gtype = gDimensions * 1000 + gType;
    int sdo_srid  = gSRID;

    fg = "SDO_GEOMETRY(" + sdo_gtype + ", ";
    if (sdo_srid == 0)
      fg = fg + "NULL, ";
    else
      fg = fg + sdo_srid + ", ";
    if (gPoint == null)
      fg = fg + "NULL), ";
    else {
      fg = fg + "SDO_POINT_TYPE(" + gPoint[0]+", "+gPoint[1]+", ";
      if (gPoint.length < 3)
        fg = fg + "NULL), ";
      else if (java.lang.Double.isNaN(gPoint[2]))
        fg = fg + "NULL), ";
      else
        fg = fg + gPoint[2]+"), ";
    }
```

```
      if (!isPoint & gElemInfo != null) {
        fg = fg + "SDO_ELEM_INFO_ARRAY( ";
        for (int i=0; i<gElemInfo.length-1; i++)
          fg = fg +  gElemInfo[i]+", ";
        fg = fg +  gElemInfo[gElemInfo.length-1] + "), ";
      }
      else
        fg = fg + "NULL, ";
      if (!isPoint & gOrdinates != null) {
        fg = fg + "SDO_ORDINATE_ARRAY( ";
        for (int i=0; i<gOrdinates.length-1; i++)
          fg = fg +  gOrdinates[i]+", ";
        fg = fg +  gOrdinates[gOrdinates.length-1] + ")";
      }
      else
        fg = fg + "NULL";
      fg = fg + ")";

      return (fg);
    }
  }
```

Using the SdoPrint Program

Once you have compiled the example program, invoke it from the command line. You need to pass it a JDBC connection string, a user name and password, the name of the table to read, and the name of the geometry column followed by an optional `WHERE` clause. The last argument specifies the level of detail to print.

■ **Tip** Make sure to include the JDBC driver (`$ORACLE_HOME/jdbc/lib/classes12.jar`) in the classpath as well as the spatial Java library (`$ORACLE_HOME/md/lib/sdoapi.jar`) before starting the program.

Listing 7-14 shows how to invoke the program to print out the details of one of our branches.

Listing 7-14. *Invoking* `SdoPrint`

```
java SdoPrint jdbc:oracle:thin:@127.0.0.1:1521:orcl101 spatial spatial branches ➥
   location "where id=10" 2

SdoPrint - Oracle Spatial (SDO) read
Connecting to database 'jdbc:oracle:thin:@127.0.0.1:1521:orcl101'
Got a connection: oracle.jdbc.driver.T4CConnection
```

```
Executing query: 'SELECT location FROM branches where id=10'
Geometry # 1:
 Type:            1
 SRID:            8307
 Dimensions:      2
 NumPoints:       1
 Size:            40
 isPoint:         true
 isCircle:        false
 hasCircularArcs: false
 isGeodeticMBR:   false
 isLRSGeometry:   false
 isMultiPoint:    false
 isRectangle:     false
 MBR:             (-77.003476936374 38.8875640280567)
                  (-77.003476936374 38.8875640280567)
 First Point:     [2] (-77.003476936374, 38.8875640280567)
 Last Point:      [2] (-77.003476936374, 38.8875640280567)
 Label Point:     [2] (-77.003476936374, 38.8875640280567)
 Point:           [2] (-77.003476936374, 38.8875640280567)
 Java Point:      [2] (-77.003476936374, 38.8875640280567)
 Java Points List: NULL
 Elements:        [0 elements]
 Points List:     [1 points]

Done - 1 geometries extracted
 1 points
 40 bytes
```

Dissecting the SdoPrint Program

The program connects to the database with JDBC, using the information provided. It then constructs a `SELECT` statement, executes it, and fetches the results from its result set. The `getObject()` method of the result set extracts the geometry object for each row into a `STRUCT`:

```
STRUCT dbObject = (STRUCT) ors.getObject(1);
```

Converting the geometry into a `JGeometry` object is simply a matter of invoking the static `load()` method of `JGeometry`:

```
JGeometry geom = JGeometry.load(dbObject);
```

We can now use one of the many get() methods to extract information from the geometry object. The main methods are summarized in Table 7-1. The additional is() methods listed in Table 7-2 detail the nature of the geometry.

Table 7-1. *Main* JGeometry get() *Methods*

Method	Information Returned
getType()	Type of geometry (1 for a point, 2 for a line, etc.)
getDimensions()	Dimensionality
getSRID()	Spatial reference system ID
getNumPoints()	Number of points in the geometry
getPoint()	Coordinates of the point object (if the geometry is a point)
getFirstPoint()	First point of the geometry
getLastPoint()	Last point of the geometry
getMBR()	MBR of the geometry
getElemInfo()	Content of the SDO_ELEM_INFO array
getOrdinatesArray()	Content of the SDO_ORDINATES array
getJavaPoint()	For a single point object, returns the coordinates of the point as a java.awt.geom.Point2D object
getJavaPoints()	For a multipoint object, returns an array of java.awt.geom.Point2D objects
createShape()	Converts the geometry into a java.awt.Shape object, ready for use by the drawing and manipulation facilities of the java.awt package

Table 7-2. *Main JGeometry* is() *Methods*

Method	Information Returned
isPoint()	Is this a point?
isCircle()	Is this a circle?
isGeodeticMBR()	Is this a geodetic MBR?
isMultiPoint()	Is this a multipoint?
isRectangle()	Is this a rectangle?
hasCircularArcs()	Does the geometry contain any arcs?
isLRSGeometry()	Is this a “linear referenced” geometry?

Here is how the SdoPrint program uses those methods:

```
// extract details from JGeometry object
int gType =              geom.getType();
int gSRID =              geom.getSRID();
int gDimensions =        geom.getDimensions();
long gNumPoints =        geom.getNumPoints();
long gSize =             geom.getSize();
```

```
boolean isPoint =          geom.isPoint();
boolean isCircle =         geom.isCircle();
boolean hasCircularArcs =  geom.hasCircularArcs();
boolean isGeodeticMBR =    geom.isGeodeticMBR();
boolean isLRSGeometry =    geom.isLRSGeometry();
boolean isMultiPoint =     geom.isMultiPoint();
boolean isRectangle =      geom.isRectangle();

// point
double gPoint[]  =         geom.getPoint();
// element info array
int gElemInfo[] =          geom.getElemInfo();
int gNumElements =         (gElemInfo == null ? 0 : gElemInfo.length / 3);
// ordinates array
double gOrdinates[] =      geom.getOrdinatesArray();
// other information
double[] gFirstPoint =     geom.getFirstPoint();
double[] gLastPoint =      geom.getLastPoint();
double[] gMBR =            geom.getMBR();

// Java graphics
Point2D gJavaPoint =       geom.getJavaPoint();
Point2D[] gJavaPoints =    (isMultiPoint ? geom.getJavaPoints():null);
Shape gShape =             geom.createShape();
```

Creating Geometries

Creating a new geometry requires that you create a new JGeometry object, convert it into a STRUCT using the static JGeometry.store() method, and then pass the STRUCT to an INSERT or UPDATE statement.

There are two ways you can construct new JGeometry objects. One way is to use one of the constructors listed in Table 7-3. The other way is to use one of the static methods that create various geometries. Those methods are listed in Table 7-4.

Table 7-3. JGeometry *Constructors*

Constructor	Purpose
JGeometry (double x, double y, int srid)	Constructs a point
JGeometry (double x, double y, double z, int srid)	Constructs a three-dimensional point
JGeometry (double minX, double minY, double maxX, double maxY, int srid)	Creates a rectangle
JGeometry (int gtype, int srid, int[] elemInfo, double[] ordinates)	Constructs a generic geometry

Table 7-4. *Static* `JGeometry` *Creation Methods*

Creation Method	Purpose
`createPoint(double[] coord, int dim, int srid)`	Creates a point
`createLinearLineString(double[] coords, int dim, int srid)`	Creates a simple line string
`createLinearPolygon(double[] coords, int dim, int srid)`	Creates a simple polygon
`createMultiPoint(java.lang.Object[] coords, int dim, int srid)`	Creates a multipoint object
`createLinearMultiLineString (java.lang.Object[] coords, int dim, int srid)`	Creates a multiline string object
`createLinearPolygon(java.lang.Object[] coords, int dim, int srid)`	Creates a multipolygon
`createCircle(double x1, double y1, double x2, double y2, double x3, double y3, int srid)`	Creates a circle using three points on its circumference
`createCircle(double x, double y, double radius, int srid)`	Creates a circle using a center and radius

The `SdoLoad` program in Listing 7-15 illustrates the process. It reads the definition of a polygon shape from a text file and uses the information to construct a polygon `JGeometry` object, which it then writes to the database in a table and column passed as arguments to the program.

Listing 7-15. `SdoLoad` *Program*

```
/*
 * @(#)SdoLoad.java 1.0 12-Jul-2003
 *
 * This program reads a geometry from an ASCII text file and inserts
 * it in a database table.
 *
 * It uses the Java API for Oracle Spatial supplied with
 * version 10.1 or the Oracle Server (class JGeometry)
 *
 * The program lets you specify connection parameters to a database, as
 * well as the name of the table and the name of the geometry column to
 * load into. It also lets you specify the name of an identification
 * column (a number) to identify the row to insert or update.
 *
 * The input file is structured as described in the Region class.
 *
 */
```

```
import java.io.*;
import java.sql.*;
import java.util.*;
import java.awt.geom.*;
import oracle.jdbc.driver.*;
import oracle.sql.STRUCT;
import oracle.spatial.geometry.JGeometry;

public final class SdoLoad
{
  public static void main(String args[]) throws Exception
  {
    System.out.println ("SdoLoad - Oracle Spatial (SDO) load example");

    // Check and process command-line arguments
    if (args.length != 9) {
      System.out.println ("Parameters:");
      System.out.println ("<Connection>:  JDBC connection string");
      System.out.println ("               e.g: jdbc:oracle:thin:@server:port:sid");
      System.out.println ("<User>:        User name");
      System.out.println ("<Password>:    User password");
      System.out.println ("<Table name>:  Table to import");
      System.out.println ("<Geo column>:  Name of geometry column");
      System.out.println ("<ID column>:   Name of geometry id column");
      System.out.println ("<ID value>:    Value of geometry ID");
      System.out.println ("<Input File>:  Name of input file");
      System.out.println ("<Action>:      I for insert or U for pdate");
      return;
    }
    String  connectionString  = args[0];
    String  userName          = args[1];
    String  userPassword      = args[2];
    String  tableName         = args[3];
    String  geoColumn         = args[4];
    String  idColumn          = args[5];
    int     idValue           = Integer.parseInt(args[6]);
    String  inputFileName     = args[7];
    boolean insertAction      = (args[8].compareTo("I")==0 ? true : false);

    // Open input file
    System.out.println ("Opening file '" + inputFileName + "'");
    BufferedReader inputFile =
       new BufferedReader(new FileReader(inputFileName));

    // Register the Oracle JDBC driver
    DriverManager.registerDriver(new oracle.jdbc.driver.OracleDriver());
```

```
    // Get a connection to the database
    System.out.println ("Connecting to database '"+connectionString+"'");
    Connection dbConnection = DriverManager.getConnection(connectionString,
      userName, userPassword);

    // Load the geometry from the file
    loadGeometry(dbConnection, tableName, geoColumn, idColumn, idValue,
      inputFile, insertAction);

    // Close database connection
    dbConnection.close();

    // Close input file
    inputFile.close();
  }

  static void loadGeometry(Connection dbConnection, String tableName,
    String geoColumn, String idColumn, int idValue, BufferedReader inputFile,
    boolean insertAction)
    throws SQLException, IOException
  {
    // Construct the SQL statement
    String SqlStatement;
    if (insertAction)
      SqlStatement = "INSERT INTO " + tableName + " (" + geoColumn + ","
        + idColumn + ") " +  "VALUES (?, ?)";
    else
      SqlStatement = "UPDATE " + tableName + " SET " + geoColumn + " = ? "
        + "WHERE " + idColumn + " = ?";
    System.out.println ("Executing query: '"+SqlStatement+"'");

    // Prepare the SQL statement
    PreparedStatement stmt = dbConnection.prepareStatement(SqlStatement);

    // Load geometry Region from input file
    Region polygon = new Region(inputFile);
    System.out.println ("Region geometry loaded ("
      + polygon.getNrOfPoints() + " points)");

    // Get the list of points of the region
    double ordinates[] = polygon.getOrdinates();

    // Construct new JGeometry object
    JGeometry geom = JGeometry.createLinearPolygon(ordinates, 2, 8307);

    // Convert object into Java STRUCT
    STRUCT dbObject = JGeometry.store (geom, dbConnection);
```

```
    // Insert or update row in the database table
    stmt.setObject (1,dbObject);
    stmt.setInt (2, idValue);
    stmt.execute();
    stmt.close();
  }

  /* Class Region

     This class defines the geometry of a region as obtained from
     an ASCII file.

     The input is a list of records:

       NUM_POINTS 26
       POINT 1 -77.120201 38.9342
       POINT 2 -77.101501 38.910999
       ......
       POINT 26 -77.120201 38.9342

     The first line defines the number of points that follow.
     Then each point is defined on a separate line.

     The program performs minimal parsing and validation of the
     input file.
  */
  static class Region {

    int nrOfPoints = 0;
    Point2D points[] = null;

    public Region(BufferedReader inputFile)
      throws IOException {
      this.loadFromFile (inputFile);
    }

    public void loadFromFile (BufferedReader inputFile)
      throws IOException {

      String s;
      while((s = inputFile.readLine())!= null) {
        StringTokenizer st = new StringTokenizer (s);
        int n = st.countTokens();
        if (n > 0) {
          String tk = st.nextToken();
          if (tk.compareTo ("NUM_POINTS") == 0) {
            nrOfPoints = Integer.parseInt(st.nextToken());
            points = new Point2D[nrOfPoints];
          }
```

```
          if (tk.compareTo ("POINT") == 0) {
            int pn = Integer.parseInt(st.nextToken());
            double x = Double.parseDouble(st.nextToken());
            double y = Double.parseDouble(st.nextToken());
            points[pn-1] = new Point2D.Double(x,y);
          }
        }
      }
    }
    public Point2D[] getPoints() {
      return points;
    }
    public double[] getOrdinates() {
      double ordinates[] = new double[nrOfPoints * 2];
      for (int i=0; i<points.length; i++) {
        ordinates [i*2] = points[i].getX();
        ordinates [i*2+1] = points[i].getY();
      }
      return ordinates;
    }

    public int getNrOfPoints() {
      return nrOfPoints;
    }

  }
}
```

Note that the largest parts of this program are the parsing of input arguments, and the reading and parsing of the input file. The part that actually constructs the `JGeometry` object and writes or updates the database is short.

First, we construct the proper SQL statement and prepare it for execution:

```
String SqlStatement;
if (insertAction)
  SqlStatement = "INSERT INTO " + tableName + " (" + geoColumn + ","
    + idColumn + ") " + "VALUES (?, ?)";
else
  SqlStatement = "UPDATE " + tableName + " SET " + geoColumn + " = ? "
    + "WHERE " + idColumn + " = ?";
PreparedStatement stmt = dbConnection.prepareStatement(SqlStatement);
```

Then we parse the input file and extract the points that define the contour of the polygon:

```
// Load geometry Region from input file
Region polygon = new Region(inputFile);
System.out.println ("Region geometry loaded ("
  + polygon.getNrOfPoints() + " points)");
// Get the list of points of the region
double ordinates[] = polygon.getOrdinates();
```

We can now construct the JGeometry object using the coordinates read from the input file:

```
JGeometry geom = JGeometry.createLinearPolygon(ordinates, 2, 8307);
```

We convert JGeometry into a STRUCT object:

```
STRUCT dbObject = JGeometry.store (geom, dbConnection);
```

We set the STRUCT object into the prepared SQL statement:

```
stmt.setObject (1,dbObject);
```

Finally, we execute the SQL statement:

```
stmt.execute();
```

Modifying Existing Geometries

The JGeometry class does not provide any method that lets you modify a geometry. For example, there is no method to remove a point from a line or to add one more point to a line. To perform those updates, you need to extract the list of points using a method such as getOrdinatesArray(), then update the resulting Java arrays, and create a new JGeometry object with the results.

To write the modified geometries to the database, proceed as discussed previously: convert the JGeometry object into a STRUCT using the store() method, and then pass the STRUCT to your SQL INSERT or UPDATE statement.

Manipulating Geometries in C Using OCI

The lowest-level API you can use to access Oracle databases is the *Oracle Call Interface* (OCI). OCI is extremely rich and powerful. It lets you access all database features, including the processing of SQL statements, LOBs, objects, and queues. It supports multithreading and connection pooling, object caching and notifications, and array fetches and inserts. OCI is also fairly complex—the *OCI Programmer's Guide* manual contains over 1,300 pages! Using the OCI API can seem daunting at first, but you are unlikely to use all its facilities at once.

OCI is C oriented. You can use it from C as well as C++. We assume that you are familiar with how to write OCI programs. For further details, you can study the Oracle documentation and you can look at the numerous examples provided with the database (in $ORACLE_HOME/oci/samples).

In the discussion that follows, we examine only the specifics of reading and writing SDO_GEOMETRY objects. You can find a set of complete example programs in the Downloads area of the Apress website (www.apress.com). The code fragments that follow are extracted from those programs.

We begin by looking at how the SDO_GEOMETRY objects are mapped to C structures. We then discuss how to read a geometry into a C structure.

Note Remember that you do not need to use objects at all when dealing with point geometries. You can extract the x and y coordinates using dot notation, as discussed at the beginning of the chapter.

Mapping Oracle Objects to C Structures

Oracle objects (including SDO_GEOMETRY objects) are passed in OCI programs as structures (C struct) with a format specific to the object type being processed. The C definition of this structure is generated using the ott tool provided with your Oracle installation. The following command generates the necessary C structures:

```
ott userid=spatial/spatial code=c intype=sdo_geometry.typ hfile=sdo_geometry.h
```

You must provide the sdo_geometry.typ file. It should list all the object types to process. Do not forget to include all the types used internally by the SDO_GEOMETRY type. Here is an example of an "intype" file:

```
CASE = UPPER
TYPE MDSYS.SDO_GEOMETRY
TYPE MDSYS.SDO_POINT_TYPE
TYPE MDSYS.SDO_ELEM_INFO_ARRAY
TYPE MDSYS.SDO_ORDINATE_ARRAY
```

The resulting C structure (in the file sdo_geometry.h) must be included in all programs that use geometry types. It contains the following structures:

```
struct SDO_GEOMETRY
{
   OCINumber SDO_GTYPE;
   OCINumber SDO_SRID;
   struct SDO_POINT_TYPE SDO_POINT;
   SDO_ELEM_INFO_ARRAY * SDO_ELEM_INFO;
   SDO_ORDINATE_ARRAY * SDO_ORDINATES;
};
typedef struct SDO_GEOMETRY SDO_GEOMETRY;
```

and

```
typedef OCIArray SDO_ELEM_INFO_ARRAY;
typedef OCIArray SDO_ORDINATE_ARRAY;

struct SDO_POINT_TYPE
{
   OCINumber X;
   OCINumber Y;
   OCINumber Z;
};
typedef struct SDO_POINT_TYPE SDO_POINT_TYPE;
```

It also contains structures for null indicators (SDO_GEOMETRY_ind, which is not shown here).

Reading Geometries

Reading objects in OCI involves a number of additional steps that are not needed when reading native types such as NUMBER and VARCHAR. Objects need descriptors, so we must first set up the proper descriptor for the SDO_GEOMETRY type. We then set up variables to receive the data fetched by the SELECT statement and link them to the statement.

Next, we can execute the SELECT statement and fetch the results, and then convert the results into C structures and variables. We will look at each of step in turn in the sections that follow.

Getting Type Descriptors

We use the OCITypeByName() call to fetch the descriptor of the SDO_GEOMETRY type. This is done once only in our program.

```
#include "sdo_geometry.h"
...
/* Type descriptor for geometry object type */
OCIType             *geometry_type_desc;
...
/* Get the descriptor for SDO_GEOMETRY */
status = OCITypeByName (
  (dvoid *)envhp,           /* (in)  Environment Handle */
  errhp,                    /* (in)  Error Handle */
  svchp,                    /* (in)  Service Context Handle */
  "MDSYS",                  /* (in)  Type owner name */
  strlen("MDSYS"),          /* (in)  (length) */
  "SDO_GEOMETRY",           /* (in)  Type name */
  strlen("SDO_GEOMETRY"),   /* (in)  (length) */
  0,                        /* (in)  Version name (NOT USED) */
  0,                        /* (in)  (length) */
  OCI_DURATION_SESSION,     /* (in)  Pin duration */
  OCI_TYPEGET_HEADER ,      /* (in)  Get option */
  &geometry_type_desc       /* (out) Type descriptor */
);
```

Setting Bind Variables

We need to perform several steps here. First, we define the bind variables proper using the types produced by the ott tool and included by sdo_geometry.h. We also need to define a *handle* for the variable:

```
/* Host variables */
SDO_GEOMETRY        *geometry_obj = NULL;
SDO_GEOMETRY_ind    *geometry_ind = NULL;
...
/* Handles for host variables */
OCIDefine           *geometry_hp;
```

Then we use the OCIDefineByPos() function to associate the host variable handle (geometry_hp) with the handle of the prepared SELECT statement (select_stmthp):

```
/* Define the host variable */
status = OCIDefineByPos(
  select_stmthp,          /* (in)  Statement Handle */
  &geometry_hp,           /* (out) Define Handle */
  errhp,                  /* (in)  Error Handle */
  (ub4)1,                 /* (in)  Bind variable position */
  (dvoid *)0,             /* (in)  Value Pointer (NOT USED) */
  0,                      /* (in)  Value Size (NOT USED) */
  SQLT_NTY,               /* (in)  Data Type */
  (dvoid *)0,             /* (in)  Indicator Pointer (NOT USED) */
  (ub2 *)0,               /* (out) Length of data fetched (NOT USED)*/
  (ub2 *)0,               /* (out) Column return codes (NOT USED) */
  (ub4)OCI_DEFAULT        /* (in)  Operating mode */
);
```

Finally, we use the OCIDefineObject() function to link the handle with the object descriptor and the host variable proper:

```
/* Define the object */
status = OCIDefineObject(
  geometry_hp,            /* (in)  Define handle */
  errhp,                  /* (in)  Error handle */
  geometry_type_desc,     /* (in)  Geometry type descriptor */
  (dvoid **) &geometry_obj, /* (in)  Value Pointer */
  (ub4 *)0,               /* (in)  Value Size (NOT USED) */
  (dvoid **) &geometry_ind, /* (in)  Indicator Pointer */
  (ub4 *)0                /* (in)  Indicator Size */
);
```

Fetching the Geometries

We can now execute the SELECT statement, using the normal OCIStmtExecute() and OCIStmtFetch() calls. The content of the SDO_GEOMETRY object is now available in the structures that we defined and passed to the OCIDefineObject() call (geometry_obj and geometry_ind in the previous code fragment).

Decoding the Geometries

The SDO_GEOMETRY structure just filled cannot be used directly, as it still contains OCI-specific data types such as OCINumber and OCIArray, which we must now convert into equivalent C data types, in the following structure:

```
struct point {
   double x;
   double y;
   double z;
```

```
};
typedef struct point point_struct;

struct geometry
{
    int gtype;
    int srid;
    struct point *point;
    int n_elem_info;
    int *elem_info;
    int n_ordinates;
    double *ordinates;
};
typedef struct geometry geometry_struct;

geometry_struct *geometry;
```

Let's first look at the scalar elements in the SDO_GEOMETRY structure: SDO_GTYPE and SDO_SRID. We will use the OCINumberToInt() call to convert them from OCINumber into C int.

```
/* Extract SDO_GTYPE */
OCINumberToInt (
  errhp,
  &(geometry_object->SDO_GTYPE),
  (uword) sizeof (int),
  OCI_NUMBER_SIGNED,
  (dvoid *) & geometry->gtype);

/* Extract SDO_SRID */
OCINumberToInt (
  errhp,
  &(geometry_object->SDO_SRID),
  (uword) sizeof (int),
  OCI_NUMBER_SIGNED,
  (dvoid *) & geometry->srid);
```

Then we need to convert the SDO_POINT structure. The added difficulty here is that we need to check for NULLs. The entire SDO_POINT structure may be NULL, or individual elements (X, Y, or Z) could be NULL.

```
/* Extract SDO_POINT */
geometry->point = 0;
if (geometry_object_ind->SDO_POINT._atomic == OCI_IND_NOTNULL) {
  x = y = z = 0;
  /* Allocate space for point structure */
  geometry->point = malloc (sizeof(point_struct));
  /* Extract X */
  if (geometry_object_ind->SDO_POINT.X == OCI_IND_NOTNULL)
    OCINumberToReal(
```

```
      errhp, &(geometry_object->SDO_POINT.X), (uword)sizeof(double), (dvoid *)&x);
  /* Extract Y */
  if (geometry_object_ind->SDO_POINT.Y == OCI_IND_NOTNULL)
    OCINumberToReal(
      errhp, &(geometry_object->SDO_POINT.Y), (uword)sizeof(double), (dvoid *)&y);
  /* Extract Z */
  if (geometry_object_ind->SDO_POINT.Z == OCI_IND_NOTNULL)
    OCINumberToReal(
      errhp, &(geometry_object->SDO_POINT.Z), (uword)sizeof(double), (dvoid *)&z);
  /* Fill point structure */
  geometry->point->x = x;
  geometry->point->y = y;
  geometry->point->z = z;
}
```

Finally, we need to convert the array structures SDO_ELEM_INFO and SDO_ORDINATES. This is a fairly complex operation. We need to range over each array, extracting one element at a time, and then convert each of the extracted elements to a C type.

First we do this for SDO_ELEM_INFO, which we convert to an array of ints:

```
/* Get the size of the array */
OCICollSize (envhp, errhp,
  (OCIColl *)(geometry_object->SDO_ELEM_INFO),
  &geometry->n_elem_info);

if (geometry->n_elem_info > 0) {

  /* Allocate memory for the array */
  geometry->elem_info = malloc (sizeof(int)*geometry->n_elem_info);

  /* Get all elements in the array */
  /* Loop over array elements and process one by one */
  for (i=0; i<geometry->n_elem_info; i++) {
    /* Extract one element from the VARRAY */
    OCICollGetElem(envhp, errhp,
      (OCIColl *) (geometry_object->SDO_ELEM_INFO),
      (sb4)       (i),
      (boolean *) &exists,
      (dvoid **)  &oci_number,
      (dvoid **)  0
    );
    /* Convert the element to int */
    OCINumberToInt(errhp, oci_number,
      (uword)sizeof(int),
      OCI_NUMBER_UNSIGNED,
      (dvoid *)&geometry->elem_info[i]);
  }
}
```

Then we convert the SDO_ORDINATES array, which we turn into an array of doubles. Since the SDO_ORDINATES array can be very large for complex geometries, the conversion to a C array can also require a large number of OCI calls for extracting and converting the elements. To optimize this process, Oracle 10*g* provides new calls that extract and convert all elements in the SDO_ORDINATES array in just two calls.

```
/* Get the size of the array */
OCICollSize(envhp, errhp,
  (OCIColl *)(geometry_object->SDO_ORDINATES), &geometry->n_ordinates);

if (geometry->n_ordinates > 0) {

  /* Allocate memory */
  geometry->ordinates = malloc (sizeof(double)*geometry->n_ordinates);

  /* Get all elements in the array */

  /* (Re)allocate space for intermediate vectors */
  global_oci_number
    = (OCINumber *)malloc(sizeof(OCINumber *) * geometry->n_ordinates);
  global_exists
    = (boolean *)malloc(sizeof(boolean) * geometry->n_ordinates);

  /* Extract all elements from the VARRAY */
  OCICollGetElemArray (envhp, errhp,
    (OCIColl *) geometry_object->SDO_ORDINATES,
    (sb4) (0),
    (boolean *) global_exists,
    (dvoid **) &global_oci_number,
    (dvoid **) 0,
    &(geometry->n_ordinates)
  );

  /* Convert all extracted elements to doubles */
  OCINumberToRealArray (errhp,
    (const OCINumber **) &global_oci_number,
    geometry->n_ordinates,
    (uword) sizeof (double),
    (dvoid *) geometry->ordinates);
}
```

Writing Geometries

Writing objects in OCI really means that we need to define the proper structures for the object to be written, populate them, and pass them as a bind variable to an INSERT or UPDATE statement. In the following discussion, we assume that we will execute a statement such as the following:

```
INSERT INTO SALES_REGIONS (ID, GEOM) VALUES (:ID, :GEOMETRY)
```

where the values for the ID and GEOM columns are provided in bind variables at runtime.

Setting Bind Variables

This process is very similar to that for reading geometries. First, we define the bind variable proper using the types produced by the ott tool and included by sdo_geometry.h. We also need to define a handle for the variable:

```
/* Host variables */
SDO_GEOMETRY       *geometry_obj = NULL;
SDO_GEOMETRY_ind   *geometry_ind = NULL;
...
/* Handles for host variables */
OCIDefine          *geometry_hp;
```

Then we use the OCIBindByName() function to associate the host variable handle (geometry_hp) with the handle of the prepared INSERT statement (insert_stmthp):

```
/* Bind the host variable */
status = OCIBindByName(
  insert_stmthp,                /* (in)  Statement Handle */
  &geometry_hp,                 /* (out) Bind Handle */
  errhp,                        /* (in)  Error Handle */
  (text *) ":GEOMETRY",         /* (in)  Placeholder */
  strlen(":GEOMETRY"),          /* (in)  Placeholder length */
  (ub1 *) 0,                    /* (in)  Value Pointer (NOT USED) */
  0,                            /* (in)  Value Size (NOT USED) */
  SQLT_NTY,                     /* (in)  Data Type */
  (dvoid *) 0,                  /* (in)  Indicator Pointer (NOT USED) */
  (ub2 *) 0,                    /* (out) Actual length (NOT USED) */
  (ub2) 0,                      /* (out) Column return codes (NOT USED) */
  (ub4) 0,                      /* (in)  (NOT USED) */
  (ub4 *) 0,                    /* (in)  (NOT USED) */
  (ub4)OCI_DEFAULT              /* (in)  Operating mode */
);
```

Finally, we use the OCIBindObject() function to link the handle with the object descriptor and the host variable proper:

```
status = OCIBindObject(
  geometry_hp,                  /* (in)  Bind handle */
  errhp,                        /* (in)  Error handle */
  geometry_type_desc,           /* (in)  Geometry type descriptor */
  (dvoid **) &geometry_obj,     /* (in)  Value Pointer */
  (ub4 *)0,                     /* (in)  Value Size (NOT USED) */
  (dvoid **) &geometry_ind,     /* (in)  Indicator Pointer */
  (ub4 *)0                      /* (in)  Indicator Size */
);
```

Constructing the Geometries

Constructing the geometry to write means that you need to populate the geometry_obj structure with the proper information. However, you have seen that this structure contains OCI-specific types (OCINumber and OCIArray). Use functions such as OCINumberFromInt() and OCINumberFromReal() to convert the numeric values from C types (int, real) into the OCINumber type. Use OCICollAppend() to populate the array structures.

Writing the Geometries

All we need to do now is execute the INSERT statement, using the OCIStmtExecute() call.

■ **Tip** In the examples, we use the standard malloc() and free() calls. You may consider using the equivalent calls provided by OCI, OCIMemoryAlloc() and OCIMemoryFree(), which allocate memory from Oracle-managed memory.

OCI Examples

If you want to find out more about using OCI for geometry objects, you can obtain a set of fully operational examples from the Downloads area of the Apress website (www.apress.com). All examples take a user name, password, and database name from command-line arguments.

OCI_SAMPLE.C and OCI_SAMPLE_ARRAY.C

This program illustrates the basic operation of an OCI program. It does not use any spatial concepts; it just fetches regular column data from the US_CITIES table. The OCI_SAMPLE_ARRAY.C variant illustrates the use of array fetches (the size of the array is passed as the last command-line argument).

READ_POINTS.C and READ_POINTS_ARRAY.C

This second program illustrates the fetching of spatial information (points) without using object types (i.e., by extracting the x and y values of each point). It shows how to dynamically construct SQL statements from user input. The READ_POINTS_ARRAY.C variant uses array fetches.

READ_GEOM.C and READ_GEOM_ARRAY.C

This program contains a complete example of how to read and decode geometry objects. It can read any geometry objects from any table. Each object is first loaded into a C structure, from which it is then printed out.

The input to the program is a SELECT statement that returns a single column of type SDO_GEOMETRY.

The READ_GEOM_ARRAY.C variant uses array fetches.

SELECT_POIS.C

This program shows how to select spatial objects using a spatial query. It selects all objects from the US_POIS table that lie within a chosen distance from a given point passed as an input argument. The selected objects are ordered by distance from the starting point.

LOAD_GEOM.C

This program loads geometry objects into a table in the database. The geometries are read from a text file. Each object is first loaded into a C structure, from which it is stored into the SDO_GEOMETRY OCI structure and finally inserted into the destination table.

Manipulating Geometries in C Using Pro*C

As you have seen, using OCI can be fairly complex. The API requires many steps for basic operations, such as connecting to the database or executing a SQL query. Pro*C makes those tasks somewhat easier.

Pro*C allows you to mix and match SQL and the C language—you just write your SQL statements inside your C code, and the Pro*C precompiler takes care of generating the proper basic OCI code and calls to execute the SQL statements.

As with OCI, a detailed study of Pro*C is outside the scope of this book. We will look at only those aspects of Pro*C that deal with objects.

Reading Geometry Objects

Before reading objects, we have to allocate structures to read them into. Fetching is done the usual way. Then, just as with OCI, we need to convert the content of the object into C variables and structures. Those steps are detailed in the sections that follow.

Allocating Objects in the Object Cache

Before you can do anything with an object, you need to allocate it in the object cache. Use the ALLOCATE statement, for example:

```
EXEC SQL ALLOCATE :geometryObject :geometryObjectInd ;
```

To free an object, use this:

```
EXEC SQL FREE :geometryObject;
```

Fetching the Geometries

Use a regular SELECT INTO statement:

```
EXEC SQL SELECT GEOM
  INTO :geometryObject
  FROM US_COUNTIES
 WHERE ID = :id;
```

Decoding the Geometries

Just as with OCI, the objects returned by the SELECT statement are not directly usable; we need to convert them into C structures. That conversion is, however, much easier with Pro*C than with OCI. The EXEC SQL OBJECT GET statement extracts a value from the object type and, if applicable, converts it into a C variable.

We declare variables to hold the converted object. Note that the object structures (SDO_GEOMETRY and so on) are the same as those we used for OCI.

```
EXEC SQL BEGIN DECLARE SECTION ;
#include "geometry.h"
EXEC SQL END   DECLARE SECTION ;
...
EXEC SQL BEGIN DECLARE SECTION;
  SDO_GEOMETRY              *geometryObject ;
  SDO_POINT_TYPE            *pointObject;
  SDO_ELEM_INFO_ARRAY       *elemInfoArrayObject ;
  SDO_ORDINATE_ARRAY        *ordinateArrayObject ;
  SDO_GEOMETRY_ind          *geometryObjectInd ;
  SDO_POINT_TYPE_ind        *pointObjectInd;
  int                       gType;
  int                       srId;
  double                    x, y, z;
  long                      nOrdinates;
  long                      nElemInfo;
  int                       elementInfoValue;
  double                    *ordinateArray;
EXEC SQL END DECLARE SECTION;
```

First we extract the scalar attributes (SDO_GTYPE and SDO_SRID):

```
EXEC SQL OBJECT GET SDO_GTYPE FROM :geometryObject INTO :gType ;
EXEC SQL OBJECT GET SDO_SRID FROM :geometryObject INTO :srId ;
```

Then we convert the SDO_POINT structure:

```
pointObject = &(geometryObject->SDO_POINT);
pointObjectInd = &(geometryObjectInd->SDO_POINT);
if (pointObjectInd->_atomic == 0) {
  if (pointObjectInd->X == 0)
      EXEC SQL OBJECT GET X FROM :pointObject INTO :x;
  if (pointObjectInd->Y == 0)
      EXEC SQL OBJECT GET Y FROM :pointObject INTO :y;
  if (pointObjectInd->Z == 0)
      EXEC SQL OBJECT GET Z FROM :pointObject INTO :z;
}
```

Next we convert the SDO_ELEM_INFO array. For that, we need to allocate an array object in the cache and extract the array into that object. We then use the COLLECTION DESCRIBE statement to get the size of the array.

Finally, we range over the elements of the array, using COLLECTION GET to extract each into a C variable:

```
EXEC SQL ALLOCATE :elemInfoArrayObject;
EXEC SQL OBJECT GET SDO_ELEM_INFO FROM :geometryObject INTO :elemInfoArrayObject ;
EXEC SQL COLLECTION DESCRIBE :elemInfoArrayObject GET SIZE INTO :nElemInfo;
for (i=1; i<=nElemInfo; i++) {
  EXEC SQL COLLECTION GET :elemInfoArrayObject INTO :elementInfoValue;
}
```

The conversion process for the SDO_ORDINATE array is similar, except that we extract all the numbers in the array in a single operation, using the EXEC SQL FOR ... COLLECTION GET statement:

```
EXEC SQL ALLOCATE :ordinateArrayObject;
EXEC SQL OBJECT GET SDO_ORDINATES FROM :geometryObject  INTO :ordinateArrayObject ;
EXEC SQL COLLECTION DESCRIBE :ordinateArrayObject GET SIZE INTO :nOrdinates;
ordinateArray = (double *) calloc (nOrdinates,(size_t)sizeof(double));
EXEC SQL FOR :nOrdinates
  COLLECTION GET :ordinateArrayObject INTO :ordinateArray;
}
```

Writing Geometry Objects

Just as with reading geometries, we first need to allocate a variable in the object cache. We then populate the geometry variable, and finally we write it out to the database using an EXEC SQL INSERT statement.

We use the EXEC SQL OBJECT SET statement to load the scalar attributes (SDO_GTYPE and so on), and then we use EXEC SQL FOR ... COLLECTION SET and EXEC SQL FOR ... COLLECTION APPEND to populate the arrays (SDO_ORDINATES and SDO_ELEM_INFO).

We do not detail the full process here. If you are interested in the details, refer to the example code for this book provided in the Downloads section of the Apress website (www.apress.com).

Pro*C Examples

From the Downloads section of the Apress website (www.apress.com) you can obtain two complete example programs, PREADGEOM.PC and PWRITEGEOM.PC, that illustrate reading and writing geometries using Pro*C.

Summary

In this chapter, you learned how to map geometry types into data structures that you can use in application programs for PL/SQL, Java, and C, to read, write, and manipulate them. Note that there are a few occasions when you will need to perform such manipulations, and Oracle Spatial provides a rich set of operators and functions that should cover the majority of cases. We will examine those operators and functions in the next two chapters.

PART 3

Analysis and Visualization

CHAPTER 8

Spatial Indexes and Operators

To run the examples in this chapter, you need to import the following datasets:

```
imp spatial/spatial file=app_with_loc.dmp full=y indexes=n
imp spatial/spatial file=map_large.dmp full=y
```

In previous chapters, we examined how to store location information in Oracle tables. We augmented existing tables, such as `branches`, `customers`, and `competitors`, with an `SDO_GEOMETRY` column to store locations of data objects. In this chapter, we describe how to use this spatial information to perform proximity analysis.

Proximity analysis refers to query/analysis using the locations of data objects. Specifically, in a business application, you might be interested in (but not limited to) the types of proximity analysis shown in Table 8-1.

Table 8-1. *Types of Proximity Analyses in a Business Application*

Analysis Type	Description
Customer analysis	Identify customers nearest to, or within a specified radius from, a branch or a competitor. For customers close to a competitor, you might provide certain promotions to retain them. You may specifically target this analysis on `GOLD` customers whom you want to retain at any cost.
Sales region analysis	Build sales regions (i.e., quarter-mile buffers) around branch and competitor locations. Identify which of these overlap with one another or with state and county boundaries. If sales regions of branches overlap substantially, you could merge such branches.

We describe how to perform these (and additional) varieties of proximity analysis in detail in this chapter. To perform efficient proximity analysis, you will make use of three basic elements of Oracle's spatial technology:

- *Spatial operators*: Just as you can specify relational operators in a SQL statement, such as < (less than), > (greater than), or = (equal to), and so on, you can likewise use a spatial operator to search the location (`SDO_GEOMETRY`) columns of a table for proximity with respect to a query location.

The following SQL shows how to search the customers table using a spatial operator:

```
SELECT COUNT(*)
FROM branches b, customers c
WHERE b.id=1
AND SDO_WITHIN_DISTANCE
   (c.location, b.location, 'DISTANCE=0.25 UNIT=MILE')='TRUE';
```

This example counts the customers within a quarter-mile of a specified store (id=1). The equality operator, b.id=1, selects only the row that has an ID of 1 from the branches table. You then specify a spatial predicate using the SDO_WITHIN_DISTANCE operator, with which you identify the customers that are within a quarter-mile of the specified store.

- *Spatial indexes*: Analogous to B-tree indexes, spatial indexes facilitate fast execution of spatial operators on SDO_GEOMETRY columns of Oracle tables. A B-tree index on the id column of the branches table would facilitate searches based on branch ID. Similarly, a spatial index on the location column of the customers table would facilitate fast execution of the SDO_WITHIN_DISTANCE operator.
- *Geometry processing functions*: These functions perform a variety of operations, including computation of the spatial interaction of two or more SDO_GEOMETRY objects. Spatial functions do not use spatial indexes, and they enable a more rigorous analysis of spatial data than is possible with spatial operators.

In this chapter, we focus on only the first two topics listed previously: *spatial indexes* and *spatial operators*. We will describe the third topic, *geometry processing functions*, in Chapter 9. A majority of the functionality of spatial indexes and spatial operators is part of Oracle Locator (included in all editions of the Oracle Database). This means all Oracle applications can leverage the functionality described in this chapter.

The remainder of the chapter is structured as follows:

- First, we discuss how to create spatial indexes on SDO_GEOMETRY columns.
- Then, we describe spatial operators that perform different types of proximity analysis and how to use these operators in a SQL statement.
- In the last section, we cover more advanced topics regarding spatial indexing and spatial queries. These include *function-based spatial indexing*, *parallel* and *partitioned* indexing, and *spatial joins*. Function-based spatial indexing allows spatial indexes to be created on functions that return SDO_GEOMETRY values. Partitioned indexing allows local indexes to be created for each partition of a partitioned table. Parallel indexing allows the creation of a spatial index in parallel. Spatial joins enable fast joining of multiple tables based on a spatial criterion. Some of these advanced topics, such as partitioned indexes, are included only in the Enterprise Edition of Oracle (as priced options).

Spatial Indexes

Spatial operators enable proximity analysis on SDO_GEOMETRY columns. Listing 8-1 shows how to search for customers within a half-mile of a branch location.

Listing 8-1. `SDO_WITHIN_DISTANCE` *Spatial Operator in SQL*

```
SQL> SELECT COUNT(*)
FROM branches b , customers c
WHERE  b.id=1
  AND SDO_WITHIN_DISTANCE
  (c.location, b.location,  'DISTANCE=0.5 UNIT=MILE')='TRUE';
ERROR at line 1:
ORA-13226: interface not supported without a spatial index
ORA-06512: at "MDSYS.MD", line 1723
ORA-06512: at "MDSYS.MDERR", line 8
ORA-06512: at "MDSYS.SDO_3GL", line 387
```

The error in Listing 8-1 indicates that to use spatial operators, we first need to create a spatial index on the `location` column of the `customers` table. As an application developer, creating spatial indexes on the `SDO_GEOMETRY` columns is one of the first steps to undertake when enabling proximity analysis in your application.

As noted earlier, spatial indexes in Oracle are analogous to conventional indexes such as B-trees. Just as a B-tree index on a name column speeds up queries of the sort `where name = 'Larry'`, so do spatial indexes enable fast searching on the indexed `SDO_GEOMETRY` columns. Spatial indexes are required to ensure effective response times for queries that use spatial operators, such as the one in Listing 8-1.

Just like B-tree indexes, spatial indexes are created using SQL. For instance, you can create a spatial index on the `location` column of the `customers` table, as shown in Listing 8-2.

Listing 8-2. *Creating an Index*

```
SQL> CREATE INDEX customers_spatial_idx ON customers(location)
INDEXTYPE  IS MDSYS.SPATIAL_INDEX;
```

Note that the statement is similar to creating a B-tree index, except that the `INDEXTYPE IS MDSYS.SPATIAL_INDEX` clause specifies that the index to be created is a spatial index instead of a regular B-tree index.

However, this statement may fail as illustrated in the following code, if you have not already populated the appropriate metadata for the spatial layer (corresponding to `<customers table, location column>`):

```
ERROR at line 1:
ORA-29855: error occurred in the execution of ODCIINDEXCREATE routine
ORA-13203: failed to read USER_SDO_GEOM_METADATA view
ORA-13203: failed to read USER_SDO_GEOM_METADATA view
ORA-06512: at "MDSYS.SDO_INDEX_METHOD_10I", line 10
ORA-06512: at line 1
```

■ **Caution** Always insert metadata for a spatial layer (`table_name, column_name`) prior to creating a spatial index.

You may recall that we discussed how to add spatial metadata for a spatial layer in Chapter 3. We briefly recap that discussion in the next section.

Inserting Metadata for a Spatial Layer Prior to Indexing

Spatial metadata for a spatial layer (identified by `<table_name, column_name>`) is inserted in the `USER_SDO_GEOM_METADATA` view. This view has the fields shown in Listing 8-3 that need to be populated appropriately.

Listing 8-3. `USER_SDO_GEOM_METADATA` *View*

```
SQL> DESCRIBE USER_SDO_GEOM_METDATA;
 Name                             Null?        Type
 -----------------------          --------     -------------------
TABLE_NAME                        NOT NULL     VARCHAR2(32)
COLUMN_NAME                       NOT NULL     VARCHAR2(1024)
DIMINFO                                        MDSYS.SDO_DIM_ARRAY
SRID                                           NUMBER
```

We can populate these fields as shown in Listing 8-4.

Listing 8-4. *Inserting Metadata for the Spatial Layer Corresponding to the* `location` *Column of the* `customers` *Table*

```
SQL> INSERT INTO  user_sdo_geom_metadata
(table_name, column_name, srid, diminfo)
VALUES
(
  'CUSTOMERS',          -- TABLE_NAME
  'LOCATION',           -- COLUMN_NAME
  8307,                 -- SRID specifying a geodetic coordinate system
  SDO_DIM_ARRAY         -- DIMINFO attribute for storing dimension bounds, tolerance
  (
    SDO_DIM_ELEMENT
    (
      'LONGITUDE',      -- DIMENSION NAME for first dimension
      -180,             -- SDO_LB for the dimension: -180 degrees
      180,              -- SDO_UB for the dimension: 180 degrees
      0.5               -- Tolerance of 0.5 meters (not 0.5 degrees: geodetic SRID)
    ),
    SDO_DIM_ELEMENT
    (
      'LATITUDE',       -- DIMENSION NAME for second dimension
      -90,              -- SDO_LB for the dimension: -90 degrees
      90,               -- SDO_UB for the dimension: 90 degrees
      0.5               -- Tolerance of 0.5 meters (not 0.5 degrees: geodetic SRID)
    )
  )
 );
```

The table_name and column_name fields, which identify the spatial layer, are set to customers and location, respectively. The srid field is set to 8307 to indicate a geodetic coordinate system. The diminfo field specifies the bounds and tolerance for each dimension. It is set using an SDO_DIM_ARRAY object containing two elements. The first element specifies the longitude dimension as the dimension_name, and –180 (degrees) and 180 (degrees) as the lower and upper bounds for this dimension. The tolerance is set to 0.5 (meters). The second element specifies the latitude dimension as the dimension_name, and –90 (degrees) and 90 (degrees) as the lower and upper bounds for this dimension. The tolerance is set again to 0.5 (meters).

Creating a Spatial Index

Now that we have populated the metadata, we can create the spatial index. However, if the index creation failed earlier, we first need to drop the index that failed. Note that this behavior is different from that of a B-tree (when B-tree index creation fails, we don't need to explicitly drop the B-tree index). The command to drop a spatial index, shown in Listing 8-5, is the same as that for other indexes, such as B-trees.

Listing 8-5. *Dropping a Spatial Index*

```
SQL> DROP INDEX customers_sidx;
```

Now we are ready to re-create a spatial index on the location column of the customers table, as shown in Listing 8-6.

Listing 8-6. *Creating a Spatial Index on the* location *Column of the* customers *Table*

```
SQL> CREATE INDEX customers_spatial_idx ON customers(location)
INDEXTYPE  IS MDSYS.SPATIAL_INDEX;
```

■ Note During index creation, Oracle checks whether the SDO_SRID in the column being indexed matches the SRID in the USER_SDO_GEOM_METADATA for the corresponding spatial layer. If these values do not match, Oracle raises the ORA-13365 error. Oracle, however, does not run any validation checks during index creation. You need to explicitly run validation (see Chapter 5 for details) if you are unsure of the validity of the spatial data.

Spatial Indexing Concepts

We have created a spatial index on the `location` column of the `customers` table, and we know that this will facilitate fast execution of spatial operator queries. However, before we move on to look at some more examples, it is important to understand how a spatial index works.

The `spatial_index` is internally implemented as an *R-tree* index,[1] a B-tree-like hierarchical structure that stores rectangle approximations of geometries as key values. Figure 8-1 shows an example of an R-tree `spatial_index` for customer locations represented by points.

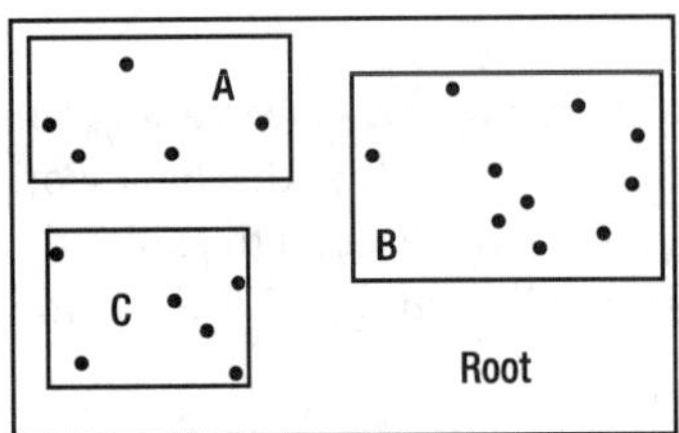

Rectangles: Index Approximations
• (dots): Point Geometries from Table

ROWIDs and MBRs from Data Table

Figure 8-1. *Example of an R-tree for a set of points*

Say that the black dots in Figure 8-1 represent the locations of customers stored as point geometries in the `location` (`SDO_GEOMETRY`) column of the `customers` table. For each `SDO_GEOMETRY` in the `location` column, the R-tree computes a *minimum bounding rectangle* (MBR) enclosing the `SDO_GEOMETRY`, and it creates a hierarchy of MBRs.

For instance, in Figure 8-1, the point locations are clustered into three nodes: A, B, and C. Each node is associated with an MBR that encloses the locations of the data in the subtree. The left side of Figure 8-1 shows the points and the MBRs for nodes A, B, and C. These nodes are further clustered into a single "root" node. In this manner, an R-tree constructs a hierarchical tree structure using the MBRs of the `SDO_GEOMETRY` data in a table. It then uses this hierarchy of MBRs to guide queries to appropriate branches of the tree and finally to the rows of the data table.

Figure 8-2 illustrates how the R-tree index is stored in Oracle. The logical tree structure is stored as an Oracle table that starts with the prefix `MDRT`. Each node of the tree structure is stored as a separate row in this table.

1. Norbert Beckmann, Hans-Peter Kriegel, Ralf Schneider, and Bernhard Seeger. "The R*-tree: An Efficient and Robust Access Method for Points and Rectangles." Proceedings of the ACM SIGMOD International Conference on the Management of Data, 1990, p. 322–31.

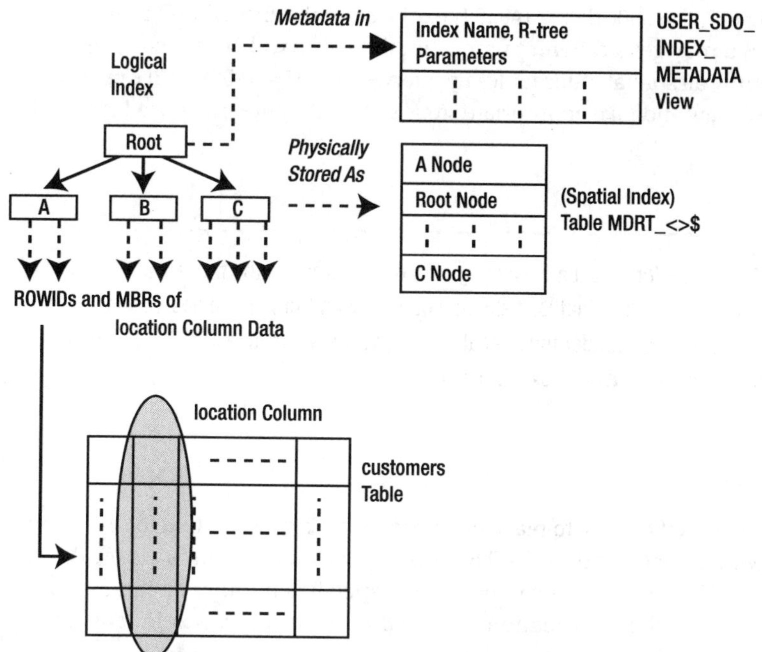

Figure 8-2. *Storage of a spatial (R-tree) index*

The metadata for the spatial index is stored in the view USER_SDO_INDEX_METADATA. (You should not confuse this view with the USER_SDO_GEOM_METADATA view that stores information about spatial layers.) This view stores the spatial index name (as SDO_INDEX_NAME), the table storing the index (as SDO_INDEX_TABLE), the root ROWID for the R-tree index, the branching factor or *fanout* of an R-tree node, and other relevant parameters. You can consult this view to identify the spatial index (MDRT) table (or SDO_INDEX_TABLE) corresponding to a specific spatial index. As an alternative, you can consult the simpler USER_SDO_INDEX_INFO view.

Listing 8-7. *Identifying the* SDO_INDEX_TABLE *That Stores the Spatial Index on the* customers *Table*

```
SQL> SELECT SDO_INDEX_TABLE FROM USER_SDO_INDEX_INFO
WHERE  TABLE_NAME = 'CUSTOMERS' AND COLUMN_NAME='LOCATION';
SDO_INDEX_TABLE
--------------------------------
MDRT_D81F$
```

■Note The USER_SDO_INDEX_INFO and USER_SDO_INDEX_METADATA views store all the VARCHAR2 fields in uppercase. You should compare these fields with uppercase literals (as in Listing 8-7).

As shown in Listing 8-7, the SDO_INDEX_TABLE (i.e., the spatial index table) has the name MDRT_D81F$. Note that you may get a different name, but the name will always start with the prefix MDRT. You can identify all spatial index tables by querying the SDO_INDEX_TABLE column in the USER_SDO_INDEX_INFO view and take appropriate steps so that they are not moved around by an unwary DBA.

■ **Caution** The SDO_INDEX_TABLE for a spatial index (e.g., the one returned in the preceding SQL) should never be treated as a regular Oracle table—that is, it should not be moved from one tablespace to another, dropped, copied, etc. Otherwise, this will render the spatial index invalid and could lead to the failure of subsequent spatial query operators or spatial index rebuilding.

Spatial Index Parameters

In B-tree indexes, you can specify where to place the index data. Can you do that for the spatial index table associated with a spatial index? Yes. The CREATE INDEX statement in Listing 8-6 can take an additional PARAMETERS clause that can be used to specify a number of parameters, including where to store the index information. Listing 8-8 shows the syntax for creating a spatial index, including the PARAMETERS clause (in bold).

Listing 8-8. *Syntax for Creating a Spatial Index*

```
CREATE INDEX <indexname> ON <tablename>(<columnname>)
INDEXTYPE IS MDSYS.SPATIAL_INDEX
PARAMETERS ('parameter_string');
```

The parameter_string is a list of parameter_name=value pairs. Let's examine some important parameters that you're likely to use in applications.

TABLESPACE Parameter

You can specify which tablespace to use for storing the spatial index table with this parameter. For instance, TABLESPACE=TBS_3 puts the spatial index table in the TBS_3 tablespace. Listing 8-9 shows an example.

Listing 8-9. *Creating a Spatial Index in Tablespace* TBS_3

```
SQL> CREATE INDEX customers_sidx ON customers(location)
INDEXTYPE IS MDSYS.SPATIAL_INDEX
PARAMETERS ('TABLESPACE=TBS_3');
```

You can specify the INITIAL and NEXT extents in addition to the TABLESPACE parameter, as shown in Listing 8-10.

Listing 8-10. *Creating an Index with the* `INITIAL` *and* `NEXT` *Extents for an Index Table*

```
SQL> CREATE INDEX customers_sidx ON customers(location)
INDEXTYPE IS MDSYS.SPATIAL_INDEX
PARAMETERS ('TABLESPACE=TBS_3 NEXT=5K INITIAL=10K');
```

If your tablespaces are *locally managed* (see the *Oracle Reference* for more details), you do not need these parameters, and Oracle will ignore them even if specified.

WORK_TABLESPACE Parameter

During index creation, the R-tree index performs sorting operations on the entire dataset. As a result, it creates some working tables that are dropped at the end of index creation. Creating and dropping many tables with different sizes can fragment the space in a tablespace. To avoid this, you can specify a separate tablespace for these working tables using the `WORK_TABLESPACE` parameter, as shown in Listing 8-11.

Listing 8-11. *Creating an Index with* `WORK_TABLESPACE` *As* `TBS_3`

```
SQL> CREATE INDEX  customers_sidx ON  customers(location)
INDEXTYPE  IS MDSYS.SPATIAL_INDEX
PARAMETERS ('WORK_TABLESPACE=TBS_3');
```

In this example, `WORK_TABLESPACE=TBS_3` places all working tables in tablespace `TBS_3`. This ensures the existing tablespaces holding the index and/or data are not fragmented due to index creation work. The total size (in bytes) used in such a "work tablespace" will be approximately 200–300 times the number of rows in the `customers` table.

■ **Note** These working tables are regular tables and not "temporary" tables. You cannot use the temporary tablespace in Oracle for this purpose. Also note that if `WORK_TABLESPACE` is not specified, the working tables are created in the same tablespace as the index.

LAYER_GTYPE Parameter

You can use this parameter to specify that the geometry data in the `location` column of the `customers` table are *specific*-type geometries such as points (by default, all types are permitted). This will help in integrity checking and sometimes in speeding up the query operators.

For instance, as shown in Listing 8-12, we can set the parameter string to `LAYER_GTYPE = POINT` to indicate that the `customers` table has only point data. Trying to insert a line geometry into this column will raise an error. In general, you can set the value to the names of the `SDO_GTYPE`s (point, line, polygon, and so on), as discussed in Chapter 4.

Listing 8-12. *Creating an Index for Specific-Type (Point) Geometries*

```
SQL> CREATE INDEX  customers_sidx ON  customers(location)
INDEXTYPE  IS MDSYS.SPATIAL_INDEX
PARAMETERS ('LAYER_GTYPE=POINT');
```

SDO_INDX_DIMS Parameter

This parameter specifies that the dimensionality of the `spatial_index`. By default, this is set to 2. The R-tree can index three- and four-dimensional geometries. Listing 8-13 shows an example for setting the index dimensionality explicitly to 2. You can set this parameter to 3 or 4 to create a three- or four-dimensional R-tree index.

Listing 8-13. *Creating an R-tree Index with Dimensionality Specified*

```
SQL> CREATE INDEX  customers_sidx ON  customers(location)
INDEXTYPE  IS MDSYS.SPATIAL_INDEX
PARAMETERS ('SDO_INDX_DIMS=2');
```

SDO_DML_BATCH_SIZE Parameter

Inserts and deletes to a table containing a spatial index are not directly incorporated in the spatial index. Instead, they are incorporated in the index at commit time in batches. This parameter specifies the batch size for the batched insert/delete/update in a transaction. (For transactions with large number of inserts, set this parameter to 5000 or 10000.) Listing 8-14 shows an example.

Listing 8-14. *Creating an Index with the* `SDO_DML_BATCH_SIZE` *Parameter*

```
SQL> CREATE INDEX  customers_sidx ON  customers(location)
INDEXTYPE  IS MDSYS.SPATIAL_INDEX
PARAMETERS ('SDO_DML_BATCH_SIZE=5000');
```

This parameter, if not specified, is internally set to 1000. This means inserts in a transaction are incorporated in the index in batches of 1,000. This is a good value for most transactions that have a mix of queries and inserts, deletes, and updates. However, if your transactions have a large number of inserts, deletes, and updates (say on the order of 5,000 or 10,000 or more), you may want to set the `SDO_DML_BATCH_SIZE` parameter to a higher value, for example 5000 or 10000. This will substantially improve the performance of the commit operation (i.e., the incorporation of the updates in the index at commit time). Note, however, that this might consume more memory and other system resources. In general, you should always set this parameter to be in the range of 1 to 10000.

Tip If you expect to perform substantial number of insert (or delete or update) operations within a transaction on a table having a spatial index, set the `SDO_DML_BATCH_SIZE` parameter to 5000 or 10000 in the `CREATE INDEX` statement.

SDO_LEVEL Parameter

Instead of an R-tree index (which is the default), you can create a quadtree index by specifying the SDO_LEVEL parameter in the PARAMETERS clause (search the documentation for "Oracle Spatial Quadtree Indexing"). Quadtrees, unlike R-trees, need explicit tuning (the SDO_LEVEL parameter needs to be tuned for best performance) and are discouraged. Quadtrees can index only two-dimensional nongeodetic data. Listing 8-15 shows an example.

Listing 8-15. *Creating a Quadtree Type of Spatial Index*

```
SQL> CREATE INDEX customers_sidx ON customers(location)
INDEXTYPE  IS MDSYS.SPATIAL_INDEX
PARAMETERS ('SDO_LEVEL=8');
```

USER_SDO_INDEX_METADATA View

All of the previously described parameters that can be used in the CREATE INDEX statement are stored in the USER_SDO_INDEX_METADATA view. For instance, after creating a spatial index, you can check the SDO_DML_BATCH_SIZE value for this index as shown in Listing 8-16.

Listing 8-16. *Examining the* USER_SDO_INDEX_METADATA *View for Index Parameters*

```
SQL> SELECT SDO_DML_BATCH_SIZE  FROM USER_SDO_INDEX_METADATA
WHERE  SDO_INDEX_NAME = 'CUSTOMERS_SIDX';
SDO_DML_BATCH_SIZE
------------------
              1000
```

Note Again, observe that the USER_SDO_INDEX_METADATA view stores all its VARCHAR2 fields in uppercase. You should compare these fields with uppercase literals (as in Listings 8-7 and 8-16).

Listing 8-16 shows that the SDO_DML_BATCH_SIZE parameter is set to the default value of 1,000. Likewise, you can examine the SDO_TABLESPACE parameter (and other parameters) in the USER_SDO_INDEX_METADATA view to verify that the index is stored in the tablespace you specified.

Spatial Index Size Requirements

For a set of *N* rows in a table, the R-tree spatial index roughly requires 100 × *N* bytes of storage space for the spatial index table. Also, during index creation, it requires an additional 200 × *N* to 300 × *N* bytes for temporary worktables. You can use the utility function in Listing 8-17 to roughly estimate the size (in megabytes) of an R-tree spatial index table.

Listing 8-17. *Estimating the Size of a Spatial Index on the* `location` *Column of the* `customers` *Table*

```
SQL> SELECT   sdo_tune.estimate_rtree_index_size
(
  'SPATIAL',      -- schema name
  'CUSTOMERS',    -- table name
  'LOCATION'      -- column name on which the spatial index is to be built
) sz
FROM dual;

        SZ
----------
         1
```

The first parameter specifies the schema name, the second the table name, and the third the column name on which the spatial index is to be built. For building a spatial index on the `location` column of the `customers` table, this function indicates that you need roughly 1MB of space. Note that this is the final index size. You may need two to three times this space during the index creation process

In addition, when you create a spatial index, the Oracle database parameter `SORT_AREA_SIZE` should to be set to 1MB to optimize the index creation process.

Given this background on spatial indexes, let's move on to look at associated spatial operators and how to perform proximity analysis using such operators.

Spatial Operators

In this section, we describe the different spatial operators that Oracle Spatial supports for performing spatial analysis. We start with an overview of spatial operators, their general syntax, their semantics (along with any required privileges), and their evaluation using spatial indexes. Next, we take a closer look at different spatial operators and describe how to perform different kinds of proximity analyses (including those discussed in Table 8-1) using those operators. In the third part of this section, we describe how specifying appropriate "hints" can ensure faster evaluation of spatial operators.

Oracle Spatial supports a variety of spatial operators for performing proximity analysis. Just like the relational operators <, >, and =, the spatial operators can be used in the `WHERE` clause of a regular SQL statement. Let's examine the syntax and the semantics of these operators.

Syntax of Spatial Operators

These operators have the generic syntax described in Listing 8-18.

Listing 8-18. *General Syntax of Spatial Operators*

```
<spatial_operator>
(
```

```
  table_geometry         IN SDO_GEOMETRY,
  query_geometry         IN SDO_GEOMETRY
  [, parameter_string  IN VARCHAR2
   [, tag                IN NUMBER ]]
)
='TRUE'
```

In Listing 8-18,

- `table_geometry` is the `SDO_GEOMETRY` column of the table on which the operator is applied.
- `query_geometry` is the query location. This could be an `SDO_GEOMETRY` column of another table, a bind variable, or a dynamically constructed object.
- `parameter_string` specifies the parameters specific to the spatial operator. As the opening square bracket indicates, this argument is optional in some operators.
- `tag` specifies a number used only in specific spatial operators. Again, the opening square bracket indicates that this argument is optional. This argument can be specified only in conjunction with the `parameter_string` argument.

We should note two things in the preceding syntax and explanation. First, the `table_geometry` column *must* be spatially indexed. Spatial operators raise an error otherwise. Second, the operator is always equated to the string `'TRUE'` in the preceding signature. This makes it a *predicate* to be evaluated with respect to every row of the indexed table. Oracle Spatial stipulates that a spatial operator should always be equated to `'TRUE'`.

Semantics of Spatial Operators

When you specify a spatial operator in a SQL statement, Oracle selects only those rows for which the operator evaluates to `TRUE`. This means the operator selects only those rows of the associated table where the corresponding `table_geometry` (`SDO_GEOMETRY` column) values satisfy a specified operator relationship with respect to the `query_geometry` (query location). This type of selection is analogous to selection with relational operators using a specific predicate such as `id>=10`.

Let's look at an example of spatial operator usage. Listing 8-19 shows our first spatial query using the `SDO_WITHIN_DISTANCE` operator in the `WHERE` clause.

Listing 8-19. *Spatial Operator Usage in a SQL Statement*

```
SQL> SELECT COUNT(*)
FROM branches b, customers c
WHERE  b.id=1
  AND SDO_WITHIN_DISTANCE
  (c.location, b.location, 'DISTANCE=0.5 UNIT=MILE') = 'TRUE';
  COUNT(*)
----------
       108
```

The first column of the SDO_WITHIN_DISTANCE operator specifies the column name (i.e., the location column) that is indexed in the customers table. The second column specifies a query location. In this case, the query location is selected from the branches table. The third argument specifies the parameters for the operator. In the case of the SDO_WITHIN_DISTANCE operator, this parameter specifies the distance (and the units) to search. The operator returns all rows of the customers table where the location column satisfies the spatial-operator relationship with respect to the query location. In this example, it returns all customers within 0.5 miles of the query location.

All spatial operators, including the SDO_WITHIN_DISTANCE operator in the previous example, use the spatial index (associated with their first argument, the table_geometry) to prune irrelevant rows. Unlike the geometry processing functions described in Chapter 9, spatial operators are *tied* to the spatial index. In other words, they *require* that a spatial index exist on the table_geometry column specified as the first argument of an operator. For instance, if you executed the SQL in Listing 8-6 after dropping the customers_sidx index, you would get an ORA-13226 ("Interface not supported without a spatial index") error.

Evaluation of Spatial Operators

Next, we briefly discuss how spatial operators are evaluated. An understanding of this will help to ensure the best execution strategies for a spatial operator.

Since spatial operators are tied to the spatial index, they are, in most cases, evaluated in a two-stage filtering mechanism involving the spatial index. As shown in Figure 8-3, a spatial operator is first evaluated using the spatial index. This evaluation using the index is referred to as the *primary filter*. Here, the approximations in the index (the MBRs stored in the spatial index table) are used to identify a candidate set of rows that satisfies the operator relationship with respect to the query location. The identified rows are then passed through the Geometry Engine, referred to as the *secondary filter*, to return the correct set of rows for the specified operator. Note that all of this processing is transparent to the user: just specifying the operator in the WHERE clause of a SQL statement will internally invoke the appropriate index (primary filter) and the Geometry Engine (secondary filter) functionality to identify the correct set of rows.

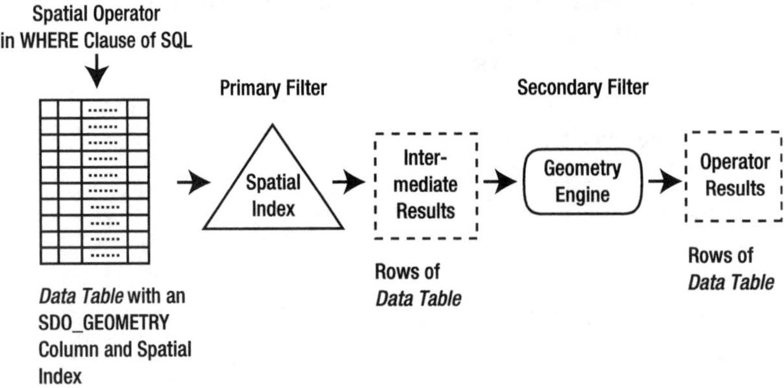

Figure 8-3. *Spatial operator evaluation using an associated spatial index*

In some cases, however, the optimizer may decide to bypass the spatial index. It then invokes the secondary filter (i.e., the Geometry Engine functions) directly on appropriate rows of the table. (This might happen for a variety of reasons, including insufficient cost estimates for the spatial operator. Note that Oracle Spatial provides only rough estimates for the spatial operator evaluation with and without spatial indexes.) Not using the spatial index has the following implications:

- It might result in inefficient execution strategies whenever the SQL involves multiple tables or spatial and nonspatial predicates on the same table. Such cases might need tuning by providing explicit hints to use appropriate indexes.
- Oracle Spatial requires that the SDO_NN operator be evaluated using a spatial index. Sometimes you need explicit hints to ensure the use of a spatial index.

We discuss these cases and the remedies using explicit hints later in the "Hints for Spatial Operators" section.

A Closer Look at Spatial Operators

Now that you have some background on how spatial operators are evaluated in Oracle, we next describe the semantics of different spatial operators. Oracle Spatial provides different operators to perform the following types of proximity analyses. These operators can be used to enable the different analyses listed in Table 8-1 for a business application.

- *Find all data within a specified distance from a query location*: This operator is called SDO_WITHIN_DISTANCE or simply the *within distance* operator. This operator will enable customer analysis, as described in Table 8-1.
- *Find the nearest neighbors to a query location*: This operator is called SDO_NN or simply the *nearest neighbor* operator. This operator can be useful in performing customer analysis, as described in Table 8-1.
- *Find neighbors that interact with or relate to a query location*: The primary operator to solve this purpose is called SDO_RELATE. There are other variants for determining specific types of relation. If only the index approximations are to be used, you can use a simpler variant (operator) called SDO_FILTER. These operators enable sales region analysis, as described in Table 8-1.

In this section of the chapter, we discuss each of these operators in sequence and how to use them for performing analysis in a business application.

SDO_WITHIN_DISTANCE Operator

First, we will describe the SDO_WITHIN_DISTANCE operator. This operator is one of the simplest spatial operators, and you can start your proximity analysis with it. This operator facilitates analysis such as the identification of customers within a quarter-mile radius of a store site.

Given a set of locations, the SDO_WITHIN_DISTANCE operator returns all locations that are within a specified distance from a query location. Figure 8-4 shows an example. The

SDO_WITHIN_DISTANCE operator specifies a distance *d* from the query location Q. The spatial index will retrieve the objects A, B, and C that are within this specified distance *d*. Objects D and E are eliminated, as they are farther than distance *d* from query location Q.

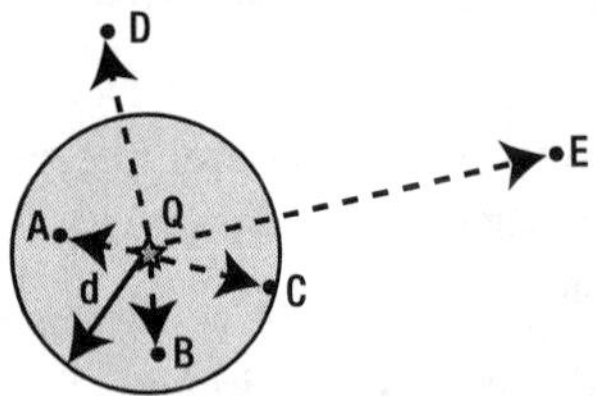

Figure 8-4. *The* SDO_WITHIN_DISTANCE *operator specifies a maximum distance* d.

The SDO_WITHIN_DISTANCE operator has the following syntax. You can observe that this operator conforms to the generic spatial_operator syntax in Listing 8-18. The cut-off distance *d* is specified in the third argument, parameter_string, using the parameter distance=d. Note that Oracle Spatial stipulates that the operator always be evaluated to the string 'TRUE'.

```
SDO_WITHIN_DISTANCE
(
  table_geom        IN SDO_GEOMETRY,
  query_geom        IN SDO_GEOMETRY,
  parameter_string  IN VARCHAR2
)
='TRUE'
```

where

- table_geom is the SDO_GEOMETRY column of the table that is searched.
- query_geom is the SDO_GEOMETRY specifying the query location. This could be a column of another table, a bind variable, or a dynamically constructed object.
- parameter_string specifies the parameter *distance* and optionally the parameter *unit* (for the distance specified). The string will be of the form 'DISTANCE=<numeric value> [UNIT=<string>]'.

NOTE The default unit for geodetic data is meter.

Listing 8-20 shows the usage of the SDO_WITHIN_DISTANCE operator. Here, the customers within a quarter-mile distance of a specific competitor store (store id=1) are identified.

Listing 8-20. `SDO_WITHIN_DISTANCE` *Operator Retrieving All Customers Within a Quarter-Mile Radius of a Competitor Store*

```
SQL> SELECT ct.id, ct.name
FROM competitors comp, customers ct
WHERE comp.id=1
  AND SDO_WITHIN_DISTANCE
  (ct.location, comp.location, 'DISTANCE=0.25 UNIT=MILE ' )='TRUE'
ORDER BY ct.id;
        ID NAME
---------- -----------------------------------
        25 BLAKE CONSTRUCTION
        28 COLONIAL PARKING
        34 HEWLETT-PACKARD DC GOV AFFAIRS
        41 MCGREGOR PRINTING
        48 POTOMAC ELECTRIC POWER
        50 SMITH HINCHMAN AND GRYLLS
       270 METRO-FARRAGUT NORTH STATION
       271 METRO-FARRAGUT WEST STATION
       468 SAFEWAY
       809 LINCOLN SUITES
       810 HOTEL LOMBARDY
      1044 MUSEUM OF THE THIRD DIMENSION
      1526 INTERNATIONAL FINANCE
      1538 MCKENNA AND CUNEO
      2195 STEVENS ELEMENTARY SCHOOL
      6326 HOTEL LOMBARDY
      7754 EXECUTIVE INN
      7762 PHILLIPS 66
      7789 SEVEN BUILDINGS
      7821 RENAISSANCE MAYFLOWER HOTEL
      8138 ST GREGORY HOTEL
      8382 EXXON
      8792 DESTINATION HOTEL & RESORTS

23 rows selected.
```

Can you also report the distance of these returned customers from the corresponding store? Yes, but you have to use a spatial function called `SDO_GEOM.SDO_DISTANCE` for this purpose. Listing 8-21 shows the corresponding SQL.

Listing 8-21. `SDO_WITHIN_DISTANCE` *Operator Retrieving All Customers in a Quarter-Mile Radius of a Competitor Store and Also Reporting Their Distances*

```
SQL> col dist format 999
SELECT ct.id, ct.name,
SDO_GEOM.SDO_DISTANCE(ct.location, comp.location, 0.5, ' UNIT=YARD ') dist
FROM competitors comp, customers ct
```

```
WHERE comp.id=1
  AND SDO_WITHIN_DISTANCE
    (ct.location,  comp.location, 'DISTANCE=0.25 UNIT=MILE' )='TRUE'
ORDER BY  ct.id;
        ID NAME                                  DIST
---------- ----------------------------------- ----
        25 BLAKE CONSTRUCTION                   319
        28 COLONIAL PARKING                     398
        34 HEWLETT-PACKARD DC GOV AFFAIRS       428
        41 MCGREGOR PRINTING                    350
        48 POTOMAC ELECTRIC POWER               355
        50 SMITH HINCHMAN AND GRYLLS            252
       270 METRO-FARRAGUT NORTH STATION         345
       271 METRO-FARRAGUT WEST STATION          272
       468 SAFEWAY                              252
       809 LINCOLN SUITES                       104
       810 HOTEL LOMBARDY                       313
      1044 MUSEUM OF THE THIRD DIMENSION        153
      1526 INTERNATIONAL FINANCE                236
      1538 MCKENNA AND CUNEO                     97
      2195 STEVENS ELEMENTARY SCHOOL            305
      6326 HOTEL LOMBARDY                       329
      7754 EXECUTIVE INN                        375
      7762 PHILLIPS 66                          303
      7789 SEVEN BUILDINGS                      355
      7821 RENAISSANCE MAYFLOWER HOTEL          322
      8138 ST GREGORY HOTEL                     359
      8382 EXXON                                326
      8792 DESTINATION HOTEL & RESORTS          159

23 rows selected.
```

Note that the SDO_GEOM.SDO_DISTANCE function takes as the first two arguments the locations of a customer and a store that satisfy the SDO_WITHIN_DISTANCE predicate. The third argument specifies the tolerance, and the fourth argument specifies the optional units parameter to retrieve the distances in appropriate units. In this case, the unit is set to yard. You will learn about this function in more detail in Chapter 9.

■ **Note** The SDO_GEOM.SDO_DISTANCE function is part of Locator.

SDO_NN Operator

The SDO_WITHIN_DISTANCE operator retrieves all objects within a specified distance *d* from a query location. What if there are no objects within distance *d*? What if the nearest object is at distance 2 × *d*? The SDO_WITHIN_DISTANCE operator is not appropriate when you need to obtain a specific number of neighbors, no matter how far they are from the query location. For these cases, the SDO_NN operator is appropriate.

Given a set of locations, the SDO_NN operator retrieves data in order of their distance to a query location. Figure 8-5 shows an example. A, B, C, D, and E are locations in a table that is spatially indexed. Q is a query location. The SDO_NN operator orders the items A, B, C, D, and E based on their distance to Q and returns them in the order of distance. If only one neighbor is requested, then A is returned. If two neighbors are requested, A and B are returned.

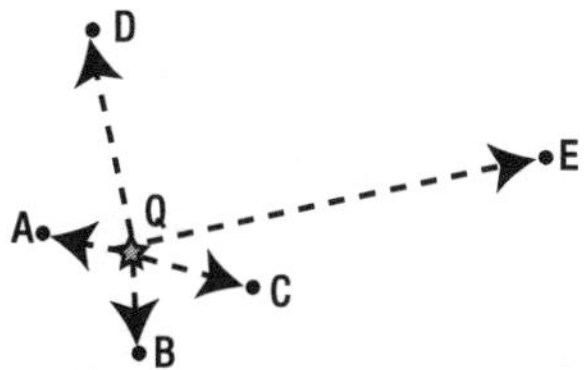

Figure 8-5. SDO_NN *on five locations: A, B, C, D, and E*

The SDO_NN operator has the following syntax. Observe that this syntax conforms to the generic signature (for any <spatial_operator>) in Listing 8-6, with some minor modifications. Note again that Oracle Spatial requires that the operator always evaluate to 'TRUE'.

```
SDO_NN
(
  table_geometry        IN SDO_GEOMETRY,
  query_geometry        IN SDO_GEOMETRY
  [, parameter_string  IN VARCHAR2
  [, tag                IN NUMBER ]]
)
='TRUE'
```

where

- table_geom specifies the SDO_GEOMETRY column of the table whose spatial index is to be used.
- query_geom specifies the SDO_GEOMETRY for the query location. This could be a column of another table or a bind variable.
- parameter_string, an optional argument, specifies one of two tuning parameters, SDO_BATCH_SIZE or SDO_NUM_RES. We discuss these parameters in the next sections.
- tag, another optional argument, allows the SDO_NN operator to be bound to an ancillary distance operator. We discuss it in the later part of this section. Note that this tag can be specified only if parameter_string is specified.

The SDO_NN operator facilitates proximity analysis in the business application. For instance, we can use it to identify the nearest customers to a competitor store (whose ID is 1). Listing 8-22 shows a simple example.

Listing 8-22. *A Simple Example of the SDO_NN Operator*

```
SQL> SELECT ct.id, ct.name
FROM competitors comp, customers ct
WHERE comp.id=1
  AND SDO_NN(ct.location,  comp.location)='TRUE' ;
        ID NAME
---------- -----------------------------------
      1538 MCKENNA AND CUNEO
    .......
3173 rows selected.
```

The query in Listing 8-22 returns all 3,173 customer ids (from the customers table) in order of their distance from the location of the specified competitor store (id=1). But in general, we do not want to look at all the customers; rather, we want to select only the closest five or ten. To enforce this restriction, we specify ROWNUM<=N in the preceding SQL, where N is the number of neighbors that we are interested in. Listing 8-23 shows the SQL when N is 5 (i.e., it retrieves the five nearest customers to the competitor id=1).

Listing 8-23. SDO_NN *Operator Retrieving the Five Nearest Customers to a Specific Competitor*

```
SQL> SELECT ct.id, ct.name, ct.customer_grade
FROM competitors comp, customers ct
WHERE comp.id=1
  AND SDO_NN(ct.location,  comp.location)='TRUE'
  AND ROWNUM<=5
ORDER BY ct.id;

        ID NAME                                CUSTOMER_GRADE
---------- ----------------------------------- ---------------
       809 LINCOLN SUITES                      GOLD
      1044 MUSEUM OF THE THIRD DIMENSION       SILVER
      1526 INTERNATIONAL FINANCE               SILVER
      1538 MCKENNA AND CUNEO                   SILVER
      8792 DESTINATION HOTEL & RESORTS         GOLD

5 rows selected.
```

Note that the customers have been graded into GOLD, SILVER, PLATINUM, and other categories. We want to retain the GOLD customers at any cost and should not let our competitors decrease our market share by poaching these important customers. So how do we identify these customers? One mechanism is to focus on the nearest GOLD customers to each competitor. We can modify Listing 8-23 to return the five nearest GOLD customers instead of any nearest five customers.

Listing 8-24 shows the SQL for competitor id=1. Note that the customer_grade='GOLD' predicate is added to the WHERE clause.

Listing 8-24. SDO_NN *Operator Retrieving the Five* GOLD *Customers Nearest to a Specific Competitor*

```
SQL> SELECT ct.id, ct.name, ct.customer_grade
FROM competitors comp, customers ct
WHERE comp.id=1
  AND ct.customer_grade='GOLD'
  AND SDO_NN(ct.location,  comp.location)='TRUE'
  AND ROWNUM<=5
ORDER BY ct.id;
        ID NAME                               CUSTOMER_GRADE
---------- ---------------------------------- --------------
       809 LINCOLN SUITES                     GOLD
       810 HOTEL LOMBARDY                     GOLD
      6326 HOTEL LOMBARDY                     GOLD
      7821 RENAISSANCE MAYFLOWER HOTEL        GOLD
      8792 DESTINATION HOTEL & RESORTS        GOLD

5 rows selected.
```

Note that all the customers returned are GOLD customers. The SILVER customers are filtered out.

In general, you can use the SDO_NN operator in different applications. For instance, Chapter 2 has some examples for obtaining the five nearest restaurants (or, more specifically, the five nearest Pizza Hut restaurants) to a certain highway.

The SDO_NN operator, as shown in Listing 8-24, can be used with other predicates in the same SQL statement. However, there are some restrictions.

- The SDO_NN operator *must always* be evaluated using the spatial index. Otherwise, an Oracle error is raised.
- If there is a nonspatial predicate on the same table (e.g., customer_grade='GOLD') and this column (customer_grade) has an index, then that index should not be used in the execution.

Specifying appropriate hints such as ORDERED and INDEX will help ensure that the spatial index is used. We look at how to specify these hints in the "Hints for Spatial Operators" section later in this chapter.

SDO_BATCH_SIZE Tuning Parameter

Note that in the query in Listing 8-24, the five nearest GOLD customers are not the five nearest customers to the specified competitor (see Listing 8-23). As a result, the spatial index will iteratively return neighbors in *batches* until all the predicates in the WHERE clause are satisfied. For example, to find the five nearest GOLD customers, the index will first return the ten nearest customers. If there are fewer than five GOLD customers among these ten nearest customers, then the index will return the next batch of the next ten customers. It continues returning the customers in batches until all the predicates in the SQL are satisfied, including customer_grade='GOLD' and ROWNUM<=10.

The size of these batches is determined by the index. However, you can set this "batch" size using the SDO_BATCH_SIZE parameter. For instance, if we know that the five nearest GOLD customers are within the first 100 nearest customers, we can pass this information to the index by specifying 'SDO_BATCH_SIZE=100'. This may speed up the query processing.

Listing 8-25 shows the SQL of Listing 8-24 with the SDO_BATCH_SIZE parameter specified. Note that even if the estimate is incorrect (i.e., the fifth GOLD customer is the one-hundred-first neighbor), the query returns correct results. SDO_BATCH_SIZE is set to 100.

Listing 8-25. SDO_NN *Operator Retrieving the Five* GOLD *Customers Nearest to a Competitor*

```
SQL> SELECT ct.id, ct.name, ct.customer_grade
FROM  competitors comp, customers ct
WHERE comp.id=1
  AND ct.customer_grade='GOLD'
  AND SDO_NN(ct.location,  comp.location, 'SDO_BATCH_SIZE=100' )='TRUE'
  AND ROWNUM<=5
ORDER BY ct.id;
        ID NAME                               CUSTOMER_GRADE
---------- ---------------------------------- ---------------
       809 LINCOLN SUITES                     GOLD
       810 HOTEL LOMBARDY                     GOLD
      6326 HOTEL LOMBARDY                     GOLD
      7821 RENAISSANCE MAYFLOWER HOTEL        GOLD
      8792 DESTINATION HOTEL & RESORTS        GOLD

5 rows selected.
```

SDO_NUM_RES Tuning Parameter

In most cases, you do not have to qualify the neighbors being retrieved—that is, you may just be interested in five nearest customers instead of five nearest GOLD customers. You already saw in Listing 8-23 how to obtain the nearest neighbors in such cases. However, by specifying the SDO_NUM_RES=<N> parameter, the SDO_NN operator returns exactly N neighbors and may be evaluated faster than without the parameter (as in Listing 8-23).

Note Since the spatial index returns exactly N neighbors, you do not have to prune the search with the ROWNUM<=N predicate in the SQL.

Listing 8-26 shows the equivalent for Listing 8-23. Notice that there is no rownum<=5 predicate, as the spatial index retrieves exactly five neighbors because of the additional parameter SDO_NUM_RES=5 in the SDO_NN invocation. Also note that the order of the neighbors returned in Listing 8-26 is not the same as in Listing 8-23 (although the same neighbors are returned in both).

Listing 8-26. SDO_NN *Operator Retrieving the Five Customers Nearest to a Specific Competitor*

```
SQL> SELECT ct.id, ct.name, ct.customer_grade
FROM  competitors comp, customers ct
WHERE comp.id=1
  AND SDO_NN(ct.location,  comp.location, 'SDO_NUM_RES=5')='TRUE' ;

        ID NAME                                CUSTOMER_GRADE
---------- ----------------------------------- ---------------
       809 LINCOLN SUITES                      GOLD
      1044 MUSEUM OF THE THIRD DIMENSION       SILVER
      1526 INTERNATIONAL FINANCE               SILVER
      1538 MCKENNA AND CUNEO                   SILVER
      8792 DESTINATION HOTEL & RESORTS         GOLD

5 rows selected.
```

■ **Caution** Using SDO_NUM_RES=<N> returns the N nearest neighbors to a specified query location, but the order of neighbors in the result set may not correspond to their distance to the query location.

SDO_NN with the Ancillary SDO_NN_DISTANCE Operator

In Listings 8-23 and 8-26, you saw how to obtain the five customers nearest to a competitor. In Listing 8-25, you saw how to obtain the five GOLD customers nearest to a competitor. In other words, you saw how to combine the SDO_NN operator with other predicates in the same SQL statement.

Instead of just identifying the nearest customers, why don't we find out how far away they are? In some cases, the first neighbor could be within 1 mile, but the next one could be 25 miles away. Knowing the distances will help us better understand the results. Fortunately, we can know the distances without paying any additional cost. The SDO_NN operator internally computes the distances to identify the customers. These distances can be retrieved by using the SDO_NN_DISTANCE ancillary operator.

To fully use the nearest neighbor functionality, we augment the SDO_NN operator with an ancillary operator to provide the distance of each neighbor. This ancillary operator, called SDO_NN_DISTANCE, is specified as part of the SELECT list and is bound to an SDO_NN operator in the WHERE clause. Listing 8-27 shows how to augment the SQL of Listing 8-26 to retrieve the distances of the neighbors.

■ **Caution** To use the ancillary operator, you will have to specify one of the tuning parameters, either SDO_NUM_RES or SDO_BATCH_SIZE. In other words, you cannot use the SDO_NN_DISTANCE operator with the two-argument signature in Listing 8-23. If you do not know to what value to set SDO_BATCH_SIZE, then set it to 0 and the index will use the appropriate batch size internally.

Listing 8-27. SDO_NN *Operator Retrieving the Five Customers Nearest to a Specific Competitor Along with Their Distances*

```
SQL> col dist format 999
SELECT ct.id, ct.name, ct.customer_grade, SDO_NN_DISTANCE(1) dist
FROM competitors comp, customers ct
WHERE comp.id=1
  AND SDO_NN(ct.location,  comp.location, 'SDO_NUM_RES=5',1)='TRUE'
ORDER BY ct.id;
        ID NAME                                CUSTOMER_GRADE  DIST
---------- ----------------------------------- --------------- ----
       809 LINCOLN SUITES                      GOLD              95
      1044 MUSEUM OF THE THIRD DIMENSION       SILVER           140
      1526 INTERNATIONAL FINANCE               SILVER           216
      1538 MCKENNA AND CUNEO                   SILVER            89
      8792 DESTINATION HOTEL & RESORTS         GOLD             146

5 rows selected.
```

Note that SDO_NN_DISTANCE(1) specifies a *numeric tag*, 1, in braces. This numeric tag is also specified as the fourth argument to the SDO_NN operator. This tag serves the purpose of binding the SDO_NN_DISTANCE ancillary operator to an instance of the SDO_NN operator in the WHERE clause. As a result, the SQL in Listing 8-27 returns the distances (to competitor id=1) along with the customer ids. Likewise, we can augment Listing 8-25 to return the distances of the five nearest GOLD customers and their distances. The resulting SQL is shown in Listing 8-28.

Listing 8-28. SDO_NN *Operator Retrieving the Five* GOLD *Customers Nearest to a Specific Competitor Along with Their Distances*

```
SQL> SELECT ct.id, ct.name, ct.customer_grade, SDO_NN_DISTANCE(1) dist
FROM competitors comp, customers ct
WHERE comp.id=1
  AND ct.customer_grade='GOLD'
  AND SDO_NN(ct.location,  comp.location, 'SDO_BATCH_SIZE=100', 1  )='TRUE'
  AND ROWNUM<=5
ORDER BY ct.id;
```

```
        ID NAME                                   CUSTOMER_GRADE  DIST
---------- ----------------------------------- --------------- ----
       809 LINCOLN SUITES                      GOLD              95
       810 HOTEL LOMBARDY                      GOLD             286
      7821 RENAISSANCE MAYFLOWER HOTEL         GOLD             295
      6326 HOTEL LOMBARDY                      GOLD             301
      8792 DESTINATION HOTEL & RESORTS         GOLD             146

5 rows selected.
```

By the way, in which units are the distances? Meters, kilometers, or miles? In general, the distances returned will be in the units for the coordinate system (refer to the information on `SRID` of the geometries and the `MDSYS.CS_SRS` tables in Chapter 4). Since the `SRID` for this dataset is 8307, a geodetic coordinate system, the distances returned are in meters. However, we can specify the desired units, such as miles, in the third argument, the `parameter_string` part of the query. Listings 8-29 and 8-30 correspondingly modify the SQL in Listings 8-27 and 8-28 to return the distances in miles. The `'UNIT=MILE'` parameter is added to the parameter string of the `SDO_NN` operator in these examples.

Listing 8-29. *Rewriting Listing 8-27 with Mile As the Distance Unit*

```
SQL> col dist format 9.99
SELECT ct.id, ct.name, ct.customer_grade, SDO_NN_DISTANCE(1) dist
FROM competitors comp, customers ct
WHERE comp.id=1
  AND SDO_NN(ct.location,  comp.location, 'SDO_NUM_RES=5 UNIT=MILE',1)='TRUE'
ORDER BY ct.id;
        ID NAME                                   CUSTOMER_GRADE  DIST
---------- ----------------------------------- --------------- ----
       809 LINCOLN SUITES                      GOLD             .06
      1044 MUSEUM OF THE THIRD DIMENSION       SILVER           .09
      1526 INTERNATIONAL FINANCE               SILVER           .13
      1538 MCKENNA AND CUNEO                   SILVER           .06
      8792 DESTINATION HOTEL & RESORTS         GOLD             .09

5 rows selected.
```

Listing 8-30. *Rewriting Listing 8-28 with Mile As the Distance Unit*

```
SQL> col dist format 9.99
SELECT ct.id, ct.name, ct.customer_grade, SDO_NN_DISTANCE(1) dist
FROM competitors comp, customers ct
WHERE comp.id=1
  AND ct.customer_grade='GOLD'
  AND SDO_NN
    (ct.location,  comp.location, 'SDO_BATCH_SIZE=100 UNIT=MILE', 1 )='TRUE'
  AND ROWNUM<=5
ORDER BY ct.id;
```

```
        ID NAME                               CUSTOMER_GRADE  DIST
---------- ---------------------------------- --------------- ----
       809 LINCOLN SUITES                     GOLD             .06
       810 HOTEL LOMBARDY                     GOLD             .18
      6326 HOTEL LOMBARDY                     GOLD             .19
      7821 RENAISSANCE MAYFLOWER HOTEL        GOLD             .18
      8792 DESTINATION HOTEL & RESORTS        GOLD             .09

5 rows selected.
```

Operators for Spatial Interactions (Relationships)

Until now, we have discussed how to identify interesting locations based on their distance to a query location. Next let's look at operators to find locations/geometries that interact with a query geometry. Such operators are used frequently in applications for analysis using buffer zones.

For example, we could precompute quarter-mile to 2-mile buffer zones around existing branch or competitor locations. Say we have constructed quarter-mile buffer zones around competitor locations using the `SDO_GEOM.SDO_BUFFER` function, as shown in Listing 8-31.

■ **Note** We discuss the `SDO_GEOM.SDO_BUFFER` function in detail in Chapter 9.

This function takes the location of each competitor as the first argument and buffers it by 0.25 (the second argument) miles (specified in fourth argument). It takes the tolerance of 0.5 meters as the third argument. Let this buffer region denote the sales region (or *area of influence*) of each competitor. Likewise, we can compute the area of influence (or sale region) of each branch. Listing 8-31 shows the SQL for creating these tables.

Listing 8-31. *Creating the Sales Region (Area of Influence) for Each Competitor/Branch*

```
SQL> CREATE TABLE COMPETITORS_SALES_REGIONS AS
SELECT id, name, SDO_GEOM.SDO_BUFFER
(a.location, 0.25, 0.5, 'UNIT=MILE ARC_TOLERANCE=0.005') geom
FROM competitors a;

SQL> CREATE TABLE SALES_REGIONS AS
SELECT id, name, SDO_GEOM.SDO_BUFFER
(a.location, 0.25, 0.5, 'UNIT=MILE ARC_TOLERANCE=0.005') geom
FROM branches a;
```

Listing 8-32 shows the SQL to create spatial indexes on these tables.

Listing 8-32. *Creating Indexes on Sales Regions of Competitors/Branches*

```
Rem Metadata for Sales_regions table
SQL> INSERT INTO USER_SDO_GEOM_METADATA
SELECT 'SALES_REGIONS','GEOM', DIMINFO, SRID
FROM USER_SDO_GEOM_METADATA
WHERE TABLE_NAME='BRANCHES';

Rem Metadata for Competitors_regions table
SQL> INSERT INTO USER_SDO_GEOM_METADATA
SELECT 'COMPETITORS_SALES_REGIONS','GEOM', DIMINFO, SRID
FROM USER_SDO_GEOM_METADATA
WHERE TABLE_NAME='COMPETITORS';

Rem Index-creation for Sales_regions table
SQL> CREATE INDEX sr_sidx ON sales_regions(geom)
INDEXTYPE IS MDSYS.SPATIAL_INDEX;

Rem Index-creation for Competitors_sales_regions table
SQL> CREATE INDEX cr_sidx ON competitors_sales_regions(geom)
INDEXTYPE IS MDSYS.SPATIAL_INDEX;
```

We can then identify how many customers are inside the buffer regions of each competitor (and target them for explicit promotions). Note that this functionality can also be accomplished by the SDO_WITHIN_DISTANCE operator that you saw in Listing 8-20. However, this buffer region–based approach offers more rigorous analysis, such as how many customers are "inside"; how many, if any, customers are on the border (i.e., exactly at a distance of a quarter-mile); and so on. Note that this supplements all types of analyses in Table 8-1.

Additionally, we can perform analysis using demographic or transportation data such as city and state boundaries, and highway and transportation networks. For instance, we can identify which sales regions intersect each another or city/county/state boundaries, and possibly compute the area of intersection, the number of customers in each such intersection area, and so on (see Chapter 9 for details). This will help in detailed analysis, such as how many customers are from New Hampshire versus how many are from Massachusetts for a specific branch. From among several candidates, we can choose the region with best metrics. This enables the sales region analysis described in Table 8-1.

Figure 8-6 shows an example of a circular buffer zone query Q. A, B, C, D, and E are arbitrarily shaped data geometries. Using the interaction-based operators with Q as the query geometry, we can identify geometries that *intersect* Q (A, C, and D), that are *inside* Q (A), and that *touch* Q (C).

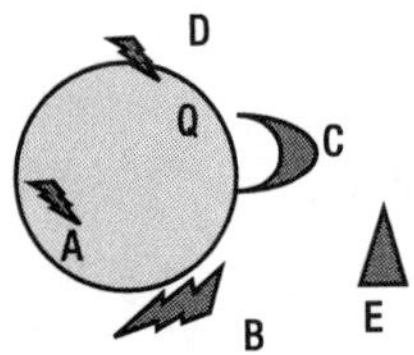

Figure 8-6. *Arbitrarily shaped data geometries (A, B, C, D, and E) are shown in black. A circular query geometry (Q) is shown in gray.*

There are two primary spatial operators for such interaction detection. Like the SDO_NN and SDO_WITHIN_DISTANCE operators, these operators are evaluated using the index-based model of Figure 8-3 and use the syntax of Listing 8-18.

- SDO_FILTER: This operator identifies all geometries whose MBRs intersect with the MBR of a query geometry. This operator primarily uses the spatial index without invoking a Geometry Engine function.
- SDO_RELATE: This operator identifies all geometries that interact in a specified manner with a query geometry. The specified type of interaction could involve intersection, touching the boundaries, being completely inside, etc.
- SDO_ANYINTERACT, SDO_CONTAINS, SDO_COVERS, SDO_COVEREDBY, SDO_EQUAL, SDO_INSIDE, SDO_ON, SDO_OVERLAPS, and SDO_TOUCH: These operators are simplified variants of the SDO_RELATE operator for specific types of interactions. Instead of specifying the SDO_RELATE operator with an appropriate parameter to identify a specific relationship, you can directly use the corresponding simplified variant.

Next, we examine each of these operators in further detail.

SDO_FILTER Operator

The SDO_FILTER operator identifies all rows of a table where the MBRs of the column geometry intersect with the MBR of a specified query geometry. This operator always returns a superset of results for other interaction-based operators. In that sense, this operator is an approximation of other interaction-based operators.

Figure 8-7 shows how the SDO_FILTER operator evaluates for the data of Figure 8-6. It computes the MBRs around the data and the query geometries. It returns the data geometries A, B, C, and D as the result, as their MBRs intersect the MBR of the circular query Q.

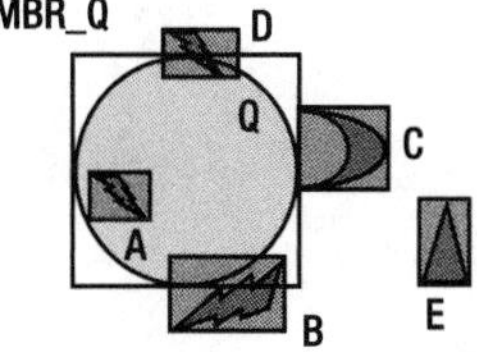

Figure 8-7. *In* SDO_FILTER, *the MBRs of data/query geometries are compared.*

The SDO_FILTER operator has the following syntax:

```
SDO_FILTER
(
  table_geometry        IN SDO_GEOMETRY,
  query_geometry        IN SDO_GEOMETRY
  [, parameter_string   IN VARCHAR2 ]
)
= 'TRUE'
```

where

- table_geometry is the column name of the table whose spatial index is to be used.
- query_geometry is the query location. This could be a column of another table or a bind variable.
- parameter_string is always set to querytype=window. This parameter is optional (as indicated by the enclosing square brackets in the preceding syntax) and can be safely omitted in Oracle 10*g*. However, in prior releases, this parameter is mandatory.

Listing 8-33 shows the use of the SDO_FILTER operator to identify all customers within a competitor's area of influence. Note that this query may return more customers than those that actually fall within a competitor's service area.

Listing 8-33. SDO_FILTER *Operator Retrieving All Customers Within a Competitor's Service Area*

```
SQL> SELECT  ct.id, ct.name
FROM competitors_regions comp, customers ct
WHERE comp.id=1
  AND SDO_FILTER(ct.location,  comp.geom)='TRUE'
ORDER BY ct.id;
```

```
        ID NAME
---------- -----------------------------------
        25 BLAKE CONSTRUCTION
        28 COLONIAL PARKING
        34 HEWLETT-PACKARD DC GOV AFFAIRS
        38 KIPLINGER WASHINGTON EDITORS
        41 MCGREGOR PRINTING
        42 MCI COMMUNICATIONS
        48 POTOMAC ELECTRIC POWER
        50 SMITH HINCHMAN AND GRYLLS
       270 METRO-FARRAGUT NORTH STATION
       271 METRO-FARRAGUT WEST STATION
       468 SAFEWAY
       809 LINCOLN SUITES
       810 HOTEL LOMBARDY
      1044 MUSEUM OF THE THIRD DIMENSION
      1081 GEORGE WASHINGTON UNIVERSITY
      1178 AVIS RENT-A-CAR
      1526 INTERNATIONAL FINANCE
      1538 MCKENNA AND CUNEO
      1901 CLUB QUARTERS WASHINGTON
      2195 STEVENS ELEMENTARY SCHOOL
      6326 HOTEL LOMBARDY
      7387 ELLIPSE
      7754 EXECUTIVE INN
      7762 PHILLIPS 66
      7789 SEVEN BUILDINGS
      7821 RENAISSANCE MAYFLOWER HOTEL
      8138 ST GREGORY HOTEL
      8382 EXXON
      8792 DESTINATION HOTEL & RESORTS
      8793 LOEWS HOTELS REGIONAL

30 rows selected.
```

In general, the SDO_FILTER operator returns more candidates—30 rows in Listing 8-33—than those that actually intersect a query geometry (23 rows, as you will see in Listing 8-35). Why would anyone use this operator? The reasons are it is very fast (compared to other spatial operators) and it does prune a majority of the geometries (except the 30 returned out of 3,100+ rows) in the customers table that do not fall in the neighborhood of the query geometry. In that sense, the SDO_FILTER operator works as a fast approximation of other interaction-detecting operators such as SDO_RELATE.

Applications such as map visualizers, which can tolerate such approximations in the result set, use the SDO_FILTER operator to render maps. A typical query from Oracle MapViewer would look like Listing 8-34.

Listing 8-34. *Typical Query from MapViewer Using the* `SDO_FILTER` *Operator*

```
SELECT location
FROM customers
WHERE SDO_FILTER
  (
  location,
  SDO_GEOMETRY
  (
    2003, 8307, null,
    SDO_ELEM_INFO_ARRAY(1, 1003, 3),  -- Rectangle query window
    SDO_ORDINATE_ARRAY(-122.43886,37.78284,-122.427195,37.79284)
  )
) = 'TRUE';
```

Typically, the query window in such map-rendering applications would be a rectangle corresponding to the window displayed on the screen. This window will be modified as the user navigates (e.g., zooms in and out, and pans) on the map.

■ **Tip** Unlike all other operators, which work only for two-dimensional geometries, `SDO_FILTER` can work with two-, three-, and four-dimensional geometries. The index can be set to three- or four-dimensional by setting the `SDO_INDX_DIMS` parameter in the `CREATE INDEX` statement (see Listing 8-14).

SDO_RELATE Operator

As shown earlier in Figure 8-7, not all objects returned by the `SDO_FILTER` operator intersect with the query geometry Q (e.g., object B). The `SDO_FILTER` operator always returns the exact result set and possibly more geometries (a superset). How do you find geometries that interact with the query in a specified manner? The `SDO_RELATE` operator provides this functionality.

For example, as shown in Figure 8-6, we can specify the interaction to be `ANYINTERACT` (intersection), and the `SDO_RELATE` operator will return A, C, and D. If we specify the interaction to be `INSIDE`, it returns A. If we specify the interaction to be `TOUCH`, it returns C. In general, the `SDO_RELATE` operator has the following syntax. Note that the `SDO_RELATE` operator, as with other spatial operators, should be compared to the string `'TRUE'`.

```
SDO_RELATE
(
  table_geometry      IN SDO_GEOMETRY,
  query_geometry      IN SDO_GEOMETRY,
  parameter_string    IN VARCHAR2
)
= 'TRUE'
```

where

- `table_geometry` is the column name of the table whose spatial index is to be used.
- `query_geometry` is the query location. This could be a column of another table or a bind variable.
- `parameter_string` is set to `'querytype=window MASK=<interaction-type>'`. The `SDO_RELATE` operator is true if `table_geometry` has an `<interaction-type>` relation with `query_geometry` (the query). The `interaction-type` or `mask-type` could be one of several types, which we discuss next.

Before we describe the different interactions for an `SDO_RELATE` operator, you should understand what constitutes a geometry. Every geometry is composed of three parts:

- *Boundary*: This is the outer border for the geometry. Figure 8-8 shows the boundary in solid black for different types of geometries. For a point geometry, there is only a boundary point. For a line-string geometry, the two endpoints are the boundary. For a polygon (with or without voids), the rings forming the polygon are the boundary.
- *Interior*: Everything in the geometry inside the boundaries is considered interior. This is shown in gray in Figure 8-8.
- *Exterior*: This is everything outside the geometry. This is implicitly white in Figure 8-8.

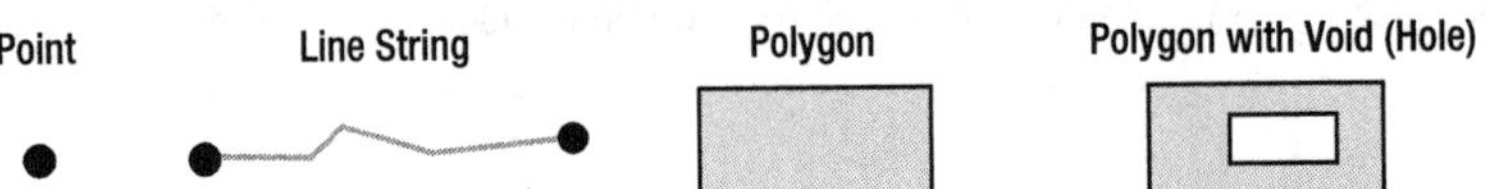

Figure 8-8. *The boundary is solid black and the interior is gray for different types of geometries.*

Interactions in SDO_RELATE

Now that you understand the interior and boundary parts of geometries, we'll resume our discussion on the different interaction types for the `SDO_RELATE` operator. These interactions are illustrated in Figure 8-9. The two geometries Q and A in Figure 8-9 correspond to `query_geometry` and `table_geometry`, respectively, in the preceding signature for `SDO_RELATE`.

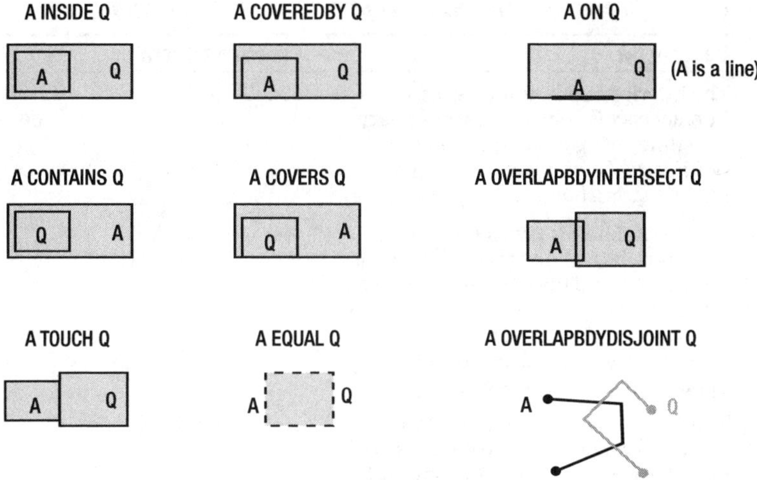

Figure 8-9. *Interactions between a data geometry A and a query geometry Q for* `SDO_RELATE` *operator*

The different relationships/interactions between Q and A are due to different interactions between the interior and boundary of one geometry with those of the other. Note that each of these interactions has an equivalent simplified operator. You can use either the `SDO_RELATE` operator with the appropriate mask specification or the corresponding simplified operator in your queries, as shown in Table 8-2. Like all other operators, the `SDO_RELATE` and equivalent simplified operators need to be evaluated to the string `'TRUE'`.

Table 8-2. *Names, Semantics, and Operators of the Interactions in Figure 8-9*

Interaction	Description	Simplified Operator
`INSIDE`	This interaction holds if the boundary and interior of geometry A (data geometries) are inside the interior of the query Q. In Figure 8-5, geometry A is *inside* query Q.	`SDO_INSIDE` (A, Q)
`CONTAINS`	This holds if the boundary and interior of Q are inside the interior of A (data geometry). This relationship is the reverse of `INSIDE` (i.e., if A is inside Q, then Q contains A).	`SDO_CONTAINS` (Q, A)
`COVEREDBY`	A is `COVEREDBY` Q if the interior and boundary of A (data geometries) are inside the interior of Q (query), except that the boundaries overlap.	`SDO_COVEREDBY` (A, Q)

(continued)

Table 8-2. *Names, Semantics, and Operators of the Interactions in Figure 8-9 (continued)*

Interaction	Description	Simplified Operator
ON	The interior and boundaries of A interact exclusively with the boundary of Q (line string completely on the boundary of a polygon). Note that A is a line string here.	SDO_ON (A, Q)
COVERS	This interaction is true if the interior and boundary of query Q is inside the interior of A and the boundaries overlap. This is the reverse of COVEREDBY (i.e., if Q is covered by A, then A covers Q). Alternatively, you can use the following operator for the same semantics.	SDO_COVERS (A, Q)
TOUCH	This holds if the boundaries of two geometries touch, but the interiors do not intersect. In Figure 8-5, geometry C *touches* query Q.	SDO_TOUCH (C, Q)
OVERLAPBDYINTERSECT	This holds if the boundaries and interiors of A and query Q intersect.	SDO_OVERLAPBDYINTERSECT (A, Q)
OVERLAPBDYDISJOINT	This holds if the interior of one intersects the interior and boundary of the other, but the two boundaries do not intersect.	SDO_OVERLAPBDYDISJOINT (A, Q)
EQUAL	This holds if the interior and boundary of A exactly match those of Q.	SDO_EQUAL (A, Q)
ANYINTERACT	This interaction is true if either the boundary or interior of A intersects with the boundary or interior of Q. In other words, if there is any intersection between the two geometries (i.e., any of the previous interactions are true). In Figure 8-5, geometries A, C, and D have an ANYINTERACT relation with query Q.	SDO_ANYINTERACT(A, Q)

SQL/MM (where *MM* stands for multimedia) is the *extended* standard for specifying spatial and multimedia operators in SQL statements. This standard specifies a standard set of query relationships that start with the prefix ST. Table 8-3 shows the SQL/MM relationships (ISO IEC 13249) and the corresponding masks in Oracle Spatial.

Table 8-3. *SQL/MM Spatial Relationship and the Equivalent Oracle Spatial Mask*

SQL/MM Relationship	Oracle Spatial SDO_RELATE Relationship Mask
ST_Contains	CONTAINS+COVERS
ST_Within	INSIDE+COVEREDBY
ST_Overlaps	OVERLAPBDYDISJOINT
ST_Crosses	OVERLAPBDYINTERSECT

SQL/MM Relationship	Oracle Spatial SDO_RELATE Relationship Mask
ST_Intersects	ANYINTERACT
ST_Touches	TOUCH
ST_Equals	EQUAL
ST_Disjoint	Negation of ANYINTERACT (use MINUS to subtract ANYINTERACT results from the entire set)

Now that we've covered the different spatial relationships determined by the SDO_RELATE operator (or the equivalent simplified operators), we'll move on to describe how to use this operator to perform customer analysis and sales region analysis, as described in Table 8-1.

First, we'll use the SDO_RELATE operator for customer analysis. We'll identify all customers *inside* or *on the boundary of* the buffer zones of each competitor store using the ANYINTERACT interaction mask. Listing 8-35 shows the SQL for a specific competitor (id=1).

Listing 8-35. SDO_RELATE *Operator Retrieving All Customers in a Quarter-Mile Buffer Zone of a Competitor Store*

```
SQL> SELECT  ct.id, ct.name
FROM competitors_sales_regions comp, customers ct
WHERE comp.id=1
  AND SDO_RELATE(ct.location,  comp.geom, 'MASK=ANYINTERACT ' )='TRUE'
ORDER BY ct.id;

        ID NAME
---------- -----------------------------------
        25 BLAKE CONSTRUCTION
        28 COLONIAL PARKING
        34 HEWLETT-PACKARD DC GOV AFFAIRS
        41 MCGREGOR PRINTING
        48 POTOMAC ELECTRIC POWER
        50 SMITH HINCHMAN AND GRYLLS
       270 METRO-FARRAGUT NORTH STATION
       271 METRO-FARRAGUT WEST STATION
       468 SAFEWAY
       809 LINCOLN SUITES
       810 HOTEL LOMBARDY
      1044 MUSEUM OF THE THIRD DIMENSION
      1526 INTERNATIONAL FINANCE
      1538 MCKENNA AND CUNEO
      2195 STEVENS ELEMENTARY SCHOOL
      6326 HOTEL LOMBARDY
      7754 EXECUTIVE INN
      7762 PHILLIPS 66
      7789 SEVEN BUILDINGS
      7821 RENAISSANCE MAYFLOWER HOTEL
```

```
     8138 ST GREGORY HOTEL
     8382 EXXON
     8792 DESTINATION HOTEL & RESORTS

23 rows selected.
```

To identify the DISJOINT relationship, use *negation* of ANYINTERACT (i.e., subtract the results of ANYINTERACT from the entire set). Listing 8-36 shows the SQL to identify all customers that are disjoint from competitor region (id=1):

Listing 8-36. *Identifying a DISJOINT relationship*

```
SELECT  ct.id, ct.name
FROM  customers ct
WHERE ct.rowid NOT IN
(
  SELECT ct.rowid
  FROM competitors_sales_regions comp, customers ct
  WHERE comp.id=1
    AND SDO_RELATE(ct.location, comp.geom, 'MASK=ANYINTERACT')='TRUE'
);
```

Note that Listing 8-35 is the exact equivalent of Listing 8-20, except it executes a little slower than Listing 8-20. In general, the following tip should be useful.

■ **Tip** Specifying the ANYINTERACT mask in an SDO_RELATE query (with buffered regions) as in Listing 8-35 is equivalent to Listing 8-20 with the SDO_WITHIN_DISTANCE operator. The question that arises is which usage is better and when. The solution is to use SDO_WITHIN_DISTANCE wherever possible. The SDO_WITHIN_DISTANCE operator, in most cases, will be faster since it prunes based on distance rather than trying to check if a customer is inside, as in SDO_RELATE.

The next question to ask is when the SDO_RELATE operator is useful. The SDO_RELATE operator offers much more power than the SDO_WITHIN_DISTANCE operator. Instead of specifying the ANYINTERACT relationship, you can specify a variety of other relationships such as INSIDE, TOUCH, OVERLAPBDYDISJOINT, and so on. These relationships are especially useful while performing analysis with nonpoint data that occur in geographic datasets such as the us_states or us_counties table. We referred to such analysis as “sales region analysis” in Table 8-1.

For instance, we can analyze the influence of our competitors inside and outside the District of Columbia (D.C.) region. Some competitor branches extend their area of influence to neighboring states. First, we’ll look at how many competitor regions intersect the D.C. region. Listing 8-37 shows an example.

Listing 8-37. SDO_RELATE *Operator Identifying All Competitors in the D.C. Region*

```
SQL> SELECT COUNT(*)
FROM us_states st, competitors_sales_regions comp
WHERE st.state_abrv='DC'
  AND SDO_RELATE(comp.geom,  st.geom, 'MASK=ANYINTERACT ' )='TRUE';
  COUNT(*)
----------
       286

1 row selected.
```

Not all of these competitors sales regions are inside D.C. To get the competitors whose influence is completely inside the D.C. area, we should use the SDO_RELATE operator with the INSIDE relationship. Listing 8-38 shows the SQL.

Listing 8-38. SDO_RELATE *Operator Identifying All Competitors Inside the D.C. Region*

```
SQL> SELECT COUNT(*)
FROM us_states st, competitors_sales_regions comp
WHERE st.state_abrv='DC'
  AND SDO_RELATE(comp.geom,  st.geom, 'MASK=INSIDE ' )='TRUE';

  COUNT(*)
----------
       268

1 row selected.
```

For those competitors whose influence extends beyond but also overlaps the D.C. area, we should use the SDO_RELATE operator with the OVERLAPBDYINTERSECT relationship. Listing 8-39 shows the corresponding SQL.

Listing 8-39. SDO_RELATE *Operator Identifying All Competitors That Overlap the D.C. Region*

```
SQL> SELECT COUNT(*)
FROM us_states st, competitors_sales_regions comp
WHERE st.state_abrv='DC'
  AND SDO_RELATE(comp.geom,  st.geom, 'MASK=OVERLAPBDYINTERSECT ' )='TRUE'  ;
  COUNT(*)
----------
        18

1 row selected.
```

From the examples in Listings 8-37 to 8-39, we note that there are 286 competitor regions in the D.C. area, of which 268 are completely inside and 18 overlap. We could use this analysis to target the 18 competitors and the customers in their area of influence as we pursue business expansion outside the D.C. area. Within D.C., we can target the 268 competitor regions.

■ Caution In general, if the underlying tolerance associated with a table in the `USER_SDO_GEOM_METADATA` view is modified, some of the relationships may change. For instance, a `TOUCH` relationship may become `DISJOINT`. Always set the tolerance value to suit your application (see related discussion in Chapter 3).

Next, we will analyze which sales regions overlap. After identifying such sales regions, we can possibly merge the corresponding branches if the overlap is significant. To this end, we will identify all sales regions that overlap or touch the sales region of a specific branch (`id=51`). We can perform similar analysis for other branches. Instead of specifying multiple masks, we can perform this analysis using the `ANYINTERACT` mask in `SDO_RELATE`. Listing 8-40 shows the SQL to identify all sales regions that intersect a specified sales region.

Listing 8-40. *Identifying Sales Regions That Intersect a Specific Sales Region (*`id=51`*)*

```
SQL> SELECT a.id
FROM sales_regions b, sales_regions a
WHERE b.id=51
  AND a.id <> 51
  AND SDO_RELATE(a.geom,  b.geom, 'MASK=ANYINTERACT' )='TRUE';

     A.ID
----------
        63
        54
        72
        69
        43
        66
        50
        75
        76

9 rows selected.
```

■ Tip In Oracle, specifying `ANYINTERACT` in `SDO_RELATE` (or using `SDO_ANYINTERACT`) is recommended over specifying `SDO_RELATE` with the equivalent combination of multiple masks. Oracle optimizes the processing for the `ANYINTERACT` mask.

Multiple Masks in SDO_RELATE

Before considering merging the sales regions returned in Listing 8-40 with the query sales region (`id=51`), we should do further analysis to determine how many of these sales regions are "touching" and how many are "overlapping" the query sales region (`id=51`). (Note that they won't be inside or contain the query region, as all sales regions are of the same size—that is, they're constructed using quarter-mile radius buffers.) We can determine the exact relationship by using the `SDO_GEOM.RELATE` function that we discuss in Chapter 9. Here, we describe an alternate approach using just the `SDO_RELATE` operator and appropriate masks to determine the type of intersection.

First, we will see how many sales regions *overlap* the query sales region (`id=51`). This involves specifying two masks, `OVERLAPBDYDISJOINT` and `OVERLAPBDYINTERSECT`, in the `parameter_string` of the `SDO_RELATE` operator. We can combine multiple such masks using a plus sign (+) in the mask specification. Listing 8-41 shows an example.

Listing 8-41. *Identifying All Sales Regions That Overlap a Specific Sales Region (*`id=51`*)*

```
SQL> SELECT a.id
FROM sales_regions b, sales_regions a
WHERE b.id=51
  AND a.id <> 51
  AND SDO_RELATE
  (a.geom,  b.geom, 'MASK=OVERLAPBDYDISJOINT+OVERLAPBDYINTERSECT')='TRUE' ;
        ID
----------
        63
        54
        72
        69
        43
        66
        50
        75

8 rows selected.
```

Note that only eight out of the nine returned in Listing 8-40 are overlapping. This means the other region, which intersected the query sales region (`id=51`), was actually "touching" it. We can verify this using the query in Listing 8-42.

Listing 8-42. *Verifying That a Sales Region Touches Another Sales Region (*`id=51`*)*

```
SQL> SELECT a.id
FROM sales_regions b, sales_regions a
WHERE b.id=51
  AND a.id <> 51
  AND SDO_RELATE(a.geom, b.geom, 'MASK=TOUCH' )='TRUE' ;
        ID
----------
        76
```

Another very useful combination is that of the INSIDE and COVEREDBY masks. For instance, we can use the INSIDE+COVEREDBY mask in Listing 8-38 instead of just the INSIDE mask. This will retrieve all sales regions of competitors that are inside and may also touch the border of the D.C. boundary.

■ **Tip** In Oracle, the combination of INSIDE and COVEREDBY is optimized. The combination of CONTAINS and COVERS is also optimized.

Together with the SDO_FILTER operator, the SDO_RELATE operator provides a rich set of functionality for use in a wide variety of applications. Whereas the SDO_NN and SDO_WITHIN_DISTANCE operators provide simple and easy-to-use distance-based analysis, the SDO_RELATE operator provides a detailed analysis of query geometry-data geometry relationships.

Tuning Parameter for SDO_RELATE on Non-geodetic Data Tables

During the evaluation of an SDO_RELATE query on non-geodetic data, an R-tree index in Oracle Spatial uses the MBR of the query to internally compute tiles (by recursively subdividing the MBR) that cover the query geometry (in that sense, the R-tree of Oracle Spatial is much different from the ones published in research literature[2]). It then uses the tiles to eliminate candidate data geometries without performing the expensive secondary filter (Geometry Engine) operations (see Figure 8-3). The user does not have to do anything to invoke this optimization. The R-tree automatically invokes this optimization. However, for some query geometries, there may be a need for fine-tuning. Figure 8-10 shows an example.

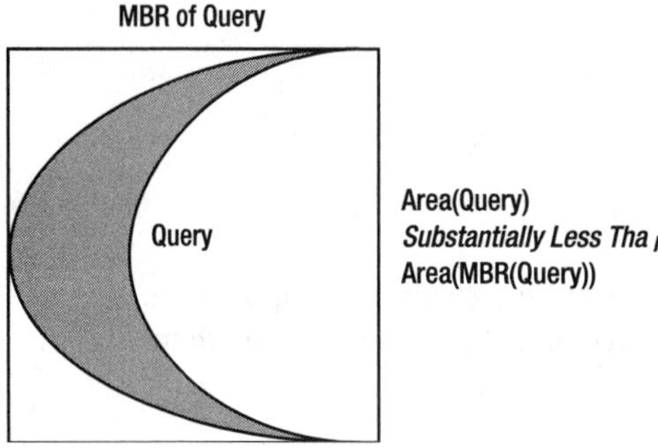

Figure 8-10. *Example of a query geometry*

---

2. For an overview of the Oracle R-tree, see Ravikanth V. Kothuri and Siva Ravada. "Efficient Processing of Large Spatial Queries Using Interior Approximations." Proceedings of the 7th International Symposium on Spatial and Temporal Databases (SSTD), 2001.

Consider the query geometry in Figure 8-10. The area of the query geometry is substantially (say 75 percent) less than the area of the MBR for the query geometry. In this case, specifying SDO_LEVEL=6 in the parameter_string of the SDO_RELATE operator may improve the response time for this operator. This is due to the elimination of more data prior to the expensive secondary filter. Note that we should not specify the SDO_LEVEL as 7 or higher, as this is likely to degrade the performance due to an increase in the cost of tile generation. Listing 8-43 shows an example that adds the tuning parameter to Listing 8-38.

Listing 8-43. *Adding the* SDO_LEVEL=6 *Parameter to an* SDO_RELATE *Query*

```
SQL> SELECT COUNT(*)
FROM  us_states st, competitors_sales_regions comp
WHERE st.state_abrv='DC'
  AND SDO_RELATE(comp.geom,  st.geom, 'MASK=INSIDE SDO_LEVEL=6' )='TRUE'  ;
```

Hints for Spatial Operators

Recall that during our discussion on operator evaluation, we noted that the optimizer may not choose the spatial index. This might happen when the spatial operator is used in conjunction with other nonspatial operators (on the same table) or in a multitable join. Oracle Spatial does not provide cost and selectivity estimates for spatial operators that are comparable to other operators in SQL. As a result, the choice made by the optimizer to use or not to use the spatial index may be incorrect. Specifying explicit hints will ensure an appropriate execution plan. In this section, we look at specific cases where you may need appropriate hints and how to specify these hints.

To determine whether or not a spatial operator is evaluated using the spatial index, we can trace the execution plan for the SQL statement involving the operator. Before tracing, we first have to load the utlxplan package (once). We can then use SET AUTOTRACE ON to view the execution plan output (see the *Oracle Reference* for more information). Alternatively, we can use the EXPLAIN PLAN statement. Listing 8-44 illustrates this with an example.

Listing 8-44. *Explaining the Execution Plan for a SQL Statement*

```
SQL> @$ORACLE_HOME/rdbms/admin/utlxplan  -- Load only once
SQL> SET AUTOTRACE ON
SQL> SELECT ct.id
FROM  customers ct
WHERE SDO_WITHIN_DISTANCE
(
  ct.location,
  ( SELECT location FROM competitors WHERE id=1),
  'DISTANCE=0.25 UNIT=MILE '
)='TRUE' ;
```

The plan looks like the following:

```
Execution Plan
----------------------------------------------------------
   0      SELECT STATEMENT Optimizer=ALL_ROWS (Cost=5 Card=4 Bytes=153
          56)

   1    0   TABLE ACCESS (BY INDEX ROWID) OF 'CUSTOMERS' (TABLE) (Cost
          =3 Card=4 Bytes=15356)

   2    1     DOMAIN INDEX OF 'CUSTOMERS_SIDX' (INDEX (DOMAIN))
   3    2       TABLE ACCESS (BY INDEX ROWID) OF 'COMPETITORS' (TABLE)
           (Cost=2 Card=1 Bytes=3832)

   4    3         INDEX (RANGE SCAN) OF 'COMPETITORS_ID' (INDEX) (Cost
          =1 Card=1)
```

If you see a statement like `DOMAIN INDEX of <index_name>`, it means the optimizer is using the spatial index referred to by `<index_name>`. The spatial index and other non-native indexes like the context index are referred to as *domain indexes* in Oracle. In most cases, you do not have to specify any hints—the optimizer automatically picks the spatial domain index whenever it sees a spatial operator. However, there are exceptions:

- When the SQL has multiple predicates on the same table
- When the SQL has multiple tables being joined

Let's look at each of these cases and how the `NO_INDEX`, `ORDERED`, and `INDEX` hints can help.

Spatial Operator with Other Predicates on the Same Table

Say the spatial operator is not an `SDO_NN` operator—that is, the operator is, for instance, an `SDO_WITHIN_DISTANCE` operator. You do not have to do anything here. Otherwise, if the SQL has an `SDO_NN` operator and one or more additional nonspatial predicates such as `customer_grade='GOLD'` on the same table, you may need to specify explicit hints. Let's look at this in detail in the following section.

Spatial Operator Is an SDO_NN Operator

Consider the examples in Listings 8-24, 8-25, and 8-28. Here we want to identify the five nearest customers whose grade is `GOLD`. (Note that we cannot use the `SDO_NUM_RES=5` parameter, as in Listing 8-26 or 8-27, to answer this query correctly because that query will return the five nearest customers, of which two are not `GOLD` customers. In effect, it returns only three `GOLD` customers instead of the required five.) Listings 8-24, 8-25, and 8-28 answer the query correctly and return the customers in order of their distance to the query. Listing 8-45 repeats the SQL in Listing 8-28 for ease of reference.

Listing 8-45. SDO_NN *Operator Retrieving the Five* GOLD *Customers Nearest to a Specific Competitor Along with Their Distances*

```
SQL> col dist format 999
SELECT ct.id, ct.customer_grade, SDO_NN_DISTANCE(1) dist
FROM competitors comp, customers ct
WHERE comp.id=1
  AND ct.customer_grade='GOLD'
  AND SDO_NN(ct.location,  comp.location, 'SDO_BATCH_SIZE=100', 1  )='TRUE'
  AND ROWNUM<=5
ORDER BY ct.id;

        ID     CUSTOMER_GRADE           DIST
----------     ---------------          ----
       809     GOLD                     95
       810     GOLD                     286
      7821     GOLD                     295
      6326     GOLD                     301
      8792     GOLD                     146

5 rows selected.
```

The query works fine as long as there is no index on the customer_grade column (i.e., on the column involved in the *equality* predicate). Now, say we have created an index on the customer_grade column of the customers table. Then we re-execute the example in Listing 8-45, as shown in Listing 8-46.

Listing 8-46. *Creating an Index on* customer_grade *and Rerunning Listing 8-45*

```
SQL> CREATE INDEX cust_grade ON customers(customer_grade);
SQL> col dist format 9999
SELECT ct.id, ct.name, SDO_NN_DISTANCE(1) dist
FROM competitors comp, customers ct
WHERE comp.id=1
  AND ct.customer_grade='GOLD'
  AND SDO_NN(ct.location,  comp.location, 'SDO_BATCH_SIZE=100', 1  )='TRUE'
  AND ROWNUM<=5
ORDER BY ct.id;

        ID      CUSTOMER_GRADE          DIST
  ---------- ---------------          ----------
      1154     GOLD                   545
      1155     GOLD                   3072
      1157     GOLD                   860
      1158     GOLD                   792
      1159     GOLD                   1068

5 rows selected.
```

```
Execution Plan
----------------------------------------------------------
   0      SELECT STATEMENT Optimizer=ALL_ROWS (Cost=8 Card=2 Bytes=153
          60)

   1    0   COUNT (STOPKEY)
   2    1     TABLE ACCESS (BY INDEX ROWID) OF 'CUSTOMERS' (TABLE) (Co
          st=8 Card=2 Bytes=7696)

   3    2       NESTED LOOPS (Cost=8 Card=2 Bytes=15360)
   4    3         TABLE ACCESS (BY INDEX ROWID) OF 'COMPETITORS' (TABL
          E) (Cost=2 Card=1 Bytes=3832)

   5    4           INDEX (RANGE SCAN) OF 'COMPETITORS_ID' (INDEX) (Co
          st=1 Card=1)

   6    3         BITMAP CONVERSION (TO ROWIDS)
   7    6           BITMAP AND
   8    7             BITMAP CONVERSION (FROM ROWIDS)
   9    8               INDEX (RANGE SCAN) OF 'CUST_GRADE' (INDEX) (Co
          st=0)

  10    7             BITMAP CONVERSION (FROM ROWIDS)
  11   10               SORT (ORDER BY)
  12   11                 DOMAIN INDEX OF 'CUSTOMERS_SIDX' (INDEX (DOM
          AIN))
```

Listing 8-46 gives incorrect results (in fact, it may give different results at different times too). This erroneous behavior happens for the following reason: the SDO_NN returns, say, the 100 nearest neighbors in order of their distance to query geometry. The order, however, is lost when they are bitmap-merged with the results of the B-tree index on `customer_grade`. This behavior is documented in the *Oracle Spatial User's Guide*.

The preceding erroneous behavior can be avoided by ensuring the following hints in the sidebar titled "Hints for the SDO_NN Operator."

HINTS FOR THE SDO_NN OPERATOR

Here are some hints for the optimizer to ensure correct execution of SDO_NN:

- Force the optimizer to use the associated spatial index for the SDO_NN operator. This is required because the SDO_NN operator is actually a distance-ordering operator and cannot be evaluated (in current releases) without the spatial index (an Oracle error ORA-13249 will be raised if index is not chosen).
- Force the optimizer to *not use* indexes on other predicates on the same table as the SDO_NN operator operates on. (Otherwise, it may return incorrect results, as shown in Listing 8-46.)

We can rewrite Listing 8-46 as shown in Listing 8-47 to ensure the preceding two criteria are satisfied. Specify the INDEX/NO_INDEX hints with the table alias (or table name) as the first argument and the index name as the second. Listing 8-47 executes correctly and returns the customers in distance order. Note that these results are identical to those of Listing 8-45 (or Listing 8-28).

Listing 8-47. *Usage of Hints with* SDO_NN *and Other Operators on the Same Table*

```
SQL> SELECT /*+ NO_INDEX(ct cust_grade) INDEX(ct customers_sidx) */
ct.id, ct.customer_grade, SDO_NN_DISTANCE(1) dist  FROM
competitors comp, customers ct
WHERE comp.id=1
  AND ct.customer_grade='GOLD'
  AND SDO_NN(ct.location,  comp.location, 'SDO_BATCH_SIZE=100', 1  )='TRUE'
  AND ROWNUM<=5
ORDER BY ct.id;
        ID      CUSTOMER_GRADE             DIST
----------      ---------------            ----
       809      GOLD                       95
       810      GOLD                       286
      7821      GOLD                       295
      6326      GOLD                       301
      8792      GOLD                       146

5 rows selected.

Execution Plan
----------------------------------------------------------
   0       SELECT STATEMENT Optimizer=ALL_ROWS (Cost=7 Card=2 Bytes=153
           60)

   1    0    COUNT (STOPKEY)
   2    1      NESTED LOOPS (Cost=7 Card=2 Bytes=15360)
   3    2        TABLE ACCESS (BY INDEX ROWID) OF 'COMPETITORS' (TABLE)
            (Cost=2 Card=1 Bytes=3832)

   4    3          INDEX (RANGE SCAN) OF 'COMPETITORS_ID' (INDEX) (Cost
           =1 Card=1)

   5    2        TABLE ACCESS (BY INDEX ROWID) OF 'CUSTOMERS' (TABLE) (
           Cost=7 Card=2 Bytes=7696)

   6    5          DOMAIN INDEX OF 'CUSTOMERS_SIDX' (INDEX (DOMAIN))
```

Spatial Operator with Multiple Tables in a SQL Statement

If the operator is an SDO_NN operator, the criteria and hints in the sidebar titled "Hints for the SDO_NN Operator" should be applied. In addition, the following general guidelines apply for all spatial operators.

When a SQL statement has more than one table, the optimizer may or may not choose the spatial index. If we want the spatial index to be used (for performance reasons), we should specify the table whose spatial index is to be used as the *inner* table. We can enforce this by specifying this table to be the last in the FROM clause of the SELECT statement and specifying the ORDERED hint. Listing 8-48 shows the usage with the customers and competitors tables. Note that we want to use the spatial index on the customers table, so we specify it as the inner table (i.e., the last table in the FROM clause).

Listing 8-48. *Spatial Operator with Multiple Hints in a SQL Statement with Two Tables*

```
SQL>  SELECT /*+ ORDERED */ ct.id, ct.name
FROM competitors comp, customers ct
WHERE comp.id=1
  AND SDO_WITHIN_DISTANCE
  (ct.location, comp.location, 'DISTANCE=0.25 UNIT=MILE ' )='TRUE'
ORDER BY ct.id ;
        ID NAME
---------- -----------------------------------
        25 BLAKE CONSTRUCTION
        28 COLONIAL PARKING
        34 HEWLETT-PACKARD DC GOV AFFAIRS
        41 MCGREGOR PRINTING
        48 POTOMAC ELECTRIC POWER
        50 SMITH HINCHMAN AND GRYLLS
       270 METRO-FARRAGUT NORTH STATION
       271 METRO-FARRAGUT WEST STATION
       468 SAFEWAY
       809 LINCOLN SUITES
       810 HOTEL LOMBARDY
      1044 MUSEUM OF THE THIRD DIMENSION
      1526 INTERNATIONAL FINANCE
      1538 MCKENNA AND CUNEO
      2195 STEVENS ELEMENTARY SCHOOL
      6326 HOTEL LOMBARDY
      7754 EXECUTIVE INN
      7762 PHILLIPS 66
      7789 SEVEN BUILDINGS
      7821 RENAISSANCE MAYFLOWER HOTEL
      8138 ST GREGORY HOTEL
      8382 EXXON
      8792 DESTINATION HOTEL & RESORTS
23 rows selected.
```

```
Execution Plan
----------------------------------------------------------
   0      SELECT STATEMENT Optimizer=ALL_ROWS (Cost=5 Card=32 Bytes=92
          48)

   1    0   SORT (ORDER BY) (Cost=5 Card=32 Bytes=9248)
   2    1     NESTED LOOPS (Cost=4 Card=32 Bytes=9248)
   3    2       TABLE ACCESS (BY INDEX ROWID) OF 'COMPETITORS' (TABLE)
           (Cost=2 Card=1 Bytes=137)

   4    3         INDEX (UNIQUE SCAN) OF 'COMPETITORS_PK' (INDEX (UNIQ
          UE)) (Cost=1 Card=1)

   5    2       TABLE ACCESS (BY INDEX ROWID) OF 'CUSTOMERS' (TABLE) (
          Cost=4 Card=32 Bytes=4864)

   6    5         DOMAIN INDEX OF 'CUSTOMERS_SIDX' (INDEX (DOMAIN))
```

Note the order of the tables in Listing 8-48. The customers table, whose index needs to be used, is specified last (i.e., as the *inner* table). In general, if the first argument of the spatial_operator is from table A, and the second is from table B, always ensure that table B precedes table A in the FROM clause of the SQL statement. The ORDERED hint, in such a SQL, informs the optimizer to use table B as the *outer* table and table A as the *inner* table.

You can generalize the preceding guidelines and specify the ORDERED, INDEX, and/or NO_INDEX hints in a SQL with multiple tables or multiple *indexed* operators (domain index, B-tree, bitmap, IOT operators) to ensure an appropriate execution.

Advanced Spatial Index Features

In this section, we cover some advanced spatial indexing features that are useful for large spatial repositories. These include function-based indexing, parallel indexing, and partitioned indexing. For each of these features, we describe how to create the associated spatial index and how to use spatial operators.

Function-Based Spatial Indexes

Oracle allows us to create a B-tree index on a function operating on one or more columns of a table. We can do the same with a spatial index. Instead of creating indexes on a column of SDO_GEOMETRY, we can create indexes on *any deterministic function* that returns an SDO_GEOMETRY using existing columns of a table. For instance, we can indirectly use the SDO_GCDR.GEOCODE_AS_GEOMETRY function that returns an SDO_GEOMETRY from the address fields of the customers table as described in Chapters 3 and 6. (Note that the SDO_GCDR package is available only in the priced option of Spatial—it is not available in Locator.) This means we do not have to explicitly materialize the location from the address fields of the customers table to create spatial indexes. Instead, we can create functions that return SDO_GEOMETRY from existing columns of a table.

Note that the SDO_GCDR.GEOCODE_AS_GEOMETRY function is not defined as a deterministic function. So, we create a *deterministic* function, called gcdr_geometry, around the SDO_GCDR.GEOCODE_AS_GEOMETRY as shown in Listing 8-49. We can then use gcdr_geometry as the function in the function-based spatial index.

Listing 8-49. *Creating a Deterministic Function to Return an* SDO_GEOMETRY *Using Address Attributes of the* customers *Table*

```
CREATE or REPLACE FUNCTION gcdr_geometry(street_number varchar2,
street_name varchar2, city varchar2, state varchar2, postal_code varchar2)
RETURN MDSYS.SDO_GEOMETRY DETERMINISTIC is
BEGIN
   RETURN (sdo_gcdr.geocode_as_geometry('SPATIAL',
                    sdo_keywordarray(street_number || ' ' ||street_name ,
                    city || ' ' || state || ' ' || postal_code), 'US'));
END;
/
```

As a sidenote, declaring a function to be deterministic helps with performance if the function is called multiple times in the same SQL statement. Listing 8-50 shows a SQL statement with two invocations of the gcdr_geometry function. The optimizer will evaluate this function just once if it is declared as DETERMINISTIC.

Listing 8-50. *Declaring the* gcdr_geometry *Function As* DETERMINISTIC

```
SQL> SELECT
gcdr_geometry(street_number,street_name,city,state,postal_code).sdo_point.x,
gcdr_geometry(street_number,street_name,city,state,postal_code).sdo_point.y
FROM customers WHERE id=1;
```

We also need to populate the USER_SDO_GEOM_METADATA view that has the TABLE_NAME, COLUMN_NAME, DIMINFO, and SRID columns. All columns except the column_name field can be populated as described in Listing 8-4. The column_name to be inserted is not a regular column of the table. Instead, it is a pseudo-column, obtained using the GCDR_GEOMETRY function. So, we set the column_name to be an invocation of the function with associated arguments. The SQL for inserting this information into the metadata is shown in Listing 8-51.

Listing 8-51. *Inserting the Metadata for a* <table, function-based pseudo-column>

```
SQL> INSERT INTO user_sdo_geom_metadata VALUES
(
  'CUSTOMERS',
  'SPATIAL.GCDR_GEOMETRY(street_number,street_name,city,state,postal_code)',
  MDSYS.SDO_DIM_ARRAY
```

```
  (
    MDSYS.SDO_DIM_ELEMENT('X', -180, 180, 0.5),
    MDSYS.SDO_DIM_ELEMENT('Y', -90, 90, 0.5)
  ),
  8307
);
```

■ **Caution** While inserting into the metadata view, do not include any spaces between the arguments of the GCDR_GEOMETRY function—that is, do not have the arguments as `street_number, <space> street_name`. This will cause errors during index creation. Also, make sure to put the schema owner of the function in the column name, i.e., set the column name to `'spatial.gcdr_geometry...'` and not as `'gcdr_geometry...'`.

Now we can create an index on the customers table using the function-based virtual column. This virtual column is a function, GCDR_GEOMETRY, that returns an SDO_GEOMETRY using the street_number, street_name, city, state, and postal_code columns of the table. Listing 8-52 shows the corresponding SQL.

Listing 8-52. *Creating a Spatial Index on a Function Returning an* SDO_GEOMETRY

```
SQL> CREATE INDEX customers_spatial_fun_idx ON  customers
(
  gcdr_geometry(street_number, street_name, city,  state, postal_code)
)
INDEXTYPE  IS MDSYS.SPATIAL_INDEX
PARAMETERS ('LAYER_GTYPE=POINT');
```

Note that you can augment the preceding CREATE INDEX with a parameter string to specify appropriate parameters as in Listings 8-8 through 8-15. Specifically, 'LAYER_GTYPE=POINT' should be used since the geocoded addresses will always be points.

As in the case of function-based indexes on B-trees, to create and use function-based spatial indexes, the user needs to have the QUERY REWRITE privilege (GLOBAL QUERY REWRITE if creating index in another schema). Besides, the QUERY_REWRITE_ENABLED parameter must be set to TRUE, and the QUERY_REWRITE_INTEGRITY parameter must be set to TRUSTED. You can set them either in the parameter file used at database start-up or in a particular session as shown in Listing 8-53.

Listing 8-53. *Setting Session Parameters to Enable Query Rewrite on Function-Based Indexes*

```
SQL> ALTER SESSION SET QUERY_REWRITE_INTEGRITY = TRUSTED;
SQL> ALTER SESSION SET QUERY_REWRITE_ENABLED = TRUE;
```

Once an index is created using a function-based index, the function will serve as the virtual column for the table. We can use this column in spatial operators just like a regular SDO_GEOMETRY column in a table. The SQL in Listing 8-54 shows an example using the SDO_NN operator. This example is the equivalent of Listing 8-26, except it uses the function-based virtual column. The function is specified as the first argument (i.e., as the indexed column) to the spatial operator.

Listing 8-54. SDO_NN *Operator Retrieving the Five Customers Nearest to Each Competitor Using the Function-Based Index*

```
SQL>  SELECT /*+ ORDERED */ ct.id, ct.name, ct.customer_grade
FROM  competitors comp, customers ct
WHERE comp.id=1
  AND SDO_NN
  (
    gcdr_geometry
      (ct.street_number,ct.street_name, ct.city, ct.state, ct.postal_code),
    comp.location,
    'SDO_NUM_RES=5'
  )='TRUE'
ORDER BY ct.id;

        ID NAME                                CUSTOMER_GRADE
---------- ----------------------------------- ---------------
       809 LINCOLN SUITES                      GOLD
      1044 MUSEUM OF THE THIRD DIMENSION       SILVER
      1526 INTERNATIONAL FINANCE               SILVER
      1538 MCKENNA AND CUNEO                   SILVER
      8792 DESTINATION HOTEL & RESORTS         GOLD

5 rows selected.
```

■ **Tip** Always specify 'LAYER_GTYPE=POINT' in the CREATE INDEX statement if you are creating a spatial index on a function that geocodes addresses to SDO_GEOMETRY objects. If you do not specify this parameter, queries will be slow. A better alternative, then, would be to explicitly store the geocoded addresses as SDO_GEOMETRY columns and index them.

To summarize, functional-based indexing could be used whenever the location data cannot be explicitly materialized for various reasons (e.g., if existing table definitions cannot be changed), but the power and functionality of Oracle Spatial is desired.

Partitioned Spatial Indexes

Table partitioning, a priced option of Oracle, is an important Oracle feature to achieve scalability and manageability in large databases. For instance, we can have the customers table partitioned on the customer_grade attribute as illustrated in Listing 8-55.

Listing 8-55. *Creating a Partitioned Table*

```
SQL> CREATE TABLE customers
(
  NAME                    VARCHAR2(64),
  ID                      NUMBER,
  STREET_NUMBER           VARCHAR2(14),
  STREET_NAME             VARCHAR2(80),
  CITY                    VARCHAR2(64),
  STATE                   VARCHAR2(64),
  POSTAL_CODE             VARCHAR2(16),
  CUSTOMER_GRADE          VARCHAR2(15),
  LOCATION                SDO_GEOMETRY
)
PARTITION by RANGE(CUSTOMER_GRADE)
(
  PARTITION GOLD         VALUES LESS THAN ('GOLDZZZZZZ'),
  PARTITION PLATINUM     VALUES LESS THAN ('PLATINUMZZZZZZ'),
  PARTITION SILVER       VALUES LESS THAN ('SILVERZZZZZZ')
);
```

In Listing 8-55 partitions are created based on *ranges*. For instance, the first partition GOLD will have all customers whose grade will be less than 'GOLDZZZZZZ'. This means the customer grade GOLD (less than 'GOLDZZZZZZ') will be in this partition. We define other partitions analogously.

Creating Local Indexes on Partitioned Tables

If we create an index using the SQL in Listing 8-6, this will create a single global spatial index on all the partitions. Alternatively, we can create a local index, one for each partition, by specifying the keyword LOCAL at the end of the CREATE INDEX statement in Listing 8-6 and specifying some optional partition-specific parameters. Listing 8-56 shows the SQL syntax for a local partitioned index.

Listing 8-56. *Creating a Local Partitioned Spatial Index*

```
CREATE INDEX customers_spatial_idx ON customers(location)
INDEXTYPE  IS MDSYS.SPATIAL_INDEX
[PARAMETERS ('parameter_string')]
LOCAL  [PARAMETERS(sequence of 'partition-specific parameters')] ;
```

Caution You can create local spatial indexes only on *range*-partitioned tables (created as in Listing 8-55). You cannot create local spatial indexes on *list*- or *hash*-partitioned tables.

What is the advantage of creating *local* indexes as opposed to creating one *global* index for all the partitions? Manageability and scalability are two primary advantages of local partitioned indexing.

- *Manageability*: You can rebuild the local index associated with a specific partition without affecting other partitions. As with B-tree indexes, you can take advantage of all the partitioning features, such as exchange partitions and split partitions, while maintaining the associated spatial indexes.
- *Scalability*: Queries can be targeted to specific partitions, improving performance. This means you will be searching only a subset of the data as opposed to the entire set.
  - By specifying different tablespaces for each partition and mapping each tablespace to a different I/O device, you can obtain I/O parallelism in queries.
  - Likewise, spatial indexes can be created on each partition in parallel.

In addition to the LOCAL keyword, you can specify partition-specific parameters. These parameters will override the default parameters specified before the LOCAL keyword. Listing 8-57 shows an example.

Listing 8-57. *Creating a Local Partitioned Spatial Index with Partition-Specific Parameters*

```
SQL> CREATE INDEX customers_spatial_idx ON customers(location)
INDEXTYPE  IS MDSYS.SPATIAL_INDEX
PARAMETERS ('TABLESPACE=USERS')
LOCAL
(
  PARTITION IP1 PARAMETERS('TABLESPACE=TBS_3'),
  PARTITION IP2,
  PARTITION IP3
);
```

Note that in the preceding CREATE INDEX statement, index partition names IP1, IP2, and IP3 correspond to the table partitions GOLD, SILVER, and PLATINUM, respectively (matched based on the order/sequence of specification). The index for partition IP1 is placed in tablespace TBS_3, whereas the indexes for all other partitions are placed in the default tablespace USERS specified before the LOCAL keyword.

■ **Caution** Parameters specified per partition must be compatible (the same type of index: R-tree or quadtree), with the default parameters and the parameters for other partitions.

Querying Using Local Partitioned Indexes

If a table is partitioned and you have created a local partitioned index on it, there is nothing specific to be done at the time of queries. There's very little overhead if the SQL contains only the spatial operator without any partition key. If a partitioned key is specified in the `WHERE` clause of the SQL statement along with a spatial operator, Oracle automatically prunes irrelevant partitions using the partition key and applies the spatial operator only on relevant partitions. Listing 8-58 includes the partition key in the query of Listing 8-20.

Listing 8-58. `SDO_WITHIN_DISTANCE` *Operator on a Partitioned Table*

```
SQL> SELECT /*+ ORDERED */ ct.id, ct.name
FROM competitors comp, customers ct
WHERE comp.id=1
  AND customer_grade='GOLD'
  AND SDO_WITHIN_DISTANCE
    (ct.location,  comp.location, 'DISTANCE=0.25 UNIT=MILE ' )='TRUE'
  ORDER BY ct.id;
        ID NAME
---------- -----------------------------------
       809 LINCOLN SUITES
       810 HOTEL LOMBARDY
      6326 HOTEL LOMBARDY
      7821 RENAISSANCE MAYFLOWER HOTEL
      8138 ST GREGORY HOTEL
      8792 DESTINATION HOTEL & RESORTS
6 rows selected.
```

This query, instead of returning 23 rows as in Listing 8-20, returns only 6 rows. Since the majority of the rows are eliminated in the search, the query may also execute faster. This example demonstrates how local spatial indexes extend the performance advantages of table partitioning to spatial analysis.

For all partitions that satisfy the partitioning key (or all the partitions if there is no partition pruning), the spatial operators execute using the local indexes on each partition, aggregate the results, and return them to the user. As a consequence, the results for the `SDO_WITHIN_DISTANCE`, `SDO_FILTER`, and `SDO_RELATE` operators would be the same as the results if the table *were* not partitioned.

The results for the SDO_NN operator differ, however. The SDO_NN operator will return the specified number of neighbors for each partition (instead of for all the partitions satisfying the query). For example, if the query specifies SDO_NUM_RES=5 in the parameter string of the SDO_NN operator, then each partition that satisfies the SQL returns the five nearest neighbors from its associated local index. This means if there are three partitions, SDO_NN will return a total of 3 × 5 = 15 results when SDO_NUM_RES=5 is specified. To get the five nearest neighbors, the SQL has to be modified as shown in Listing 8-59. Note that the results match those in Listing 8-24.

Listing 8-59. *Obtaining the Five Customers Nearest to Each Competitor When the* customers *Table Has a Local Partitioned Index*

```
SQL> SELECT id, name FROM
(
  SELECT /*+ ORDERED */ a.id , a.name, SDO_NN_DISTANCE(1) dist
  FROM  competitors b, customers a
  WHERE b.id=1
  AND SDO_NN(a.location,  b.location, 'SDO_NUM_RES=5' , 1)='TRUE' ORDER BY dist
)
WHERE ROWNUM<=5
ORDER BY id;
        ID NAME
---------- -----------------------------------
       809 LINCOLN SUITES
      1044 MUSEUM OF THE THIRD DIMENSION
      1526 INTERNATIONAL FINANCE
      1538 MCKENNA AND CUNEO
      8792 DESTINATION HOTEL & RESORTS

5 rows selected.
```

Parallel Indexing

Just as in the case of B-trees, you can create spatial indexes in parallel. For this, you can specify the PARALLEL clause with an optional parallel_degree parameter at the end of the CREATE INDEX statement, as shown in Listing 8-60.

Listing 8-60. *Creating a Spatial Index with the* PARALLEL *Keyword*

```
CREATE INDEX customers_spatial_idx ON customers(location)
INDEXTYPE IS MDSYS.SPATIAL_INDEX
[PARAMETERS ('parameter_string')]  [LOCAL [Partition-specific parameters]]
PARALLEL [parallel_degree];
```

All optional parameters are specified in square brackets. The parallel_degree parameter, which is also optional, specifies the degree of parallelism. This degree specifies the number of slaves to work in parallel to create the index. If `parallel_degree` is omitted, Oracle uses the degree associated with the table (this is stored in the `USER_TABLES` dictionary view). You can alter the degree to 2 (or more) for a table using the SQL in Listing 8-61. You can do the same for a specific index too.

Listing 8-61. *Setting the Degree of Parallelism to 2 for a Table*

```
SQL> ALTER TABLE customers PARALLEL 2 ;
```

Whether the index being created is a local partitioned index or a global index, index creation is performed in parallel if the *parallel degree* is more than 1. However, that is not the case with queries.

Spatial indexes do not perform any explicit parallel processing at query time (except for the parallelism for the underlying table scans). However, if the spatial index is a local partitioned index, then the query processing on multiple partitions is performed in parallel. This means partitioning and parallelism go hand in hand. Using partitioning and setting the table degree to more than 1 (as in Listing 8-61) implicitly improves the performance of proximity analysis operations using spatial indexes.

You will learn about some of the best practices relating to partitioning in Chapter 14.

Spatial Joins

Listing 8-20 identified all customers inside a quarter-mile of a specific competitor (`id=1`). Say we now want to look at all customers within 200 meters of all competitors. What if we wanted to perform this operation for all competitors instead of just the one with `id=1`? We could remove the `comp.id=1` predicate in Listing 8-20 (and set the distance to 200 meters). This would result in the SQL shown in Listing 8-62.

Listing 8-62. `SDO_RELATE` *Operator Retrieving All Customers Inside (and Touching the Border of) Each Competitor Region*

```
SQL> SELECT COUNT(DISTINCT ct.id)
FROM competitors comp, customers ct
WHERE SDO_WITHIN_DISTANCE
    (ct.location,  comp.location, 'DISTANCE=200 UNIT=METER ' )='TRUE';

COUNT(DISTINCTCT.ID)
--------------------
                1145
```

This query executes in a *nested loop*, performing the `SDO_WITHIN_DISTANCE` operation for each row in the `competitors` table. What if there is a spatial index on the `competitors` table? We can use this index in addition to the index on the customers in the preceding operation. This will speed up the query significantly for large datasets.

To use both indexes, we need to use the `SDO_JOIN` table function. This function has the following syntax:

```
SDO_JOIN
(
  table1                     IN VARCHAR2,
  col1                       IN VARCHAR2,
  table2                     IN VARCHAR2,
  col2                       IN VARCHAR2
  [, parameter_string        IN VARCHAR2
  [, preserve_join_order     IN NUMBER]]
)
RETURNS SDO_ROWIDSET
```

where

- table1 and col1 refer to the first table name and the corresponding geometry column name.
- table2 and col2 refer to the second table name and the corresponding geometry column name.
- parameter_string is optional. Just as in the SDO_RELATE and SDO_WITHIN_DISTANCE operators, this parameter can specify either MASK=<mask-type> or DISTANCE=<val> [UNIT=<unit-spec>]. If the parameter_string is not specified, then SDO_JOIN will operate only as the primary filter (i.e., it will be equivalent to SDO_FILTER).
- preserve_join_order can be either 0 or 1. If the tables are of different sizes, then SDO_JOIN may internally reorder the tables for join processing. You may set this to 1 only if you prefer to override this reordering. For all practical purposes, just leave it as the default value of 0 (or do not specify this parameter).
- The SDO_JOIN returns an SDO_ROWIDSET. This is *table* of rowid pairs of the form <rowid1, rowid2>. The first rowid, rowid1, corresponds to the rows of table1, and the second rowid, rowid2, corresponds to the rows of the second table, table2.

Using this syntax for the SDO_JOIN, we can rewrite Listing 8-62 to use the indexes of both tables. This query, shown in Listing 8-63, is likely to be faster than the query in Listing 8-62.

Listing 8-63. SDO_JOIN *Operator Analyzing the Number of Customers Inside All the Competitor Regions*

```
SQL> SELECT COUNT(DISTINCT ct.id)
FROM competitors comp, customers ct,
  TABLE
  (
    SDO_JOIN
      (
      'competitors', 'location',  -- first table and the SDO_GEOMETRY column
      'customers', 'location',    -- second table and the SDO_GEOMETRY column
```

```
      'DISTANCE=200 UNIT=METER'                  -- specify mask relationship
    )
  ) jn
WHERE  ct.rowid=jn.rowid2 and  comp.rowid = jn.rowid1;
COUNT(DISTINCTCT.ID)
--------------------
                1145
```

Note that SDO_JOIN is a table function and is included in the FROM clause of the SQL. In contrast, the SDO_WITHIN_DISTANCE operator in Listing 8-62 is included in the WHERE clause of a SQL statement. In general, the SDO_JOIN function will execute faster than the equivalent SDO_RELATE or the SDO_WITHIN_DISTANCE operators, as SDO_JOIN uses both the spatial indexes.

Note that if the parameter_string is omitted, SDO_JOIN operates just like an SDO_FILTER operation. Listing 8-64 is therefore equivalent to Listing 8-65. However, since SDO_JOIN uses two spatial indexes instead of one in SDO_FILTER, the SQL in Listing 8-65 (using SDO_JOIN) may run significantly faster than that in Listing 8-64.

Listing 8-64. SDO_FILTER *Operator Retrieving All Customers Whose MBRs Intersect Those of Competitor Regions*

```
SQL> SELECT COUNT(DISTINCT ct.id)
FROM competitors_sales_regions comp, customers ct
WHERE SDO_FILTER(ct.location,  comp.geom)='TRUE';
  COUNT(*)
----------
      2171
```

Listing 8-65. SDO_JOIN *Operator Retrieving All Customers Whose MBRs Intersect the MBRs of Competitor Regions (Filter Operation Is Used)*

```
SQL> SELECT COUNT(DISTINCT ct.id)
FROM competitors_sales_regions comp, customers ct,
  TABLE
  (
    SDO_JOIN
    (
      'competitors_sales_regions', 'geom',  -- first table and column
      'customers', 'location'               -- second table and column
    )
  ) jn
WHERE  ct.rowid=jn.rowid2 AND comp.rowid = jn.rowid1;
  COUNT(*)
----------
      2171
```

Summary

In this chapter, we discussed how to perform proximity analysis using spatial indexes and associated operators. We explained how to create spatial indexes on SDO_GEOMETRY columns of Oracle tables. Once these indexes are created, they help in the fast processing of several spatial operators that are useful in proximity analysis. These operators include SDO_NN and SDO_WITHIN_DISTANCE, which provide distance-based analysis, and SDO_RELATE and SDO_FILTER, which provide interaction-based analysis.

The majority of the functionality described in this chapter (except that in the "Advanced Spatial Index Features" section) is part of Locator, which is included with the Oracle Database Server. As a result, most applications running on Oracle can readily leverage this functionality for supporting proximity analysis. In the next chapter, we will complement this analysis with additional functions on SDO_GEOMETRY objects.

CHAPTER 9

■ ■ ■

Geometry Processing Functions

To run the examples in this chapter, you need to import the following datasets:

```
imp spatial/spatial file=app_data_with_loc.dmp ignore=y full=y
imp spatial/spatial file=map_large.dmp full=y ignore=y
```

In Chapter 8, we discussed how to perform proximity analysis using a spatial index and associated spatial operators. In this chapter, we describe *geometry processing* functions, which are also referred to as *spatial functions* (whenever there is no ambiguity), that complement this functionality. In contrast to the spatial operators, these geometry processing functions

- Do not require a spatial index
- Provide more detailed analyses than the spatial operators associated with a spatial index
- Can appear in the SELECT list (as well as the WHERE clause) of a SQL statement

We supplement the "customer analysis" and "sales region analysis" of Chapter 8 with the additional types of analyses presented in Table 9-1, which use the spatial functions described in this chapter. The new analyses are shown in bold in the table.

Table 9-1. *Augmenting Proximity Analyses from Table 8-1 Using Geometry Processing Functions*

Analysis Type	Description
Customer analysis	Identify customers nearest to, or within a specified radius from, a branch or a competitor. For customers close to a competitor, you might provide certain promotions to retain them. You may specifically target this analysis on GOLD customers whom you want to retain at any cost. **Identify appropriate regions to start a new branch (i.e., a new business unit) to cater to a group of customers.**
Sales region analysis	Build sales regions (i.e., quarter-mile buffers) around branch and competitor locations. Identify which of these overlap with one another or with state and county boundaries. If sales regions of branches overlap substantially, you could merge such branches. **Create buffers around branches and competitors to indicate sales regions or coverage.** **Identify the overlapping portion of two sales regions, determine the area of the overlapping portion, examine the customer population in this portion, and so on. If the area exceeds a threshold and the number of customers is significant, you may consider merging the sales regions (i.e., merging the corresponding branches).** **Determine the total coverage of all the branches (or store locations). This indicates in which parts of the city/country the business has a presence and in which parts the business is not represented.** **Identify the coverage of competitors (or a specific competitor), and target customers that are in exclusive regions of the coverage.**

New Analysis shown in bold.

The analyses in Table 9-1 are much more detailed than was possible in Table 8-1 using spatial indexes and associated operators. In this chapter, you will learn about spatial functions that enable such complex analysis on SDO_GEOMETRY objects. These spatial functions can be classified into the following broad categories:

- *Buffering functions*: The SDO_BUFFER function creates a buffer around an existing SDO_GEOMETRY object. The object can be of any type—point, line, polygon, or collection. For instance, we can create buffers around the point locations in the branches table. The buffers created around such business/branch locations may represent the *sales regions* for those businesses/branches.

- *Relationship analysis functions*: These functions determine the relationship between two SDO_GEOMETRY objects. For example, using these functions, we can compute the distance between a potential customer and a branch (business) location (then we can know whether the customer is within a quarter-mile from the branch location). Alternatively, we can determine if a customer or a supplier is *inside* a specified buffer zone around a branch location.

- *Geometry combination functions*: These functions perform intersection, union, and other geometry combination functions on pairs of geometries. We can use these functions to identify pairs of sales regions that intersect (or overlap) and find the intersection areas. We can target customers in these intersection areas for specific promotions.

- *Geometric analysis functions*: These functions perform analysis such as area calculations on individual geometric objects. For instance, for the overlap region of two sales regions, we can compute the area and check if this area (of the overlap region) is significantly large. If it is, then the corresponding branch locations can be marked as potential candidates for *merging*.
- *Aggregate functions*: The preceding analysis functions analyze individual or pairs of geometries. Spatial also has *aggregate* functions that perform *aggregation* analyses on an arbitrary set of geometries instead of individual or pairs of geometries. These sets of geometries can result from any arbitrary selection criterion in the `WHERE` clause of a SQL statement.

With the exception of the spatial aggregate functions, all other spatial functions discussed in this chapter are part of the `SDO_GEOM` package. This means you can use them as `SDO_GEOM.<function_name>` in SQL statements. These functions can appear wherever a user-defined function can occur in a SQL statement. The spatial aggregate functions, on the other hand, can appear only in the `SELECT` list of a SQL statement.

Most of the spatial functions described previously take one or two `SDO_GEOMETRY` arguments, a `tolerance` argument, and other optional arguments. The `tolerance` argument has the same meaning as described in Chapter 8. To recap, tolerance in a geometry reflects the distance that two points must be apart to be considered different (e.g., to accommodate rounding errors). The tolerance for *geodetic* geometries (where interpolation between points is the shortest distance on the surface of the Earth; to determine if a geometry is geodetic, look at the `SRID` value and compare it with those in the `MDSYS.GEODETIC_SRIDS` table) is specified in meters and is usually set to 0.1 or 0.5. For nongeodetic geometries, this tolerance will be set based on the application.

In this chapter, we discuss each of the spatial functions in turn. We use these functions to perform analyses on two sets of data:

- The `branches` and `customers` tables of the business application
- The `us_states`, `us_counties`, and `us_parks` tables that constitute the geographic data in the business application

Buffering Functions

The first function we discuss is `SDO_BUFFER`. This function constructs a buffer around a specified geometric object or a set of geometric objects. For instance, we can use this function to create a quarter-mile buffer around a delivery site location. This buffer geometry will be a circle around the delivery site with a radius of a quarter mile. Likewise, a buffer around an L-shaped road will be the merged area of two sausage shapes (flattened ovals), one for each segment of the road.

Figure 9-1 shows examples of the constructed buffers for different types of geometries, with the pre-buffered geometries shown. Note that only simple geometries are shown here. The `SDO_BUFFER` function can work with complex `SDO_GEOMETRY` objects, such as voided polygons, compound polygons, and collections. Note that if the input geometric object has a large enough interior hole, the resultant buffer zone may also have an interior hole.

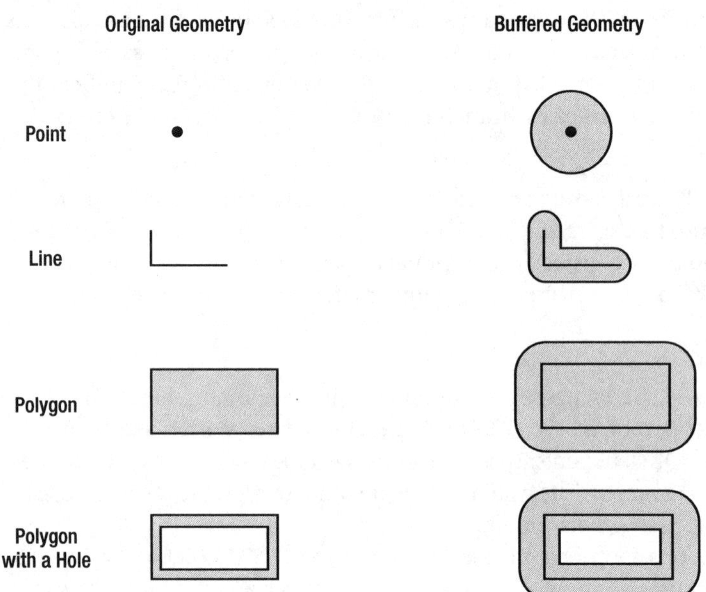

Figure 9-1. *Geometric objects and buffered geometries for some simple types*

Next, let's examine how to construct these buffers using the SDO_BUFFER function. This function has the following syntax:

```
SDO_BUFFER
(
  geometry      IN SDO_GEOMETRY,
  distance      IN NUMBER,
  tolerance     IN NUMBER
  [, params     IN VARCHAR2]
)
RETURNS an SDO_GEOMETRY
```

where

- geometry is a parameter that specifies an SDO_GEOMETRY object to be buffered.
- distance is a parameter that specifies a numerical distance to buffer the input geometry.
- tolerance is a parameter that specifies the tolerance.
- params is the optional fourth argument that specifies two parameters, unit=<value_string> and arc_tolerance=<value_number>.

The unit=<value_string> parameter specifies the unit in which the distance is specified. You can obtain possible values for the units by consulting the MDSYS.SDO_DIST_UNITS table.

The arc_tolerance=<value_number> parameter is required if the geometry is geodetic (i.e., the SDO_SRID in the geometry is set to a geodetic SRID such as 8307 or 8265). In geodetic space, arcs are not permitted. Instead, they are represented using straight-line approximations. The arc tolerance parameter specifies the maximum distance between an arc and its straight-line approximation. Figure 9-2 shows this arc tolerance.

Figure 9-2. *The arc tolerance is the maximum distance between the arc and the lines approximating the arc.*

You should note the following:

- The arc_tolerance always has to be greater than the tolerance for the geometry.
- The tolerance is specified in units of meters for geodetic data. The arc_tolerance, however, is always in the units specified in the parameter_string.
- The units parameter, if specified, applies to both the arc_tolerance and the buffer distance.

Using this signature, we can construct a quarter-mile buffer around each branch location in the branches table as shown in Listing 9-1. We store these buffers in a sales_regions table for use in subsequent analysis.

Listing 9-1. *Creating Buffers Around Branches*

```
SQL> CREATE TABLE sales_regions AS
SELECT id,
SDO_GEOM.SDO_BUFFER(a.location, 0.25, 0.5, 'arc_tolerance=0.005 unit=mile') geom
FROM branches a;
```

Note that the first parameter is the geometry to be buffered. The second parameter specifies the buffer distance as 0.25. The third parameter specifies the tolerance to be 0.5 meters, the tolerance unit for geodetic geometries. The parameter_string in the fourth argument specifies the units for the buffer distance (of 0.25). In this case, the units are miles. The buffer distance, then, is 0.25 miles. Additionally, the parameter_string also specifies an arc tolerance of 0.005. Since the units are miles, the arc tolerance will be interpreted as 0.005 miles (equivalent to 26.4 feet or 8.1 meters).

Likewise, we can create buffers around competitor stores, as shown in Listing 9-2.

Listing 9-2. *Creating Buffers Around Competitor Locations*

```
SQL>  CREATE TABLE COMPETITORS_SALES_REGIONS AS
SELECT id,
SDO_GEOM.SDO_BUFFER(a.location, 0.25, 0.5, 'unit=mile arc_tolerance=0.005') geom
FROM competitors a;
```

Note that we need to create spatial indexes for both tables. You can refer to Chapter 8 for details on how to create the metadata and the spatial index. Here, we provide the script to do just that:

```
Rem Metadata for Sales_regions table
SQL> INSERT INTO user_sdo_geom_metadata
SELECT 'SALES_REGIONS',
'GEOM', diminfo, srid FROM user_sdo_geom_metadata
WHERE table_name='BRANCHES';

Rem Metadata for Competitors_sales_regions table
SQL> INSERT INTO user_sdo_geom_metadata
SELECT 'COMPETITORS_SALES_REGIONS',
'GEOM', diminfo, srid FROM user_sdo_geom_metadata
WHERE table_name='COMPETITORS';

Rem Index-creation for Sales_regions table
SQL> CREATE INDEX sr_sidx ON sales_regions(geom)
INDEXTYPE IS mdsys.spatial_index;

Rem Index-creation for Competitors_sales_regions table
SQL> CREATE INDEX cr_sidx ON competitors_sales_regions(geom)
INDEXTYPE IS mdsys.spatial_index;
```

Relationship Analysis Functions

In this section, we examine two functions to analyze the relationship between two SDO_GEOMETRY objects. The first function is SDO_DISTANCE. This function determines how far apart two geometries are. The second function is RELATE. This function determines whether two geometries interact in any specified manner. For instance, we can use this function to identify if there are any customers *inside* the buffers created in Listing 9-2.

SDO_DISTANCE

The SDO_DISTANCE function computes the *minimum* distance between any two points on the two geometries. Figure 9-3 shows some examples. This distance computation takes into account both vertices and the interpolated curves of each geometry. In the line geometry example, one of the vertices of the line is closest to the second (point) geometry. In the polygon example, one of the curves is closest to the second (point) geometry.

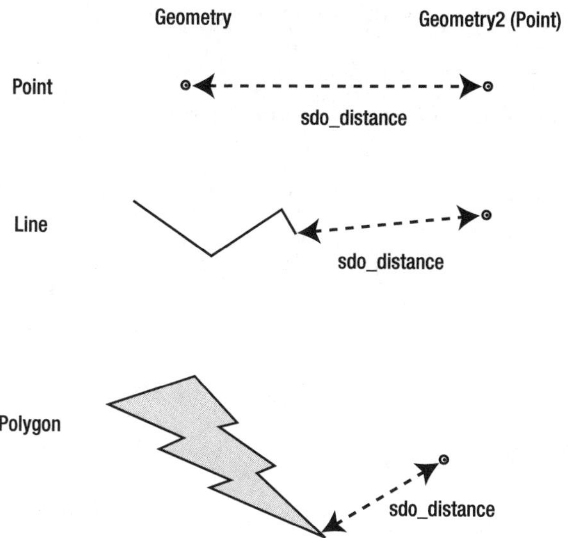

Figure 9-3. *The* SDO_DISTANCE *function for different pairs of geometric objects*

The SDO_DISTANCE function has the following syntax:

```
SDO_DISTANCE
(
  geometry1          IN SDO_GEOMETRY,
  geometry2          IN SDO_GEOMETRY,
  tolerance          IN NUMBER
  [, params          IN VARCHAR2]
)
  RETURNS a NUMBER
```

where

- geometry1 and geometry2 are the first two arguments, and they specify SDO_GEOMETRY objects.
- tolerance specifies the tolerance for the dataset. For geodetic data, this is usually 0.5 or 0.1 (0.5 meters or 0.1 meters). For nongeodetic data, this is set appropriately to avoid rounding errors (see Chapter 8 for details).
- params is the optional fourth parameter in a string of the form 'unit=<value_string>'. This specifies the units in which the distance should be returned. You can obtain possible values for the units by consulting the MDSYS.SDO_DIST_UNITS table.

This function returns the minimum distance between geometry1 and geometry2 in the units specified. If no unit is specified, the default unit for the coordinate system is used (this can be determined by inspecting the SDO_SRID attribute in the SDO_GEOMETRY objects and looking at the WKTEXT in the MDSYS.CS_SRS table for that SRID).

Using this function, we can identify the customers within a quarter-mile radius of a competitor location, as shown in Listing 9-3.

Listing 9-3. *Identifying Customers Within a Quarter-Mile of a Competitor Location*

```
SQL> SELECT ct.id, ct.name
FROM competitors comp, customers ct
WHERE comp.id=1
AND SDO_GEOM.SDO_DISTANCE(ct.location, comp.location, 0.5, 'unit=mile') < 0.25
ORDER BY ct.id;
        ID NAME
---------- -----------------------------------
        25 BLAKE CONSTRUCTION
        28 COLONIAL PARKING
        34 HEWLETT-PACKARD DC GOV AFFAIRS
        41 MCGREGOR PRINTING
        48 POTOMAC ELECTRIC POWER
        50 SMITH HINCHMAN AND GRYLLS
       270 METRO-FARRAGUT NORTH STATION
       271 METRO-FARRAGUT WEST STATION
       468 SAFEWAY
       809 LINCOLN SUITES
       810 HOTEL LOMBARDY
      1044 MUSEUM OF THE THIRD DIMENSION
      1526 INTERNATIONAL FINANCE
      1538 MCKENNA AND CUNEO
      2195 STEVENS ELEMENTARY SCHOOL
      6326 HOTEL LOMBARDY
      7754 EXECUTIVE INN
      7762 PHILLIPS 66
      7789 SEVEN BUILDINGS
      7821 RENAISSANCE MAYFLOWER HOTEL
      8138 ST GREGORY HOTEL
      8382 EXXON
      8792 DESTINATION HOTEL & RESORTS

23 rows selected.
```

Note that the preceding query will have the same semantics as Listing 8-20, which uses the SDO_WITHIN_DISTANCE operator. The SDO_WITHIN_DISTANCE operator in Listing 8-20 uses the spatial index, but the SDO_GEOM.SDO_DISTANCE function does not. As a result, Listing 9-3 will be much slower in comparison. You should use the SDO_WITHIN_DISTANCE operator wherever possible. You should use the SDO_DISTANCE function only

- To operate on nonindexed tables
- To augment the SDO_WITHIN_DISTANCE operator

Here is an example of where the SDO_DISTANCE function will come in handy. In Listing 9-4, the SDO_WITHIN_DISTANCE operator identifies the rows that are within a specified distance. The SDO_DISTANCE in the SELECT list of the SQL identifies the exact distance of each of these rows to the query geometry. Note that the unit is specified as yard in the SDO_DISTANCE function. As a result, the distances are returned in yards.

Listing 9-4. *Using the* SDO_DISTANCE *Function with the* SDO_WITHIN_DISTANCE *Spatial Operator in SQL*

```
SQL> SELECT ct.id, ct.name,
SDO_GEOM.SDO_DISTANCE(ct.location, comp.location, 0.5, 'unit=yard')  distance
FROM competitors comp, customers ct
WHERE comp.id=1
  AND SDO_WITHIN_DISTANCE
  (ct.location, comp.location, 'distance=0.25 unit=mile')='TRUE'
ORDER BY ct.id;
        ID NAME                                 DISTANCE
---------- ---------------------------------- ----------
        25 BLAKE CONSTRUCTION                 319.038526
        28 COLONIAL PARKING                   398.262506
        34 HEWLETT-PACKARD DC GOV AFFAIRS     427.660664
        41 MCGREGOR PRINTING                  350.463038
        48 POTOMAC ELECTRIC POWER             354.721567
        50 SMITH HINCHMAN AND GRYLLS          252.366911
       270 METRO-FARRAGUT NORTH STATION       344.955038
       271 METRO-FARRAGUT WEST STATION        271.905717
       468 SAFEWAY                            252.001358
       809 LINCOLN SUITES                     103.915921
       810 HOTEL LOMBARDY                     313.088568
      1044 MUSEUM OF THE THIRD DIMENSION      152.658273
      1526 INTERNATIONAL FINANCE              235.987835
      1538 MCKENNA AND CUNEO                  96.9728115
      2195 STEVENS ELEMENTARY SCHOOL          304.662483
      6326 HOTEL LOMBARDY                     329.301433
      7754 EXECUTIVE INN                      374.571287
      7762 PHILLIPS 66                        302.628637
      7789 SEVEN BUILDINGS                    354.721567
      7821 RENAISSANCE MAYFLOWER HOTEL        322.143941
      8138 ST GREGORY HOTEL                   359.219279
      8382 EXXON                              326.165809
      8792 DESTINATION HOTEL & RESORTS        159.234843

23 rows selected.
```

RELATE

In Listing 9-2, we created buffers around competitor locations. What do we do with these buffers around the branch locations and competitor locations? We can perform relationship analysis to identify customers inside these sales regions and competitor regions. We can do this using either the SDO_RELATE operator (as in described in Chapter 8) or the RELATE function in the SDO_GEOM package. The RELATE function has the following syntax:

```
RELATE
(
  Geometry_A       IN SDO_GEOMETRY,
  mask,            IN VARCHAR2,
  Geometry_Q,      IN SDO_GEOMETRY,
  Tolerance        IN NUMBER
)
RETURNS a relationship of type VARCHAR2
```

where

- Geometry_A and Geometry_Q are arguments that specify geometric objects.
- The mask argument can take one of the following values:
  - DETERMINE: This determines the relationship or interaction Geometry_A has with Geometry_Q.
  - Any relationship specified in Figure 8-8, including
    - INSIDE, COVEREDBY, COVERS, CONTAINS, EQUAL, OVERLAPBDYDISJOINT, OVERLAPBDYINTERSECT, ON, and TOUCH
    - ANYINTERACT: If any of the preceding relationships holds
    - DISJOINT: If none of the preceding relationships holds

This RELATE function returns

- 'TRUE' if the geometries intersect and the ANYINTERACT mask is specified
- The value of mask if Geometry_A satisfies the specified mask-type relationship with Geometry_Q
- 'FALSE' if the relationship between the geometries does not match the relationship specified in the second argument, mask
- The type of relationship, if the mask is set to 'DETERMINE'

Using this signature for the RELATE function, we can perform proximity analyses using our buffer zones around branches and competitors. We can identify all customers that are inside the competitors_sales_regions (i.e., the buffer zones around competitors), as shown in Listing 9-5.

Listing 9-5. *Identifying Customers* Inside *a Competitor's Sales Region*

```
SQL> SELECT ct.id, ct.name
FROM customers ct, competitors_sales_regions comp
WHERE SDO_GEOM.RELATE (ct.location, 'INSIDE',  comp.geom, 0.1) = 'INSIDE'
  AND comp.id=1
ORDER BY ct.id;
        ID NAME
---------- -----------------------------------
        25 BLAKE CONSTRUCTION
        28 COLONIAL PARKING
        34 HEWLETT-PACKARD DC GOV AFFAIRS
        41 MCGREGOR PRINTING
        48 POTOMAC ELECTRIC POWER
        50 SMITH HINCHMAN AND GRYLLS
       270 METRO-FARRAGUT NORTH STATION
       271 METRO-FARRAGUT WEST STATION
       468 SAFEWAY
       809 LINCOLN SUITES
       810 HOTEL LOMBARDY
      1044 MUSEUM OF THE THIRD DIMENSION
      1526 INTERNATIONAL FINANCE
      1538 MCKENNA AND CUNEO
      2195 STEVENS ELEMENTARY SCHOOL
      6326 HOTEL LOMBARDY
      7754 EXECUTIVE INN
      7762 PHILLIPS 66
      7789 SEVEN BUILDINGS
      7821 RENAISSANCE MAYFLOWER HOTEL
      8138 ST GREGORY HOTEL
      8382 EXXON
      8792 DESTINATION HOTEL & RESORTS

23 rows selected.
```

Note that this query returns only those customers at a distance of less than 0.25 miles from (i.e., that are inside the sales region of) the specified competitor (id=1). This does not, however, return the customers that are exactly 0.25 miles from the competitor (i.e., those that touch or are on the boundary of the competitor buffer zone). To include those, we can simply specify the ANYINTERACT mask, as shown in Listing 9-6. Note that the function is compared with 'TRUE' instead of 'ANYINTERACT'.

Listing 9-6. *Identifying Customers That* Interact *with a Competitor's Sales Region*

```
SQL> SELECT ct.id, ct.name
FROM customers ct, competitors_sales_regions comp
WHERE SDO_GEOM.RELATE (ct.location, 'ANYINTERACT',  comp.geom, 0.5) = 'TRUE'
  AND comp.id=1
ORDER BY ct.id;

        ID NAME
---------- -----------------------------------
        25 BLAKE CONSTRUCTION
        28 COLONIAL PARKING
        34 HEWLETT-PACKARD DC GOV AFFAIRS
        41 MCGREGOR PRINTING
        48 POTOMAC ELECTRIC POWER
        50 SMITH HINCHMAN AND GRYLLS
       270 METRO-FARRAGUT NORTH STATION
       271 METRO-FARRAGUT WEST STATION
       468 SAFEWAY
       809 LINCOLN SUITES
       810 HOTEL LOMBARDY
      1044 MUSEUM OF THE THIRD DIMENSION
      1526 INTERNATIONAL FINANCE
      1538 MCKENNA AND CUNEO
      2195 STEVENS ELEMENTARY SCHOOL
      6326 HOTEL LOMBARDY
      7754 EXECUTIVE INN
      7762 PHILLIPS 66
      7789 SEVEN BUILDINGS
      7821 RENAISSANCE MAYFLOWER HOTEL
      8138 ST GREGORY HOTEL
      8382 EXXON
      8792 DESTINATION HOTEL & RESORTS

23 rows selected.
```

When to Use the RELATE Function

Note that the query in Listing 9-6 is the exact equivalent of Listing 8-35. This query uses the SDO_GEOM.RELATE spatial function, whereas the query in Listing 8-35 uses the SDO_RELATE operator. As operators are evaluated using the spatial index, Listing 8-35 will execute faster. In contrast, the SDO_GEOM.RELATE function in Listing 9-6 does not use any index and is evaluated for every row of the customers table. This might result in a much slower evaluation. Why and when should the SDO_GEOM.RELATE function be used? The RELATE function is never to be used if the SDO_RELATE operator can serve the same purpose.

However, the SDO_GEOM.RELATE function can be useful in certain scenarios—for example, to operate on nonindexed tables or subsets of geometries such as the suppliers table in Listing 9-7. Note that the suppliers table does not have a spatial index.

Listing 9-7. *Identifying Suppliers in a Quarter-Mile Buffer Around a Competitor*

```
SQL> SELECT  a.id
FROM suppliers a, competitors_sales_regions b
WHERE SDO_GEOM.RELATE (a.location, 'ANYINTERACT',  b.geom, 0.5) = 'TRUE'
AND b.id=1;
```

The SDO_GEOM.RELATE function can also be used to complement the SDO_RELATE operator. For instance, we can use the SDO_RELATE operator with the ANYINTERACT mask (or a combination of masks) to identify a candidate set of rows. We can then use the SDO_GEOM.RELATE function to determine the relationship for each row that is returned. Listing 9-8 shows how to complement the functionality of Listing 8-35 using the SDO_GEOM.RELATE function.

Listing 9-8. *Identifying Customers in Quarter-Mile Buffer Around a Competitor*

```
SQL> SELECT  ct.id, ct.name,
SDO_GEOM.RELATE (ct.location, 'DETERMINE',  comp.geom, 0.5)  relationship
FROM customers ct, competitors_sales_regions comp
WHERE comp.id=1
  AND SDO_RELATE(ct.location, comp.geom, 'mask=anyinteract')='TRUE';

    ID NAME                                  RELATIONSHIP
------ -----------------------------------   ------------------------------------
    25 BLAKE CONSTRUCTION                    INSIDE
  7821 RENAISSANCE MAYFLOWER HOTEL           INSIDE
  8138 ST GREGORY HOTEL                      INSIDE
  8382 EXXON                                 INSIDE
  6326 HOTEL LOMBARDY                        INSIDE
  1526 INTERNATIONAL FINANCE                 INSIDE
   810 HOTEL LOMBARDY                        INSIDE
    50 SMITH HINCHMAN AND GRYLLS             INSIDE
   271 METRO-FARRAGUT WEST STATION           INSIDE
  7762 PHILLIPS 66                           INSIDE
    34 HEWLETT-PACKARD DC GOV AFFAIRS        INSIDE
  1538 MCKENNA AND CUNEO                     INSIDE
  1044 MUSEUM OF THE THIRD DIMENSION         INSIDE
    28 COLONIAL PARKING                      INSIDE
    41 MCGREGOR PRINTING                     INSIDE
  7754 EXECUTIVE INN                         INSIDE
   270 METRO-FARRAGUT NORTH STATION          INSIDE
  2195 STEVENS ELEMENTARY SCHOOL             INSIDE
   809 LINCOLN SUITES                        INSIDE
  8792 DESTINATION HOTEL & RESORTS           INSIDE
   468 SAFEWAY                               INSIDE
    48 POTOMAC ELECTRIC POWER                INSIDE
  7789 SEVEN BUILDINGS                       INSIDE

23 rows selected.
```

Another interesting analysis that we can perform in our business application is the identification of sales regions that intersect each other. We can use the combination of the SDO_RELATE operator to identify pairs of sales regions that intersect each other and then perform the SDO_GEOM.RELATE to determine whether they just *touch* or *overlap* with each other. Listing 9-9 shows the SQL to retrieve all sales regions that intersect a sales region with id=51.

Listing 9-9. RELATE *Function Complementing the* SDO_RELATE *Operator*

```
SQL> SELECT a.id,
SDO_GEOM.RELATE(a.geom, 'DETERMINE', b.geom, 0.5) relationship
FROM sales_regions b, sales_regions a
WHERE b.id=51 AND a.id<>51 AND
  SDO_RELATE
  (a.geom, b.geom,
  'mask=TOUCH+OVERLAPBDYDISJOINT+OVERLAPBDYINTERSECT'
  )='TRUE'
ORDER BY a.id;
        ID      RELATIONSHIP
----------      ----------------------------------
        43      OVERLAPBDYINTERSECT
        50      OVERLAPBDYINTERSECT
        54      OVERLAPBDYINTERSECT
        63      OVERLAPBDYINTERSECT
        66      OVERLAPBDYINTERSECT
        69      OVERLAPBDYINTERSECT
        72      OVERLAPBDYINTERSECT
        75      OVERLAPBDYINTERSECT
        76      TOUCH

9 rows selected.
```

Instead of doing two queries as in Listing 8-41 and Listing 8-42, Listing 9-10 will tell us, in a single SQL query, which sales regions overlap and which touch.

■ **Tip** Use SDO_GEOM.RELATE and SDO_RELATE in combination to identify specific types of interactions.

Listing 9-9 shows the sales regions that overlap with a specific sales region (with id=51). But can we extract just the overlap (or intersection) region—that is, the area that is common to both sales regions? Based on the size of these intersection regions and the number of customers in these intersection regions, we can designate the corresponding pair of branch locations as potential candidates for merging. In the next section, we discuss functions to extract the intersection regions of overlapping geometric objects.

Geometry Combination Functions

In mathematics, two *sets of items*, A and B, can be combined using different *set-theory* operations such as A minus B, A union B, and A intersection B. Here, we examine similar functions that act on a pair of geometries instead of a pair of sets. If A and B are two geometries, the semantics of each of the geometry combination functions are illustrated in Figure 9-4.

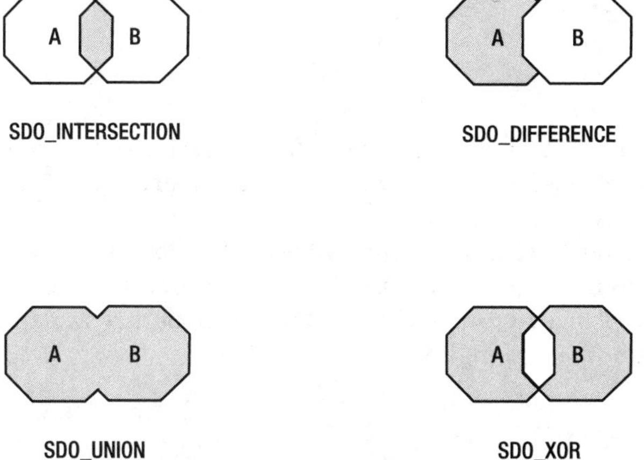

Figure 9-4. *Semantics of geometry combination functions for octagon-shaped polygon geometries A and B. The shaded region shows the result of each specific function.*

The values retuned by each function described in Figure 9-4 as follows:

- A SDO_INTERSECTION B: Returns the region of A that is also shared by B.
- A SDO_UNION B: Returns the region covered by A or B.
- A SDO_DIFFERENCE B: Returns the region covered by A that is not also covered by B.
- A SDO_XOR B: Returns the region of A and B that is not shared by both. This function is equivalent to (A SDO_UNION B) SDO_DIFFERENCE (A SDO_INTERSECTION B).

Each of these functions has the following signature:

```
SDO_<set_theory_fn>
(
  Geometry_A         IN SDO_GEOMETRY,
  Geometry_B         IN SDO_GEOMETRY,
  Tolerance          IN NUMBER
)
  RETURNS SDO_GEOMETRY
```

where

- Geometry_A and Geometry_B are SDO_GEOMETRY objects (with the same SRIDs).
- Tolerance is the tolerance value for the geometric objects.

The function returns an SDO_GEOMETRY that computes the appropriate geometry combination function for Geometry_A with respect to Geometry_B.

Now that you understand the semantics and syntax, let's look at examples of how to use these functions to perform proximity analysis.

SDO_INTERSECTION

In Listing 9-9, we identified all sales regions that overlapped (or touched) a specific sales region (with id=51). Here, we can perform more rigorous analysis with each such pair of overlapping sales regions and determine whether they are good candidates for merging.

Consider sales regions with ids 51 and 63. Listing 9-10 shows the SQL for identifying the intersection geometry for each pair of overlapping sales regions. The sales_intersection_zones table stores these intersection regions. Listing 9-11 shows the ids of sales regions that overlap with sales region 51 (the ids are the same as in Listing 9-9).

Listing 9-10. SDO_INTERSECTION *of Two Geometries*

```
SQL> CREATE TABLE sales_intersection_zones AS
SELECT a.id id1, b.id id2,
SDO_GEOM.SDO_INTERSECTION(a.geom, b.geom, 0.5) intsxn_geom
FROM sales_regions b, sales_regions a
WHERE a.id<> b.id
AND SDO_RELATE(a.geom,  b.geom, 'mask=anyinteract' )='TRUE' ;
```

Listing 9-11. *Sales Regions Intersecting the Sales Region with* id=51

```
SQL> SELECT id2 FROM sales_intersection_zones WHERE id1=51;
   ID2
------
    43
    50
    54
    63
    66
    69
    72
    75
    76

9 rows selected.
```

We can use the *intersection geometry* (the `intsxn_geom` column) stored in the `sales_intersection_zones` table for subsequent analysis on sales regions. Listing 9-12 shows how to use this geometry to identify customers inside the intersection area of two specific sales regions with `ids` 51 and 43. The result of this SQL indicates that there are only two customers common to both sales regions.

Listing 9-12. *Identifying Customers in* `sales_ intersection_zones`

```
SQL> SELECT count(*)
FROM sales_intersection_zones b, customers a
WHERE b.id1=51 AND  b.id2=43
AND SDO_RELATE(a.location, b.intsxn_geom, 'mask=anyinteract')='TRUE';
  COUNT(*)
----------
         2
```

We can perform the preceding intersection analysis without materializing the intersection regions in a separate table. Listing 9-13 shows the corresponding SQL to identify customers in the intersection of sales regions 51 and 43. Note that the result is the same as that of Listing 9-12.

Listing 9-13. *Identifying Customers in the Intersection of Sales Regions 51 and 43*

```
SQL> SELECT COUNT(*)
FROM customers ct
WHERE SDO_RELATE
(
  ct.location,
  (
    SELECT SDO_GEOM.SDO_INTERSECTION(a.geom, b.geom, 0.5)
    FROM sales_regions a, sales_regions b
    WHERE a.id = 51 and b.id = 43
  ),
  'mask=anyinteract'
)='TRUE';
  COUNT(*)
----------
         2
```

SDO_UNION

We can use the `SDO_UNION` function to compute the geometry covered by two sales regions. We can then use the resulting union geometry to identify the total number of customers. Listing 9-14 shows the SQL for sales regions 43 and 51.

Listing 9-14. `SDO_UNION` *of Two Geometries*

```
SQL> SELECT  count(*)
FROM
(
  SELECT SDO_GEOM.SDO_UNION (a.geom, b.geom, 0.5) geom
  FROM sales_regions b, sales_regions a
  WHERE a.id=51 and b.id=43
) b, customers a
WHERE SDO_RELATE(a.location, b.geom, 'mask=anyinteract')='TRUE';
  COUNT(*)
----------
       124

1 row selected.
```

The number of customers returned is 124. Compare this with the two customers returned in Listing 9-13 using the intersection region. This means there are 122 customers that are not common to both sales regions. Since not more than 2 percent of the customers are common to both sales regions, we may decide not to combine the two sales regions with `id`s 51 and 43.

What if we want to know the coverage of all our businesses in the Washington, D.C., area? This will involve not just two sales region geometries, but all geometries in the `sales_regions` table. We can repeatedly perform the union in an iterative fashion, as the PL/SQL procedure in Listing 9-15 demonstrates.

Listing 9-15. *Coverage of the Sales Regions: Performing a Union of All the Sales Regions*

```
DECLARE
   Geom mdsys.sdo_geometry
   coverage mdsys.sdo_geometry := null;
BEGIN
   OPEN cur FOR SELECT geom FROM sales_regions;

  LOOP
     EXIT WHEN cur%NOTFOUND;
     FETCH cur INTO geom;
     coverage := SDO_GEOM.SDO_UNION(coverage, geom);
  END LOOP;
  EXECUTE IMMEDIATE 'INSERT INTO sales_region_coverage values (:1)'
    USING coverage;
  COMMIT;
END;
```

Note that the procedure in Listing 9-15 computes the coverage by performing a union of all the sales regions and inserts the coverage geometry into the `sales_region_coverage` table. It assumes the table exists and contains only one column of type `SDO_GEOMETRY`. Later in the chapter, we will look at alternate methods using spatial aggregate functions to perform exactly the same task.

SDO_DIFFERENCE

The SDO_DIFFERENCE function subtracts the second geometry from the first geometry. In effect, it returns the region that is exclusive to the first geometry. Note that this is meaningful only in the following situations:

- Both the first and second geometries have area (i.e., polygons or multipolygons, and so on).
- The second geometry is a polygon or a line and the first geometry is a line.
- The first geometry is a point.

If the preceding conditions are not met, the SDO_DIFFERENCE operation returns the first geometry as the result.

Using the SDO_DIFFERENCE function, we can compare the sales regions with the competitor regions, as shown in Listing 9-16. For instance, we want to target customers exclusively served by a specific competitor (with id=2). First, we identify all sales regions that intersect this competitor region using a simple SDO_RELATE query (left as an exercise to the reader). There is only one sales region (id=6) that intersects competitor region 2. To find customers exclusive to competitor region 2, we first compute the difference of the competitor region with respect to sales region 6. The resulting region is exclusive to competitor region 2.

Listing 9-16. SDO_DIFFERENCE *of Competitor Region 2 with Sales Region 6*

```
SQL> CREATE TABLE exclusive_region_for_comp_2 AS
SELECT SDO_GEOM.SDO_DIFFERENCE(b.geom, a.geom, 0.5) geom
FROM sales_regions a, competitors_sales_regions b
WHERE b.id=2 and a.id=6  ;
```

Once we construct the region that is exclusive to competitor region 2, we can identify customers in this exclusive zone, as shown in Listing 9-17. We probably can target such customers with special promotions to wean them from the specific competitor (id=2).

Listing 9-17. *Identifying Customers in an Exclusive Zone of a Competitor*

```
SQL> SELECT ct.id, ct.name
FROM exclusive_region_for_comp_2 excl, customers ct
WHERE SDO_RELATE(ct.location, excl.geom, 'mask=anyinteract')='TRUE'
ORDER BY ct.id;

    ID NAME
------ -----------------------------------
    51 STUDENT LOAN MARKETING
   487 GETTY
   795 FOUR SEASONS HOTEL WASHINGTON DC
   796 HOTEL MONTICELLO-GEORGETOWN
   798 GEORGETOWN SUITES
   821 LATHAM HOTEL
```

```
  1022 C AND O CANAL BOAT TRIPS
  1161 GEORGETOWN SUITES HARBOR BLDG
  1370 BIOGRAPH THEATRE
  1377 FOUNDRY
  1558 US OFFICE PRODUCTS
  2067 WASHINGTON INTERNATIONAL SCHOOL
  6685 SONESTA INTERNATIONAL HOTELS
  6953 FOUNDRY MALL
  6956 WASHINGTON HARBOUR
  6957 WASHINGTON HARBOUR
  7163 GEORGETOWN VISITOR CENTER
  7164 GEORGETOWN VISITOR CENTER
  7176 CHESAPEAKE & OHIO CANAL
  7601 MASONIC LODGE

20 rows selected.
```

Note that we can combine Listings 9-16 and 9-17 into a single SQL statement as shown in Listing 9-18. We obtain the same 20 customers as in Listing 9-17.

Listing 9-18. *Combining Listings 9-16 and 9-17*

```
SQL> SELECT  ct.id, ct.name
FROM sales_regions sr, competitors_sales_regions csr, customers ct
WHERE csr.id=2 AND sr.id=6
  AND SDO_RELATE
  (
    ct.location,
    (SDO_GEOM.SDO_DIFFERENCE(csr.geom, sr.geom, 0.5)),
    'mask=anyinteract'
  )='TRUE'
ORDER BY ct.id;
    ID NAME
------ -----------------------------------
    51 STUDENT LOAN MARKETING
   487 GETTY
   795 FOUR SEASONS HOTEL WASHINGTON DC
   796 HOTEL MONTICELLO-GEORGETOWN
   798 GEORGETOWN SUITES
   821 LATHAM HOTEL
  1022 C AND O CANAL BOAT TRIPS
  1161 GEORGETOWN SUITES HARBOR BLDG
  1370 BIOGRAPH THEATRE
  1377 FOUNDRY
  1558 US OFFICE PRODUCTS
  2067 WASHINGTON INTERNATIONAL SCHOOL
  6685 SONESTA INTERNATIONAL HOTELS
```

```
  6953 FOUNDRY MALL
  6956 WASHINGTON HARBOUR
  6957 WASHINGTON HARBOUR
  7163 GEORGETOWN VISITOR CENTER
  7164 GEORGETOWN VISITOR CENTER
  7176 CHESAPEAKE & OHIO CANAL
  7601 MASONIC LODGE

20 rows selected.
```

SDO_XOR

This function can be rewritten as the SDO_DIFFERENCE of the SDO_UNION and the SDO_INTERSECTION of the two geometries. This function can be used as an alternate mechanism to identify if two overlapping sales regions need to be merged. For instance, if sales regions 1 and 2 overlap, we can compare the number of customers in the SDO_XOR of these regions with those in the SDO_UNION of these regions. If the number in the SDO_XOR is close to that in the SDO_UNION, then these two sales regions, although overlapping, have few common customers. This is the case in Listing 9-19. The result of 122 customers is close to that from the SDO_UNION (as in Listing 9- 14). As a result, these sales regions need not be merged.

Listing 9-19. SDO_XOR *of Sales Regions 43 and 51 to Identify Customers That Are Not Shared Between Them*

```
SQL> SELECT count(*)
FROM
(
  SELECT SDO_GEOM.SDO_XOR (a.geom, b.geom, 0.5) geom
  FROM sales_regions b, sales_regions a
  WHERE a.id=51 and b.id=43
) b, customers a
WHERE SDO_RELATE(a.location, b.geom, 'mask=anyinteract')='TRUE';
    COUNT(*)
----------
       122

1 row selected.
```

Geometric Analysis Functions

In the previous section, we examined how to construct geometries that represent the intersection, union, or difference of a pair of geometries. In this section, we describe how to perform further analysis on individual geometries. These individual geometries can be columns of existing tables, or they can be the result of other operations such as unions and intersections. For instance, we can compute the area of the intersection region for each pair of overlapping sales regions. Next, we can identify the pair (of sales regions) that has the maximum area for the overlap. The pair can then be marked as a potential candidate for merging of associated business units.

Area and Length Functions

We will start off with area and length calculations. Then we will examine other geometric functions. These functions have the following generic syntax:

```
Function_name
(
  Geometry          IN SDO_GEOMETRY,
  tolerance         IN NUMBER
  [, units_params   IN VARCHAR2]
)
RETURN NUMBER
```

where

- Geometry specifies the geometry object to be analyzed.
- tolerance specifies the tolerance to be used in this analysis.
- units_params is an optional third argument that specifies the units in which the area/length is to be returned. This argument is of the form 'unit=<value_string>'. You can obtain possible values for the units by consulting the MDSYS.SDO_DIST_UNITS table for length functions and the MDSYS.SDO_AREA_UNITS table for area functions.

Accuracy of Area and Length Computations

The area and length functions take the curvature of the Earth into account during calculations. For a geodetic geometry, the accuracy of the area function varies based on geometry size and how much it varies in latitude.

- For small geometries such as New Hampshire, the area function is accurate to within 0.0001 percent.
- For larger geometries of the size of India, the accuracy is within 0.001 percent.
- For much larger geometries, the accuracy is within 0.1 percent.

The length function, on the other hand, is accurate to within 0.00000001 percent. This also holds true for distance calculations between point geometries using the SDO_DISTANCE function.

Next, let's look at examples of the area and the length functions.

SDO_AREA

This function computes the area of an SDO_GEOMETRY object. For instance, if a rectangle object has a length of 10 units and a width of 20 units, the area would be 10 × 20 = 200 square units. Likewise, for arbitrary geometric objects, this function returns the area covered by them.

Listing 9-20 shows how to compute the area of the intersection of sales region 51 with sales region 43 in the sales_regions table (this could be used in addition to the analysis in Listing 9-12 to determine whether or not to merge these sales regions). Note that the unit is specified as 'sq_yard' to indicate square yards.

Listing 9-20. *Area of the Intersection Region of Sales Region 1 and Sales Region 2*

```
SQL> SELECT SDO_GEOM.SDO_AREA
(SDO_GEOM.SDO_INTERSECTION(a.geom, b.geom, 0.5), 0.5, ' unit=sq_yard ' ) area
FROM sales_regions b, sales_regions a
WHERE a.id=51 and b.id=43;
      AREA
-----------
 26243.3702
```

The area function makes sense only for a polygon geometry. For a point or a line string, the area will always be 0. For a line string, there is another useful function, SDO_LENGTH, that we can use for analysis.

SDO_LENGTH

This function returns the *length* for a line string and the *perimeter* for a polygon. For points, this function returns 0.

We can use this function to identify connectors between multiple interstates. Usually, these connectors are very short in length, on the order of 1 or 2 miles. Opening a new store close to these connectors is ideal, as the location would be close to multiple main interstates. Listing 9-21 shows the interstates (connectors) that are not more than 1 mile in length. These interstates usually connect multiple major interstates and are ideal sites for new businesses.

Listing 9-21. *Identifying Interstates Shorter Than 1 Mile*

```
SQL> SELECT interstate
FROM us_interstates
WHERE SDO_GEOM.SDO_LENGTH(geom, 0.5, 'unit=mile') < 1;
INTERSTATE
-----------------------------------
I10/I45
I40/I65
I30/I35E
I564
I71/I670
I55B
I90/I87
I94S
I94/I35E
I94/I35W
I670/315
I96S

12 rows selected.
```

MBR Functions

If you want to show geometry on a map, you usually need to specify the *extent*—that is, the lower bound and upper bound in each dimension. You can use the *minimum bounding rectangle* (MBR) for this purpose. This rectangle is usually specified by the lower-left (all the minimum values) and upper-right (all the maximum values) corner vertices. Figure 9-5 shows an example of the MBR for different geometries.

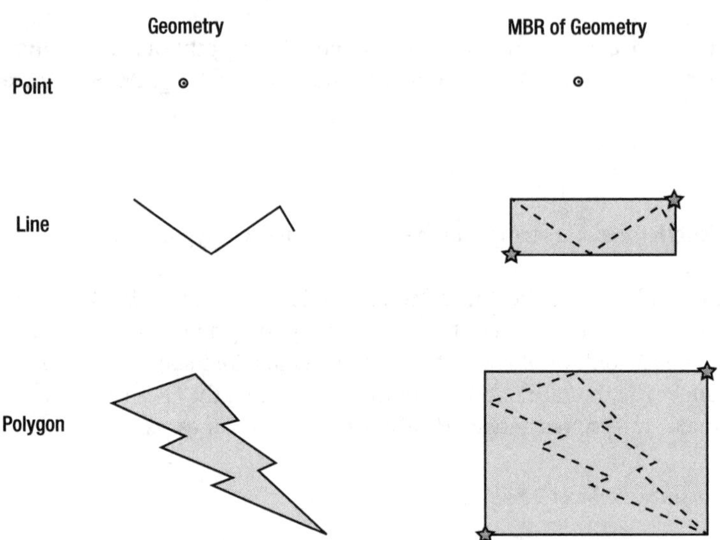

Figure 9-5. `SDO_MBR` *for different geometries. The stars mark the lower-left and upper-right corners of the MBRs.*

Note that the MBR of a geometry will usually cover more area than the original geometry. For a point geometry, the MBR is also a point (i.e., a degenerate MBR where the lower-left and upper-right corners are the same).

Spatial provides several functions to compute the MBR and associated components.

SDO_MBR

The `SDO_MBR` function takes an `SDO_GEOMETRY` as an argument and computes the MBR for the geometry. It returns an `SDO_GEOMETRY` object.

- If the input is a *point*, then the `SDO_MBR` function returns the point geometry.
- If input is a *line string* parallel to the x- or y-axis, then the function returns a linear geometry.
- Otherwise, the function returns the MBR of the input geometry as an `SDO_GEOMETRY` object.

Listing 9-22 shows how to get the extent or the MBR for a specific sales region in the sales_regions table.

Listing 9-22. *Computing the MBR of a Geometry*

```
SQL> SELECT SDO_GEOM.SDO_MBR(a.geom) mbr FROM sales_regions a WHERE
a.id=1;



MBR(SDO_GTYPE, SDO_SRID, SDO_POINT(X, Y, Z), SDO_ELEM_INFO,
SDO_ORDINATES)
----------------------------------------------------------------------------
SDO_GEOMETRY(2003, 8307, NULL, SDO_ELEM_INFO_ARRAY(1, 1003, 3),
SDO_ORDINATE_ARR
AY(-77.049535, 38.8970816, -77.040259, 38.90433))

1 row selected.
```

SDO_MIN_MBR_ORDINATE and SDO_MAX_MBR_ORDINATE

Instead of getting the extent in both dimensions, sometimes you may be interested in the extent in a specific dimension. You can obtain this using the SDO_MIN_MBR_ORDINATE and SDO_MAX_MBR_ORDINATE functions, which return the minimum and maximum ordinates of a geometry in a specified dimension, respectively. Listing 9-23 shows how to get the extent in the first dimension.

Listing 9-23. *Obtaining the* MIN_ORDINATE*s and* MAX_ORDINATE*s in a Specific Dimension*

```
SQL> SELECT SDO_GEOM.SDO_MIN_MBR_ORDINATE(a.geom, 1) min_extent,
SDO_GEOM.SDO_MAX_MBR_ORDINATE(a.geom, 1) max_extent
FROM sales_regions a WHERE a.id=1;
MIN_EXTENT     MAX_EXTENT
----------     ----------
-77.049535     -77.040259

1 row selected.
```

Miscellaneous Geometric Analysis Functions

In addition to the MBR functions are several other functions to perform simple *geometric* analyses such as computing the centroid or computing the convex hull.[1] Each of these functions has the following generic signature:

```
<Function_name>
(
  Geometry        IN SDO_GEOMETRY,
  Tolerance       IN NUMBER
)
RETURNS SDO_GEOMETRY
```

where the first argument is an SDO_GEOMETRY object and the second specifies the tolerance for the geometry.

Let's look at each of these functions in turn.

SDO_CONVEXHULL

The MBR is a very coarse approximation of a geometric object. A finer approximation is the convex hull of that object. A geometric set is *convex* if for every pair of points in the set, the line joining those two points is contained completely within the geometry. The convex hull of a geometry is the smallest convex set that contains all of that geometry. Thus, a convex hull of a polygon simplifies by eliminating the concave vertices (where the boundary bends inward) in its boundary. Figure 9-6 shows the convex hull for different types of geometries.

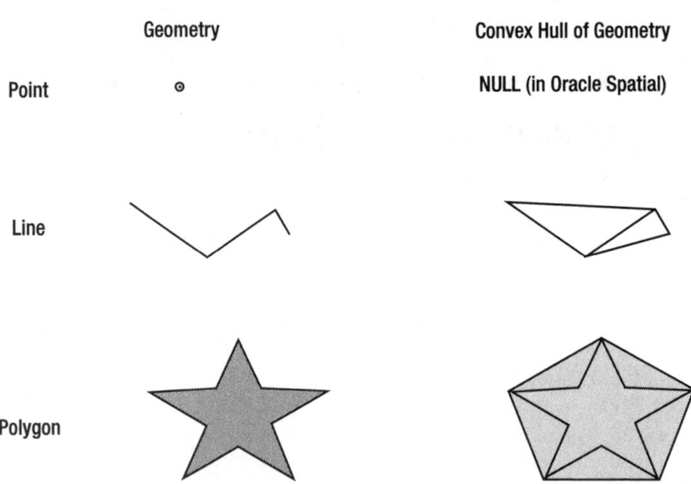

Figure 9-6. *Example of* SDO_CONVEXHULL *for different geometry objects*

---

1. For a variety of applications of these functions, refer to Mark de Berg, Marc van Krevald, Mark Overmars, and Otfried Schwarzopf, *Computational Geometry: Algorithms and Applications, Second Edition* (New York: Springer-Verlag, 2000).

The SDO_CONVEXHULL function computes the convex hull of an SDO_GEOMETRY. Listing 9-24 illustrates this for the state of New Hampshire. Note that the geometry for the state of New Hampshire has 709 vertices. In contrast, the convex hull shown in Listing 9-24 reduces it to 30 (i.e., a total of 60 numbers in the SDO_ORDINATE_ARRAY attribute of the resulting SDO_GEOMETRY). In this case, the convex hull simplifies the geometry without compromising too much on its shape. It can be used as a finer approximation of the geometry than the MBR in applications involving computational geometry algorithms.

Listing 9-24. *Computing the Convex Hull for the State of New Hampshire*

```
SQL> SELECT SDO_GEOM.SDO_CONVEXHULL(a.geom, 0.5) cvxhl
FROM us_states a
WHERE a.state_abrv='NH';

CVXHL(SDO_GTYPE, SDO_SRID, SDO_POINT(X, Y, Z), SDO_ELEM_INFO,
SDO_ORDINATES)
--------------------------------------------------------------------------------
SDO_GEOMETRY
(
  2003, 8307, NULL,
  SDO_ELEM_INFO_ARRAY(1, 1003, 1),      -- A Polygon
  SDO_ORDINATE_ARRAY                    -- Vertices of polygon
  (
    -71.294701, 42.6968992, -71.182304, 42.7374992, -70.817787, 42.8719901,
      -70.712257, 43.042324, -70.703026, 43.057457, -70.7052, 43.0709,
    -71.084816, 45.3052478, -71.285332, 45.3018647, -71.301582, 45.2965197,
    -71.443062, 45.2383418, -72.068199, 44.273666, -72.379906, 43.5740009,
      -72.394676, 43.5273279, -72.396866, 43.5190849, -72.553307, 42.8848878,
      -72.556679, 42.8668668, -72.557594, 42.8524128, -72.542564, 42.8075558,
      -72.516022, 42.7652279, -72.458984, 42.7267719, -72.412491, 42.7253529,
      -72.326614, 42.722729, -72.283455, 42.721462, -71.98188, 42.7132071,
      -71.773003, 42.7079012, -71.652107, 42.7051012, -71.630905, 42.7046012,
   -71.458282, 42.7004362, -71.369682, 42.6982082, -71.294701, 42.6968992
  )
)

1 row selected.
```

Caution The SDO_CONVEXHULL function is not defined—that is, it returns NULL for any geometry with less than three noncolinear points or if all the points are collinear.

The convex hull function is traditionally used to calculate the smallest convex geometry covering a set of points or a set of polygons. However, the function in Listing 9-24 generates the hull for a single geometry. How do you operate on sets of geometries? One option is to perform a union of geometries as in Listing 9-15 and then compute the convex hull for the resulting union. An alternative and easier approach is to use the equivalent spatial aggregate function that operates on sets of geometries. We discuss this aggregate function later in the chapter.

SDO_CENTROID

Suppose you want to label each intersection region with a name on a map. Where do you put the label? One place to put the label is at the *centroid* (i.e., the "center of mass or gravity") for the geometry. Mathematically speaking, the centroid of a geometric object is defined by an average position of all points within the object. If the number of points is finite, such as a set of points, the centroid's x-value is the average of all the point's x-values, and the centroid's y-value is the average of all the point's y-values. For an infinite number of points (such as a curve or polygon), you use this equivalent integral from calculus:

$$\int_g p\,d\mu \Big/ \int_g d\mu$$

where g is the geometry, p is the point value, and μ is any uniform integral measure.

The SDO_CENTROID function computes the geometric centroid of an SDO_GEOMETRY object. Figure 9-7 shows examples of centroids for different geometries. Note that the centroid is not defined for lines in Oracle Spatial. The centroid for inverted C-shaped polygons can be outside the polygon.

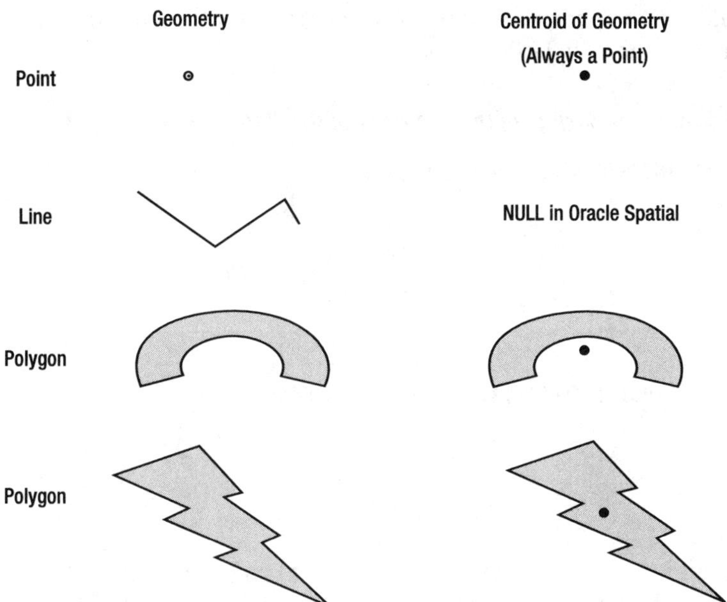

Figure 9-7. `SDO_CENTROID` *for different geometries*

The centroid of any geometry is always a point. This centroid may or may not lie on the geometry itself. The inverted C-shaped polygon in Figure 9-7 is one such example. The `SDO_CENTROID` function also returns `NULL` for linear geometries.

Listing 9-25 shows how to compute the centroid for the state of New Hampshire using the `SDO_CENTROID` function. We can use the location of the centroid to place a label for the state while displaying it on a map.

Listing 9-25. *Computing the Centroid for the State of New Hampshire*

```
SQL> SELECT SDO_GEOM.SDO_CENTROID(a.geom, 0.5) ctrd
FROM us_states a WHERE state_abrv='NH';
CTRD(SDO_GTYPE, SDO_SRID, SDO_POINT(X, Y, Z), SDO_ELEM_INFO,
SDO_ORDINATES)
--------------------------------------------------------------------------------
SDO_GEOMETRY
(2001, 8307, SDO_POINT_TYPE(-71.580917, 43.6792049, NULL), NULL, NULL)

1 row selected.
```

SDO_POINTONSURFACE

Since the centroid of a polygon may or may not lie within that polygon, it may be useful to put a label on some other point on the surface of the geometry. This is not only useful, but also necessary in creating some types of polygonal maps. We can get one such point using the SDO_POINTONSURFACE function as shown in Listing 9-26.

Listing 9-26. *Obtaining a Point on the Surface of the Geometry of the State of Massachusetts*

```
SQL> SELECT SDO_GEOM.SDO_POINTONSURFACE(a.geom, 0.5) pt
FROM us_states a
WHERE state_abrv='MA';

PT(SDO_GTYPE, SDO_SRID, SDO_POINT(X, Y, Z), SDO_ELEM_INFO,
SDO_ORDINATES)
--------------------------------------------------------------------------
SDO_GEOMETRY(2001, 8307, SDO_POINT_TYPE(-73.265411, 42.745861, NULL),
NULL, NULL)

1 row selected.
```

■ **Caution** The only assurance for the SDO_POINTONSURFACE function is that the returned point will be in the boundary/interior of the polygon passed in. (In the current implementation, it actually returns the first point in the SDO_ORDINATE_ARRAY of the polygon geometry.) No other assumptions can be made.

Aggregate Functions

Until now, you have seen spatial functions that operate either on a single geometric object or on a pair of geometric objects. Next, we describe *spatial aggregate* functions that operate on a set of SDO_GEOMETRY objects. Like other aggregate functions in Oracle, these spatial aggregates are specified in the SELECT list of a SQL statement.

Aggregate MBR Function

Suppose we want to find out the extent covered by a set of SDO_GEOMETRY objects. (Usually, we will need this information to populate the USER_SDO_GEOM_METADATA view before creating an index.) Figure 9-8 shows the aggregate MBR for a set of point geometries.

Figure 9-8. SDO_AGGR_MBR *for a set of points. The stars mark the lower-left and upper-right vertices of the computed MBR.*

We can compute the MBR of a collection using the SDO_AGGR_MBR function. Listing 9-27 illustrates its usage by computing the aggregate MBR for all the locations in the branches table.

Listing 9-27. *Finding the Extent of a Set of Geometries Using* SDO_AGGR_MBR

```
SQL> SELECT  SDO_AGGR_MBR(a.location) extent FROM branches a;

EXTENT(SDO_GTYPE, SDO_SRID, SDO_POINT(X, Y, Z), SDO_ELEM_INFO,
SDO_ORDINATES)
--------------------------------------------------------------------------------
SDO_GEOMETRY
(
  2003, 8307, NULL,
  SDO_ELEM_INFO_ARRAY(1, 1003, 3),  -- A Rectangle-type polygon
  SDO_ORDINATE_ARRAY(-122.49836, 37.7112075, -76.950947, 38.9611552)
)
```

Note that this returns the coordinate extent or the MBR of the set of geometries as an SDO_GEOMETRY object. You may need to use the SDO_MIN_MBR_ORDINATE and SDO_MAX_MBR_ORDINATE functions on the resulting MBR to appropriately set the SDO_DIM_ARRAY elements in the USER_SDO_GEOM_METADATA view.

Other Aggregate Functions

In addition to the MBR, we may want to compute the union or the convex hull of a set of geometries. You can use the SDO_AGGR_UNION or SDO_AGGR_CONVEXHULL function for this purpose. Unlike the SDO_AGGR_MBR function, which takes an SDO_GEOMETRY as the argument, these functions take an SDOAGGRTYPE as the argument. The SDOAGGRTYPE has the following structure.

```
SQL> DESCRIBE SDOAGGRTYPE;
Name                   Null?     Type

GEOMETRY                         MDSYS.SDO_GEOMETRY
TOLERANCE                        NUMBER
```

SDO_AGGR_UNION

The aggregate function SDO_AGGR_UNION computes the union of a set of geometries. The union is returned as an SDO_GEOMETRY object. Figure 9-9 shows the union for a set of points.

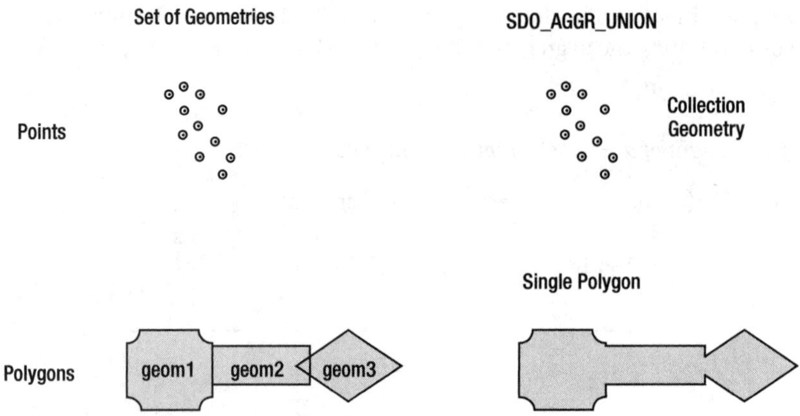

Figure 9-9. *Two examples of* SDO_AGGR_UNION

For a set of point geometries, the union is a geometry *collection.* For a set of three overlapping polygon geometries, the union is a single polygon. Note the interior edges vanish on the union polygon shown at the right of Figure 9-9.

We can create a union of all the locations in the branches table to identify the coverage of stores, as shown in Listing 9-28. This creates a collection of all 77 point locations for the branches.

Listing 9-28. *Finding the Coverage of* sales_regions *Using* SDO_AGGR_UNION

```
SQL>SELECT SDO_AGGR_UNION(SDOAGGRTYPE(a.location, 0.5)) coverage
FROM branches a;

COVERAGE(SDO_GTYPE, SDO_SRID, SDO_POINT(X, Y, Z), SDO_ELEM_INFO,
SDO_ORDINATES)
-------------------------------------------------------------------------------
SDO_GEOMETRY
(
  2005, 8307, NULL,
  SDO_ELEM_INFO_ARRAY(1, 1, 77),    -- collection of 77 points
  SDO_ORDINATE_ARRAY
  (
    -122.41915, 37.7751038, -122.39489, 37.793174, -122.39686, 37.793595,
    -77.02601, 38.8945028, -77.033619, 38.8991971, -122.40839, 37.788633,
    -122.49045, 37.7339297, -122.43403, 37.7511713, -122.40361, 37.7839342,
    -122.40007, 37.7998365, -122.40415, 37.7702542, -122.4025, 37.791987,
    -122.46898, 37.7380652, -122.40473, 37.730593, -122.4076, 37.7845683,
    -122.39796, 37.7438371, -122.40876, 37.7991795, -122.43855, 37.7440736,
    -122.47552, 37.726909, -122.42232, 37.7906913, -122.4308, 37.7974994,
    -122.47685, 37.7429851, -122.40781, 37.794415, -122.40864, 37.788168,
    -122.4359, 37.7238284, -122.4886, 37.75362, -122.40145, 37.7881653,
    -122.40255, 37.792281, -122.44138, 37.7160032, -122.42035, 37.744667,
    -122.41864, 37.753694, -122.40391, 37.7112075, -122.4787, 37.763452,
    -122.46635, 37.7640397, -122.40599, 37.7933898, -122.4783, 37.7803596,
```

```
    -122.44957, 37.7821163, -122.43418,37.7907946, -122.43879, 37.7738425,
    -122.41713, 37.7392079, -122.46537, 37.7828694, -122.4395, 37.800408,
    -122.43495, 37.7607737, -122.45275, 37.78649, -122.41914, 37.7751346,
    -122.39652, 37.7782523, -122.40047, 37.7958989, -122.49836, 37.7756795,
    -122.40905, 37.7527288, -122.39119, 37.7330824, -77.032016, 38.8993045,
    -77.033679, 38.8987586, -76.950947, 38.8925976, -77.006755, 38.93653,
    -77.042079, 38.9026399, -77.037653, 38.9295113, -76.989522, 38.8655141,
    -76.993059, 38.9001983, -77.033158, 38.9035919, -77.023716, 38.9331479,
    -77.062822, 38.9431214, -77.09677, 38.9442554, -77.083759, 38.9570281,
    -77.009721, 38.9611552, -76.995893, 38.90018, -77.001773, 38.8215786,
    -77.017477, 38.8765101, -77.003477, 38.887564, -77.02956, 38.8982647,
    -77.039476, 38.9012157, -77.046673, 38.9037307, -77.06342, 38.9075175,
    -77.044112, 38.9092715, -77.043592, 38.9214703, -77.051909, 38.9242888,
    -77.057711, 38.9344998, -77.044897, 38.9007058
  )
)
```

Note that the union returns a geometry *collection* where each element is a point in the input set. This is because the individual points do not intersect. Let's look at another example where there is a union of two overlapping polygons, sales regions 51 and 43, and a third disjoint, region 2. This will return a collection of two polygon elements: one element after merging overlapping regions 1 and 7, and another element for disjoint region 2. This is illustrated in Listing 9-29. Compare this with Listing 9-14, where we could only perform union of two regions (1 and 7) at a time using the SDO_UNION function.

Listing 9-29. *Union of Three Sales Regions (ids 43, 51, and 2)*

```
SQL> SELECT SDO_AGGR_UNION(SDOAGGRTYPE(a.geom, 0.5)) union_geom
FROM sales_regions a
WHERE id=51 or id=43 or id=2 ;
UNION_GEOM(SDO_GTYPE, SDO_SRID, SDO_POINT(X, Y, Z), SDO_ELEM_INFO,
SDO_ORDINATES
-------------------------------------------------------------------------------
SDO_GEOMETRY
(
  2007, 8307, NULL,                              -- Collection Geometry
  SDO_ELEM_INFO_ARRAY(1, 1003, 1, 35, 1003, 1), -- Two polygonal rings
  SDO_ORDINATE_ARRAY                             -- Vertices of the polygons
  (
    -77.061998, 38.9358866, -77.062351, 38.9344997, -77.061997,
    38.9331128, -77.060992, 38.9319371, -77.059486, 38.9311515, -77.057711,
    38.9308756,-77.055935, 38.9311515, -77.05443, 38.9319371, -77.053424,
    38.9331128, -77.05307, 38.9344997, -77.053423, 38.9358866, -77.054429,
    38.9370624, -77.055935, 38.9378481, -77.057711, 38.938124, -77.059486,
    38.9378481, -77.060992, 38.9370624, -77.061998, 38.9358866, -122.41056,
    37.7933897, -122.41021, 37.7920025, -122.40922,37.7908265, -122.40774,
    37.7900408, -122.40599, 37.7897649, -122.40541, 37.7898563, -122.40567,
    37.7895524, -122.40602, 37.7881652, -122.40567, 37.7867781, -122.40468,
```

```
        37.7856021, -122.4032, 37.7848164, -122.40145, 37.7845404, -122.3997,
        37.7848164, -122.39822, 37.7856021, -122.39723, 37.7867781, -122.39688,
        37.7881652, -122.39723, 37.7895524, -122.39822, 37.7907285, -122.3997,
        37.7915143, -122.40145, 37.7917902, -122.40203, 37.7916988, -122.40177,
        37.7920025, -122.40142, 37.7933897, -122.40177, 37.7947769, -122.40276,
        37.7959529, -122.40424, 37.7967387, -122.40599, 37.7970147, -122.40774,
        37.7967387, -122.40922, 37.7959529, -122.41021, 37.7947769, -122.41056,
        37.7933897
    )
)

1 row selected.
```

Likewise, we can compute the coverage (i.e., the union of all the sales_regions) as in the following example. Note that this will be the equivalent of the coverage obtained in Listing 9-15. Unlike Listing 9-15, the following usage is much simplified without the need for PL/SQL code. Listing 9-30 illustrates the power of spatial aggregate functions.

Listing 9-30. *Union of All Sales Regions to Obtain Business Coverage*

```
SQL> SELECT  SDO_AGGR_UNION(SDOAGGRTYPE(a.geom, 0.5)) coverage
FROM sales_regions a;
-- output too big to be shown: result geometry more than 100 vertices
```

SDO_AGGR_CONVEXHULL

The resulting unions in Listings 9-29 and 9-30 are complex geometries with some concave vertices. As an alternative, we can compute the SDO_AGGR_CONVEXHULL to compute the convex hull from the set of sales_regions. Figure 9-10 shows the aggregate convex hull for the point set in Figure 9-8. Listing 9-31 shows the code for computing the coverage of sales regions using the SDO_AGGR_CONVEXHULL function.

Set of Geometries SDO_AGGR_CONVEXHULL

Figure 9-10. SDO_AGGR_CONVEXHULL *for a set of points*

Listing 9-31. *Finding the Coverage of* sales_regions *Using* SDO_AGGR_CONVEXHULL

```
SQL> SELECT SDO_AGGR_CONVEXHULL(SDOAGGRTYPE(a.geom, 0.5)) coverage
FROM sales_regions a;
COVERAGE(SDO_GTYPE, SDO_SRID, SDO_POINT(X, Y, Z), SDO_ELEM_INFO,
```

```
SDO_ORDINATES)
--------------------------------------------------------------------------------
SDO_GEOMETRY
(
  2003, 8307, NULL,                          -- Polygon type geometry
  SDO_ELEM_INFO_ARRAY(1, 1003, 1),
  SDO_ORDINATE_ARRAY                         -- Vertices of the polygon
  (
    -122.48595, 37.6881575, -76.865425, 38.7930326, -76.86362, 38.7927488,
    -76.861815, 38.7930202, -76.860283, 38.7938054, -76.85926, 38.7949851,
    -76.80744, 38.8662751, -76.807079, 38.8676696, -76.807438, 38.8690665,
    -76.808461, 38.8702533, -76.868265, 38.9394471, -76.869798, 38.9402428,
    -122.55129, 37.7783805, -122.62661, 37.7497019, -122.62812, 37.7489059,
    -122.62913, 37.7477192, -122.62948, 37.7463226, -122.62912, 37.7449286,
    -122.62811, 37.7437496, -122.62661, 37.742965, -122.51969, 37.6946774,
    -122.48949, 37.6881485, -122.48772, 37.687876, -122.48595, 37.6881575
  )
)

1 row selected.
```

Note that as opposed to the union geometry in Listing 9-30 (or the union of the branches in 9-25), the aggregate convex hull computed has fewer vertices. This might result in a significant speeding up in computation if the convex hull approximation of the coverage is used (instead of the actual union) in further proximity analyses.

Caution The SDO_AGGR_CONVEXHULL returns NULL if all the vertices of all the input geometries are collinear or if there is only one vertex (one point).

SDO_AGGR_CENTROID

Assume that we have identified that a group of customers in the customers table is too far from existing branch locations. We may want to start a new store to cater to this group of customers. What might be the best location for this new store? The *centroid* of the group is a reasonable choice. The centroid of the customer locations minimizes the average distance from the customers to the new store location. Figure 9-11 illustrates the centroid for a set of points.

Set of Geometries

SDO_AGGR_CENTROID

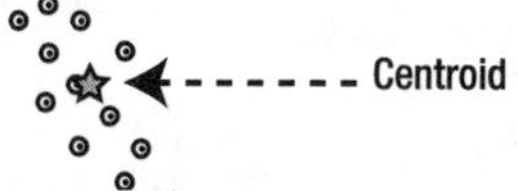

Figure 9-11. SDO_AGGR_CENTROID *for a set of points*

The SDO_AGGR_CENTROID function allows us to compute this centroid for an arbitrary group of customers as shown in Listing 9-32.

Listing 9-32. *Finding the Centroid of Customer Locations Using* SDO_AGGR_CENTROID

```
SQL> SELECT SDO_AGGR_CENTROID(SDOAGGRTYPE(a.location, 0.5)) ctrd
FROM customers a
WHERE  id>100;
CTRD(SDO_GTYPE, SDO_SRID, SDO_POINT(X, Y, Z), SDO_ELEM_INFO,
SDO_ORDINATES)
--------------------------------------------------------------------------------
SDO_GEOMETRY
(2001, 8307, SDO_POINT_TYPE(-103.19018, 38.0963807, NULL), NULL, NULL)
```

As shown in Listing 9-32, we can have any arbitrary spatial or attribute filtering in the WHERE clause of the SQL statement. The aggregate function, CENTROID in this case, operates only on the subset of the geometries that satisfy the WHERE clause as collected by the GROUP BY clause, if any.

Summary

In this chapter, we described how to perform proximity analysis using spatial functions to solve real application problems. We described functions to perform relationship analysis, unions, intersections, and other geometry combination functions on pairs of geometric objects. We covered how to create buffers around geometric objects and use them in relationship analysis with other geometries. We also examined how to identify the extents, centroids, and convex hulls of individual geometric objects or groups of geometric objects.

Together, these functions aid in the analysis of business demographics, such as number of customers in appropriate buffers and intersecting regions. Such analysis is vital to making strategic decisions, such as starting new businesses at appropriate locations, merging existing businesses, or targeting specific customers with additional promotions.

CHAPTER 10

Network Modeling

In the previous chapters, we described geographical objects as points, lines, and polygons. In Chapters 8 and 9, you saw how to search geographical objects based on the way they are positioned with respect to other objects. In particular, you learned how to find objects that are within some distance from another object (with the `SDO_WITHIN_DISTANCE` operator) or simply to find the object nearest to another one (with the `SDO_NN` operator).

Those operations are useful, no doubt. However, they find and select objects based solely on the shortest absolute distance ("as the crow flies") between them. This may be very different from the actual distance you would need to travel to reach your destination. Unless you are a bird, you are obliged by nature (if not by law!) to travel only along well-defined paths—that is, you follow streets and roads, and you obey traffic regulations such as one-way streets and speed limits.

Consider the set of points illustrated in Figure 10-1. The point nearest to point D is point B. However, if the points are placed on a network, as illustrated in Figure 10-2, then the point nearest to point D is now point E.

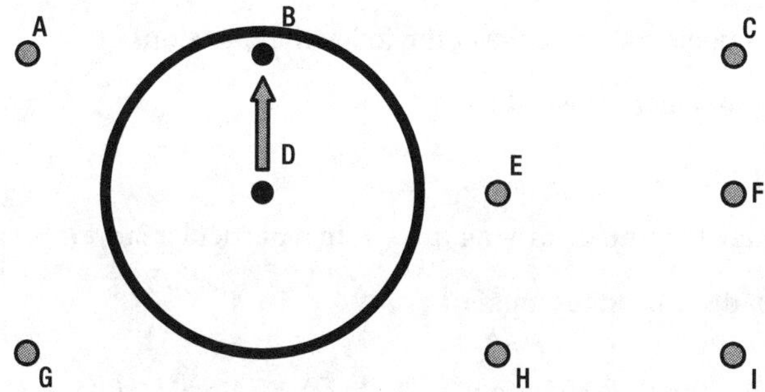

Figure 10-1. *Nearest point "as the crow flies"*

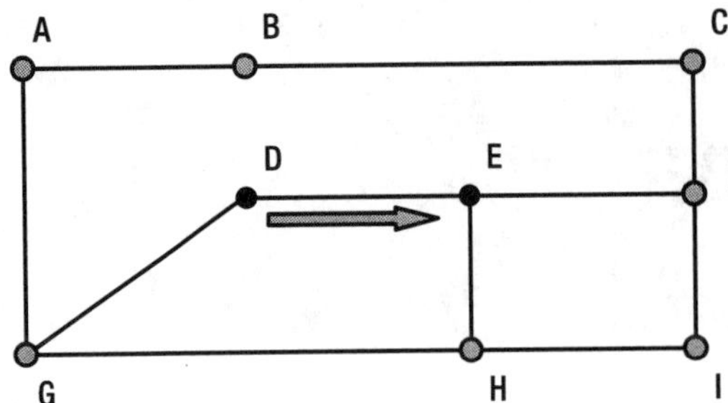

Figure 10-2. *Nearest point along a network*

Things get complicated if we introduce one-way streets, as illustrated in Figure 10-3. Then the nearest point to D is G.

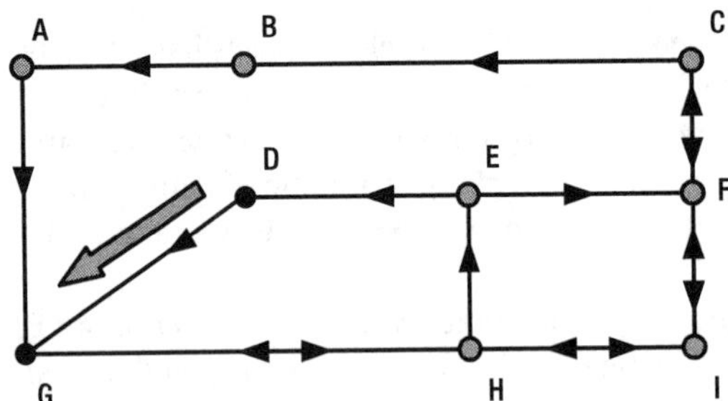

Figure 10-3. *Nearest point along a directed network*

By representing the links between objects, we can answer the following questions:

- What is the shortest or fastest route between two cities?
- What is the closest hotel to an airport?
- How many customers live less than 30 minutes driving time from a particular store?
- How can we reroute traffic if a road is closed for repairs?

More specifically, we can now revisit the types of analyses that you studied in previous chapters. Table 10-1 shows some examples of analyses we can perform on our business data (customers, stores, and branches) once we have positioned them on a road network.

Table 10-1. *Examples of Network-Based Proximity Analyses*

Type of Network Analysis	Usage
Nearest neighbor	Identify the branch nearest to a specific customer.
Route computation	Determine the optimal route from a branch to a customer location. Determine the optimal route for a salesperson to visit a series of customers.
Within distance	Identify customers that live within 30 minutes driving distance of a specific branch.

These analyses are similar to those in Tables 8-1 and 9-1, except they use *network* distances instead of *spatial* distances. In this chapter, we describe how to perform these types of network analyses. In Chapter 12, we use some of those of analyses in the example application.

In this chapter, we first cover the general concepts and terminology of network modeling, and describe how they are used in the Oracle Network Data Model. We also look at the data structures. Next, we move on to describe how to define and load networks in the Oracle database. We then show how to use the Java API to perform network analyses. Finally, we apply all the concepts we describe to our business data.

General Network Modeling Concepts

We all have an intuitive understanding of what constitutes a network. Nevertheless, we think it useful to start with some generic formal definitions of networking concepts. Those concepts are illustrated in Figure 10-4. The figure shows a set of city streets, with a network representation of those streets.

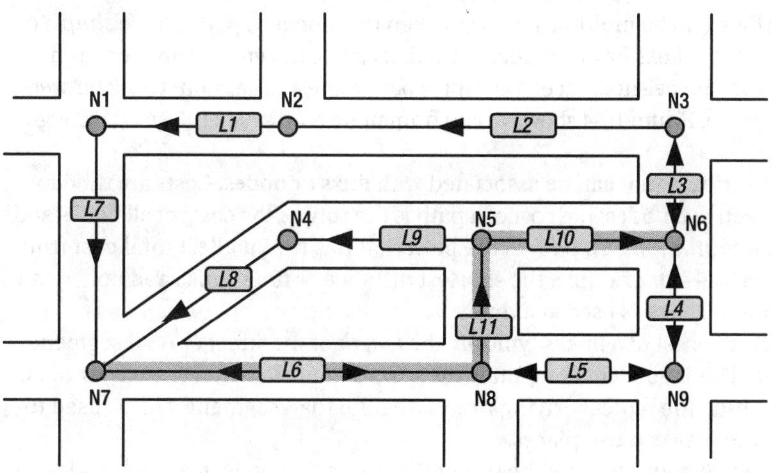

Figure 10-4. *Network concepts: nodes and links*

A *network* is a type of mathematical graph that captures relationships between objects using connectivity. A network consists of nodes and links.

A *node* represents an object of interest on the network. For a road network, nodes are the intersections, as illustrated in Figure 10-4.

A *link* represents a relationship between two nodes. Each link connects two and only two nodes. Multiple links can leave from and meet at the same node. Two nodes can be connected by multiple links. Links can be *directed* or *undirected.* An undirected link can be traversed in either direction, whereas a directed link allows traffic in only one direction. Nodes define the direction of a link: a directed link is considered to "flow" from its *start node* to its *end node.* The *colink* of a directed link is the link that "flows" between the same nodes, in the opposite direction.

On a road network, links represent road and street segments between intersections. A directed link represents a one-way street. In Figure 10-4, links L1 and L2 represent one-way streets. Links L3 and L4 represent two-way streets.

Network elements (links and nodes) may have geometric information associated with them. A *logical network* contains connectivity information but no geometric information. A *spatial network* contains both connectivity information and geometric information.

In Oracle Spatial, in a spatial network, the nodes and links are `SDO_GEOMETRY` objects representing points and lines, respectively.

Note A spatial network can also use other kinds of geometry representations. One variant lets you use linear-referenced geometries. Another lets you use topology objects. We do not cover these possibilities in this chapter. Linear referencing is covered in Appendix B, and topology is discussed in Appendix C.

A *path* represents a route through the network. It is formed by a sequence of nodes and links between two nodes. There can be multiple paths between two nodes. A path can be *simple* or *complex.* In a simple path, the links form an ordered list that can be traversed from the start node to the end node, with each link visited once. A complex path represents a subnetwork between a start and destination node. Figure 10-4 shows a path from node N7 to node N6, going through links L6, L11, and L10.

Cost is a numeric attribute that can be associated with links or nodes. Costs are used for computing paths between two nodes: the cost of a path is the sum of the costs of all nodes and links on that path. The *minimum cost path* is the path that has the smallest total cost from a start node to an end node—for example, the shortest distance or time. Links and nodes can have multiple costs, but only one is used at a time.

On a road network, the cost of a link is typically the *length* of the street or road segment represented by that link. This is good for computing the *shortest* route between two places. Most road networks also include the typical driving *time* along the road segment. This is used to compute the *fastest* route between two places.

Reachable nodes are all nodes that can be reached from a given node. *Reaching* nodes are all nodes that can reach a given node.

The *spanning tree* of a network is a tree (i.e., a graph with no cycles) that connects all nodes of the network. (The directions of links are ignored in a spanning tree.) The *minimum cost spanning tree* (MCST) is a tree that connects all nodes and has the minimum total cost. Spanning trees are commonly used to find the optimal way to build transportation networks (road, rail, and air) to connect a number of places. See Figure 10-18 later in this chapter for an example of an MCST.

Finally, network *constraints* are restrictions defined on network searches. On a road network, for example, driving routes may be required to include only roads that are accessible to trucks or to avoid toll roads. Other constraints can be time based, such as mountain-pass closures during the winter, ferry operation hours, or turns prohibited during peak traffic hours.

Examples of Networks

Networks are used to solve many different problems. In this book, we concentrate on networks that represent spatial objects (roads, rivers, etc.). The following sections present a sampling of network applications.

Road Networks

In a typical road network, the intersections of roads are nodes, and the road segments between two intersections are links. The spatial representation of a road is not inherently related to the nodes and links in the network. For example, a shape point in the spatial representation of a road (reflecting a sharp turn in the road) is not a node in the network if that shape point is not associated with an intersection, and a single spatial object may make up several links in a network (such as a straight segment intersected by three crossing roads).

An important operation with a road network is to find the path from a start point to an end point, minimizing either the travel time or distance. There may be additional constraints on the path computation, such as having the path go through a particular landmark or avoiding a particular intersection.

Train Networks

The subway network of any major city is probably best modeled as a logical network, assuming that precise spatial representation of the stops and tracks is unimportant. In such a network, all stops on the system constitute the nodes of the network, and a link is the connection between two stops if a train travels directly between these two stops. Important operations with a train network include finding all stations that can be reached from a specified station, finding the number of stops between two specified stations, and finding the travel time between two stations.

Utility Networks

Utility networks, such as power lines or cable networks, must often be configured to minimize cost. An important operation with a utility network is to determine the connections among nodes, using MCST algorithms, to provide the required quality of service at the minimum cost. Another important operation is reachability analysis so that, for example, if a station in a water network is shut down, you know which areas will be affected and how the affected areas can be supplied with water from other stations.

Biochemical Networks

Biochemical processes can be modeled as biochemical networks to represent reactions and regulations in living organisms. For example, metabolic pathways are networks involved in enzymatic reactions, while regulatory pathways represent protein-protein interactions. In this example, a pathway is a network; genes, proteins, and chemical compounds are nodes; and reactions among nodes are links. Important operations for a biochemical network include computing paths and the degrees of nodes.

Finance Networks

Many multinational companies with subsidiaries in multiple countries are linked together in a financial network, which is used to transport funds (dividends, royalties, and interests) between them. Tax rates in the various countries and tax treaties between countries are modeled as "costs" on the network links. Various network operations can help find the best way to transfer capital and optimize tax costs.

Project Networks

Our final network example relates to project plans. A *project* is really a network with activities and dependencies represented as links and nodes. Activities have costs (e.g., the time to complete an activity or the resources needed).

Oracle Network Data Model

The network support in Oracle 10*g* is composed of the following elements:

- A data model to store networks inside the database as a set of network tables. This is the *persistent* copy of a network.
- SQL functions to define and maintain networks (the `SDO_NET` package).
- Network analysis functions in Java. The Java API works on a copy of the network loaded from the database. This is the *volatile* copy of the network. Results of analyses (i.e., computed network paths) and network changes can be written back to the database.

The relationship between these elements is illustrated in Figure 10-5. We examine each element in this chapter.

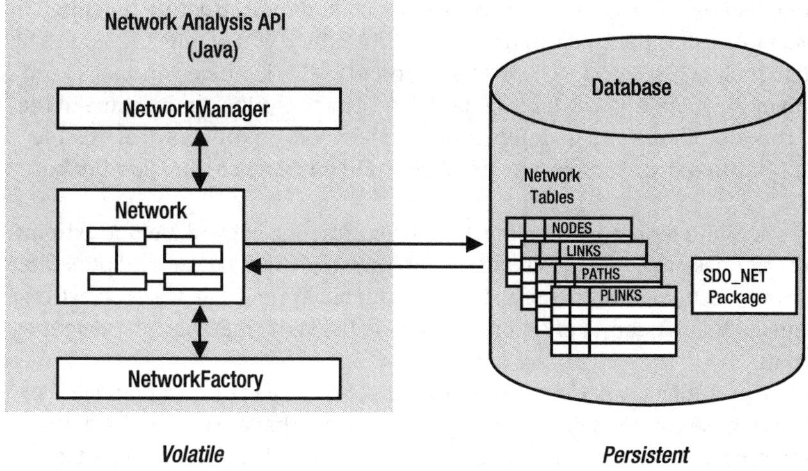

Figure 10-5. *Oracle Network Data Model*

Data Structures: The Network Tables

We will first examine the way you define your network elements as tables. A network is defined using two tables: a *node* table and a *link* table. You must provide those tables with the proper structure and content to model your network.

A network can also have a *path* table and a *path link* table. These tables are optional and are filled with the results of analyzes performed in the Java API, such as the shortest path between two nodes. They are needed only if applications want to make analysis results available to other applications by storing them inside the database.

Figure 10-6 shows the relationships between the tables that describe a network.

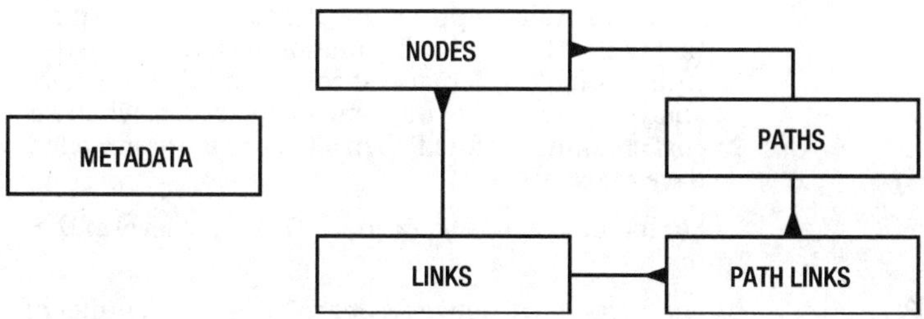

Figure 10-6. *Network tables*

The tables can be named in any way you like, but they must follow a well-defined structure. Or, to be more precise, they must contain a certain minimum number of columns, some with predefined names.

You have a large degree of flexibility in structuring the tables—some columns can be named in any way you like (the *geometry* and *cost* columns, in particular), and their order is unimportant. You can also include any other columns to hold additional information. And finally, the tables could actually be views over existing tables.

The actual naming of the tables that constitute a network and their structure is defined in a separate metadata table called USER_SDO_NETWORK_METADATA, which you update the same way as the basic spatial metadata (USER_SDO_METADATA). In particular, this is where you specify the name of the column in the *node* and *link* tables that defines the *cost* value, or the name of the *geometry* column. This also allows you to define multiple networks on the same set of tables, using different cost columns—for example, one network based on distances and another based on travel times.

There are several techniques for defining the data structures for a network. At one extreme, a simple procedure call does everything; it creates all tables with default names and populates the metadata. At the other extreme, you create all the tables manually (or create views on existing tables) and fill the metadata manually. Functions are provided to verify that the data structures are valid and coherent.

In this section, we present an overview of the structure of each of the network tables. For each table, we indicate those columns that are required and those that are optional. Columns with names in lowercase can have any name. Their actual name is defined in the metadata.

Node Table

The *node* table, as shown in Table 10-2, describes all nodes in the network. Each node has a unique numeric identifier (the NODE_ID column). This is the only required column—all others are actually optional.

Table 10-2. *The* Node *Table*

Column	Data Type	Meaning
NODE_ID*	NUMBER	Unique identification for that node in the network. This is also the primary key of the table.
geometry_column	SDO_GEOMETRY	A point geometry object that contains the coordinates of the node. This is only present for spatial networks. Logical networks contain no geometries.
cost_column	NUMBER	A numeric value representing the cost for traversing that node. There could be multiple costs associated with a node. The actual cost column used for network analysis is defined in the network metadata. When no cost column is defined, then all nodes are assumed to have a cost of 0.
HIERARCHY_LEVEL	NUMBER	For hierarchical networks only. This is the level of the node.
PARENT_NODE_ID	NUMBER	For hierarchical networks only. This is the identifier of the parent node for this node.
ACTIVE	CHAR(1)	Defines whether the node is active (visible in the network or not)—'Y' or 'N'. An inactive node will not be used by the network analysis functions. When the column is not defined, then all nodes are considered to be active.
NODE_NAME	VARCHAR2(32)	Name of the node. Fill this with any descriptive name (not used by the network analysis functions).
NODE_TYPE	VARCHAR2(24)	Type of node. Fill this with any descriptive code or text.

** This column is required. The remaining columns in the table are optional.*

Link Table

The *link* table, as shown in Table 10-3, describes all links in the network. Each link has a unique numeric identifier (the LINK_ID column) and contains the identifiers of the two nodes it connects. All other columns are optional.

Table 10-3. *The* Link *Table*

Column	Data Type	Meaning
LINK_ID*	NUMBER	Unique identification for that link in the network. This is also the primary key of the table.
START_NODE_ID*	NUMBER	Unique identifier of the node from which the link originates.
END_NODE_ID*	NUMBER	Unique identifier of the node at which the link terminates.
geometry_column	SDO_GEOMETRY	A line geometry object that describes the shape of the link. This is present only for spatial networks. Logical networks contain no geometries.
cost_column	NUMBER	A numeric value representing the cost for traversing that link. There could be multiple costs associated with a link. The actual cost column used for network analysis is defined in the network metadata. When no cost column is defined, then all links are assumed to have a cost of 1.
PARENT_LINK_ID	NUMBER	For hierarchical networks only. This is the identifier of the parent link for this node.
ACTIVE	CHAR(1)	Defines whether the link is active (visible in the network or not)—'Y' or 'N'. An invisible link will not be used by the network analysis functions. When the column is not defined, then all nodes are considered to be active.
LINK_LEVEL	NUMBER	Priority of the link.
LINK_NAME	VARCHAR2	Name of the link. Fill this with any descriptive name (not used by the network analysis functions).
LINK_TYPE	VARCHAR2	Type of link. Fill this with any descriptive code or text.

* *These columns are required. All others are optional.*

Path Table

The *path* table, as shown in Table 10-4, stores the start and end node of a path, and its total cost. Note that the *cost* column is always present and is named COST. The list of the links that describe a path is in the *path link* table (described in the next section). Remember that the *path* and *path link* tables are optional—you need to create them only if you want to retain paths computed by the network analysis Java API.

Table 10-4. *The* Path *Table*

Column	Data Type	Meaning
PATH_ID*	NUMBER	Unique identification for that path in the network. This is also the primary key of the table.
START_NODE_ID*	NUMBER	Unique identifier of the node from which the path originates.
END_NODE_ID*	NUMBER	Unique identifier of the node at which the path terminates.
COST*	NUMBER	A numeric value representing the total cost for the path.
SIMPLE*	CHAR(1)	Contains Y if the path is simple path or N if it is complex. If the column does not exist, then all paths are considered simple. Note that all paths produced by the Java API are simple.
geometry_column	SDO_GEOMETRY	A line geometry object that describes the shape of the path, formed by linking together the geometries of all links in the path. This is present only when the network is *spatial*.
PATH_NAME	VARCHAR2	Name of the path. Fill this with any descriptive name.
PATH_TYPE	VARCHAR2	Type of path. Fill this with any descriptive code or text.

* *These columns are required. All others are optional.*

Path Link Table

The *path link* table, as shown in Table 10-5, stores the list of all links that define a path. The PATH_ID and LINK_ID form the primary key of the table. All columns are required.

Table 10-5. *The* Path Link *Table*

Column	Data Type	Meaning
PATH_ID	NUMBER	Path identification
LINK_ID	NUMBER	Link identification
SEQ_NO	NUMBER	Sequence of that link in the path

Network Metadata

The view USER_SDO_GEOM_METADATA, as shown in Table 10-6, describes the elements that compose a network: the names of the tables and the names of optional columns such as costs and geometries.

Table 10-6. *The* USER_SDO_GEOM_METADATA *View*

Name	Data Type	Meaning
NETWORK	VARCHAR2(24)	Unique name of the network. Note that this is limited to 24 characters.
NETWORK_ID	NUMBER	Unique network number (optional).
NETWORK_CATEGORY	VARCHAR2(12)	The network category is SPATIAL if the network nodes and links are associated with spatial geometries and LOGICAL if the network nodes and links are not associated with spatial geometries.
GEOMETRY_TYPE	VARCHAR2(24)	Type of spatial geometry if the network category is SPATIAL. This is typically set to SDO_GEOMETRY, but it could also be set to LRS_GEOMETRY or TOPO_GEOMETRY (not covered in this book).
NETWORK_TYPE	VARCHAR2(24)	User-defined string to describe the type of network.
NO_OF_HIERARCHY_LEVELS	NUMBER	Number of levels in the network hierarchy. It contains 1 if there is no hierarchy.
NO_OF_PARTITIONS	NUMBER	Number of partitions in the network. It is set to 1 (Oracle 10*g* release 1 supports only nonpartitioned networks).
LINK_DIRECTION	VARCHAR2(12)	Specifies whether or not the links of the network are directed (DIRECTED or UNDIRECTED).
NODE_TABLE_NAME	VARCHAR2(32)	Name of the *node* table.
NODE_GEOM_COLUMN	VARCHAR2(32)	Name of the geometry column in the *node* table (if the network category is SPATIAL).
NODE_COST_COLUMN	VARCHAR2(1024)	Name of the cost column in the *node* table. If this is not specified, then network analysis does not use any node costing (i.e., all nodes have a cost of 0).
LINK_TABLE_NAME	VARCHAR2(32)	Name of the *link* table.
LINK_GEOM_COLUMN	VARCHAR2(32)	Name of the geometry column in the *link* table (if the network category is SPATIAL).
LINK_COST_COLUMN	VARCHAR2(1024)	Name of the cost column in the *link* table. If this is not specified, then network analysis does not use any link costing (i.e., all links have a cost of 1).
PATH_TABLE_NAME	VARCHAR2(32)	Name of the *path* table. This is optional. If it is not specified, then the network does not use any *path* table.
PATH_LINK_TABLE_NAME	VARCHAR2(32)	Name of the *path link* table. This is optional. Only specify it if the network uses a *path* table.
PATH_GEOM_COLUMN	VARCHAR2(32)	Name of the geometry column in the *path* table.
LRS_TABLE_NAME	VARCHAR2(32)	Name of the table that contains the LRS geometries (only when GEOMETRY_TYPE is LRS_GEOMETRY).
LRS_GEOM_COLUMN	VARCHAR2(32)	Name of the geometry column in the LRS table.
PARTITION_TABLE_NAME	VARCHAR2(32)	Not currently used (Oracle 10*g* release 1 supports only nonpartitioned networks).

The simplest possible network is one that contains a *node* table with only a NODE_ID column and a *link* table that contains LINK_ID, START_NODE_ID, and END_NODE_ID columns. This is a logical network, undirected and without costs.

Defining Networks

As mentioned earlier, you have several ways to define the data structures for a network. At one extreme, a simple procedure call will do everything. At the other extreme, you create all the tables manually.

All operations are provided by procedures and functions of the SDO_NET package.

"Automatic" Network Definition

You can use the CREATE_SDO_NETWORK or CREATE_LOGICAL_NETWORK procedure to create all the structures of a network.

The example in Listing 10-1 creates a spatial network called US_ROADS. The links are directed, and the nodes have no cost. No names are provided for the various tables; they will receive default generated names. In this and the following example, we use the *named* notation for parameters. This notation is more verbose, but it makes your code easier to read and maintain. It is especially useful for calling procedures or functions that have a long list of parameters.

Listing 10-1. *Creating a Spatial Network Using Default Table Names*

```
SQL> BEGIN
       SDO_NET.CREATE_SDO_NETWORK (
         NETWORK => 'US_ROADS',
         NO_OF_HIERARCHY_LEVELS => 1,
         IS_DIRECTED => TRUE,
         NODE_WITH_COST => FALSE
     );
     END;
     /
```

The call can be shortened to the following (using the *positional* parameter notation):

```
SQL> EXEC SDO_NET.CREATE_SDO_NETWORK ('US_ROADS',1,TRUE,FALSE)
```

The procedure creates four network tables called US_ROADS_NODE$, US_ROADS_LINK$, US_ROADS_PATH$, and US_ROADS_PLINK$, and it adds information to the network metadata. The geometry columns in the *node*, *link*, and *path link* tables are called GEOMETRY. The *link* table has a cost column called COST. The *path* and *path link* tables are created, even if you do not want any. Listing 10-2 shows the structure of the resulting tables.

Listing 10-2. *Structure of Default Network Tables*

```
SQL> describe US_ROADS_NODE$
 Name                                      Null?    Type
 ----------------------------------------- -------- --------------------
 NODE_ID                                   NOT NULL NUMBER
 NODE_NAME                                          VARCHAR2(32)
 NODE_TYPE                                          VARCHAR2(24)
 ACTIVE                                             VARCHAR2(1)
 PARTITION_ID                                       NUMBER
 GEOMETRY                                           MDSYS.SDO_GEOMETRY

SQL> describe US_ROADS_LINK$
 Name                                      Null?    Type
 ----------------------------------------- -------- --------------------
 LINK_ID                                   NOT NULL NUMBER
 LINK_NAME                                          VARCHAR2(32 CHAR)
 START_NODE_ID                             NOT NULL NUMBER
 END_NODE_ID                               NOT NULL NUMBER
 LINK_TYPE                                          VARCHAR2(24 CHAR)
 ACTIVE                                             VARCHAR2(1 CHAR)
 LINK_LEVEL                                         NUMBER
 GEOMETRY                                           MDSYS.SDO_GEOMETRY
 COST                                               NUMBER

SQL> describe US_ROADS_PATH$
 Name                                      Null?    Type
 ----------------------------------------- -------- --------------------
 PATH_ID                                   NOT NULL NUMBER
 PATH_NAME                                          VARCHAR2(32 CHAR)
 PATH_TYPE                                          VARCHAR2(24 CHAR)
 START_NODE_ID                             NOT NULL NUMBER
 END_NODE_ID                               NOT NULL NUMBER
 COST                                               NUMBER
 SIMPLE                                             VARCHAR2(1 CHAR)
 GEOMETRY                                           MDSYS.SDO_GEOMETRY

SQL> describe US_ROADS_PLINK$
 Name                                      Null?    Type
 ----------------------------------------- -------- --------------------
 PATH_ID                                   NOT NULL NUMBER
 LINK_ID                                   NOT NULL NUMBER
 SEQ_NO                                             NUMBER
```

Note that the tables have primary keys defined (using default constraint names). No foreign key constraints are defined, however.

Note The network creation function is not atomic. If it fails to complete, then you may be left with a half-created network (i.e., some tables are created). Before you try to create the network again, you must first manually drop the existing network using the DROP_NETWORK procedure.

Our second example (see Listing 10-3) illustrates the creation of the same US_ROADS network with explicit table and column names. The example also shows the complete list of parameters you can pass to the procedure.

Listing 10-3. *Network Creation with Explicit Table and Column Names*

```
SQL> BEGIN
  SDO_NET.CREATE_SDO_NETWORK (
    NETWORK => 'US_ROADS',
    NO_OF_HIERARCHY_LEVELS => 1,
    IS_DIRECTED => TRUE,
    NODE_TABLE_NAME  => 'US_INTERSECTIONS',
    NODE_GEOM_COLUMN => 'LOCATION',
    NODE_COST_COLUMN => NULL,
    LINK_TABLE_NAME  => 'US_STREETS',
    LINK_GEOM_COLUMN => 'STREET_GEOM',
    LINK_COST_COLUMN => 'STREET_LENGTH',
    PATH_TABLE_NAME  => 'US_PATHS',
    PATH_GEOM_COLUMN => 'PATH_GEOM',
    PATH_LINK_TABLE_NAME => 'US_PATH_LINKS'
  );
END;
/
```

When no name is given for a *geometry* column, it is named GEOMETRY. When no name is given for a *cost* column, then no cost column is created.

"Manual" Network Definition

The "automatic" creation method you just saw is not flexible. It gives you very little control over the actual structuring of the tables, and it gives you no control at all over their physical storage (tablespaces, space management, partitioning, etc.). But it is easy to use. In particular, it automatically populates the network metadata and makes sure the table structures are consistent.

The alternative is to create the network tables manually. This gives you total flexibility over the table structures, but you must manually update the network metadata and ensure that the table structures are consistent with the metadata.

Listing 10-4 illustrates the process for manually creating the US_ROADS spatial network with only the columns we need. Note that for simplicity, we do not include any storage parameters for the tables, and we define the primary key constraints inline. A better practice is to create explicit indexes and use them to define the constraints.

Note that the us_streets table contains two columns that can be used as cost: street_length represents the length of the street segment, whereas travel_time contains the time needed to drive along that street segment.

■ Note Travel times are usually derived from the type of street segment (interstate or motorway, local road, etc.). This is often referred to in road-navigation databases as the *functional class* of the street segment. Travel times may also include local specific speed limits.

Listing 10-4. *Manual Network Creation*

```
SQL> -- Create the node table
SQL> CREATE TABLE us_intersections (
 node_id         NUMBER,
 location        SDO_GEOMETRY,
 CONSTRAINT us_intersections_pk PRIMARY KEY (node_id)
     );
SQL> -- Create the link table
     CREATE TABLE us_streets (
       link_id          NUMBER,
       start_node_id    NUMBER NOT NULL,
       end_node_id      NUMBER NOT NULL,
       active           CHAR(1),
       street_geom      SDO_GEOMETRY,
       street_length    NUMBER,
       travel_time      NUMBER,
       CONSTRAINT us_streets_pk PRIMARY KEY (link_id)
     );
SQL> -- Create path table
SQL> CREATE TABLE us_paths (
       path_id          NUMBER,
       start_node_id    NUMBER NOT NULL,
       end_node_id      NUMBER NOT NULL,
       cost             NUMBER,
       simple           VARCHAR2(1),
       path_geom        SDO_GEOMETRY,
       CONSTRAINT us_paths_pk PRIMARY KEY (path_id)
     );
SQL> -- Create path link table
SQL> CREATE TABLE us_path_links (
       path_id          number,
       link_id          number,
```

```
    seq_no          number,
    CONSTRAINT us_path_links_pk PRIMARY KEY (path_id, link_id)
  );
```

This code only creates the tables that define our network. We still need to "glue" them together as an actual network, which we will do by manually by inserting the proper information into the network metadata (USER_SDO_NETWORK_METADATA), as illustrated in Listing 10-5.

Listing 10-5. *Setting Up Network Metadata*

```
SQL> INSERT INTO USER_SDO_NETWORK_METADATA (
       NETWORK,
       NETWORK_CATEGORY,
       GEOMETRY_TYPE,
       NO_OF_HIERARCHY_LEVELS,
       NO_OF_PARTITIONS,
       LINK_DIRECTION,
       NODE_TABLE_NAME,
       NODE_GEOM_COLUMN,
       NODE_COST_COLUMN,
       LINK_TABLE_NAME,
       LINK_GEOM_COLUMN,
       LINK_COST_COLUMN,
       PATH_TABLE_NAME,
       PATH_GEOM_COLUMN,
       PATH_LINK_TABLE_NAME
     )
     VALUES (
       'US_ROADS',           -- network (primary key)
       'SPATIAL',            -- network_category
       'SDO_GEOMETRY',       -- geometry_type
       1,                    -- no_of_hierarchy_levels
       1,                    -- no_of_partitions
       'DIRECTED',           -- link_direction
       'US_INTERSECTIONS',   -- node_table_name
       'LOCATION',           -- node_geom_column
       NULL,                 -- node_cost_column (no cost at node level)
       'US_STREETS',         -- link_table_name
       'STREET_GEOM',        -- link_geom_column
       'STREET_LENGTH',      -- link_cost_column
       'US_PATHS',           -- path_table_name
       'PATH_GEOM',          -- path_geom_column
       'US_PATH_LINKS'       -- path_link_table_name
     );
SQL> COMMIT;
```

This insert can be tricky. Because of the large number of columns to fill, it is easy to make mistakes. So, it is important that you verify that your definitions are consistent using the validation functions provided by Oracle. We will discuss those functions shortly.

■ **Note** You can also create the network tables individually, using the SDO_CREATE_xxx_TABLE procedures (where xxx stands for NODE, LINK, etc.). Those procedures are of little interest, as they give no option to control the storage parameters for the tables, and you must still manually update the network metadata and make sure it is consistent with the tables you created. We do not discuss those procedures here.

Defining Multiple Networks on the Same Tables

In the preceding example, the us_streets table contains two cost columns: street_length and travel_time. We defined the US_ROADS network as using street_length for the cost column. This means that we can use this network for computing the *shortest* routes between nodes.

But we may also want to compute the *fastest* routes between nodes. For this, all we need to do is define a second network on the same tables, this time using travel_time as the cost column for the links. This is illustrated in Listing 10-6, where we define a new network called US_ROADS_TIME.

Listing 10-6. *Setting Up Metadata for a Time-Based Road Network*

```
SQL> INSERT INTO USER_SDO_NETWORK_METADATA (
       NETWORK,
       NETWORK_CATEGORY,
       GEOMETRY_TYPE,
       NO_OF_HIERARCHY_LEVELS,
       NO_OF_PARTITIONS,
       LINK_DIRECTION,
       NODE_TABLE_NAME,
       NODE_GEOM_COLUMN,
       NODE_COST_COLUMN,
       LINK_TABLE_NAME,
       LINK_GEOM_COLUMN,
       LINK_COST_COLUMN,
       PATH_TABLE_NAME,
       PATH_GEOM_COLUMN,
       PATH_LINK_TABLE_NAME
     )
     VALUES (
       'US_ROADS_TIME',        -- network (primary key)
       'SPATIAL',              -- network_category
       'SDO_GEOMETRY',         -- geometry_type
       1,                      -- no_of_hierarchy_levels
       1,                      -- no_of_partitions
       'DIRECTED',             -- link_direction
       'US_INTERSECTIONS',     -- node_table_name
```

```
        'LOCATION',          -- node_geom_column
        NULL,                -- node_cost_column (no cost at node level)
        'US_STREETS',        -- link_table_name
        'STREET_GEOM',       -- link_geom_column
        'TRAVEL_TIME',       -- link_cost_column
        'US_PATHS',          -- path_table_name
        'PATH_GEOM',         -- path_geom_column
        'US_PATH_LINKS'      -- path_link_table_name
    );
SQL> COMMIT;
```

Notice that the US_ROADS_TIME network uses the same *path* and *path link* tables as the US_ROADS network. If you want, you can create and use different tables. That way, you can keep separate the results of distance-based searches and time-based searches.

Defining a Network over Existing Structures

In the previous example, we were able to define our network structures entirely from scratch. What if we already have a network defined (as *node* and *link* tables) and used in existing applications?

One way is to create a copy of the existing network into tables suitable for the Oracle Network Data Model. This approach has drawbacks: it doubles the storage costs and adds complexities to maintaining the two copies of the network in sync.

A simpler approach is to define a network directly on the existing tables, by just setting up the network metadata to point to the existing tables. That may, however, not be directly possible. Even though the structure of network tables is flexible, there are still some constraints—for example, the primary key of the node table must be called NODE_ID.

The solution is to create views over the existing tables, and rename columns in the views so that they match the naming conventions of the network tables. This approach is illustrated in the following simple example. Consider that an existing application already uses a water distribution network, defined as a set of pipes and valves. Those tables were created by the application as shown in Listing 10-7.

Listing 10-7. *Existing Water Network Tables*

```
SQL> CREATE TABLE valves (
        valve_id      NUMBER PRIMARY KEY,
        valve_type    VARCHAR2(20),
        location      SDO_GEOMETRY
        -- ... other columns ...
    );
SQL> CREATE TABLE pipes (
        pipe_id       NUMBER PRIMARY KEY,
        diameter      NUMBER,
        length        NUMBER,
        start_valve   NUMBER NOT NULL REFERENCES valves,
        end_valve     NUMBER NOT NULL REFERENCES valves,
        pipe_geom     SDO_GEOMETRY
        -- ... other columns ...
    );
```

Our first step is to define views over the existing tables, as illustrated in Listing 10-8. Notice that column valve_id in the original valves table is renamed to node_id in the net_pipes view. Similar renaming takes place in the net_pipes view.

Listing 10-8. *Views over Existing Tables*

```
SQL> CREATE VIEW net_valves (node_id, valve_type, location) AS
       SELECT valve_id,
              valve_type,
              location
              -- ...other columns ...
       FROM   valves;
SQL> CREATE VIEW net_pipes
       (link_id, start_node_id, end_node_id, length, pipe_geom)
     AS
       SELECT pipe_id,
              start_valve,
              end_valve,
              length,
              pipe_geom
              -- ... other columns ...
       FROM pipes;
```

The second step is optional. If we want to keep the results of any network traces or analyses, then we need to also create *path* and *path link* tables (see Listing 10-9). There is little flexibility in creating those tables—all we can do is choose the name of the tables and choose a name for the SDO_GEOMETRY column in the *path* table.

Listing 10-9. *Creating the* Path *and* Path Link *Tables*

```
SQL> CREATE TABLE net_paths (
       path_id         NUMBER,
       start_node_id   NUMBER NOT NULL,
       end_node_id     NUMBER NOT NULL,
       cost            NUMBER,
       simple          VARCHAR2(1),
       path_geom       SDO_GEOMETRY,
       CONSTRAINT net_paths_pk PRIMARY KEY (path_id)
     );
SQL> CREATE TABLE net_path_links (
       path_id         NUMBER,
       link_id         NUMBER,
       seq_no          NUMBER,
       CONSTRAINT net_path_links_pk PRIMARY KEY (path_id, link_id)
     );
```

The final step is to set up the network metadata for the water network. This is shown in Listing 10-10. Notice that this is an *undirected* network—in a pipe, water can flow in any direction.

Listing 10-10. *Metadata for a Network on Existing Structures*

```
SQL> INSERT INTO USER_SDO_NETWORK_METADATA (
       NETWORK,
       NETWORK_CATEGORY,
       GEOMETRY_TYPE,
       NO_OF_HIERARCHY_LEVELS,
       NO_OF_PARTITIONS,
       LINK_DIRECTION,
       NODE_TABLE_NAME,
       NODE_GEOM_COLUMN,
       NODE_COST_COLUMN,
       LINK_TABLE_NAME,
       LINK_GEOM_COLUMN,
       LINK_COST_COLUMN,
       PATH_TABLE_NAME,
       PATH_GEOM_COLUMN,
       PATH_LINK_TABLE_NAME
     )
     VALUES (
       'WATER_NET',          -- network (primary key)
       'SPATIAL',            -- network_category
       'SDO_GEOMETRY',       -- geometry_type
       1,                    -- no_of_hierarchy_levels
       1,                    -- no_of_partitions
       'UNDIRECTED',         -- link_direction
       'NET_VALVES',         -- node_table_name
       'LOCATION',           -- node_geom_column
       NULL,                 -- node_cost_column (no cost at node level)
       'NET_PIPES',          -- link_table_name
       'PIPE_GEOM',          -- link_geom_column
       'LENGTH',             -- link_cost_column
       'NET_PATHS',          -- path_table_name
       'PATH_GEOM',          -- path_geom_column
       'NET_PATH_LINKS'      -- path_link_table_name
     );
SQL> COMMIT;
```

Validating Network Structures

You may make mistakes when defining all network structures and metadata manually. We recommend that you verify the correctness of your definitions using one of the functions provided.

The main function is VALIDATE_NETWORK. It verifies the consistency between the metadata and the network tables, and it verifies that the tables are correctly defined (i.e., that they contain the right columns with the right data types). The function takes only one argument: the name of the network to validate.

The result of the function is a string that can take the following values:

- NULL if the network does not exist
- TRUE if the network is correctly defined
- A string with diagnostics if the network is not correctly defined

For example, if the us_streets table in the previous example was created without the street_length column, the validation of network US_ROADS would fail, as illustrated in Listing 10-11.

Listing 10-11. *Validating a Network Definition*

```
SQL> select sdo_net.validate_network('us_roads') from dual;
SDO_NET.VALIDATE_NETWORK('US_ROADS')
------------------------------------------------------------------------------
  Link Schema Error:  [COST]
```

You can also use individual VALIDATE_xxxx_SCHEMA functions (where xxxx stands for NODE, LINK, or PATH) to verify the correctness of each table in a network.

Populating Network Tables

You can populate network tables (*link* and *node* tables) using any tool: inserts from an application program, SQL*Loader, and so on.

Dropping a Network

To drop a network, use the DROP_NETWORK procedure. It will drop all tables related to a network and remove the definition of the network from the metadata. The example in Listing 10-12 removes the US_ROADS network.

Listing 10-12. *Dropping a Network*

```
SQL> EXEC SDO_NET.DROP_NETWORK ('US_ROADS');
PL/SQL procedure successfully completed.
```

The procedure locates the tables that compose a network as indicated in the network metadata. If the metadata is incorrect—for example, if it contains the wrong name for a *node* table—then the procedure will attempt to drop the table whose name is in the metadata. Note that it also automatically removes any spatial metadata from USER_SDO_GEOM_METADATA.

■ **Caution** If you only want to modify the network definition, do not use the DROP_NETWORK procedure, since it will also drop the complete network data. Instead, simply delete the definition from USER_SDO_NETWORK_METADATA and reinsert the new one. If the network is defined using views (such as WATER_NET), then the procedure only removes the views without touching the tables the views are based on.

Spatial Indexes on Network Tables

For spatial networks in which tables contain SDO_GEOMETRY columns, it may be necessary to set up spatial indexes. This is not a requirement; network analysis functions do not need spatial indexes.

Spatial indexes need spatial metadata in the USER_SDO_GEOM_METADATA table. You can insert the metadata manually, or you can use the INSERT_GEOM_METADATA procedure to set the metadata for all tables that are part of the network and that contain an SDO_GEOMETRY column. This is illustrated in Listing 10-13. The function takes the name of the network as an input parameter, followed by the bounds definitions and the SRID.

Listing 10-13. *Adding Spatial Metadata to Network Tables*

```
SQL> BEGIN
       SDO_NET.INSERT_GEOM_METADATA (
         'US_ROADS',
         SDO_DIM_ARRAY (
           SDO_DIM_ELEMENT ('Long', -180, +180, 1),
           SDO_DIM_ELEMENT ('Lat',   -90,  +90, 1)
         ),
         8307
       );
     END;
     /
SQL> COMMIT;
```

Getting Information About a Network

To find out the details about the structure of a network (the name of the *link* table, the name of the *cost* column in the *node* table, etc.), just query the USER_SDO_NETWORK_METADATA view. Be aware that the output may be hard to read.

You can alternatively use one of the many functions in the SDO_NET package that return an individual piece of information. The functions' names are self-descriptive. They all take one argument: the name of the network to examine. We do not list them in detail here.

Listing 10-14 shows a convenient procedure that uses all those functions in order to display information about a network in a readable way. Listing 10-15 shows the results of executing the procedure on the US_ROADS network.

Listing 10-14. *Convenient Procedure for Getting Network Details*

```
CREATE OR REPLACE PROCEDURE SHOW_NET_DETAILS (NETWORK_NAME VARCHAR2) AS
BEGIN
  DBMS_OUTPUT.PUT_LINE ('NETWORK_EXISTS() =                 ' ||
    SDO_NET.NETWORK_EXISTS(NETWORK_NAME));
  DBMS_OUTPUT.PUT_LINE ('IS_HIERARCHICAL() =                ' ||
    SDO_NET.IS_HIERARCHICAL(NETWORK_NAME));
  DBMS_OUTPUT.PUT_LINE ('IS_LOGICAL() =                     ' ||
    SDO_NET.IS_LOGICAL(NETWORK_NAME));
```

```
  DBMS_OUTPUT.PUT_LINE ('IS_SPATIAL() =                   ' ||
    SDO_NET.IS_SPATIAL(NETWORK_NAME));
  DBMS_OUTPUT.PUT_LINE ('GET_NETWORK_CATEGORY() =         ' ||
    SDO_NET.GET_NETWORK_CATEGORY(NETWORK_NAME));
  DBMS_OUTPUT.PUT_LINE ('SDO_GEOMETRY_NETWORK() =         ' ||
    SDO_NET.SDO_GEOMETRY_NETWORK(NETWORK_NAME));
  DBMS_OUTPUT.PUT_LINE ('GET_NETWORK_TYPE() =             ' ||
    SDO_NET.GET_NETWORK_TYPE(NETWORK_NAME));
  DBMS_OUTPUT.PUT_LINE ('GET_GEOMETRY_TYPE() =            ' ||
    SDO_NET.GET_GEOMETRY_TYPE(NETWORK_NAME));
  DBMS_OUTPUT.PUT_LINE ('GET_NO_OF_HIERARCHY_LEVELS() = ' ||
    SDO_NET.GET_NO_OF_HIERARCHY_LEVELS(NETWORK_NAME));
  DBMS_OUTPUT.PUT_LINE ('GET_LINK_DIRECTION() =           ' ||
    SDO_NET.GET_LINK_DIRECTION(NETWORK_NAME));
  DBMS_OUTPUT.PUT_LINE ('GET_NODE_TABLE_NAME() =          ' ||
    SDO_NET.GET_NODE_TABLE_NAME(NETWORK_NAME));
  DBMS_OUTPUT.PUT_LINE ('GET_NODE_COST_COLUMN() =         ' ||
    SDO_NET.GET_NODE_COST_COLUMN(NETWORK_NAME));
  DBMS_OUTPUT.PUT_LINE ('GET_NODE_GEOM_COLUMN() =         ' ||
    SDO_NET.GET_NODE_GEOM_COLUMN(NETWORK_NAME));
  DBMS_OUTPUT.PUT_LINE ('GET_LINK_TABLE_NAME() =          ' ||
    SDO_NET.GET_LINK_TABLE_NAME(NETWORK_NAME));
  DBMS_OUTPUT.PUT_LINE ('GET_LINK_COST_COLUMN() =         ' ||
    SDO_NET.GET_LINK_COST_COLUMN(NETWORK_NAME));
  DBMS_OUTPUT.PUT_LINE ('GET_LINK_GEOM_COLUMN() =         ' ||
    SDO_NET.GET_LINK_GEOM_COLUMN(NETWORK_NAME));
  DBMS_OUTPUT.PUT_LINE ('GET_PATH_TABLE_NAME() =          ' ||
    SDO_NET.GET_PATH_TABLE_NAME(NETWORK_NAME));
  DBMS_OUTPUT.PUT_LINE ('GET_PATH_GEOM_COLUMN() =         ' ||
    SDO_NET.GET_PATH_GEOM_COLUMN(NETWORK_NAME));
  DBMS_OUTPUT.PUT_LINE ('GET_PATH_LINK_TABLE_NAME() =     ' ||
    SDO_NET.GET_PATH_LINK_TABLE_NAME(NETWORK_NAME));
END;
```

Listing 10-15. *Getting Network Details*

```
SQL> EXEC show_net_details ('US_ROADS');
NETWORK_EXISTS() =              TRUE
IS_HIERARCHICAL() =             FALSE
IS_LOGICAL() =                  FALSE
IS_SPATIAL() =                  TRUE
GET_NETWORK_CATEGORY() =        SPATIAL
SDO_GEOMETRY_NETWORK() =        TRUE
GET_NETWORK_TYPE() =
GET_GEOMETRY_TYPE() =           SDO_GEOMETRY
GET_NO_OF_HIERARCHY_LEVELS() = 1
GET_LINK_DIRECTION() =          DIRECTED
GET_NODE_TABLE_NAME() =         US_INTERSECTIONS
```

```
GET_NODE_COST_COLUMN() =
GET_NODE_GEOM_COLUMN() =       LOCATION
GET_LINK_TABLE_NAME() =        US_STREETS
GET_LINK_COST_COLUMN() =       STREET_LENGTH
GET_LINK_GEOM_COLUMN() =       STREET_GEOM
GET_PATH_TABLE_NAME() =        US_PATHS
GET_PATH_GEOM_COLUMN() =       PATH_GEOM
GET_PATH_LINK_TABLE_NAME() =   US_PATH_LINKS
PL/SQL procedure successfully completed.
```

Verifying Network Connectivity

The SDO_NET package provides some other functions, summarized in Table 10-7, to help you locate any errors inside the network data such as isolated nodes or dangling links. All the functions take a network name as parameter.

Table 10-7. *Network Verification Functions*

Function	Usage
SDO_NET.GET_NO_OF_NODES()	Returns the number of nodes in the network
SDO_NET.GET_NO_OF_LINKS()	Returns the number of links in the network
SDO_NET.GET_ISOLATED_NODES()	Returns the nodes that are not related to any link
SDO_NET.GET_INVALID_LINKS()	Returns the links with nonexistent start or end nodes
SDO_NET.GET_INVALID_PATHS()	Returns the paths with nonexistent start or end nodes, or with nonexistent links

■ **Note** You can prevent errors such as isolated nodes or dangling links using referential integrity constraints in the *link* table, as illustrated in the definition of the `pipes` table in Listing 10-7.

Some other functions, listed in Table 10-8, allow you to find out details about individual nodes in the network. They all take two parameters: the name of the network and the identifier of the node to examine.

Table 10-8. *Node Detail Functions*

Function	Usage
SDO_NET.GET_NODE_DEGREE()	Returns the number of links that originate and terminate at that node
SDO_NET.GET_NODE_IN_DEGREE()	Returns the number of links that terminate at that node (i.e., those links that have this node's ID as END_NODE_ID)
SDO_NET.GET_NODE_OUT_DEGREE()	Returns the number of links that originate at that node (i.e., those links that have this node's ID as START_NODE_ID)
SDO_NET.GET_IN_LINKS()	Returns a list containing the IDs of all notes that terminate at that node (as an SDO_NUMBER_ARRAY type)
SDO_NET.GET_OUT_LINKS()	Returns a list containing the IDs of all notes that originate at that node (as an SDO_NUMBER_ARRAY type)

Example Networks

We will now create and load two very simple networks called UNET and DNET. We will use those networks extensively later on to illustrate network analysis functions.

UNET: A Simple Undirected Network

Figure 10-7 shows a simple network (UNET) with undirected links. Links have a cost proportional to their length; the cost of each link is shown in parentheses. Listing 10-16 shows the creation of the network, and Listing 10-17 shows the loading of the network. Note that the ordering of the nodes in the `start_node_id` and `end_node_id` columns in the `unet_links` table is unimportant.

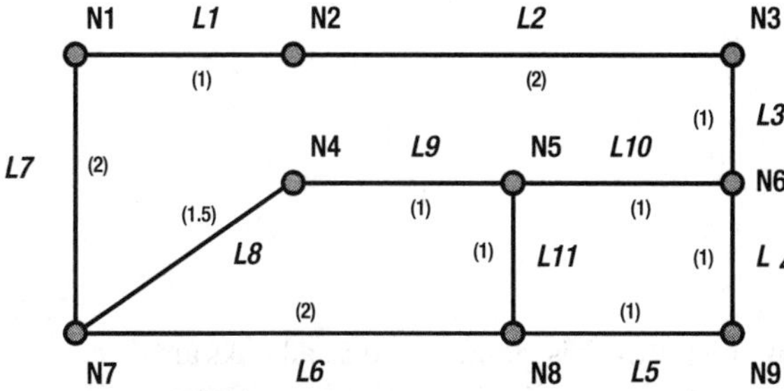

Figure 10-7. *A simple undirected network*

Listing 10-16. *Defining the UNET Network*

```
SQL> BEGIN
       SDO_NET.CREATE_SDO_NETWORK (
         NETWORK => 'UNET',
         NO_OF_HIERARCHY_LEVELS => 1,
         IS_DIRECTED => FALSE,
         NODE_TABLE_NAME => 'UNET_NODES',
         NODE_GEOM_COLUMN => 'GEOM',
         NODE_COST_COLUMN => NULL,
         LINK_TABLE_NAME => 'UNET_LINKS',
         LINK_COST_COLUMN => 'COST',
         LINK_GEOM_COLUMN => 'GEOM',
         PATH_TABLE_NAME => 'UNET_PATHS',
         PATH_GEOM_COLUMN => 'GEOM',
         PATH_LINK_TABLE_NAME => 'UNET_PLINKS'
       );
     END;
     /
```

Listing 10-17. *Loading the UNET Network*

```
SQL> -- Populate the node table
SQL> INSERT INTO unet_nodes (node_id, node_name, geom)
       VALUES (1, 'N1',
         SDO_GEOMETRY (2001, NULL, SDO_POINT_TYPE (1,3,NULL), NULL, NULL));
  ...
SQL> COMMIT;
SQL> -- Populate the link table
SQL> INSERT INTO unet_links
       (link_id, link_name, start_node_id, end_node_id, cost, geom)
       VALUES ( 1, 'L1',  1,  2,  1,
          SDO_GEOMETRY (2002, NULL, NULL,
            SDO_ELEM_INFO_ARRAY (1,2,1),
            SDO_ORDINATE_ARRAY (1,3, 2,3))
       );
...
SQL> COMMIT;
```

DNET: A Simple Directed Network

In Oracle, the directed/undirected nature of the network is global—that is, all links are directed. Therefore, bidirectional links must be represented as two links, one in each direction: a link and a colink, as illustrated in Figure 10-8.

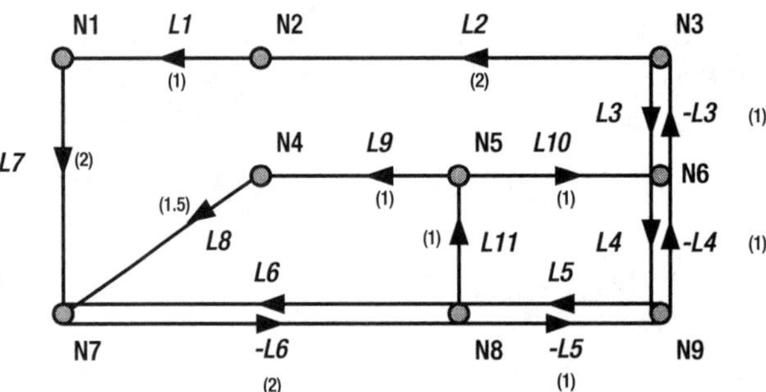

Figure 10-8. *Directed network with bidirectional links*

The usual convention in network modeling is to identify a link and its colink using the same number with opposite signs. For example, link L6 goes from node N8 to node N7, whereas link –L6 goes from node N7 to node N8. Note that in our example, a link and its colink have the same cost. In the real world, however, they could have different costs or types. An example would be a one-way street, with a bus lane going in the opposite direction.

Listing 10-18 shows the creation of the network, and Listing 10-19 shows the loading of the network. Note that the ordering of the nodes in the `start_node_id` and `end_node_id` columns in the `dnet_links` table is very important—it determines the direction of the link.

Listing 10-18. *Defining the DNET Network*

```
SQL> BEGIN
       SDO_NET.CREATE_SDO_NETWORK (
         NETWORK => 'DNET',
         NO_OF_HIERARCHY_LEVELS => 1,
         IS_DIRECTED => TRUE,
         NODE_TABLE_NAME => 'DNET_NODES',
         NODE_GEOM_COLUMN => 'GEOM',
         NODE_COST_COLUMN => NULL,
         LINK_TABLE_NAME => 'DNET_LINKS',
         LINK_COST_COLUMN => 'COST',
         LINK_GEOM_COLUMN => 'GEOM',
         PATH_TABLE_NAME => 'DNET_PATHS',
         PATH_GEOM_COLUMN => 'GEOM',
         PATH_LINK_TABLE_NAME => 'DNET_PLINKS'
       );
     END;
     /
```

Listing 10-19. *Loading the DNET Network*

```
SQL> -- Populate The Node Table
SQL> INSERT INTO dnet_nodes (node_id, node_name, geom)
       VALUES (1, 'N1',
         SDO_GEOMETRY (2001, NULL, SDO_POINT_TYPE (1,3,NULL), NULL, NULL));
...
SQL> COMMIT;
SQL> -- Populate The Link Table
SQL> INSERT INTO dnet_links
       (link_id, link_name, start_node_id, end_node_id, cost, geom)
       VALUES ( 1, 'L1', 2, 1, 1,
         SDO_GEOMETRY (2002, NULL, NULL,
           SDO_ELEM_INFO_ARRAY (1,2,1),
           SDO_ORDINATE_ARRAY (2,3, 1,3))
       );
...
SQL> COMMIT;
```

■ **Note** The geometric representation does not have to match the logical representation exactly. In particular, the orientation of the line geometry for a link does not have to match the direction of the link. In this section's example, link L1 goes from node N2 to node N1, whereas the line string goes in the opposite direction. It is, however, a good idea to make the physical orientation of a link (its digitizing order) match its logical direction.

Analyzing and Managing Networks Using the Java API

Network analysis uses a Java API that provides a range of analysis functions. This is actually where the value of the network data model truly lies. You use that API to find the cheapest path between nodes, the nearest nodes to a node, and so on.

The Java API is very rich. We will list only the most important methods here. For a complete reference, see the Javadoc documentation for the API in `$ORACLE_HOME/md/doc/sdonm.zip`. Note that there is no other documentation of the Java API.

The Java API is provided as a package called `oracle.spatial.network` in a Java Archive (JAR) file called `sdonm.jar`. You will find it in your Oracle installation at `$ORACLE_HOME/md/lib`. To use it in your Java applications, just include it in your classpath. Note that you also need other packages to use the Java API. All necessary packages are summarized in Table 10-9.

Table 10-9. *Packages Needed to Use the Network Java API*

Package	JAR File	Usage	Location
`oracle.spatial.network`	`sdonm.jar`	Network analysis	`$ORACLE_HOME/md/lib`
`oracle.spatial.geometry`	`sdoapi.jar`	`JGeometry` object	`$ORACLE_HOME/md/lib`
(multiple)	`classes12.jar`	JDBC driver	`$ORACLE_HOME/jdbc/lib`

The API is composed of three main sets of classes:

- `Network`, `Node`, `Link`, and `Path`: These classes store and maintain networks and network elements.
- `NetworkManager`: This class performs network analysis, and it also reads networks from the database and writes them back.
- `NetworkFactory`: This class creates networks and network elements.

We will now look at each of the classes in turn. We will start with `NetworkManager`, as this is the class that is at the heart of network analysis.

Analyzing Networks: The NetworkManager Class

The fundamental use of the Network Data Model is to find paths between nodes. There can be many paths between any two nodes, and the model can help find them all or choose the "best" one (i.e., the one with the lowest cost).

The analysis functions are all provided by methods of the `NetworkManager` class. The methods operate on a memory-resident copy of the network. Therefore, the first step in a program is to load the network from the database.

Loading a Network

The `readNetwork()` method loads a network from the database into a `Network` object. The method needs a connection to a database and the name of the network to load. By default, it loads the entire network, but you can also specify a subset of the network: either a certain level or all elements in a chosen rectangular window.

The following loads the complete network called UNET from the database:

```
Network UNet =
  NetworkManager.readNetwork(dbConnection, "UNET");
```

Updating a Network

The `writeNetwork()` method writes a network back to the database. The method's name is a misnomer: it actually takes all changes you made to the memory-resident network and applies them to the persistent copy stored in the database.

The main use of the `writeNetwork()` method is to store the paths calculated by the analysis functions into the *path* and *path link* tables inside the database.

Finding the Shortest Path Between Nodes

A very common operation on a network is to find the shortest path between two nodes. The `shortestPath()` method does just this; it returns the "best" path between two nodes in a network. The inputs to the method are the network on which to perform the analysis, and the start and end nodes. This is probably the *most useful analysis function*, and it is the building block for all routing engines and others that provide driving directions.

The best path between two nodes is the one with the smallest cost. Remember that the cost of a node or link is a numeric value defined in the network tables. That cost can represent anything, for example, the length of a road segment or the time needed to travel along that road segment. When no cost column is present, then all links are considered to have a cost of 1, and nodes have a cost of 0. Only active nodes and links are considered—in other words, those that have an `ACTIVE` column set to `'Y'`.

The code in Listing 10-20 returns the shortest path from node N4 to node N3 on the UNET undirected network shown in Figure 10-7. Figure 10-9 shows the resulting path. The `shortestPath()` method returns a `Path` object. We use a number of methods of the `Path` object to extract various pieces of information, such as the cost of the path and the number of links. We also extract the detailed structure of the path as an array of `Link` objects. We then proceed to extract details from each of the `Link` objects.

Note We detail how to use the `Path`, `Link`, and `Node` objects later in this chapter.

Listing 10-20. *Using the* `shortestPath()` *Method*

```
// Get shortest path from node N4 to N3
Network testNet = uNet;
startNodeId = 4;
endNodeId = 3;
Path path = NetworkManager.shortestPath (testNet, startNodeID ,endNodeId);
```

```
// Show path cost and number of links
System.out.println ("Path cost: " + path.getCost() );
System.out.println ("Number of links: "+ path.getNoOfLinks());
System.out.println ("Simple path? "+ path.isSimple());

// Show the links traversed
System.out.println ("Links traversed:");
Link[] linkArray = path.getLinkArray();
for (int i = 0; i < linkArray.length; i++)
  System.out.println ("  Link " + linkArray[i].getID() + "\t"
    + linkArray[i].getName() +"\t" + linkArray[i].getCost());

// Show the nodes traversed
System.out.println ("  Nodes traversed:");
Node [] nodeArray = path.getNodeArray();
for (int i = 0; i < nodeArray.length; i++)
  System.out.println ("    Node " + nodeArray[i].getID() + "\t"
    + nodeArray[i].getName() +"\t" + nodeArray[i].getCost());
```

Here are the results of executing the code in Listing 10-20:

```
Path cost: 3.0
Number of links: 3
Simple path? true
Links traversed:
  Link 9     L9     1.0
  Link 10    L10    1.0
  Link 3     L3     1.0
Nodes traversed:
  Node 4     N4     0.0
  Node 5     N5     0.0
  Node 6     N6     0.0
  Node 3     N3     0.0
```

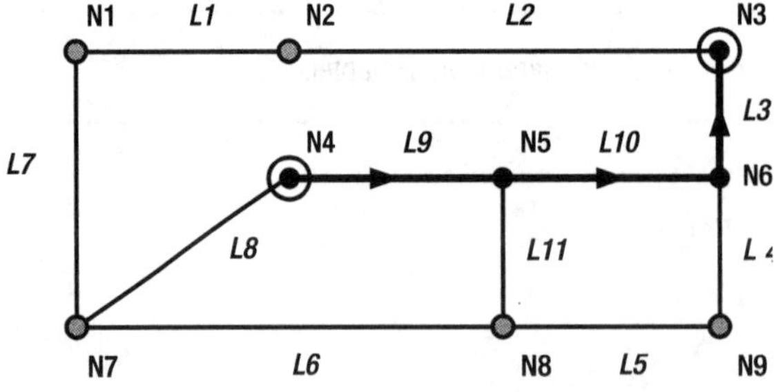

Figure 10-9. *The path from node N4 to node N3 (undirected network)*

Performing the same operation on the directed network DNET (from Figure 10-8) gives the following results (depicted in Figure 10-10):

```
Path cost: 6.5
Number of links: 5
Simple path? true
Links traversed:
  Link 8      L8      1.5
  Link -6     L6      2.0
  Link 11     L11     1.0
  Link 10     L10     1.0
  Link -3     L3      1.0
Nodes traversed:
  Node 4      N4      0.0
  Node 7      N7      0.0
  Node 8      N8      0.0
  Node 5      N5      0.0
  Node 6      N6      0.0
  Node 3      N3      0.0
```

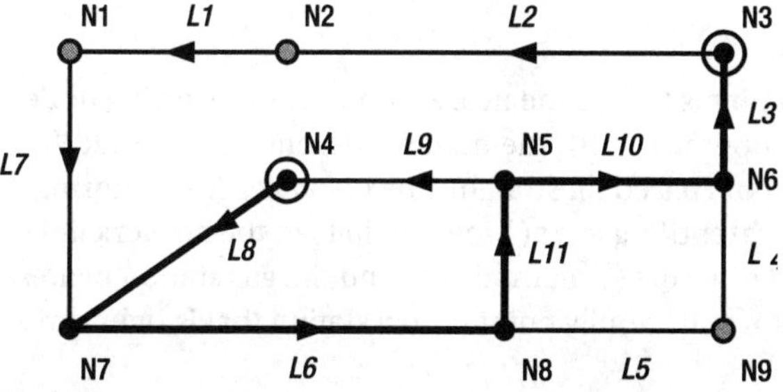

Figure 10-10. *The path from node N4 to node N3 (directed network)*

You can see that the shortest path is no longer as straightforward as in the previous example. It now has to follow the one-way links in the right direction!

The `shortestPath()` method uses the A* algorithm to find the shortest path between the nodes. You can also use the `shortestPathDijkstra()` method, which uses the algorithm developed by Professor E. W. Dijkstra. Discussing the relative merits of the two algorithms is beyond the scope of this book.

Saving the Computed Path

The `Path` object obtained by running one of the preceding functions is a stand-alone object; it is not related to any network. To store that path into the database, you need to complete it with some information before adding it to the network and writing it to the database, as illustrated in the following code example:

```
// Give a name to the path - construct it using the path id.
path.setName ("P" + path.getID() + " Friday excursion");

// Compute the geometry of the path
path.computeGeometry(0.05);

// add the path to the network
network.addPath(path);
```

Notice that the path has automatically received a unique ID (a sequential number), which you can override if you want. Note also the `computeGeometry()` method generates a geometry object that will make it easy to display the resulting path graphically on a map.

The `addPath()` method only adds the path into the memory-resident copy of the network. To store the path in the database tables, you still need to use the `NetworkManager.writeNetwork()` method.

The path returned by the `shortestPath()` method is sufficient to find a route through a water or electricity network. The list of the pipes traversed is sufficient to locate the network elements (the pipes and valves). For a road network, it will list the street segments traversed, in the right order.

Finding the Nearest Neighbors

Another common network analysis operation is to find the nearest node(s) to a starting node. This is very similar to the SDO_NN spatial operator, with the major difference being that the SDO_NN operator locates the nearest neighbors based on straight-line distances (i.e., ignoring any road travel constraints), whereas the `nearestNeighbors()` method follows the network links.

An example of the use of the `nearestNeighbors()` method is to find the gas station nearest to our current location. The SDO_NN operator will happily point us to a station that is right across a canal, with no bridge in sight.

The code in Listing 10-21 finds the two nearest nodes from node N4 on the undirected network UNET. The `nearestNeighbors()` method returns an array of `Path` objects. Not only does it tell us who the nearest nodes are, but it also tells us how to reach them.

Listing 10-21. *Using the* `nearestNeighbors()` *Method*

```
// Find the two nearest neighbors of node N4
Network testNet = uNet;
startNodeId = 4;
numNeighbors = 2;
Path[] pathArray =
  NetworkManager.nearestNeighbors (testNet, startNodeId, numNeighbors);

// Display the resulting paths
System.out.println ("  " + pathArray.length + " nearest neighbors of node "
  + startNodeId + " in network " + testNet.getName());
for (int i = 0; i < pathArray.length; i++)
```

```
{
  Path path = pathArray[i];
  System.out.println("    node " + path.getEndNode().getID() +
    ", path cost " + path.getCost());
}
```

Running the code in Listing 10-21 gives the following results, which are illustrated in Figure 10-11:

```
2 nearest neighbors of node 4 in network UNET
  node 5, path cost 1.0
  node 7, path cost 1.5
```

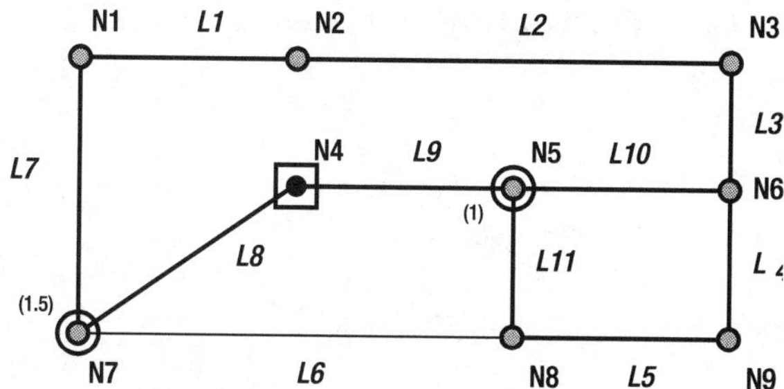

Figure 10-11. *The two nearest nodes to node N4 (undirected network)*

Performing the same operation on the directed network DNET (from Figure 10-8) gives the following results, which are illustrated in Figure 10-12:

```
2 nearest neighbors of node 4 in network DNET
  node 7, path cost 1.5
  node 8, path cost 3.5
```

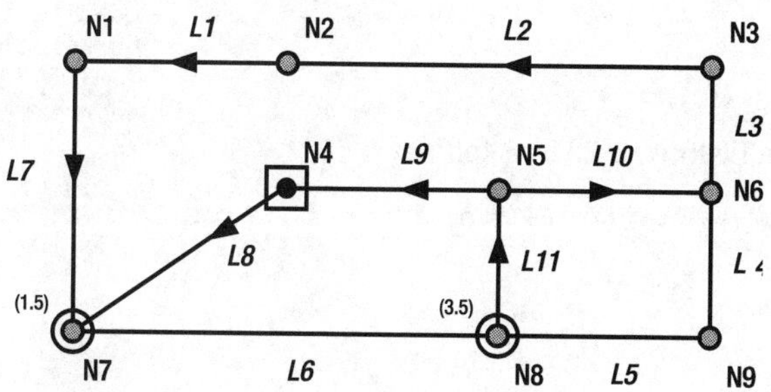

Figure 10-12. *The two nearest nodes to node N4 (directed network)*

The directions on the network links change our results: node N5 is no longer the nearest.

Finding All Nodes Within Some Distance

Another common network analysis operation selects nodes based on the distance that separates them from a starting node. This is comparable to the SDO_WITHIN_DISTANCE spatial operator, with the difference being that SDO_WITHIN_DISTANCE uses straight-line distances, whereas the withinCost() method uses distances along the network.

A typical example of using the withinCost() method is to find the network nodes (road intersections) that are within a certain driving distance or driving time from a given store. The polygon that includes all those points represents the *traction zone* of the store. It would not include customers that are directly across a river from the store, but have no means to cross the river because the nearest bridges are far away. Multiple analyses using different driving times produce polygons that represent *isochrones* (i.e., zones that are at the same distance [in time] from a location).

The code in Listing 10-22 finds the nodes that are at a distance of less than three "cost units" from node N4 on the UNET network. Just like nearestNeighbors(), the withinCost() method returns an array of Path objects.

Listing 10-22. *Using the* withinCost() *Method*

```
// Find nodes that are less than 3 'cost units' from node N2
Network testNet = uNet;
startNodeId = 2;
maxCost = 3;
Path[] pathArray =
  NetworkManager.withinCost (testNet, startNodeId, maxCost);

// Display the resulting paths
System.out.println ("  " + pathArray.length + " nodes from node "
  + startNodeId + " in network " + testNet.getName() +
  " within a cost of " + maxCost + ": ");
for (int i = 0; i < pathArray.length; i++)
{
  Path path = pathArray[i];
  System.out.println("    node " + path.getEndNode().getID() +
    ", path cost " + path.getCost());
}
```

The output from running the code in Listing 10-22 is as follows:

```
4 nodes from node 2 in network UNET within a cost of 3.0:
  node 1, path cost 1.0
  node 3, path cost 2.0
  node 6, path cost 3.0
  node 7, path cost 3.0
```

Figure 10-13 shows the results graphically.

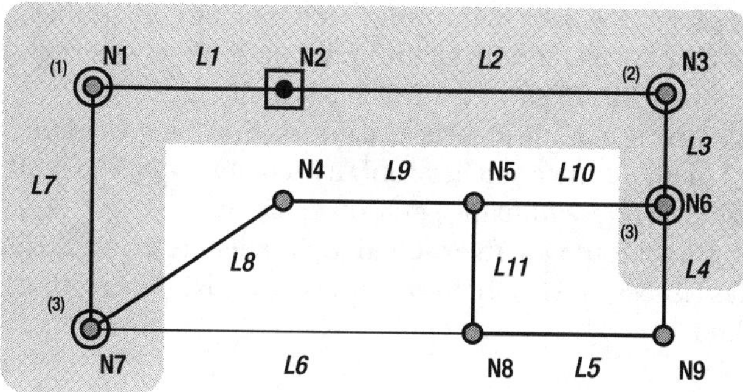

Figure 10-13. *Nodes less than three "cost units" from node N4 (undirected network)*

Performing the same operation on the directed network DNET gives the following results, as shown in Figure 10-14.

```
2 nodes from node 2 in network DNET within a cost of 3.0:
  node 1, path cost 1.0
  node 7, path cost 3.0
```

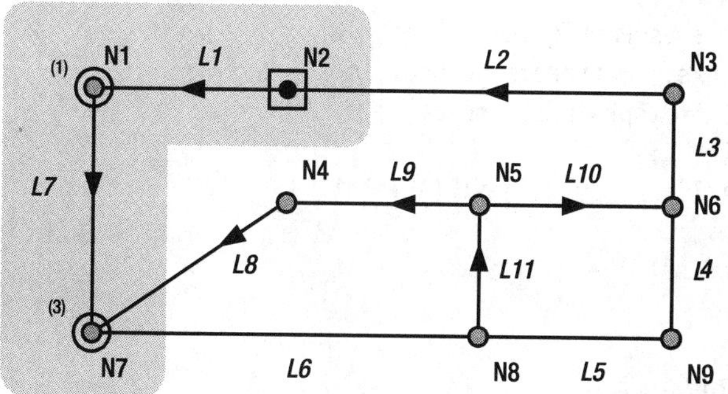

Figure 10-14. *Nodes less than three "cost units" from node N4 (directed network)*

Traveling Salesperson Problem

A traveling salesperson visits many customers in a day. The customers are spread out geographically. The salesperson really does not want to go crisscrossing the country from one visit to the other. He or she does not want to waste unnecessary time driving up and down roads. He or she would like to visit customers in the most optimal order so as to minimize travel time.

The `tspPath()` method is available to solve the *traveling salesperson problem* (TSP). You pass it the list of the nodes to visit, and the method returns the shortest path that passes through all the nodes you specified. You can optionally specify that you want to return to your starting point.

You also need a way to get the list of nodes to visit in the order proposed. Of course, they are all in the returned Path object, but they are mixed with all the nodes that you traverse on the way. The tspOrder() method will return the nodes on the TSP in the right order.

The tspOrder() method requires an array of node objects (Node[]) as input, as well as the Path object produced by the tspPath() method. Since you have only a list of *node IDs*, you must first construct the node array by fetching all nodes from the Network object.

The following code obtains the optimal route for an example trip on network UNET. We start at node N7 and need to visit nodes N2, N3, and N5. Then we come back to N7. Listing 10-23 shows how to use the tspPath() method.

Listing 10-23. *Using the* tspPath() *Method*

```
// Traveling Salesperson Problem: nodes N7, N2, N3, N5, then back to N7
Network testNet = uNet;
int[] nodeIds = {2,3,5};
boolean isClosed = true;
boolean useExactCost = true;
Path tspPath = NetworkManager.tspPath (testNet, nodeIds, isClosed,
  useExactCost, null);

// Display the resulting path
Link[] linkArray = tspPath.getLinkArray();
System.out.println ("  Path cost: " + tspPath.getCost() );
System.out.println ("  Number of links: "+ tspPath.getNoOfLinks());
System.out.println ("  Simple path? "+ tspPath.isSimple());
for (int i = 0; i < linkArray.length; i++)
  System.out.println ("    Link " + linkArray[i].getID() + "\t"
    + linkArray[i].getName()
    + "\t(cost: " + linkArray[i].getCost() + ")" );

// Construct input node array
Node[] inputNodes =  new Node[nodeIds.length];
for (int i = 0; i < nodeIds.length; i++)
  inputNodes[i] = network.getNode(nodeIds[i]);

// Display the visitation order
Node[] outputNodes =  NetworkManager.tspOrder(inputNodes, tspPath);
System.out.println ("  Actual node visitation order : " );
for (int i = 0; i < outputNodes.length; i++)
  System.out.println ("    Node " + outputNodes[i].getID() + "\t" +
     outputNodes[i].getName());
```

The result of executing the code in Listing 10-23 is as follows:

```
Path cost: 9.5
Number of links: 7
Simple path? true
  Link 7      L7      (cost: 2.0)
  Link 1      L1      (cost: 1.0)
  Link 2      L2      (cost: 2.0)
  Link 3      L3      (cost: 1.0)
  Link 10     L10     (cost: 1.0)
  Link 9      L9      (cost: 1.0)
  Link 8      L8      (cost: 1.5)
Actual node visitation order :
  Node 7      N7
  Node 2      N2
  Node 3      N3
  Node 5      N5
  Node 7      N7
```

Figure 10-15 shows the path chosen. The large circles are the nodes to visit. The square (N7) is our starting and ending point.

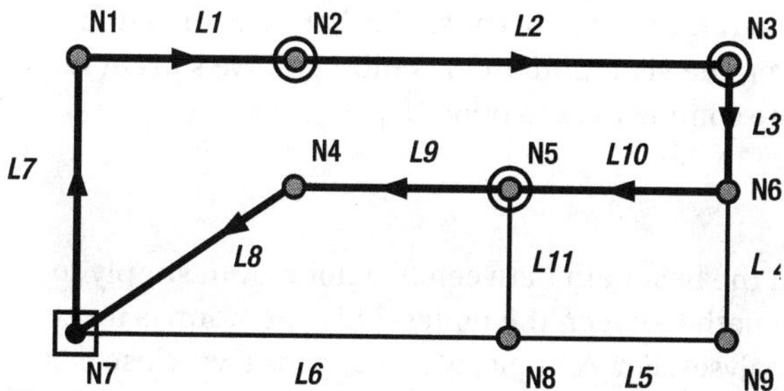

Figure 10-15. *Solution for the TSP*

Let's try the same operation on the directed network DNET. We get a different path, which is expected since we now have to consider the one-way links. Here are the results, with the path shown in Figure 10-16:

```
Path cost: 10.0
Number of links: 7
Simple path? true
  Link -6     L6      (cost: 2.0)
  Link 11     L11     (cost: 1.0)
  Link 10     L10     (cost: 1.0)
  Link -3     L3      (cost: 1.0)
  Link 2      L2      (cost: 2.0)
  Link 1      L1      (cost: 1.0)
  Link 7      L7      (cost: 2.0)
```

```
Actual node visitation order :
  Node 7       N7
  Node 5       N5
  Node 3       N3
  Node 2       N2
  Node 7       N7
```

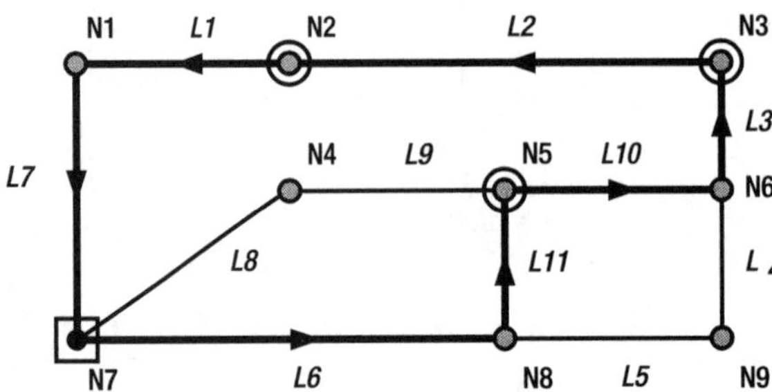

Figure 10-16. *TSP and one-way streets*

Notice that there's one important difference between the two examples: the nodes are not visited in the same order. In the first case, we actually visit the nodes in the order in which they are listed in the `nodeIds` parameter, but that is just because this happens to match the optimal path. In the second case, however, the visitation order is different. We start at node N7, then visit nodes N5, N3, and N2, before coming back to node N7.

Discovering Reachability

A different kind of problem is not to find the best path between two nodes, but simply to determine whether there indeed exists a path between the nodes. This operation is most useful in utility networks and "what-if" analyses. For example, what happens if we close this valve or if this circuit breaker trips? Will some customers no longer be serviced?

There are three methods available to determine reachability:

- `findReachableNodes()` returns all nodes that can be reached from the source node.
- `findReachingNodes()` returns all nodes that can reach the target node.
- `isReachable()` checks if the source node can reach the target node.

Consider the network shown in Figure 10-17. It is the same network we have been playing with (UNET), except that two links are no longer accessible.

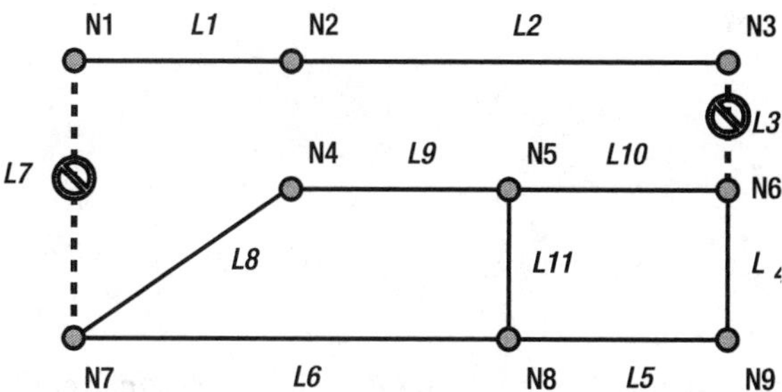

Figure 10-17. *UNET network with two links disabled*

The two links may have been removed from the network entirely, but a more likely scenario is that they still exist but are no longer active (i.e., the `ACTIVE` attribute has been set to `'N'`). For example, they could represent roads that are closed for repairs.

You can change the status of a link or node by updating the network tables in the database:

```
update unet_links set active = 'N' where link_id in (7,3);
commit;
```

You can also change the state directly on the memory-resident copy:

```
testNet.getLink(7).setState(false);
testNet.getLink(3).setState(false);
```

The code in Listing 10-24 illustrates the use of the `findReachableNodes()` method. The method returns an array of `Node` objects.

Listing 10-24. *Using the* `findReachableNodes()` *Method*

```
// Find nodes that can be reached from node N4
Network testNet = uNet;
nodeId = 4;
Node[] nodeArray = NetworkManager.findReachableNodes (testNet, nodeId);

// Display the results
System.out.println ("  " + nodeArray.length + " nodes in network "
  + testNet.getName() + " are reachable from node " + nodeId);
for (int i = 0; i < nodeArray.length; i++)
  System.out.println("    node " + nodeArray[i].getID());
```

The code in Listing 10-24 produces the following results. Note that nodes N1, N2, and N3 are not reachable because of the inactive links L3 and L7.

```
5 nodes in network UNET are reachable from node 4
  node 9      N9
  node 8      N8
  node 7      N7
  node 6      N6
  node 5      N5
```

The `findReachingNodes()` method works the same way.

In a large, fully connected network, those methods can return many nodes. As a matter of fact, they would return *all* nodes in the network, since they are all ultimately connected to one another. Such a result would not be very useful.

So, both methods let you limit the scope of the search by including either (or both) of the following parameters:

- *A rectangular geographical area*: Only those nodes inside the rectangle will be searched for reachability.
- *A maximum search depth, as a number of links to traverse*: Only those nodes less than the specified number of links away from the search node are considered.

Minimum Cost Spanning Tree

A *spanning tree* is a tree that connects all nodes in a graph. A *minimum cost spanning tree* (MCST) is the spanning tree with the minimum cost. Practically speaking, it tells you how you should wire together all nodes in your network at the lowest cost.

Typical applications are in the design of actual networks (utilities, telecommunications, transportation, etc.). For example, designing a gas pipeline in such a way that it follows an MCST approach can save a great deal money in equipment, construction, and operation costs.

There are two methods for obtaining the MCST of a network: `mcstLinkArray()` and `mcst()`. The `mcstLinkArray()` method returns an array containing all the `Link` objects in the tree. The `mcst()` method returns a new `Network` object that contains only those links and nodes that form the spanning tree. This is helpful because you can now use this new network for performing direct searches, such as shortest paths or nearest neighbors. You can write this new network to the database and use it for further analyses.

The code in Listing 10-25 gets the MCST for our undirected test network (UNET).

Listing 10-25. *Using the* `mcst()` *Method*

```
// Compute the Minimum Spanning Cost Tree
Network mcstNet = NetworkManager.mcst(uNet);

// Inspect the resulting network
System.out.println ("  Nodes: " + mcstNet.getNoOfNodes());
System.out.println ("  Links: " + mcstNet.getNoOfLinks());

// Display MCST network links
Link[] linkArray = mcstNet.getLinkArray();
double treeCost = 0;
for (int i = 0; i < linkArray.length; i++) {
```

```
    System.out.println ("    Link " + linkArray[i].getID() + "\t"
      + linkArray[i].getName()+ "\t"
      + linkArray[i].getCost());
    treeCost = treeCost + linkArray[i].getCost();
  }
  System.out.println ("  Total cost: \t\t" + treeCost);
```

The results of the code in Listing 10-25 are as follows. Figure 10-18 shows the resulting tree.

```
Nodes: 9
Links: 8
  Link 2      L2      2.0
  Link 4      L4      1.0
  Link 8      L8      1.5
  Link 9      L9      1.0
  Link 1      L1      1.0
  Link 3      L3      1.0
  Link 10     L10     1.0
  Link 5      L5      1.0
Total cost:           9.5
```

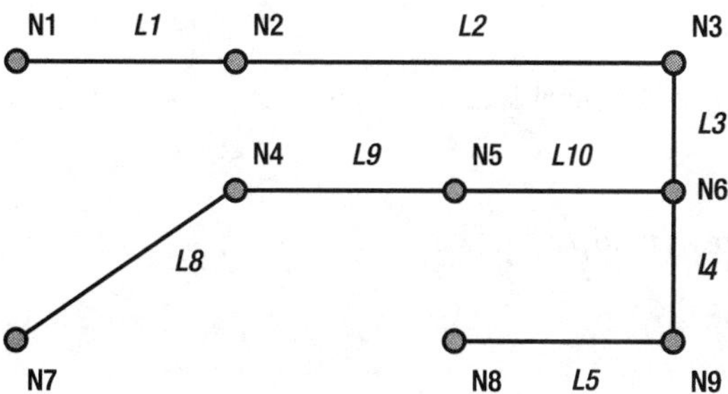

Figure 10-18. *MCST on network UNET*

Multiple Path Searches

We have two more methods to examine: `allPaths()` and `shortestPaths()`. The `allPaths()` method returns *all* possible paths between two nodes, and the `shortestPaths()` method (notice the plural) returns the shortest paths from one node to *all* the other nodes. Both methods return an array of `Path` objects.

Finding All Paths Between Two Nodes

Obviously, on a large, fully connected network, the `allPaths()` method could return a very large number of responses, and the computation could take a long time. So this method lets you limit the search space by specifying one or more of the following bounds:

- `Depth`: Only return the solutions that have less than the specified number of links.
- `Cost`: Only return the solutions whose cost is less than the specified value.
- `Solutions`: Only return the `N` best solutions.

The example in Listing 10-26 illustrates the search for all paths between nodes N3 and N4 on the undirected network (UNET). The bounds are set to a high value to get all possible solutions.

Listing 10-26. *Using the* `allPaths()` *Method*

```
// Get all paths between nodes 3 and 4
maxDepth = 1000;
maxCost = 1000;
maxSolutions = 1000;
Path[] pathArray =
   NetworkManager.allPaths(uNet, 3, 4, maxDepth, maxCost, maxSolutions);;

// Display the solutions found
for (int i = 0; i < pathArray.length; i++)
{
  Path p = pathArray[i];
  int numLinks = p.getNoOfLinks();
  double cost = p.getCost();
  System.out.println ("    path["+i+"] links:" + numLinks + ", path cost "+ cost);
}
```

The results of the code in Listing 10-26 are as follows:

```
path[0] links:3, path cost 3.0
path[1] links:5, path cost 5.0
path[2] links:4, path cost 6.5
path[3] links:5, path cost 6.5
path[4] links:5, path cost 6.5
path[5] links:6, path cost 9.0
path[6] links:8, path cost 11.0
```

To limit the results to only those solutions with four or fewer links, set the `maxDepth` parameter in the code to 4. The results then become

```
path[0] links:3, path cost 3.0
path[1] links:4, path cost 6.5
```

Finding All Shortest Paths from a Node

The `shortestPaths()` method returns the shortest path between a chosen node and each of the reachable nodes in the network. It takes no search restrictions, so it will return one solution for each reachable node. The results are ordered by cost, with the "nearest" nodes returned first.

Listing 10-27 shows how to use this method on node N4 in network UNET.

Listing 10-27. *Using the* `shortestPaths()` *Method*

```
// Get the shortest paths between node 4 and all other nodes
Path[] pathArray = NetworkManager.shortestPaths(uNet, 4);
for (int i = 0; i < pathArray.length; i++)
{
  Path p = pathArray[i];
  int endNodeId = p.getEndNode().getID();
  int numLinks = p.getNoOfLinks();
  double cost = p.getCost();
  System.out.println ("    path["+i+"] to node " + endNodeId + ", links:"
    + numLinks + ", path cost "+ cost);
}
```

The results of Listing 10-27 are as follows:

```
path[0] to node 5, links:1, path cost 1.0
path[1] to node 7, links:1, path cost 1.5
path[2] to node 6, links:2, path cost 2.0
path[3] to node 8, links:2, path cost 2.0
path[4] to node 3, links:3, path cost 3.0
path[5] to node 9, links:3, path cost 3.0
path[6] to node 1, links:2, path cost 3.5
path[7] to node 2, links:3, path cost 4.5
```

On a complex, fully connected network, this method will return a large number of results. We need a way to limit the number of results. We can do this using *network constraints*.

Limiting the Search Space: The SystemConstraint Class

The `SystemConstraint` class is a specific example of a network constraint. It lets you define a set of constraints to limit the search space for *any* of the methods you have seen so far.

Specifically, the `SystemConstraint` class lets you define the following constraints:

- `MaxCost`: The maximum cost.
- `MaxDepth`: The maximum search depth (the number of links in the paths).
- `MaxDistance`: The maximum geographical distance from the start node and any candidate node (i.e., only consider those nodes that are within that distance from that start node).
- `MaxMBR`: Only consider those nodes that are inside the MBR.
- `MustAvoidLinks`: A list of links to avoid.
- `MustAvoidNodes`: A list of nodes to avoid.

To use the class, just create a `SystemConstraint` object and configure it with one or more of the preceding constraints using specific methods such as `setMaxDepth()`. You can then pass it as the last parameter to any of the analysis methods you have seen so far, with the exception of the `mcst()` method.

Listing 10-28 shows how to set up a constraint that avoids node N5 and limits the cost of any solution to ten "cost units." Then use the `shortestPath()` method to find the optimal path between nodes N3 and N4, and pass it the `SystemConstraint` just defined.

■ **Note** When you set up a list of nodes to avoid, the links associated to those nodes are automatically put on the list of links to avoid.

Listing 10-28. *Using the* `SystemConstraint` *Class*

```
// Set up a system constraint with a list of nodes to avoid and a cost limit
int[] avoidNodes = {5};        // Nodes to avoid
myConstraint = new SystemConstraint (uNet, avoidNodes);
myConstraint.setMaxCost(10);

// Get shortest path from node N4 to N3 considering the constraint
Path path = NetworkManager.shortestPath (uNet, 3, 4, myConstraint);

// Show path cost and number of links
System.out.println ("Path cost: " + path.getCost() );
System.out.println ("Number of links: "+ path.getNoOfLinks());
System.out.println ("Simple path? "+ path.isSimple());

// Show the links traversed
System.out.println ("Links traversed:");
Link[] linkArray = path.getLinkArray();
for (int i = 0; i < linkArray.length; i++)
  System.out.println ("  Link " + linkArray[i].getID() + "\t"
    + linkArray[i].getName() +"\t" + linkArray[i].getCost());

// Show the nodes traversed
System.out.println ("  Nodes traversed:");
Node [] nodeArray = path.getNodeArray();
for (int i = 0; i < nodeArray.length; i++)
  System.out.println ("    Node " + nodeArray[i].getID() + "\t"
    + nodeArray[i].getName() +"\t" + nodeArray[i].getCost());
```

Because node N5 is now prohibited, we get a different answer from the one in Listing 10-20. Figure 10-19 shows the new path.

```
Path cost: 6.5
Number of links: 4
Simple path? true
Links traversed:
  Link 8      L8      1.5
  Link 7      L7      2.0
  Link 1      L1      1.0
  Link 2      L2      2.0
Nodes traversed:
  Node 4      N4      0.0
  Node 7      N7      0.0
  Node 1      N1      0.0
  Node 2      N2      0.0
  Node 3      N3      0.0
```

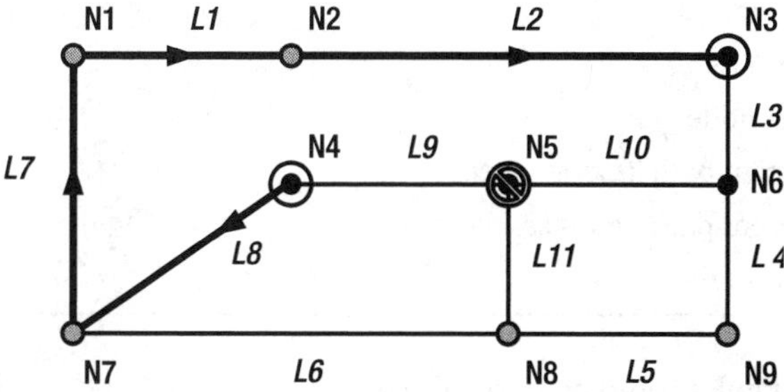

Figure 10-19. *The path from node N4 to node N3, avoiding node N5*

Advanced Analysis: Network Constraints

The analyses we have performed so far only consider relatively simple variables: network connectivity, link directions, node and link state, and costs. However, many real-life scenarios require more sophisticated choices.

Route calculations on a road network need to consider restricted maneuvers. One-way streets can easily be modeled using directed links. The dynamic aspect of the road network (such as streets closed due to repairs) can be modeled using the active/inactive states.

But some restrictions may be seasonal or time dependent—for instance, a mountain pass is open only during the summer months, and a ferry operates only at certain times of year. Other restrictions may be legal—for example, a left turn on a busy boulevard or a U-turn. Those restrictions may apply only at certain times (e.g., the left turn is prohibited during peak traffic hours, but allowed otherwise).

Finally, the restrictions may apply differently to different classes of vehicles. For example, a private access road cannot be used to carry public traffic, but it is always open to emergency vehicles. Or a low tunnel or weak bridge prevents trucks but not cars from using a road. Or on a canal network, barges can travel only on those sections that are wide and deep enough, whereas small boats can go anywhere.

Similar issues exist for other kinds of networks. In an electrical or telecommunications network, nodes may represent complex equipment whose behavior is more sophisticated than a simple On/Off status.

You can implement those kinds of constraints using the `NetworkConstraint` interface, specifically with the `isSatisfied()` method. This method is passed an `AnalysisInfo` object that provides sufficient context information for you to decide whether to accept or reject the constraint. Use one of the methods shown in Table 10-1 to find out the current state of the solution being computed.

Table 10-10. `AnalysisInfo` *Methods*

Method	Meaning
`getCurrentCost()`	Returns the current path cost
`getCurrentDepth()`	Returns the current path depth
`getCurrentLink()`	Returns the current link
`getCurrentNode()`	Returns the current node
`getNextLink()`	Returns the next link
`getNextNode()`	Returns the next node
`getPathLinkVec()`	Returns the current path links as a `Vector`
`getPathNodeVec()`	Returns the current path nodes as a `Vector`
`getStartNode()`	Returns the start node

Return `false` to indicate that the next link should be skipped.

We will now illustrate the use of network constraints using a simple example. Suppose that our UNET network represents a canal network. Each link in our network has a `link_level` column, which we use to define the class of each canal as a number from 1 to 3. A class 1 canal is very wide and deep; any boat can travel through such a canal. Class 2 canals are narrower and not as deep as class 1 canals. Class 3 canals are still smaller and can accept only very small boats.

Boats also have a size. Size 1 boats are large and heavy, and they can only travel through class 1 canals. Size 2 boats are smaller than size 1 boats, and they can travel through class 1 or class 2 canals. Size 3 boats are smaller still and can travel on any class of canal (1, 2, or 3).

The code in Listing 10-29 sets the `link_level` column in the `unet_links` table. The resulting UNET network is shown in Figure 10-20.

Listing 10-29. *Setting Link Levels for the UNET Network*

```
SQL> UPDATE unet_links SET link_level = 1 WHERE link_id IN (1, 2, 3, 5, 6, 7, 10);
SQL> UPDATE unet_links SET link_level = 2 WHERE link_id IN (4, 11);
SQL> UPDATE unet_links SET link_level = 3 WHERE link_id IN (8, 9);
SQL> COMMIT;
```

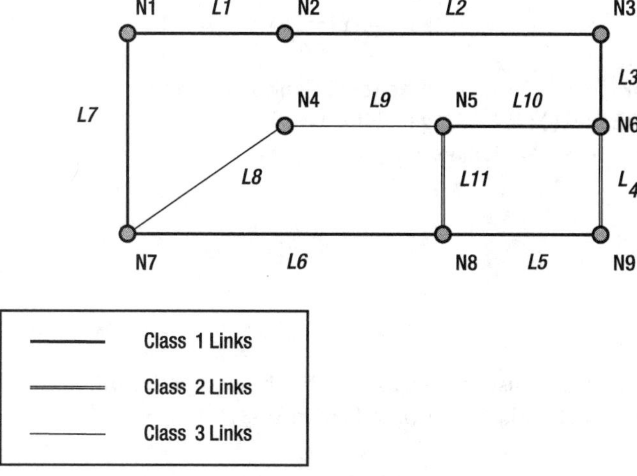

Figure 10-20. *Network with multiple link levels*

We can now write a network constraint that will make sure that boats only travel through the canals that can accommodate them. The code for the `LinkLevelConstraint` class is shown in Listing 10-30.

Listing 10-30. *Network Constraint*

```
import java.util.*;
import oracle.spatial.network.*;
/**
 * The following network constraint assumes that
 * 1. each link has a link level (stored as LINK_LEVEL in { 1,2,3 })
 * 2. for a given target level (in { 1,2,3 } ), the following must hold:
 *    target Level 1 can only travel on link Level 1
 *    target Level 2 can travel on link Level 1 and 2
 *    target Level 3 can travel on link Level 1, 2, and 3
 */
public class LinkLevelConstraint implements NetworkConstraint {

  int p_targetLevel = 0;                    // Default; no restriction

  public LinkLevelConstraint (int targetLevel) {
    p_targetLevel = targetLevel;
  }

  public boolean requiresPathLinks() {
    return false ;
  }
```

```
  public boolean isSatisfied (AnalysisInfo info) {
    if ( p_targetLevel == 0 )                // no restriction
      return true ;
    Link link = info.getNextLink() ;         // potential link candidate
    int linkLevel = link.getLinkLevel();     // get link Level
    if ( link != null && p_targetLevel >= linkLevel )
      return true;
    else
      return false;
  }
}
```

We can now use the network constraint just created to find the shortest path from node N7 to node N5 on the modified UNET network, as shown in Listing 10-31.

Listing 10-31. *Using the Network Constraint*

```
// Set up network constraint
int targetLevel = 1;
LinkLevelConstraint netConstraint = new LinkLevelConstraint (targetLevel);

// Get shortest path from node N7 to N5
Network testNet = uNet;
startNodeId = 7;
endNodeId = 5;
Path path = NetworkManager.shortestPath (testNet, startNodeID ,endNodeId);

// Show path cost and number of links
System.out.println ("Path cost: " + path.getCost() );
System.out.println ("Number of links: "+ path.getNoOfLinks());
System.out.println ("Simple path? "+ path.isSimple());

// Show the links traversed
System.out.println ("Links traversed:");
Link[] linkArray = path.getLinkArray();
for (int i = 0; i < linkArray.length; i++)
  System.out.println ("    Link " + linkArray[i].getID() + "\t"
   + linkArray[i].getName() +"\t"
   + linkArray[i].getLinkLevel() + "\t"
   + linkArray[i].getCost() );
// Show the nodes traversed
System.out.println ("  Nodes traversed:");
Node [] nodeArray = path.getNodeArray();
for (int i = 0; i < nodeArray.length; i++)
  System.out.println ("    Node " + nodeArray[i].getID() + "\t"
    + nodeArray[i].getName() +"\t"
    + nodeArray[i].getCost());
```

You can now try to find the shortest path between nodes N7 and N3 with various settings of the targetLevel parameter. You should see the following results. Remember that the targetLevel value passed to the constraint represents the size of the boat; the smaller the value, the larger the boat. With targetLevel set to 1 (i.e., for a *large* boat), the result of running the code in Listing 10-31 is as follows. The path is long because the boat can travel only through the largest (class 1) canals.

```
Path cost: 7.0
Number of links: 5
Simple path? true
Links traversed:
  Link 7      L7      1       2.0
  Link 1      L1      1       1.0
  Link 2      L2      1       2.0
  Link 3      L3      1       1.0
  Link 10     L10     1       1.0
Nodes traversed:
  Node 7      N7      0.0
  Node 1      N1      0.0
  Node 2      N2      0.0
  Node 3      N3      0.0
  Node 6      N6      0.0
  Node 5      N5      0.0
```

Running the same code with the targetLevel set to 2, which indicates a *medium* boat, you should get the following results. The path is shorter, indicating the boat can travel through class 1 and class 2 canals.

```
Path cost: 3.0
Number of links: 2
Simple path? true
Links traversed:
  Link 6      L6      1       2.0
  Link 11     L11     2       1.0
Nodes traversed:
  Node 7      N7      0.0
  Node 8      N8      0.0
  Node 5      N5      0.0
```

With targetLevel set to 3 (for a *small* boat), we can travel on any link:

```
Path cost: 2.5
Number of links: 2
Simple path? true
Links traversed:
  Link 8      L8      3       1.5
  Link 9      L9      3       1.0
```

```
Nodes traversed:
  Node 7     N7     0.0
  Node 4     N4     0.0
  Node 5     N5     0.0
```

The same constraint could be used for a road network, where the `link_level` could be used to indicate the type of vehicles that can pass a link. Level 3 links could be used to indicate bridges or tunnels that heavy trucks cannot use.

More sophisticated constraints, such as time-based turn restrictions, need additional information. That information can be fetched from the database when the network constraint object is instantiated.

Network Structures: The Network, Node, Link, and Path Classes

The `Network` class stores and maintains networks. The classes `Node`, `Link`, and `Path` define individual network elements.

Network Class

The methods of the `Network` class let you select, add, modify, and delete network elements, as well as find out general information about the network.

A `Network` object is either created from scratch using the `NetworkFactory` class or instantiated from the database using the `readNetwork()` method of the `NetworkManager` class.

Note that you cannot instantiate the `Node`, `Link`, and `Path` classes (they are actually interfaces). To create any of them, use the proper methods of the `NetworkFactory` class.

Maintaining the Network

The `addNode()`, `addLink()`, and `addPath()` methods add node, link, and path elements, respectively, to a network. Their inputs are `Node` and `Link` objects produced by the `NetworkFactory` class. The `Path` objects are typically produced by analysis functions of the `NetworkManager` class.

For example, the following adds node `n1` to network `graph`:

```
graph.addNode(n1);
```

The `deleteNode()`, `deleteLink()`, and `deletePath()` methods remove elements from a network. You can pass them either a `Node`, `Link`, or `Path` object, or their numeric identifier.

The `setState()` method allows you to turn network elements "on" and "off." The method alters the `ACTIVE` state of the link of node. An inactive link or node is not considered by any network analysis operation.

The `Network` class remembers the changes you make. When you write it back to the database (using the `writeNetwork()` method of the `NetworkManager` class), only the changes are applied to the database. The method performs an automatic commit.

Extracting Network Elements

A large number of methods extract elements from a network. Examples of these elements are single nodes, links, or paths (based on their identifier), or collections of nodes or links based on various criteria: all active nodes or links; all elements at a certain hierarchy level; all elements of a certain type; or simply all of the nodes, links, and paths in the network.

You can also extract the entire network at a given hierarchy level or the network contained inside a given rectangular window.

Finding Information About the Network

Methods are available to extract metadata information: name, type, and name of the network structures in the database (table and column names).

Other methods return element counts: the number of nodes, links, or paths in the network; a count of those elements at a certain hierarchy level; or only the active elements.

Yet more methods return the current maximum identifier for nodes, links, and paths. Since identifiers must be unique, this is useful to generate new identifiers for new elements.

Node and Link Classes

These classes are used to describe elements in the network. A number of *get* and *set* methods enable you to obtain details on each element and modify it. The major *get* methods on the `Node` and `Link` classes are shown in Tables 10-11 and 10-12. *Set* methods (not listed here) allow you to modify nodes and links.

Table 10-11. *Main* get *Methods on the* `Node` *Object*

Method	Meaning
`getCost()`	Returns the stored cost for the node
`getID()`	Returns the unique numeric identifier of the node (from the column `NODE_ID` in the `NODE` table)
`getName()`	Returns the name of the node (from the column `NODE_NAME` in the `NODE` table)
`isActive()`	Returns `true` if the node is active (derived from the column `ACTIVE` in the `NODE` table)
`getGeometry()`	Returns the geometric point for the node
`getInLinks()`	Returns an array of the links that terminate at this node
`getOutLinks()`	Returns an array of the links that originate from this node

Table 10-12. *Main* get *Methods on the* `Link` *Object*

Method	Meaning
`getCost()`	Returns the stored cost for the link
`getID()`	Returns the unique numeric identifier of the link (from the column `LINK_ID` in the `LINK` table)
`getName()`	Returns the name of the link (from the column `LINK_NAME` in the `LINK` table)
`isActive()`	Returns `true` if the link is active (derived from the column `ACTIVE` in the `LINK` table)

(Continues)

Table 10-12. *Main* get *Methods on the* `Link` *Object (Continued)*

Method	Meaning
`getGeometry()`	Returns the geometric line for the link
`getStartNode()`	Returns the start node for that link
`getEndNode()`	Returns the end node for the link
`getCoLink()`	Returns the *colink* of the link (i.e., the link that goes in the opposite direction)

Path Class

`Path` objects are primarily used to store the results of analysis functions—for example, the result of the `shortestPath()` method of the `NetworkManager` class.

The main method of the `Path` class is `getLinkArray()`, which returns a list of all links that compose the path, as an array. Alternate notations return the list of links as an `Iterator` or a `Vector`.

The `Path` class has many other useful methods:

- The `getXxxx()` and `isXxxx()` methods return various information about the path: whether or not it is closed, whether it is simple or complex, its total cost and the number of links that compose it, the start and end nodes, and so on. The list goes on and on. The main methods are listed in Table 10-13.
- The path search method `contains()` finds out whether a path contains a specific `Node` or `Link`, and the `getLinkAt()` and `getNodeAt()` methods extract specific path elements.
- The path editing methods are `clip()`, `split()`, `insertLink()`, `removeLink()`, and `concatenate()` (to join two paths).
- The `computeGeometry()` method computes the geometry of the complete path from the geometries of all the links that form the path.

Table 10-13. *Main* get *Methods on the* `Path` *Object*

Method	Meaning
`getCost()`	Returns the total computed cost for the path
`getNoOfLinks()`	Returns the total number of links in the path
`getLinkArray()`	Returns an array of the links in the path
`getGeometry()`	Returns the geometric shape of the path

Creating Networks: The NetworkFactory Class

Use the `NetworkFactory` class to create new networks and networks elements (nodes, links, and paths). Those elements are transient; the `NetworkManager` class lets you write them to the database.

Creating Networks

The createLogicalNetwork() and createSDONetwork() methods create an empty network (logical or spatial). You can optionally specify the names of the tables for storing the network in the database.

For example, the following code creates a new spatial network called NH_ROADS, single level, directed, using an SRID of 8307 and two-dimensional geometries:

```
Network nhRoads = NetworkFactory.createSDONetwork("NH_ROADS", 1, true, 8307, 2);
```

The tables for this network will use default names (i.e., NH_ROADS_NODE$).

Creating Network Elements

The createNode(), createLink(), and createPath() methods create nodes, links, and paths. Those are stand-alone elements. Methods of the Network class enable you to add them to a network.

For example, the following code creates node n1 with the identifier 1. No other information is given—the node has no cost and no geometry.

```
Node n1 = NetworkFactory.createNode(1);
```

Creating Network Tables

Other methods let you create the physical table structures inside the database. createNetworkTables() will create all the tables for a network (using the names that you specified when creating the network, or default names if you did not specify any). Methods such as createNodeTable() let you create individual tables.

The preceding methods create empty tables. To actually populate the tables with the network data, use the writeNetwork() method of the NetworkManager class.

Network Creation Example

The code in Listing 10-32 illustrates how to create and populate a network using the Java interface. It produces the same network as the simple undirected logical network (UNET) illustrated in Figure 10-7 that we defined and created in the database using SQL statements in Listings 10-16 and 10-17.

Listing 10-32. *Creating a Network Using the Java API*

```
// Create the network object
String networkName = "MY_NET";
Network myNet = NetworkFactory.createLogicalNetwork(
  networkName,                // networkName
  1,                          // noOfHierarchyLevels
  true,                       // isDirected
  networkName+"_NODE",        // nodeTableName
  "COST",                     // nodeCostColumn
  networkName+"_LINK",        // linkTableName
```

```
  "COST",                       // linkCostColumn
  networkName+"_PATH",          // pathTableName
  networkName+"_PLINK"          // pathLinkTableName
);

// Create the nodes
Node n1 = NetworkFactory.createNode (1, "N1");
Node n2 = NetworkFactory.createNode (2, "N2");
Node n3 = NetworkFactory.createNode (3, "N3");
Node n4 = NetworkFactory.createNode (4, "N4");
Node n5 = NetworkFactory.createNode (5, "N5");
Node n6 = NetworkFactory.createNode (6, "N6");
Node n7 = NetworkFactory.createNode (7, "N7");
Node n8 = NetworkFactory.createNode (8, "N8");
Node n9 = NetworkFactory.createNode (9, "N9");

// Create the links
Link l1  = NetworkFactory.createLink ( 1, "L1",  n1, n2, 1);
Link l2  = NetworkFactory.createLink ( 2, "L2",  n2, n3, 2);
Link l3  = NetworkFactory.createLink ( 3, "L3",  n3, n6, 1);
Link l4  = NetworkFactory.createLink ( 4, "L4",  n6, n9, 1);
Link l5  = NetworkFactory.createLink ( 5, "L5",  n9, n8, 1);
Link l6  = NetworkFactory.createLink ( 6, "L6",  n8, n7, 2);
Link l7  = NetworkFactory.createLink ( 7, "L7",  n7, n1, 2);
Link l8  = NetworkFactory.createLink ( 8, "L8",  n7, n4, 1.5);
Link l9  = NetworkFactory.createLink ( 9, "L9",  n4, n5, 1);
Link l10 = NetworkFactory.createLink (10, "L10", n5, n6, 1);
Link l11 = NetworkFactory.createLink (11, "L11", n5, n8, 1);

// Add the nodes to the network
myNet.addNode (n1);
myNet.addNode (n2);
myNet.addNode (n3);
myNet.addNode (n4);
myNet.addNode (n5);
myNet.addNode (n6);
myNet.addNode (n7);
myNet.addNode (n8);
myNet.addNode (n9);

// Add the links to the network
myNet.addLink (l1);
myNet.addLink (l2);
myNet.addLink (l3);
myNet.addLink (l4);
myNet.addLink (l5);
myNet.addLink (l6);
```

```
myNet.addLink (l7);
myNet.addLink (l8);
myNet.addLink (l9);
myNet.addLink (l10);
myNet.addLink (l11);

// Create the network tables in the database
NetworkFactory.createNetworkTables (dbConnection, myNet);

// Write the network (this also writes the metadata)
NetworkManager.writeNetwork (dbConnection, myNet);
```

Debugging Network Structures

All classes have a `toString()` method that formats their content in a readable way. For example, the following dumps the `myNet` network just created:

```
System.out.println (myNet);
```

and produces the following output:

```
User    Name:   [null]
Network Name:   [MY_NET]
Network Category:   [LOGICAL]
Geometry Type:  []
No. Of Hierarchy Levels: [1]
Link    Dir.  :   [DIRECTED]
Node    Table :  MY_NET_NODE[null ]:(DIM:0,SRID:0)
Link    Table :  MY_NET_LINK[null ]:(DIM:0,SRID:0)
LRS     Table :  null
Path    Table :  MY_NET_PATH[null ]:(DIM:0,SRID:0)
Path-Link Table: MY_NET_PLINK
Link Cost Column: [COST]
Node Cost Column: [COST]

Network Node Table:
NodeID: 2[H:1] , Name: N2, Type: null, Cost: 0.0 InLinks: 1  OutLinks: 2
NodeID: 4[H:1] , Name: N4, Type: null, Cost: 0.0 InLinks: 8  OutLinks: 9
NodeID: 9[H:1] , Name: N9, Type: null, Cost: 0.0 InLinks: 4  OutLinks: 5
NodeID: 8[H:1] , Name: N8, Type: null, Cost: 0.0 InLinks: 5 11  OutLinks: 6
NodeID: 6[H:1] , Name: N6, Type: null, Cost: 0.0 InLinks: 3 10  OutLinks: 4
NodeID: 1[H:1] , Name: N1, Type: null, Cost: 0.0 InLinks: 7  OutLinks: 1
NodeID: 3[H:1] , Name: N3, Type: null, Cost: 0.0 InLinks: 2  OutLinks: 3
NodeID: 7[H:1] , Name: N7, Type: null, Cost: 0.0 InLinks: 6  OutLinks: 7 8
NodeID: 5[H:1] , Name: N5, Type: null, Cost: 0.0 InLinks: 9  OutLinks: 10 11
```

```
Network Link Table:
LinkID: 2[H:1] , Name: L2, Type: null, State: true, Cost: 2.0, Level: 1,
StartNode: 2, EndNode: 3,
CoLink ID:none
LinkID: 4[H:1] , Name: L4, Type: null, State: true, Cost: 1.0, Level: 1,
StartNode: 6, EndNode: 9,
CoLink ID:none
LinkID: 9[H:1] , Name: L9, Type: null, State: true, Cost: 1.0, Level: 1,
StartNode: 4, EndNode: 5,
CoLink ID:none
LinkID: 8[H:1] , Name: L8, Type: null, State: true, Cost: 1.5, Level: 1,
StartNode: 7, EndNode: 4,
CoLink ID:none
LinkID: 11[H:1] , Name: L11, Type: null, State: true, Cost: 1.0, Level: 1,
StartNode: 5, EndNode: 8,
CoLink ID:none
LinkID: 6[H:1] , Name: L6, Type: null, State: true, Cost: 2.0, Level: 1,
StartNode: 8, EndNode: 7,
CoLink ID:none
LinkID: 1[H:1] , Name: L1, Type: null, State: true, Cost: 1.0, Level: 1,
StartNode: 1, EndNode: 2,
CoLink ID:none
LinkID: 3[H:1] , Name: L3, Type: null, State: true, Cost: 1.0, Level: 1,
StartNode: 3, EndNode: 6,
CoLink ID:none
LinkID: 10[H:1] , Name: L10, Type: null, State: true, Cost: 1.0, Level: 1,
StartNode: 5, EndNode: 6,
CoLink ID:none
LinkID: 7[H:1] , Name: L7, Type: null, State: true, Cost: 2.0, Level: 1,
StartNode: 7, EndNode: 1,
CoLink ID:none
LinkID: 5[H:1] , Name: L5, Type: null, State: true, Cost: 1.0, Level: 1,
StartNode: 9, EndNode: 8,
CoLink ID:none
```

The Network Editor

All the examples you have seen so far have used either SQL or Java, but with no actual graphical results and little interaction. Oracle provides a nice graphical editor that lets you experiment visually with actual data and try out all the network analysis functions.

Starting the Editor

The editor is a Java program supplied as a JAR file, `sdondme.jar`. Make sure to include all the required JAR files in the Java classpath (see Table 10-14).

Table 10-14. *JAR Files Used by the Network Editor*

JAR File	Usage	Location
sdondme.jar	Network editor	$ORACLE_HOME/md/lib
sdoapi.jar	Spatial SDO API	$ORACLE_HOME/md/lib
sdonm.jar	Network Java API	$ORACLE_HOME/md/lib
sdoutl.jar	Spatial utilities	$ORACLE_HOME/md/lib
classes12.jar	JDBC driver	$ORACLE_HOME/jdbc/lib
xmlparserv2.jar	XML parser	$ORACLE_HOME/lib

Since the network API loads networks in memory, you may want to provide sufficient memory to Java using the -Xms and -Xmx options.

The main class of the editor is oracle.spatial.network.editor.NetworkEditor. Listing 10-33 shows how you can start the editor in a Windows environment.

Listing 10-33. *Starting the Network Editor*

```
set JAVA_ORACLE_HOME=D:\Oracle\Ora101
set JAR_LIBS=%JAVA_ORACLE_HOME%/md/lib/sdondme.jar;
%JAVA_ORACLE_HOME%/lib/xmlparserv2.jar; %JAVA_ORACLE_HOME%/jdbc/lib/classes12.jar;
%JAVA_ORACLE_HOME%\md/lib/sdonm.jar; %JAVA_ORACLE_HOME%/md/lib/sdoapi.jar;
%JAVA_ORACLE_HOME%/md/lib/sdoutl.jar
java -Xms512M -Xmx512M -cp %JAR_LIBS% oracle.spatial.network.editor.NetworkEditor
```

You should now see the window shown in Figure 10-21.

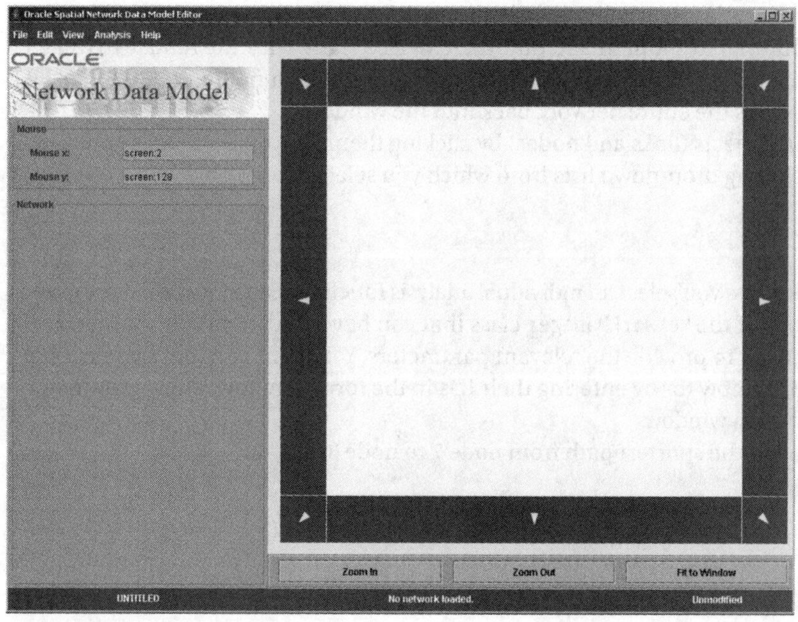

Figure 10-21. *Main window of the network editor*

Caution The editor window will occupy your entire screen. It is not resizable. To see it entirely, you may have to set your window so it does not sit in front of the editor window; otherwise, the status window of the editor will be hidden behind the task bar.

Connecting to the Database

Select the Connect to Database option from the File menu, and then fill the next dialog box with the usual JDBC connection information: host name, port, database name, user name, and password.

Loading a Network from the Database

Select the Read Network from Database option from the File menu. This brings up a dialog box much like the connection box, where you can select the network to load from the Network Name drop-down list.

Depending on the size of the network you load, this may take some time. For the networks we used in the preceding examples, this will be fast, of course.

Note The network editor can manipulate only spatial networks.

Using the Loaded Network

Once the network has loaded, you will see it entirely in the main map window. Use the Zoom In and Zoom Out buttons to zoom in and out. You can also right-click the mouse to drag a rectangle to zoom into. You can pan using the arrow buttons all around the window. The Fit to Window button brings the entire network back into the window.

Select individual objects (links and nodes) by clicking them. The object details appear in the left window, including drop-down lists from which you select related objects.

Network Analysis

The `Analysis` function lets you select an individual analysis function. Each function corresponds to one of the methods of the `NetworkManager` class that you have studied in this chapter. For each function, you need to provide the relevant parameters. You identify nodes by selecting them from the map window (or by entering their IDs in the form window). Other parameters are entered into the form window.

Figure 10-22 shows the shortest path from node 7 to node 3.

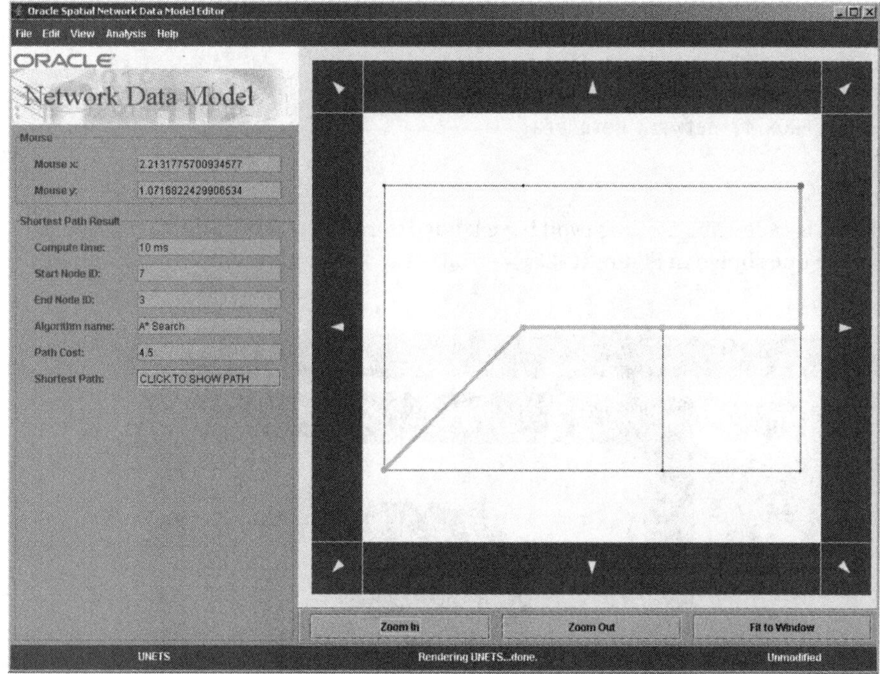

Figure 10-22. *Shortest path from node 7 to node 3 on network UNET*

Network Editing

From the Edit menu, you can modify the network by adding and removing nodes and links.

To add a node, click the spot on the screen where you want the new node to be placed. The left window is then filled with the x and y coordinates of the node, as well as with a new ID for the node. You just need to fill the other information, such as node cost and status, before clicking the Create button.

You can add links only between existing nodes. Click the start node and then the end node. The IDs of the two nodes appear in the left window (but you can also enter them manually). Fill in the rest of the form and click the Create button.

You can delete links or nodes by selecting them and then using the Delete Selected option of the Edit menu.

Once you have finished changing the network, you can write it back to the database using the Write Network to Database option from the File menu. If you forget to do this before exiting the editor or loading another network, you will be reminded.

Example Data: The Streets of San Francisco

The network analysis on the simple networks (UNET and DNET) we have been working with is interesting, but not very spectacular.

In the Downloads area of the Apress website (`www.apress.com`), you will find a dataset that contains a street network for San Francisco, California. This network contains some 31,000 links and 11,000 nodes. Use the Oracle Import tool to load it, as shown in Listing 10-34. Notice the additional step to insert the network metadata in `USER_SDO_NETWORK_METADATA`.

Listing 10-34. *Loading the Network Data*

```
imp spatial/spatial file=net.dmp full=y
SQL> INSERT INTO USER_SDO_NETWORK_METADATA
       SELECT * FROM my_network_metadata;
SQL> commit;
```

The network is called `NET_SF`. Once you have loaded it in the Network Editor, you will see a window like the one shown in Figure 10-23.

Figure 10-23. *The streets of San Francisco*

Zoom in until you see the links and nodes in sufficient detail. Each link represents a street segment between two intersections. Nodes are intersections. This is a directed network, and arrows indicate the direction of each link.

Try performing some analysis functions. For example, select the "Nearest N Nodes from a given node choice" from the Analysis menu, select a node by clicking it, enter the number of neighbors to search, and click the Compute button. A typical result should look like Figure 10-24.

Figure 10-24. *A nearest neighbors search in San Francisco*

Caution Some analysis functions may need to process a great deal of information—this is the case for the functions that return all paths between two nodes or those that find all nodes that are reachable or that can reach a given node. By default, those functions perform unbounded searches that can take a long time to complete. Make sure to limit the results by providing a maximum depth, cost, or number of solutions. The MCST function has no limit; it always runs on the complete network.

Summary

In this chapter, you learned how to define and load networks. You also learned how to use the Java API provided with the Oracle Network Data Model to perform such network-based analyses as finding the shortest path between two nodes, finding all nodes within some distance from a node, and discovering the nearest neighbors to a node.

In Chapter 12, you will use some of the techniques you learned in this chapter in a complete application.

CHAPTER 11

Generating Maps Using MapViewer

So far, you have seen how to use spatial-based queries and how to manipulate spatial objects. However, one important aspect is still missing: visualization of spatial objects using maps. After all, location information is all about maps, and to paraphrase a common saying, a map is certainly worth a thousand words. In this chapter, you will see how to enable map-based visualization of spatial data in your applications using Oracle MapViewer.

MapViewer is a Java servlet that constructs maps by reading appropriate database views and tables, and returns the maps to the client applications in appropriate formats. Each map constructed is specified using one or more layers, or *themes*. Each theme represents a logical grouping of geographic spatial features, such as roads, customer locations, rivers, and so on. These features are rendered with specific *styles*. In this chapter, we will describe in detail how to create these maps using Oracle MapViewer (Oracle Application Server MapViewer, to use its full name), covering the following topics:

- The need for maps in Spatial applications, and an overview of Oracle MapViewer
- How to install, deploy, and configure MapViewer
- How to define maps with themes and styles, and store their definitions in the database using the map definition (MapDef) tool
- How to use MapViewer and the maps that you have defined in your applications, via the available XML and Java APIs
- How to manage and administer the MapViewer server (i.e., how to manage data sources, caches, map definitions, etc.)

Why Use Maps in Location-Enabled Applications?

We are all familiar with maps. We used maps in geography classes. We currently use maps to decide where to go for our vacations or to find our way when we are lost on the road. In this section, you will see how maps enable visualization of location data in your applications.

To start, consider the query in Listing 11-1, which selects all our branches in San Francisco.

Listing 11-1. *Branches in San Francisco*

```
SQL> SELECT street_number num,
            street_name,
            city,
            postal_code
       FROM branches
      WHERE city = 'SAN FRANCISCO';

NUM   STREET_NAME                CITY          POSTAL_CODE
----- -------------------------- ------------- ------------
420   POST ST                    SAN FRANCISCO 94102
944   STOCKTON ST                SAN FRANCISCO 94108
1007  TARAVAL ST                 SAN FRANCISCO 94116
1995  UNION ST                   SAN FRANCISCO 94123
1640  VAN NESS AVE               SAN FRANCISCO 94109
245   WINSTON DR                 SAN FRANCISCO 94132
5268  DIAMOND HEIGHTS BLVD       SAN FRANCISCO 94131
1455  STOCKTON ST                SAN FRANCISCO 94133
2090  JERROLD AVE                SAN FRANCISCO 94124
1     POWELL ST                  SAN FRANCISCO 94102
2485  SAN BRUNO AVE              SAN FRANCISCO 94134
288   W PORTAL AVE               SAN FRANCISCO 94127
315   MONTGOMERY ST              SAN FRANCISCO 94104
680   8TH ST                     SAN FRANCISCO 94103
915   FRONT ST                   SAN FRANCISCO 94111
150   4TH ST                     SAN FRANCISCO 94103
4098  24TH ST                    SAN FRANCISCO 94114
1515  SLOAT BLVD                 SAN FRANCISCO 94132
445   POWELL ST                  SAN FRANCISCO 94102
50    CALIFORNIA ST              SAN FRANCISCO 94111
45    SPEAR ST                   SAN FRANCISCO 94105
1200  MONTGOMERY ST              SAN FRANCISCO 94133
5000  3RD ST                     SAN FRANCISCO 94124
2850  24TH ST                    SAN FRANCISCO 94110
3701  BALBOA ST                  SAN FRANCISCO 94121
500   BATTERY ST                 SAN FRANCISCO 94111
501   BRANNAN ST                 SAN FRANCISCO 94107
1525  MARKET ST                  SAN FRANCISCO 94102
3565  CALIFORNIA ST              SAN FRANCISCO 94118
501   CASTRO ST                  SAN FRANCISCO 94114
2200  CHESTNUT ST                SAN FRANCISCO 94123
600   CLEMENT ST                 SAN FRANCISCO 94118
433   CORTLAND AVE               SAN FRANCISCO 94110
1275  FELL ST                    SAN FRANCISCO 94117
```

```
2310  FILLMORE ST              SAN FRANCISCO  94115
2835  GEARY BLVD               SAN FRANCISCO  94118
5500  GEARY BLVD               SAN FRANCISCO  94121
701   GRANT AVE                SAN FRANCISCO  94108
800   IRVING ST                SAN FRANCISCO  94122
1945  IRVING ST                SAN FRANCISCO  94122
6     LELAND AVE               SAN FRANCISCO  94134
2701  MISSION ST               SAN FRANCISCO  94110
3250  MISSION ST               SAN FRANCISCO  94110
5150  MISSION ST               SAN FRANCISCO  94112
345   MONTGOMERY ST            SAN FRANCISCO  94104
33    NEW MONTGOMERY ST        SAN FRANCISCO  94105
2325  NORIEGA ST               SAN FRANCISCO  94122
15    OCEAN AVE                SAN FRANCISCO  94112

48 rows selected.
```

Compare this textual response with Figure 11-1, which positions those branches on a map of San Francisco, and Figure 11-2, which compares those branch positions with positions of competitors. Notice how the map clearly points out the placement of our branches and those of our competitors.

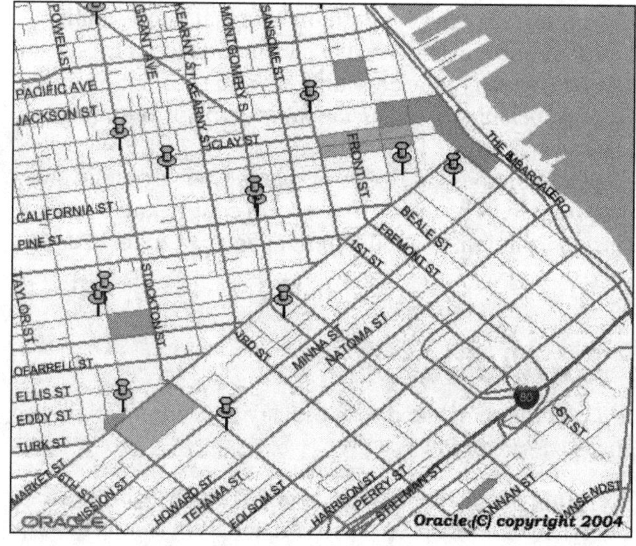

Figure 11-1. *A map showing the position of our branches*

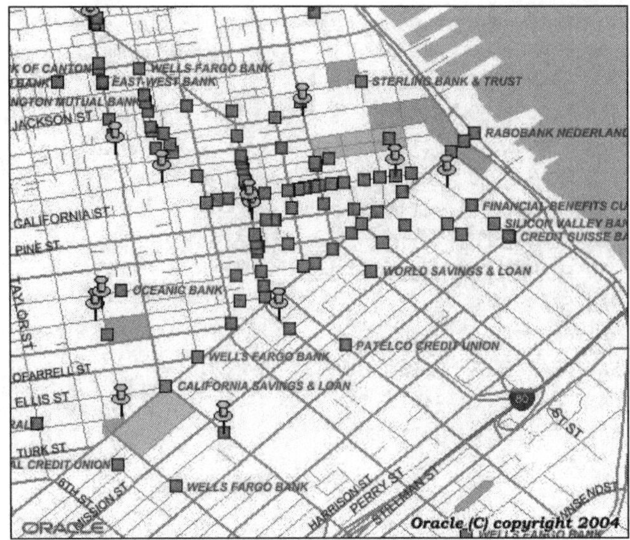

Figure 11-2. *A map showing the position of our branches and those of our competitors*

As you can see from these images, maps are meaningful geometric representations of the world rendered in a human-readable size and format. Maps are so fundamental to the way in which we perceive the world that they predate everything but the cave paintings humans created in an attempt to understand the world and to find ways to communicate that understanding. Whether scratched in the sand with a stick, printed on papyrus or paper, or displayed on a screen, a map can convey an understanding of the shape of the environment and the relationships among things within it in a manner more efficient and understandable than any number of spoken or written words.

Computer-generated maps are much like paper maps, except that they are dynamically generated from information stored in databases. They allow us a level of control and interaction: we can choose to see more or less information, to see different regions, to zoom in and out, and so on.

Overview of Oracle MapViewer

MapViewer is a pure Java server-side component included with Oracle Application Server. The main components, illustrated in Figure 11-3, are as follows:

- *The MapViewer servlet running inside Oracle Application Server*: The servlet processes *requests* sent by client applications, fetches the proper information from spatial tables, and constructs maps in a variety of graphical formats (GIF, PNG, or JPEG), which it then returns to the requesting client.
- *Map definitions*: The map definitions are stored inside the database. This is where you describe your maps: which tables to use, how the maps should be rendered (colors, line thickness, fonts, etc.), and so on.

- *A Java client API*: Java applications will use this API to simplify their development by avoiding the need for manually constructing and parsing XML requests and responses. The Java API also includes JavaServer Pages (JSP) tags to ease the inclusion of maps in JSP.
- *A Map Definition Manager tool*: This is a stand-alone program that helps users manage the map definitions stored inside the database.

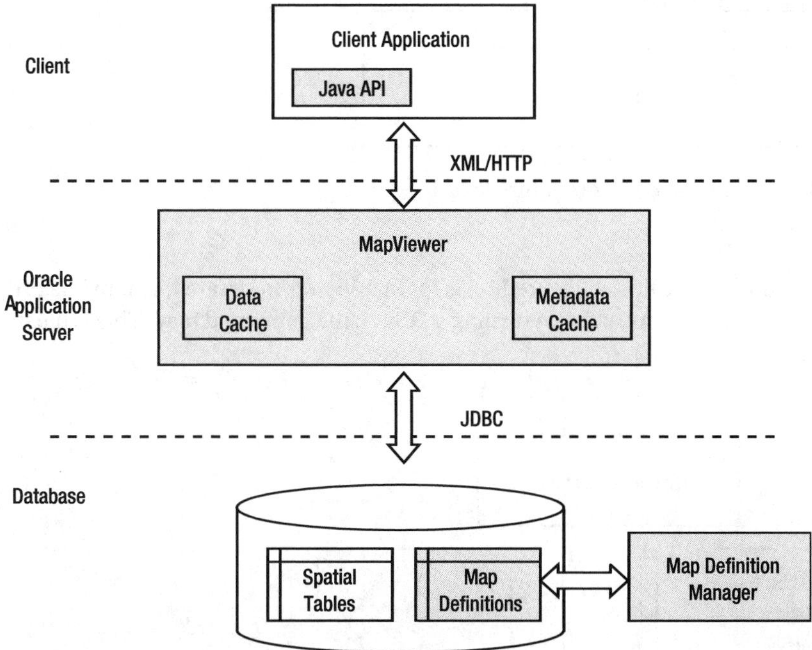

Figure 11-3. *Oracle MapViewer architecture*

The client applications talk to the MapViewer servlet over HTTP in a request/response model, as illustrated in Figure 11-4. Requests and responses are encoded in XML. Java clients can use the Java API, which takes care of constructing and sending the XML requests, as well as reading and parsing the XML responses.

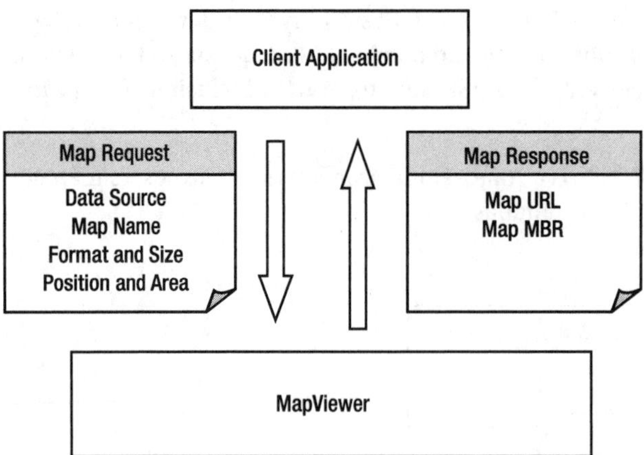

Figure 11-4. *MapViewer request/response flow*

An alternative to the flow in Figure 11-4 is for MapViewer to stream the map image directly to the client application instead of returning a URL to the generated map. This is illustrated in Figure 11-5.

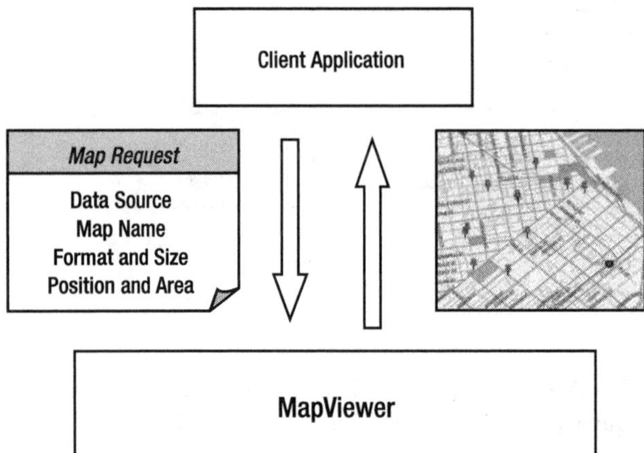

Figure 11-5. *MapViewer request/response flow with image streaming*

Since MapViewer is a pure Java tool, it can run on any platform where Java is available. However, that does not mean it can be used only from Java applications. Its lowest level API (XML over HTTP) allows any application to use its services.

MapViewer is not an end-user tool; rather, it is a component that developers use to add maps into their applications. With that in mind, let's move on and see how to use MapViewer to create maps such as these, and then how to use them in an application. The first step is to install and configure MapViewer for use.

Getting Started with MapViewer

MapViewer is provided as a standard J2EE archive (EAR) format. You can deploy MapViewer either in a full Oracle Application Server environment or in a stand-alone installation of Oracle Application Server Containers for J2EE (OC4J), the core component of the Application Server. We will concentrate on the installation of MapViewer using the stand-alone OC4J.

As discussed, MapViewer is a pure Java component, as is OC4J, so you can install MapViewer and OC4J on any platform that has a suitable Java environment. MapViewer needs a Java 2 Platform Standard Edition Software Development Kit from Sun Microsystems (J2SE SDK) 1.4 or later, with SDK 1.4.2_04 being the recommended Java version.

■Tip MapViewer needs a graphical environment in order to generate maps. The "headless" mechanism in J2SE SDK 1.4 enables MapViewer to run on Linux or UNIX systems without setting any X11 `DISPLAY` variable. To enable AWT headless mode on Linux or UNIX systems, specify the following in the command line to start the OC4J server: `-Djava.awt.headless=true`.

Installing OC4J

OC4J is available for download from the Oracle Technology Network website at `http://otn.oracle.com`. Go to the Downloads area for Oracle Application Server (Services ➤ Downloads ➤ Application Server), then go to Oracle iAS J2EE Downloads, and select Oracle iAS Containers for J2EE Standalone v9.0.4. The result is a file called `oc4j_extended.zip` (approximately 30MB in size).

For your convenience, we also provide a link to this file in the Downloads section of the Apress website (`www.apress.com`). Once you have downloaded the file, follow these steps:

1. Unpack the `oc4j_extended.zip` archive into a new directory on your file system. We will call this directory `$OC4J_HOME` from now on.
2. Go to this directory and change directory (`cd`) to `j2ee/home`.
3. Enter the command `java -jar oc4j.jar -install` and provide an administrative password when prompted.

Your OC4J environment is now ready for use. Start it by entering `java -jar oc4j.jar`. To verify that everything is correct, go to `http://`*`oc4j_server`*`:8888` using your web browser, where *`oc4j_server`* is the name or IP address of the machine where you just installed OC4J. For example, you would use `http://127.0.0.1:8888` if you installed OC4J on your desktop machine. You should see the page shown in Figure 11-6.

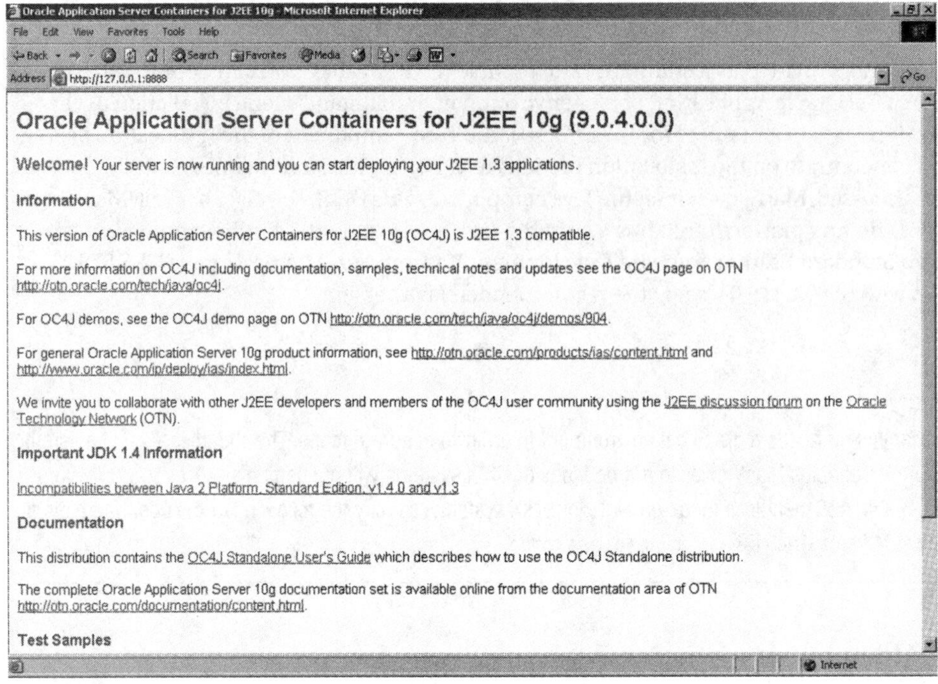

Figure 11-6. *Verifying the OC4J installation*

To stop the OC4J server, just kill the Java process that runs it—for example, by pressing Ctrl+C in the terminal window where you started it.

Installing MapViewer

MapViewer is also available for download from the Oracle Technology Network website at `http://otn.oracle.com`. Go to the Downloads area for the Oracle Database, then to Oracle Spatial, then to Oracle Application Server MapViewer. Select Oracle Application Server 10*g* (9.0.4) MapViewer. The result is an archive file called `mapviewer_904.zip` (approximately 7MB).

Just like for OC4J, for your convenience, we provide a link to this file in the Downloads section of the Apress website (`www.apress.com`). Follow these steps to install MapViewer:

1. Make sure the OC4J server is not started. If it is, stop it.

2. In the directory where you extracted OC4J, create a directory called `/lbs`.

3. Extract the file `mapviewer.ear` from the archive you just downloaded, and put it into the directory `$OC4J_HOME/lbs`.

4. Add a definition of the MapViewer application to the server configuration file of OC4J. This is file `$OC4J_HOME/j2ee/home/config/server.xml`. Add the following `<application>` element inside the `<application-server>` element:

```
<application name="MapViewer"
  path="../../../lbs/mapviewer.ear" auto-start="true" />
```

5. Add a definition of the MapViewer application to the web configuration file of OC4J. This is file `$OC4J_HOME/config/http-web-site.xml`. Add the following `<web-app>` element inside the `<web-site>` element:

```
<web-app application="MapViewer"
  name="web" root="/mapviewer" load-on-startup="true" />
```

You can now start the OC4J server again. OC4J will automatically deploy the MapViewer application and start it. Verify that MapViewer was successfully installed by going to `http://`*`oc4j_server`*`:8888/mapviewer` in your web browser (e.g., `http://127.0.0.1:8888/mapviewer` if you installed OC4J on your own desktop system). You should see the home page of MapViewer, as shown in Figure 11-7.

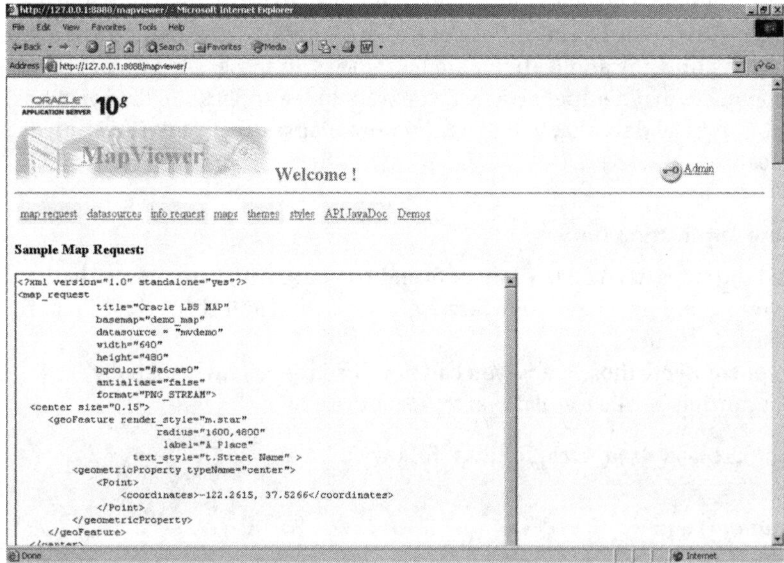

Figure 11-7. *MapViewer home page*

What really happened? The OC4J server noticed the presence of a new application, automatically unpacked the `mapviewer.ear` file, and then unpacked the `web.war` file it found inside the `mapviewer.ear` file. You will see a new folder, `$OC4J_HOME/lbs/mapviewer`, with a number of subfolders and files.

Caution When you edit the XML configuration files, make sure to insert the new definitions in the proper places. In particular, make sure that you *do not* put them inside existing comments. We recommend that you use a text editor that is able to recognize and color-code XML syntax elements or an XML-aware editor such as XMLSpy. We also recommend that you make backup copies of any configuration file you modify, just in case.

Viewing Predefined Maps

At this point, MapViewer is ready for use. The default settings are adequate for you to start using it, although a little later in the chapter we will examine some of the configuration settings. We have yet to discuss how to define new maps, but you are already in a position to display a first predefined map. To do this, perform these steps:

1. Load the sample data into your database, together with predefined map definitions.
2. Define a MapViewer data source.
3. Install the sample maps so that they can be retrieved using your OC4J server.

Load the Sample Data

To work through all the examples shown in this chapter, you need to populate your database with the sample data provided in the Downloads section of the Apress website (`www.apress.com`). So far, we have been using only the application data (`customers`, `branches`, and `competitors` tables) without any references to other spatial data. If you want to see application data on maps, you also need the geographical data that will appear on the maps: streets, administrative boundaries, natural features, and so on.

Location-Enabling the Application Data

If you have performed the steps detailed in Chapter 6, and you have run the examples in the following chapters, you should now have your `customers`, `branches`, and `competitors` tables spatially enabled and ready for use.

In case you did not complete those steps, you can now load them in the "spatially enabled" format by importing the file `app_data_with_loc.dmp` as follows:

```
imp spatial/spatial file=app_data_with_loc.dmp full=y
```

Loading the Geographical Data

For clarity and ease of use, we provide the data as several Oracle dump files (you can find details on the tables and their structure in Appendix E):

- Large-scale data (countries, states, counties, etc.) are provided in the file `map_large.dmp`.
- Detailed data (city streets, etc.) are provided in file `map_detailed.dmp`.

Load the data using the Oracle Import tool as illustrated in the following code. Note that this will create the tables, load the tables with data, load the spatial metadata, and create the spatial indexes. Once the import is complete, the tables are ready for use.

```
imp spatial/spatial file=map_large.dmp full=y
imp spatial/spatial file=map_detailed.dmp full=y
```

Loading Maps, Themes, and Style Definitions for MapViewer

Maps, themes, and style definitions are provided ready for use. To use them, you simply need to perform these steps:

1. Import them into the database. This creates and populates three tables: `my_maps`, `my_themes`, and `my_styles`.
2. Load the definitions into the dictionary tables used by MapViewer.

The full process is illustrated in Listing 11-2.

Listing 11-2. *Loading Maps, Themes, and Style Definitions*

```
imp spatial/spatial file=styles.dmp full=y

SQL> INSERT into user_sdo_styles
       select * from my_styles;
SQL> insert into user_sdo_themes
       select * from my_themes;
SQL> insert into user_sdo_maps
       select * from my_maps;
SQL> commit;
```

Define a Data Source

The next step is to define a permanent data source in MapViewer's configuration file. This is not strictly necessary, since you could also add a data source via MapViewer's administration page, but having a permanent data source makes it easier for you when you stop and start OC4J and MapViewer.

To add the data source, you edit the configuration file, as explained in the previous section. The file is located at `$OC4J_HOME/lbs/mapviewer/web/WEB-INF/conf/MapViewerConfig.xml`. Add the following definition inside the main `<MapperConfig>` element:

```
<map_data_source name="spatial10g"
                 jdbc_host="127.0.0.1"
                 jdbc_port="1521"
                 jdbc_sid="orcl101"
                 jdbc_user="spatial"
                 jdbc_password="!spatial"
                 jdbc_mode="thin"
                 max_connections="5"
                 number_of_mappers="3"
/>
```

Replace the JDBC connection details (`host`, `port`, `sid`, `user`, and `password`) with your own information. The user name should be the one you loaded the example data into.

If your OC4J server is not up and running, then start it now by going to `$OC4J_HOME/j2ee/home` and entering the command `java -jar oc4j.jar`.

Install and Load Examples

The MapViewer examples provided with this book are available in a file called `web-examples.zip`. Expand it into `$OC4J_HOME/lbs/mapviewer/web/spatial-book`.

■ **Note** In all the examples, it is assumed that you installed OC4J on your desktop machine, so you will access it using the `localhost` address (`127.0.0.1`).

In your browser, go to the home page for the book examples at `http://127.0.0.1:8888/mapviewer/spatial-book`. You should see the page shown in Figure 11-8.

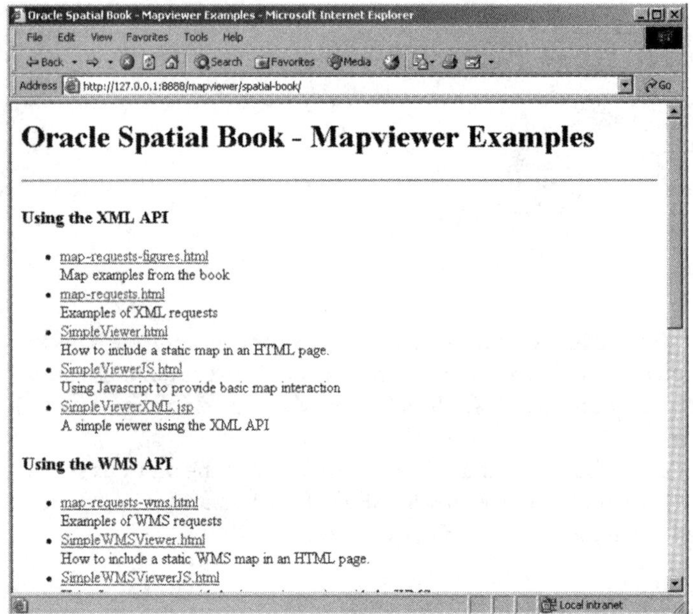

Figure 11-8. *Home page for the MapViewer examples*

Click the `map-requests.html` link. You should now see the page shown in Figure 11-9.

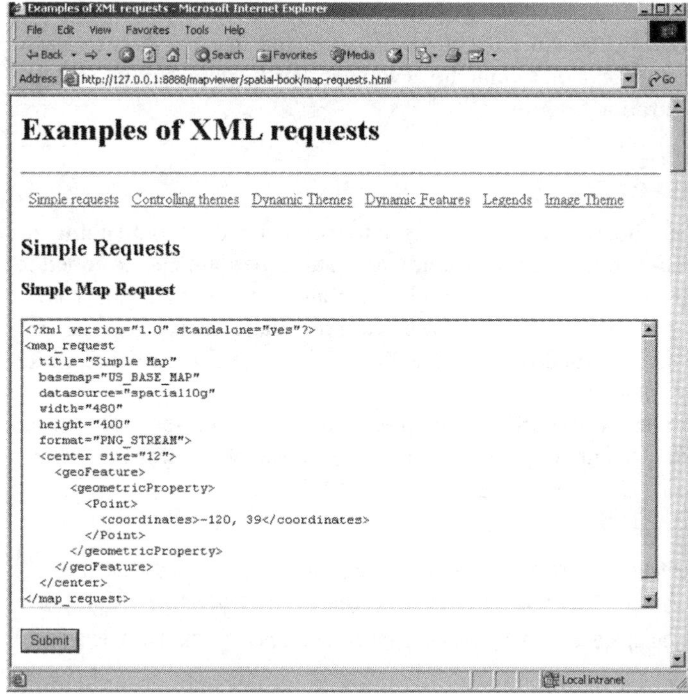

Figure 11-9. *XML request for getting a map*

Click the Submit button. You should now see the map shown in Figure 11-10.

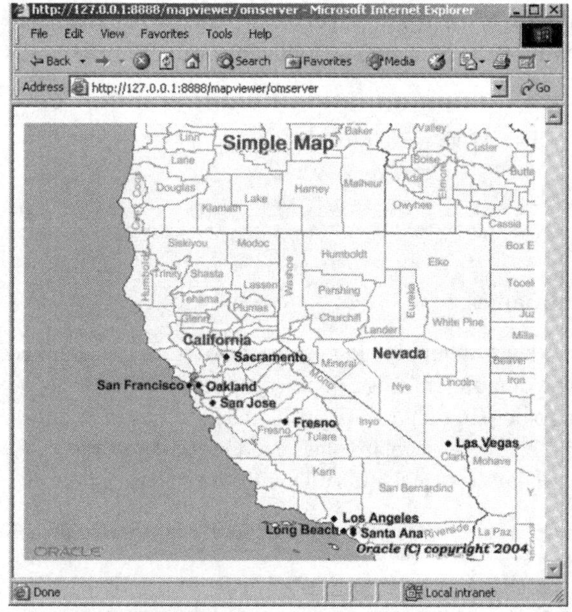

Figure 11-10. *Your first map*

In the rest of this chapter, you will learn how this map was defined and how to define your own maps. Then you will learn how to embed maps in your applications and allow users to interact with the maps. Before we move on to that, however, it is worth taking a quick look at some of the MapViewer configuration options.

Configuring MapViewer

While the MapViewer default settings are adequate for you to start using it, at some point you will probably want to change some configuration parameters. Those parameters are coded in XML. You can find the configuration file at `$OC4J_HOME/lbs/mapviewer/web/WEB-INF/conf/mapViewerConfig.xml`. You can change parameters by editing this file, preferably using an XML-aware editor, but Notepad or vi will do as well. The file contains many comments, which make it easier for you to apply changes.

Note that MapViewer will apply the changes only when you restart it, either by stopping and starting the entire OC4J component or by restarting MapViewer via the administrative API.

■ **Caution** The location of the configuration file for MapViewer version 10.1.2 (which we use here) is different from that used in previous versions. The configuration file used to be in `$OC4J_HOME/lbs/mapviewer/conf/mapViewerConfig.xml`. If you upgrade from a previous version of MapViewer, make sure to adjust any relative file specification.

The next sections cover the main MapViewer configuration options.

Logging

MapViewer can generate a log of its operation. The `<logging>` element enables you to control how detailed this logging should be and where it should go. The following is an example setting:

```
<logging log_level="info" log_thread_name="true" log_time="true">
<log_output name="System.err"/>
<log_output name="../log/mapviewer.log"/>
</logging>
```

The element contains the following attributes:

- `log_level`: This attribute defines the level of detail to log. It can range from less detailed (`fatal`) to very detailed (`finest`). The default (`info`) is a good compromise. The `debug` and `finest` settings are only useful to help in diagnosing problems or to better understand the operation of MapViewer. The `finest` level involves each request getting logged, together with each and every database SQL query. Do not use it in production.
- `log_thread_name`: When this attribute is set to `true`, the name of each MapViewer thread is logged with each message.
- `log_time`: When this attribute is set to `true`, a timestamp is logged with each message.

The <logging> element contains one or more <log_output> elements. Each <log_output> element defines one log destination. The destination System.err corresponds to the console of the OC4J container.

Note All file specifications are relative to the location of the configuration file. For example, ../log/mapviewer.log is equivalent to $OC4J_HOME/lbs/mapviewer/web/WEB-INF/log/mapviewer.log. This makes your configuration files portable between different installations. Notice that you can write the file specifications in the configuration file using forward slashes (/), even if you use a Windows platform.

Caution MapViewer starts a new log file each time the application server (or OC4J container) starts. Files are named by appending a number at the end (e.g., mapviewer_35.log). The log files are not automatically removed.

Map Image Lifetime

The map images generated by MapViewer are stored in the file system on the application server. The <save_images_at> element enables you to control the lifetime of those files. The following is a typical setting:

```
<save_images_at file_prefix="omsmap"
                url="/mapviewer/images/"
                path="../../../web/images"
                life= "5"
                recycle_interval="10" />
```

The element uses XML attributes to define the following parameters:

- file_prefix is the prefix of the generated map files. Maps are numbered sequentially, and this number is appended to the prefix you choose. The default is omsmap, and we see no reason to change this.
- url is used to produce the URL that points to the generated maps, which is relative to the URL used to reach the MapViewer servlet. The default is /mapviewer/images, which corresponds to $OC4J_HOME/lbs/mapviewer/web/images. Again, we see no reason to change this.
- path is the folder in which images are stored. By default, the images go to ../../../web/images, which is the same as $OC4J_HOME/lbs/mapviewer/web/images. There is no reason to change this.

- `life` specifies how long (in minutes) a generated map should remain on the server. By default, it is set to 0, which means that images are *never* deleted. This is probably not a good idea, since images will accumulate quickly.
- `recycle_interval` specifies how frequently the recycling thread will start and remove old maps. By default, this happens every 8 hours. In production systems, this process will probably need to happen more often.

Caching

When MapViewer reads data from spatial tables, it automatically keeps a copy of the geometries in a JDBC object cache, thereby avoiding the need to read them again for subsequent map requests on the same geographical area. The cache is memory resident.

The `<spatial_data_cache>` element enables you to control the size of the cache. The following is an example setting:

```
<spatial_data_cache
  max_cache_size="32"
report_stats="false"
/>
```

where

- `max_cache_size` is a parameter that specifies the size (in megabytes) of the memory cache. The default is 64MB.
- `report_stats` provides cache statistics. When this parameter is set to `true`, MapViewer will periodically (approximately every 5 minutes) report the current cache size and the number of cached objects as a log message.

■Note Previous versions of MapViewer also included a disk-based cache. This is no longer the case. The old parameters `max_disk_cache_size` and `disk_cache_path` that used to control the size and location of the disk cache are now ignored.

Permanent Data Sources

MapViewer accesses databases via JDBC. A data source defines the parameters for a JDBC connection: host name, port, database name, user name, and password. Each data source has a unique name.

Data sources can be defined dynamically, using the administrative API, or they can be defined statically in the configuration file. A data source is defined in a `<map_data_source>` element. Here is an example that defines a data source over a database that runs on the same system as MapViewer:

```
<map_data_source name="spatial10g"
jdbc_host="127.0.0.1"
jdbc_port="1521"
jdbc_sid="orcl101"
jdbc_user="spatial"
jdbc_password="!spatial"
jdbc_mode="thin"
max_connections="10"
number_of_mappers="3"
/>
```

where

- `name` is the name of the data source. It must be unique.
- `jdbc_host` is the name or IP address of the system hosting the Oracle database.
- `jdbc_port` is the port on which the database is listening. By default, databases listen on port 1521.
- `jdbc_sid` is the name of the database.
- `jdbc_user` is the user name to connect to the database.
- `jdbc_password` is the password of the user connecting to the database. The password must be written with a leading ! symbol. MapViewer will automatically encrypt this password and replace it in the configuration file with the encrypted result.
- `number_of_mappers` defines the maximum number of concurrent map requests that this data source can handle.
- `max_connections` limits the number of connections used for the data source. MapViewer will use as many concurrent connections as needed for a request, and then it will close them up to the maximum number specified.

You can also tell MapViewer to use one of the data sources defined for OC4J. Those data sources are defined in configuration file `$OC4J_HOME/j2ee/home/config/data-sources.xml`. For example, here is an OC4J data source definition:

```
<data-source
    class="com.evermind.sql.DriverManagerDataSource"
    name="spatial10g"
    location="jdbc/spatial10gCore"
    xa-location="jdbc/xa/spatial10gXA"
    ejb-location="jdbc/spatial10g"
    connection-driver="oracle.jdbc.driver.OracleDriver"
    username="spatial"
    password="spatial"
    url="jdbc:oracle:thin:@localhost:1521:orcl101"
    inactivity-timeout="30"
/>
```

You can use that data source for MapViewer by defining it as follows in the MapViewer configuration file:

```
<map_data_source name="spatial10g"
                 container_ds="jdbc/spatial10g"
                 max_connections="5"
                 number_of_mappers="3"
/>
```

Global Map Options

The <global_map_config> element enables you to define some settings that control the general look and feel of the produced maps. In particular, you can use it to set a copyright notice and logo on all the maps produced by your server. Here is a typical setting:

```
<global_map_config>
    <title text="MapViewer Demo" font="Courier" position="NORTH"/>
  <note text="Oracle (C) copyright 2004"
     font="Bookman Old Style Bold Italic"
     position="SOUTH_EAST"/>
  <logo image_path="../../../web/myicons/orcl_logo_test.gif"
     position="SOUTH_WEST"/>
  <rendering
     allow_local_adjustment="false"
     use_globular_projection="false" />
</global_map_config>
```

where

- title defines the position of map titles on the generated maps. You can also specify a default title that will appear when a map is requested without any explicit title.
- note defines a text string that will appear on all maps—typically a copyright notice. The text and font parameters are self-explanatory. The position parameter lets you specify where the text should appear on the map using a keyword such as NORTH, SOUTH, EAST, WEST, NORTH_WEST, SOUTH_EAST, and so on. In the preceding example, the copyright notice appears at the lower right of the image.
- logo is a GIF logo that will appear on all maps. The position of the logo is specified the same way as it is for the note. The image_path parameter specifies the file specification of the logo. Like all other file specifications, it is relative to the location of the configuration file itself.
- rendering represents advanced settings for controlling the appearance of maps on geodetic data.

Constructing Maps

A map is constructed from one or more themes, which refer to styles. A theme is based on a table. Figure 11-11 illustrates these relationships.

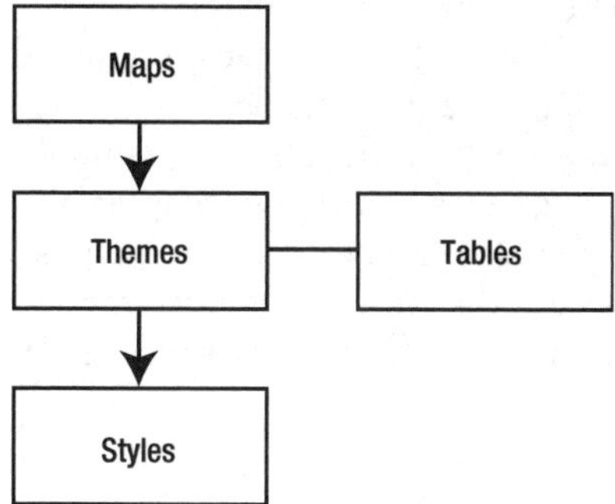

Figure 11-11. *Elements of map definitions*

Styles describe *how* the information shown on a map should look: color, symbols, and so on. Themes define *what* information should appear on a map and the style to use. We will examine those concepts in greater detail at the same time we explain how to define them.

Figure 11-11 is a simplification; multiple maps can use the same theme, and multiple themes can use the same style. A theme can use many different styles. Also, multiple themes can be based on the same table. A table could also be a view or a dynamically defined SQL query.

The definitions are stored in the database, in a set of three dictionary views: USER_SDO_MAPS, USER_SDO_THEMES, and USER_SDO_STYLES. Like all Oracle dictionary views, they come in three variants: USER, ALL, and DBA. Only the USER views are updateable—you define new styles (or themes, or maps) by inserting into the corresponding USER view. You can also remove styles (or themes, or maps), or update them by deleting or updating the USER views. The ALL views include all objects (styles, themes, or maps) that you are allowed to access. The DBA views include all objects in the database, but only DBAs are allowed to access them.

The relationships between the various elements are not implemented via referential integrity constraints; rather, a MAP definition contains a list of themes, and a THEME refers to a list of styles. Those lists are coded inside the definition elements using an XML notation.

You can directly update the tables where map, theme, and style definitions are stored, but this requires that you understand precisely the structure of the tables, as well as the XML syntax.

A better way is to use the map definition tool called MapDef that is provided with MapViewer. At the time of this writing, this tool is not provided with the MapViewer software—you need to download it separately from the Oracle Technology Network website. This tool is far from perfect, and you may find it cumbersome at times. Oracle plans to provide a new and improved tool after the release of Oracle 10*g*.

Styles

Spatial information is stored inside the database as geometric shapes: points, lines, and polygons. To draw those shapes on a map, you need to tell MapViewer how to do this (i.e., what *style* to use). To do this, you associate each theme with a style.

A style is a visual attribute that represents a spatial feature. Basic map symbols and labels for representing point, line, and area features are defined and stored as individual styles. Symbology on a map can be simple and informal, or it can follow guidelines based on standard usages. Those graphical charts are typically defined by national mapping agencies, such the U.S. Federal Geographic Data Committee or the Ordnance Survey of Great Britain. Symbols should be chosen to reflect the culture, common understanding, and sensitivities of map viewers.

Proper use of styles can have a large impact on map readability and usability. For example, compare the two maps shown in Figure 11-12. Both maps show the same content, but the left map uses no styling rules to speak of, whereas the right map uses a rich set of styles that allows us to clearly identify the features shown on the map.

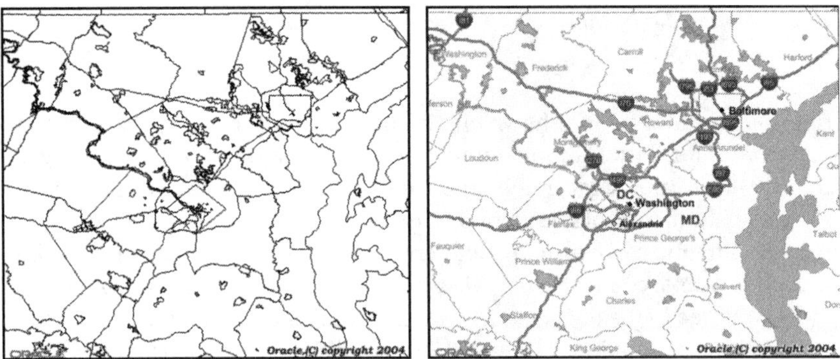

Figure 11-12. *Comparing styling rules*

Note The association of themes and styles may need to be dynamic, as different cultures are used to different map style conventions. For example, a French Michelin map, a British Ordnance Survey map, and an American Rand McNally atlas do not use the same conventions.

In the following sections, we will take a look at the various style types that are used for different geographic features that comprise maps, and then we will discuss how they are stored in the Oracle database.

Point Styles

Points are represented as graphic shapes: a cross, a star, a square, or a pictogram (e.g., a small house or a church). These pictograms are often represented as small bitmap images, for example, with a plane representing an airport, a skier representing a ski resort, an ambulance representing a hospital, and so on.

Line Styles

Lines can be very complex to define. They are used to represent a variety of linear objects: highways, railroads, canals, rivers, electricity lines, sewers, and so on. A line typically needs many parameters: thickness, color, center and side lines, and hash marks, among others.

Area Styles

Areas are represented using a *fill* color (e.g., the color of the interior of a polygon) and a *stroke* color (e.g., the color of the boundary of the polygon).

Text Styles and Labeling

Objects shown on maps correspond to real-world features. Many of those features are named: cities, parks, streets, customers, stores, and so on. Labels containing those names may be used to identify the features.

Efficient labeling of map features is an art in itself. Labels must be placed so that they can be clearly and unambiguously associated with the features they describe, and in a manner that doesn't obscure symbols or other labels. If labels overlap, some may need to be moved or even omitted.

MapViewer automatically places labels on maps, but you still need to define the font and color to use for those labels.

Defining Styles: The USER_SDO_STYLES View

Styles are stored in the `USER_SDO_STYLES` view. This is the view you will update to define and maintain your *private* styles. The `ALL_SDO_STYLES` view lists all styles defined by all users in the database. In other words, this makes it easy for multiple users to share styles. Note that there are no privileges on styles—once you define a style in your `USER_SDO_STYLES` view, anyone can use that style in a map or application.

Each style has a unique name and defines one or more graphical elements using XML syntax. There are six types of styles:

- *Color*: Coloring for the fill (inside) and stroke (contour) of area features.
- *Marker*: A geometric shape (with a fill and stroke color) or an image for point features.
- *Line*: Used to represent linear features, defining width, color, center and edge lines, and hash marks. It also defines how lines end and how they join.
- *Area*: Fill patterns for areas.
- *Text*: Font, color, and highlighting for text labels.
- *Advanced*: A composite style used for thematic mapping.

Table 11-1 lists the columns of the `USER_SDO_STYLES` view. The `ALL` and `DBA` variants contain an additional `OWNER` column.

Table 11-1. *Structure of the* USER_SDO_STYLES *View*

Column Name	Data Type	Description
NAME	VARCHAR2	Name of the style
TYPE	VARCHAR2	Type of style (COLOR, MARKER, LINE, AREA, TEXT, or ADVANCED)
DESCRIPTION	VARCHAR2	Description of the style
DEFINITION	CLOB	XML definition of the style
IMAGE	BLOB	Image for marker styles

Managing Styles Using the Map Definition Tool

Download the MapDef tool from the Oracle Technology Network website, at the same location from which you downloaded the MapViewer kit. For convenience, we also provide it with the code download for this book as a Java JAR file called `mapdef.jar`. Save it anywhere you like on your disk.

The MapDef tool uses JDBC to connect to the database, so you must have JDBC drivers available on your machine. JDBC drivers are provided with all Oracle database installations in `$ORACLE_HOME/jdbc/lib/classes12.jar`.

To start the tool, go to the folder where you downloaded the JAR file and run the following command:

```
java -cp $ORACLE_HOME/jdbc/lib/classes12.jar;mapdef.jar
oracle.eLocation.console.GeneralManager
```

You will see the window in Figure 11-13 appear.

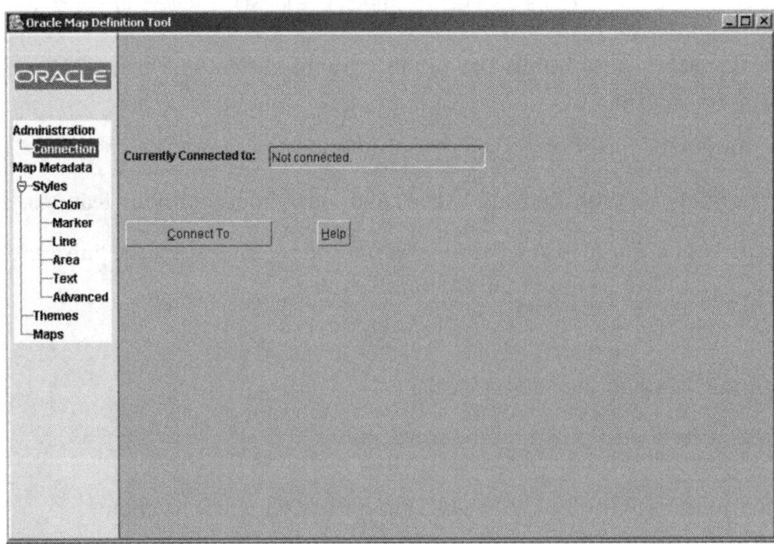

Figure 11-13. *Starting the MapDef tool*

Click the Connect To button and fill in the box that appears (shown in Figure 11-14) with the usual JDBC connection information: host name, database name (SID), port, user name, and password.

Figure 11-14. *Connecting to the database*

You can also choose which styles you want to use by selecting from the Style View drop-down list. The default is set to `USER_SDO_STYLES`. This means that you will see only your own private styles, and you will be able to modify them.

If you change to `ALL_SDO_STYLES`, then you will see *all* the styles defined in the database. You will *not* be able to define or make any change to any styles, but you will be able to use them to define your themes.

You can tell the MapDef tool to "prefill" the connection box by passing additional parameters on the command line when you start it:

```
java -cp "D:\Oracle\ora101B2\jdbc\lib\classes12.jar;mapdef.jar"
  -Dhost=localhost -Dsid=ORCL101 -Dport=1521 -Duser=spatial -Dpassword=spatial
  oracle.eLocation.console.GeneralManager
```

Once you are connected, you can select the type of definition you want to modify from the menu on the left side of the window. Before making actual changes, you may want to make a copy of your definitions. See the section "Exporting and Importing Map Definitions" later in this chapter for the way to do so.

All screens for managing styles use a similar logic:

- To create a new style, click the New button. This brings up a new form that you need to fill. Click the Insert button when you are done.
- To update a style, select it from the list on the left side. Then modify the settings and click the Update button when you are done.
- To delete a style, select it, and then click the Delete button.

Your styles must have unique names. However, different users can define their own styles using the same names.

■ **Note** The styles provided with MapViewer as well as those provided with the book examples have names that begin with `C.` for colors, `M.` for markers, and so on, but this is just a convention. You can name your styles any way you like.

Color Styles

Color styles are primarily used to render area features. A color is defined by the following primitive constructs:

- A *fill* color (i.e., the coloring of the inside of the feature)
- A *stroke* color (i.e., the coloring of the contour of the feature)

Both settings are optional. If no fill is set, then the interior of the area features will be empty. If no stroke is set, then adjacent areas will merge without any visible separation.

In addition, you can set the *opacity* of the area. This lets you control how much of the underlying features is seen through this area. When the opacity is set to 255 (the default), the area is totally opaque. If you set the opacity to 0, the area is totally transparent.

You have several techniques for choosing colors: a picker, a hue-saturation-brightness model, and a red-green-blue model. You can also enter colors manually using the hexadecimal encoding.

Figure 11-15 shows the definition of a new color.

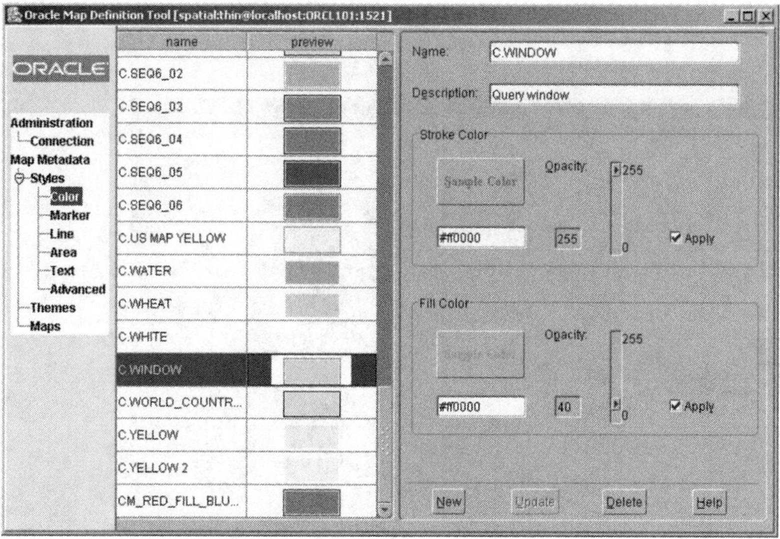

Figure 11-15. *Defining a color*

Marker Styles

Markers define symbols for point features. You can define them in two ways:

- *As vector drawings (circles, polygons, etc.)*: See Figure 11-16 for an example of a circle marker. The actual shape is described by a set of coordinates (for a generic polygon) or by a radius (for a circle). You can specify a fill and stroke color.

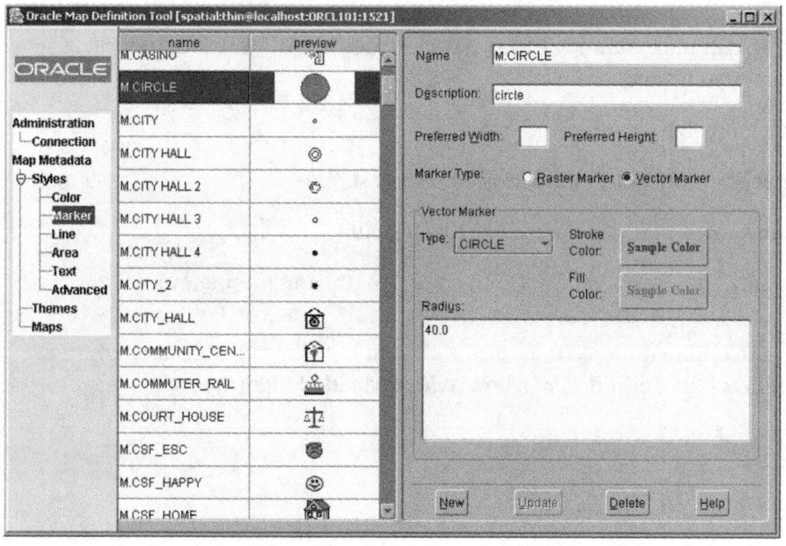

Figure 11-16. *Defining a circle marker*

- *As bitmap images*: See Figure 11-17 for an example of a bitmap symbol.

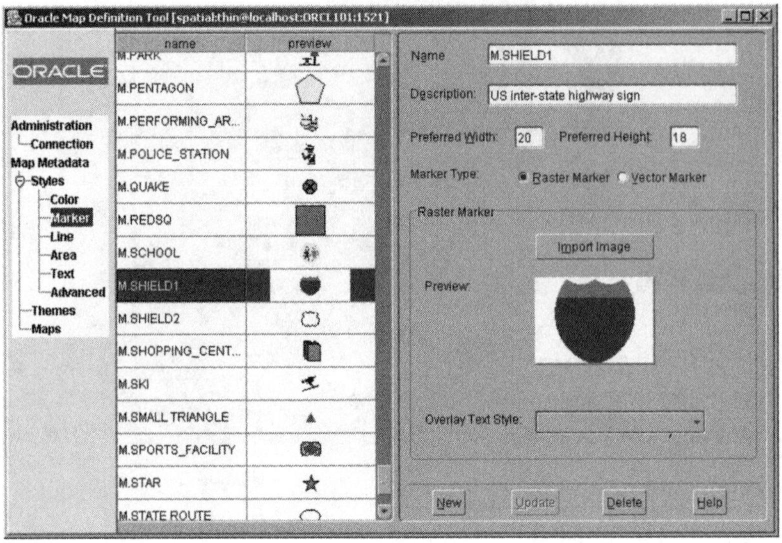

Figure 11-17. *Defining a bitmap symbol*

You can also use markers as styles for rendering labels. For example, the bitmap symbol illustrated in Figure 11-17 will be used to render the interstate numbers.

Line Styles

Lines are rather complex graphic objects. They are defined by the combination of several characteristics (all optional):

- A general color, thickness, and opacity
- A center line, with color, thickness, and dash styling
- Side lines, with color, thickness, and dash styling
- Hash marks on the center line, with color, length, and frequency

You can also define the way lines terminate and the way multiple lines connect. Figure 11-18 shows the definition of a line style for divided highways.

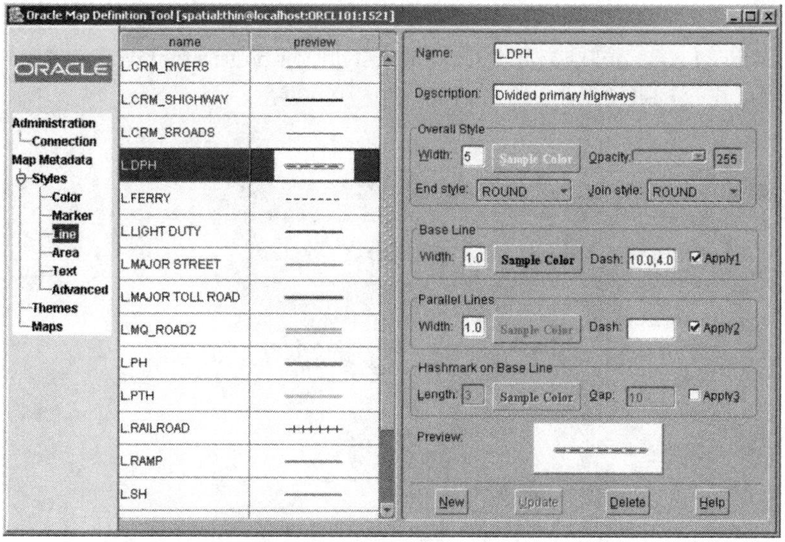

Figure 11-18. *Defining a line style*

Area Styles

Area styles are bitmaps used for filling an area with some patterns instead of a color style. They are loaded from bitmaps. Figure 11-19 shows the definition of a pattern.

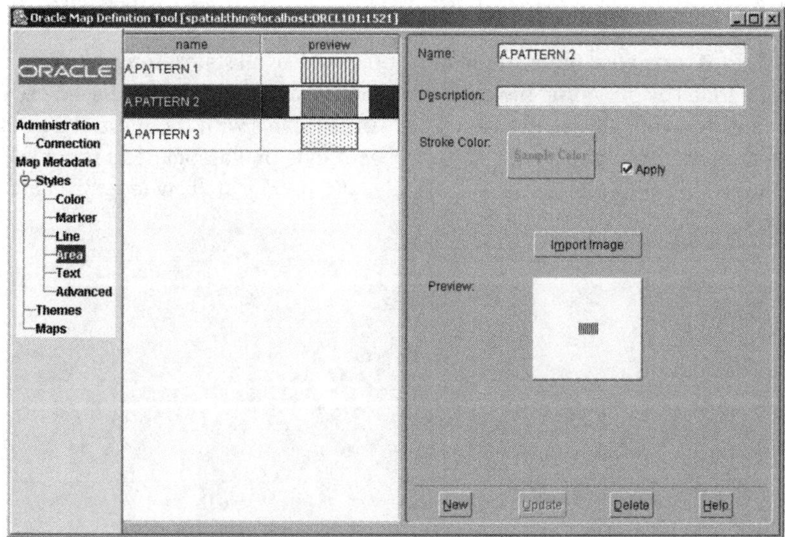

Figure 11-19. *Defining an area pattern style*

Text Styles

Text styles define the way labels should be rendered. A text style combines a font with a color, size, and bolding and/or italicizing. See Figure 11-20 for an example.

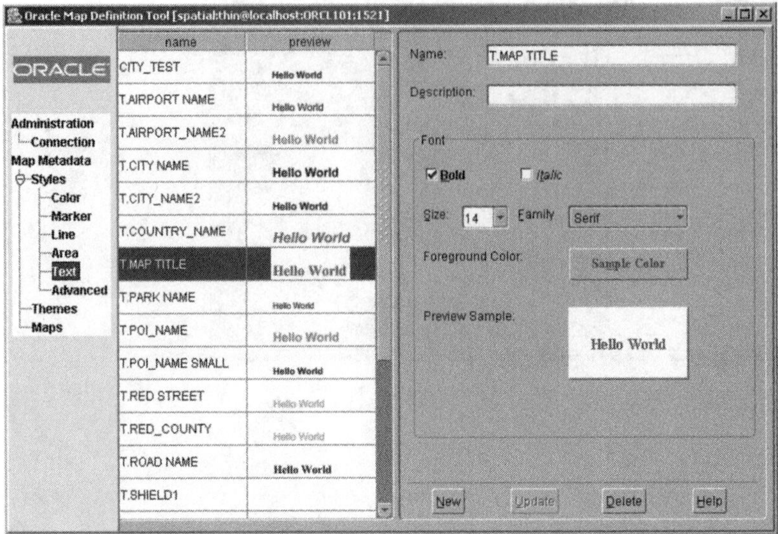

Figure 11-20. *Defining a text style*

Advanced Styles

Advanced styles are the most complex, but also the most powerful, of all styles. You can use them to define thematic maps by providing the ability to render features differently based on a user-selectable value. Later, you will see how to use advanced styles with thematic styles.

Figure 11-21 shows an example of a *variable color scheme* style that associates a range of colors to a range of values. Figure 11-22 illustrates a *variable size marker* style, where the value of an attribute is represented using circles of varying sizes.

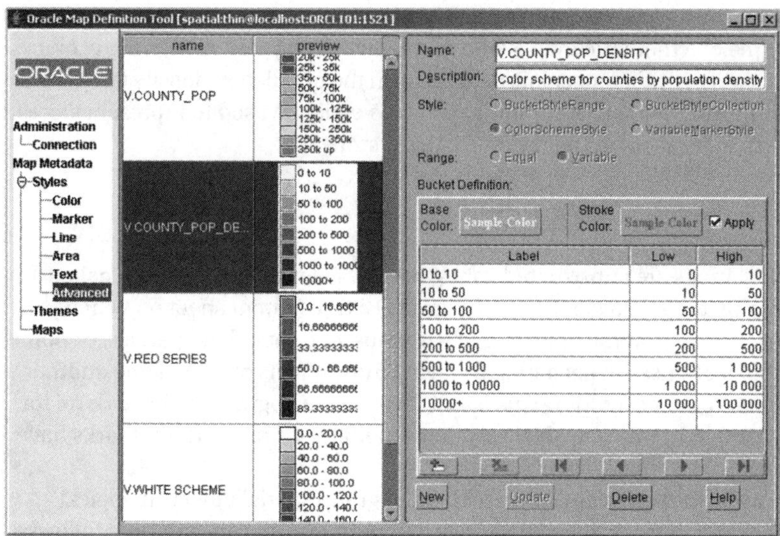

Figure 11-21. *Variable color scheme style*

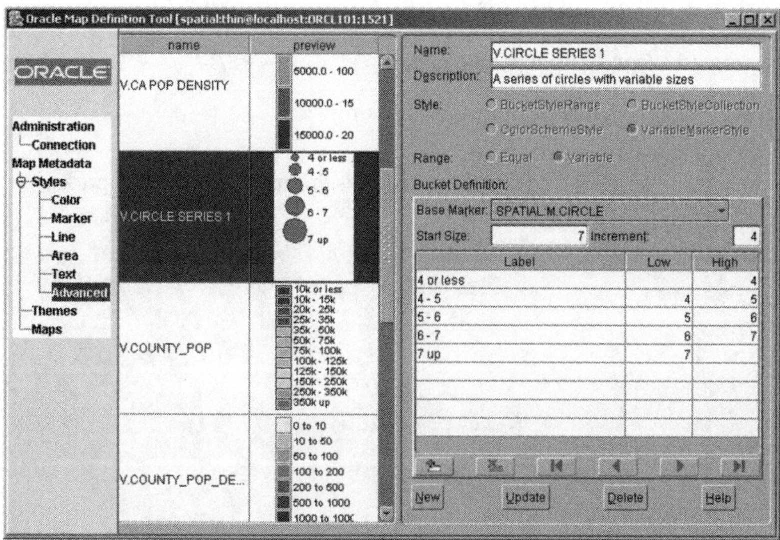

Figure 11-22. *Variable size marker style*

Thematic maps are often used in conjunction with statistical analysis of geographical information. An example of a thematic map is one that shows the type of underlying geology or one that presents counties in different colors depending in the population density (an example of this is shown later in Figure 11-27). Other thematic maps could be used to represent stores with different sized symbols based on the revenue of each store.

Themes

As previously discussed, maps are constructed using themes. Themes are also often called *layers* in GIS and mapping tools. You can think of a layer as a transparent sheet on which you have drawn a set of related geographic objects, such as roads, or a set of land parcels, or points representing customer locations. You get a map by laying those sheets on top of one another (and, of course, aligning them correctly). This is exactly what cartographers have done for more than a century, and light tables with transparent media with registration marks have been the tools of geographic analysis since the late 1800s.

Themes are a very powerful concept. You use them to group spatial objects in logical subsets. Typical examples of themes that you will see in mapping applications are as follows:

- Political boundaries (countries, country subdivisions, states, provinces, counties, city limits, etc.)
- Natural features (rivers, forests, lakes, etc.)
- Transportation networks (roads, streets, railways, etc.)
- Customer or store locations, truck positions, and so on

Figure 11-23 shows a map composed of five themes: cities, interstates, national parks, counties, and states.

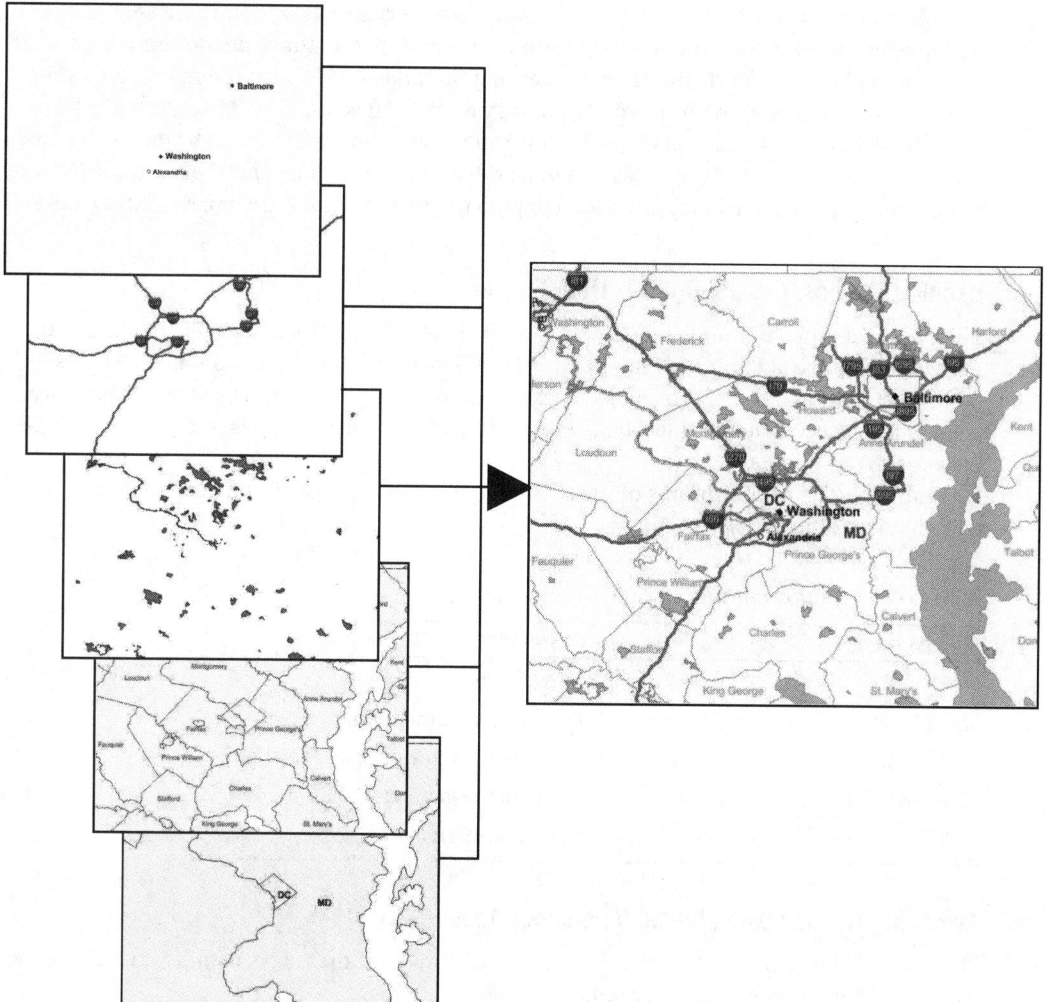

Figure 11-23. *A map with multiple themes*

The way you group your spatial objects in themes is important. This grouping will determine the way users interact with your maps. Users can decide which data they want to see on a map by selecting complete themes (turning them "on" or "off"). You could, for example, mix rivers and railroads in the same layer, but that would mean that users would never be able to see rivers without also seeing railroads.

Themes do not have to be homogeneous. In other words, a theme can contain different types of spatial objects—for example, lines and polygons. A typical example is a "hydro" theme that combines lakes (which are polygons) and rivers (which are lines).

You can define multiple themes on the same table essentially by defining a sequence of SQL queries, one for each theme. For example, assume that all roads are defined in a single spatial table. You can define multiple themes on that table, where each theme selects a subset of the table: motorways, national roads, country roads, and so on.

As another example, if you are especially interested in roads that cross bridges of a certain character, you can separate them as a theme and define a symbology for them. This is a handy visual tool for the spatial analysis needed to plan the routes of oversize or very heavy trucks.

Defining Themes: The USER_SDO_THEMES View

Themes are defined in the `USER_SDO_THEMES` view. This is the view you update to define and maintain your private themes. The `ALL_SDO_THEMES` view lists the themes defined by users on tables that you can access. You will see a theme in your `ALL_SDO_THEMES` view only if you have been granted access on the underlying table (i.e., if that table also appears in your `ALL_TABLES` view).

Table 11-2 lists the columns of the `USER_SDO_THEMES` view. The `ALL` and `DBA` variants contain an additional `OWNER` column.

Table 11-2. *Structure of the* `USER_SDO_THEMES` *View*

Column Name	Data Type	Description
NAME	VARCHAR2	Name of the theme
DESCRIPTION	VARCHAR2	Description of the theme
BASE_TABLE	VARCHAR2	Name of the table used by this theme
GEOMETRY_COLUMN	VARCHAR2	Name of the geometry column
STYLING_RULES	CLOB	XML definition of the theme

Managing Themes Using the Map Definition Tool

To define a theme, you first need to give it a unique name. Other users could, however, define their own themes with the same name.

Next, you need to choose the base table (or view) this theme should use by selecting it from the Base Table drop-down list. After that, you can choose the name of the geometry column from the Geometry Column drop-down list. You can then start filling the styling rules. A theme could have multiple styling rules, with each rule applying to different rows in the underlying table.

Consider the simple theme illustrated in Figure 11-24.

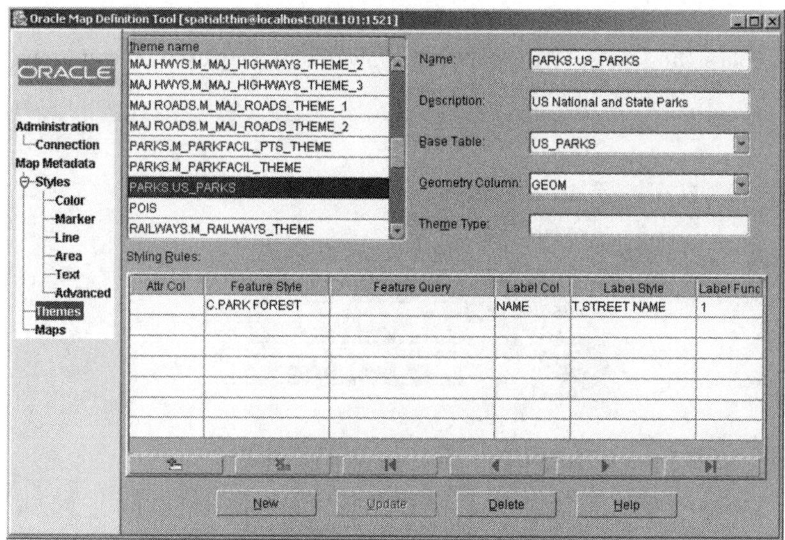

Figure 11-24. *Simple theme for the* `US_PARKS` *table features*

This theme describes the rendering for the features in the `US_PARKS` table, which stores national and state parks. The theme uses only one styling rule, which is also the most common case.

Choosing a Feature Style

You must choose a feature style from the Feature Style drop-down list that lets you choose one of the styles defined in the database. If you originally connected using the `ALL_STYLES` option, then you will be able to choose from all the styles that anyone defined. If you connected using the `USER_STYLES` option, then you will see only your own private styles.

Notice that style names are prefixed with the name of their owner (i.e., the user who created them). For example, `SPATIAL:C.PARK_FOREST` is a style defined by user `SPATIAL`.

Labeling

Labeling of features is optional. If you want your features to be labeled, you need to specify the following in the styling rule:

- *The name of the column that provides the label*: You choose this from the Label Col drop-down list.
- *The text style to use*: You choose this from the Label Style drop-down list.
- *A label function*: Set this to 1 (or any positive value) if you want all features to be labeled. You also could specify a SQL expression or function that returns a numeric value. If that value is zero or negative, then the corresponding feature will not be labeled.

Multiple Styling Rules

When you define multiple styling rules, MapViewer will apply different styles to different rows in the table. See Figure 11-25 for an example.

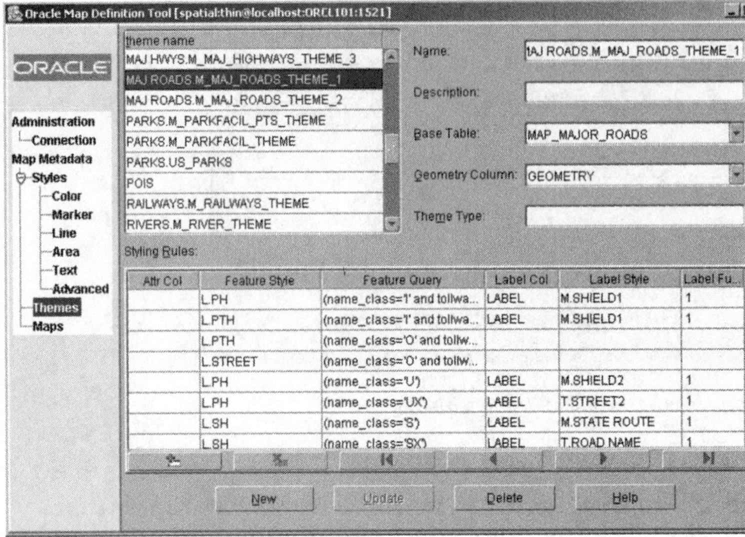

Figure 11-25. *Theme with multiple styling rules*

This theme describes the rendering for the `MAP_MAJOR_ROADS` table. That table contains road segments of different kinds that need to be displayed using different colors and thicknesses, and different labeling styles. One styling rule is defined for each kind of road, and each rule uses a different feature and label style. Some rules do not have any labeling at all.

To identify which rule should be applied to which rows, you just need to provide a SQL expression in the Feature Query column to select the relevant rows. MapViewer will include this expression in the `WHERE` clause of the `SELECT` statement it generates to read the table for this theme.

Buttons at the bottom of the window let you insert a new rule, remove a rule, or move rules in the list. Note that the order of the rules is unimportant.

Thematic Mapping: Using Advanced Styles

Another way to get MapViewer to render features depending on some attribute value is to use an advanced style. This technique is called *thematic mapping*. See Figure 11-26 for an example of a theme that uses an advanced style.

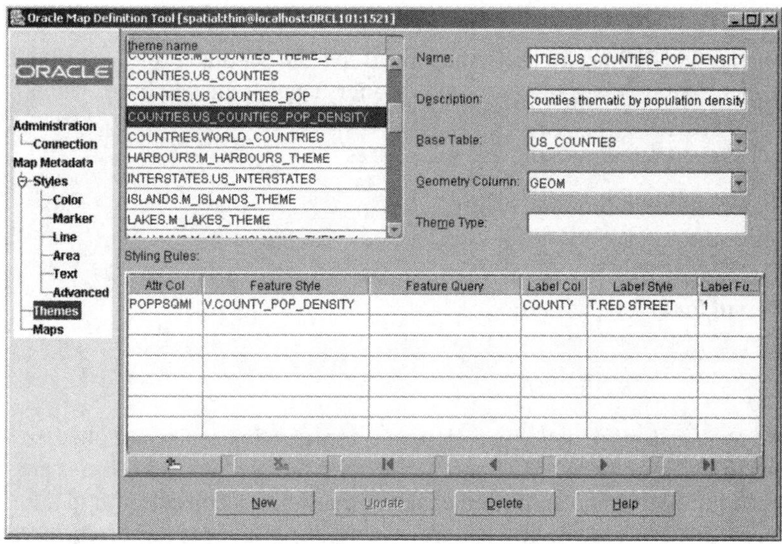

Figure 11-26. *Thematic mapping using an advanced style*

For this theme, U.S. counties should be rendered in such a way that the color of each county varies with the population density in that county.

To achieve this, we will use the advanced style we defined previously (see Figure 11-21). In addition, we need to specify the name of the attribute whose value will control the rendering. Here we use the column `poppsqmi`, which contains the average population per square mile in each country. We choose this column from the Attr Col drop-down list.

Figure 11-27 shows an example of a map that uses this style.

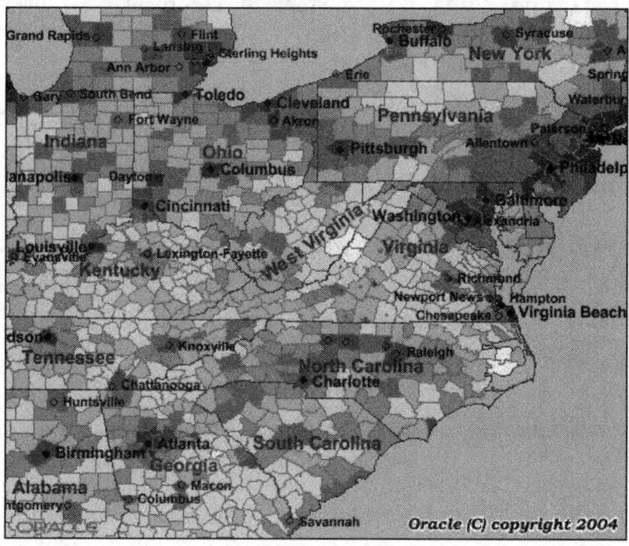

Figure 11-27. *Population density of the eastern United States*

Advanced Style vs. Multiple Styling Rules

Whenever possible, you should define and use an advanced style rather than multiple styling rules. This is because each styling rule generates a spatial query against the database, whereas an advanced style requires only one query, so it is more efficient.

You must use multiple styling rules in the following cases:

- The styling is based on a combination of attributes.
- The styling is not based on a range of values.
- Labeling is different for different features.

Defining Maps

As you have seen, a map is a collection of themes. However, constructing a map is more than just listing the themes that should appear on that map. The order in which the themes are listed is important. In addition, the map definition enables you to control the amount of information to include, depending on the scale of the map. Both concepts are very important, and we will examine them in the sections that follow.

Theme Ordering

The themes in a map must be assembled in the correct order depending on the type of symbology for each layer and its relative importance. To go back to our transparent sheets metaphor, if the counties are drawn as colored polygons, then the "counties" sheet should be placed at the bottom of the stack, so that the "roads" sheet and the "customers" sheet can be seen. If the "counties" sheet is placed on the top, then it will obscure (hide) the other sheets.

For computer-generated maps, the order in which the themes are defined controls the *rendering* or *display* order of those themes. The first theme to appear is rendered, and then the others are rendered successively on top of one another, until you have the complete map. This is illustrated in Figure 11-23.

For MapViewer, the themes are listed in the order of rendering—that is, the first theme in the list is rendered first, then the second, and so on. The theme at the end of the list is rendered last.

Note Most mapping tools list the themes in the opposite order: the theme that appears at the bottom of the list is the one rendered first, and the others are layered on top of one another. The topmost theme is rendered last. MapViewer uses the opposite convention.

Note that you can define one or more themes to use transparent styles. Such a theme can be defined as the last theme to be rendered (i.e., at the end of the theme list) and allow other themes to be partially seen.

Map Scale and Zoom Level

One important advantage of generating maps on the fly is to show more or less information depending on the current scale of the map. Let's examine what this means.

The scale of a map determines the size of the geographical area shown on that map. The scale represents the ratio of a distance on the map to the actual distance on the ground. For example, if 2 cm on the map represents 1 km on the ground, then the scale would be 2 cm/1 km, which is the same as 2 cm/100,000 cm, or 1/50,000. The scale is then 1:50,000.

Geographers talk commonly about *large-* and *small-*scale maps. A large-scale map—for example, 1:1,000 (remember, this is the fraction 1/1,000)—shows a small area with great detail and is useful for analysis that deals with small area, such as site planning for construction or a walk in the park. A small-scale map, such as 1:250,000 (1/250,000), shows a large area with little detail and is useful for large-area application such as routing a truck or a flying an airplane. The *larger* the denominator in the scale expression, the *smaller* the scale of the map and the *larger* the area of coverage for a particular display size, and vice versa.

Zooming in or out is nothing but changing the scale of a map—that is, asking for a new map to be produced at a different scale.

The amount of information shown on a map depends on the scale of that map. Maps at a small scale (e.g., showing the entire United States) will show less detail than maps at a large scale (e.g., showing the southern tip of Manhattan). It would be meaningless for a map of the continental United States to show the details on each street in every city and town, as well as each and every gas station and ATM. Not only would the map be hard to read, but it would also take a long time to produce because of the amount of data to read and render. A map at that scale would reasonably include only the boundaries of the U.S. states, some major cities, and the major interstate highways.

Then as you zoom in, you should see gradually more details: counties start to appear, then secondary highways, then major roads, then streets, then building outlines, and so on. This is a fundamental concept in cartography often referred to as *scale-dependent content* or *scale-dependent symbology*. On the other hand, when you zoom in very closely, it probably makes no sense to show country or state boundaries anymore.

To make this possible, you associate a *scale range* to individual themes. A theme will only appear on a map when the scale of the map is inside that range. Setting scale ranges correctly is important—it determines how readable and useful your maps will be. It can also determine the performance of your application.

USER_SDO_MAPS View

Maps are defined in the `USER_SDO_MAPS` view. This is the view you will update to define and maintain your maps. The `ALL_SDO_MAPS` view lists all maps in the database.

Table 11-3 lists the columns of the `USER_SDO_MAPS` view. The `ALL` and `DBA` variants contain an additional `OWNER` column.

Table 11-3. *Structure of the* `USER_SDO_MAPS` *View*

Column Name	Data Type	Description
NAME	VARCHAR2	Name of the map
DESCRIPTION	VARCHAR2	Optional description of the map
DEFINITION	CLOB	XML definition of the map

Managing Maps Using the Map Definition Tool

To define a map, you first need to give it a unique name. Other users could define their own maps with the same name.

Then you need to specify the themes to appear on that map, as illustrated in Figure 11-28, which shows the definition of the map whose construction is shown in Figure 11-23. You choose each theme from the Theme Name drop-down list in each entry. That list includes all the themes that you can access (i.e., themes that anyone defined that are based on tables you are authorized to access; in other words, the themes listed in the ALL_SDO_THEMES view).

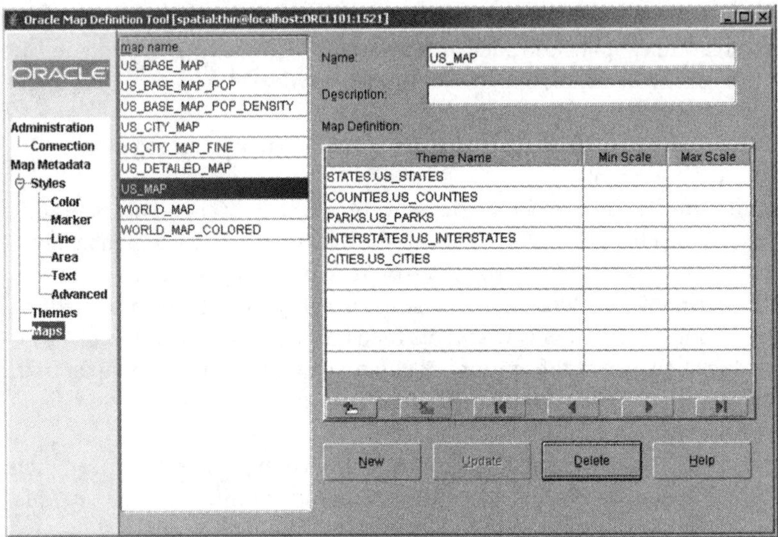

Figure 11-28. *Defining a map*

Themes are listed in the order of rendering; the first theme in the list is rendered first, then the second, and so on. The theme at the end of the list is rendered last. You can control and change the ordering of the themes using the buttons at the bottom of the form. For the map shown in the example, MapViewer will first render the US_STATES theme, then the US_COUNTIES, US_PARKS, and US_INTERSTATES themes. The US_CITIES theme is rendered last.

Scale Dependency

The Min Scale and Max Scale parameters define the visible scale range of each theme. They control whether or not the theme is displayed, depending on the current map scale. When no values are specified, then the theme is always visible.

MapViewer defines the scale of a map as the distance on the ground that corresponds to 1 inch on the map. That distance is expressed in the units of the coordinate system of the spatial tables. With data in a geodetic coordinate system (i.e., in latitude, longitude), the scale represents the number of decimal degrees that correspond to 1 inch on the map.

A high Min Scale value is associated with less map detail and a smaller scale in cartographic terms, whereas a high Max Scale value is associated with greater map detail and a larger scale in cartographic terms. (Note that the MapViewer meaning of "map scale" is different from the popular meaning of cartographic map scale.)

- *Min Scale* is the value to which the display must be zoomed in for the theme to be displayed. For example, if parks have a Min Scale value of 2 and if the current map scale value is 2 or less (but greater than the Max Scale value), parks will be included in the display. However, if the display is zoomed out so that the map scale value is greater than 2, parks will not be included in the display.
- *Max Scale* is the value beyond which the display must be zoomed in for the theme to not be displayed. For example, if states have a Max Scale value of 5, and the current map scale value is 5 or less, states will not be included in the display. However, if the display is zoomed in so that the map scale value is greater than 5 (but less than the Min Scale value), states will be included in the display.

Figure 11-29 illustrates the use of scale dependency. Map `US_BASE_MAP` contains two themes based on the `US_STATES` table: `US_STATES` and `US_STATE_LINES`. The `US_STATE_LINES` theme uses a style without any fill color (i.e., it shows only the border of the states). This means that states can be rendered on top of the counties, without hiding them. Notice also the two themes for cities: `US_CITIES` and `US_MAJOR_CITIES`. Both are defined on the `US_CITIES` table, but `US_MAJOR_CITIES` includes only those cities with a population over 250,000.

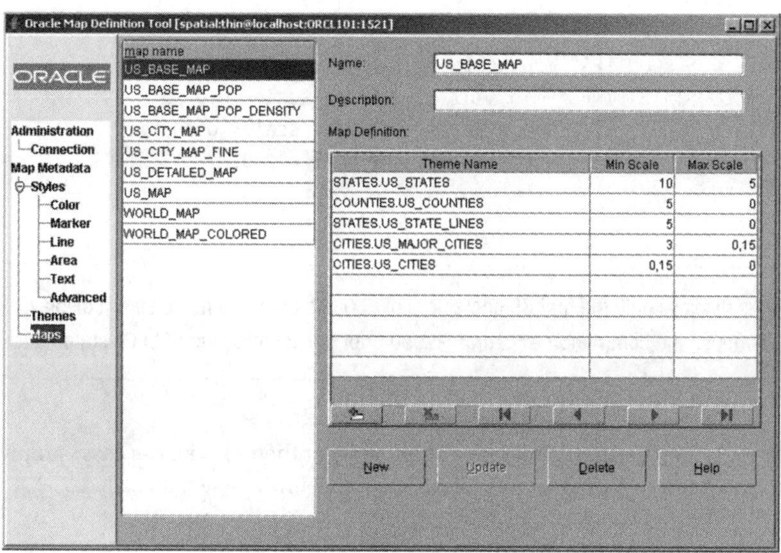

Figure 11-29. *Defining a map with scale-dependent content*

On the initial small-scale map, you see only the states (theme US_STATES). Then as you zoom in, you stop seeing the states and see only the counties (theme US_COUNTIES) with the state boundaries (theme US_STATE_LINES). As you zoom in further, you begin to see the major cities (theme US_MAJOR_CITIES), which are finally replaced by all cities (theme US_CITIES).

■ **Tip** When you modify any map definitions (maps, themes, or styles), the changes will not automatically be visible to the applications. This is because MapViewer keeps a copy of those definitions in a memory cache. To get the applications to use the new settings, you must instruct MapViewer to clear its cache. Do this using the administration API described at the end of the chapter.

Viewing and Updating Map Definitions

In addition to using the MapDef tool, you can also update the map, theme, and style definitions by directly updating the USER_SDO_MAPS, USER_SDO_THEMES, and USER_SDO_STYLES views using standard SQL statements.

Viewing the definitions is simple: just use a SELECT statement. For example, here is how to view the XML definition of map US_BASE_MAP:

```
SQL> select definition from user_sdo_maps where name = 'US_BASE_MAP';

<?xml version="1.0" standalone="yes"?>
<map_definition>
  <theme name="STATES.US_STATES" max_scale="5.0"/>
  <theme name="COUNTIES.US_COUNTIES" min_scale="5.0" max_scale="0.0"/>
  <theme name="STATES.US_STATE_LINES" min_scale="5.0" max_scale="0.0"/>
  <theme name="CITIES.US_MAJOR_CITIES" min_scale="3.0" max_scale="0.15"/>
  <theme name="CITIES.US_CITIES" min_scale="0.15" max_scale="0.0"/>
</map_definition>
```

■ **Tip** By default, SQL*Plus displays only the first 80 characters of CLOB columns. To make sure it displays the complete XML definition, use the command `set long 32000` prior to executing the SELECT statement.

Creating or updating a map definition element (map, style, or theme) is just as easy: simply use an INSERT or UPDATE statement. For example, here is how to define a new map called US_MAP:

```
insert into user_sdo_maps (name, description, definition)
  values (
'US_MAP','',
'<?xml version="1.0" standalone="yes"?>
<map_definition>
  <theme name="STATES.US_STATES" min_scale="10.0" max_scale="5.0"/>
  <theme name="COUNTIES.US_COUNTIES" min_scale="5.0" max_scale="0.0"/>
  <theme name="PARKS.US_PARKS" min_scale="2.0" max_scale="0.0"/>
```

```
  <theme name="INTERSTATES.US_INTERSTATES" min_scale="2.0" max_scale="0.0"/>
  <theme name="CITIES.US_CITIES" min_scale="3.0" max_scale="0.0"/>
</map_definition>
');
```

Exporting and Importing Map Definitions

Map definitions are stored in dictionary tables, so they will not be included when you export data from one database to another. To transfer map definitions successfully using the Oracle Export tool, you can use the following technique:

1. In the source database, before running the export, save a copy of the map definitions in regular tables:

```
create table my_styles as select * from user_sdo_styles;
create table my_themes as select * from user_sdo_themes;
create table my_maps as select * from user_sdo_maps;
```

2. In the target database, load the definitions back in the dictionary:

```
insert into user_sdo_styles select * from my_styles;
insert into user_sdo_themes select * from my_themes;
insert into user_sdo_maps select * from my_maps;
```

3. If definitions already exist in the target database, you may need to remove the old definitions first:

```
delete from user_sdo_maps where name in (select name from my_maps);
delete from user_sdo_themes where name in (select name from my_themes);
delete from user_sdo_styles where name in (select name from my_styles);
```

Using MapViewer in Applications

At the beginning of this chapter, you saw the overall architecture of MapViewer, and we presented a brief overview of the request/response flow between the client applications and the MapViewer server. Let's now examine this flow in greater detail.

The flow of operation for requesting a map is as follows:

1. The client application constructs a web service request to obtain a map. That request can be generated directly in XML or via a number of Java methods. The request contains the name of the data source (database) to read, the name of the map to generate, its format (GIF, PNG, or JPEG), its size in pixels, and the area covered by the map. The application can construct the XML request manually, or it can use the Java client API to generate it.

2. The client calls the MapViewer servlet over HTTP, passing the XML request as a parameter. Again, this can be done manually or via the Java client API.

3. The MapViewer servlet parses the request, reads the necessary map definitions from the database, selects from the spatial tables, and generates a map in GIF, PNG, or JPEG format. The map is written out as a file. Note that map definitions are cached by the servlet. The servlet can also optionally cache part or all of the spatial data it reads.

4. The servlet constructs an XML response that includes the URL to the generated image file and returns it to the client.

5. The client then parses the XML and extracts the map image URL, which it then forwards to the client browser. If the client uses the client Java API, it only needs to invoke the proper method to extract the URL.

An alternative to step 5 is for MapViewer to return the resulting map directly by streaming it to the client instead of returning an XML document. This is only possible when using the XML API directly. In this case, no image file is generated on the server.

In the following section, we proceed with a study on how to encode the map requests in XML. Then we review the principles and techniques for interacting with maps. After that, we demonstrate how you can use the three techniques available to client applications for accessing the MapViewer servlet:

- *XML API*: Can be used from any environment.
- *Java API*: Good for use in Java programs (servlets, applets, and JSP pages)
- *JSP tags*: Good for use in JSP pages

Map Requests and Responses

The exchanges between the client application and the MapViewer server are simple. The application sends a request, coded in XML, and the MapViewer sends a response back (also in XML) pointing to the map it produced.

In this section, we will first walk through a number of map requests and show you how to write those requests in XML. You will find the requests at `http://127.0.0.1:8888/mapviewer/spatial-book/map-requests.html`. The XML requests are shown in a set of forms. Clicking the Submit button on each form sends the request for execution by the MapViewer servlet. The forms let you experiment by modifying the XML requests. Later, we will look at some applications that use the XML API.

There are two ways in which you can interact with the MapViewer server using the XML API, depending on the format you specify for the resulting map:

- If the format is `GIF_URL` (the default), `PNG_URL`, or `JPEG_URL`, then you are returned an XML form that contains a URL to the generated map.
- If the format is `GIF_STREAM`, `PNG_STREAM`, or `JPEG_STREAM`, then the image is returned directly. No XML parsing is needed. The examples in the `map-requests.html` page use the "stream" technique so that you can easily see the results.

■ **Note** Map requests return XML. To view this XML correctly, you must use a browser that is able to show an XML document in a tree structure, such as Microsoft Internet Explorer 6 or Netscape Navigator 7.

Simple Map Request

Let's first examine a simple map request. It looks like this:

```
<map_request
  title="Simple Map"
  basemap="US_BASE_MAP"
  datasource="spatial10g"
  width="480"
  height="400"
  format="PNG_STREAM">
  <center size="12">
    <geoFeature>
      <geometricProperty>
        <Point>
          <coordinates>-120, 39</coordinates>
        </Point>
      </geometricProperty>
    </geoFeature>
  </center>
</map_request>
```

As its name implies, the `<map_request>` element describes a request to MapViewer. Its parameters define the generic format and aspect of the map:

- `datasource` is the name of the JDBC data source to get the map from. That data source can be a permanent one (defined in the configuration file) or one that was dynamically added via the administrative API. This is a required parameter.
- `basemap` is the name of the base map to display. This corresponds to a map defined in the `USER_SDO_MAPS` table in the database. This is actually an optional parameter, since a map can also be constructed from a list of themes (as we will show in the next example).
- `width` and `height` represent the size (in pixels) of the resulting image.
- `format` is the format of the image to produce. MapViewer is able to produce maps in the GIF, PNG, or JPEG graphic format. In addition, it can return the image in one of the following two ways:
    - *As a URL in an XML response*: Specify `GIF_URL`, `PNG_URL`, or `JPEG_URL`.
    - *As a directly streamed image*: Specify `GIF_STREAM`, `PNG_STREAM`, or `JPEG_STREAM`.

  The default is `GIF_URL`.
- `title` is an optional string that will appear on the map as a title. The title is positioned as specified in the configuration file. By default, it goes at the top of the map. If no title is specified, then the default title from the configuration file is used. If you do not want the default title to appear, then pass an empty string.

Some other parameters not mentioned in the preceding example are as follows:

- `bgcolor` is the color to use for the background. The default is to use an "ocean blue" backdrop. To get a white background instead, set it to `#FFFFFF`.
- `antialiasing` can be `true` or `false` (the default). When this parameter is set to `true`, MapViewer renders the map image in an antialiased manner. This usually provides the map with better graphic quality, but it may take longer for the map to be generated.

We still need to specify the area to be included in the map. We do this by specifying the center point of the map and its size, using the `<center>` element. The `<center>` element contains a `<geoFeature>` element, which contains a `<geometricProperty>` element, which itself contains a `<Point>` element, which finally contains a `<coordinates>` element that defines the x and y coordinates of the map center point.

Note The `<geometricProperty>` element is coded using the OGC GML v1.0 specification.

The `size` parameter of the `<center>` element sets the size of the map (actually, the height of the map). It is expressed in the units of the spatial tables used for the map. In the preceding example, we use geodetic data, so the size is expressed in decimal degrees. The value 180 means that we want a map that goes from the South Pole to the North Pole.

When you run the preceding example, you should get the map shown in Figure 11-30 as a result.

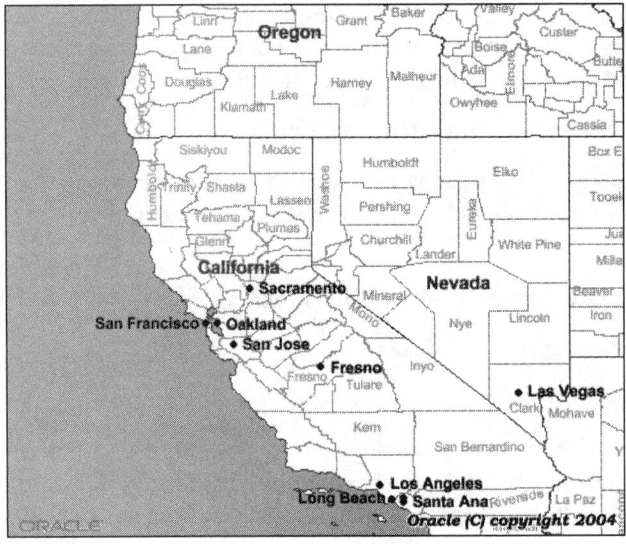

Figure 11-30. *A simple map*

If you modify the format parameter to be PNG_URL, then the map image is generated as a file on the OC4J server, and you are returned an XML form that contains the URL to the generated image, as shown in Figure 11-31.

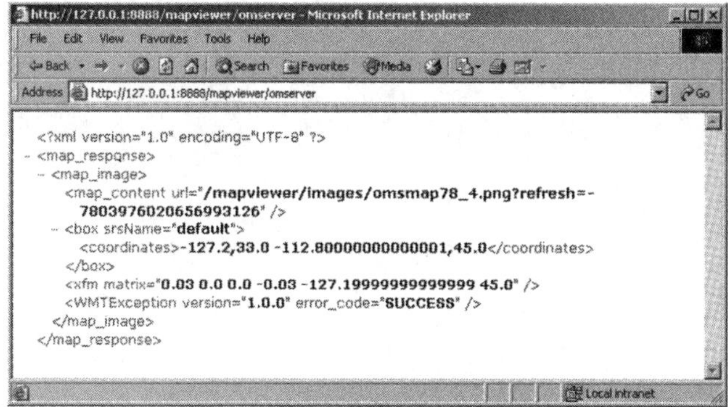

Figure 11-31. *XML response*

Another possibility is to use a <box> element instead of a <center> element. In this case, you specify the exact geographical area to display, by specifying the coordinates of the lower-left and upper-right corners of that area. The XML request becomes

```
<?xml version="1.0" standalone="yes"?>
<map_request
  title="Box query"
  basemap="US_BASE_MAP"
  datasource="spatial10g"
  width="400"
  height="400"
  format="PNG_STREAM">
  <box>
     <coordinates>-126,33 -114,45</coordinates>
  </box>
</map_request>
```

Caution You must make sure to set the map size (width and height) to the same aspect ratio as the spatial window in the <box> element. Failure to do so will result in distorted output.

Adding Themes to a Base Map

You can complement your map with additional themes that are not defined in the base map. This lets you control which themes appear on the map. Consider the following example. It is identical to our first simple map, but we now ask for interstates and parks to appear on top of the base information.

```
<?xml version="1.0" standalone="yes"?>
<map_request
  title="Base Map with Additional Themes"
  basemap="US_BASE_MAP"
  datasource="spatial10g"
  width="480"
  height="400"
  format="PNG_STREAM">
  <center size="12">
    <geoFeature>
      <geometricProperty>
        <Point>
          <coordinates>-120.0,39.0</coordinates>
        </Point>
      </geometricProperty>
    </geoFeature>
  </center>
  <themes>
    <theme name="PARKS.US_PARKS"  />
    <theme name="INTERSTATES.US_INTERSTATES"  />
  </themes>
</map_request>
```

When you run the preceding example, you should get the map shown in Figure 11-32 as a result.

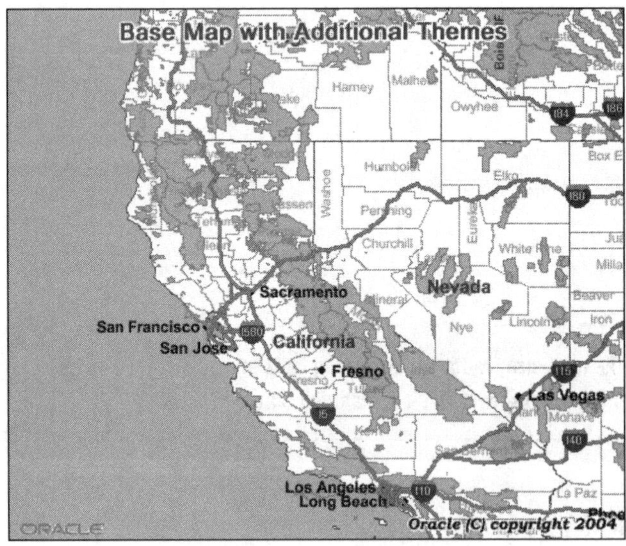

Figure 11-32. *A simple map with additional themes*

Note that the order in which you specify the additional themes is important. The themes in the base map are rendered first (in the order they are defined in the map definition), and then the additional layers are rendered in the order they appear. In the preceding example, parks are rendered first, and then interstates are rendered on top of the parks.

Using Multiple Data Sources

The preceding example assumes that all the data needed to produce a map exist in a single data source. In real applications, it is common to separate application data (e.g., the `branches` and `competitors` tables) from the base geographical data tables (e.g., `US_STATES`). Use the `datasource` parameter in the `<theme>` element to indicate where each theme comes from. If no data source is specified, then the theme is assumed to come from the main data source (defined by the `datasource` parameter in the top-level `<map_request>` element).

This technique is illustrated in the following example. The data source for each additional theme is explicitly specified. The resulting map is identical to that from the previous example.

```
<?xml version="1.0" standalone="yes"?>
<map_request
  title="Base Map with Additional Themes"
  basemap="US_BASE_MAP"
  datasource="spatial10g"
  width="480"
  height="400"
  format="PNG_STREAM">
  <center size="12">
    <geoFeature>
      <geometricProperty>
        <Point>
          <coordinates>-120.0,39.0</coordinates>
        </Point>
      </geometricProperty>
    </geoFeature>
  </center>
  <themes>
    <theme name="PARKS.US_PARKS" datasource="spatial10g" />
    <theme name="INTERSTATES.US_INTERSTATES" datasource="spatial10g" />
  </themes>
</map_request>
```

Constructing a Map from Themes

You can construct a map entirely from individual themes. In this case, there is no `basemap` parameter in the map request; instead, you list the themes to appear on the map. The themes must be listed in the order in which they should be rendered—that is, the first theme listed gets rendered first, and then the others are rendered one after the other. The last theme listed is rendered last.

As you just saw, each theme could come from a different data source:

```
<?xml version="1.0" standalone="yes"?>
<map_request
  title=""
  datasource="spatial10g"
  width="480"
  height="400"
  format="PNG_STREAM">
  <center size="1.5">
    <geoFeature>
      <geometricProperty>
        <Point>
          <coordinates>-77.0,39.0</coordinates>
        </Point>
      </geometricProperty>
    </geoFeature>
  </center>
  <themes>
    <theme name="STATES.US_STATES"  />
    <theme name="COUNTIES.US_COUNTIES" />
    <theme name="RIVERS.US_RIVERS" />
    <theme name="PARKS.US_PARKS" />
    <theme name="INTERSTATES.US_INTERSTATES" />
    <theme name="CITIES.US_CITIES" />
  </themes>
</map_request>
```

This technique is useful to let the application (or the user of the application) control which themes should be displayed. The Java examples will show an application that lets the end user select the themes to display.

Note that in the preceding example, all themes are always rendered, irrespective of the zoom level. This may not be what you want. If you want the themes to be rendered only at the appropriate zoom level, you then need to include scale limits in the theme definitions, like this:

```
<theme name="STATES.US_STATES" min_scale="10.0" max_scale="5.0"/>
<theme name="COUNTIES.US_COUNTIES" min_scale="5.0" max_scale="0.0"/>
<theme name="RIVERS.US_RIVERS" min_scale="0.6" max_scale="0.0"/>
<theme name="PARKS.US_PARKS" min_scale="2.0" max_scale="0.0"/>
<theme name="INTERSTATES.US_INTERSTATES" min_scale="2.0" max_scale="0.0"/>
<theme name="CITIES.US_CITIES" min_scale="0.15" max_scale="0.0"/>
```

The map produced by submitting the preceding request appears in Figure 11-33.

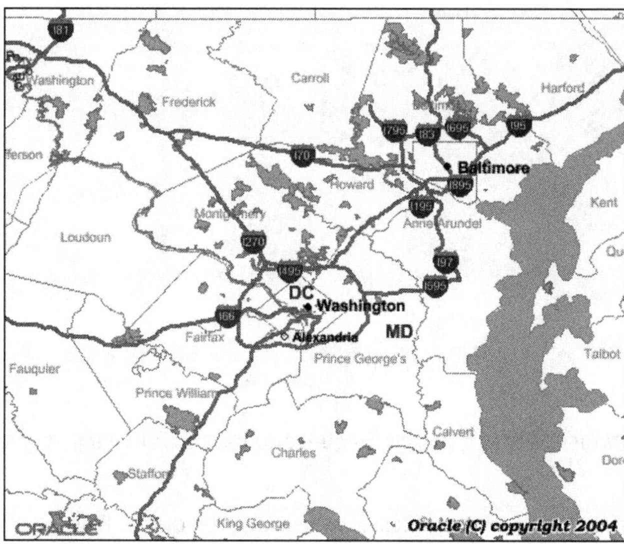

Figure 11-33. *A map constructed only from themes*

Dynamic Themes

The examples you have seen so far construct maps from predefined theme definitions. We will now add information from themes that we will dynamically define for a specific map request. We do this using a `<jdbc_query>` element inside a `<theme>` element. The `<jdbc_query>` element includes a SQL query that selects the additional information to display on the map.

Consider the following example:

```
<?xml version="1.0" standalone="yes"?>
<map_request
  title=" "
  basemap="US_CITY_MAP_FINE"
  datasource="SPATIAL10G"
  width="480"
  height="400"
  format="PNG_STREAM">
  <center size="0.02">
    <geoFeature>
      <geometricProperty>
        <Point>
          <coordinates>-122.40, 37.79</coordinates>
        </Point>
      </geometricProperty>
    </geoFeature>
  </center>
```

```
  <themes>
    <theme name="Branches">
      <jdbc_query
        datasource="SPATIAL10G"
        spatial_column="LOCATION"
        render_style="M.CYAN PIN"
        jdbc_srid="8307">
          select * from branches
      </jdbc_query>
    </theme>
  </themes>
</map_request>
```

The `<jdbc_query>` element contains the SQL query to execute and has the following parameters:

- `datasource` is the name of a JDBC data source to use for executing the query. This is a required setting.
- `spatial_column` is the name of the spatial column (of type `SDO_GEOMETRY`) returned by the SQL query.
- `jdbc_srid` is the coordinate system of the geometries returned by the SQL query.
- `render_style` is the name of the style to apply.
- `label_column` is the name of the column used for labeling the features in this theme.
- `label_style` is the name of the style to use for labeling.

This assumes that the table processed by the SQL statement is in a data source known to MapViewer. You can also get data from any other database by specifying the JDBC connection details:

- `jdbc_host`: Server name
- `jdbc_port`: Database port (1521 is the default)
- `jdbc_sid`: Database name
- `jdbc_user`: User name for the connection
- `jdbc_password`: Password for the user name
- `jdbc_mode`: Driver type (OCI8 or thin)

See Figure 11-34 for the map produced by running the preceding request. It overlays our branches on top of a map of San Francisco. This is the same as the map in Figure 11-1 at the start of the chapter.

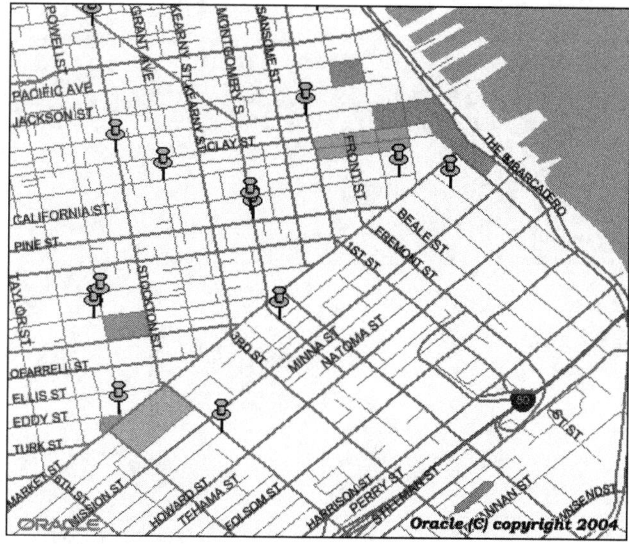

Figure 11-34. *A map with a dynamically constructed theme*

You can include any number of dynamic and static themes in a map request. You must, however, make sure that all dynamic themes have names, and that those names are unique (i.e., no two themes should have the same name).

There is no limit to the number of dynamic themes you can include in a map. The following example shows the same map as the preceding example, but this time we include the location of our branches as well as the competitors. This results in the map shown in Figure 11-2 at the beginning of the chapter.

```
<?xml version="1.0" standalone="yes"?>
<map_request
  title=" "
  basemap="US_CITY_MAP_FINE"
  datasource="SPATIAL10G"
  width="480"
  height="400"
  format="PNG_STREAM">
  <center size="0.02">
    <geoFeature>
      <geometricProperty>
        <Point>
          <coordinates>-122.40, 37.79</coordinates>
        </Point>
      </geometricProperty>
    </geoFeature>
  </center>
```

```
  <themes>
    <theme name="Competitors">
       <jdbc_query
         datasource="SPATIAL10G"
         spatial_column="LOCATION"
         render_style="M.BUSINESS RED SQUARE"
         label_column="NAME"
         label_style="T.BUSINESS NAME RED"
         jdbc_srid="8307">
           select * from competitors
       </jdbc_query>
    </theme>
    <theme name="Branches">
       <jdbc_query
         datasource="SPATIAL10G"
         spatial_column="LOCATION"
         render_style="M.CYAN PIN"
         jdbc_srid="8307">
           select * from branches
       </jdbc_query>
    </theme>
  </themes>
</map_request>
```

■ **Note** Contrary to static (predefined) themes, the information fetched by dynamic themes is never cached.

Dynamic Features

In addition to having a map display features extracted from a database, you can also add manually defined features onto the map. These are generally constructed by the client application, for example, to visualize the place where a user clicked the map.

You do this with the `<geoFeature>` element. This element includes a `<geometricProperty>` element that describes the geometric shape (using GML v1.0 notation), as well as parameters for rendering and labeling styles.

Our first example is to visualize the center of the current map. All we need to do is add some rendering information to the existing `<geoFeature>` element that defines the map center, like this:

```
<?xml version="1.0" standalone="yes"?>
<map_request
  title=" "
  basemap="US_BASE_MAP"
  datasource="SPATIAL10G"
```

```
  width="480"
  height="400"
  format="PNG_STREAM">
  <center size="4">
    <geoFeature
      render_style="M.CYAN PIN"
      label="Map center" label_always_on="true"
      text_style="T.TITLE"
      radius="100000,150000,200000">
      <geometricProperty>
        <Point srsName="SDO:8307">
          <coordinates> -82.0,35.0 </coordinates>
        </Point>
      </geometricProperty>
    </geoFeature>
  </center>
</map_request>
```

Here are the parameters we supply to the `<geoFeature>` element:

- `render_style` is the style to use for rendering the map's center point.
- `label` is hard-coded text to use as a label for the center point.
- `text_style` is the style to use for rendering the label.
- `label_always_on` is optional. It tells MapViewer to always show the center label, even if it collides with other labels.
- `radius` is a comma-separated list of radius values. MapViewer will draw a circle around the center point at each of the radiuses you specify.

See Figure 11-35 for the map produced by running the preceding request.

Note Make sure to specify the coordinate system used to specify the map center. In this section's first example, it is passed to the `<Point>` element as the parameter `srsName`. That way, you can specify the radius values in meters.

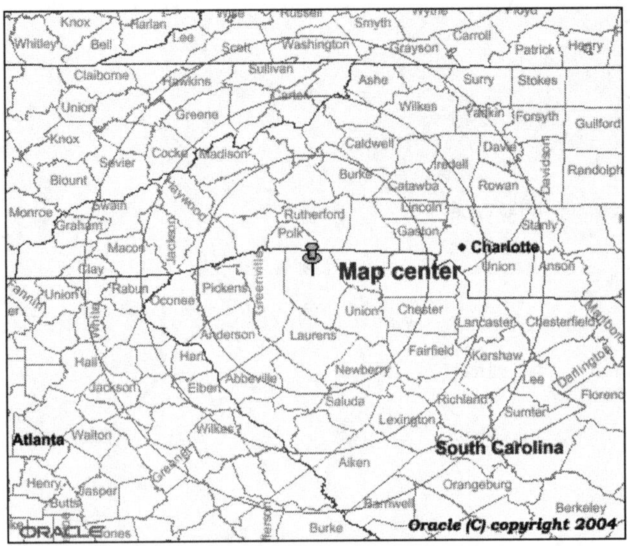

Figure 11-35. *Circles around the map center*

Our second example draws a polygon on top of a map:

```
<?xml version="1.0" standalone="yes"?>
<map_request
  title=" "
  basemap="US_BASE_MAP"
  datasource="SPATIAL10G"
  width="480"
  height="400"
  format="PNG_STREAM">
  <center size="6">
    <geoFeature>
      <geometricProperty>
        <Point>
          <coordinates> -82.0,35.0 </coordinates>
        </Point>
      </geometricProperty>
    </geoFeature>
  </center>
  <geoFeature
    label="Query Window"
    text_style="T.WINDOW_NAME"
    render_style="C.WINDOW">
    <geometricProperty>
      <Polygon>
        <outerBoundaryIs>
          <LinearRing>
```

```
          <coordinates>
          -84.0,35.0 -83.0,34.0 -81.0,34.0 -80.0,35.0 -80.0,36.0
          -82.0,37.0 -84.0,35.0
          </coordinates>
        </LinearRing>
      </outerBoundaryIs>
    </Polygon>
  </geometricProperty>
 </geoFeature>
</map_request>
```

We described the label, text_style, and render_style parameters of the <geoFeature> element earlier. The <geometricProperty> element is used to describe the geometric shape in GML v1.0 notation. In the preceding example, we draw a polygon shape. A MapViewer request can include any number of <geoFeature> elements. See Figure 11-36 for the map produced by running the preceding request.

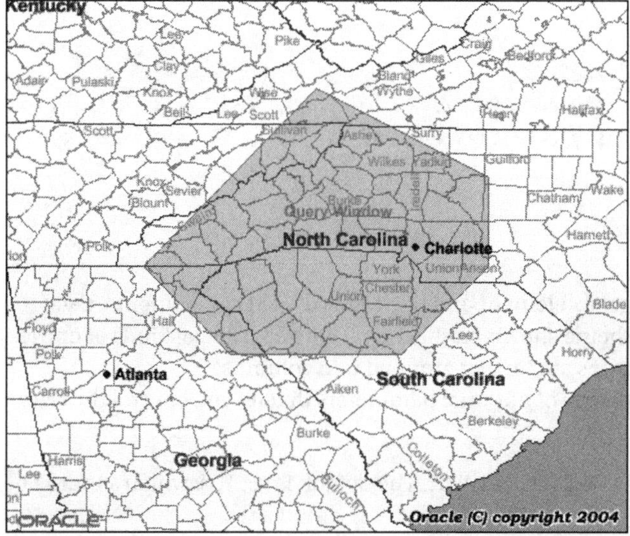

Figure 11-36. *A map with a polygon overlay*

Legends

Legends are an important aid to make maps readable. Here is an example of a map request that includes a legend:

```
<?xml version="1.0" standalone="yes"?>
<map_request
  title=" "
  basemap="US_BASE_MAP"
  datasource="spatial10g"
```

```
  width="480"
  height="400"
  format="GIF_STREAM">
  <center size="8.0">
    <geoFeature>
      <geometricProperty>
        <Point>
          <coordinates>-94.0,37.0</coordinates>
        </Point>
      </geometricProperty>
    </geoFeature>
  </center>
  <legend profile="MEDIUM" position="SOUTH_EAST">
    <column>
      <entry text="Map Legend" is_title="true" />
      <entry text="Counties"     style="C.FUNNY COLOR" />
      <entry text="Rivers"       style="C.RIVER" />
      <entry text="Parks"        style="C.PARK FOREST" />
    </column>
    <column>
      <entry text=" " is_title="true" />
      <entry text="Interstates"  style="L.PH" />
      <entry text="Major Cities" style="M.CITY HALL 4" />
    </column>
  </legend>
</map_request>
```

The legend is defined in a <legend> element and by groups of <entry> elements. Each <entry> element corresponds to a theme shown on the map. There are special kinds of entries to represent titles or separators. Entries are further grouped into columns.

The <legend> element has a number of optional parameters that let you control the size, position, and background of the legend:

- size can be specified as SMALL, MEDIUM, or LARGE. The default is MEDIUM, which should be adequate for most cases.
- position is one of NORTH, SOUTH, EAST, or WEST, or a corner such as NORTH_EAST or SOUTH_WEST. The default is SOUTH_EAST (i.e., the lower-right corner of the map).
- bgstyle lets you specify the background of the legend. You code this using an SVG notation. For example, "fill:#ffffff;stroke:#ff0000" sets the legend to a white background with a red boundary.

Each <entry> element should correspond to a layer on the map. For each entry, you specify two parameters:

- text: A text string to appear on the legend (it should be the name of a theme)
- style: A style name (it should be the style for that theme)

Figure 11-37 shows the map produced by running the preceding request.

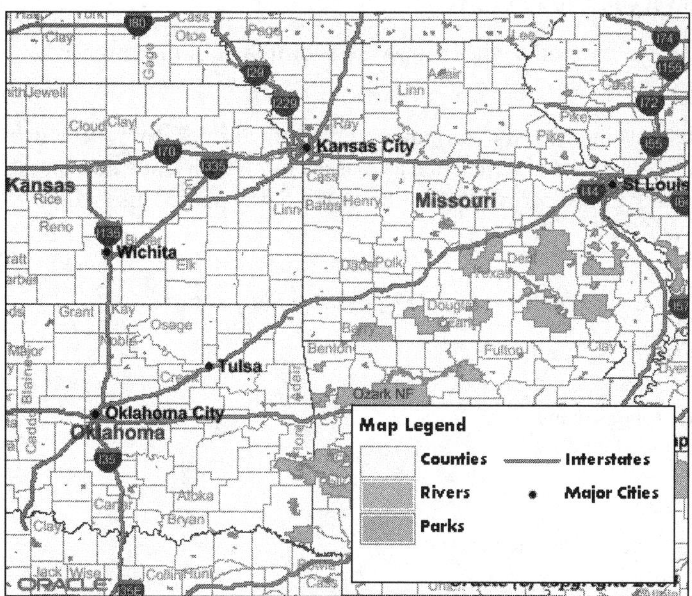

Figure 11-37. *A map with a legend*

The XML Map Response

Unless you asked for MapViewer to return a map image directly to you (in the format `GIF_STREAM`, `PNG_STREAM`, or `JPEG_STREAM`), you need to parse the XML map response to extract the URL to the map that MapViewer generated on the server.

A typical map response looks like this:

```
<?xml version="1.0" encoding="UTF-8"?>
<map_response>
 <map_image>
  <map_content url="/mapviewer/images/omsmap63.png?refresh=-399141980181404304" />
  <box srsName="default">
     <coordinates> -18.0,-15.0  18.0,15.0 </coordinates>
  </box>
  <xfm matrix="0.075 0.0 0.0 -0.075 -18.0 15.0" />
  <WMTException version="1.0.0" error_code="SUCCESS">
  </WMTException>
 </map_image>
</map_response>
```

The `<map_response>` element contains only one element, `<map_image>`, which itself contains the following main elements:

- `<map_image>` contains the `url` parameter, which in turn contains the relative URL to the generated map image (constructed using the `url` parameter of the `<save_images_at>` element in the MapViewer configuration file).
- `<box>` defines the actual area covered by the map as the coordinates of the lower-left and upper-right corners of the map.
- `<xfm>` represents the matrix values that are the parameters for an `AffineTransform`, which you can use to convert a screen coordinate (such as a user's mouse click position on the returned map image) back to the coordinate in the user's data space. This is done automatically in the Java API.

In case the request failed, you will receive an error response similar to this:

```
<?xml version="1.0" encoding="UTF-8"?>
<oms_error>
  Message:[oms] : data source not found.
  Sat Jan 24 00:41:35 CET 2004
  Severity: 0
  Description:
     at oracle.lbs.mapserver.oms.doPost(oms.java:273)
     ...
     at java.lang.Thread.run(Thread.java:536)
</oms_error>
```

Interacting with Maps

The examples you have seen so far in this chapter produce *static* maps—all you can do is look at the map. What if you want to see more detail, or less detail, or a different area? In this section, we will review the techniques you can use to enable users to interact with maps.

Controlling the Level of Detail: Zoom In and Zoom Out

The most frequently used movement controls are zoom in and zoom out. *Zooming in* means that you focus in on a smaller area in greater detail. When you *zoom out*, you see a larger area and less detail. From a mapping point of view, zooming in and out is easily performed by changing the scale of the current map.

MapViewer does not provide any specific method for zooming in or zooming out—this is all under the control of the client application. To zoom in by a chosen factor, the application just resubmits the same map request but specifies a size reduced (or enlarged) by the desired factor. MapViewer then generates a new map. Note that MapViewer will automatically adjust the amount of information that appears on the map; it includes only those themes that should be visible at the current scale, based on the `min_scale` and `max_scale` parameters of the theme definition.

A simple approach to implement zoom controls in applications is to use two buttons: one for zooming in (by a fixed factor) and one for zooming out (by the same factor). Whenever one of the buttons is clicked, the application simply computes a new map size (by multiplying or dividing the current size by the chosen factor) and requests a new map at that size. More sophisticated techniques use a range of buttons, each associated with a fixed scale factor, a slider bar, or an edit box where you type in the desired factor or scale.

A yet more sophisticated technique is to let the user select a rectangular window on the map using a mouse *drag*. This approach requires some intelligence in the user application, typically via an applet. We do not cover this technique in this book.

Controlling the Area Seen on the Map: Pan and Recenter

The next most frequently used movement is a lateral pan. *Panning* is the action of shifting the map window so that another part of the map is shown.

As with zoom in and zoom out, MapViewer does not provide any specific method for panning—again, this is all under the control of the client application. The application simply needs to decide on a new center and resubmit the same map request with that new center position. The map content and size remain the same. MapViewer then generates a new map covering the new location.

A common approach to implement panning is to use a set of four (up, down, left, and right) or eight buttons (at corners). Whenever one of the buttons is clicked, the application computes a new center, by offsetting one or both coordinates (x and y) by a fixed factor (e.g., half the current width or height of the map). It then submits a request for a new map, centered on the computed point.

Another common approach is to *recenter* the map on the spot where a user clicked. This technique requires that the application capture the coordinates of the click and use those coordinates to compute a new center. Note that this requires a conversion from *image* coordinates to the equivalent *ground* coordinates. Image coordinates are in pixels, with an origin at the upper-left corner of the image, whereas ground coordinates are in the units of the coordinate system of the map. MapViewer's Java API provides methods to perform this transformation.

A more sophisticated technique is to use a mouse drag to move the map. Click in the map, hold, and move the map around. This approach requires some intelligence in the user application, typically via an applet, and we do not cover it in this book.

Note that scrollbars are rarely seen in mapping applications since they usually imply by their size the maximum area available. The earth is pretty big, so this can be confusing.

Selecting Features: Identify

The *identify* operation lets the user select a spatial object graphically, via a mouse click, and obtain additional information about that object, such as coordinates (usually latitude, longitude is the default) or attribute information not displayed on the map. The user also needs to specify from which theme to select from.

The common approach is for the application to capture the coordinates of the mouse click, convert them from image coordinates to ground coordinates, and then use this information to perform a spatial search. One difficulty is to select point or line objects. Clicking *exactly* on the point or on the line is almost impossible, so the application needs to convert the clicked point into a square region of a few pixels around the clicked point. MapViewer's Java API provides a number of methods to easily perform those spatial searches.

More sophisticated techniques (not covered in this book) let the user select a rectangular window on the map using a mouse drag and select all objects that interact with this window.

Choosing the Information to Appear on the Map: Layer Control

The application may let the user choose the amount of information that should appear on the maps, by allowing the user to select the themes to include.

The common simple approach is to use a check box–like select list constructed from a list of available themes. The user picks from the list those themes that should appear on the map, and the application includes those themes on the subsequent map requests.

Applications may provide more sophisticated user interfaces, and let the user also select the order in which the themes appear on the map, or let the user dynamically associate a style to the themes.

Finally, the application may let the user construct new dynamic themes on the fly. The application can, for example, construct SQL statements based on user input and add them to the map as dynamic themes.

Using the XML API

Let's now examine how to write applications that use MapViewer using the native XML API. As you have already seen, this is the most basic technique to use MapViewer, and you can use it from any application development environment. Our examples will examine HTML, JavaScript, and JavaServer Pages (JSP), but other environments such as applets or servlets, C and C++, or even PL/SQL can be used as well.

Static Map Embedded in HTML

Embedding a map request in a static HTML page is not difficult—you just need to define an `<image>` element and hard-code the XML request in the `src` parameter, like this:

```
<image
  name="mapImage"
  src="http://127.0.0.1:8888/mapviewer/omserver?xml_request=..."
  alt="Map Image" >
```

■ **Note** See `http://127.0.0.1:8888/mapviewer/spatial-book/SimpleViewer.html`.

This does obviously not provide any user interaction, as all the user can do is refresh the map by reloading the HTML page. However, this may be sufficient if all you need is, for example, to show the current position of your delivery trucks on a map. A simple page refresh will trigger a regeneration of the map, which then reflects the current position of the trucks.

Note that embedding XML code inside HTML is not totally straightforward. You must make sure to escape the angle brackets and other signs that may otherwise confuse your browser.

Simple Interaction Using JavaScript

You can allow users to interact with the map in a simple way by using JavaScript on your HTML page. Figure 11-38 shows the resulting HTML page.

Note See `http://127.0.0.1:8888/mapviewer/spatial-book/SimpleViewerJS.html`.

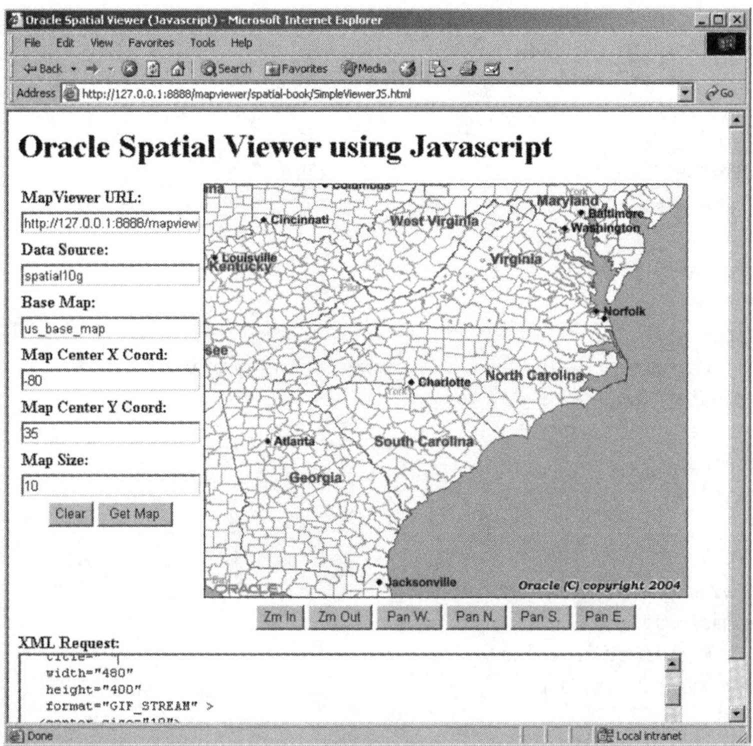

Figure 11-38. *Interacting with MapViewer using JavaScript*

The HTML page contains the following elements:

- A form that lets you specify the name of the data source to use as well as the name of the map to display. It also allows you to specify the x and y coordinates of the center of the map and its size. Click the Get Map button to get a new map.
- The map image.
- A set of navigation buttons for zooming and panning.
- A form that shows the XML sent to MapViewer.

The main work of the application is done in the JavaScript procedure `requestMap()` shown in the following code listing. That function gets the values for all form fields and constructs an XML request, which it then puts into the `src` parameter of the main `<image>` element.

```
function requestMap() {
  // Check that all form fields have been filled in
  checkForm()
  // Generate XML request
  document.viewerForm.mapRequest.value =
    "<?xml version=\"1.0\" standalone=\"yes\" ?>\n" +
    "<map_request \n" +
    "    basemap=\"" + viewerForm.baseMap.value + "\"\n" +
    "    datasource=\"" + viewerForm.dataSource.value + "\"\n" +
    "    width=\"480\"\n" +
    "    height=\"400\"\n" +
    "    format=\"GIF_STREAM\" >\n" +
    "  <center size=\"" + viewerForm.mapSize.value + "\">\n" +
    "    <geoFeature>\n" +
    "      <geometricProperty typeName=\"center\">\n" +
    "        <Point>\n" +
    "          <coordinates>\n" +
    "            " + viewerForm.cx.value + ", " + viewerForm.cy.value + "\n" +
    "          </coordinates>\n" +
    "        </Point>\n" +
    "      </geometricProperty>\n" +
    "    </geoFeature>\n" +
    "  </center>\n" +
    "</map_request>\n";
  // Update image URL with new XML request
  document.viewerForm.mapImage.src =
    document.viewerForm.MapViewerURL.value + "?xml_request=" +
    document.viewerForm.mapRequest.value
}
```

Zooming and panning is controlled by a set of buttons. Each button is associated with a JavaScript procedure that updates the center and size of the map, before requesting a new map with the new parameters.

```
<td><input type="button" name="action" value="Zm In"  onclick="zoom(1/2)">     </td>
<td><input type="button" name="action" value="Zm Out" onclick="zoom(2)">       </td>
<td><input type="button" name="action" value="Pan W." onclick="pan(-0.5, 0)"> </td>
<td><input type="button" name="action" value="Pan N." onclick="pan(0, 0.5)">  </td>
<td><input type="button" name="action" value="Pan S." onclick="pan(0, -0.5)"> </td>
<td><input type="button" name="action" value="Pan E." onclick="pan(0.5, 0)">  </td>
```

The `zoom()` function changes the size of the map by a chosen factor but leaves the center of the map unchanged.

```
function zoom(zoomFactor) {
  document.viewerForm.mapSize.value
    = document.viewerForm.mapSize.value * zoomFactor;
  requestMap()
}
```

The `pan()` function moves the x or y coordinate of the map center by chosen factors but leaves the size unchanged.

```
function pan(xFactor, yFactor) {
  document.viewerForm.cx.value =
    1*document.viewerForm.cx.value + document.viewerForm.mapSize.value * xFactor;;
  document.viewerForm.cy.value =
    1*document.viewerForm.cy.value + document.viewerForm.mapSize.value * yFactor;;
  requestMap()
}
```

That is all there is to it. You will see pretty much the same interaction logic in all the examples that follow in this chapter.

Using the XML API in a JSP Page

The JavaServer Pages (JSP) technology is a powerful way to create applications that perform complex operations and allow rich user interactions. Consider the HTML page in Figure 11-39.

■ **Note** See `http://127.0.0.1:8888/mapviewer/spatial-book/SimpleViewerXML.jsp`.

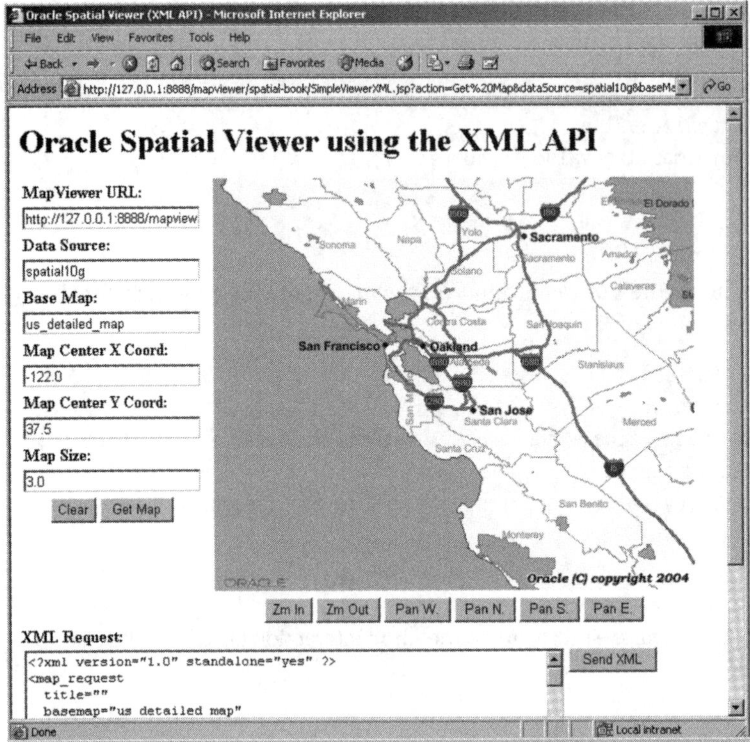

Figure 11-39. *Interacting with MapViewer using JSP*

The HTML page contains much the same basic elements as the JavaScript example:

- A form that lets you specify the name of the data source to use as well as the name of the map to display. It also lets you specify the x and y coordinates of the center of the map and its size. Use the Get Map button to get a new map.
- The map image.
- A set of navigation buttons for zooming and panning.
- A form that shows the XML sent to MapViewer.

It also provides the following capabilities:

- The ability to recenter the map by clicking it
- The ability to see the response XML
- The ability to modify the request XML

The logic of the Java code in the JSP page is as follows:

1. Extract the input parameters from the HTTP request object. These parameters include the name of the data source and the base map, and the center and size of the map.

```
dataSource = request.getParameter("dataSource");
baseMap = request.getParameter("baseMap");
cx = request.getParameter("cx") != null ?
  Double.valueOf(request.getParameter("cx")).doubleValue() : 0.0;
cy = request.getParameter("cy") != null ?
  Double.valueOf(request.getParameter("cy")).doubleValue() : 0.0;
mapSize = request.getParameter("mapSize") != null ?
  Double.valueOf(request.getParameter("mapSize")).doubleValue() : 0.0;
```

2. Process the requested user action (zoom or pan button). The logic is similar to the JavaScript example: the zoom operations change the map size by a fixed factor (2*x* or 1/2*x*), and the pan operations shift the x or y coordinate of the map center by half the map size.

```
if (userAction.equals("Get Map")) {
  // User clicked the 'Get Map' button and
  // chose a new datasource or map name,
  // or manually entered a new map center and size
  // Nothing to do: new settings already
  // extracted from request parameters
}
// User clicked one of the 'Zoom' buttons:
// Zoom in or out by a fixed factor (2x)
else if (userAction.equals("Zm In"))
  mapSize = mapSize/2;
else if (userAction.equals("Zm Out"))
  mapSize = mapSize*2;
// User clicked one of the 'Pan' buttons:
// shift map 50% in the desired direction.
else if (userAction.equals("Pan W."))
  cx = cx - mapSize/2;
else if (userAction.equals("Pan N."))
  cy = cy + mapSize/2;
else if (userAction.equals("Pan S."))
  cy = cy - mapSize/2;
else if (userAction.equals("Pan E."))
  cx = cx + mapSize/2;
```

3. If the user clicked the map, extract the x and y coordinates of the click, and convert them to the corresponding ground coordinates (i.e., to a new map center). Note that we need to know the actual bounds of the map; we have extracted them from the XML response to our previous map request (as shown in the following code).

```
// User clicked on the map. Get the coordinates of the clicked point
// convert to map coordinates, and use it as new map center
else if (userAction.equals("reCenter")) {
  imgCX = Integer.valueOf(request.getParameter("mapImage.x")).intValue();
  imgCY = Integer.valueOf(request.getParameter("mapImage.y")).intValue();
  cx = boxLLX+imgCX/mapWidth*(boxURX-boxLLX);
  cy = boxURY-imgCY/mapHeight*(boxURY-boxLLY);
}
```

4. Construct a new XML map request based on those parameters and the user action.

```
mapRequest =
        "<?xml version=\"1.0\" standalone=\"yes\" ?>\n"    +
        "<map_request \n"                                   +
        "  title=\""       + mapTitle      + "\"\n"         +
        (baseMap.trim().length()!=0 ?
         ("  basemap=\""     + baseMap    + "\"\n") : "")  +
        "   datasource=\"" + dataSource + "\"\n"            +
        "   width=\""       + mapWidth      + "\"\n"        +
        "   height=\""      + mapHeight     + "\"\n"        +
        "   format=\"PNG_URL\" >\n"                         +
        "  <center size=\"" + mapSize + "\">\n"             +
        "    <geoFeature>\n"                                +
        "      <geometricProperty typeName=\"center\">\n"  +
        "        <Point>\n"                                 +
        "          <coordinates>\n"                         +
        "            " + cx + ", " + cy + "\n"              +
        "          </coordinates>\n"                        +
        "        </Point>\n"                                +
        "      </geometricProperty>\n"                      +
        "    </geoFeature>\n"                               +
        "  </center>\n"                                     +
        "</map_request>\n";
```

5. Send the XML map request to the MapViewer servlet via an HTTP request.

```
// Get a connection to the MapViewer server
URL url = null;                       // URL to MapViewer servlet
HttpURLConnection hurlc = null;       // HTTP connection
url = new URL(MapViewerURL);
hurlc = (HttpURLConnection) url.openConnection();
hurlc.setDoOutput(true);
hurlc.setDoInput(true);
```

```
hurlc.setUseCaches(false);
hurlc.setRequestMethod("POST");
// Send the map request to the MapViewer server
os = hurlc.getOutputStream();
os.write(("xml_request=" + mapRequest).getBytes());
os.flush();
os.close();
```

6. Parse the XML response and extract the URL to the generated map as well as the bounds of the new map.

7. Update the HTML form with the URL of the generated map.

Using the Java API

The XML API is powerful, but it can be difficult to use. For using MapViewer from Java environments (servlets, JSP, or any Java application), there is a better and simpler alternative that involves using a simple Java interface that takes care of all the XML manipulations and the exchanges with the MapViewer server.

■ Note See `http://127.0.0.1:8888/mapviewer/spatial-book/SimpleViewerJava.jsp`.

The Java API to MapViewer is distributed as a JAR file located in your MapViewer installation (at `$OC4J_HOME/lbs/mapviewer/web/WEB-INF/lib/mvclient.jar`). It consists of a single class: `oracle.lbs.mapclient.MapViewer`. To use the API in your applications, make sure to include `mvclient.jar` into your classpath. This will already be the case when you use the API from Java applications (servlets or JSPs) that execute inside in the same OC4J instance that is running MapViewer.

The documentation (Javadoc) is available in your MapViewer installation as well, at `$OC4J_HOME/lbs/mapviewer/web/mapclient`, and you can access it directly at `http://127.0.0.1:8888/mapviewer/mapclient`. Please refer to Javadoc for the precise syntax of the various methods.

We will now examine the various features of the API. We will begin by looking at simple map requests, and then we will examine various interactions: zooming and panning, theme and style control, and adding dynamic features and legends.

See Figure 11-40 for an example of the output of the `SimpleViewerJava.jsp` page. Note that there is little visible difference between this page and the one that uses the XML API.

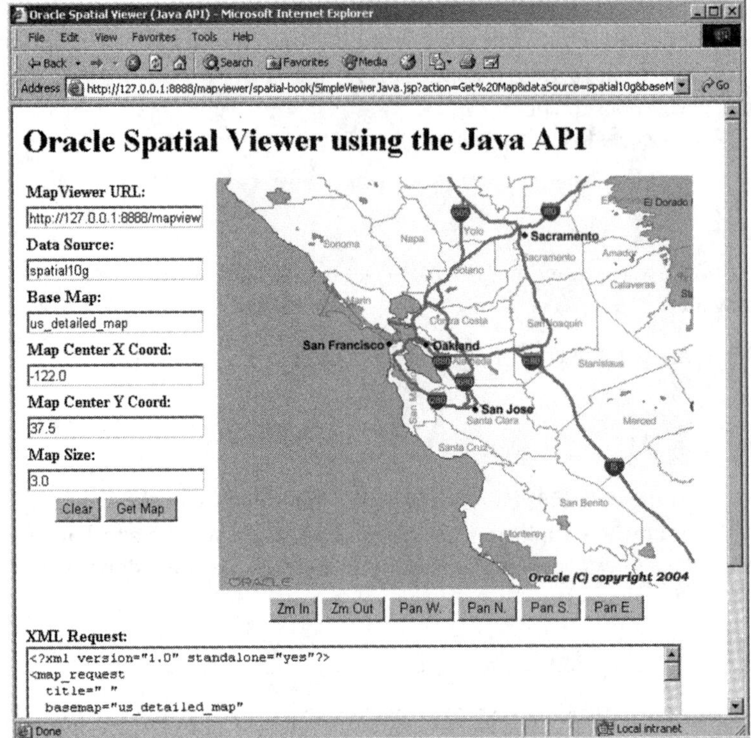

Figure 11-40. *JSP page that uses the Java API*

Sending Map Requests

Let's first consider the construction and execution of a simple map request. The basic flow of operation when using the MapViewer bean is as follows:

1. Create a MapViewer object.
2. Set up request parameters in the MapViewer object (using various `set()` methods).
3. Send the request to the server (invoking the `run()` method).
4. Extract the results from the object (using `get()` methods).

Create a MapViewer Object

Your application needs to import the `oracle.lbs.mapclient.MapViewer` package and create a MapViewer object. Before you can use the object, you must pass it the URL of the MapViewer servlet, which establishes the connection with the MapViewer server. You can do this at the time you create the object, like this:

```
MapViewer mv = new MapViewer(MapViewerURL);
```

Alternatively, you can pass it later on using the `setServiceURL` method, like this:

```
MapViewer mv = new MapViewer();
...
mv.setServiceURL(MapViewerURL);
```

The service URL has the form `http://<host>:<port>/mapviewer/omserver`. When you use the API from a JSP page or servlet, and your JSP page or servlet runs in the same container as the MapViewer servlet, then you can construct the URL from the request parameters:

```
mapViewerURL = "http://"
  + request.getServerName()+":"
  + request.getServerPort()
  + request.getContextPath()
  + "/omserver";
```

Set Up the Map Request

The MapViewer class provides a number of "set" methods that let you control the parameters for a map request: data source, base map, and so on.

First, you define the general parameters for the map:

- `setDataSourceName()` sets the name of the data source to use.
- `setBaseMapName()` sets the name of the base map to display. This is optional.
- `setImageFormat()` selects the format of the image to produce. For servlets or JSP pages, this must be `FORMAT_GIF_URL`, `FORMAT_PNG_URL`, or `FORMAT_JPEG_URL`. For "thick" clients, you can also set this to `FORMAT_RAW_COMPRESSED`, which instructs MapViewer to return the image in `java.awt.Image` format.
- `setDeviceSize()` defines the size of the requested map in pixels.
- `setMapTitle()` sets the map title. Set it to a blank string (not an empty string) if you want no title at all.

Then you define the area to be covered by the map:

- `setCenter()` sets the center (x and y coordinates).
- `setSize()` sets the height of the map.
- `setCenterAndSize()` sets both center and size in one operation.
- `setBox()` sets the box to query, as the coordinates of the lower-left and upper-right corners.

You can also specify some processing options:

- `setAntiAliasing()` is either `true` or `false` (the default).
- `setBackgroundColor()` should be used only if you want a background different from the default "ocean blue" color.

There are many other methods you can use to set or add legends, select the themes to display, add dynamic themes, add features, and so on, which we will examine in the following sections.

Note that the parameters are not verified by the API when you set them. For example, if you specify an invalid data source, you will only get an error when you attempt to send the request to the MapViewer service. Also note that most "set" methods have a corresponding "get" method.

The following extract from SimpleViewerJava.jsp shows the basic steps of setting up a map request:

```
// Set up map request
mv.setDataSourceName(dataSource);                    // Data source
mv.setBaseMapName(baseMap);                          // Base map
mv.setMapTitle(" ");                                 // No title
mv.setImageFormat(MapViewer.FORMAT_PNG_URL);         // Map format
mv.setDeviceSize(
  new Dimension(mapWidth, mapHeight));               // Map size
mv.setCenterAndSize(cx, cy, mapSize);
```

Send the Request to the MapViewer Server

The main method for sending a request is run(). This method constructs the XML request from the properties currently set in the MapViewer object, sends it to the MapViewer service, reads the XML response, and parses the response. All failures are signaled via Java exceptions.

```
// Send map request
mv.run();
```

Extract Information from the Map Response

Once a request has completed, you can extract its results from the MapViewer object using "get" methods. Mostly, you will extract the URL of the generated image.

- getGeneratedMapImageURL() extracts the URL of the image generated by MapViewer on the server, provided you asked for an image in FORMAT_PNG_URL or FORMAT_GIF_URL format. This is the normal case for all servlets and JSP pages.
- getGeneratedMapImage() extracts the image in java.awt.Image format, provided you asked for an image in FORMAT_RAW_COMPRESSED format.
- getMapMBR() extracts the minimum bounding rectangle (MBR) of the generated map. The result is an array of doubles that contains the xmin, ymin, xmax, and ymax of the current map's MBR.
- getMapRequestString() and getMapResponseString() return the XML string sent to the MapViewer and the XML response. This is mostly useful for debugging purposes.

The following code shows how to extract information returned by the MapViewer server:

```
// Get URL to generated Map
imgURL = mv.getGeneratedMapImageURL();
```

```
// Get the XML request sent to the server
mapRequest = mv.getMapRequestString();

// Get the XML response received from the server
mapResponse = mv.getMapResponseString();

// Get size and center of new map
mapSize = mv.getSize();
Point2D center = mv.getCenter();
cx = center.getX();
cy = center.getY();

// Get the MBR of the map
double box[] = mv.getMapMBR();
boxLLX = box[0];
boxLLY = box[1];
boxURX = box[2];
boxURY = box[3];
```

Zooming and Panning

There are two techniques you can use for controlling the zooming and panning. The first approach is identical to the one illustrated in the XML API example. You compute a new map center and size based on user actions, and request a new map using the `run()` method. This technique is good for "stateless" applications. The MapViewer object is rebuilt from scratch for each map request, and there is no need to save it in servlet session. This is illustrated in the following code example:

```
if (userAction.equals("Get Map")) {
  // User clicked the 'Get Map' button and
  // chose a new datasource or map name,
  // or manually entered a new map center and size
  // Nothing to do: new settings already
  // extracted from request parameters
}

// User clicked one of the 'Zoom' buttons:
// Zoom in or out by a fixed factor (2x)
else if (userAction.equals("Zm In"))
  mapSize = mapSize/2;
else if (userAction.equals("Zm Out"))
  mapSize = mapSize*2;

// User clicked one of the 'Pan' buttons:
// shift map 50% in the desired direction.
else if (userAction.equals("Pan W."))
  cx = cx - mapSize/2;
```

```
else if (userAction.equals("Pan N."))
  cy = cy + mapSize/2;
else if (userAction.equals("Pan S."))
  cy = cy - mapSize/2;
else if (userAction.equals("Pan E."))
  cx = cx + mapSize/2;

// User clicked on the map. Get the coordinates of the clicked point
// convert to map coordinates, and use it as new map center
else if (userAction.equals("reCenter")) {
  imgCX = Integer.valueOf(request.getParameter("mapImage.x")).intValue();
  imgCY = Integer.valueOf(request.getParameter("mapImage.y")).intValue();
  cx = boxLLX+imgCX/mapWidth*(boxURX-boxLLX);
  cy = boxURY-imgCY/mapHeight*(boxURY-boxLLY);
}
```

The second technique is to use the `run()` method only when requesting a new map, and then use the `zoomIn()`, `zoomOut()`, or `pan()` method for zooming or panning. This technique requires that the MapViewer object be retained between successive invocations of the JSP page or servlet. In other words, it must be saved in session context and restored on each execution.

Note that the parameters of those methods are always expressed in *device coordinates*—that is, they are in pixels on the map image (their origin is at the upper-left corner of the image). This means that you can use directly the coordinates you receive from a click on the image.

You can use the `zoomIn()` method in several ways:

- `zoomIn(double factor)` zooms in by the chosen factor.
- `zoomIn(int x, int y, double factor)` recenters the map on the chosen point (in device coordinates) and zooms by the chosen factor. This combines a zoom and pan.
- `zoomIn(int x1, int y1, int x2, int y2)` zooms in on the specified device rectangle.

Here is how you can use the `zoomOut()` method:

- `zoomOut(double factor)` zooms out by the chosen factor.
- `zoomOut(int x, int y, double factor)` recenters the map on the chosen point (in device coordinates) and zooms out by the chosen factor.

Here is how you can use the `pan()` method:

- `pan(int x, int y)` recenters the map on the chosen point (in device coordinates).

The following code example illustrates the use of the `zoomIn()`, `zoomOut()`, and `pan()` methods.

■ **Note** See `http://127.0.0.1:8888/mapviewer/spatial-book/SimpleViewerJavaSession.jsp`.

```
// Fetch saved MapViewer object from session (if any)
MapViewer mv = (MapViewer) session.getAttribute("mvhandle");
if (mv==null) {
  // No MapViewer object found - must create and initialize it
  mv = new MapViewer(MapViewerURL);
  session.setAttribute("mvhandle", mv);      // keep client handle in the session
}

if (userAction.equals("Get Map")) {
  // User clicked the 'Get Map' button and
  // choose a new datasource or map name,
  // or manually entered a new map center and size
  // Initialize the MapViewer object with the entered
  // information
  mv.setDataSourceName(dataSource);                     // Data source
  mv.setBaseMapName(baseMap);                           // Base map
  mv.setMapTitle("  ");                                 // No title
  mv.setImageFormat(MapViewer.FORMAT_PNG_URL);          // Map format
  mv.setDeviceSize(new Dimension(mapWidth, mapHeight)); // Map size
  mv.setCenterAndSize(cx, cy, mapSize);
  // Send map request
  mv.run();
}

// User clicked one of the 'Zoom' buttons:
// Zoom in or out by a fixed factor (2x)
else if (userAction.equals("Zm In"))
  mv.zoomIn(2);
else if (userAction.equals("Zm Out"))
  mv.zoomOut(2);

// User clicked one of the 'Pan' buttons:
// shift map 50% in the desired direction.
else if (userAction.equals("Pan W."))
  mv.pan (0, mapHeight/2);
else if (userAction.equals("Pan N."))
  mv.pan (mapWidth/2, 0);
else if (userAction.equals("Pan S."))
  mv.pan (mapWidth/2, mapHeight);
else if (userAction.equals("Pan E."))
  mv.pan (mapWidth, mapHeight/2);

// User clicked on the map. Get the coordinates of the clicked point
// convert to map coordinates, and use it as new map center
else if (userAction.equals("reCenter")) {
  imgCX = Integer.valueOf(request.getParameter("mapImage.x")).intValue();
  imgCY = Integer.valueOf(request.getParameter("mapImage.y")).intValue();
  mv.pan (imgCX, imgCY);
}
```

Theme Control

The MapViewer bean gives you extensive control over the themes in a map. Themes are kept in an ordered list inside the map request. This ordering of themes is very important: it determines the order in which the themes are rendered on the map. As we mentioned earlier, the first theme in the list gets rendered first, and then the others are rendered one after the other. The last theme listed gets rendered last.

The following methods add and delete themes:

- `addPredefinedTheme()` adds a predefined theme to the current map request. You can optionally specify the position at which the theme should be added in the list of existing themes. If you do not specify a position, then the theme is added at the end of the list of themes. The first theme in the list is number 0.
- `addThemesFromBaseMap()` lets you compose a map only with themes (i.e., without any base map). It adds to the current map request all themes defined for the specified base map. This is equivalent to finding out all the themes listed in the base map, and then calling `addPredefinedTheme()` and `setThemeScale()` for each theme in the list. Note that this actually sends an "administrative" request to the MapViewer server to get the theme list. The themes are loaded in the order in which they appear in the base map, but you are able to change that order if you desire.
- `addImageTheme()` adds an image theme for which you must supply the query string for retrieving the image data to be rendered as part of the map.
- `addJDBCTheme()` adds a JDBC theme for which you must supply a SQL query. There are two main variants of that method: one that uses a data source name to identify the database to connect to and one that needs explicit JDBC connection parameters (host, port, database, user name, and password). You can optionally specify the position at which the theme should be added in the list of existing themes. If you do not specify a position, then the theme is added at the end of the list of themes.
- `deleteTheme()` removes a theme from the current map request.

The following methods are for enabling and disabling themes (note that all themes are originally enabled):

- `setThemeEnabled()` enables or disables one specific theme.
- `enableThemes()` enables a list of themes.
- `setAllThemesEnabled()` enables or disables all themes in the map request.

These methods are for controlling the order of the themes:

- `moveThemeDown()` moves a specific theme down one position in the list of themes. The theme to move is identified by its sequence in the list of themes.
- `moveThemeUp()` moves a theme up one position in the list.

These methods are for controlling theme and label visibility:

- `setThemeScale()` sets the minimum and maximum scale values for displaying a theme. Note that this is not needed for themes added from a base map using the `addThemesFromBaseMap()` method; those themes have the scale values defined in the base map definition.
- `setLabelAlwaysOn()` controls whether or not MapViewer labels all features in a theme even if two or more labels will overlap.

Use these methods to find information about themes:

- `hasThemes()` checks to see if the current map request has any explicitly added themes. If the map request contains only a base map, then this method returns `FALSE`.
- `getThemeNames()` returns the list of all themes in the map request.
- `getEnabledThemes()` returns the list of all themes that are currently enabled in the map request.
- `getThemePosition()` gets the position of a theme in the list of themes in the map request.
- `getActiveTheme()` gets the name of the topmost theme (i.e., the one at the end of the theme list).

Note See `http://127.0.0.1:8888/mapviewer/spatial-book/SpatialViewer.jsp`.

See Figure 11-41 for an example of the output of the `SpatialViewer.jsp` page that lets you select the themes to display. The selection is done via a series of check boxes that is dynamically constructed from the list returned by the `getThemeNames()` method.

The initial list of themes is set when the MapViewer object is constructed:

```
mv.addThemesFromBaseMap(baseMap);                // Themes from base map
mv.setAllThemesEnabled(true);                    // Enable all themes
```

Here is how the check-box list is constructed in the HTML code:

```
<table>
    <% String[] ts = mv.getThemeNames(); %>
    <% for(int i=0; i<ts.length; i++) {%>
    <tr><td>
      <input type="checkbox"
        name="checkedThemes"
        value="<%=ts[i]%>"
        <%=mv.getThemeEnabled(ts[i])?"checked":""%>
      >
      <%= ts[i] %>
    </td></tr>
  <%}%>
</table>
```

The result of selecting check boxes is then passed back to the JSP page. The following statement extracts the checked themes in an array of strings:

```
String[] checkedThemes = request.getParameterValues("checkedThemes");
```

Finally, enabling the themes on the map is done like this:

```
// Enable the themes selected by the user
if (checkedThemes != null)
  mv.enableThemes(checkedThemes);
else
  mv.setAllThemesEnabled(false);
```

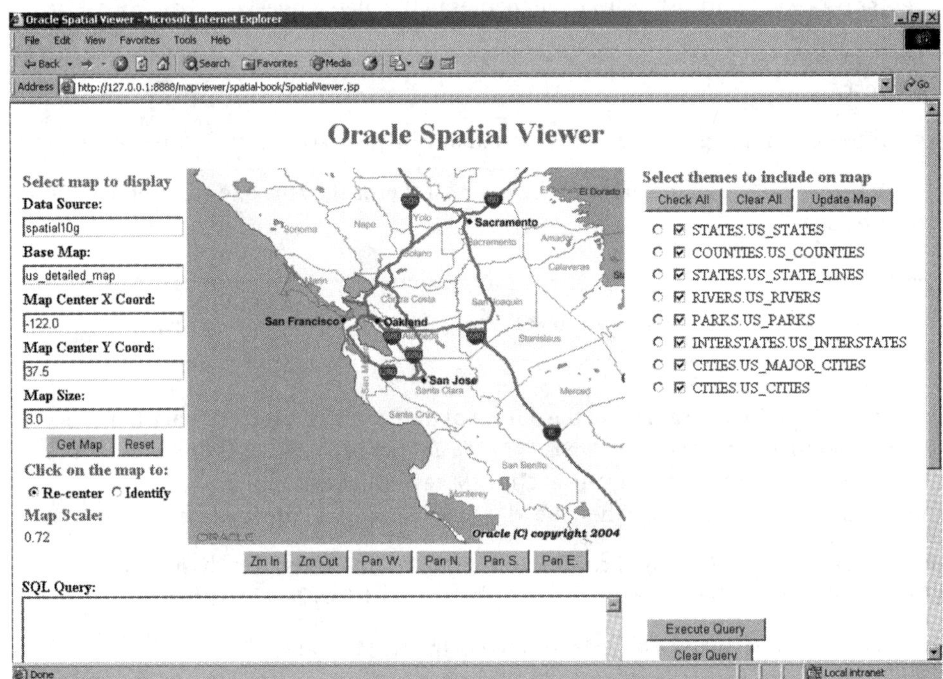

Figure 11-41. *Selecting the themes to display*

Dynamic Themes

As just explained, you use the `addJDBCTheme()` method to add dynamic themes (i.e., themes based on the results of JDBC queries).

The `SpatialViewer.jsp` page lets you enter a SQL statement, which it then adds as a theme called `SQL_QUERY`. See Figure 11-42 for an example that generates a buffer around a selected county. Here is the code that achieves this:

```
// If necessary, run the SQL query entered by the user
if (sqlQuery != null && sqlQuery.length() > 0) {
  // Add a JDBC theme for the query
  mv.addJDBCTheme (
      dataSource,                 // dataSource
      "[SQL_QUERY]",              // Theme name
      sqlQuery.replace(';',' '), // SQL Query (remove trailing semicolon if any)
      null,                       // Name of spatial column
      null,                       // srid
      "SQL_QUERY",                // renderStyle
      null,                       // labelColumn
      null,                       // labelStyle
      true);                      // passThrough
}
```

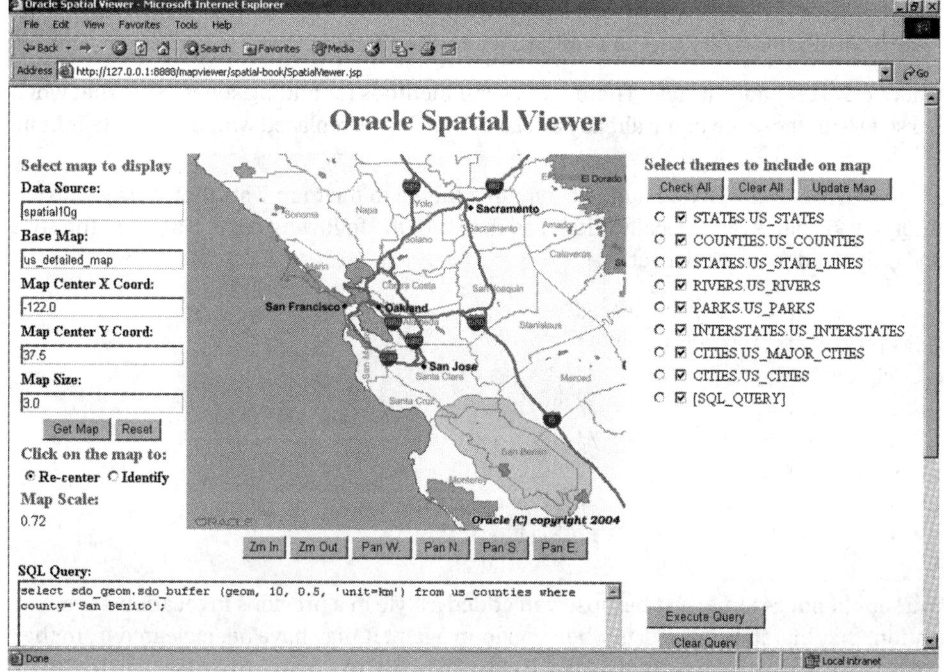

Figure 11-42. *Adding a dynamic query to a map*

Note that the JDBC theme appears as a regular theme in the map. You can therefore turn it "on" or "off" just like any other theme.

Style Control

Styles are defined in the database, but you can also dynamically define new styles. Note that those styles are temporary only—they are not written to the database, so they will disappear when the MapViewer service is shut down or when its metadata cache gets cleared.

Note When you define a style with the same name as a permanent style, your definition overrides the permanent style in MapViewer's metadata cache. All subsequent map requests will then use the new style. To revert back to the permanent style, you just need to delete the dynamic style.

The following methods let you control styles:

- `styleExists()` returns `TRUE` if the style with the given name already exists in MapViewer's style cache on the server.
- `deleteStyle()` deletes the named style from MapViewer's cache. This deletes only dynamically added styles—you cannot delete a permanent style.
- `addXxxStyle()` adds a style. There are several methods for adding styles. Note that when a style with the same name already exists, it silently gets replaced with the new definition.

In the previous example, we added a dynamic theme to the map. This theme uses a style called `SQL_QUERY` that is dynamically added, as shown in the following code. Note that the style is added only if it does not exist yet.

```
// Add style for overlay if needed
if (!mv.styleExists ("SQL_QUERY"))
  mv.addColorStyle (
    "SQL_QUERY",              // Style name
    "red",                    // Stroke color
    "red",                    // Fill color
    255,                      // Stroke opacity
    40);                      // Fill opacity
```

You should not assume, just because you added a style in a previous invocation of your application, that this style still exists when you loop again. It may have been cleared from the MapViewer style cache as a result of a "cache clear" request, or it may have been deleted by another user.

Identification and Queries

Identification is the ability to select a spatial object graphically, via a mouse click, and obtain additional information about that object. The JSP file `SpatialViewer.jsp` illustrates how to do this. Figure 11-43 shows the result of selecting one county. Notice that the radio button for the `US_COUNTIES` theme is selected. Also, the radio button on the left ("Click on the map to:") is set to Identify. A blue pin is set on the map to indicate the point clicked, and information about the county is displayed under the map.

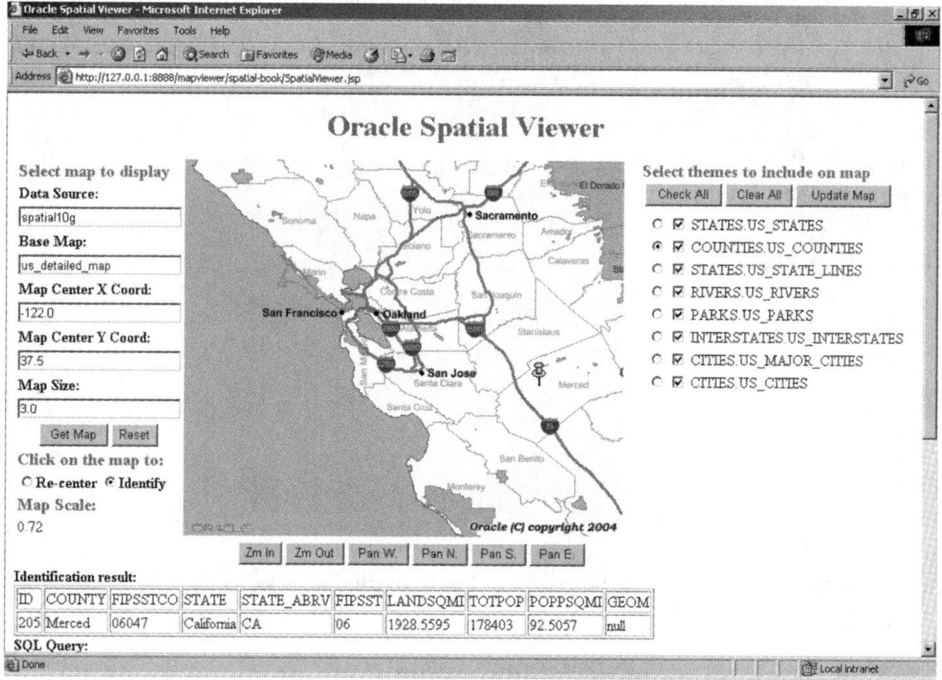

Figure 11-43. *Identifying spatial objects*

The main method to use is `identify()`. Its main drawback is that it works on *tables*, not *themes*. Also, you need to pass it the name of the geometry column to query.

Other methods are available to perform various queries. They all select from a chosen theme and can use image (pixel) or ground coordinates.

- `queryAtPoint()` selects features at a chosen point. Note that this works fine for polygons (areas), but not for points or lines, since it is impossible to guarantee that the mouse click falls exactly on the point or line.
- `queryWithinRadius()` selects all features that are completely inside a chosen radius from a point.
- `queryWithinRectangle()` selects all features that are completely inside a chosen rectangle (defined using the lower-left and upper-right corners).
- `queryWithinArea()` selects features that are inside a chosen polygon area.
- `queryNN()` selects the nearest features to a point.

A common parameter to all methods is the list of columns to select. This is passed as an array of strings (`String[]`). Passing a single string, *, is the same as passing the names of all columns.

All methods return their results as an array of string arrays (`String[][]`). The first row of strings contains the names of the columns. Each subsequent row contains the values for each column in each matching row. This format is easy to output in an HTML table.

Let's examine how the example in Figure 11-43 is programmed. First, the radio button for choosing the themes to select is constructed in much the same way as the theme selector you saw in an earlier example:

```
<table>
    <% String[] ts = mv.getThemeNames(); %>
    <% for(int i=0; i<ts.length; i++) {%>
    <tr><td>
    <input type="radio"
       name="identifyTheme"
       value="<%=ts[i]%>"
       <%=ts[i].equals(identifyTheme)?"checked":""%>
    >
    <%= ts[i] %>
    </td></tr>
  <%}%>
</table>
```

The result of checking the radio box is passed back to the JSP page. Here is how the name of the selected theme is extracted:

```
String identifyTheme = request.getParameter("identifyTheme");
```

The actual identification is performed as follows. First, we need to extract the coordinates of the mouse click:

```
imgCX = Integer.parseInt(request.getParameter("mapImage.x"));
imgCY = Integer.parseInt(request.getParameter("mapImage.y"));
```

Then we query the feature at that point:

```
String[] colsToSelect = new String[]{"*"};
String[][] featureInfo = mv.queryAtPoint (
    dataSource,              // Datasource
    identifyTheme,           // Theme name
    colsToSelect,            // Names of columns to select
    imgCX, imgCY,            // Mouse click
    null,                    // No extra conditions
    true);                   // Coords are in pixels
```

And we add a point at the place we clicked:

```
Point2D p = mv.getUserPoint(imgCX,imgCY);
mv.addPointFeature (p.getX(), p.getY(), 8307,"M.CYAN PIN", null, null, null);
```

Finally, we format the results as an HTML <table>:

```
<table border="1">
  <% for (int i=0; i<featureInfo.length; i++) {%>

    <tr>
    <% String[] row = featureInfo[i];
       for (int k=0; k<row.length; k++) {%>
        <td><%= row[k] %></td>
      <% } %>
    </tr>
  <% } %>
</table>
```

Dynamic Features

Some methods enable you to draw features on top of the map:

- addPointFeature() adds a point feature to the current map request.
- addLinearFeature() adds a line feature to the current map request.
- getNumGeoFeatures() returns the number of dynamic features added to the current map request.
- removeAllLinearFeatures() removes all the line features from the map request.
- removeAllPointFeatures() removes all the point features from the map request.

The features are defined by a list of coordinates, a rendering style, and a label style. The style names refer to styles that must exist on the MapViewer server, either as permanent styles or as dynamic styles that you created previously. For point features, you can optionally specify the radius for a number of circles to be drawn around the point.

You need to call the preceding methods before sending the map request to the MapViewer service—that is, before you call the run() method, or any of the zoom and pan methods.

Legend

The following methods let you control the legend of the map:

- setMapLegend() sets the map legend. There are two ways to define a legend. One is to construct the legend specification in XML according to the syntax of the <legend> element covered earlier in the chapter. The other is to construct the legend in a Java String array and pass that.
- getMapLegend() gets the map legend.
- deleteMapLegend() deletes the legend.

Here is how to generate the legend shown in Figure 11-44:

```
String legendSpec =
  "<legend profile=\"MEDIUM\" position=\"SOUTH_EAST\">\n"+
  "  <column>\n"+
  "    <entry text=\"Map Legend\" is_title=\"true\" />\n"+
  "    <entry text=\"Counties\"     style=\"C.FUNNY COLOR\" />\n"+
  "    <entry text=\"Rivers\"       style=\"C.RIVER\" />\n"+
  "    <entry text=\"Parks\"        style=\"C.PARK FOREST\" />\n"+
  "  </column>\n"+
  "  <column>
  "    <entry text=\" \" is_title=\"true\" />\n"+
  "    <entry text=\"Interstates\"  style=\"L.PH\" />\n"+
  "    <entry text=\"Major Cities\" style=\"M.CITY HALL 4\" />\n"+
  "  </column>\n"+
  "</legend>\n";
mv.setMapLegend(legendSpec);
```

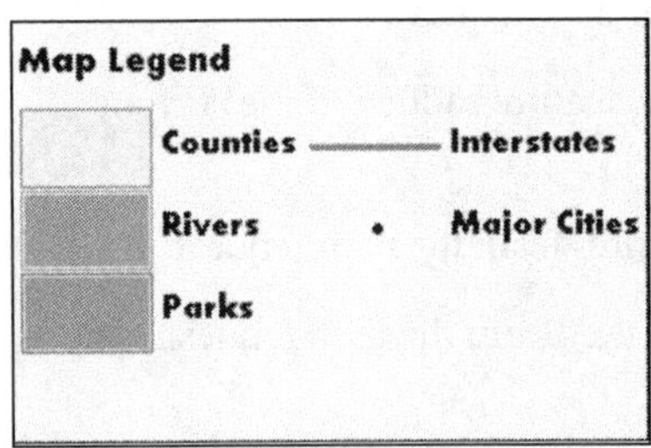

Figure 11-44. *Example of a legend*

Data Sources

So far, we have assumed that you know which data sources are available, which maps are defined, which themes exist, and so on. However there may be times when you need to discover dynamically what information exists. This is what the following methods let you do.

- `getDataSources()` gets the names of the data sources defined on the server. Those can be permanent data sources (defined in MapViewer's configuration file) or data sources dynamically added using the administrative API.
- `getBaseMapNames()` gets the names of all base maps defined in a data source.
- `getPredefinedThemes()` gets the name of all themes defined in a data source. A variant lets you find the themes used by a specific base map.
- `getPermanentStyles()` gets the list of styles defined in a data source.
- `dataSourceExists()` determines whether a data source exists on the server.

You can also dynamically define a new data source using the `addDataSource()` method. You need to pass the usual information needed for setting up a JDBC connection to an Oracle database (i.e., host name, port number, database name, user name, and password).

Using JSP Tags

Some applications may not need the full flexibility of the MapViewer Java API. For such applications, you can use a set of JSP tags that let you embed maps in JSP with minimal programming. Note that tags use the MapViewer Java API internally, which enables you to combine the use of the tags and the Java API in the same application.

■ **Note** See `http://127.0.0.1:8888/mapviewer/spatial-book/SimpleViewerTags.jsp`.

The definition of the JSP tags is in your MapViewer installation (at `$OC4J_HOME/lbs/mapviewer/web/WEB-INF/mvtaglib.tld`). You need to include a pointer to this file in your JSP pages.

Figure 11-45 shows the output of the `SimpleViewerTags.jsp` page. The center of the page shows the map produced by MapViewer. Interacting with the map uses a different technique from the previous examples: all interactions take place via mouse clicks on the map. A radio button underneath the map defines what happens when you click on the map:

- *Re-center*: A new map is produced, centered on the point clicked.
- *Zoom In*: The new map is centered on the point clicked, zoomed-in by a factor of two.
- *Zoom Out*: The new map is centered on the point clicked, zoomed-out by a factor of two.
- *Identify*: The application fetches the details about the county in which the mouse click is located and displays those details at the bottom of the page.

Under the radio buttons are the coordinates of the current center of the map, as well as the scale of the current map.

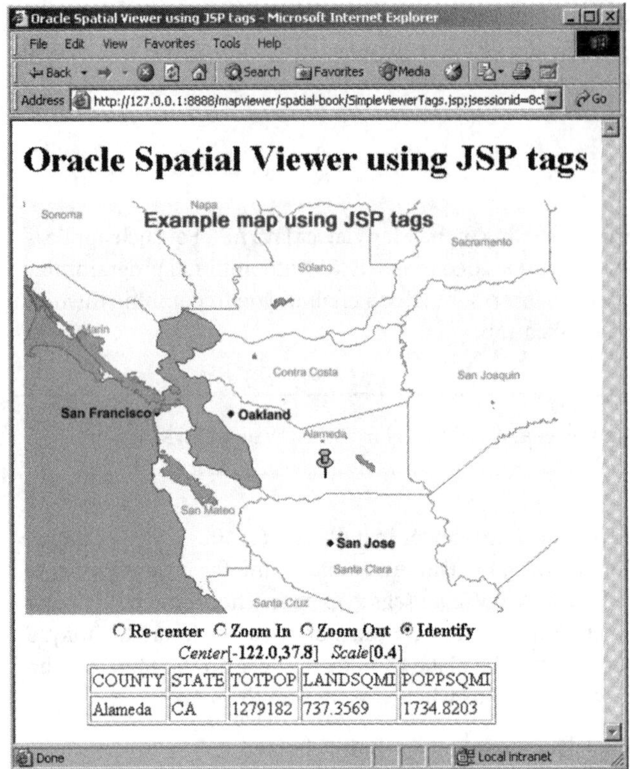

Figure 11-45. *JSP page that uses the MapViewer JSP tags*

Table 11-4 lists the JSP tags available.

Table 11-4. *JSP Tags for MapViewer*

Tag Name	Usage
`init`	Creates the MapViewer bean and places it in the current session. This tag must appear before any other MapViewer JSP tags.
`setParam`	Specifies one or more parameters for the current map request.
`importBaseMap`	Adds the predefined themes that are in the specified base map to the current map request.
`addPredefinedTheme`	Adds a predefined theme to the current map request.
`addJDBCTheme`	Adds a dynamically defined theme to the map request.
`makeLegend`	Creates a legend (map inset illustration) drawn on top of the generated map.
`run`	Submits the current map request to the MapViewer service for processing. The processing can be to zoom in or out, to recenter the map, or to perform a combination of these operations.
`getParam`	Gets the value associated with a specified parameter for the current map request.

Tag Name	Usage
getMapURL	Gets the HTTP URL for the currently available map image, as generated by the MapViewer service.
identify	Gets nonspatial attribute (column) values associated with spatial features that interact with a specified point or rectangle on the map display, and optionally uses a marker style to identify the point or rectangle.

We will now examine the main JSP tags and the way they are used in the example application.

Initialization and Setup: The init Tag

Your JSP application must include a pointer to the JSP tags library. It also must indicate that the JSP uses sessions to keep context. Finally, you may import the definitions of the MapViewer Java API if you want to use some of its features in conjunction with the JSP tags, as is the case in the example.

```
<%@ taglib uri="/WEB-INF/mvtaglib.tld" prefix="mv" %>
<%@ page session="true" %>
<%@ page import="oracle.lbs.mapclient.MapViewer" %>
```

Use the init tag to initialize the connection with the MapViewer servlet: it creates a MapViewer object and saves it in the session for the JSP page.

```
<!-- Initialize MapViewer handle and save it in the session -->
<mv:init
  url="<%=mapViewerURL%>"
  datasource="spatial10g"
  id="mvHandleSimpleViewerTags" />
```

- The url argument specifies the URL to the MapViewer server. Note that it is provided by a JSP substitution from variable mapViewerURL. This allows you to construct it dynamically from the request parameters, as shown in the discussion of the Java API.
- The datasource argument defines the name of the data source. This could also come from a substituted variable.
- The id argument is the name used to save the MapViewer object into the session for the JSP page. It must be constant (no substituted variable).

Setting Up the Map

Several tags are available to specify the format and content of the map. Here is how they are used in the example page.

First, we define the general size of the map in pixels, as well as the title to show on the map:

```
<!-- Set map format and size -->
<mv:setParam
  title="Example map using JSP tags"
  width="480"
  height="360"/>
```

Then we define the name of the base map to display together with any additional predefined themes:

```
<!-- Add themes from the base map -->
<mv:importBaseMap name="us_base_map"/>
<!-- Additional themes -->
<mv:addPredefinedTheme name="parks.us_parks"/>
```

Finally, we set the center and size of the map:

```
<!--  Set initial map center and size -->
<mv:setParam
  centerX="-122.0"
  centerY="37.8"
  size="1.5" />
```

In addition, you can use the addJDBCTheme tag to add themes based on SQL queries. This technique is not used in the example.

Interacting with the Map: The run Tag

The previously discussed tags only define the parameters for the map. To actually generate the map, use the run tag. The run tag does more than just generate a new map—it also allows you to dynamically interact with the map.

```
<mv:run
  action="<%=userAction%>"
  x="<%= imgCX %>"
  y="<%= imgCY %>" />
```

- The action argument defines the action to take against the current map. It can be specified as recenter, zoomin, or zoomout.
- The x and y arguments define the coordinates of the center of the new map. They are passed as image coordinates (i.e., they represent the coordinates of the mouse click in the map image).

In the preceding example, the action argument is provided by the userAction variable, which contains the current setting of the radio button displayed underneath the map image on the HTML page.

```
String userAction = request.getParameter("userAction");
```

The userAction request parameter contains the current setting of the radio button. Here is the HTML definition of the button:

```
<!-- Map click action  -->
<tr>
  <td align="center">
    <input type="radio" name="userAction" value="recenter"
      <%= "recenter".equals(userAction)?"checked":""%> ><B>Re-center</B>
    <input type="radio" name="userAction" value="zoomin"
      <%= "zoomin".equals(userAction)?"checked":""%> ><B>Zoom In</B>
    <input type="radio" name="userAction" value="zoomout"
      <%= "zoomout".equals(userAction)?"checked":""%> ><B>Zoom Out</B>
    <input type="radio" name="userAction" value="identify"
      <%= "identify".equals(userAction)?"checked":""%> ><B>Identify</B>
  </td>
</tr>
```

The x and y arguments are set from variables (imgCX and imgCY) that contain the coordinates of the mouse click:

```
String imgCX = request.getParameter("userClick.x");
String imgCY = request.getParameter("userClick.y");
```

Displaying the Map: The getMapURL Tag

This tag returns the URL of the map image produced by the run tag. Use it in your HTML code to display the map in an <img> tag or in an <input type="image"> tag, as follows:

```
<!-- Map display  -->
<tr>
  <td valign="top" align="center" >
  <input type="image"
     border="1"
     src="<mv:getMapURL />"
     name="userClick"
     alt="Click on the map for selected action"
  >
  </td>
</tr>
```

Getting Feature Details: The identify Tag

The identify tag lets you extract details about a selected feature and flag it on the map:

```
<mv:identify
  id="identifyResults"
  table="us_counties"
  spatial_column="geom"
  srid="8307"
```

```
  x="<%= imgCX %>" y="<%= imgCY %>"
  style="M.CYAN PIN">
  county, state_abrv state, totpop, landsqmi, poppsqmi
</mv:identify>
```

- id is the name of the variable (of type String[][]) that receives the results of the identification query. The first row of strings contains the names of the columns. Each subsequent row contains the values for each column in each matching row. This format is easy to output in an HTML table.
- table is the name of the table to query.
- spatial_column is the name of the spatial column to query in that table (of type SDO_GEOMETRY).
- srid is the coordinate system for that spatial column.
- x and y are the coordinates of the mouse click (in image coordinates).
- style is optional. If specified, it indicates the style to use for the symbol that marks the spot clicked on the resulting map. If omitted, then no mark is set on the map.

The content of the tag (county, etc.) represents the names of the columns to read from the specified table. Notice that the state_abrv column is renamed to state.

The results of the query are formatted as an HTML <table> as follows:

```
<!-- Identification result -->
<% if (featureInfo !=null && featureInfo.length>0) {%>
  <tr><td align="center">
  <table border="1">
    <% for (int i=0; i<featureInfo.length; i++) {%>
      <tr>
      <% String[] row = featureInfo[i];
         for (int k=0; k<row.length; k++) {%>
          <td><%= row[k] %></td>
         <% } %>
      </tr>
    <% } %>
  </table>
  </td></tr>
<% } %>
```

Combining MapViewer JSP Tags and the Java API

Since the JSP tags use a MapViewer object, you can combine the tags with MapViewer's Java API. This is particularly useful to extract various pieces of information from the MapViewer object not accessible through the JSP tags.

Before using MapViewer's Java API, you need to extract the MapViewer object saved in the page session:

```
MapViewer mvHandle = (MapViewer) session.getAttribute("mvHandleSimpleViewerTags");
```

The following HTML code displays the coordinates of the center of the current map, as well as the scale of that map, using the getRequestCenter() and getMapScale() methods of the MapViewer object:

```
<!-- Current position -->
<tr>
  <td align="center">
    <i>Center</i>[<b>
      <%=mvHandle.getRequestCenter().getX()+ ","+
        mvHandle.getRequestCenter().getY()%></b>]
    <i>Scale</i>[<b><%=mvHandle.getMapScale()%></b>]
  </td>
</tr>
```

Using the Administrative API

In addition to the map request APIs (XML and Java) described previously, MapViewer also provides an administrative API, which lets applications perform such actions as discovering data sources, maps, themes, and styles, or managing data sources and caches.

Browsing Map Definitions

The functions in the administrative API are useful to build generic applications that enable users to discover what map definitions exist. They let you find out the data sources defined on the MapViewer server, as well as browse the maps, themes, and styles defined in a data source. You can access those functions via the MapViewer home page (http://host:port/mapviewer).

Listing Data Sources

The following XML request returns a list of the data sources known by the server:

```
<?xml version="1.0" standalone="yes"?>
<non_map_request>
  <list_data_sources />
</non_map_request>
```

The response is an XML form that looks like this:

```
<?xml version="1.0" ?>
<non_map_response>
  <map_data_source_list succeed="true">
    <map_data_source name="spatial10g />
    <map_data_source name="mvdemo" />
  </map_data_source_list>
</non_map_response>
```

Note that this gives you only the names of the data sources. To obtain further details, such as JDBC connection details, you need to use a secure variant, which we discuss shortly.

You can also verify the existence of a data source:

```
<?xml version="1.0" standalone="yes"?>
<non_map_request>
  <data_source_exists data_source="mvdemo"/>
</non_map_request>
```

Listing Maps

The following XML request returns a list of the base maps defined for a data source:

```
<?xml version="1.0" standalone="yes"?>
<non_map_request>
  <list_maps data_source="spatial10g" />
</non_map_request>
```

The response is an XML form like this:

```
<?xml version="1.0" ?>
<non_map_response>
  <map_list succeed="true">
    <map name="CITY_MAP" />
    <map name="US_BASE_MAP" />
    <map name="US_CITY_MAP" />
    <map name="US_DETAILED_MAP" />
    <map name="WORLD_MAP" />
    <map name="WORLD_MAP_COLORED" />
  </map_list>
</non_map_response>
```

Listing Themes

Use the following request to get the list of all themes defined in a data source:

```
<?xml version="1.0" standalone="yes"?>
<non_map_request>
  <list_predefined_themes data_source="spatial10g" />
</non_map_request>
```

The response is an XML form that contains the names of the themes:

```
<?xml version="1.0" ?>
<non_map_response>
  <predefined_theme_list succeed="true">
    <predefined_theme name="COUNTRIES.WORLD_COUNTRIES" />
    <predefined_theme name="COUNTIES.US_COUNTIES" />
    <predefined_theme name="RIVERS.US_RIVERS" />
    <predefined_theme name="STATES.US_STATES" />
```

```
    <predefined_theme name="WORLD.WORLD_CONTINENTS" />
    <predefined_theme name="WORLD.WORLD_COUNTRIES" />
    <predefined_theme name="WORLD.WORLD_COUNTRIES_COLORED" />
  </predefined_theme_list>
</non_map_response>
```

You can also get the themes used in specific base map:

```
<?xml version="1.0" standalone="yes"?>
<non_map_request>
  <list_predefined_themes data_source="spatial10g" map="US_BASE_MAP"/>
</non_map_request>
```

The response lists the themes with their scale limits:

```
<?xml version="1.0" ?>
<non_map_response>
  <predefined_theme_list succeed="true">
    <predefined_theme name="STATES.US_STATES"
       min_scale="10.0" max_scale="5.0" />
    <predefined_theme name="COUNTIES.US_COUNTIES"
       min_scale="5.0" max_scale="0.0" />
    <predefined_theme name="STATES.US_STATE_LINES"
       min_scale="5.0" max_scale="0.0" />
    <predefined_theme name="CITIES.US_MAJOR_CITIES"
      min_scale="3.0" max_scale="0.15" />
    <predefined_theme name="CITIES.US_CITIES"
       min_scale="0.15" max_scale="0.0" />
  </predefined_theme_list>
</non_map_response></non_map_response>
```

Listing Styles

Use the following request to get the names of all styles defined in a data source. This list contains only the permanent styles (i.e., those stored in the database). Dynamically created styles do not appear.

```
<?xml version="1.0" standalone="yes"?>
<non_map_request>
  <list_styles data_source="spatial10g" />
</non_map_request>
```

The response is an XML form that looks like this:

```
<?xml version="1.0" ?>
<non_map_response>
  <style_list succeed="true">
    <style name="A.PATTERN 1" />
    ...
```

```
    <style name="V.WORLD_COUNTRIES" />
  </style_list>
</non_map_response>
```

You can restrict the list to specific style types by adding a `style_type` parameter.

Managing the MapViewer Server

Other functions in the Administrate API let you exercise some control over the MapViewer server. You can do the following:

- Manage data sources (JDBC connections) by adding, removing, and listing data sources.
- Manage caches by clearing data and metadata caches.
- Restart MapViewer after you change its configuration settings.

MapViewer comes with an HTML page that provides you access to the administrative API. You can get to that page by clicking the Admin button at the top right of the MapViewer home page (`http://host:port/mapviewer`). See Figure 11-46 for an example of the administration page.

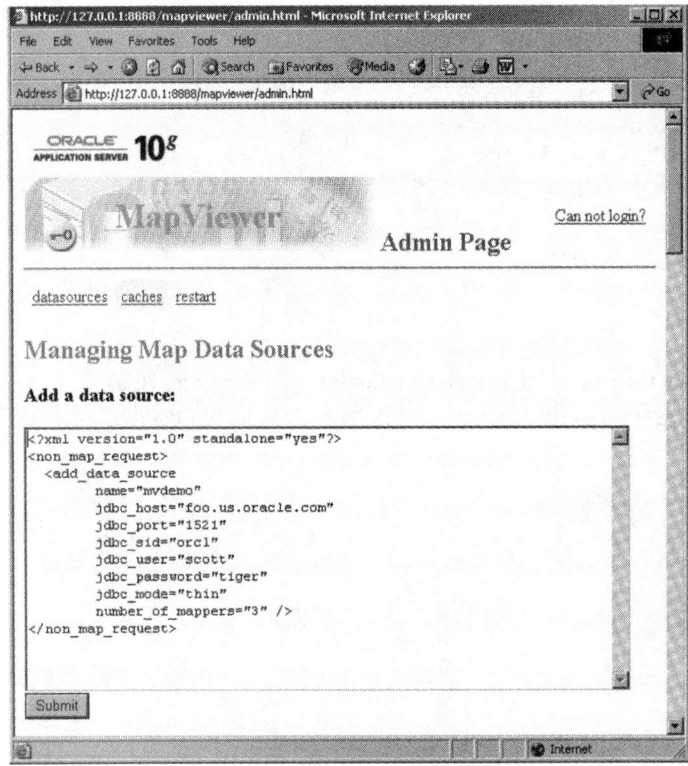

Figure 11-46. *MapViewer administration page*

Security and Access Control

The management functions are protected. When you attempt to call one, you will be asked to specify a user name and password.

If MapViewer is deployed in a stand-alone OC4J, then the user name will be "admin". The password is the admin password you specified when you installed the OC4J instance (at the prompt after you typed in `java -jar oc4j.jar -install`). If you have forgotten the password, you can repeat this installation command again, which will prompt for a new admin password.

When MapViewer is deployed in the Oracle Internet Application Server, you need to create an administration user in the OC4J instance where MapViewer is running and map this administration user to MapViewer's built-in security role, `map_admin_role`.

Managing Data Sources

One of the major functions of the administrative API is that it lets you dynamically manage the data sources. You can define new data sources, redefine existing data sources, and remove data sources. Those changes are temporary; they take place only in the running MapViewer server. Any new data source you define disappears if the MapViewer server is restarted.

Adding a Data Source

Here is the XML request you submit to define a new data source:

```
<?xml version="1.0" standalone="yes"?>
<non_map_request>
  <add_data_source
        name="spatial10g"
        jdbc_host="127.0.0.1"
        jdbc_port="1521"
        jdbc_sid="orcl101"
        jdbc_user="spatial"
        jdbc_password="spatial"
        jdbc_mode="thin"
        number_of_mappers="3" />
</non_map_request>
```

The data source will be available to all users of the MapViewer server. However, its definition is not persistent; the data source definition will disappear at the next shutdown of the server.

Listing Data Sources

The following XML request returns a list of the data sources known by the server:

```
<?xml version="1.0" standalone="yes"?>
<non_map_request>
  <list_data_sources />
</non_map_request>
```

The response is an XML form that looks like this:

```
<?xml version="1.0" ?>
  <non_map_response>
    <map_data_source_list succeed="true">
      <map_data_source name="spatial10g" host="127.0.0.1" sid="orcl101"
        port="1521" user="spatial" mode="thin" numMappers="3" />
      <map_data_source name="mvdemo" host="127.0.0.1" sid="orcl101"
        port="1521" user="mvdemo" mode="thin" numMappers="3" />
    </map_data_source_list>
  </non_map_response>
```

Note that this request can also be sent in a "nonprivileged" mode—that is, without being logged as the MapViewer administrator. In that case, the XML response lists only the data source names.

Modifying a Data Source

The following XML request changes the number of *mappers* (the maximum number of concurrent threads) and the maximum number of connections for a data source:

```
<?xml version="1.0" standalone="yes"?>
<non_map_request>
  <redefine_data_source
        name="spatial10g"
        jdbc_host="127.0.0.1"
        jdbc_port="1521"
        jdbc_sid="orcl101"
        jdbc_user="spatial"
        jdbc_password="spatial"
        jdbc_mode="thin"
        number_of_mappers="4"
        max_connections="40" />
</non_map_request>
```

Note that you cannot change the host, port, user name, or password. Those must match exactly the values specified when the data source was defined. If they do not, then you will receive an error indicating that the data source cannot be found.

To modify any of those parameters, you need to remove the data source and re-create it with the new parameters. You can modify the parameters for a permanent data source (one defined in MapViewer's configuration file), but those changes will disappear when MapViewer is restarted.

Removing a Data Source

To remove a data source, you must provide the JDBC password for that data source:

```
<?xml version="1.0" standalone="yes"?>
<non_map_request>
  <remove_data_source data_source="spatial10g" jdbc_password="spatial" />
non_map_request>
```

You can remove a permanent data source (one defined in MapViewer's configuration file), but it will come back when MapViewer is restarted.

Managing Caches

The MapViewer server maintains a cache for the data it reads from the database, as well as a cache for the map definitions, the *metadata cache*. The following commands enable you to clear those caches.

Clearing the Data Cache

Use this request to clear the data cache for a named theme in a named data source:

```
<?xml version="1.0" standalone="yes"?>
<non_map_request>
  <clear_theme_cache data_source="spatial10g" theme="us_states" />
</non_map_request>
```

Clearing the Metadata Cache

The following request clears the styles, maps, and themes from the cache of the MapViewer server for a given data source:

```
<?xml version="1.0" standalone="yes"?>
<non_map_request>
  <clear_cache data_source="spatial10g" />
</non_map_request>
```

This operation is necessary if you change any style, theme, or map definition in the database. It forces MapViewer to reload the definitions from the database the next time they are needed.

Restarting MapViewer

The following restarts the MapViewer server. All data and metadata caches are cleared, all data sources are closed, and all dynamically added data sources are removed. MapViewer then rereads the configuration file and starts up again.

```
<?xml version="1.0" standalone="yes"?>
<non_map_request>
  <restart/>
</non_map_request>
```

This operation is necessary if you change settings in MapViewer's configuration file, for example, if you add a new permanent data source, or if you modify the logging parameters.

Summary

In this chapter, you learned how to define maps, themes, and styles, and how to add maps to your applications. MapViewer is a very powerful product, and we touched on only the most important aspects of it. In the next chapter, we will use many of the techniques we presented here to build a complete application.

CHAPTER 12

■ ■ ■

A Sample Application

To create the sample application in this chapter, you need to load the following datasets and run the following scripts:

```
imp spatial/spatial file=app_data.dmp full=y
imp spatial/spatial file=gc.dmp full=y
imp spatial/spatial file=map_large.dmp full=y
imp spatial/spatial file=map_detailed.dmp full=y
imp spatial/spatial file=net.dmp full=y
imp spatial/spatial file=styles.dmp full=y
```

Throughout this book, you have learned many techniques relating to spatial technology: how to location-enable an application, how to perform spatial analysis, and how to view the results using dynamically generated maps.

The time has come to use all of these techniques in a single application that integrates spatial analysis and visualization. This chapter presents and dissects such an application. Table 12-1 lists the main requirements for the application, along with the features of Oracle Spatial exercised and the chapters that discuss those features.

Table 12-1. *Sample Application Requirements*

Application Requirement	Features Used
Display a map showing the locations of customers, competitors, and branches, along with additional geographical information such as streets, public buildings, administrative boundaries, and so on.	Map generation (Chapter 11)
Select the information to appear on the map, and allow the usual map navigation: zoom in and out, pan, and recenter.	Map generation (Chapter 11)
Enter a street address and center the map on that address.	Geocoding (Chapter 6)
Find all customers, competitors, or branches within a specified distance from a location on the map. This location could be the location of a branch, a customer, or a competitor, or a street address. The results are highlighted on the map.	Proximity analysis and geometry processing (Chapters 8 and 9)
Find a specified number of neighboring customers, competitors, or branches closest to a specified location on this map. This location could be the location of a customer, a competitor, or a branch, or a street address. The results are highlighted on the map.	Proximity analysis and geometry processing (Chapters 8 and 9)
Show the route between the origin location and the nearest neighbor returned by the preceding analysis.	Network modeling (Chapter 10)

We begin this chapter with a study of the data needed by the application. Much of that data should have been loaded and prepared as you proceeded through the examples in the preceding chapters.

We then walk you through the application, showing you how to install and run it, how to use it, and how the various functions of the application were implemented.

The complete source code is at the end of this chapter. It is also provided in the Downloads section of the Apress website (`www.apress.com`).

Data Preparation and Setup

The application requires several types of data before you can actually run it:

- *Geographical data*: This is the data that will appear as a "backdrop" on our map. Without it, you would see only colored dots, without anything to relate them to. This data includes the definition of a street network used for computing the shortest path between places, as well as the data used by the geocoder.
- *Location-enabled application tables*: The `branches`, `customers`, and `competitors` tables contain only street addresses. To use them in the application, they must first be extended with a spatial column (`SDO_GEOMETRY`), and this column must be populated.
- *Map definitions and styles*: The application uses a predefined map, themes, and styles.

Loading the Geographical Data

If you have not done so yet, now is the time to load your database with the base geographical data. For clarity and ease of use, we provide the data as several Oracle dump files.

You need to import those files using the Oracle Import tool. The code shown in Listing 12-1 performs the following actions:

- Loads the large-scale data (countries, states, counties, etc.).
- Loads the detailed data (city streets, etc.).
- Loads the street network.
- Loads the geocoding data.
- Loads the metadata required for the network definition into the metadata table, `USER_SDO_NETWORK_METADATA` (the metadata is imported together with the network data, but you still need to load it). See Chapter 10 for details.

Listing 12-1. *Loading the Geographical Data*

```
imp spatial/spatial file=map_large.dmp full=y
imp spatial/spatial file=map_detailed.dmp full=y
imp spatial/spatial file=net.dmp full=y
imp spatial/spatial file=gc.dmp full=y

SQL> INSERT INTO USER_SDO_NETWORK_METADATA
       SELECT * FROM my_network_metadata;
SQL> commit;
```

Location-Enabling the Application Tables

The three application tables, `branches`, `customers`, and `competitors`, must also be loaded, and then *spatially enabled*. We explained this process in Chapter 3 and detailed it further in Chapter 6. Listing 12-2 shows the process for the `branches` table only, but the process is identical for the other two tables (`customers` and `competitors`). Here's an outline of the basic steps:

1. Load the application tables.
2. Add a spatial column to each application table.
3. Geocode each table. Remember to commit the update.
4. Set up the spatial metadata for each table.
5. Create a spatial index on each table.

Listing 12-2. *Loading and Location-Enabling the Business Data*

```
imp spatial/spatial file=app_data.dmp full=y
SQL> ALTER TABLE branches ADD (location SDO_GEOMETRY);
SQL> UPDATE branches
```

```
    SET location = SDO_GCDR.GEOCODE_AS_GEOMETRY (
      'SPATIAL',
      SDO_KEYWORDARRAY (
         street_number || ' ' || street_name,
         city  || ' ' || postal_code),
      'US'
    );
SQL> COMMIT;
SQL> INSERT INTO USER_SDO_GEOM_METADATA (
       TABLE_NAME, COLUMN_NAME, DIMINFO, SRID)
     VALUES (
       'BRANCHES',
       'LOCATION',
       SDO_DIM_ARRAY(
         SDO_DIM_ELEMENT('Longitude', -180, 180, .5),
         SDO_DIM_ELEMENT('Latitude',   -90,  90, .5)),
       8307);
SQL> CREATE INDEX branches_sx ON branches (location)
       indextype is mdsys.spatial_index;
```

Loading Map and Style Definitions for MapViewer

Maps, themes, and style definitions are provided ready for use. All you need to do is to import them into the database. Importing the styles dump file creates and populates three tables: my_maps, my_themes, and my_styles. The definitions must still be loaded into the dictionary tables used by MapViewer. Listing 12-3 illustrates this process.

Listing 12-3. *Loading Map Definitions*

```
imp spatial/spatial file=styles.dmp full=y

SQL> INSERT into user_sdo_styles
       select * from my_styles;
SQL> insert into user_sdo_themes
       select * from my_themes;
SQL> insert into user_sdo_maps
       select * from my_maps;
SQL> commit;
```

PL/SQL Tools

The application needs to extract the longitude and latitude coordinates of the geocoded application tables. The usual way to do this is to extract the coordinates from the SDO_GEOMETRY objects—a technique that was described in Chapter 7—like this:

```
SQL> SELECT name, c.location.SDO_POINT.X x, c.location.SDO_POINT.Y y
     FROM customers c;
NAME                                        X          Y
----------------------------------- ---------- ----------
A CAPITOL PLACE BED &BREAKFAST       -76,99022  38,888654
A NA AUTO SERVICE                   -77,015277   38,90242
...
```

However, that technique requires that the query use a table alias (c in the preceding example), which MapViewer does not currently support. So, you will need to use a couple of simple stored functions instead. Create them as shown in Listing 12-4.

Listing 12-4. *Functions to Extract x and y Coordinates*

```
SQL> CREATE OR REPLACE FUNCTION get_point_x(g SDO_GEOMETRY) RETURN
NUMBER IS
     BEGIN
       RETURN g.SDO_POINT.X;
     END;
     /
SQL> CREATE OR REPLACE FUNCTION get_point_y(g SDO_GEOMETRY) RETURN
NUMBER IS
     BEGIN
       RETURN g.SDO_POINT.Y;
     END;
     /
```

The functions are used like this:

```
SQL> SELECT name, get_point_x(location) x, get_point_y(location) y
     FROM customers;
NAME                                        X          Y
----------------------------------- ---------- ----------
A CAPITOL PLACE BED &BREAKFAST       -76,99022  38,888654
A NA AUTO SERVICE                   -77,015277   38,90242
...
```

Application Walk-Through

Let's first walk through the application from a user's perspective and see what it can do. Then we will look under the hood to see how the various features and functions are implemented.

Setting Up the Application

The first step is to make sure that you have a running Oracle Application Server or, at a minimum, the stand-alone Oracle Containers for Java (OC4J) software. You also need to have the MapViewer component up and running.

If you ran any of the examples presented in Chapter 11, then you should be all set. If not, just refer back to Chapter 11; specifically, review the section titled "Getting Started with MapViewer." This section includes instructions on how to install and set up the OC4J software.

All you then need to do is copy the file `SampleApplication.jsp` into `$OC4J_HOME/lbs/mapviewer/web/spatial-book/sample-app`, where `$OC4J_HOME` is the root folder where you installed OC4J.

Starting the Application

Enter the following URL in your browser:

```
http://127.0.0.1:8888/mapviewer/spatial-book/sample-app/SampleApplication.jsp
```

Note that this URL assumes you installed OC4J on your local machine. If you installed it on some other machine, then just replace IP address `127.0.0.1` with that of your server.

If your setup is correct, you should now see a page like the one shown in Figure 12-1.

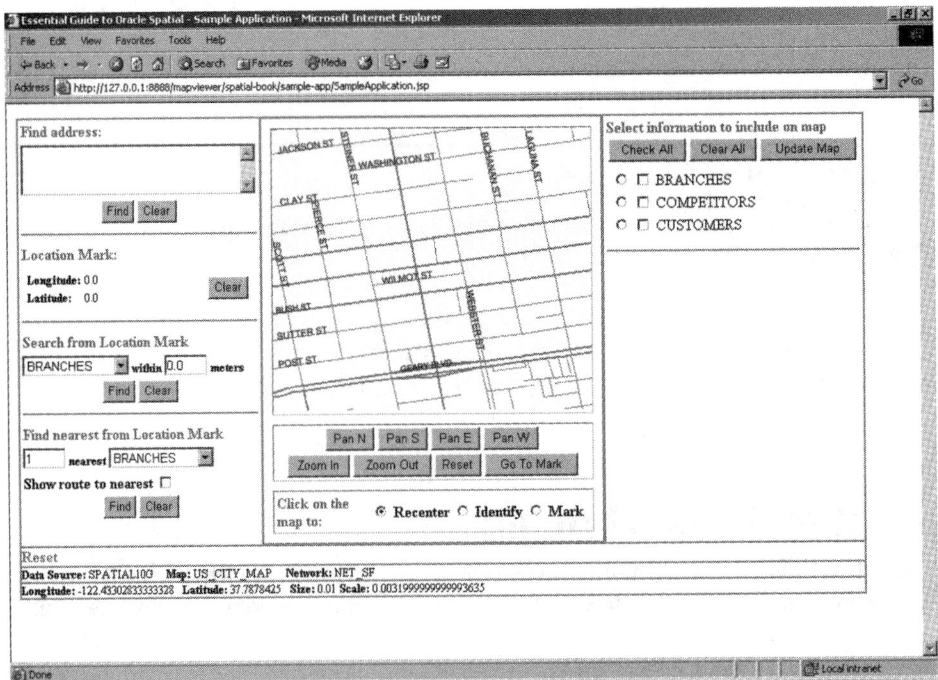

Figure 12-1. *Home page of the sample application*

Notice that the map is centered on downtown San Francisco. The initial center and size of the map is actually controlled by parameters you can pass to the application. For example, the following URL positions the initial map on downtown Washington, D.C.:

```
http://127.0.0.1:8888/mapviewer/spatial-book/sample-app/SampleApplication.jsp➥
?initialCx=-77.03497825&initialCy=38.90819015
```

Application Home Page

The home page of the application consists of three main windows:

- The center window contains the map proper, with navigation buttons and controls. This is also where you indicate what should happen when you click on the map.
- The left window lets you enter an address on which to position the map. It also shows the current position of the location mark (see the next section for details) and lets you perform searches around it.
- The right window lets you control what application data should appear on the map—that is, which application themes (branches, customers, or competitors) should be enabled. Once a theme is displayed on a map, the application will allow you to click that theme (e.g., a particular branch) and display details specific to that theme. This information will also appear in the right window (though it is not visible in Figure 12-1).

The bottom of the page contains a status window (where the word "Reset" appears). This window is where the application displays the SQL statements it sends to the database. It also uses the status window to report any errors.

A second status window shows various pieces of information, such as the name of the data source used to connect to the database, the name of the base map used, and the name of the network. The second row shows the current center and size of the map, as well as the current scale.

Location Mark

The left window shows the current position (longitude and latitude) of a *location mark*. Initially, there is no mark set, and the coordinates are shown as zero.

The location mark is the pivotal concept of the application: you use functions provided by the application to set the location mark, and other functions to perform searches and analyses from that mark.

You can set the location mark by entering a street address; by selecting a branch, customer, or competitor; or simply by clicking on the map. This logic is illustrated in Figure 12-2.

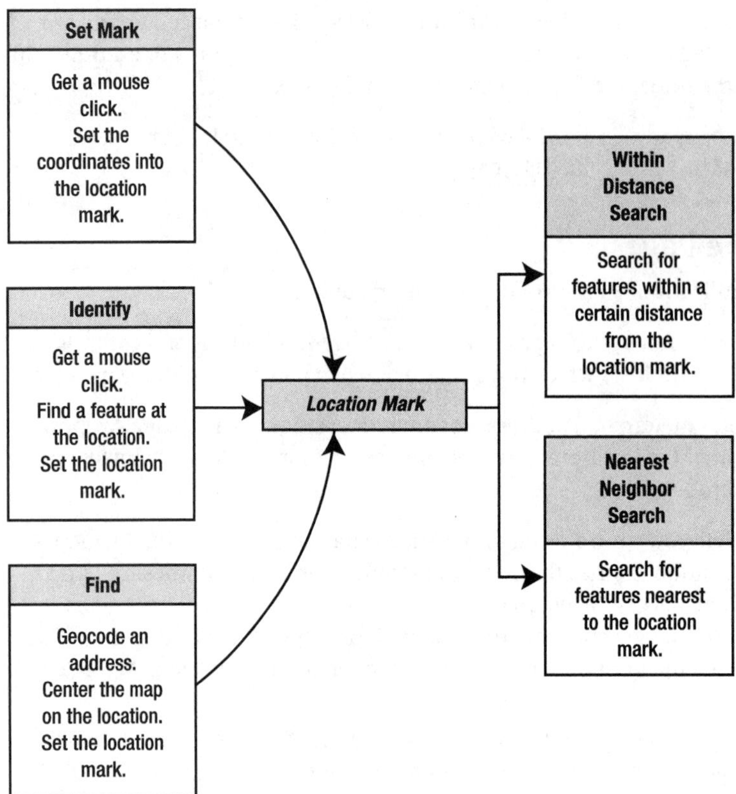

Figure 12-2. *Using the location mark*

The current position of the location mark is shown on the map using a yellow pin. The Clear button next to the Location Mark setting resets it to zero. It also removes the yellow pin marker from the map.

Zooming, Panning, and Recentering

The application provides buttons for navigating around the map and adjusting the zoom level:

- The Pan buttons are used to shift the map in the indicated direction.
- The Zoom In and Zoom Out buttons do exactly what you would expect them to do.
- The Reset button essentially restarts the application. It resets the map to the origin settings and clears all query and search results as well as the location mark.
- The Go To Mark button is an easy way to recenter the map on the current coordinates of the location mark.

You can also reposition the map by simply clicking on it. Make sure the radio button below the map is set to Recenter.

Adding Application Data to the Map

The window on the right side of the page shows a list of business tables, from which you can select data to incorporate into the map. Next to each table name is a radio button and a check box. Select the check box for each of the tables that you want to use to populate the map, and click the Update Map button.

The map in the center window is then refreshed with the tables you have chosen. Branches appear as green triangles, customers appear as blue lozenges, and competitors appear as red squares. Notice that not all these elements are labeled. This is because MapViewer tries its best to not overlay labels, as shown in Figure 12-3 in the next section.

The Clear All and Check All buttons clear and set all application themes, respectively. Note that you still need to click the Update Map button to refresh the map.

Positioning on a Street Address

You can reposition the map at any time by simply entering a valid street address in the window at the top left and clicking the Find button. Be sure to format the address on two lines. For example, you can enter the following address:

```
600 Stockton Street
San Francisco, CA
```

The address is marked with a yellow pin. The right-side window shows the normalized and corrected address.

■ **Note** The first time you position the map to a street address after starting up the application server, you will notice a delay. This is because the Oracle geocoder initializes itself by reading and parsing the address-description parameters in the database.

If the address you entered is incorrect or could not be found, the status window at the bottom of the page will indicate this to you. Otherwise, you will see the SQL statement sent to the database to call the geocoding function.

Note that the yellow pin indicates the current position of your location mark. The coordinates (longitude and latitude) of that location mark are shown in the left window. This mark is important: you will use it as a starting point for searches.

Figure 12-3 shows the result of positioning the map on the preceding address and showing the branches.

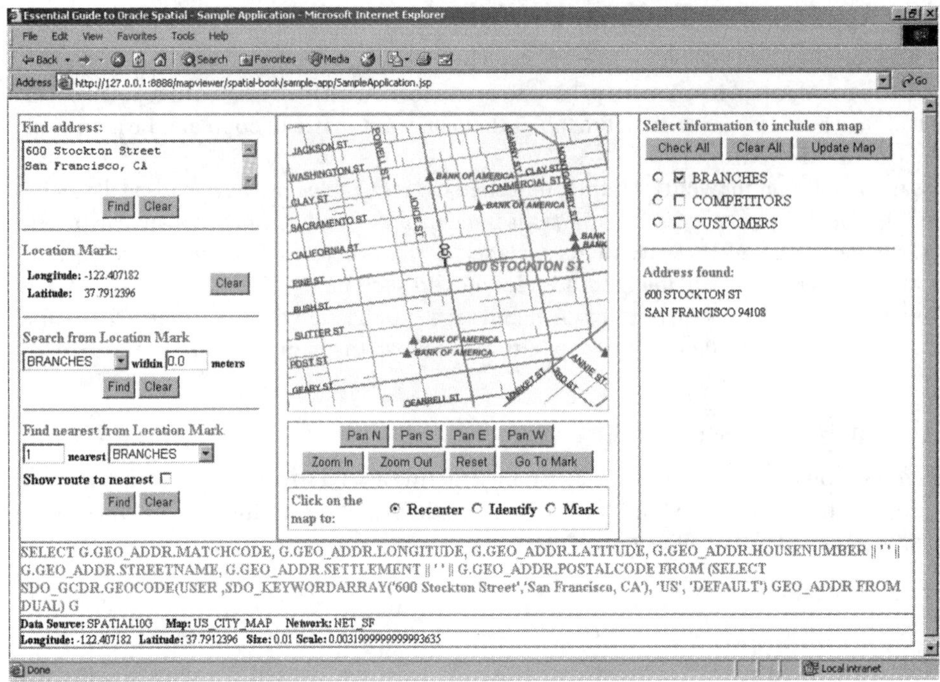

Figure 12-3. *Map positioned on an address*

Identifying a Branch, Customer, or Competitor

Now that you see all the application data (branches and so forth), let's find out more about them by selecting one of them using the mouse.

Before doing so, you need to tell the application which of the application themes you will be selecting from. For example, select the radio button in front of the `branches` table in the selection window.

You also need to tell the application what it should do when you click on the map. For example, you should indicate that when you next click on the map, you do not want to reposition it on the point you clicked; rather, you want to get information on the application theme object (the branch) that is on the map on that point. For that, make sure to select the Identify option.

Now to select a branch, simply move the mouse on the symbol for that branch (the green triangle) and click. The branch is marked with a yellow pin, and details on the branch are shown inside the right window.

Figure 12-4 shows the results of identifying a branch.

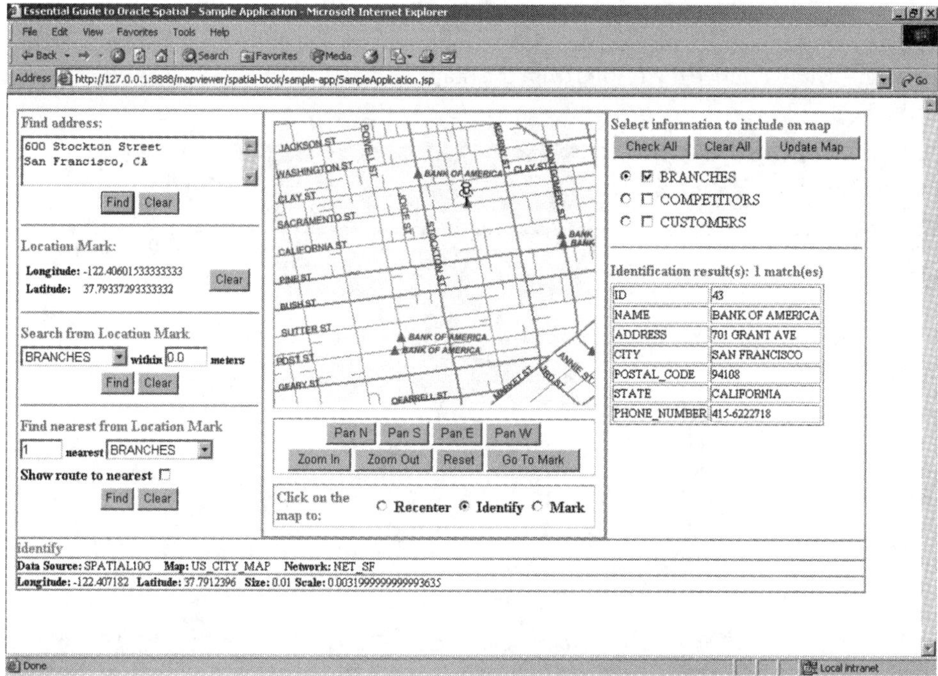

Figure 12-4. *Identifying a branch*

The location mark is now set to the location of the branch you just selected. You can use this mark to search from the selected branch. The process is identical to select a customer or a competitor.

■ **Note** The selection could actually return multiple matches (multiple customers or competitors) if they are at the same address or are very close together.

Searching "Within Distance"

The application only lets you search for visible information. In other words, the table you want to search (`branches`, `customers`, or `competitors`) must be shown on the map.

Remember that to make a table visible, you need to select the check box directly in front of the table's name in the right window, and then click the Update Map button.

Next, go to the "Search from Location Mark" area of the left window. Select the `competitors` table from the drop-down list and enter a distance (e.g., 150 meters). Then click the Find button.

The new map marks all competitors within 150 meters with a blue pin. The competitors' details are shown in the right window, as illustrated in Figure 12-5. Notice the new SEARCH RESULTS theme that appears in the right window to represent the dynamic results of the search. You can uncheck it to remove the results from the map.

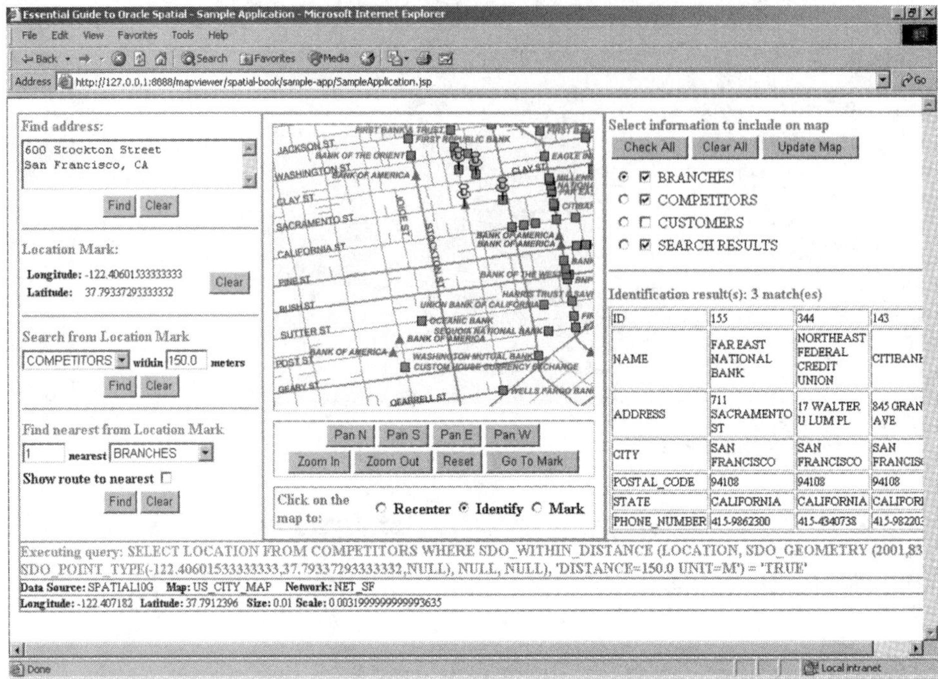

Figure 12-5. *Results of a "within distance" search*

Note that the search radius could be larger than the area currently shown on the map. All matches will be returned, even those that are outside the current map window. However, you will have to zoom out manually to make those matches appear on the map.

The SQL query used to find those competitors is shown in the status window. Clicking the Clear button in the search area removes the query results from the map.

You can repeat this operation for customers. First add the customers to the map, and then select the `customers` table from the drop-down list and click the Find button.

Setting a Mark on the Map

You can also set the location mark directly on the map. This lets you perform searches from anyplace. All you need to do is select the Mark option under the map window, and then click anywhere on the map.

The location mark, identified by the yellow pin, is now set to the place you clicked.

Searching for Nearest Neighbors

Navigate to the "Find nearest from Location Mark" area of the left window. Select the `branches` table from the drop-down list and enter the number of branches to show. Then click the Find button.

The result is much like the one from the previous search: the three nearest branches to the location mark you set are marked with blue pins, and their details are shown in the window on the right.

Note that the nearest branch may actually be far away and outside the area currently shown on the map. You will see it by zooming out.

The status window shows the SQL query used to find the nearest branches.

Route Calculation

Select the "Show route to nearest" check box in the "Find nearest from Location Mark" area of the left window, and then repeat the search by clicking the Find button again. The map will now highlight the route to the first branch returned by the query. Figure 12-6 shows the three nearest branches to the current location mark, with the route to the nearest one highlighted.

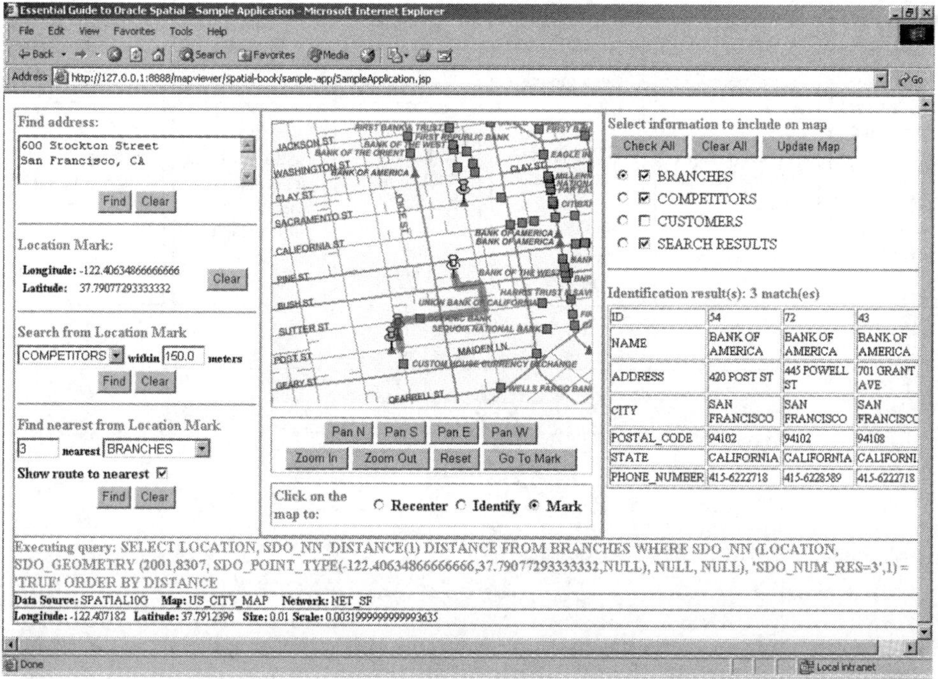

Figure 12-6. *Results of a "nearest neighbor" search*

Under the Hood

The general logic of the application is fairly simple, as shown in Figure 12-7. The application is written as a single JavaServer Page (JSP), which contains the application logic proper (in Java) as well as the HTML output.

The HTML page contains a single form. All user actions (e.g., button presses and mouse clicks on the map) are posted back to the JSP as request parameters.

The main logic of the application is therefore as follows:

- Parse the request parameters.
- Process the user request.
- Display the HTML output.

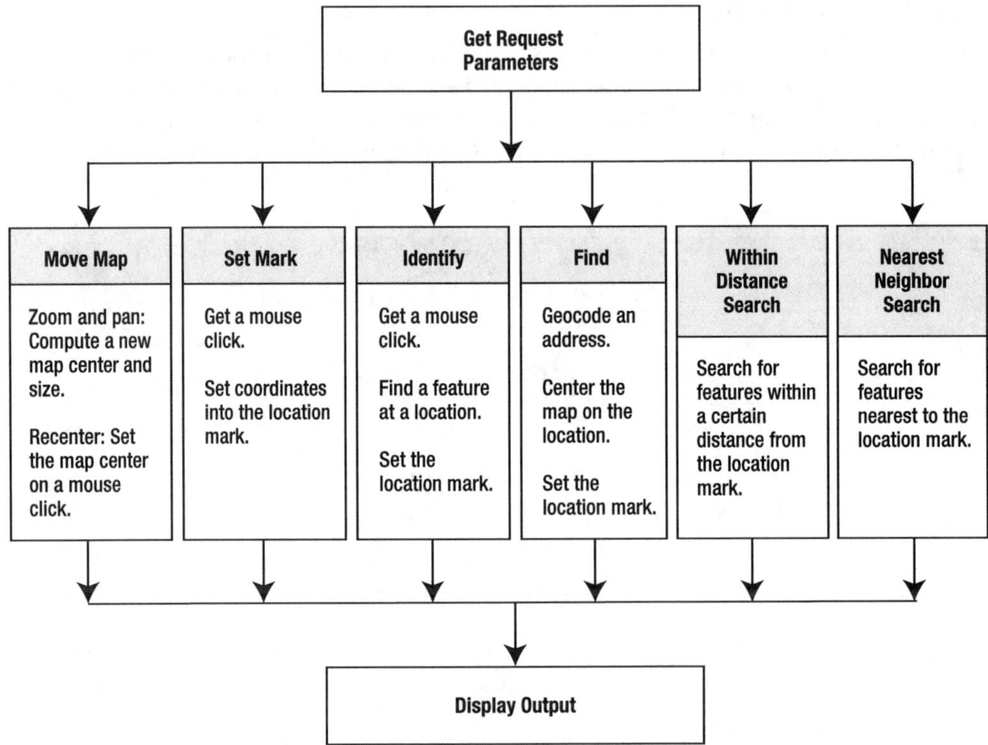

Figure 12-7. *Flow of the sample application*

The complete source code for the application is at the end of this chapter, in Listing 12-16. We will now look at the major functions implemented by the application.

Initialization: The "Reset" Action

This is where you initialize the `MapViewer` and `Network` objects and save them in your session. Here, you also set up and request the initial map. See Listing 12-5 for the source code.

Note that this action is called under three circumstances:

- When the application is launched the first time
- When the user clicks the Reset button
- If the `MapViewer` object is no longer in the session, which means the session expired

The name of the base map, as well as the data source, the initial center and size of the map, and the size of the map in pixels are all defined in variables. The defaults are such that the initial map is positioned on downtown San Francisco.

Listing 12-5. Reset *Action*

```
// ---------------------------------------------------------------------------
// [Reset] button clicked
// Initialize the MapViewer object with the original center and size
// Load the network representation
// ---------------------------------------------------------------------------
if (userAction.equals("Reset")) {

  // Create and initialize new MapViewer object)
  mv = new MapViewer(mapViewerURL);
  mv.setDataSourceName(dataSource);                       // Data source
  mv.setBaseMapName(baseMap);                             // Base map
  for(int i=0; i<appThemes.length; i++) {                 // Additional themes
    mv.addPredefinedTheme(appThemes[i]);                  // Theme name
    mv.setThemeScale(appThemes[i],
      appThemeMinScale, 0.0);                             // Scale limits
  }
  mv.setAllThemesEnabled(false);                          // Themes disabled
  mv.setMapTitle("  ");                                   // No title
  mv.setImageFormat(MapViewer.FORMAT_PNG_URL);            // Map format
  mv.setDeviceSize(new Dimension(mapWidth, mapHeight)); // Map size

  // Save MapViewer object in session
  session.setAttribute("MapviewerHandle", mv);

  // Get JDBC database connection
  InitialContext ic  = new InitialContext();
  DataSource ds = (DataSource) ic.lookup(dataSource);
  Connection conn = ds.getConnection();

  // Load network
  net = NetworkManager.readNetwork(conn, networkName);

  // Save Network object in session
  session.setAttribute("NetworkHandle", net);

  // Release database connection
  conn.close();

  // Set initial map position and display it
  mv.setCenterAndSize(initialCx, initialCy, initialSize);
  mv.run();
```

```
    // Set default options
    clickAction = "recenter";
    showRoute = false;
    markX = 0;
    markY = 0;
  }
```

Zooming, Panning, and Recentering

Zooming is straightforward. We just use the `zoomIn()` or `zoomOut()` method of the `MapViewer` object. Those methods take a zoom factor value as argument. To make the application more flexible, this factor is defined in a variable:

```
double zoomFactor = 1.5;            // Zoom factor
```

The `zoomIn()` and `zoomOut()` methods behave like the `run()` method: they submit a map request to the MapViewer server and process the response. The source code for using these methods is shown in Listing 12-6.

Listing 12-6. Zoom *Actions*

```
// ----------------------------------------------------------------------
// [Zoom XXX] button clicked
// Zoom in or out by a fixed factor
// ----------------------------------------------------------------------
else if (userAction.equals("Zoom In"))
  mv.zoomIn(zoomFactor);
else if (userAction.equals("Zoom Out"))
  mv.zoomOut(zoomFactor);
```

Panning is just as straightforward as zooming. The `pan()` method of the `MapViewer` object recenters the map to a new location. Note that the coordinates `pan()` expects should be in image coordinates (not in geographical coordinates).

Like the `zoomIn()` and `zoomOut()` methods, `pan()` submits a new map request to the MapViewer server and processes the response. The source code is shown in Listing 12-7.

Listing 12-7. Pan *Actions*

```
// ----------------------------------------------------------------------
// [Pan XXX] button clicked
// Shift map 50% in the desired direction.
// ----------------------------------------------------------------------
else if (userAction.equals("Pan W"))
  mv.pan (0, mapHeight/2);
else if (userAction.equals("Pan N"))
  mv.pan (mapWidth/2, 0);
```

```
else if (userAction.equals("Pan S"))
  mv.pan (mapWidth/2, mapHeight);
else if (userAction.equals("Pan E"))
  mv.pan (mapWidth, mapHeight/2);
```

Recentering the map to the point identified by a mouse click is easy as well. All you need to do is extract the coordinates of the mouse click. They are passed as subattributes `.x` and `.y` of the attribute that corresponds to the map image on the HTML page (defined as an input element of type image).

Again, the fact that the `pan()` method uses image coordinates makes the repositioning easy to write—just pass it the coordinates of the mouse click directly. It will convert the coordinates to geographical coordinates and submit a new map request. The source code is shown in Listing 12-8.

Listing 12-8. reCenter *Action*

```
// -----------------------------------------------------------------
// Map clicked to recenter
// Use the coordinates of the clicked point as new map center
// -----------------------------------------------------------------
else if (userAction.equals("reCenter")) {
  // Extract coordinates of mouse click
  int imgCX = Integer.parseInt(request.getParameter("mapImage.x"));
  int imgCY = Integer.parseInt(request.getParameter("mapImage.y"));
  // Pan to that position
  mv.pan (imgCX, imgCY);
}
```

Adding Application Data to the Map

The application themes (whose names are defined in the variable `appThemes`) are initially not visible. Their visibility is controlled using the `enableThemes()` method of the `MapViewer` object, as shown in Listing 12-9.

The list of themes to be enabled is in the variable `checkedThemes[]`. This is a string array that is populated from the request parameter of the same name, which itself gets set via a `<checkbox>` element in the HTML page. If that list is empty, then you use the `setAllThemesEnabled(false)` method to disable all the application themes. Finally, the `run()` method requests a refresh of the map.

Listing 12-9. updateMap *Action*

```
// -----------------------------------------------------------------
// [Update Map] button clicked
// Enable the themes selected by the user and refresh the map
// -----------------------------------------------------------------
else if (userAction.equals("Update Map")) {
  if (checkedThemes == null)
    mv.setAllThemesEnabled(false);
```

```
    else
      mv.enableThemes(checkedThemes);
    mv.run();
  }
```

Positioning on a Street Address

Let's now examine how to position the map on a street address. For that, you call the geocoder and use the resulting coordinates. The format of the address must be acceptable to the geocoder: the application passes it to the geocoder exactly as you type it. For U.S. addresses, you can write the address on two, three, or more lines. See Chapter 6 for details.

After splitting the input address, you construct the SQL statement to call the geocoder. Here you will submit the query using the `doQuery()` method of the `MapViewer` object. However, just like `identify()`, the `doQuery()` method returns the result as arrays of strings—it cannot return objects. You therefore need to write the query in a slightly convoluted way to extract individual results from the `SDO_GEO_ADDR` object returned by the call to the geocoder.

A typical query sent to the database looks like this:

```
SELECT G.GEO_ADDR.MATCHCODE,
       G.GEO_ADDR.LONGITUDE,
       G.GEO_ADDR.LATITUDE,
       G.GEO_ADDR.HOUSENUMBER || ' ' || G.GEO_ADDR.STREETNAME,
       G.GEO_ADDR.SETTLEMENT || ' ' || G.GEO_ADDR.POSTALCODE
FROM (
  SELECT SDO_GCDR.GEOCODE(
           USER,
           SDO_KEYWORDARRAY(
              '600 Stockton Street','San Francisco, CA'),
           'US', 'DEFAULT')
           GEO_ADDR
  FROM DUAL) G
```

Once the query is completed, you extract the results: the match code, the longitude and latitude, and the first address line.

You then add a point feature (a yellow pin) at the location returned and save the coordinates as the new value for the location mark. Note that the point feature is also labeled with the corrected address returned by the geocoder.

Listing 12-10 shows the source code.

Listing 12-10. Find *Action*

```
// ------------------------------------------------------------------
// [Find] button clicked:
// Geocode the entered address.
// Center map on the resulting coordinates.
// Set mark on that point.
// ------------------------------------------------------------------
else if (userAction.equals("Find")) {
```

```
// Extract address details
String[] addressLines = findAddress.split("\r\n");

// Construct query to geocoder
String gcQuery =
  "SELECT "+
  "G.GEO_ADDR.MATCHCODE, G.GEO_ADDR.LONGITUDE, "+
  "G.GEO_ADDR.LATITUDE, " +
  "G.GEO_ADDR.HOUSENUMBER || ' ' || G.GEO_ADDR.STREETNAME, " +
  "G.GEO_ADDR.SETTLEMENT || ' ' || G.GEO_ADDR.POSTALCODE " +
  "FROM (SELECT SDO_GCDR.GEOCODE(USER ,SDO_KEYWORDARRAY(";
for (int i=0; i<addressLines.length; i++) {
  gcQuery = gcQuery + "'" + addressLines[i] + "'";
  if (i < addressLines.length-1)
    gcQuery = gcQuery + ",";
}
gcQuery = gcQuery + "), 'US', 'DEFAULT') " +
"GEO_ADDR FROM DUAL) G";

// Send query
String[][] f = mv.doQuery(dataSource, gcQuery);

// Extract match code. Proceed only if > 0
int matchCode = Integer.parseInt(f[1][0]);
if (matchCode > 0) {

  // Extract X and Y coordinates from geocode result
  double destX = Double.valueOf(f[1][1]).doubleValue();
  double destY = Double.valueOf(f[1][2]).doubleValue();

  // Extract full street address from result
  String streetAddress = f[1][3];

  // Transform result from row-major to column-major
  geocodeInfo = new String[f[0].length-3];
  for (int i=0; i<f[0].length-3; i++)
    geocodeInfo[i] = f [1][i+3];

  // Center map on the new address and zoom in
  mv.setCenterAndSize(destX, destY, markerMapSize);

  // Remove any existing marker
  mv.removeAllPointFeatures();

  // Remove any route from that mark
  mv.removeAllLinearFeatures();
```

```
      // Add a marker at the point clicked and label it
      // with the first address line
      mv.addPointFeature (
        destX, destY,
        mapSrid,
        markerStyle,
        streetAddress,
        markerLabelStyle,
        null,
        true);

      // Save new mark
      markX = destX;
      markY = destY;

      // Show SQL statement
      mapError = gcQuery;

      // Refresh map
      mv.run();
    }
    else
      mapError = "Address not found";
  }
```

Identifying a Branch, Customer, or Competitor

Here is how you get details about business data shown on the map: branches, customers, and competitors.

The first step is, as for other map click actions, to get the coordinates of the point clicked on the map. You also verify that a theme (branches, customers, or competitors) is selected for identification, and that the theme is also shown on the map.

You then use the `identify()` method of the `MapViewer` object. This method is passed the name of the theme to select from as well as the list of columns to return. It also needs the coordinates of the mouse click.

Since you are selecting points, it is impossible to click exactly on the point to identify. You therefore enlarge the area of the click by passing a small rectangular region to the method. This rectangle is constructed by specifying the coordinates of the lower-left and upper-right corners as 4 pixels away from the user click.

The `colsToSelect` argument defines the name of the columns to return:

```
String[] colsToSelect                // Columns to select for application themes
  = new String[]{
    "ID",
    "NAME",
    "STREET_NUMBER||' '||STREET_NAME ADDRESS",
```

```
        "CITY",
        "POSTAL_CODE",
        "STATE",
        "PHONE_NUMBER",
        "GET_POINT_X(LOCATION) LONGITUDE",
        "GET_POINT_Y(LOCATION) LATITUDE"
    };
```

Note that you ask for the street_number and street_name columns to be concatenated. Notice also the last two columns, where you use the get_point_x() and get_point_y() functions to return the coordinates of the selected object. Those functions are described in Listing 12-4 at the beginning of this chapter.

The result of the identify() method is an array of string arrays (String[][]). The first row of strings contains the names of the columns, and the following row contains the value returned for each column. You transpose this result into another array, so that the first *column* contains the column names, and the subsequent columns contain the corresponding values.

Finally, proceed the same way as for the manual setting of the mark: add a point feature on the object found and save the coordinates as the new value for the location mark.

Listing 12-11 shows the source code.

Listing 12-11. identify *Action*

```
// ----------------------------------------------------------------------
// Map clicked to identify a feature.
// Get the coordinates of the clicked point
// use them to query the feature from the selected theme
// ----------------------------------------------------------------------
else if (userAction.equals("identify")) {

  // Extract coordinates of mouse click
  int imgCX = Integer.parseInt(request.getParameter("mapImage.x"));
  int imgCY = Integer.parseInt(request.getParameter("mapImage.y"));

  if (identifyTheme == null)
    mapError = "No theme selected to identify";
  else if (!mv.getThemeEnabled(identifyTheme))
    mapError = "Theme "+identifyTheme+" is not visible";
  else {

    // Locate the feature and get details
    // Notes:
    //   1. The identify() method needs a TABLE NAME, not a theme name.
    //      We just assume that the theme and table name are the same.
    //   2. We query a rectangle of 4 pixels around the user click. Notice,
    //      however, that pixels have their origin at the UPPER-LEFT corner
    //      of the image, whereas ground coordinates use the LOWER-LEFT
    //      corner.
```

```
    String[][] f = mv.identify(dataSource, identifyTheme, colsToSelect,
      geoColumn, mapSrid,
      imgCX-4, imgCY+4,
      imgCX+4, imgCY-4,
      false);

    // The result is one row per matching record, but we want to display
    // results as one column per record.
    if (f!= null && f.length > 0) {
      featureInfo = new String[f[0].length][f.length];
      for (int i=0; i<f.length; i++)
        for (int j=0; j<f[i].length; j++)
          featureInfo[j][i] = f [i][j];
      featuresFound = f.length-1;
    } else
      mapError = "No matching " + identifyTheme + " found";

    if (featuresFound > 0) {

      // Remove any existing marker
      mv.removeAllPointFeatures();

      // Remove any route from previous mark
      mv.removeAllLinearFeatures();

      // Add a marker at the point clicked
      Point2D p = mv.getUserPoint(imgCX,imgCY);
      mv.addPointFeature (p.getX(), p.getY(),
        mapSrid, markerStyle, null, null, null);

      // Save new mark
      markX = p.getX();
      markY = p.getY();

      // Refresh map
      mv.run();
    }
  }
}
```

■ **Note** The `identify()` method needs a *table name* as input, not a *theme name*. MapViewer does not provide a method to retrieve the name of the table associated with a theme. For this application, you assume that the themes to identify have the same names as the tables they use: the `competitors` theme is defined on the `competitors` table.

Setting a Mark on the Map

As for the *reCenter* action, you first must get the coordinates of the point just clicked for this action. You then use the `addPointFeature()` method to define a new point feature to the map.

However, the `addPointFeature()` method wants geographical coordinates, so you must first convert the mouse click from image to geographical coordinates, using the `getUserPoint()` method:

```
Point2D p = mv.getUserPoint(imgCX,imgCY);
```

This method returns a `java.awt.geom.Point2D` object, from which you extract the x and y coordinates, and pass them to `addPointFeature()`. You also save those coordinates as the location mark (i.e., in the `markX` and `markY` variables).

The `markerStyle` argument defines the style to be used for rendering the location mark on the map. It is defined as follows:

```
String markerStyle ="M.YELLOW PIN"; // Style for location mark
```

The source code is shown in Listing 12-12.

Listing 12-12. setMark *Action*

```
// ----------------------------------------------------------------------
// Map clicked to set a mark
// Get the coordinates of the clicked point and use them to set a mark
// at that point
// ----------------------------------------------------------------------
else if (userAction.equals("setMark")) {

  // Extract coordinates of mouse click
  int imgCX = Integer.parseInt(request.getParameter("mapImage.x"));
  int imgCY = Integer.parseInt(request.getParameter("mapImage.y"));

  // Remove any existing marker
  mv.removeAllPointFeatures();

  // Remove any route from previous mark
  mv.removeAllLinearFeatures();

  // Add a marker at the point clicked
  Point2D p = mv.getUserPoint(imgCX,imgCY);
  mv.addPointFeature (p.getX(), p.getY(),
    mapSrid, markerStyle, null, null, null);

  // Save new mark
  markX = p.getX();
  markY = p.getY();
```

```
    // Refresh map
    mv.run();
  }
```

Searching "Within Distance"

All the code you have seen so far deals with displaying the map and locating places, filling the location mark. The rest of the code will use the location mark as a starting point for performing searches.

The first search operation is to find all the customers, branches, or competitors that are within a chosen distance from the current location mark. The source code for this is in Listing 12-13.

First check if all the information is available to do the search: the location mark must have been set (either manually; by going to a street address; or by selecting a branch, customer, or competitor). The theme to search must be visible. You can only search for customers, for example, if they are shown on the map.

You want the results of the search in two formats:

- Highlight the matching objects on the screen (mark them with blue pins).
- Show information about each object (name, address, telephone number, etc.).

Unfortunately, MapViewer provides no method that can combine both effects. You therefore have to perform the two operations separately.

You will start by constructing a SQL query that uses the `SDO_WITHIN_DISTANCE` operator. You will then add this query to the map as a dynamic JDBC theme, using the `addJdbcTheme()` method. The `queryStyle` argument defines the style to be used for rendering the results on the map. It is defined as follows:

```
String queryStyle = "M.CYAN PIN";    // Style for query result markers
```

Continue by using the `queryWithinRadius()` method. This method returns all objects in a theme that are within a chosen radius from a starting point. Just like the `identify()` and `doQuery()` methods, the results are returned as a string array that you have to reformat.

■ **Note** The distance is entered in meters. This is because `queryWithinRadius()` has no mechanism to let the user specify a unit for the radius to search. The radius is always assumed to be in the units used for the theme being queried or meters if the theme is in a geodetic coordinate system, which is the case in this example. Allowing the user to choose a different unit is left as an exercise for the reader.

Listing 12-13. distSearch *Action*

```
// ------------------------------------------------------------------------
// [distSearch] button clicked
// Search for all neighbors within distance D from the current set mark.
// ------------------------------------------------------------------------
```

```
else if (userAction.equals("distSearch")) {
  if (markX == 0 && markY == 0)
    mapError = "No address or mark set";
  else if (!mv.getThemeEnabled(distSearchTheme))
    mapError = "Theme "+distSearchTheme+" is not visible";
  else if (distSearchParam <= 0)
    mapError = "Enter search distance";
  else {

    // Construct spatial query
    String sqlQuery = "SELECT "+geoColumn+" FROM " + distSearchTheme
      + " WHERE SDO_WITHIN_DISTANCE ("+ geoColumn + ","
      + " SDO_GEOMETRY (2001," + mapSrid + ", SDO_POINT_TYPE("
      + markX + "," + markY + ",NULL), NULL, NULL), "
      + "'DISTANCE="+distSearchParam+" UNIT=M') = 'TRUE'";
    mapError = "Executing query: "+ sqlQuery;

    // Add a JDBC theme to highlight the results of the query
    mv.addJDBCTheme (
      dataSource,                 // Data source
      "SEARCH RESULTS",           // Theme to search
      sqlQuery,                   // SQL Query
      geoColumn,                  // Name of spatial column
      null,                       // srid
      queryStyle,                 // renderStyle
      null,                       // labelColumn
      null,                       // labelStyle
      true                        // passThrough
    );

    // Perform the query
    String[][] f = mv.queryWithinRadius(
      dataSource,                 // Data source
      distSearchTheme,            // Theme to search
      colsToSelect,               // Names of columns to select
      null,                       // Extra condition
      markX, markY,               // Center point (current mark)
      distSearchParam,            // Distance to search
      false                       // Center point is in ground coordinates
    );

    if (f!= null && f.length > 0) {

      // The result is one row per matching record, but we want to display
      // results as one column per record.
      featureInfo = new String[f[0].length][f.length];
```

```
        for (int i=0; i<f.length; i++)
          for (int j=0; j<f[i].length; j++)
            featureInfo[j][i] = f [i][j];
        featuresFound = f.length-1;

        // Refresh map
        mv.run();

      } else
        mapError = "No matching " + distSearchTheme + " found";

    }
  }
```

Searching for Nearest Neighbors

The "nearest neighbor" search is similar to the previous case. The only differences are that you generate a query that uses the `SDO_NN` operator, and you use the `queryNN()` method of the `MapViewer` object instead of the `queryWithinRadius()` method. The source code is in Listing 12-14.

Listing 12-14. nnSearch *Action*

```
// ----------------------------------------------------------------------
// [nnSearch] button clicked
// Search the N nearest neighbors from the current set mark.
// ----------------------------------------------------------------------
else if (userAction.equals("nnSearch")) {
  if (markX == 0 && markY == 0)
    mapError = "No address or mark set";
  else if (!mv.getThemeEnabled(nnSearchTheme))
    mapError = "Theme "+nnSearchTheme+" is not visible";
  else if (nnSearchParam <= 0)
    mapError = "Enter number of matches to search";
  else {

    // Construct spatial query
    String sqlQuery = "SELECT "+geoColumn+", SDO_NN_DISTANCE(1) DISTANCE"
      + " FROM " + nnSearchTheme
      + " WHERE SDO_NN ("+ geoColumn + ","
      + " SDO_GEOMETRY (2001," + mapSrid + ", SDO_POINT_TYPE("
      + markX + "," + markY + ",NULL), NULL, NULL), "
      + "'SDO_NUM_RES="+nnSearchParam+"',1) = 'TRUE'"
      + " ORDER BY DISTANCE";
    mapError = "Executing query: "+ sqlQuery;
```

```
    // Add a JDBC theme to highlight the results of the query
    mv.addJDBCTheme (
      dataSource,                   // Data source
      "SEARCH RESULTS",             // Theme to search
      sqlQuery,                     // SQL Query
      geoColumn,                    // Name of spatial column
      null,                         // srid
      queryStyle,                   // renderStyle
      null,                         // labelColumn
      null,                         // labelStyle
      true                          // passThrough
    );

    // Perform the query
    String[][] f = mv.queryNN(
      dataSource,                   // Data source
      nnSearchTheme,                // Theme to search
      colsToSelect,                 // Names of columns to select
      nnSearchParam,                // Number of neighbors
      markX, markY,                 // Center point (current mark)
      null,                         // Extra condition
      false,                        // Center point is in ground coordinates
      null
    );

    if (f== null || f.length == 0)
      mapError = "No matching " + nnSearchTheme + " found";
    else {

      // The result is one row per matching record, but we want to display
      // results as one column per record.
      featureInfo = new String[f[0].length][f.length];
      for (int i=0; i<f.length; i++)
        for (int j=0; j<f[i].length; j++)
          featureInfo[j][i] = f [i][j];
      featuresFound = f.length-1;

      // Refresh map
      mv.run();
    }
  }
}
```

Route Calculation

The "nearest neighbor" search has one more feature: if the user selected the "Show route to nearest" option, then the application is expected to highlight the route from the current location mark to the nearest neighbor. The source code for this is in Listing 12-15.

The various network-based searches provided by the `NetworkManager` class only operate between nodes. In this application, you *snap* the location mark and destination to the nearest network nodes. The first step is therefore to use the `SDO_NN` operator in a SQL query to find the nearest nodes. The SQL query is submitted using the `doQuery()` method of MapViewer.

Once you have the identifiers of both nodes, getting the shortest path between them is a simple matter of calling the `NetworkManager.shortestPath()` method.

The `Path` you receive has no associated geometry yet. You use its `computeGeometry()` method to populate it, and then use the `getGeometry()` method to extract it as a `JGeometry` object.

Finally, you call the `addLinearFeature()` method of MapViewer to add it to the map. The style used is `L.TRANSPARENT`. This style is semitransparent, so the route does not obscure the underlying details on the map.

Listing 12-15. *Calculating a Route*

```
if (showRoute) {

  // Extract coordinates of destination node
  double destX = Double.valueOf(f[1][numVisibleCols]).doubleValue();
  double destY = Double.valueOf(f[1][numVisibleCols+1]).doubleValue();

  // Snap destination to nearest network node
  String qd = "SELECT NODE_ID FROM " + net.getNodeTableName()
    + " WHERE SDO_NN ("+net.getNodeGeomColumn() + ","
    + " SDO_GEOMETRY (2001," + mapSrid + ", SDO_POINT_TYPE("
    + destX + "," + destY + ",NULL), NULL, NULL), "
    + "'SDO_NUM_RES=1') = 'TRUE'";
  String [][] sd  = mv.doQuery(dataSource, qd);
  int destNodeId = Integer.parseInt(sd[1][0]);

  // Snap start (mark) to nearest network node
  String qs = "SELECT NODE_ID FROM " + net.getNodeTableName()
    + " WHERE SDO_NN ("+net.getNodeGeomColumn() + ","
    + " SDO_GEOMETRY (2001," + mapSrid + ", SDO_POINT_TYPE("
    + markX + "," + markY + ",NULL), NULL, NULL), "
    + "'SDO_NUM_RES=1') = 'TRUE'";
  String [][] ss  = mv.doQuery(dataSource, qs);
  int startNodeId = Integer.parseInt(ss[1][0]);

  // Get path from mark to destination node
  Path p = NetworkManager.shortestPath(net, startNodeId, destNodeId);

  // Check that we got a valid path back
  if (p != null && p.getNoOfLinks() > 0) {
```

```
        // Compute path geometry
        p.computeGeometry(0.5);
        JGeometry g = p.getGeometry();

        // Add route geometry to map
        mv.addLinearFeature (
          g.getOrdinatesArray(),              // Ordinates
          mapSrid,                            // SRID
          "L.TRANSPARENT",                    // Line style
          null,                               // Label column
          null                                // Label style
        );

      } else
        mapError = "Unable to compute route";

    }
```

Summary

In this chapter, we described how to create a sample application to perform a variety of spatial and network analysis, and integrate the results with visualization using MapViewer.

We explained how to set up each component, such as the geocoder and MapViewer, and how to integrate these components in a simple application. This application can be easily integrated into the business logic of most Oracle applications.

In the next chapter, we describe several case studies using Oracle Spatial technology in different applications. These case studies will give you an idea of how businesses are using and integrating different components of spatial functionality.

Application Source Code

Listing 12-16 contains the complete source code of the example application. This code is also provided in the Downloads section of the Apress website (`www.apress.com`).

Listing 12-16. *Example Application*

```
<!--

This is an application that illustrates how to integrate various
features of Oracle Spatial into a web-based application.

It supports the following actions

- display of a base map showing street-level information
- overlay the map with business data (customers, branches, and competitors)
- zoom, pan, and recenter the map
- select a customer, branch, or competitor and display details
```

```
- enter a street address and center the map on that address
- set location marks using mouse clicks
- find all customers (or branches or competitors) that are within a chosen distance
  from a location mark or customer (or branch or competitor)
- find the N nearest customers (or branches or competitors) from a location mark
  or customer (or branch or competitor)
- show the shortest route from the location mark to the nearest customer (or branch
  or competitor).

The application also shows the SQL queries it sends to the database to do the
"within distance" and "nearest neighbor" searches).

The JSP can be called with parameters to define the initial
map to display: map name, data source, initial center, and size:

  dataSource
  baseMap
  initialCx
  initialCy
  initialSize

In addition, the parameter "debug" adds a display of the XML
requests and responses.

-->

<%@ page contentType="text/html;charset=UTF-8"%>
<%@ page language="java" %>
<%@ page import="java.net.*" %>
<%@ page import="java.io.*" %>
<%@ page import="java.awt.geom.Point2D" %>
<%@ page import="java.awt.Dimension" %>
<%@ page import="javax.naming.*" %>
<%@ page import="javax.sql.*" %>
<%@ page import="java.sql.*" %>
<%@ page import="oracle.lbs.mapclient.MapViewer" %>
<%@ page import="oracle.spatial.geometry.*" %>
<%@ page import="oracle.spatial.network.*" %>

<%

  // Constants
  int    mapWidth = 350;               // Map width in pixels
  int    mapHeight = 300;              // Map height in pixels
  String defDataSource = "SPATIAL10G";// Default data source name
  String defBaseMap = "US_CITY_MAP";  // Default map name
  String defNetwork = "NET_SF";       // Default network name
```

```
double defCx = -122.43302833333328; // Default origin longitude
double defCy = 37.7878425;          // Default origin latitude
double defMapSize = 0.01;           // Initial map size
double zoomFactor = 1.5;            // Zoom factor
int    mapSrid = 8307;              // Map coordinate system
String[] appThemes                  // Application themes
  = new String [] {
    "BRANCHES",
    "COMPETITORS",
    "CUSTOMERS"
  };
double appThemeMinScale = 0.005;    // Scale at which app themes are displayed
String[] colsToSelect               // Columns to select for application themes
  = new String[]{
    "ID",
    "NAME",
    "STREET_NUMBER||' '||STREET_NAME ADDRESS",
    "CITY",
    "POSTAL_CODE",
    "STATE",
    "PHONE_NUMBER",
    "GET_POINT_X(LOCATION) LONGITUDE",
    "GET_POINT_Y(LOCATION) LATITUDE"
  };
int numVisibleCols = 7;             // Number of columns to display for searches
String geoColumn = "LOCATION";      // Name of geometry column in app themes
double markerMapSize = 0.01;        // Map size of map for address searches
String markerStyle ="M.YELLOW PIN"; // Style for location mark
String markerLabelStyle             // Style for address label
  = "T.ADDRESS_MARK_NAME";
String queryStyle = "M.CYAN PIN";   // Style for query result markers

// Name of this JSP
String jspURL = response.encodeURL(request.getRequestURI());

// URL of MapViewer servlet
String mapViewerURL  =
  "http://"+ request.getServerName()+":"
    + request.getServerPort()
    + request.getContextPath()+"/omserver";

// Static request parameters
String dataSource = null;           // Data source name
String baseMap = null;              // Map name
double initialCx = 0;               // Initial Map center X in map coordinates
double initialCy = 0;               // Initial Map center Y in map coordinates
```

```
double initialSize = 0;              // Initial Map size in map coordinates
boolean debug = false;               // Debug mode
String networkName = null;           // Name of network for network-based searches

// Current map and search parameters
double cx = 0;                       // Current map center X in map coordinates
double cy = 0;                       // Current map center Y in map coordinates
double mapSize = 0;                  // Current map size in map coordinates

double mapScale = 0;                 // Scale of the current map
String[] checkedThemes;              // List of checked themes
String identifyTheme;                // Name of theme to identify
double markX = 0;                    // Mark X
double markY = 0;                    // Mark Y
String findAddress;                  // Street address to find
int nnSearchParam;                   // Number of matches for NN search

String nnSearchTheme;                // Theme to search for nearest neighbors
boolean showRoute;                   // Show route to nearest neighbor
double distSearchParam;              // Distance for within distance search
String distSearchTheme;              // Theme to search for within distance search

// User action
String userAction = null;            // User requested action
String clickAction = null;           // Action to perform on mouse click

// HTML output
String imgURL = "";                  // URL of returned map
String mapRequest = "";              // Map request (XML)
String mapResponse = "";             // Map response (XML)
String mapError = "";                // Error or information message
int featuresFound = 0;               // Number of features found
String[][] featureInfo = null;       // Attributes of selected features
String[] geocodeInfo = null;         // Result of geocode operation

// Load static request parameters
dataSource = request.getParameter("dataSource");
if (dataSource != null)
  dataSource = dataSource.toUpperCase();
else
  dataSource = defDataSource;
baseMap = request.getParameter("baseMap");
if (baseMap != null)
  baseMap = baseMap.toUpperCase();
else
  baseMap = defBaseMap;
initialCx = request.getParameter("initialCx") != null ?
```

```
  Double.valueOf(request.getParameter("initialCx")).doubleValue() : defCx;
initialCy = request.getParameter("initialCy") != null ?
  Double.valueOf(request.getParameter("initialCy")).doubleValue() : defCy;
initialSize = request.getParameter("initialSize") != null ?
  Double.valueOf(request.getParameter("initialSize")).doubleValue() : defMapSize;
debug = request.getParameter("debug") != null ?
  Boolean.valueOf(request.getParameter("debug")).booleanValue(): false;
networkName = request.getParameter("networkName");
if (networkName != null)
  networkName = networkName.toUpperCase();
else
  networkName = defNetwork;

// Load dynamic request parameters:

// - Current location mark
markX = request.getParameter("markX") != null ?
  Double.valueOf(request.getParameter("markX")).doubleValue() : 0;
markY = request.getParameter("markY") != null ?
  Double.valueOf(request.getParameter("markY")).doubleValue() : 0;

// - List of checked themes and theme to identify
checkedThemes = request.getParameterValues("checkedThemes");
identifyTheme = request.getParameter("identifyTheme");

// - Address to find
findAddress = request.getParameter("findAddress");
if (findAddress == null)
  findAddress = "";

// - Nearest neighbor search parameters
nnSearchParam = request.getParameter("nnSearchParam") != null ?
  Integer.parseInt(request.getParameter("nnSearchParam")) : 1;
nnSearchTheme = request.getParameter("nnSearchTheme");
showRoute = request.getParameter("showRoute") != null ?
  Boolean.valueOf(request.getParameter("showRoute")).booleanValue(): false;

// - Within distance search parameters
distSearchParam = request.getParameter("distSearchParam") != null ?
  Double.valueOf(request.getParameter("distSearchParam")).doubleValue() : 0;
distSearchTheme = request.getParameter("distSearchTheme");

// Reload MapViewer from session (if present)
MapViewer mv = (MapViewer) session.getAttribute("MapviewerHandle");
// Reload Network from session (if present)
Network net = (Network) session.getAttribute("NetworkHandle");
```

```
// Get user action. Default is "Reset"
userAction = request.getParameter("userAction");
if (userAction == null || mv == null)
  userAction = "Reset";
clickAction = request.getParameter("clickAction");
if (clickAction == null)
  clickAction = "reCenter";
if (request.getParameter("mapImage.x") != null)
  userAction = clickAction;
if (request.getParameter("distSearch") != null)
  userAction = "distSearch";
if (request.getParameter("nnSearch") != null)
  userAction = "nnSearch";
if (request.getParameter("clearSearch") != null)
  userAction = "Clear Search";
mapError = userAction;

// Dispatch and process user action
if (userAction != null) {

  // ---------------------------------------------------------------------
  // [Reset] button clicked
  // Initialize the MapViewer object with the original center and size
  // Load the network representation
  // ---------------------------------------------------------------------
  if (userAction.equals("Reset")) {

    if (mv == null)
      mapError = "Session lost - Resetting";

    // Create and initialize new MapViewer object)
    mv = new MapViewer(mapViewerURL);
    mv.setDataSourceName(dataSource);                    // Data source
    mv.setBaseMapName(baseMap);                          // Base map
    for(int i=0; i<appThemes.length; i++) {              // Additional themes
      mv.addPredefinedTheme(appThemes[i]);               // Theme name
      mv.setThemeScale(appThemes[i],
        appThemeMinScale, 0.0);                          // Scale limits
    }
    mv.setAllThemesEnabled(false);                       // Themes disabled
    mv.setMapTitle("  ");                                // No title
    mv.setImageFormat(MapViewer.FORMAT_PNG_URL);         // Map format
    mv.setDeviceSize(new Dimension(mapWidth, mapHeight)); // Map size

    // Save MapViewer object in session
    session.setAttribute("MapviewerHandle", mv);
```

```
    // Get JDBC database connection
    InitialContext ic = new InitialContext();
    DataSource ds = (DataSource) ic.lookup(dataSource);
    Connection conn = ds.getConnection();

    // Load network
    net = NetworkManager.readNetwork(conn, networkName);

    // Save Network object in session
    session.setAttribute("NetworkHandle", net);

    // Release database connection
    conn.close();

    // Set initial map position and display it
    mv.setCenterAndSize(initialCx, initialCy, initialSize);
    mv.run();

    // Set default options
    clickAction = "reCenter";
    showRoute = false;
    markX = 0;
    markY = 0;
  }

  // ------------------------------------------------------------------------
  // [Zoom XXX] button clicked
  // Zoom in or out by a fixed factor
  // ------------------------------------------------------------------------
  else if (userAction.equals("Zoom In"))
    mv.zoomIn(zoomFactor);
  else if (userAction.equals("Zoom Out"))
    mv.zoomOut(zoomFactor);

  // ------------------------------------------------------------------------
  // [Pan XXX] button clicked
  // Shift map 50% in the desired direction.
  // ------------------------------------------------------------------------
  else if (userAction.equals("Pan W"))
    mv.pan (0, mapHeight/2);
  else if (userAction.equals("Pan N"))
    mv.pan (mapWidth/2, 0);
  else if (userAction.equals("Pan S"))
    mv.pan (mapWidth/2, mapHeight);
  else if (userAction.equals("Pan E"))
    mv.pan (mapWidth, mapHeight/2);
```

```
// ------------------------------------------------------------------------
// Map clicked to recenter
// Use the coordinates of the clicked point as new map center
// ------------------------------------------------------------------------
else if (userAction.equals("reCenter")) {
  // Extract coordinates of mouse click
  int imgCX = Integer.parseInt(request.getParameter("mapImage.x"));
  int imgCY = Integer.parseInt(request.getParameter("mapImage.y"));
  // Pan to that position
  mv.pan (imgCX, imgCY);
}

// ------------------------------------------------------------------------
// [Update Map] button clicked
// Enable the themes selected by the user and refresh the map
// ------------------------------------------------------------------------
else if (userAction.equals("Update Map")) {
  if (checkedThemes == null)
    mv.setAllThemesEnabled(false);
  else
    mv.enableThemes(checkedThemes);
  mv.run();
}

// ------------------------------------------------------------------------
// Map clicked to set a mark
// Get the coordinates of the clicked point and use them to set a mark
// at that point
// ------------------------------------------------------------------------
else if (userAction.equals("setMark")) {

  // Extract coordinates of mouse click
  int imgCX = Integer.parseInt(request.getParameter("mapImage.x"));
  int imgCY = Integer.parseInt(request.getParameter("mapImage.y"));

  // Remove any existing marker
  mv.removeAllPointFeatures();

  // Remove any route from previous mark
  mv.removeAllLinearFeatures();

  // Add a marker at the point clicked
  Point2D p = mv.getUserPoint(imgCX,imgCY);
  mv.addPointFeature (p.getX(), p.getY(),
    mapSrid, markerStyle, null, null, null);
```

```
    // Save new mark
    markX = p.getX();
    markY = p.getY();

    // Refresh map
    mv.run();
  }

  // ---------------------------------------------------------------------------
  // Map clicked to identify a feature.
  // Get the coordinates of the clicked point
  // use them to query the feature from the selected theme
  // ---------------------------------------------------------------------------
  else if (userAction.equals("identify")) {

    // Extract coordinates of mouse click
    int imgCX = Integer.parseInt(request.getParameter("mapImage.x"));
    int imgCY = Integer.parseInt(request.getParameter("mapImage.y"));

    if (identifyTheme == null)
      mapError = "No theme selected to identify";
    else if (!mv.getThemeEnabled(identifyTheme))
      mapError = "Theme "+identifyTheme+" is not visible";
    else {

      // Locate the feature and get details
      // Notes:
      //   1. The identify() method needs a TABLE NAME, not a theme name.
      //      We just assume that the theme and table name are the same.
      //   2. We query a rectangle of 4 pixels around the user click. Notice,
      //      however, that pixels have their origin at the UPPER-LEFT corner
      //      of the image, whereas ground coordinates use the LOWER-LEFT
      //      corner.
      String[][] f = mv.identify(dataSource, identifyTheme, colsToSelect,
        geoColumn, mapSrid,
        imgCX-4, imgCY+4,
        imgCX+4, imgCY-4,
        false);

      // The result is one row per matching record, but we want to display
      // results as one column per record.
      if (f!= null && f.length > 0) {
        featureInfo = new String[f[0].length][f.length];
        for (int i=0; i<f.length; i++)
          for (int j=0; j<f[i].length; j++)
            featureInfo[j][i] = f [i][j];
```

```
        featuresFound = f.length-1;
      } else
        mapError = "No matching " + identifyTheme + " found";

      if (featuresFound > 0) {

        // Remove any existing marker
        mv.removeAllPointFeatures();

        // Remove any route from previous mark
        mv.removeAllLinearFeatures();

        // Add a marker at the point clicked
        Point2D p = mv.getUserPoint(imgCX,imgCY);
        mv.addPointFeature (p.getX(), p.getY(),
          mapSrid, markerStyle, null, null, null);

        // Save new mark
        markX = p.getX();
        markY = p.getY();

        // Refresh map
        mv.run();
      }
    }
  }

  // ---------------------------------------------------------------------
  // [Clear] button clicked:
  // Remove the mark and refresh map
  // ---------------------------------------------------------------------
  else if (userAction.equals("Clear")) {

    if (markX != 0 || markY != 0) {

      // Clear current address
      findAddress = "";

      // Remove any existing marker
      mv.removeAllPointFeatures();

      // Remove any route from that mark
      mv.removeAllLinearFeatures();

      // Reset mark
      markX = 0;
      markY = 0;
```

```
    // Refresh map
    mv.run();

  }
}

// ---------------------------------------------------------------------------
// [Go to Mark] button clicked
// Center map on mark
// ---------------------------------------------------------------------------
else if (userAction.equals("Go To Mark")) {
  if (markX == 0 && markY == 0)
    mapError = "No address or mark set";
  else {
    mv.setCenter(markX, markY);
    mv.run();
  }
}

// ---------------------------------------------------------------------------
// [Find] button clicked:
// Geocode the entered address.
// Center map on the resulting coordinates.
// Set mark on that point.
// ---------------------------------------------------------------------------
else if (userAction.equals("Find")) {

  // Extract address details
  String[] addressLines = findAddress.split("\r\n");

  // Construct query to geocoder
  String gcQuery =
    "SELECT "+
    "G.GEO_ADDR.MATCHCODE, G.GEO_ADDR.LONGITUDE, G.GEO_ADDR.LATITUDE, " +
    "G.GEO_ADDR.HOUSENUMBER || ' ' || G.GEO_ADDR.STREETNAME, " +
    "G.GEO_ADDR.SETTLEMENT || ' ' || G.GEO_ADDR.POSTALCODE " +
    "FROM (SELECT SDO_GCDR.GEOCODE(USER ,SDO_KEYWORDARRAY(";
  for (int i=0; i<addressLines.length; i++) {
    gcQuery = gcQuery + "'" + addressLines[i] + "'";
    if (i < addressLines.length-1)
      gcQuery = gcQuery + ",";
  }
  gcQuery = gcQuery + "), 'US', 'DEFAULT') " +
  "GEO_ADDR FROM DUAL) G";

  // Send query
  String[][] f = mv.doQuery(dataSource, gcQuery);
```

```
// Extract match code. Proceed only if > 0
int matchCode = Integer.parseInt(f[1][0]);
if (matchCode > 0) {

  // Extract X and Y coordinates from geocode result
  double destX = Double.valueOf(f[1][1]).doubleValue();
  double destY = Double.valueOf(f[1][2]).doubleValue();

  // Extract full street address from result
  String streetAddress = f[1][3];

  // Transform result from row-major to column-major
  geocodeInfo = new String[f[0].length-3];
  for (int i=0; i<f[0].length-3; i++)
    geocodeInfo[i] = f [1][i+3];

  // Center map on the new address and zoom in
  mv.setCenterAndSize(destX, destY, markerMapSize);

  // Remove any existing marker
  mv.removeAllPointFeatures();

  // Remove any route from that mark
  mv.removeAllLinearFeatures();

  // Add a marker at the point clicked and label it
  // with the first address line
  mv.addPointFeature (
    destX, destY,
    mapSrid,
    markerStyle,
    streetAddress,
    markerLabelStyle,
    null,
    true);

  // Save new mark
  markX = destX;
  markY = destY;

  // Show SQL statement
  mapError = gcQuery;

  // Refresh map
  mv.run();
}
```

```
  else
    mapError = "Address not found";
}

// ---------------------------------------------------------------------
// [distSearch] button clicked
// Search for all neighbors within distance D from the current set mark.
// ---------------------------------------------------------------------
else if (userAction.equals("distSearch")) {
  if (markX == 0 && markY == 0)
    mapError = "No address or mark set";
  else if (!mv.getThemeEnabled(distSearchTheme))
    mapError = "Theme "+distSearchTheme+" is not visible";
  else if (distSearchParam <= 0)
    mapError = "Enter search distance";
  else {

    // Construct point object from current location mark
    JGeometry geom = new JGeometry(markX, markY, mapSrid);

    // Construct spatial query
    String sqlQuery = "SELECT "+geoColumn+" FROM " + distSearchTheme
      + " WHERE SDO_WITHIN_DISTANCE ("+ geoColumn + ","
      + " SDO_GEOMETRY (2001," + mapSrid + ", SDO_POINT_TYPE("
      + markX + "," + markY + ",NULL), NULL, NULL), "
      + "'DISTANCE="+distSearchParam+" UNIT=M') = 'TRUE'";
    mapError = "Executing query: "+ sqlQuery;

    // Add a JDBC theme to highlight the results of the query
    mv.addJDBCTheme (
      dataSource,                // Data source
      "SEARCH RESULTS",          // Theme to search
      sqlQuery,                  // SQL Query
      geoColumn,                 // Name of spatial column
      null,                      // srid
      queryStyle,                // renderStyle
      null,                      // labelColumn
      null,                      // labelStyle
      true                       // passThrough
    );

    // Perform the query
    String[][] f = mv.queryWithinRadius(
      dataSource,                // Data source
      distSearchTheme,           // Theme to search
      colsToSelect,              // Names of columns to select
      null,                      // Extra condition
      markX, markY,              // Center point (current mark)
```

```
          distSearchParam,              // Distance to search
          false                         // Center point is in ground coordinates
        );

        if (f!= null && f.length > 0) {

          // The result is one row per matching record, but we want to display
          // results as one column per record.
          featureInfo = new String[f[0].length][f.length];
          for (int i=0; i<f.length; i++)
            for (int j=0; j<f[i].length; j++)
              featureInfo[j][i] = f [i][j];
          featuresFound = f.length-1;

          // Refresh map
          mv.run();

        } else
          mapError = "No matching " + distSearchTheme + " found";

      }
    }

    // ---------------------------------------------------------------------
    // [nnSearch] button clicked
    // Search the N nearest neighbors from the current set mark.
    // ---------------------------------------------------------------------
    else if (userAction.equals("nnSearch")) {
      if (markX == 0 && markY == 0)
        mapError = "No address or mark set";
      else if (!mv.getThemeEnabled(nnSearchTheme))
        mapError = "Theme "+nnSearchTheme+" is not visible";
      else if (nnSearchParam <= 0)
        mapError = "Enter number of matches to search";
      else {

        // Construct spatial query
        String sqlQuery = "SELECT "+geoColumn+", SDO_NN_DISTANCE(1) DISTANCE"
          + " FROM " + nnSearchTheme
          + " WHERE SDO_NN ("+ geoColumn + ","
          + " SDO_GEOMETRY (2001," + mapSrid + ", SDO_POINT_TYPE("
          + markX + "," + markY + ",NULL), NULL, NULL), "
          + "'SDO_NUM_RES="+nnSearchParam+"',1) = 'TRUE'"
          + " ORDER BY DISTANCE";
        mapError = "Executing query: "+ sqlQuery;
```

```
// Add a JDBC theme to highlight the results of the query
mv.addJDBCTheme (
  dataSource,                  // Data source
  "SEARCH RESULTS",            // Theme to search
  sqlQuery,                    // SQL Query
  geoColumn,                   // Name of spatial column
  null,                        // srid
  queryStyle,                  // renderStyle
  null,                        // labelColumn
  null,                        // labelStyle
  true                         // passThrough
);

// Perform the query
String[][] f = mv.queryNN(
  dataSource,                  // Data source
  nnSearchTheme,               // Theme to search
  colsToSelect,                // Names of columns to select
  nnSearchParam,               // Number of neighbors
  markX, markY,                // Center point (current mark)
  null,                        // Extra condition
  false,                       // Center point is in ground coordinates
  null
);

if (f== null || f.length == 0)
  mapError = "No matching " + nnSearchTheme + " found";
else {

  // The result is one row per matching record, but we want to display
  // results as one column per record.
  featureInfo = new String[f[0].length][f.length];
  for (int i=0; i<f.length; i++)
    for (int j=0; j<f[i].length; j++)
      featureInfo[j][i] = f [i][j];
  featuresFound = f.length-1;

  // Remove any existing route
  mv.removeAllLinearFeatures();

  if (showRoute) {

    // Extract coordinates of destination node
    double destX = Double.valueOf(f[1][numVisibleCols]).doubleValue();
    double destY = Double.valueOf(f[1][numVisibleCols+1]).doubleValue();
```

```
        // Snap destination to nearest network node
        String qd = "SELECT NODE_ID FROM " + net.getNodeTableName()
          + " WHERE SDO_NN ("+net.getNodeGeomColumn() + ","
          + " SDO_GEOMETRY (2001," + mapSrid + ", SDO_POINT_TYPE("
          + destX + "," + destY + ",NULL), NULL, NULL), "
          + "'SDO_NUM_RES=1') = 'TRUE'";
        String [][] sd  = mv.doQuery(dataSource, qd);
        int destNodeId = Integer.parseInt(sd[1][0]);

        // Snap start (mark) to nearest network node
        String qs = "SELECT NODE_ID FROM " + net.getNodeTableName()
          + " WHERE SDO_NN ("+net.getNodeGeomColumn() + ","
          + " SDO_GEOMETRY (2001," + mapSrid + ", SDO_POINT_TYPE("
          + markX + "," + markY + ",NULL), NULL, NULL), "
          + "'SDO_NUM_RES=1') = 'TRUE'";
        String [][] ss  = mv.doQuery(dataSource, qs);
        int startNodeId = Integer.parseInt(ss[1][0]);

        // Get path from mark to destination node
        Path p = NetworkManager.shortestPath(net, startNodeId, destNodeId);

        // Check that we got a valid path back
        if (p != null && p.getNoOfLinks() > 0) {

          // Compute path geometry
          p.computeGeometry(0.5);
          JGeometry g = p.getGeometry();

          // Add route geometry to map
          mv.addLinearFeature (
            g.getOrdinatesArray(),            // Ordinates
            mapSrid,                          // SRID
            "L.TRANSPARENT",                  // Line style
            null,                             // Label column
            null                              // Label style
          );

        } else
          mapError = "Unable to compute route";

      }

      // Refresh map
      mv.run();
    }
  }
}
```

```
    // ------------------------------------------------------------------
    // [Clear Search] button
    // Clear search results
    // ------------------------------------------------------------------
    else if (userAction.equals("Clear Search")) {

      // Remove the markers of the matching results
      mv.deleteTheme ("SEARCH RESULTS");

      // Remove any route from the current mark
      mv.removeAllLinearFeatures();

      // Refresh map
      mv.run();
    }

    // Update size and center on screen with new values
    mapSize = mv.getSize();
    Point2D center = mv.getCenter();
    cx = center.getX();
    cy = center.getY();
    mapScale = mv.getMapScale();

    // Get URL to generated Map
    imgURL = mv.getGeneratedMapImageURL();

    // Get the XML request sent to the server
    mapRequest = mv.getMapRequestString();

    // Get the XML response received from the server
    mapResponse = mv.getMapResponseString();
  }

%>

<html>
<head>
<meta http-equiv="Content-Type" content="text/html; charset=UTF-8">
<title>Essential Guide to Oracle Spatial - Sample Application</title>

<script language="JavaScript" type="text/javascript">
<!--

  function CheckAll()
  {
    var tl = document.viewerForm;
    var len = tl.elements.length;
    for (var i = 0; i < len; i++) {
```

```
      var e = tl.elements[i];
      if (e.name == "checkedThemes") {
        e.checked = true;
      }
    }
  }

  function ClearAll()
  {
    var tl = document.viewerForm;
    var len = tl.elements.length;
    for (var i = 0; i < len; i++) {
      var e = tl.elements[i];
      if (e.name == "checkedThemes") {
        e.checked = false;
      }
      if (e.name == "identifyTheme") {
        e.checked = false;
      }
    }
  }

//-->
</script>
</head>
<body>
<noscript>
<b>Your browser has JavaScript turned off.</b><br>
<hr>
</noscript>
<!-- Output the HTML content -->
<form name="viewerForm" method="post" action="<%= jspURL %>">
<table border="1" cellpadding="0" cellspacing="0">
  <tr>
    <td width="260" valign="top" align="left">

      <!-- Searches -->
      <table border="0">

        <!-- Find Address -->
        <tr><td>
          <font color="#449922"><b>Find address:</b></font>
        </td></tr>
        <tr>
          <td align="left">
            <textarea
              name="findAddress" rows="3" cols="30"
              wrap><%= findAddress%></textarea>
```

```
  </td>
</tr>
<tr>
  <td align="center">
    <input type="submit" name="userAction" value="Find">
    <input type="submit" name="userAction" value="Clear">
  </td>
</tr>
<tr><td><hr></td></tr>

<!-- Show Location mark -->
<tr><td>
  <font color="#449922"><b>Location Mark:</b></font>
</td></tr>
<tr>
  <td>
  <table>
    <tr>
      <td width="200">
        <table border="0">
          <tr><td><b><font size="-1">Longitude:</font></b></td>
          <td><font size="-1"><%= markX %></font></td></tr>
          <tr><td><b><font size="-1">Latitude: </font></b></td>
          <td><font size="-1"><%= markY %></font></td></tr>
        </table>
      </td>
  </td>
  <td>
    <input type="submit" name="userAction" value="Clear">
  </td>
  </table>
</tr>
<tr><td><hr></td></tr>

<!-- Within Distance Search -->
<tr><td>
  <font color="#449922"><b>Search from Location Mark</b></font>
</td></tr>
<tr><td><font size="-1"><b>
  <% if (appThemes !=null && appThemes.length>0) {%>
    <select name="distSearchTheme">
    <% for (int i=0; i<appThemes.length; i++) {%>
      <option <%=appThemes[i].equals(distSearchTheme)?"selected":""%>>
        <%= appThemes[i].toUpperCase() %>
      </option>
    <% } %>
    </select>
  <% } %>
```

```
        within
        <input type="text" name="distSearchParam"
          value="<%= distSearchParam %>" size="2"/>
        meters
        </b></font>
      </td></tr>
      <tr><td align="center">
      <input type="submit" name="distSearch" value="Find">
      <input type="submit" name="clearSearch" value="Clear">
      </td></tr>
      <tr><td><hr></td></tr>

      <!-- Nearest Neighbor Search -->
      <tr><td>
        <font color="#449922"><b>Find nearest from Location Mark</b></font>
      </td></tr>
      <tr><td><font size="-1"><b>
        <input type="text" name="nnSearchParam"
          value="<%= nnSearchParam %>" size="2"/>
        nearest
        <% if (appThemes !=null && appThemes.length>0) {%>
          <select name="nnSearchTheme">
          <% for (int i=0; i<appThemes.length; i++) {%>
            <option <%=appThemes[i].equals(nnSearchTheme)?"selected":""%>>
              <%= appThemes[i].toUpperCase() %>
            </option>
          <% } %>
          </select>
        <% } %>
        </b></font>
      </td></tr>
      <tr><td>
        <B>Show route to nearest</B>
        <input type="checkbox" name="showRoute" value="true"
          <%= showRoute?"checked":""%>
        >
      </td></tr>
      <tr><td align="center">
      <input type="submit" name="nnSearch" value="Find">
      <input type="submit" name="clearSearch" value="Clear">
      </td></tr>

    </table>

  <td width="300" valign="top" align="center">

    <!-- Map display and controls -->
    <table border="1" cellpadding="0" cellspacing="10">
```

```
<!-- Map Image -->
<tr>
  <td align="center" width="<%= mapWidth %>" height="<%= mapHeight %>" >
    <input type="image"
      border="0"
      name="mapImage"
      src="<%= imgURL %>"
      width="<%= mapWidth %>"
      height="<%= mapHeight %>"
      alt="Click to re-center or identify">
  </td>
</tr>

<!-- Navigation buttons -->
<tr>
  <td align="center">
    <table>
      <tr>
        <td align="center">
        <input type="submit" name="userAction" value="Pan N">
        <input type="submit" name="userAction" value="Pan S">
        <input type="submit" name="userAction" value="Pan E">
        <input type="submit" name="userAction" value="Pan W">
        </td>
      </tr>
      <tr>
        <td align="center">
        <input type="submit" name="userAction" value="Zoom In">
        <input type="submit" name="userAction" value="Zoom Out">
        <input type="submit" name="userAction" value="Reset">
        <input type="submit" name="userAction" value="Go To Mark">
        </td>
      </tr>
    </table>
  </td>
</tr>

<!-- Click action -->
<tr>
  <td>
    <table border="0">
      <tr>
        <td width="100"><font color="#449922">
          <b>Click on the map to:</b> </font></td>
        <td>
          <input type="radio" name="clickAction" value="reCenter"
            <%= clickAction.equals("reCenter")?"checked":""%> >
            <B>Recenter</B>
```

```
              <input type="radio" name="clickAction" value="identify"
                <%= clickAction.equals("identify")?"checked":""%> >
                <B>Identify</B>
              <input type="radio" name="clickAction" value="setMark"
                <%= clickAction.equals("setMark")?"checked":""%> >
                <B>Mark</B>
            </td>
          </tr>
        </table>
      </td>
    </tr>

  </table>
</td>

<td valign="top">
  <table>
    <tr>
      <!-- Theme selection -->
      <td>
       <% String[] ts = mv.getThemeNames();
          if (ts != null) { %>

         <font color="#449922">
           <b>Select information to include on map</b></font>
         <table>
           <tr>
             <td><input type="button" value="Check All"
               onClick="CheckAll()"></td>
             <td><input type="button" value="Clear All"
               onClick="ClearAll()"></td>
             <td><input type="submit" value="Update Map"
               name="userAction"></td>
           </tr>
         </table>
         <table>
           <tr>
             <td>
               <table>
               <% for(int i=0; i<ts.length; i++) {%>
                 <tr><td>
                 <input type="radio"
                    name="identifyTheme"
                    value="<%=ts[i]%>"
                    <%=ts[i].equals(identifyTheme)?"checked":""%> >
                 <input type="checkbox"
                    name="checkedThemes"
```

```
                value="<%=ts[i]%>"
                <%=mv.getThemeEnabled(ts[i])?"checked":""%> >
              <%= ts[i] %>
              </td></tr>
            <%}%>
            </table>
          </td>
        </tr>
      </table>
  <%}%>
  </td>
</tr>
<tr><td><hr></td></tr>
<tr>
  <td>

  <!-- Identification result -->
  <% if (featureInfo !=null && featureInfo.length>0) {%>
    <tr><td><font color="#449922"><b>Identification result(s):
      <%= featuresFound %> match(es) </b></font></td></tr>
    <tr><td>
    <table border="1">
      <% for (int i=0; i<numVisibleCols; i++) {%>
        <tr>
        <% String[] row = featureInfo[i];
           for (int k=0; k<row.length; k++) {%>
            <td><font size="-1"><%= row[k] %></font></td>
           <% } %>
        </tr>
      <% } %>
    </table>
    </td></tr>
  <% } %>

  <!-- Geocode result -->
  <% if (geocodeInfo !=null && geocodeInfo.length>0) {%>
    <tr><td><font color="#449922"><b>Address found:</b>
    </font></td></tr>
    <tr><td>
    <table border="0">
      <% for (int i=0; i<geocodeInfo.length; i++) {%>
        <tr><td><font size="-1"><%= geocodeInfo[i] %></font></td></tr>
      <% } %>
    </table>
    </td></tr>
  <% } %>
```

```
          </td>
        </tr>
      </table>
    </td>
  </tr>

 <!-- Error messages  -->
 <tr><td colspan="3"><font color="#FF0000"><b><%= mapError %></b></font></td></tr>

  <!-- Map Status -->
  <tr><td colspan="3">
  <font size="-1">
    <b>Data Source:</b> <%= dataSource %>    
    <b>Map:</b> <%= baseMap %>    
    <b>Network:</b> <%= networkName %>    
  </font></td></tr>
  <tr><td colspan="3">
  <font size="-1">
    <b>Longitude:</b> <%= cx %>  
    <b>Latitude:</b> <%= cy %>  
    <b>Size:</b> <%= mapSize %>
    <b>Scale:</b> <%= mapScale %>
  </font></td></tr>

  <!-- XML request and response -->
  <% if (debug) { %>
  <tr><td><b>XML Request:</b></td></tr>
  <tr>
    <td colspan="3" align="left">
      <textarea rows="6" cols="80" wrap readonly><%=mapRequest%>
      </textarea>
    </td>
  </tr>
  <tr><td><b>XML Response:</b></td></tr>
  <tr>
    <td colspan="3" align="left">
      <textarea rows="6" cols="80" wrap readonly><%=mapResponse%></textarea>
    </td>
  </tr>
  <% } %>
</table>

<SCRIPT language=JavaScript>
<!--
if (document.all) {
    document.all("mapImage").style.cursor = 'crosshair';
}
```

```
//-->
</SCRIPT>
<input type="hidden" name="markX" value="<%= markX %>">
<input type="hidden" name="markY" value="<%= markY %>">
<input type="hidden" name="debug" value="<%= debug %>">
<input type="hidden" name="dataSource" value="<%= dataSource %>">
<input type="hidden" name="baseMap" value="<%= baseMap %>">
<input type="hidden" name="networkName" value="<%= networkName %>">
</form>
</body>
</html>
```

PART 4

Advanced Spatial

CHAPTER 13

Case Studies

This chapter describes five case studies that illustrate the use of Oracle Spatial for storing, analyzing, visualizing, and integrating spatial data in business and government applications. These are large, complex applications that include several components and software tools besides Oracle Spatial, but they rely on Oracle Spatial for handling all spatial data.

The emphasis in this chapter is on the requirements and the implementation context for these applications, as well as on the way Oracle Spatial was introduced to satisfy these requirements. In each case study, we identify the main uses of Oracle Spatial and, where appropriate, provide some detailed examples. It is outside of the scope of this chapter to provide a comprehensive and detailed description of the technical implementation of Oracle Spatial in these cases. However, most of the steps illustrated in detail in Chapter 12 have been used in these applications.

All solutions described here are in use, and a number have been in use for some time already. For each case study, we introduce the context in which the application was conceived and designed, so that you may understand the needs and constraints of each implementation. We then focus on the part of the solution/system that uses Oracle Spatial and describe how, why, and with what benefits it was deployed.

Overview of the Case Studies

The first case study we examine in this chapter, *BusNet*, illustrates the use of Oracle Spatial for managing the bus network of the city of London. It serves to improve the planning and management of the bus schedules and routes, to share information with users of this information, and to integrate the system with the de facto national standard for spatial data. The case study illustrates data loading and validation (see Chapter 5), spatial analysis (see Chapter 8), and network analysis (see Chapter 10). The system extensively uses the linear referencing model of Oracle Spatial (see Appendix B).

The *P-Info* case study describes a system to provide mobile, location-enabled access to mission-critical information for police officers operating in the field. P-Info provides secure access to all databases of the Dutch police, from a handheld device that exchanges data with the servers using the GSM or UMTS telephone network. Spatial information is used for spatial selections and overlays (see Chapters 8 and 9), to visualize locations and maps (see Chapter 11), and to geocode and reverse geocode addresses (see Chapter 6).

The *Risk Repository for Hazardous Substances* is a national system in the Netherlands that gives access to information on risk and possible effects for all locations involved in the storage, processing, and transportation of hazardous substances. This information is available to citizens from the web and to professional users involved in the prevention, response, and mitigation of incidents related to hazardous substances. This case study discusses spatial analysis (see Chapters 8 and 9) and data loading and validation (see Chapter 5).

The *GeoStor* spatial data warehouse provides a single access point to spatial data for the state of Arkansas. This warehouse, which contains terabytes of data, allows users to search, visualize, and download spatial layers in a variety of formats and projections. Oracle Spatial is used for its capability to store large amounts of data, for data loading and validation (see Chapter 5), and for fast access to spatial layers (see Chapter 8). A fundamental reason for using Oracle Spatial is that it provides functional equivalence for OpenGIS specifications (see Chapter 4).

The *Location Services for UMTS* case study illustrates one of the first deployments of consumer-based location services for third-generation telecommunication networks. With these services, offered by the "3" operator, users have access to maps, points of interest, and navigation instructions from a UMTS handset. The case study illustrates the use of Oracle Spatial as the spatial data platform used during operations, as well as the reference platform for data preparation prior to using data online. This process uses loading and validation of spatial data (see Chapter 5), spatial analysis (see Chapters 8 and 9), and the linear referencing model (see Appendix B).

Notice that these applications are fully deployed and operational, and therefore utilize earlier versions of Oracle Spatial, usually 9*i*. This means that all features and capabilities discussed in the case studies are part of Oracle Spatial 10*g*, but some features of Oracle Spatial 10*g* are not visible in these case studies.

Notice also that in these case studies, Oracle Spatial is used to store and retrieve all spatial data used in the applications. The applications also use the loading mechanisms discussed in Chapter 5, and they extensively use the spatial analysis discussed in Chapters 8 and 9, but they also exploit the possibility of accessing the `SDO_GEOMETRY` objects in C/C++ or Java to implement specific functionalities required by the applications, as discussed in Chapter 7.

Spatial Information for Managing the London Bus Network

London's transport system is one of the most comprehensive, complex, and articulate urban transport systems in the world. It covers a vast area with 13,600 km of roads, 3,730 km of bus routes, 205 km of dedicated bus lanes, 329 km of subway lines, 26 km of Docklands Light Railway (DLR) lines, 28 km of new tramways, and 788 km of national rail lines in Greater London transport. Every day, over 27 million journeys are made in Greater London, 8.5 million of which take place on public transport (4.5 million by bus, 3 million by subway, and 1 million by rail). The London bus system plays a crucial role in getting and keeping London moving. About 6,500 buses are scheduled every day on over 700 different routes, amounting to about 1.5 billion passengers per year. A total of 397,000,000 km were covered by London buses in year 2003.

■Note This section is based on the work of Olliver Robinson (business analyst at Transport for London, London Buses), Prashan Rampersad, and Terry Allen. The authors wish also to thank Transport for London for making the background material available for this section of the chapter. Additional information on Transport for London can be found at `www.transportforlondon.gov.uk/tfl`.

Transport for London (TfL) is the body responsible for the management of the London transport system. TfL is accountable for the planning and delivery of transport facilities including London Buses, London Underground, DLR, and London Trams. London Buses manages the bus services in London and, along with London Underground, is the primary provider of urban public transport for the city. The extent of the bus network and the number of passengers carried makes London Buses one of the largest public transport providers in the world. The tasks of London Buses include bus route planning, service-level definition, and quality of service monitoring. London Buses does not include the bus services that are operated by private operators working under contract to London Buses. Each route is competitively tendered every 5 years.

London Buses is a success story of public transport that has been reshaped to meet the needs of twenty-first-century urban life. Thanks to a more modern, punctual, and customer-focused network, the buses of London are now carrying the highest number of passengers in over 40 years. The passenger growth rates are the highest since 1945, with a 7.3 percent passenger growth for 2002–2003 (an extra 104 million passenger trips), and a 19 percent aggregate growth between 1999 and 2003. Thanks to this performance, London Buses plays a key role in achieving the UK government's 10-year transport target, which aims to increase bus use by 10 percent by 2010.

These results can be achieved only with sophisticated management of the bus network and an appropriate information system. London Buses needs to manage and maintain a complex bus network that adapts continuously in response to changes in London's growth, spatial pattern, and economic and social developments. On average, half of the network is subject to some level of review each year. Oracle Spatial has been introduced by London Buses as the core spatial component of BusNet, the information system that supports the route network management.

BusNet

A variety of information systems are used to support London Buses' responsibilities, including systems to record passenger information and surveys, to manage contracts with operators, to support service controls, and to manage stops and shelters.

BusNet is the back-office application dedicated to bus-route network management. The system is networked to about 400 staff members and enables TfL to maintain and share reference information supporting the following:

- *Route definition*: This includes the sequence of streets for each bus run on each route (containing a list of the road names composing the run) and the sequence of transit nodes (containing a list of service access points for the runs).
- *Version control for bus-route records for past, present, and future routes*: The bus routes change for several reasons, for instance, because of changes in the route segments, start and end points, or stops. For a given route, BusNet normally contains several past expired records, the current route, and one or more proposed versions for the future.

- *Service change records that aid task workflow and enforce business rules*: Examples are the issue of a briefing or an amended route description.
- *Detailed service definition*: This includes, for instance, the operator name, the vehicles used, the day type of service (e.g., Monday–Friday nights), the time periods, the number of buses per hour, and so on.

The introduction of Oracle Spatial as a basis for BusNet came at a time when London Buses realized the need to improve the quality control of the route information, integrate the system with the de facto national reference set for road data (the Ordnance Survey's OSCAR[1]) and share route geometry definitions among internal and external stakeholders such as local authorities. The existing systems were unable to achieve these goals, and a new integrated system, BusNet, was developed to replace them. Spatial information management is at the core of BusNet, which makes it possible to

- Store route diagrams as persistent data, based accurately on London's road network. This accommodates changes not only to bus routes over time, but also to the road network itself. (A *route* is the composition of route runs, the sequence of streets composing the run, and turning points required at each extremity of the route or at intermediate points to allow buses running late to turn around and get back on schedule.)
- Establish directionality to diagrams so that sequential street names could be derived with no need for text data entry, in particular to support the route description document included in the contract with each operator to run a route.
- Support complex diagram patterns such as loops and figure eights.
- Support the recording of passenger drop-off and pick-up points at terminal and intermediate turning points on routes.
- Import and display related datasets such as bus stops owned by other systems, so that they can be displayed in conjunction with the routes they serve.

Spatial Data and Oracle Spatial in BusNet

The data model implemented in BusNet reflects the information needs illustrated in Figure 13-1. This figure identifies an operator's view and a technical planner's view. The operator's view focuses on the detailed routing of a bus route and contains information such as the sequence

---

1. *Ordnance Survey Centre Alignment of Roads* (OSCAR) is a vector-modeled network containing all motorable public and selected private roads of Great Britain. The database is updated every 6 months and is supplied in 5×5 km tiles. It provides the most common and consistent base for road-related information in the United Kingdom. As this book goes to press, the BusNet development team has successfully migrated BusNet route definitions from the OSCAR reference dataset to the Ordnance Survey's Integrated Transport Network (ITN) successor product. This is not dissimilar to total replacement of the foundations of St. Paul's Cathedral without dropping a stone! ITN is still essentially based on "link" records, as is OSCAR, but with more data attribution, and covering rail and navigable waterway networks as well as highways.

of streets traversed for each route run, the turning points, and the stands. This information allows operators to implement the bus service on the route and is part of the contract with the operator. The technical planner's view includes details of how each route is physically operated in terms of legs of service, days of the week, frequency per hour, vehicle types, and so on.

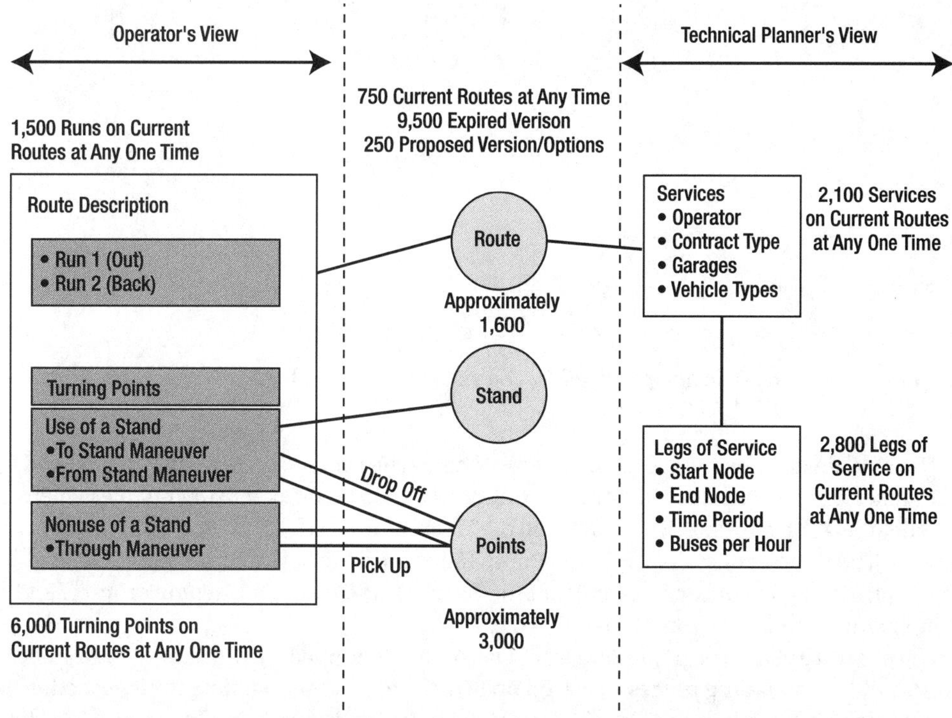

Figure 13-1. *The operator's and technical planner's view*

Figure 13-2 shows the data model used by BusNet to support just the operator's view. The road links are contained in a roads table (`oscar_road`) populated with the OSCAR road segments ("links" consisting of lines and nodes, with attributes including the road number; the road name; the form of the way, such as a divided highway or rotary; the road length; etc.). The passenger drop-off and pick-up locations associated with turning points are contained in a points table (`point`), which also provides a warehouse for different types of spatial points, such as bus-stop locations, owned by and imported from other systems. These two tables contain an `SDO_GEOMETRY` column named `geoloc` in Figure 13-2 and are the source of most spatial data used by BusNet.

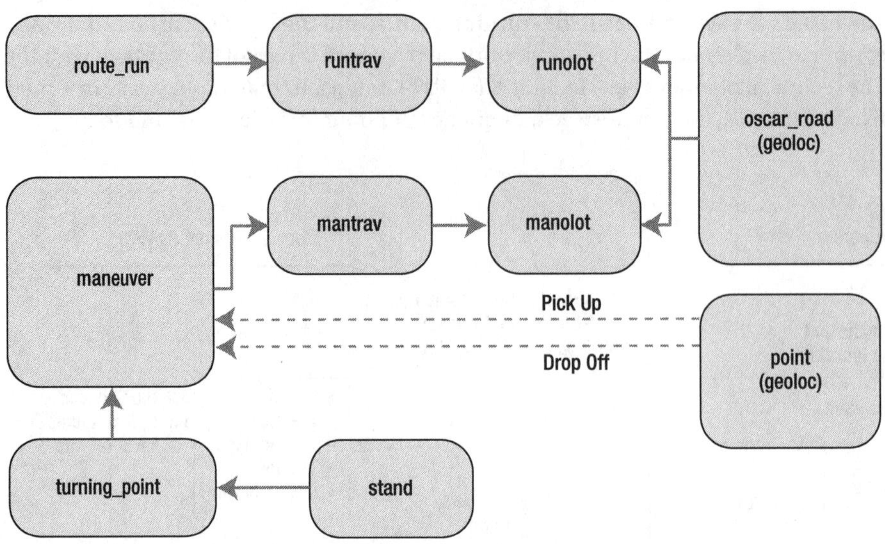

Figure 13-2. *The* `oscar_road` *and* `point` *tables contain an* `SDO_GEOMETRY`.

The road links are sequences in the `runolot` table. The `runtrav` table derives sequenced street names from the sequenced links and optionally chooses different street names where convenient (e.g., on a rotary). The `route_run` table combines all the links into a single route geometry. The same data structure is used for maneuvers, which are micro-runs associated with the turning points at each extremity of the route.[2] Maneuvers also include drop-off and pick-up point information from the `point` table.

The `oscar_road` table is populated from OSCAR files supplied by Ordnance Survey. The custom-built data-loading process is based on SQL*Loader, a bulk-loading utility used for moving data from external files into the Oracle database, in this case from the OSCAR NTF format.[3] The loading steps are as follows:

1. Create a SQL*Loader control file from the pipe-delimited NTF files, and insert blanks after each occurrence of the x, y coordinates. The blanks will be subsequently used to hold measure values.

2. Load the `oscar_road` table in BusNet from SQL*Loader.

3. Update `SDO_GEOM_METADATA` to introduce x, y and m parameters, where *m* (measure) supports the Linear Referencing System (LRS).

4. Run `SDO_LRS.REDEFINE_GEOM_SEGMENT` to calculate the measure values (i.e., the *m*s).

5. Run `SDO_GEOM.VALIDATE_LAYER`.

6. Create an R-tree index.

2. Note that to allow buses running late to turn around and get back on schedule, a number of turning points are also defined along the route.
3. The Neutral Transfer Format (NTF) was the adopted standard for spatial data transfer by the Ordnance Survey, but it looks to be superseded by Geographic Markup Language (GML).

Notice that the OSCAR database is delivered in tiles of 5×5 km. The combination of several tiles needed to cover the London area results in a certain degree of duplication for the road segments that fall in two or more tiles. The deduplication process is based on Oracle Spatial functions that exploit the LRS. For each group of two of more records that share the same `road_ID`, deduplication is carried out by the function `SDO_LRS.CONCATENATE_GEOM_SEGMENTS`, which produces a new set of concatenated segments. The function requires two inputs of type `SDO_GEOMETRY`, and it returns a new `SDO_GEOMETRY` object that corresponds to the concatenated pair.

In addition, at each delivery of OSCAR, the new and the live road datasets are compared with `SDO_GEOM.RELATE`, which returns "equals" if geometries match. If a segment exists in the live database but not in the new data, the status of the record is updated to `Withdrawn`. This prevents it from being used in new route diagrams, but allows the system to retain it as part of historic, or `Expired`, status routes. If a record exists in the new dataset but not in the live one, the new record is inserted.

BusNet is available to end users through a client interface developed in Visual Basic 6.0. The spatial functions are implemented based on MapX, which provides the GIS interface to the system. This is particularly useful, for instance, in facilitating the route definition (a record in the `route_run` table) based on selection of road links. Links can be manually selected from the screen, or they can be identified automatically with an auto trace function. The auto trace selects the minimum distance path between two points on the route network graph and applies Dijkstra's shortest path algorithm. The algorithm is implemented in the client BusNet application, but it uses the `SDO_WITHIN_DISTANCE` function to select the links to evaluate for the shortest path algorithm. It also exploits the linear referencing model to weight the links based on their length. On completion of sequencing, the `runolot` and `runtrav` records are automatically saved to the database, and the OSCAR links thus used are combined into a single geometry to populate the `geoloc` column in the `route_run` table. The function `SDO_LRS.CONCATENATE_GEOM_SEGMENTS` is again used for this purpose.

User Interface for Spatial Data in BusNet

Figure 13-3 shows the result of a polygon spatial query (highlighted in the center of the image) around a small section of road outside the TfL London Buses office. The query is created using the BusNet GIS application, which makes it possible for users to define query areas of any shape. In the User Selection pane on the right side of the screen, all spatial business objects found by Oracle Spatial within the polygon are delivered as parent "labels," including the whole of each route run that intersects the polygon. This gives the user the choice of which of these he wants to view, because it is unlikely—and unwise—to want to see everything all at once. Note the dotted line around the coach station indicating a terminus turning point maneuver for route C10 around the block. Note also the passenger pick-up and drop-off point, each near to its related bus stops icons (the small house images indicating each stop has a bus shelter with it).

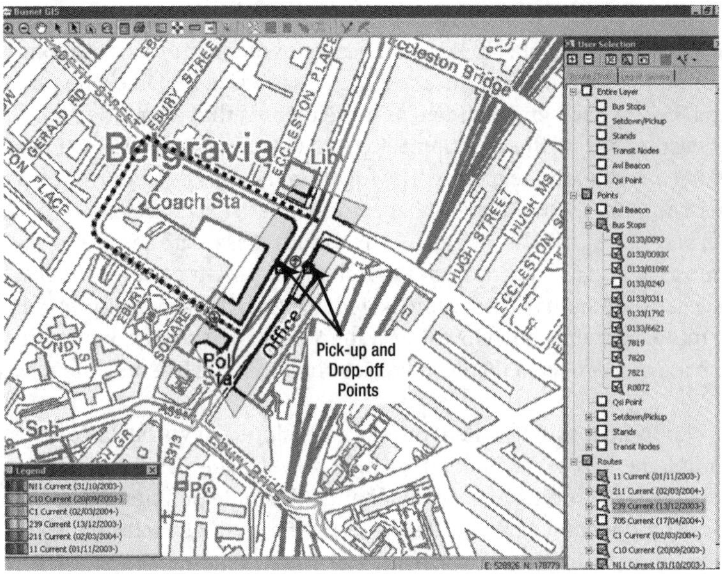

Figure 13-3. *Spatial query and visualization of route information*

Figure 13-4 shows a zoomed-out view from the same query in Figure 13-3, this time displaying bus stops in both directions (Runs 1 and 2) on Route 11. Note there is a *C* around two of the bus stop icons—one on the far left and one in the middle. This indicates a "Countdown" sign, which is the brand name of a dot-matrix indicator system showing passengers waiting at the stop when the next few buses on each route are predicted to arrive.

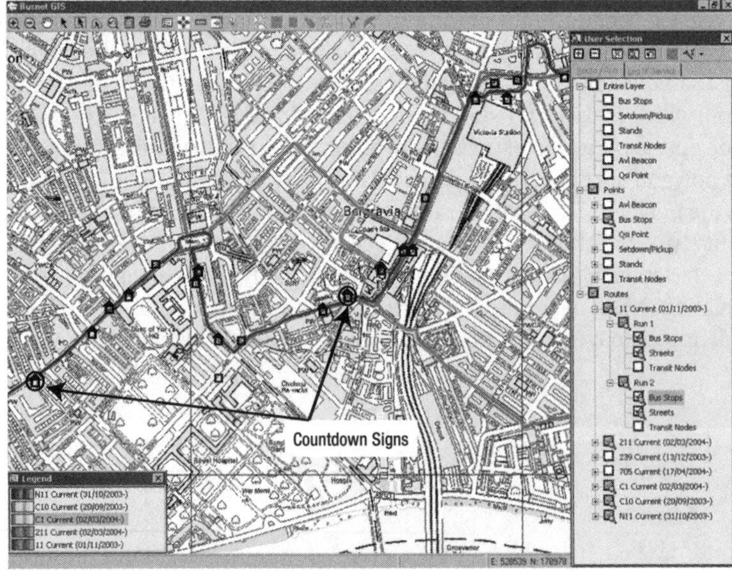

Figure 13-4. *Spatial query and visualization of route information, zoomed-out view*

Figure 13-5 shows the result of a query based on the planner's view of the BusNet object model, which enables calculation of combined buses-per-hour frequencies on a given day type and time period (in this case, Monday–Friday PM Peak) at each Service Access Point representing a bus stop or bus-stop pair. To get this result, the user must first run a polygon query, then run the function that runs a PL/SQL procedure to get all frequencies for each Leg of Service, and then add them up to produce a total for each Service Access Point. Note the different raster map background from the Ordnance Survey 1:10,000, in which the user interface has been designed to allow switching between easily during a session. All this is available to the user from a total of about five mouse clicks, whereas before this implementation, all the information presented in this way would have taken at least a day to compile. It is all immediately available from the single BusNet Oracle database and requires no more daily data maintenance by users than the predecessor systems, from which no spatial data and GIS leverage was possible.

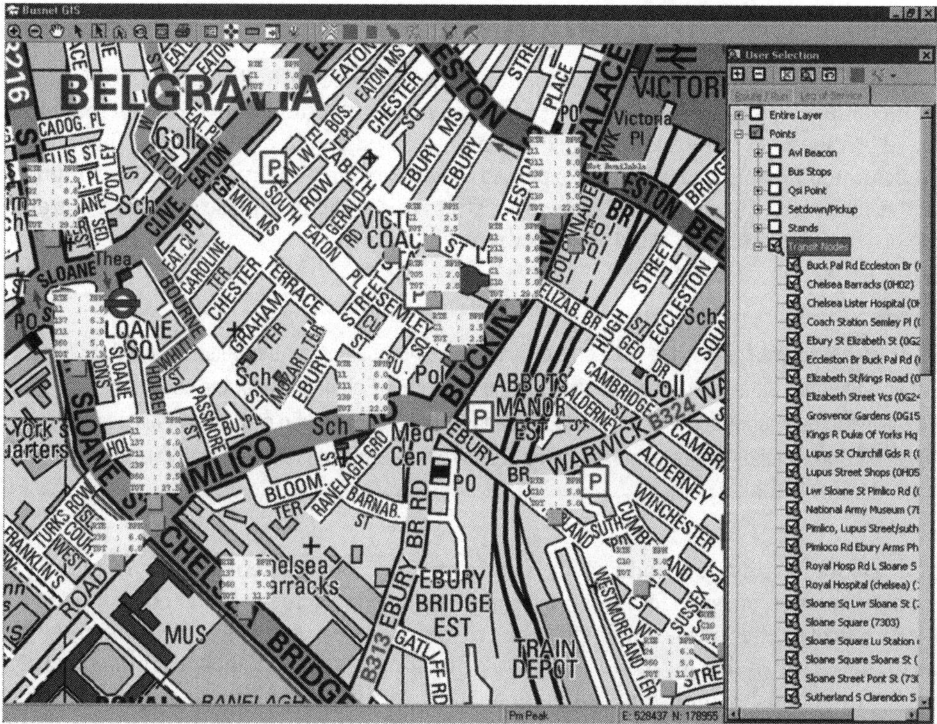

Figure 13-5. *The planner's view*

BusNet Conclusions

The introduction of BusNet makes it possible to simplify, standardize, and automate the distribution of reliable bus route information at London Buses. A key feature of the system is its data structure. It is both simple and flexible, and above all, it is strictly derived from the business logic applied by London Buses for its operations.

The spatial functionality of BusNet extensively uses the operators and functions of Spatial and the features of SDO_GEOMETRY, such as the linear referencing model. The availability of this model simplifies several operations in BusNet, such as data loading, data deduplication, and short-path searches. This was one of the reasons for choosing Oracle Spatial as a basis for BusNet. In general, BusNet benefits from the possibility of using one database for spatial and nonspatial data types, and from the use of one language (SQL) for all data operations. The availability of a vast range of spatial PL/SQL options has made it possible to implement the needs of BusNet in a neat and straightforward manner. Oracle Spatial has also allowed BusNet to implement a clear separation between data and application layers, the data model and functional logic, and application and storage layers. The structural features of Oracle Spatial, such as scalability, security, reliability, and support for OpenGIS standards, are also important factors for BusNet.

P-Info: A Mobile Application for Police Forces

The law enforcement sector faces an increasing demand for effective and efficient performance. Recent increases in urban crime, a growing concern with youth crime, and a sense of insecurity generated by the threat of terrorism have led to an increased demand for security. The police and other law enforcement agencies are expected to ensure more timely responses and improve preventive measures. These demands, however, stress the capacity of these organizations and impose on them more serious requirements than ever before.

■ **Note** P-Info was developed by the ICT Service Cooperative Association for the Dutch Police, Judicial Authorities, and Public Safety Services (ISC) and by Geodan Mobile Solutions under the coordination of the Dutch Ministry of the Interior and Kingdom Relations and with the cooperation of regional police organizations. The first P-Info initiative was launched by the police region Gelderland Midden in 2000.

Police work has always relied heavily on information management. Proper and timely information makes it possible for law enforcement agencies to achieve expected goals, and it dictates the level of effectiveness and efficiency of their operations. The growing demands on this sector have rendered many of the current information systems inadequate. Simultaneously providing timely and accurate information to the field, locating the resources deployed (vehicles and personnel), allowing data communication during operations, and integrating multiple sources of information is often beyond the capacity of current police systems.

This gap needs to be filled if the increasing requirements of law enforcement are to be met. At the same time, there is a growing awareness that simply deploying more modern IT systems does not automatically ensure benefits to the organization. IT managers are facing increasing pressure to justify the large costs of IT investments. This can result in failed implementations, huge integration costs, and never-ending upgrades. There is a growing skepticism of the maxim "IT investment equals productivity gains."

In the year 2000, the Dutch police started investigating the use of wireless technology and location services to address the needs of officers in the field and of those in the control rooms. The result of this process is the P-Info system, currently implemented by several Dutch police regions and adopted by the national police organization in support of mobile police workers.

The application focuses on mobile officers, those who operate in the field to provide citizen security, response services, and investigative capabilities. In the Netherlands, about 20,000 police personnel operate in the field either full-time or part-time. A special group of these officers operates almost exclusively in the field and performs systematic patrol and policing in urban and rural areas. By focusing on crime prevention and mobilizing citizens' support locally, their work reduces the distance between citizens and the police while increasing mutual trust and cooperation. They are assigned to, and operate in, a small area with the support and coordination of regional police offices. They operate mostly outside of the office, and the goal of the police organization is to maximize their presence in the field. Hence, these officers suffer particularly from the lack of proper information availability. In several cases, they are forced to interrupt their fieldwork and return to the office simply to gather information that is useful to the field operations.

Figure 13-6 illustrates the P-Info system at work and shows the main features of the mobile interface, in this case displayed on a PDA device, one of the many devices supported by P-Info. The figure shows a police officer (left) using P-Info during a routine check, the main interface (center) of P-Info with access to all services, and an English version of the same interface (right) together with a sample illustration of a spatial search for incidents.

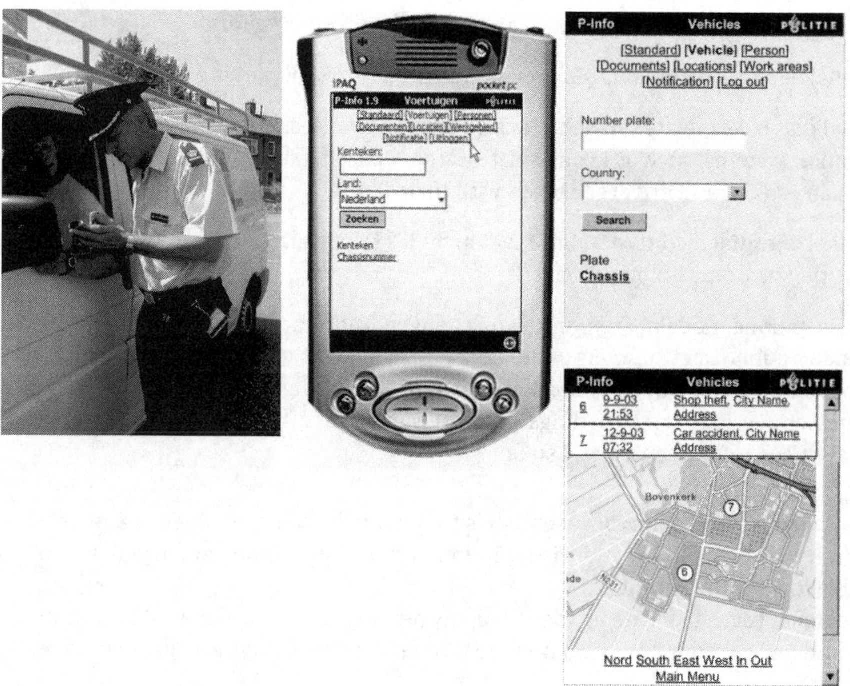

Figure 13-6. *The P-Info system at work*

P-Info Functionality

The P-Info system contains three functionality groups:

- Database and data services
- Location services
- Office automation

The central component of P-Info is the *database and data services* module. It provides integrated access to the whole range of regional, national, and international police databases. The information sources are the same as those available at the office, while information search and information provision is optimized for mobile users. Queries are predefined and the most used query forms (e.g., query by entry code, person, license plate, date, address, area, time, etc.) are predefined for easy use. With this service, simultaneous searches in multiple databases are performed in the background, and the full search results are provided in a single form. The results are an overview of a given situation—for example, information about a suspect car, collected from all databases containing the search items (car data are extracted from the national car registration system, any fines on the car are extracted from the regional databases where fines are registered, the charges to the car owner are extracted from the national databases, etc.). The databases connected to P-info include

- Regional databases that contain all reports and their mutations, such as an incident report, a theft report, and so on. They are logged and edited by the control room, or collected and edited by police staff on the basis of individual reports.
- A regional database of outstanding search warrants, fines, or parking tickets.
- National databases related to vehicles and driving licenses. They include vehicle registration systems, such as license plate numbers, ownership, annual maintenance checks, and so on, and driver's licenses with their status.
- A national criminal records database that includes information on search warrants, missing persons, and stolen vehicles.
- NSIS, the national node of the European Schengen Information System (SIS), which coordinates public safety matters under the European Schengen Convention. It contains personal data supplied by member states relating to missing persons, persons wanted as witnesses in criminal proceedings, persons wanted for arrest for extradition, aliens who have been refused entry, and so on.

The main purpose of the *location services* is to provide location-enabled searches, such as proximity or area searches, the visualization of results on a map and, in general, to location-enable the P-Info content.

Spatial searches serve to locate incidents, or any other type of record that has location information, and to rank them based on how close or far they are from the user position or any other location.

Location services include a street guide that can be consulted directly to locate an address and display it on a map, or by the P-Info server to associate a coordinates to an address string or a certain database entry.

The ability to locate any database entry in space is at the basis of location notification services. Users that register for notification receive an automatic voice message briefly describing an event (e.g., an incident) that occurred in the vicinity of the current position of the police officer.

Location functionality can also be used to locate the position of an officer on a map by applying telecom location capability (Cell ID or GPS). This can be used to optimize information and proximity searches, as well as to locate colleagues and other resources when needed. This functionality also allows the optimization of resource allocation in the field.

Office functionality includes e-mail, a calendar, contacts, and tasks. It is based on wireless access to the regular police office facilities. It is used to maintain communication between officers in the field, to check appointments made by the office assistants, and to receive documents and notifications while working in the field.

P-Info Architecture

Figure 13-7 illustrates the P-Info architecture. Mobile users access the system through a variety of handsets, such as PDAs, portable computers, or tablets. Data communication is currently based on GSM-GPRS, a standard that ensures data transfer rates of around 40Kbps. The system is designed to be bearer independent (thus it can work on, for example, GPRS, UMTS, or dedicated Tetra networks) and device independent. The interface is adapted to each device with style sheets, and it uses pure browser-based access to prevent any content from being stored on the handset. (For security reasons, information is never stored or cached in the mobile device; it is always accessed online.)

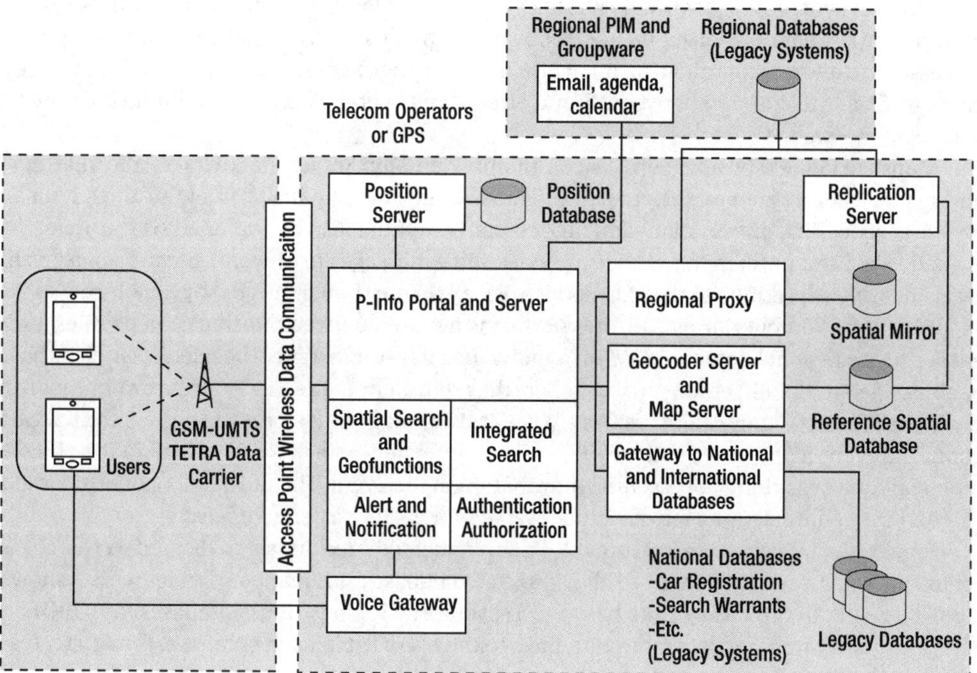

Figure 13-7. *Simplified architecture of the P-Info system*

The access point ensures that only authorized devices can access the P-Info portal and server, which in turn performs user authentication and authorization. The P-Info server and portal provides access to the underlying P-Info components. It routes the requests from the mobile users and dispatches them to the national gateway or to the regional proxy.

The national gateway includes a series of XML wrappers that serve as an interface between XML (used within P-Info) and the legacy data models of some national databases.

The regional proxy plays a similar role as the national gateway, but in this case it decides if a query can be dispatched directly to the regional databases (e.g., for details of an incident) or if it needs to access the P-Info spatial mirror. The term "spatial mirror" derives from the function of this database, which mirrors a small portion of the content of the regional databases while adding a spatial component to each record. In this way, each record in the regional database corresponds to a record in the mirror database. They share code and the name of the record, but the mirror version includes location information (the address in a standardized form and the x, y coordinates). This is necessary because the regional databases contain spatial information in the form of an address, but they do not account for x, y coordinates. Also, every address entry is a text string formatted in various slightly different ways (abbreviations, spelling mistakes, truncations, etc.). The mirror database, which is an Oracle Spatial database, makes it possible to perform spatial search and proximity analysis without accessing the regional databases, thus ensuring coherence of location information.

The mirror database and the regional database are coordinated by a replication server, which monitors entries in the regional databases and intercepts differences to the mirror database. When an addition is intercepted, the replication server invokes the geocoder to interpret and normalize the address string, and to associate it with x, y coordinates. It then copies the essential information from the regional database and creates a new entry in the mirror table, from now on synchronized with the regional repository. Notice that the geocoder needs to perform the regular normalization and geocoding activities (e.g., normalize "Bond Street, 5" and associate it to x, y coordinates), but it also needs to interpret entries such as crossroads (e.g., an incident at the crossing between "Bond Street" and "Large Street") or building locations (e.g., a railway station).

Maps are created by an OpenGIS-compliant[4] Web Map Server that extracts information and spatial features from reference spatial databases (in Oracle Spatial) containing the full road network, geocoding information, and other essential spatial display and analysis features.

The alert and notification service provides voice messages to officers operating in a given area who have subscribed to the alert service. Based on the profile selected by the officer (such as "only thefts and burglaries"), P-Info performs a match between notification profiles and entries in the regional databases. When a match occurs—for instance, because a burglary has been notified to the 112 emergency number (the equivalent of the 911 emergency number in the United States)—the system creates a VoiceXML message that stores the basic information about the event (code, time, and location). The voice gateway makes a short call to the officer's mobile phone describing the essential information of the event. The full details can be checked in a dedicated notification area of P-Info reserved for each registered officer.

Finally, the integrated search provides a sophisticated mechanism to dispatch a search—for instance, for a certain name—to all connected databases simultaneously. Figure 13-8 shows a typical result. In this case, P-Info has found several entries in various databases for "GROE". The results are organized in a table with links to the entry list in each database. P-Info creates

---

4. See www.opengis.org.

a series of nested hit lists, which contain all information available to the police regarding the search item. This mechanism saves officers a great deal of time and presents a coherent information picture to the users, independent of the database structures that contain the information.

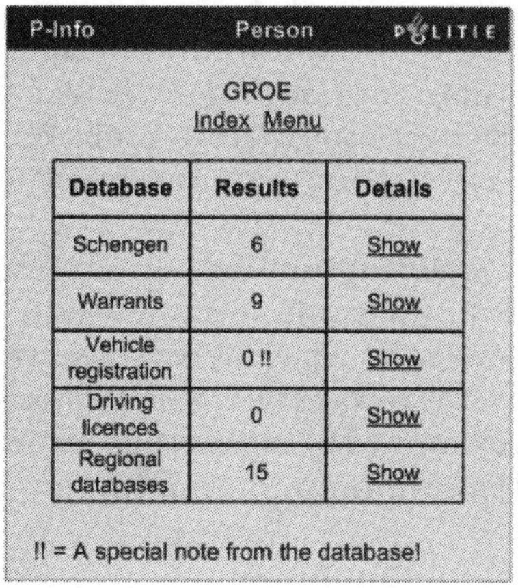

P-Info Person POLITIE

GROE
Index Menu

Database	Results	Details
Schengen	6	Show
Warrants	9	Show
Vehicle registration	0 !!	Show
Driving licences	0	Show
Regional databases	15	Show

!! = A special note from the database!

Figure 13-8. *Summary results of an integrated search*

All components of P-Info are developed in Java (J2EE and Java servlets) and run in any Java environment. Oracle Application Server is used in this case.

Use of Oracle Spatial in P-Info

Oracle Spatial is used by P-Info to store and retrieve spatial information, perform proximity analysis, and support overlay and spatial selections. The spatial mirror (see Figure 13-7) provides the basis for these operations. The main methods for selecting data from regional databases (those containing police reports) through the spatial mirror are as follows:

- Select based on proximity to a current position.
- Select based on proximity to a certain address location.
- Select based on inclusion in a certain work area.

The spatial mirror contains only point objects. The table size grows continuously, with a rate of increase of several hundreds of thousands of records per year, for each of the 25 police regions. The table size at the national level grows at a rate of several million records per year.

Listing 13-1 shows the procedure to insert the spatial object for a new record into the table `place_table` of the spatial mirror. This procedure is used by the Replication Server (see Figure 13-7). The question marks are filled in by the application and represent the incident ID and the x and y coordinates, respectively.

Listing 13-1. *Inserting Records in the Spatial Mirror*

```
INSERT INTO place_table (point_id, geo, creation_date)
VALUES(?, MDSYS.SDO_GEOMETRY(2001, 90112, MDSYS.SDO_POINT_TYPE(?, ?, NULL),
NULL, NULL), sysdate)
```

The geocoding of the incident information is complicated by the fact that officers report the location of an event in three different ways: address, crossing, and road section. Crossing and road section are often used to specify the location of a road accident. While geocoding on an address is well supported (see Chapter 6), crossing and road-section geocoding required the development of specific procedures.

Reverse geocoding is used in P-Info to associate to an x, y coordinate to a specific address. The most common use is to find the closest address to the current location of the user (e.g., based on GPS location or telecom location). Listing 13-2 shows an example. The query selects one road segment (`sdo_num_res=1`) from the table `tblstreet` (which contains the streets database) that is the closest to the current location. The location is represented by two question marks that are filled in by the application that calls the query and passes on the x, y coordinates of the current location.

Listing 13-2. *Reverse Geocoding in P-Info*

```
SELECT d.street_id id, SDO_NN_DISTANCE(1) distance
FROM tblstreet d
WHERE SDO_NN(d.geo, MDSYS.SDO_GEOMETRY(2001,90112,
  SDO_POINT_TYPE(?,?,NULL),NULL,NULL), 'SDO_NUM_RES=1', 1) = 'TRUE'
```

Officers in the field select items based on their location using either a selection of the *n* closest items (implemented using `SDO_NN`) or the items within a certain radius from the user (implemented using `SDO_WITHIN_DISTANCE`). Listing 13-3 shows an example of the first that relates to the selection of a certain number of incident locations (place codes and place names) that fall within the area of responsibility of an officer. The `place_table` table contains the objects to be selected, and the `user_location` table contains the officer's location, which can be the current position or a default position such as center of the area of responsibility. The parameter `$$nr_of_nearest_places` specifies how many places are selected.

The query uses `SDO_NN` to rank places based on distance from the user location. The first and second `AND` conditions ensure that the location is that of the user, who logs in specifying a user name (`$$user_name`) and the code of the area of responsibility (`$$regio_code`). The third `AND` condition includes an `SDO_RELATE` statement that selects only places that fall within the area of responsibility (the `geoloc` of the table `work_areas`). This query discards places that are closer but not in the area for which the officer is responsible.

Listing 13-3. *Selecting Incidents Within a Certain Work Area*

```
SELECT place_code, place_name
FROM
(
  SELECT place_code, place_name
  FROM place_table, user_location
  WHERE
    SDO_NN(place_table.geo, user_location.geo, sdo_num_res=500', 1) = 'TRUE'
    AND upper(user_location.fldid) = upper('$$user_name')
    AND upper(user_location.regio_id) = upper('$$regio_code')
    AND SDO_RELATE
      (
        place_table.geo,
        (
          SELECT geoloc FROM work_areas
          WHERE upper(areas_id) = upper('$$regio_code')
        ),
        'mask=INSIDE querytype=WINDOW'
      ) = 'TRUE'
  ORDER BY SDO_NN_DISTANCE(1)
)
WHERE rownum <= $$nr_of_nearest_places
```

Bounding boxes are used in P-Info to display certain areas on a map. For orientation purposes, an officer may request a map of a street, postal code area, administrative area, and so on. Listing 13-4 shows an example of selection of the display area for a certain postal code area, here replaced by a question mark (as earlier, this is a parameter that is passed on by the Java code that calls the query). The table `tblpostcode` contains the list of postal codes and their spatial boundaries (polygons). The query results are passed on to the web mapping application to display the full postal code area on the handheld screen.

Listing 13-4. *Selecting a Bounding Box for Display*

```
SELECT t.postcode,
  SDO_GEOM.SDO_MIN_MBR_ORDINATE(t.geo, m.diminfo, 1) left,
  SDO_GEOM.SDO_MIN_MBR_ORDINATE(t.geo, m.diminfo, 2) bottom,
  SDO_GEOM.SDO_MAX_MBR_ORDINATE(t.geo, m.diminfo, 1) right,
  SDO_GEOM.SDO_MAX_MBR_ORDINATE(t.geo, m.diminfo, 2) top,
FROM  tblpostcode t, user_sdo_geom_metadata m
  WHERE  t.postcode = ?
```

Measurable Added Value of P-Info

The Dutch police force has carried out various efficiency and effectiveness tests of P-Info. Their main goal was to determine if P-Info is able to provide a tangible benefit to the police operations. The metrics used for the tests reflected two of the original goals of the system:

to increase the visibility and presence of officers in the field, and to have the officers be able to carry out the same work in less time. Among the various measurements suitable for this purpose, tests were conducted to measure the increase in time that agents would spend in the field and the amount of time required to carry out the same operation with and without P-Info.

In the first test, a group of five police officers was monitored over a period of about 4 weeks. The officers' field presence was compared to that of other colleagues who had the same tasks but operated without P-Info (the control group). The results showed that P-Info increased the time spent in the field by about 20 percent. This means that the same amount of fieldwork could be carried out by four rather than five agents or, alternatively, that a 20 percent larger area could be patrolled at the same quality level. Considering the personnel costs and the costs of P-Info, the balance was dramatically in favor of P-Info in terms of operation costs.

The second test was a comparison of work efficiency during roadblocks. Two roadblocks were set up with the same number of personnel, with one group operating with P-Info and the other group operating in the regular way (without P-Info). At the end of the operations, the number of cars checked and fines issued were compared. The test demonstrated that about 50 percent more cars could be screened using P-Info, with a proportional increase of the number of fines.

In spite of the limitations of the tests and the necessary caution in generalizing results, there is clear evidence that P-Info improves the effectiveness and efficiency of police forces. Considering the costs of P-Info and its benefits, a clear case can be made in favor of investing in P-Info.

It is worth stressing the role of location information in P-Info. While there are some pure uses of location information in P-Info—for instance, to locate an address or a user location on a map—in the vast majority of cases, location information enables information search, provision, and visualization. P-Info is essentially a portal to multiple legacy information sources, organized to serve the specific needs of mobile officers. The combination of mobility requirements with legacy information systems put some hard requirements on the design and management of spatial data in P-Info. The result is a system that uses various forms of spatial data (reference road networks, geocoding databases, real-time user positions, and backdrop maps) and various types of services that exploit this data (such as spatial replication, visualization, and notification) within the general purpose of P-Info: providing extensive and meaningful information to officers in the field.

Risk Repository for Hazardous Substances

On May 13, 2000, two explosions in a fireworks warehouse located in the urban center of the city of Enschede in the Netherlands detonated an estimated 100 tons of explosives. The blast was felt up to 40 km away, and within minutes the surrounding residential quarter was devastated. Twenty-two people died in the accident, and over 1,000 people were injured. More than 400 houses were reduced to ashes, and another 1,000 were damaged. The material costs of the incident were estimated at between US$500 million and $1 billion.

■ **Note** This system was developed by PinkRoccade BV and Geodan IT BV for the National Institute for Public Health and the Environment (RIVM) under supervision of the Netherlands Ministry of Housing, Spatial Planning and the Environment (VROM).

In the aftermath of disasters such as this one, and also of Chernobyl (1986), Bhopal (1984), and Seveso (1976), governments in industrialized and developing countries have introduced or toughened legislation and controls over the transportation, storage, processing, and use of dangerous substances.

In the Netherlands, the Enschede disaster has triggered a number of important risk-management initiatives that are meant to improve the prevention, preparedness, and repression of industrial incidents. One of those is the obligation to report to the authorities any situation that may involve a risk related to hazardous substances. Generally speaking, these risks are the result of the storage, transport, or processing of a (bio)chemical substance.

The RRGS (Dutch acronym for Register Risk Situations Hazardous Substances) is the central repository for this information. It provides a single source for all information regarding high-risk sources countrywide. The RRGS is accessible to professional users but also to the public. For the public, the RRGS provides information to understand and assess possible risk situations in a certain neighborhood. National and local government organizations use the RRGS for spatial planning, risk management, and disaster prevention. Emergency services agencies use the information in the repository to plan and organize rescue operations and emergency response.

The example of the RRGS map interface provided in Figure 13-9 shows the location of a gas station and the related risk contours. The system is accessible through a web interface. It provides a set of forms, available to registered users, to manage the information concerning an industrial site or a transportation infrastructure, and the nature and extent of the risks associated with these objects. The map interface serves to visualize the location of risk sources, the risk contours, and the areas surrounding a facility or a transport infrastructure affected by various risk levels. The RRGS include risk sources such as

- Major industrial plants
- LPG filling stations
- Storage facilities for hazardous chemical and biochemical substances
- Storage facilities for explosives and ammunitions
- Nuclear reactors or nuclear waste storage facilities
- Railway yards for shunting trains with hazardous substances
- Containers of hazardous substances (e.g., container shipments)

As concerns transport risks, the RRGS addresses risks related to transportation by road, rail, water, or pipeline.

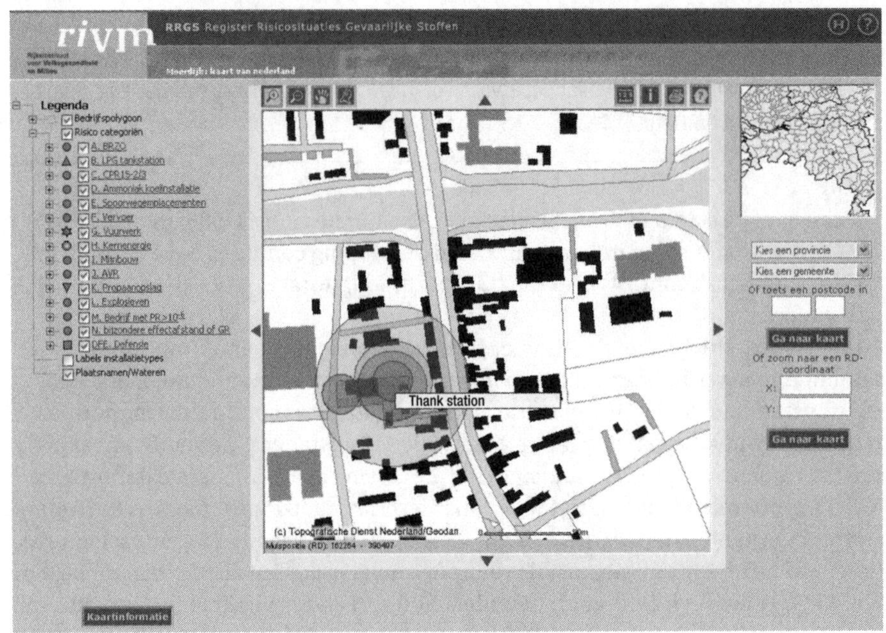

Figure 13-9. *Example of risk map for a gas station*
Image © RIVM, National Institute of Public Health and the Environment.

Table 13-1 shows the typical information included in the system. It is worth noting that risk contours and risk profiles normally require detailed studies, which are site and incident specific. In the case of RRGS, the risks are simplified representations of the actual risks and are based on generic risk models.[5] This allows a rapid risk assessment based on relatively limited information.

Table 13-1. *Example of Data Included in the RRGS*

General Data	Data on Hazardous Substances	Risk Data
Name of the installation	Name and identification numbers (e.g., CAS, UN) of the substances	Risk contours for predefined risk thresholds, such as 10^{-5}/year, 10^{-6}/year, and 10^{-8}/year, and specific consequences
Address or coordinates of a location	Nature of the hazard (i.e., toxicity, explosion, flammable)	Average population density in the area around the establishment (or transport route) Effect distances

5. According to the U.S. Department of Transportation, Office of Hazardous Material Safety, *hazard* is the characteristic of a substance that has the potential to cause harm to people, material goods, or the environment. *Consequence* is the direct effect of an event or incident. It can be a health effect (e.g., death, injury, or exposure), property loss, environmental effect, and so on. *Risk* is the combination of the likelihood and the consequence of a specified hazard being realized. *Likelihood* is expressed as a probability, such as one in 1 million.

The information in the RRGS is accessible through the system's interface, but it is also available to other systems. Other systems can use the RRGS as part of planning, logistics, or emergency management, and to overlay risk maps on other type of maps. This is one of the main requirements of the RRGS that implies an extensive adoption of open standards and web services at all levels of the system.

RRGS Technology

The RRGS is based on a web services framework. Thanks to this architecture, the system can be used stand-alone, or it can be integrated in regional and local risk-information systems, such as desktop applications for the assessment or formulation of regional plans and development plans.

The RRGS implements the OpenGIS standard interfaces and services. The open standards permit a seamless integration of external systems with the objects in the RRGS. Compliance with these standards allows a faster, more consistent, and more economical structuring of the system. Figure 13-10 provides a simplified architecture overview, completely implemented in Java (J2EE).

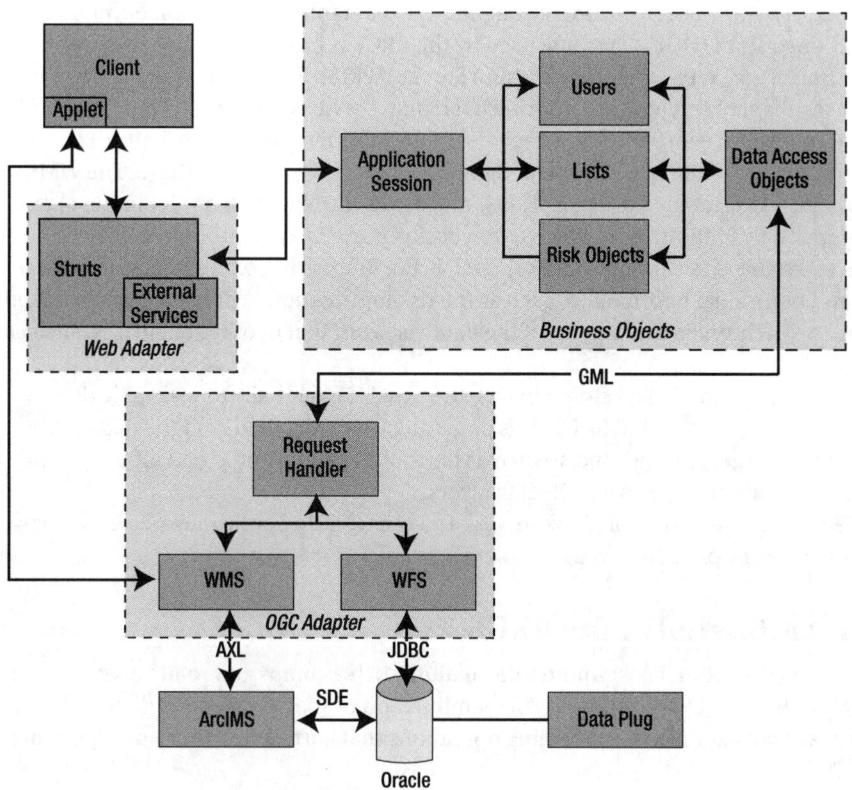

Figure 13-10. *Overview of the RRGS architecture*

The RRGS is accessible through a web interface and requires an applet for the map component of the application. The web adapter controls the main interfaces. The core of the web adapter is a Struts framework that manages the system interface and delegates tasks to the business objects.[6] Struts implements the Model View Controller (MVC) pattern. MVC organizes an interactive application into three modules. The first includes the application model, with its data representation and business logic. The second concerns the views that provide data presentation and user input. The third includes the controller that manages flows and dispatches requests. The web adapter also offers access to data services to external applications.

The business objects provide data handling, including data storage and access. The RRGS uses a Data Access Object (DAO) to communicate with the data services. A DAO abstracts and encapsulates all access to the data source and implements the access mechanism required to work with the data source (such as an RDBMS or LDAP). The business component that relies on the DAO uses the simpler interface exposed by the DAO, which hides the data source implementation details from its clients. Because the interface exposed by the DAO to clients does not change when the underlying data source implementation changes, this pattern allows the DAO to adapt to different storage schemes without affecting its business components. The DAO therefore acts as an adapter between the business object and the data source.

All communication between the DAO and the data sources is based on Geography Markup Language (GML), an XML-based encoding standard for geographic information developed by the OpenGIS Consortium (OGC). The data used by the RRGS is mediated by two OGC servers: the Web Feature Server (WFS) and the Web Map Server (WMS). The WMS allows a client to overlay maps for display served from multiple web map services on the Internet. The WFS allows a client to retrieve geospatial data encoded in GML from multiple web feature services.

The WFS accesses alphanumeric and geographic objects from the database. The WMS generates a map in a certain format (e.g., JPEG) and sends it to the map applet in the client. Maps are generated by ESRI ArcIMS, which connects to Oracle Spatial through ArcSDE.

The Oracle database, including Oracle Spatial, is the foundation of the RRGS, and stores both spatial and nonspatial information, such as the risk information. A data plug is also added to the system, to synchronize the content of the database with that of other databases, such as regional ones.

The reference geographic data stored in Oracle Spatial is essentially topographic data, at scales ranging from 1:10,000 to 1:250,000. This data can be very detailed, and the data can be used to identify single geographic objects such as parts of a building, or a road infrastructure, or a bridge. The system manages over 100 data layers.

The system runs on a cluster of Linux servers and uses Oracle Application Server as a Java container for the Java implementation.

Use of Oracle Spatial in the RRGS

Oracle Spatial is used to store background information, such as maps and road networks, and spatial information related to risk objects. All manipulation of spatial objects is done in Oracle Spatial, as well as many simple risk-modeling operations that correspond to spatial operators, such as a buffer.

The main tables with `SDO_GEOMETRY` columns are the tables containing the risk locations and the risk installations (a risk location can be, for example, a chemical plant that contains many installations, such as reactors, tanks, etc.). The geometry of risk locations is almost always

6. For more information on Struts, please visit `http://jakarta.apache.org/struts`.

a polygon, corresponding to the physical boundary of the plant or industrial premise. Risk installations, on the other hand, are always points. Each location and each installation is associated with several other SDO_GEOMETRY columns, which contain the risk and effect contours.

Risk contours for risk locations usually have specific shapes. The shape is computed by an external module (e.g., an explosion model), and it is loaded in Oracle through the WFS. The WFS receives a GML containing the risk contour and parses it to create the structure of INSERT statements for loading the spatial object (the risk contour) in the appropriate SDO_GEOMETRY column. For linear transportation infrastructures, the risk contour is calculated by a buffer function. Java code creates a SQL statement for Oracle that creates a buffer polygon in an SDO_GEOMETRY column. Remaining risk installations are associated to circular risk contours.

Listing 13-5 shows the buffer generation using SDO_BUFFER, in this case applied to an object (l_route) for a buffer of l_dist meters around the object. Notice that SDO_BUFFER returns an SDO_GEOMETRY object, which in this case is the object of a densify function. With geometries in a projected coordinate system, such as in this case, circular arcs can be *densified* into polygons. The result is straight-line polygon geometry. The arc_tolerance parameter specifies the maximum distance between the original geometry and its approximated straight-line representation, in this case 1 meter. The RRGS uses this solution to increase rendering speed.

Listing 13-5. *Example of Generating a Buffer and Densifying Its Geometry*

```
l_buffer := sdo_geom.sdo_arc_densify
(sdo_geom.sdo_buffer(l_route, l_dim, l_dist), l_dim, 'arc_tolerance = 1');
```

Once the buffer is created, the geometry can be stored in the SDO_GEOMETRY containing the risk contour. Listing 13-6 shows an example for updating the table rgs_transportroutes (major roads and highways), inserting a risk contour polygon for the p_tre_id object through the function illustrated in Listing 13-5 for geometry column risk_contour_1 of table rgs_transportroutes.

Listing 13-6. *Example of Inserting a Geometry*

```
update rgs_transportroutes tre
set tre.risk_contour_1 = l_buffer
where tre.id = p_tre_id;
```

Notice that the tables containing risk location and risk installations have multiple SDO_GEOMETRY columns to accommodate for risk contours and effect contours, and various risk and effect levels. For instance, the risk location table contains seven different SDO_GEOMETRY columns. All spatial columns are indexed.

To display spatial objects with ArcSDE, the system defines a series of views. This is necessary to separate object types in tables (points, lines, polygons, etc.) into separate views that are rendered separately. The same applies to multiple SDO_GEOMETRY columns. Different views are created for each separate column and are rendered separately.

One of the main features of the RRGS is to identify all locations and installations that contribute to the total risk of any given location. When you click a point on the map, the system detects all sources of a certain risk or effect level, based on the risk and effect contours of locations and installations. This is based on the SDO_RELATE operator. Listing 13-7 shows an example of this selection (in this case, a cursor example). The query selects the IDs of installations (irg.id) from the table of risk installations (rgs_installations), for which the risk contour (irg.risk_contour_1) contains the object b_geom.

Listing 13-7. *Example of Selecting Risk Objects Causing a Certain Risk for a Point*

```
CURSOR c_irg_rcr5(b_geom in mdsys.sdo_geometry) IS
  SELECT irg.id id
  FROM   rgs_installations irg
    WHERE  SDO_RELATE(irg.risk_countour_1, b_geom, 'MASK=CONTAINS querytype=WINDOW')
    = 'TRUE';
```

From Hazardous Substances to Risk Management

The RRGS system, which has been in operation since 2003, focuses on a specific type of risks related to hazardous substances. However, public risk managers need to address a much larger portfolio of situations that can cause serious consequences for people, material resources, and the environment. These situations include, for instance, transportation incidents (air, land, and water), earthquakes, epidemics, large fires in buildings or tunnels, floods, forest fires, and blackouts, among others. The RRGS represents only one of the sources of information needed to identify, prevent, and manage these risks.

The evolution of the RRGS is in the direction of supporting the definition of comprehensive risk maps based on multiple risk sources that interoperate and provide information to assess all types of risks. Figure 13-11 shows an example of risk sources and risk targets. Risk levels are displayed as color gradients, and risk contours (such as the 10^{-6} contour) are displayed as lines. Figure 13-12 shows the location and risk contours of several risk objects, such as tank stations (T), and the risk corridors of main road transportation infrastructures. All map information is overlaid on an aerial photograph.

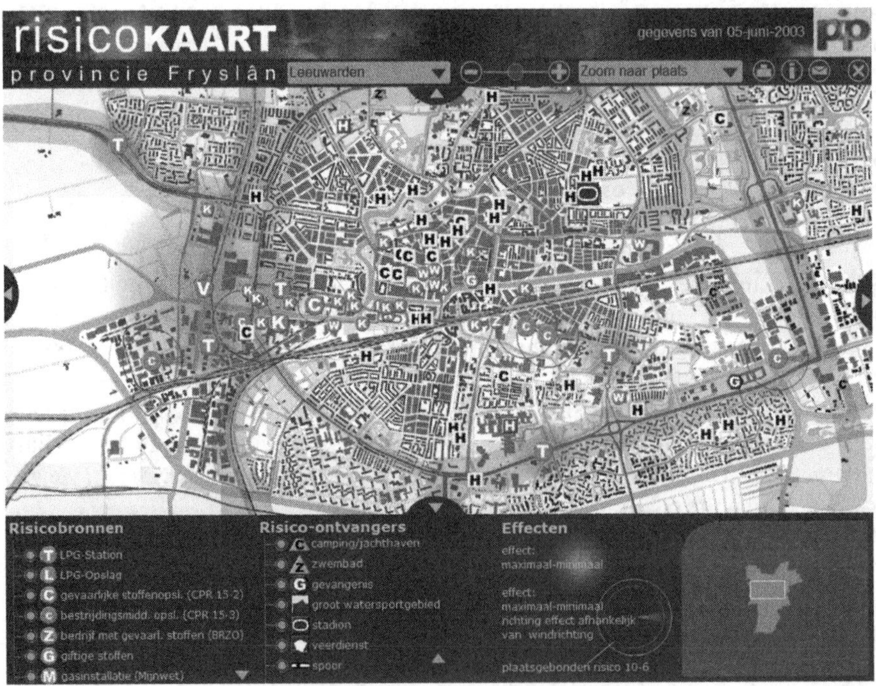

Figure 13-11. *Risk map for the province of Fryslân*
Image © Provincie Fryslân (`www.fryslan.nl`*).*

Figure 13-12. *Risk map for a portion of the Utrecht area*
Image © Provincie Utrecht (`www.provincie-utrecht.nl`*).*

These examples are publicly available from the websites of the provinces of Fryslân and Utrecht in the Netherlands. Other regional maps are also available from the sites of other regions. These maps will be replaced by uniform risk maps created based on the so-called Model RiskMap, which is currently being implemented.

It is important to notice that both maps can be extracted data from the same source (the RRGS) and integrated with other regional-specific sources. This is possible thanks to the implementation of OGC standards at all levels of the system.

GeoStor: Spatial Data Warehouse for the State of Arkansas

Access to comprehensive, accurate, and updated geospatial information has become an essential component of state and local governments, private business, and education. To meet the growing demands for effective and efficient public services, it is increasingly important to make a wide range of different data sources quickly accessible from a central facility, while ensuring coordination of local sources, data security, and easy access to the information. National security issues and the threat of terrorism have made this need even more pressing, since rapid access to transportation or healthcare facilities is crucial to those responsible for emergency response, public order, and public safety.

Note This system is managed by the Center for Advanced Spatial Technologies of the University of Arkansas and is available at `www.cast.uark.edu/cast/geostor`. This section is based on the paper titled "GeoStor Design and Operational Considerations" (`www.cast.uark.edu/cast/geostor/about_geostor/design_oper/Design_Arch_V5.zip`) by Douglas Meredith, Deborah Harmon, John Wilson, Robert Harris, James Sullins, and W. Fredrick Limp, Center for Advanced Spatial Technologies, University of Arkansas, Fayetteville.

These considerations were the basis for the development of GeoStor, a publicly accessible geospatial information system for the state of Arkansas. The system makes available more than 2TB of vector, image, and grid data though the web. The data are organized in over 650 statewide themes (such as major roads, industrial terrain, natural areas, etc.) from more than 50,000 individual data files that are the original source of this information.

Categories of information include socioeconomic data (agriculture, law, business, education, health, population, demography, and law enforcement), natural resources (plants, animals, and protected areas), climate and meteorology data, physical geography (digital elevation models, geology, landforms, and geomorphology), transportation (roads, highways, and facilities), hydrology (rivers, waterways, and hydro structures), and reference datasets (satellite images and state and district boundaries).

Users can access and download data through a web interface that provides a metadata catalog of available themes (see Figure 13-13 later in this section). The system is designed to interoperate at the level of data acquisition (to coordinate real-time data exchanges between GeoStor and data producers) and at the level of business or government applications that use GeoStor as a data source. Oracle Spatial is the foundation of GeoStor and contains all spatial data used by the system.

GeoStor Data Warehouse

Data for GeoStor are supplied by local and national organizations and are extracted from a variety of data files. The data warehouse offers a mechanism for data producers to provide current data to the system while maintaining control of the data-creation process, and at the same time it provides a mechanism for data users to access all data as if the data were derived from a single uniform entity. The data warehouse supports data searches and also a variety of applications that can use the same data collection as a foundation. This is achieved through a data warehouse design that uses interoperability and data federation principles.

Centralized spatial data repositories have always presented technical and organizational challenges at the level of data acquisition (the "input" stream from data suppliers to the repository), and at the level of data distribution and access (the "output" stream from the repository to end users).

Solutions that collect and store copies of spatial data produced by diverse organizations have the advantage of making available all data from a single coherent source. The downside is the need to harmonize diverse data standards, which can be achieved either by requiring data producers to adhere to a certain data standard or by converting data from various native formats to the format of choice of the central storage facility. Imposing data format standards on data producers has proven ineffective and difficult to achieve, as it can interfere with the data collection practices and technical requirements of these organizations. Data conversion by the data warehouse administrators, on the other hand, increases data management costs and introduces a lead time from data update at the level of the data provider and its availability from the warehouse.

From the access point of view, you should notice that central spatial data facilities should serve multiple types of users, from individual citizens, to businesses, to local and national governments. Data warehouses therefore need to be able to differentiate between levels of access (e.g., some data are available only to some users), business models (e.g., free access versus subscription), and access priority. The facilities need to implement user profiles, security, authentication, and authorization—features that are the norm in databases but that are not regular GIS features. In addition, GeoStor needs to be accessible by other applications usually residing in remote servers that use the data for specific applications, possibly in combination with other data. These distribution requirements imply a fair level of standardization in terms of data models, data storage, and access protocols.

A solution to these issues is found in the combination of database technology and web interoperability. The data warehouse is constructed based on a centralized, database-driven repository serving a variety of data services, including download, upload, search, analysis, and visualization. The concept of *data federation* underlines a certain balance between central and distributed data holdings, and the fact that institutional agreements are in place between these two levels to define and coordinate local and central activities. The structure allows multiple data providers to locally maintain their own internal information while electronically updating the central system. The users see a virtual centralized repository, while data are effectively stored partly locally and partly centrally. Software "triggers" can be installed in an individual data provider that will automatically post updates/changes to the central system as they are made. For example, in the case of an update in a transport facility (e.g., a road is closed), as soon as the change is introduced in the local database of the transportation agency, the change is propagated to the data warehouse, implying that any of its users will have the most current data available at all times. Such a mechanism assumes coordination between data suppliers and the data warehouse, in terms of data formats and data communication. A common issue in federated data systems is the optimal balance between central and local data storage. In general, a certain degree of centralization of core data holding is convenient for the system management and its performance.

GeoStor combines a central repository with interoperability schemes for connecting with local databases managed by various organizations throughout the state of Arkansas. A key aspect in the implementation of a federated geospatial clearinghouse is the definition of an interoperable data model and system architecture. Once that is achieved, the balance between centralization and distribution becomes essentially a matter of business and institutional choices, since the end user always has access to a full database that can be completely or partially virtual.

A similar level of coordination is necessary for data access and use. While individual users who download a dataset for local use are especially interested in the range of formats supported by the system, software applications that use GeoStor data remotely need to support a common data model and access protocol.

At present, examples of applications that use GeoStor include the Arkansas Economic Development Atlas (providing economic development information, such as available work force, infrastructure, and other factors); the Interoperable GeoObserver of the University of Arkansas; the Arkansas Soil Information System (a mapping application focused on mapping the soil distribution); and the U.S. Geological Survey (USGS), which uses GeoStor to populate The National Map (TNM) for the Arkansas area using OpenGIS web services.

GeoStor employs interoperability specifications developed by the OpenGIS Consortium. They allow distributed systems to exchange and integrate data based on common data and communication formats. OpenGIS specifications of relevance for GeoStor include the Coordinate Transformation Specification, the Catalog Services Specification (for metadata services), the Web Map Service Specification, and the Simple Features Specification (for spatial data). Metadata used in GeoStor is compliant with the Federal Geographic Data Committee (FGDC) Content Standard for Digital Geospatial Metadata.[7]

There are also already a number of client software applications directly connected to GeoStor for editing/updating data. These include ESRI ArcGIS and Intergraph GeoMedia applications for the Arkansas Soil and Water Conservation Commission (ASWCC) and Arkansas Geographic Information Office (AGIO), and an eSpatial-based application to edit Arkansas street centerlines and parcels by clients that are just using a browser.

GeoStor Architecture and Data Model

The architecture of GeoStor includes

- A Java client application used to browse and download data
- A set of Java servlets at the server side that interface between the client and database
- An Oracle Spatial database that contains all data centrally stored by GeoStor

Interoperability is implemented at all levels of the system, from client/server communication, to data storage, to metadata management.

The main interface of GeoSurf, the Java applet of GeoStor, is shown in Figure 13-13. GeoSurf shows the list of available map data layers, the active metadata and geographic filters, and the metadata window. For each layer, the metadata window provides a short or long description of the active map layer. For each layer, GeoStor provides a simple preview window that illustrates the content of the layer.

---

7. See `www.fgdc.gov`.

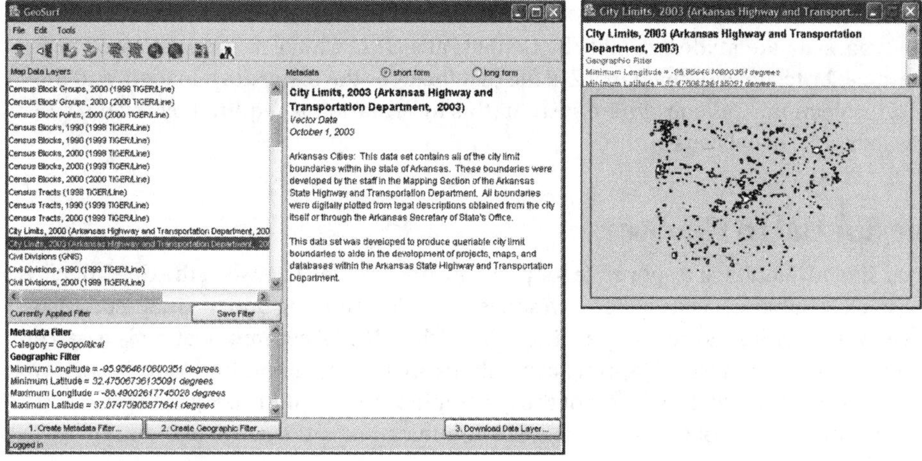

Figure 13-13. *GeoStor main interface*

Filters are used to restrict the search to layers that meet some user-defined spatial and nonspatial criteria. The metadata filter includes source criteria (e.g., only data from the U.S. Census Bureau), category conditions (e.g., only climate data for natural resource data), keyword filters, and time conditions (e.g., publication date). The geographic filter implements point and buffer constraints (i.e., it selects data within a certain buffer from a specified point), bounding box filters (i.e., it selects data within a bounding box), and polygon filters (e.g., the city limits of Little Rock, Arkansas). Web mapping with some basic map manipulation features is available for spatial filters, as shown in Figure 13-14.

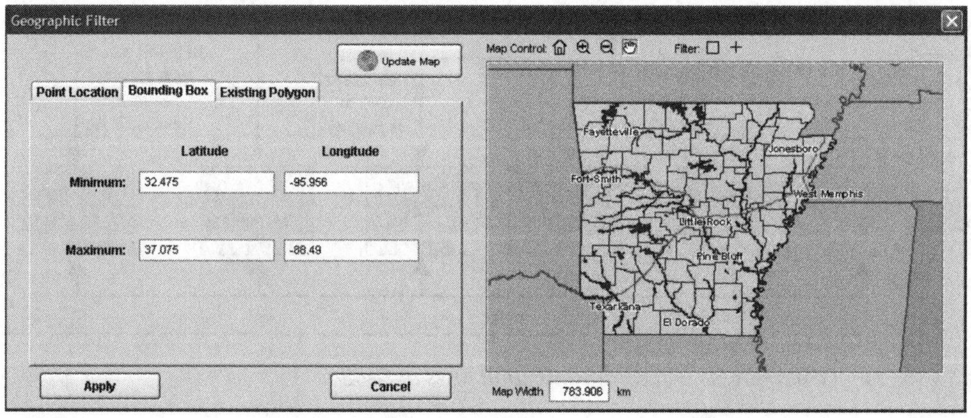

Figure 13-14. *Geographic filter*

The download wizard allows users to select datasets for download, and their projection and data type. Data are made available by GeoStor at a URL, which is communicated to the user by e-mail. Data are contained in a ZIP file that includes the file(s) downloaded, and their metadata, projection, and coordinate system (this information is required by several GIS packages to handle data layers).

Oracle Spatial in GeoStor

The server side of GeoStor is responsible for providing the interface between the GeoStor client and the Oracle database. It is designed as a series of servlets running under a J2EE-compliant web server, with each supporting a specific applet of the GUI. All communication is based on HTTP requests and responses. Mapping capabilities are based on MapInfo MapXtremeJava (MXJ), which provides visual selection of the geographic area of interest. Figure 13-15 shows all the major components of GeoSurf and the communication paths between them.

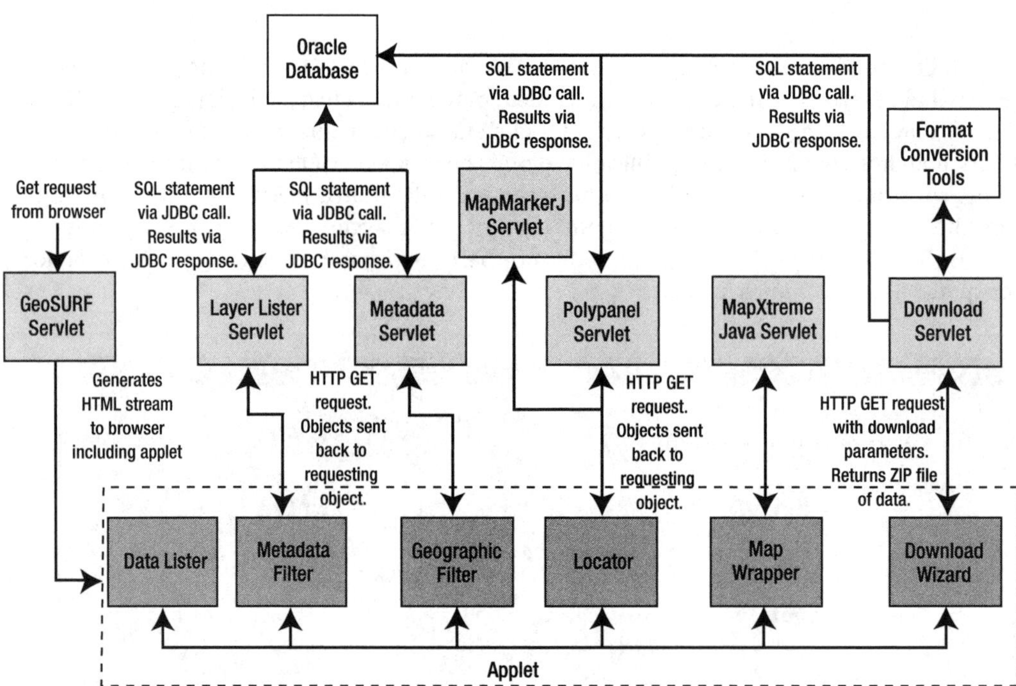

Figure 13-15. *Main components and communication lines in GeoStor*

At the database level, GeoStor uses three schemas:

- gtemp (staging area for temporary storage)
- gmeta (contains the metadata table)
- gdata (contains all data and indices)

Data tables contain one SDO_GEOMETRY column that stores all spatial elements, while all other fields are attribute information. Note that a data table is always associated with an entry in the metadata table. GeoStor uses FGDC metadata standards for describing the content of a data layer (corresponding to a data table).[8] The metadata contains information such as layer description, time period of content, spatial area covered, scale, coordinate system, and so on.

The data loading process follows a relatively simple sequence of steps. Data collected in various GIS and CAD formats is first translated by Safe Software Inc.'s Feature Manipulation Engine (FME) to Oracle Spatial and loaded in the temporary schema (gtemp). Several validation checks are run on the layer, based for instance on SDO_GEOM.VALIDATE_LAYER and visual inspection. After the checks are successfully completed, a new table is added to the gdata schema. An entry is then made in the USER_SDO_GEOM_METADATA table and the spatial index is created. To complete the process, a layer of information is added to the metadata table.

All data are stored in Universal Transverse Mercator Zone 15, North American Datum of 1983. This is the most commonly used coordinate system in Arkansas, and it reduces by as much as possible the need for end users to reproject the data downloaded from the system.

Use of GeoStor

The initial costs of GeoStor have been relatively large, but the investment will pay off in the medium and long term. For instance, the state of Arkansas has estimated that before GeoStor, an average of about 24 hours of work were necessary to search for, find, access, and retrieve a GIS file. With GeoStor, the same result can be achieved in a little over 1 hour.

The benefits of GeoStor are also indirect, for instance, in terms of supporting the economic development of Arkansas. This is the case, for instance, for about 500 jobs created in the community of Osceola that can be related to the availability of GeoStor. The industrial prospect that was evaluating various locations, including some in Arkansas, could quickly find the data necessary for making the decision through GeoStor. The nature of the prospect was such that the fast and exhaustive data availability of GeoStor helped make the difference, and the result was positive economic development. State economic development departments that learn this lesson make their states more competitive, and quick access to the data increases their chances for prosperity.

GeoStor is a living infrastructure that continuously develops and improves. The RAPID project, for instance, allows the distribution through GeoStor of GIS-ready processed satellite imagery within 10 minutes of receipt from the USGS. This very low turnaround time implies that high-resolution data can be made accessible to the public in a fraction of the time normally required for these activities.

The system has been used in support of the prevention and repression measures for the floods that affected Arkansas in March 2002, the third wettest March on record since 1880.[9]

---

8. See www.fgdc.gov/metadata/metadata.html.
9. See www.gis.state.ar.us/Programs/Projects_archive/flood_2004/Flood_index.htm

The AGIO, for example, was able to gather satellite images for the White River. The satellite data was then channeled through GeoStor, where it could be accessed, searched, and retrieved by policy makers, managers, and response decision makers such as the Arkansas Department of Emergency Management (ADEM).

Location Services for Third-Generation Mobile Networks

When the first commercial mobile phone was announced in 1983, it was evident that we were at the beginning of something radically new in personal communication: always connected, always reachable. This promise was very attractive, but the bulky and expensive devices of the time were a far cry from what seemed necessary to fulfill the promise. It seemed as though it would be a long time before small, cheap, and reliable mobile phones that could be used by everybody would become available.

■ **Note** This case study describes location services of Hutchison 3G UK limited (a Hutchison Whampoa Limited company). The authors would like to thank Hutchison 3G UK for granting permission to publish the material contained in this section. Additional information on services offered under the "3" brand can be found at `www.three.com`.

For once, it all went faster and smoother than expected. In the course of the following two decades, mobile telephones developed into ubiquitous devices. Since the introduction of the first mobile phone a little over 20 years ago, many western countries have reached a level of saturation, with penetration rates close to 85 percent of the population in Western Europe.[10] Entire industries have developed on the wave of this market growth: network manufacturers, mobile operators, phone makers, and software developers.

Most of the success of mobile phones boils down to a simple fact: standardization. The introduction of the Global System for Mobile Communication (GSM) standard in 1990 has allowed all adopting operators to offer voice and message roaming services. At present there are about 1 billion GSM users worldwide, accounting for about 80 percent of all mobile users. Figure 13-16 shows the split between voice and data spending (including messaging). The growth rate for voice is limited—around 4 percent on average—whereas the growth for data is around 24 percent.[11]

---

10. See GSM Europe at `www.gsmworld.com/gsmeurope/index.shtml`.
11. Helmut Meier, Roman Friedrich, and Hanno Blankenstein, "A master for mobile multimedia," *strategy+business*, Spring 2004.

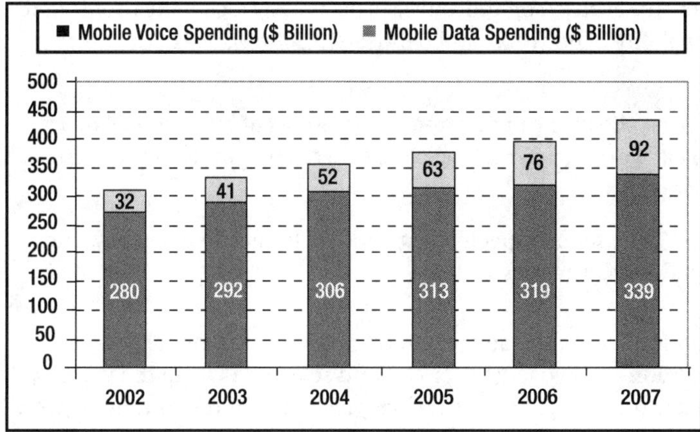

Figure 13-16. *Mobile voice and data spending for Europe, the United States, and Asia Image © Booz Allen Hamilton.*

The success of GSM is stretching the limits of this communication technology as well as the commercial possibilities of its exploitation. Several GSM markets are now nearly saturated, resulting in slower growth and fierce competition. In the period from 1995–2000, for instance, the average price decrease for 1 minute of airtime ranged between 30 percent and 70 percent. In a nearly saturated market, the industry predicts that the average revenue per user (ARPU) will steadily decrease if based on voice only. Data services therefore have an integral role in maintaining and increasing the ARPU. GSM networks, or alternative "second-generation" networks, are not suitable for rich, high-bandwidth data services.

The saturation of current GSM networks and the increasing role of mobile data services were at the basis for the introduction of third-generation (3G) mobile networks in the last few years. Universal Mobile Telecommunications System (UMTS) is currently the world's choice for 3G mobile service delivery. UMTS is based on a more efficient use of the air spectrum and endorses the standards of the Internet for data communication. UMTS will therefore facilitate the convergence between the telecommunications, information technology, media, and content industries, and it will also facilitate the delivery of new services with data rates ranging from 384Kbps up to 2Mbps.

To provide diverse location-based services (LBS) to the 3G consumer market, Hutchinson 3G has implemented a number of location-enabled applications (LEAs) that are offered to the customers of its "3" UMTS networks.[12] Hutchinson 3G is one of the first UMTS players to clearly identify LBS as one of the core features of UMTS usage. Its services, available to all "3" subscribers through the mobile portal of the operator, integrate LBS as part of a service portfolio that includes information, messaging, entertainment, and multimedia services. LBS are offered to consumers and business users, but in both cases, they use the same underlying service and content infrastructure. The location services are based on three core service types:

12. See www.three.com for additional information on "3" operators in Europe, the Middle East, and Asia.

- *Auto location and map*: This is based on the ability to accurately locate the user (thanks to the GPS-assisted capability of networks and handsets) and to visualize the user's position on a map.
- *Finder*: With these services, the user can find and locate points of interest (POIs), or search for specific POI categories (e.g., parking places) in the proximity of the current location or a given location.
- *Routing and navigation*: The user can specify start and end points for a journey, and receive map and navigation instructions.

Figure 13-17 shows two examples of the handset interface of LEA services. The image on the left shows the current position of the user (the circle) and selected POIs in the vicinity, represented by icons. The image on the right shows an overview map for the routing service. The service also includes detailed maps for every section of the journey and narrative navigation descriptions.

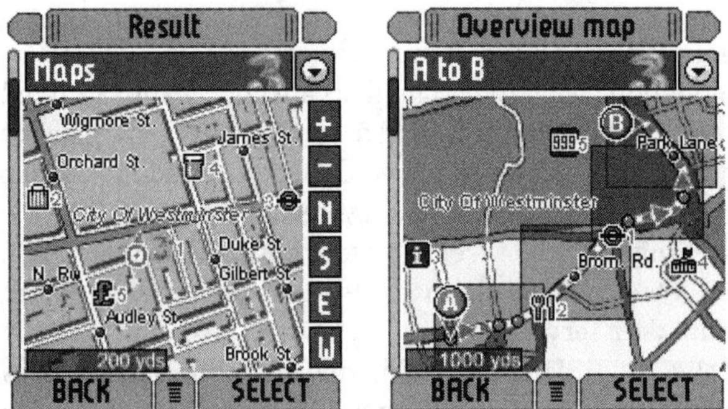

Figure 13-17. *Examples of the "3" location services*
Images © Hutchison 3G UK Limited.

Location-Enabled Applications at "3"

LEAs require the support of a diverse set of spatial and nonspatial datasets. The GeoSpatial Server (GSS) aims to deliver location-based content data to LEAs. A key component of the GSS is the content database, which allows the storage, retrieval, analysis, and update of spatial and nonspatial datasets offered to various GSS components. The GSS Repository is based on Oracle Spatial for the storage of maps, addresses, POIs, and POI attributes. The database is designed to contain a vast amount of data that can reach over 1TB. In particular, the repository contains the following:

- *Map data at various scales*: To optimize the use of bandwidth, maps are stored at various scales that are suitable for visualization, from street-level detail up to regional overview maps.
- *POI data*: This includes, for instance, the name, phone number, URL, and description of a restaurant, including the credit cards accepted, pictures of the dining rooms, guidebook reviews, and so on.
- *Address data*: This includes the full address of a POI or of a certain location, and its x, y coordinates.

The GSS serves LEAs with the appropriate map and POI features in response to a particular query. The architecture, which is based on an underlying Java implementation, identifies three main functional areas: the routing and navigation, the geocoding, and the map and POI features. The routing and navigation includes all functionality related to directions and navigation instructions. Geocoding includes normalization capabilities and the association of x, y coordinates to an address. Geocoding also includes *reverse geocoding*, the association of the closest meaningful address to a given pair of x, y coordinates. The core map and feature services include all mapping capabilities of LEAs and access to all POI information.

A typical service may include a combination of all three service categories. A user may, for instance, choose to visualize her current location (Map and Features), locate a certain address to go to (Geocoding), and get navigation instructions to the destination (Routing and Navigation).

Logical and Physical Data Models for Maps and POIs: The GSS Repository

The logical data model of the GSS Repository is based on the concept that all features within LEAs are either addresses, POIs, or map features. To illustrate the use of these features, it is useful to break down a real-world entity—a Shell gas station, for instance—into its address, POI, and map features. The address feature will record the standard address, such as "36 Magellan Road, London." The POI feature will record the name of the station, "Shell Gas Station," categorize it as a "Gas Station," and record other information relevant to its function as a POI, such as whether it serves low-emission fuel or if it has a small shop attached. The map feature will record its representation on a map base, such as the building outline polygon and the access roads.

The physical model used to implement this logical model is illustrated in Figure 13-18. The five tables illustrate the core of the physical model, which includes a variety of other tables and relations that have been omitted in this diagram for simplicity. The POI (the Shell station) corresponds to an entry in the POI table. This POI will have an address (from the address table) and an x, y coordinate (from the location table). The POI attributes, which may be structured differently for different POI classes, are stored in an attribute table, which can have any number of attributes associated with a POI (up to the limit of Oracle tables).

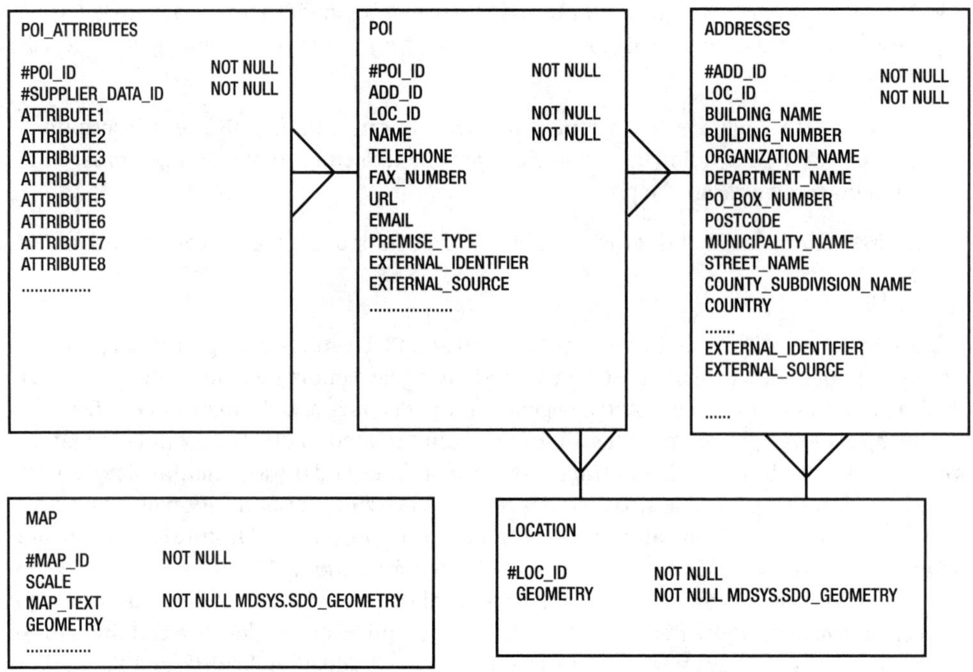

Figure 13-18. *Simplified POI and maps data model for location services: storage layer*

The location table is separated from the POI and address table. This allows, for instance, several POIs and several addresses to share the same location, and at the same time to perform reverse geocoding on the location table. Given an x, y coordinate, it is possible, for example, with a SQL statement to identify the closest item in the location table and then associate it with an address or a POI.

POIs and maps are related to each other only in terms of location. Maps provide a background to the location of the user and POIs, and include the reference information for geocoding and for the road network for routing. The map and location tables contain the `SDO_GEOMETRY` data type to store geometry features and points, respectively.

In this storage layer (SL), all information about maps, addresses, and POIs are stored independent of their actual use in LEAs. The SL acts as a general-purpose repository that contains all available current content. This model allows a certain degree of flexibility to design and deliver various types of location services by selecting and structuring the same content in different ways, each suitable for a specific service. For instance, the list of gas stations (without attribute information) may be used to provide points of reference to drivers along a certain route. The same list, fully attributed, may be offered as part of a city guide.

The selection of which content, POI, and attribute information to display to the end user is made at the presentation layer (PL) level. The PL is organized as a series of feature type tables, each corresponding to a POI table with a specific data structure. Each table feeds content to a specific LEA and is optimized to provide the content and the form of content suitable for that service. Several different PLs can be created based on the same SL, reducing the time needed to deliver various service types based on the same underlying data. The PL is created from the SL with the help of content management tools, or based on PL/SQL programs.

Data Ingestion and Preparation

The content used by LEAs is provided by several suppliers that deliver map, address, and POI content. The GSS is populated by a combination of these datasets, which undergo a data preparation process before entering the SL. The data preparation takes place in a staging environment, also based on Oracle Spatial.

The data preparation process may be manual or automated, depending on the complexity and quality of the input data, and on the frequency of its updates. In any case, each data delivery is subject to a unit test (UT) that serves to check the completeness and appropriateness of the dataset ahead of any operation. As with the data preparation process, the UT may be automatic or require manual analysis.

For each dataset, the data preparation process includes one or more of the following activities:

- *Data selection and filtering*: In many cases, input datasets contain data that are not relevant for LEAs. In the preceding example, the list of gas stations may include the construction date of a facility or the storage capacity of the tanks—information that is not relevant for mobile users.

- *Content restructuring*: The input content is often delivered in a different format from that required by LEAs. For instance, opening times and holiday periods may be contained in the same text field in the input data, while an LEA service may need to separate out the holiday period to make a certain commercial establishment unavailable during its holidays.

- *Data cleaning*: Most input data contains a certain degree of data pollution that can manifest itself in various forms, such as typos, duplication, presence of wrong characters and codes, misplaced fields, and so on. Data cleaning includes all activities that remove incorrect data and increase the quality of data before they are used in LEAs.

- *Geocoding*: Content is often delivered with incomplete address information and nonstandardized address data, and without x, y coordinates. Normalization and geocoding serve to restructure an address based on predefined reference address data, and to associate x, y coordinates with it.

- *Data integration*: Map, POI, and address information may need to be created by combining multiple sources. This may be the case in POI data, where the full POI description is extracted from two or more datasets containing data regarding the same POI. For instance, one dataset may provide the name and address, while another provides customer reviews and other relevant data. Quality requirements, standardization, and completeness may need the merging of multiple datasets to provide sufficient information regarding quality and quantity to the end user.

All these operations are carried out in a staging area, usually a different one for each content provider. The staging environment is based on Oracle and Oracle Spatial, and most data preparation procedures are based on either SQL scripts or PL/SQL programs specifically designed for each content provider. Once the data are prepared for use in the GSS, specific loading procedures are used to feed the storage layer. During these procedures, each content provider's data are mapped into the GSS SL data model, as shown in Figure 13-19.

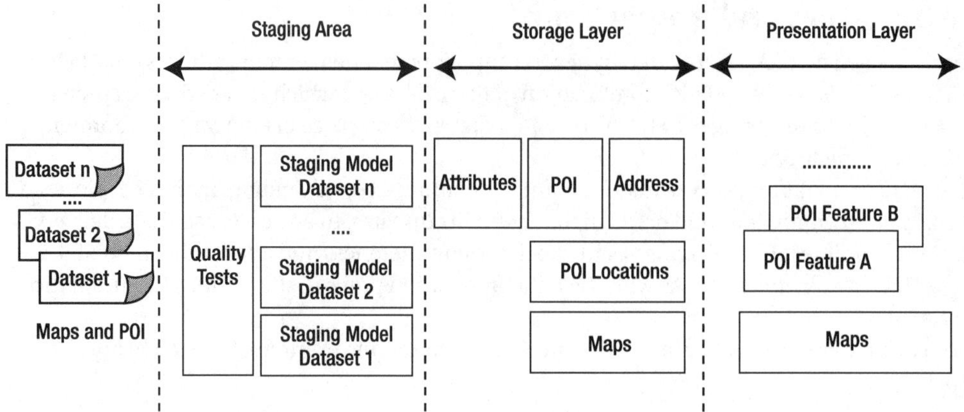

Figure 13-19. *Data ingestion and publication on the storage and presentation layers*

Map data undergoes a similar data preparation process, although the emphasis is on map feature selection and map generalization. *Map feature selection* consists of structuring and aggregating map content into layers that are useful to the mobile user. Layers may be roads, bridges, built-up areas, parks, rivers, lakes, and so on—in general, all separate map feature classes that provide visual and spatial context to a map reader.

Map generalization serves to create various versions of the same map feature, each appropriate for display at a different scale (e.g., small, medium, and large scales). The essence of map generalization is the ability to retain the visual appearance of a map while reducing its content, thus making its portrayal faster. Generalization is particularly useful when vector content is rendered on the fly by a map server to produce a bitmap for display on the device. On a very large scale (e.g., when the user visualizes a full city area), the useful detail that can be displayed is limited to major reference features, such as major roads and selected landmarks. All detailed features, such as local roads, cannot be displayed and are discarded by the portrayal engine. To speed up the rendering process, vector maps are generalized and stored with various levels of detail in the database. In this way, the portrayal engine renders only the visible spatial features at any given scale and does not waste time rendering/discarding nonvisible ones. The generalization procedures are based on PL/SQL code that for each map and for each scale decides which features to retain and their level of simplification. Typical results of generalization are the simplification of geometry—for instance, eliminating vertices, removing loops, removing small irregularities, transforming an irregular arc into a perfect arc, merging dual carriage roads into a single line, and so on.

Nonfunctional Specification

The repository data model implements the ISO standard 19115 specifications for geographic information. Hutchison 3G has also opted to implement the standards laid out by the OGC for the GSS. In particular, the Feature Server Framework exposes features retrieved from the GSS Repository in a defined object model: the Simple Features Specification defined by the OGS WFS. The GSS Repository allows data to be retrieved by an OGC-compliant WFS, and therefore it allows the creation of OGC-compliant Simple Features.

The nonfunctional characteristics of the GSS Repository cover a broad range of aspects such as availability, scalability, and portability. In some cases, nonfunctional requirements are satisfied by the inherent nature of the Oracle database environment (security, reliability, and user management). In other cases, specific solutions have been adopted to meet the Hutchinson 3G's requirements. The GSS Repository needs to be scalable to accommodate increases in users and in performance levels, and it has to ensure at least 95.95 percent availability. These requirements are satisfied by the use of Real Application Clusters (RAC), which allow the GSS Repository to run a single database on a group of servers, clustered together. RAC ensures scalability and availability by allowing multiple servers to share the work, so that in case of some server failures, the rest of the cluster can take over without service interruption.

The LEA system design and implementation needs to be portable to a range of international regions. For this reason, the UTF-8 Unicode implementation AL32UTF8 has been selected for the character set.

Summary

In this chapter, we described five case studies that demonstrate the use of Oracle Spatial in business and government applications. The *BusNet* case illustrated the use of Oracle Spatial to improve the planning and management of the bus schedules and routes for the city of London. The *P-Info* case study described a system to provide mobile, location-enabled access to mission-critical information for police officers operating in the field. The *Risk Repository for Hazardous Substances* case study illustrated a system that gives access to information on risk and possible effects of the storage, processing, and transportation of hazardous substances. The *GeoStor* spatial data warehouse case described the use of Oracle Spatial to search, visualize, and download spatial data for the state of Arkansas. The *Location Services for UMTS* case study illustrated one of the first deployments of consumer-based location services for third-generation telecommunication networks.

Oracle Spatial is used to store and retrieve all spatial data used in the applications, and the spatial analysis performed in these applications is based on the methods and tools described in this book. The applications described in this chapter rely extensively on the scalability, security, and reliability of the Oracle database—another reason for the selection of Oracle Spatial in all these applications.

Together, these case studies are meant to illustrate through real applications the variety of cases in which Oracle Spatial is used and to demonstrate the wide applicability of the Oracle Spatial technology.

CHAPTER 14

Tips, Common Mistakes, and Common Errors

This is the last chapter of the book. Now that you have studied many techniques for how to location-enable your application and how to incorporate spatial analysis and visualization tools in your application, we think it is time for a little advice.

In the first section of this chapter, we present some advice on best practices—in other words, we give some tips for location-enabling your application. In the second section, we look at some of the common pitfalls that can trap unwary users as they set out to location-enable their business application. In the third and final section of this chapter, we enumerate common errors that you may encounter in location-enabling your application and the corrective actions to sort out these errors.

Tips

In this section, we provide several tips (best practices) for data modeling, improving spatial query performance, and managing large historical/temporal spatial databases. Note that we discuss only those tips not covered in prior chapters in detail. For tips covered in earlier chapters, we refer you directly to those chapters.

Data Modeling and Loading

First, let's examine some things you should keep in mind while modeling and loading spatial data.

Always Validate Your Data

You should always validate your data before proceeding with further analysis. You can use the `SDO_GEOM.VALIDATE_*` routines to perform this validation, as discussed in Chapter 5. Chapter 5 has routines to debug/correct invalid geometries as well. You can also use the `SDO_MIGRATE.TO_CURRENT` function to correct the orientation in any invalid *polygon* geometries.

If your application involves network modeling, as described in Chapter 10, you should validate the network using the `SDO_NET.VALIDATE_NETWORK` function. See Listing 10-11 for an example.

Always Store Two- and Three-Dimensional Points in SDO_POINT

To store a two- or three-dimensional point, you should always use the SDO_POINT attribute of the SDO_GEOMETRY data type. You should set the SDO_ELEM_INFO and SDO_ORDINATES attributes to NULL. This ensures less storage and faster access for such point data. Refer to Chapter 4 for more details and examples.

Use TO_CURRENT to Correct Orientation in a Polygon

As described in Chapter 5, you can correct the orientation of a polygon using the SDO_MIGRATE.TO_CURRENT function. For instance, you can run SDO_MIGRATE.TO_CURRENT on the polygon geometry in Listing 14-1 that is oriented clockwise. (Oracle Spatial expects the ring of the polygon boundary to be oriented counterclockwise.)

Listing 14-1. *Correcting the Orientation of a Polygon Geometry Using* TO_CURRENT

```
SQL> SELECT SDO_MIGRATE.TO_CURRENT
(
  SDO_GEOMETRY
  (
    2003, NULL, NULL,
    SDO_ELEM_INFO_ARRAY(1,1003,1 ),
    SDO_ORDINATE_ARRAY
    (
      2,2,          -- Vertices specified in clockwise order
      3,3.5,
      5,2,
      2,2
    )
  ),
  SDO_DIM_ARRAY
  (
    SDO_DIM_ELEMENT('1', -180, 180, 0.0000005),
    SDO_DIM_ELEMENT('2', -90, 90, 0.0000005)
  )
) FROM DUAL;

SDO_MIGRATE.TO_CURRENT(MDSYS.SDO_GEOMETRY(2003,NULL,NULL,MDSYS.SD
O_ELEM_INFO_ARRAY
---------------------------------------------------------------------------
SDO_GEOMETRY
(
  2003, NULL, NULL,
  SDO_ELEM_INFO_ARRAY(1, 1003, 1),
  SDO_ORDINATE_ARRAY
  (
    2, 2,           -- Vertices specified in counterclockwise order
    5, 2,
```

```
      3, 3.5,
      2, 2
    )
  )
```

Use the SDO_UNION Function to Correct a Self-Crossing Polygon

In Figure 5-1 (in Chapter 5), we showed a self-crossing polygon geometry. If we modeled this geometry as a single polygon and tried to validate it as shown in Listing 5-25, Oracle throws ORA-13349 ("Polygon boundary crosses itself") error. One simple mechanism to correct this polygon geometry is to union (i.e., run `SDO_GEOM.SDO_UNION` on) the geometry with itself. Listing 14-2 shows the code to correct the invalid geometry of Listing 5-25.

Listing 14-2. *Correcting a Self-Crossing Polygon Geometry Using* `SDO_UNION`

```
SQL> SELECT SDO_GEOM.SDO_UNION
(
  SDO_GEOMETRY     -- self-crossing 'polygon' geometry
  (
    2003,          -- A polygon type geometry: invalid because edges cross
    NULL, NULL,
    SDO_ELEM_INFO_ARRAY(1,1003,1 ),
    SDO_ORDINATE_ARRAY
    (
      2,2,
      3,3.5,
      2,5,
      5,5,
      3,3.5,
      5,2,
      2,2
    )
  ),
  SDO_GEOMETRY      -- self-crossing 'polygon' geometry (repeated)
  (
    2003,
    NULL, NULL,
    SDO_ELEM_INFO_ARRAY(1,1003,1 ),
    SDO_ORDINATE_ARRAY
    (
      2,2,
      3,3.5,
      2,5,
      5,5,
      3,3.5,
      5,2,
      2,2
    )
  ),
```

```
  0.0000005
) valid_gm FROM  DUAL;

VALID_GM(SDO_GTYPE, SDO_SRID, SDO_POINT(X, Y, Z), SDO_ELEM_INFO,
SDO_ORDINATES)
--------------------------------------------------------------------------------
SDO_GEOMETRY
(
  2007,              -- Corrected to a multipolygon rather than a single polygon
  NULL, NULL,
  SDO_ELEM_INFO_ARRAY  -- Two elements, each specifying a separate polygon
  (
    1, 1003, 1,     -- First Polygon Element starting at offset 1 in SDO_ORDINATES
    9, 1003, 1      -- Second Polygon Element starting at offset 9 in SDO_ORDINATES
  ),
  SDO_ORDINATE_ARRAY
  (
    3, 3.5,         -- First vertex of first polygon element
    2, 2,           -- second vertex
    5, 2,           -- third vertex
    3, 3.5,         -- final vertex of first polygon element (same as 1st vertex)
    2, 5,           -- First vertex of second polygon element
    3, 3.5,         -- second vertex
    5, 5,           -- third vertex
    2, 5            -- final vertex of second polygon element (same as 1st vertex)
  )
)
```

Note that the preceding listing corrects the geometry to be a multipolygon with two polygon elements. The polygon elements are disjoint (i.e., the boundary does not cross). The resulting multipolygon geometry is in valid Oracle Spatial format.

Always Store Only As Many Dimensions/Digits As Needed

Some third-party tools export spatial data as three-dimensional data. The first two dimensions contain the longitude and the latitude information, and the third dimension is always set to 0. This means the SDO_ORDINATES attribute will contain *three* ordinates for each point or vertex instead of *two*. For large geometries, this will translate into some wasted storage in the SDO_ORDINATES attribute of an SDO_GEOMETRY, which could have potential implications for storage and subsequent query performance (due to a higher number of I/Os). You should clean up such data by removing every third ordinate in the SDO_ORDINATES attribute (see Chapter 7 for details).

Likewise, third-party tools may also waste space by exporting too many digits for ordinate values in an SDO_GEOMETRY. For instance, if the data is in a projected coordinate system, an ordinate value with six or more decimal digits may specify a very high precision. Applications seldom require such high precision of data. By reducing the number of decimal digits (you can use the ROUND function in Oracle for this purpose), you can reduce the storage for an SDO_GEOMETRY with potential implications on the fetch performance (I/Os) of the geometry.

Performance of Spatial Operator Query

In most applications, selection based on spatial operators is much more expensive than selection using relational operators such as ' > " , and .. The cost of spatial operators increases with the complexity of spatial data.

Use Real Data for Performance Analysis

Given the complexity of spatial data, you should always run performance tests with real data instead of synthetic/artificial data, which do not model the complexity of spatial data well. Next, we focus on how to improve the performance of spatial operator queries.

A major portion of the time to answer a spatial operator query such as SDO_RELATE or SDO_NN goes into fetching the data rows from the data table. Consider the query in Listing 14-3 for identifying the nearest customers to a branch with id=1.

Listing 14-3. *Nearest-Neighbor Query on the* customers *Table*

```
SQL> SELECT COUNT(*)
FROM branches a, customers b
WHERE a.id=1 AND SDO_NN(b.location, a.location, 'SDO_NUM_RES=100')='TRUE';
```

This query is processed by Oracle Spatial in the following sequence (see Figure 14-1):

1. The query (store) location is passed to the spatial index.
2. The spatial index returns ROWIDs of the customers table that are closest to the query (store) location.
3. Oracle then fetches the rows corresponding to the ROWIDs returned by the spatial index.

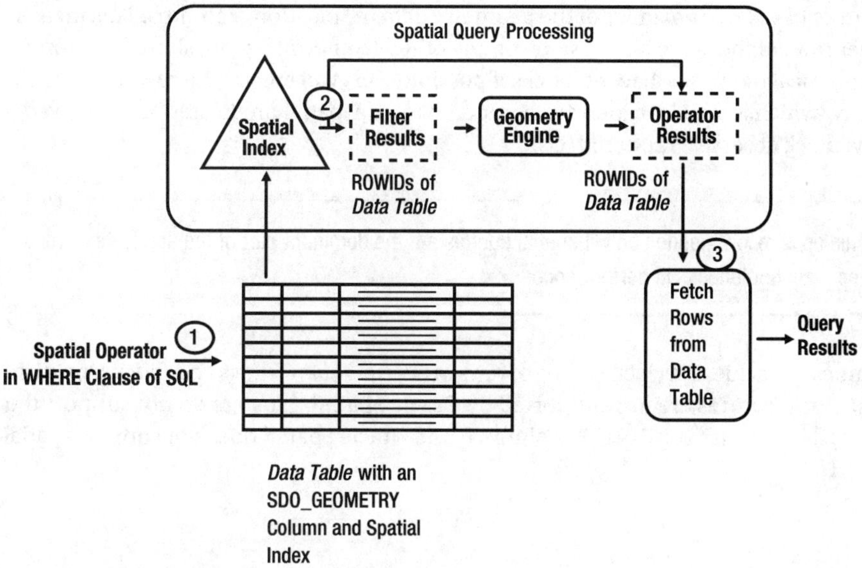

Figure 14-1. *Operator processing sequence in Oracle Spatial*

The query returns the 100 nearest customers to the specified branch location. Steps 2 and 3 may access the row data (such as ID and location columns) corresponding to these 100 customers in the `customers` table. These 100 rows may result in random disk I/Os, as there is no clustering of the `customers` table rows based on the "location" columns. The performance of the query may suffer due to a high I/O cost. This might result in a high response time for queries. In the following sections, we suggest two important tips for improving the performance.

Specify the LAYER_GTYPE Parameter

The first tip to improve query performance is to specify the `LAYER_GTYPE=POINT` parameter at the time of index creation if the table contains just point data. This will completely avoid step 3 in query processing in Figure 14-1. Instead, it will use the information in the spatial index to evaluate the query. This will substantially speed up query performance. Listing 14-4 shows how you can specify the `LAYER_GTYPE` parameter in the `CREATE INDEX` statement. Refer to Chapter 8 for more details on the `CREATE INDEX` statement.

Listing 14-4. *Specifying* `LAYER_GTYPE` *During Spatial Index Creation*

```
SQL> CREATE INDEX customers_sidx ON customers(location)
INDEXTYPE IS MDSYS.SPATIAL_INDEX PARAMETERS('LAYER_GTYPE=POINT');
```

Reorganize the Table Data to Minimize I/O

In the previous example, the spatial data in the `location` column of the `customers` table has only *point* geometries. In other tables, this may not be the case; the corresponding spatial column may contain both *point* and *nonpoint* geometries. For such tables, we cannot employ the trick shown in Listing 14-4 of specifying `LAYER_GTYPE=POINT` to improve spatial query performance. However, we can still reduce I/O in step 3 of Figure 14-1 by an alternate mechanism: cluster the rows and avoid/minimize random I/O. What we specifically need is a reclustering of the table rows based on proximity of the geometry data in "location" columns. This means that customer rows in the same city or state, or any other geometric region, should be stored in the same physical block or adjacent blocks if possible. This will ensure the rows that satisfy a spatial query (which is usually expensive compared to nonspatial predicates) are retrieved with very few block accesses (random I/Os).

■ **Caution** This tip is recommended only if spatial queries are the dominant part of the application workload and are the main bottlenecks in performance.

Two features can achieve such clustering of rows in Oracle: *Table Clusters* and *Index-Organized Tables* (IOTs). Both features are not supported by Oracle Spatial. Clusters do not support the storage of objects (such as `SDO_GEOMETRY` columns) and Oracle Spatial does not support spatial indexes on IOTs.

In this section, we describe how to achieve similar performance gains as in Oracle IOTs and Oracle Table Clusters for mostly *static* spatial data. Some experiments using similar techniques indicate record performance gains.[1] The method involves a function called `linear_key` that takes as input an `SDO_GEOMETRY` and an `SDO_DIM_ARRAY` as parameters and returns a `RAW` string. We will work with the `us_streets` table in the following example.

First, copy all the data in `us_streets` table into a new table called `us_streets_dup`. You can then truncate the original `us_streets` table as shown in Listing 14-5 and drop the associated spatial index `us_streets_sidx` on the `us_streets` table.

Listing 14-5. *Creating an Empty Table with the Same Structure As the* `us_streets` *Table*

```
SQL> CREATE TABLE us_streets_dup AS SELECT * FROM us_streets;
TRUNCATE TABLE us_streets;
DROP INDEX us_streets_sidx;
```

For each row in the `us_streets_dup` table, compute the value of the function `linear_key` (described later in this section) using the `location` column for the row. Reinsert data from the `us_streets_dup` table into the `us_streets` table by ordering the rows using the value of the `linear_key` function. This approach is likely to store the rows in the `us_streets` table in the specified order. Listing 14-6 shows the SQL. Note that we assume the metadata for the spatial layer `<us_streets, location>` is populated.

Listing 14-6. *Reinserting into the* `us_streets` *Table Based on the* `linear_key` *Order*

```
SQL> INSERT INTO us_streets
SELECT * FROM us_streets_dup a
WHERE b.table_name = 'CUSTOMERS' and b.column_name='LOCATION'
ORDER BY
  linear_key
  (
    a.location,
    (
      SELECT diminfo FROM USER_SDO_GEOM_METADATA
      WHERE table_name = 'US_STREETS' AND column_name='LOCATION'
    )
  );
```

You should be all set now. The preceding reorganization will ensure that the data in the repopulated `us_streets` table is more or less *spatially* clustered. You can now re-create the spatial index on the `location` column of the `us_streets` table. This reordering may improve the performance of subsequent queries on the table, as they might minimize random block accesses.

An alternative approach is to materialize the `linear_key` function value for each row as an additional column in the table, and then *partition* the table using the values for this materialized column. Note that to use partitioning, you will need to license the Partitioning option of Oracle.

---

1. T.P.M. Tijssen, C.W. Quak, and P.J.M. van Oosterom. "Spatial DBMS testing with data from Cadastre and TNO-NITG," `www.gdmc.nl/oosterom/kad6.pdf`, GISt Report No. 7 Delft, ISSN 1569-0245, ISBN 90-77029-02-8, March 2001.

You can code the linear_key function in a number of ways. Listing 14-7 is a simple implementation in PL/SQL. Note that this example uses the MD.HHENCODE function, which encodes a two-dimensional point (such as the CENTROID or POINTONSURFACE of a geometry) into a RAW string. This function is provided by Oracle Spatial (in both Locator and Spatial options), and it uses the lower/upper bounds in each dimension and an encoding level as additional parameters.

Listing 14-7. *Using the* linear_key *Function to Order Geometry Rows Based on a "Spatial" Ordering*

```
CREATE OR REPLACE FUNCTION linear_key
(
  location    SDO_GEOMETRY,
  diminfo     SDO_DIM_ARRAY
)
RETURN RAW DETERMINISTIC
IS
  ctr          SDO_GEOMETRY;
  rval         RAW(48);
  lvl          INTEGER;
BEGIN

  -- Compute the centroid of the geometry
  -- Alternately, you can use the 'faster' sdo_pointonsurface function
  ctr := SDO_GEOM.SDO_CENTROID(location, diminfo);

  lvl := 8;  -- Specifies the encoding level for hhcode function
  rval :=
    MD.HHENCODE
    ( -- Specify value, lower and upper bounds, encoding level for each dimension
      location.sdo_point.x, diminfo(1).sdo_lb, diminfo(1).sdo_ub, lvl,
      location.sdo_point.y, diminfo(2).sdo_lb, diminfo(2).sdo_ub, lvl
    );
  RETURN  rval;
END;
/
```

Specify Appropriate Hints in a Query

In the case of a query specifying multiple tables, you should specify appropriate hints to ensure the desired evaluation plan. Refer to Chapter 8 for details on how to use the ORDERED, INDEX, and NO_INDEX hints to suggest an appropriate plan to the optimizer.

Performance of Other Spatial Processing Functions

Next, we discuss how to improve the performance of stored functions and geometry processing functions such as SDO_AGGR_UNION (see Chapter 9 for details). Unlike the spatial operators, the geometry processing functions do not use the spatial index.

Specify DETERMINISTIC for Stored Functions

Most queries on spatial data may involve a combination of spatial operators, geometry processing functions, and user-defined stored PL/SQL functions. Here is a tip you should bear in mind when coding such stored PL/SQL functions.

If the return value of a PL/SQL function depends solely on the input parameter values (i.e., it returns the same value for the same set of parameter values, and the function does not depend on the state of the session variables and schema objects), then you should declare the function as `DETERMINISTIC`. This will allow the optimizer to avoid redundant function calls, and it may translate to a faster response time for queries. For example, in Listing 14-4 the `linear_key` function is declared as `DETERMINISTIC`.

If a `DETERMINISTIC` function is invoked multiple times with the same parameter values in a SQL statement, Oracle evaluates the function only once (and reuses the result in other invocations).

If your stored function returns an object such as an `SDO_GEOMETRY`, Oracle may evaluate this function multiple times. However, defining such a function as `DETERMINISTIC` will avoid such multiple evaluations and will improve the performance of any SQL query that uses such stored functions.

Use a Divide-and-Conquer Approach for SDO_AGGR_UNION

In some applications, you may have to compute the aggregate union of several `SDO_GEOMETRY` objects. For instance, you might want to compute the union of all the geometries in the `us_counties` table. Listing 14-8 shows the SQL to do so using the `SDO_AGGR_UNION` function (see Chapter 9 for details).

Listing 14-8. *Aggregate Union of All Geometries in the* `us_counties` *Table*

```
SQL> SELECT SDO_AGGR_UNION(SDOAGGRTYPE(a.geom, 0.5)) union_geom
FROM us_counties a;
```

The `SDO_AGGR_UNION` function is evaluated as follows. It first starts with a null value for the result (i.e., `union_geom`). It then unions (uses the `SDO_GEOM.SDO_UNION` function) every geometry in the `us_counties` table with `union_geom` in an iterative fashion.

The problem with this approach is that `union_geom` becomes larger and more complex with every union operation. Computing the union operation (using the `SDO_GEOM. SDO_UNION` function) with a complex geometry such as `union_geom` as one of the operands will be increasingly slow after each iteration.

An alternate mechanism is to divide the set of geometries to be "unioned" into disjoint groups or subsets, S1, . . ., S*n*. You can group them in any manner you like. First, compute the `SDO_AGGR_UNION` for the geometries in each subset/group, and then you can compute the union of the results of all the groups.

The SQL in Listing 14-9 shows how to compute the union of all the counties in Massachusetts by grouping them using the first letter of the county name. The county names in each group start with the same letter.

Listing 14-9. *Computing the Aggregate Unions for Multiple Groups*

```
SQL> SELECT SDO_AGGR_UNION(SDOAGGRTYPE(geom, 0.5)),  SUBSTR(county,1,1)
FROM us_counties
WHERE state_abrv='MA'
GROUP BY  (SUBSTR(county,1,1));
```

The SQL in Listing 14-9 groups all counties with the same starting letter using the SUBSTR function. For each such group, the union of the county geometries is returned. An alternate grouping could be based on the ROWNUM pseudo-column. For instance, if you want ten groups each, with approximately the same number of counties, you can use the SQL in Listing 14-10.

Listing 14-10. *Computing the Aggregate Unions Grouped by the* ROWNUM *Pseudo Column*

```
SQL> SELECT SDO_AGGR_UNION(sdoaggrtype(geom, 0.5)) union_geom
FROM us_counties
WHERE state_abrv='MA'
GROUP BY MOD(ROWNUM,10);
```

This returns the union geometries for each group. You can aggregate these geometries to obtain the aggregate union of all the counties. Listing 14-11 shows the corresponding SQL.

Listing 14-11. *Computing the Aggregate Union of Aggregate Unions Grouped by the* ROWNUM *Pseudo-Column*

```
SQL> SELECT SDO_AGGR_UNION(SDOAGGRTYPE(union_geom, 0.5))
FROM
(
  SELECT SDO_AGGR_UNION(SDOAGGRTYPE(geom, 0.5)) union_geom
  FROM us_counties
  WHERE state_abrv='MA'
  GROUP BY MOD(ROWNUM,10)
);
```

Note that Listing 14-11 uses Listing 14-10 in the FROM clause. This means the results of the SDO_AGGR_UNION in Listing 14-10 are *pipelined* to the outer-level SDO_AGGR_UNION in Listing 14-11. You can repeat this pipelining any number of times. Listing 14-12 shows a pipelining of results between three SDO_AGGR_UNION functions.

Listing 14-12. *Computing the Aggregate Union in a Pipelined Fashion*

```
SQL> SELECT SDO_AGGR_UNION(SDOAGGRTYPE(ugeom,0.5)) ugeom, state_abrv
FROM
(
```

```
   SELECT SDO_AGGR_UNION(SDOAGGRTYPE(ugeom,0.5)) ugeom
   FROM
   (
     SELECT SDO_AGGR_UNION(SDOAGGRTYPE(ugeom,0.5)) ugeom
     FROM
     (
       SELECT SDO_AGGR_UNION(SDOAGGRTYPE(geom,0.5)) ugeom
       FROM us_counties
       GROUP BY MOD (ROWNUM, 1000)
     )
     GROUP BY MOD (ROWNUM, 100)
   )
   GROUP BY MOD (ROWNUM, 10)
);
```

How many such SDO_AGGR_UNION functions should you use in this pipelined execution? We recommend that you use as many as necessary to ensure that the innermost SDO_AGGR_UNION function does not have more than ten rows. (You can easily write a stored function to apply this guideline and perform the SDO_AGGR_UNION as in Listing 14-12.) With this approach, the response time is likely to be minimized.

An analogous "divide-and-conquer" approach may help in improving the performance of the SDO_AGGR_CONVEXHULL and the SDO_AGGR_MBR aggregate functions.

Performance of Inserts, Deletes, and Updates

If a table has a spatial index on one or more of its columns, inserts, deletes, and updates on this table will take longer. This is because the associated spatial index(es) need to be kept up to date. Here are two alternatives to improve performance.

Drop the Index Before Modifying a Large Number of Rows

If you are modifying (inserting, deleting, or updating the geometry columns of) more than 30% of the total rows in a table, then it may be faster to drop the spatial indexes on columns of the table, perform the modification (either insert, delete, or update), and then re-create the spatial index.

Perform Inserts, Deletes, and Updates in Bulk

You can minimize the performance overheads of spatial indexes if you batch *multiple* inserts, deletes, and/or update operations in the same transaction. If you expect to perform more than 1,000 such operations in a typical transaction,[2] you can fine-tune the performance by specifying the parameter SDO_DML_BATCH_SIZE=<numeric_value> in the CREATE INDEX parameters. By default, this value is set to 1000 (optimal if the transaction has 1,000 inserts/deletes/updates). The SQL in Listing 14-13 shows an example of setting SDO_DML_BATCH_SIZE to 5000.

2. Note that this recommendation applies whenever "each" transaction has more than 1,000 insert, delete, or update operations.

Listing 14-13. *Setting the* SDO_DML_BATCH_SIZE *Parameter*

```
SQL> CREATE INDEX customers_sidx ON customers(location)
INDEXTYPE IS MDSYS.SPATIAL_INDEX
PARAMETERS('SDO_DML_BATCH_SIZE=5000');
```

The SDO_DML_BATCH_SIZE parameter should be in the range of 1 and 10,000. (You can inspect this value for your index in the USER_SDO_INDEX_METADATA view.) It is advisable not to increase this parameter to a value more than 10,000, as this leads to a lot of memory consumption with no discernible performance improvements.

If you have already created the spatial index, you can alter this parameter by manually changing it in the SDO_INDEX_METADATA_TABLE[3] table in the MDSYS schema for a specific spatial index. Note that you should not modify other parameters in this table. If you do, operations that use the spatial index such as spatial operators may fail (see Chapter 8 for more information).

Next, we examine the best practices for scalability and manageability of spatial data in tables with a large number of rows.

Best Practices for Scalability and Manageability of Spatial Indexes

Oracle recommends table partitioning, a licensed option, to scale with and easily manage large tables (i.e., with tens of millions of rows or larger). In fact, table partitioning is the suggested mechanism to scale to even *ultra-large databases* (on the order of *Exa-* [10^{18}] bytes).[4] You can extend the benefits of such partitioning to tables with SDO_GEOMETRY columns, too. As you saw in Chapter 8, partitioning can help in spatial query performance by pruning irrelevant partitions when the partition key is specified. Oracle combines parallelism with partitioning to efficiently process queries that access multiple partitions.

Creating a spatial index is much slower than creating a B-tree index—in some cases, by several orders of magnitude. Table partitioning will help in faster creation and easy management of spatial indexes. Specifically, we suggest using partitioning and local spatial indexes for managing large tables with tens of millions of rows, and/or managing historical, temporal, or mobile data. In this section, we illustrate the best practices for scalability and easy manageability of spatial indexes using a specific application in which new data is added continuously.

Consider an application that collects and stores weather-pattern images for different regions of the world. In such an application, you need to add data continuously on a per-day (or per-month, or per-year) basis. And, after analyzing the access patterns, you may decide to store the data on a daily basis for the current month, on a monthly basis for the prior months of the current year, and on a yearly basis for prior years. Since the current month changes with time, the challenge is to effectively maintain this data organization and to ensure all associated spatial indexes are up to date.

---

3. The USER_SDO_INDEX_METADATA and USER_SDO_INDEX_INFO dictionary views are based on this table.
4. See the following presentations for more information: "Oracle Database 10*g*: A VLDB Case Study" by Berik Davies and Xavier Lopez (www.oracle.com/openworld/archive/sf2003/solutions_bi.html), and the keynote speech titled "Journey to the Center of the Grid" given by Charles Rozwat at Oracle OpenWorld, San Francisco, September 10, 2003 (www.oracle.com/oracleworld/online/sanfrancisco/2003/keynotes.html).

Use Table Partitioning (and Local Spatial Indexes)

The solution for this problem is to use the Oracle Table Partitioning feature and create local spatial indexes for each partition. Listing 14-14 shows an example.

Listing 14-14. *Creating a Partitioned Table for Storing Temporal Weather Pattern Data*

```
SQL> CREATE TABLE weather_patterns
(
    gid NUMBER,
    geom SDO_GEOMETRY,
    creation_date VARCHAR2(32)
)
PARTITION BY RANGE(CREATION_DATE)
(
    PARTITION p1 VALUES LESS THAN ('2000-01-01')  TABLESPACE tbs_3,
    PARTITION p2 VALUES LESS THAN ('2001-01-01')  TABLESPACE tbs_3,
    PARTITION p3 VALUES LESS THAN ('2002-01-01')  TABLESPACE tbs_3,
    PARTITION p4 VALUES LESS THAN ('2003-01-01')  TABLESPACE tbs_3,
    PARTITION p5 VALUES LESS THAN ('2004-01-01')  TABLESPACE tbs_3,
    PARTITION jan VALUES LESS THAN ('2004-02-01'),  -- Month of January, 2004
    PARTITION feb VALUES LESS THAN ('2004-03-01'),  -- Month of February, 2004
    PARTITION current_month VALUES LESS THAN (MAXVALUE)
);
```

The SQL in Listing 14-14 creates a partitioned table based on the `creation_date` column. The first five partitions, `p1` to `p5`, store the data for years before 2004. You specify that these partitions go into the tablespace `TBS_3`. The next three partitions store the data for the first 3 months of 2004. There is no tablespace specified. Hence, these partitions are stored in the default tablespace, `USERS`. The last partition, `current_month`, stores the data for the `current_month` month, which, let's say, is March. You could go further and organize the data for March into days and associate partitions with these, too. But this current organization is sufficient to illustrate the concepts.

You can create a local partitioned spatial index for this table. Listing 14-15 illustrates this. Note the `LOCAL` keyword at the end of the statement. This tells Oracle to create "local" indexes—that is, a separate index for each partition (but all managed by the same name, `weather_patterns_sidx`).

Listing 14-15. *Creating a Local Partitioned Spatial Index*

```
SQL> CREATE INDEX  weather_patterns_sidx ON weather_patterns(geom)
INDEXTYPE IS MDSYS.SPATIAL_INDEX LOCAL;
```

This will create a separate spatial index for each partition of the table. The index information is stored in the corresponding tablespace associated with the partition. For example, for the first five partitions, the index is stored in tablespace `TBS_3`. You can also specify the "parallel 4" clause after the `LOCAL` keyword to indicate that the index creation should be run in parallel using four slave processes.

Let's say that, after creating the local indexes for partitions p1 to p3, the system runs out of space in the TBS_3 tablespace. At that point, you need to add more space, drop the index, and re-create the index using the SQL in Listing 14-15.

Create the Local Index As UNUSABLE for Better Manageability

An alternative option for creating local spatial indexes avoids such pitfalls and offers more flexibility. Listing 14-16 shows the alternative mechanism for creating partitioned indexes. First, you create the index as UNUSABLE. This will initialize the indexes for all partitions.

Listing 14-16. *Creating a Local Partitioned Spatial Index As "Unusable"*

```
SQL> CREATE INDEX  weather_patterns_sidx ON weather_patterns(geom)
INDEXTYPE IS MDSYS.SPATIAL_INDEX LOCAL UNUSABLE;
```

Note that the SQL in Listing 14-16 creates only a "dummy" index in each partition (more or less an instantaneous operation). After executing the SQL in Listing 14-16, Oracle marks all the partitions as UNUSABLE. Any spatial operator query, or an insert/delete/update on the table, or a specific partition will raise an error that indicates the partition is UNUSABLE. You will need to rebuild the index on the partitions before proceeding.

Rebuild the Spatial Index for Each Partition Separately

You can rebuild the index for each table partition separately (i.e., independent of one another). Listing 14-17 shows how to rebuild the local index for partition p1. Note that although we did not specify any tablespace parameter here, the index will be built in the "tablespace" specified with the table partition in the prior CREATE INDEX statement (see Listing 14-16). For partition p1, this tablespace is TBS_3. So, the index is built and stored in tablespace TBS_3.

Listing 14-17. *Rebuilding a Local Spatial Index*

```
SQL> ALTER INDEX weather_patterns_sidx REBUILD PARTITION P1;
```

Likewise, you can rebuild the local indexes for each partition separately. By rebuilding these indexes in multiple SQL*Plus sessions, you can achieve parallelism.

Rebuilding the local indexes separately gives you more control over partition index creation. If one partition fails, the whole index is not marked as failed. This means you do not have to rebuild the indexes for all partitions. Instead, you can rebuild the index only for the failed partition.

You can rebuild all UNUSABLE indexes (including the spatial index) for a partition in one attempt using the ALTER TABLE ... REBUILD UNUSBALE INDEXES command. Listing 14-18 shows the corresponding SQL. Note that this is an ALTER TABLE command instead of an ALTER INDEX command.

Listing 14-18. *Rebuilding All* UNUSABLE *Indexes for a Table Partition*

```
SQL> ALTER TABLE weather_patterns REBUIlD PARTITION P1 UNUSABLE INDEXES;
```

Use EXCHANGE PARTITION to Work on FAILED Partitions

The rebuild of the spatial index as in Listing 14-18 may fail for a variety of reasons, including lack of space in the specified tablespace for the partition or invalid geometries in the indexed column of the table partition. In the former case, if you increase the size of the tablespace and re-execute (i.e., rebuild the index as in Listing 14-18), the index will rebuild. However, if the partition has invalid geometries, then re-executing 14-18 will not help. Moreover, you may not be able to delete or update the rows corresponding to the invalid geometries. Oracle may raise the "Partition marked as `FAILED/UNUSABLE`" error for such operations.

To avoid such failures, you should always validate the spatial data before creating spatial indexes. See Chapter 5 for details on how to validate spatial data.

If you end up with an "index failed" situation, how do you recover from it? One solution is to use the `EXCHANGE PARTITION` clause of `ALTER TABLE`. You should first create a table, say `tmp`, with the same structure as the `weather_patterns` table. Then create a spatial index on this empty table `tmp` (after inserting the appropriate metadata in the `USER_SDO_GEOM_METADATA` view). Now you can execute the SQL in Listing 14-19 to exchange data between table `tmp` and partition `p1` of the `weather_patterns` table. Note that the `EXCLUDING INDEXES` clause at the end ensures that the indexes are not exchanged (only the data is exchanged).

Listing 14-19. *Exchanging* `tmp` *Data with Partition* `p1` *of* `weather_patterns` *Without Indexes*

```
SQL> ALTER TABLE weather_patterns EXCHANGE PARTITION current_month WITH
TABLE tmp EXCLUDING INDEXES;
```

If you examine the contents of the table `tmp`, you will see the rows that were earlier part of partition `p1` in `weather_patterns` table and vice versa. Since `tmp` is not a partitioned table, you can perform normal DML (delete, update, and insert) operations on this table and correct the rows with invalid geometries. (You may want to drop the spatial index if there are too many such rows.) After correcting the rows, you can re-execute Listing 14-19 to put the corrected data in partition `p1`. You can then rebuild the index on this partition as in Listing 14-17.

Use EXCHANGE PARTITION with INDEXES for New Data

You may want to use the `ALTER TABLE . . . EXCHANGE PARTITION` command for another purpose: keeping spatial indexes up to date with new data.

For instance, say you add new data to the `current_month` partition every day. How do you keep the data in the `current_month` partition up to date? One method is to add all new data to this partition directly. Inserting into partitions that have spatial indexes could be slow. Here are some tips to improve performance:

- *Add new data in large batches.* This means each insert transaction should have more than 1,000 inserts. Spatial indexes incorporate efficient algorithms to bulk load a substantial number of inserts (or deletes) within a single transaction.
- *Create a temporary table (say* `tmp`*) that has the new data along with the data in the* `current_month` *partition.* Create a spatial index on this `tmp` table. You can exchange the contents of the `tmp` table with the contents of the `current_month` partition in a split second. This will also exchange the associated spatial indexes.

Listing 14-20 shows an example of the second tip in practice.

Listing 14-20. *Adding New Data Using the* EXCHANGE PARTITION *Clause*

```
SQL> CREATE TABLE tmp (gid number, geom sdo_geometry, date varcahr2(32));
SQL> INSERT INTO TABLE tmp  VALUES (...);  --- new data

--  Also include data from current_month partition
SQL> INSERT INTO TABLE tmp
SELECT * FROM weather_partitions PARTITION(current_month);

-- Exchange table tmp with "current_month" partition of weather_patterns.
SQL> ALTER TABLE weather_patterns
EXCHANGE PARTITION current_month WITH TABLE tmp INCLUDING INDEXES;
```

Note that in Listing 14-20 we use the INCLUDING INDEXES clause. This will exchange the (already created) indexes of partition p1 and table tmp almost instantaneously. The preceding tips can help in ensuring that the current_month partition is always up to date.

Other Tips for Partition Maintenance

Next, let's examine how to split a current_month partition as you enter a new month. At the end of the year, you may also want to consolidate/merge all monthly partitions into a single yearly partition.

Splitting the current_month Partition

As you enter into the month of April, you will need to split the current_month partition into two partitions: march and current_month (which holds the current month data). You can accomplish this using the SPLIT PARTITION clause of ALTER TABLE, as shown in Listing 14-21.

Listing 14-21. *Splitting the* current_month *Partition into* march *and* current_month *Partitions*

```
SQL> ALTER TABLE weather_patterns
SPLIT PARTITION current_month AT ('2004-04-1')  INTO
(
  PARTITION march,
  PARTITION current_month
);
```

The SQL in Listing 14-21 splits the current_month partition at April 1, 2004 (the key is '2004-04-01') into the march and current_month partitions. You will need to rebuild the indexes, as shown in Listing 14-22, for each of these partitions to allow queries to succeed.

Listing 14-22. *Rebuilding the Indexes for the "Split" Partitions*

```
SQL> ALTER INDEX weather_patterns_sidx REBUILD PARTITION march;
SQL> ALTER INDEX weather_patterns_sidx REBUILD PARTITION current_month;
```

Merging Partitions

At the end of the year, you want to merge all the partitions into a single year partition. First, Listing 14-23 shows how to merge the partitions jan and feb into a single partition.

Listing 14-23. *Merging the Partitions for* jan *and* feb *into a Single Partition*

```
SQL> ALTER TABLE weather_patterns
MERGE PARTITIONS jan, feb INTO PARTITION  janfeb;
```

Note that the resulting partition is named janfeb. If you try to name it to jan in Listing 14-23, Oracle throws an error. Instead, you should first name the merged partition as janfeb as in Listing 14-23, and then later rename the janfeb partition to jan again as shown in Listing 14-24.

Listing 14-24. *Renaming a Partition*

```
SQL> ALTER INDEX weather_patterns_sidx RENAME PARTITION janfeb TO jan;
```

Likewise, using the SQL in Listings 14-23 and 14-24, you can merge partitions for other months into the jan partition. You can then rename the jan partition to an appropriate name such as p2004 using the ALTER INDEX . . . RENAME PARTITION command, as shown in Listing 14-25.

Listing 14-25. *Renaming the Merged Monthly Partition As a Year Partition*

```
SQL> ALTER INDEX weather_patterns_sidx RENAME PARTITION jan TO p2004;
```

Specify the Partition Key in the WHERE Clause

Specifying the partition key in the WHERE clause of a SELECT statement aids in pruning the number of partitions searched. If the WHERE clause does not have a predicate on the partition key, all partitions (and associated spatial indexes) are evaluated.

Specify the PARALLEL Clause to Ensure a Parallel Query on a Partitioned Index

To ensure queries on multiple partitions of a table are evaluated in parallel, you should do one of the following: (1) specify the PARALLEL clause in CREATE INDEX (see Listing 8-60 for an example), (2) alter the table by specifying a parallel degree (see Listing 8-61 for an example), or (3) alter the index by specifying a parallel degree.

To summarize, table partitioning can be an effective mechanism to ensure scalability and manageability of spatial indexes on large tables of spatial data. The partitioning features come in handy when you are managing temporal and historical spatial data.

Common Mistakes

In this section, we look at some of the common pitfalls associated with location-enabling an application. You should consult this list before you design your application.

Bounds and Tolerance for Geodetic Data

If the data in a layer is geodetic (i.e., the SRID matches one of the values in the MDSYS.GEODETIC_SRIDS table), then the corresponding DIMINFO attribute (of type SDO_DIM_ARRAY) should be set as follows:

- The first dimension in the SDO_DIM_ARRAY should correspond to the longitude dimension. The lower and upper bounds (for this dimension) should always be set to values of –180 and 180. If other values are specified for the bounds, Oracle Spatial ignores them.
- The second dimension in the SDO_DIM_ARRAY should correspond to the latitude dimension. The lower and upper bounds should always be set to values of –90 and 90. If other values are specified for the bounds, Oracle Spatial ignores them.
- The tolerance for the dimensions should always be specified in meters. The meter is the unit of distance in all geodetic coordinate systems in Oracle.

If the tolerance is set incorrectly, Oracle Spatial may return unexpected results. A value of 0.5 (0.5 meters) is suitable for most applications.

Longitude, Latitude Dimensions

For geodetic data, the first dimension should be the longitude dimension with lower and upper bounds of –180 and 180, respectively. The second dimension should be the latitude dimension with bounds of –90 and 90. You should not enter the latitude dimension first and the longitude dimension second in the DIMIFO attribute of the USER_SDO_GEOM_METADATA view. The order is important.

NULL Values for SDO_GEOMETRY

Setting the individual fields of SDO_GEOMETRY to NULL does not constitute a NULL SDO_GEOMETRY object. Instead, you should set the entire object to NULL. For example, you can set the location (SDO_GEOMETRY) column to NULL as in Listing 14-26.

Listing 14-26. *Setting the* location *Column in the* customers *Table to a* NULL *Value*

```
SQL> UPDATE customers SET location = NULL;
```

Use GEOCODE or GEOCODE_ALL

You should not use the naïve GEOCODE_AS_GEOMETRY function to convert addresses to SDO_GEOMETRY data, if you suspect that the input address may be incorrect or misspelled. The GEOCODE_AS_GEOMETRY may return incorrect SDO_GEOMETRY objects if the input address has errors. In such cases, you should use the GEOCODE or GEOCODE_ALL functions to obtain corrected address(es) along with the quality of the match(es). See Table 6-2 for more details.

Specify "INDEXTYPE is mdsys.spatial_index" in CREATE INDEX

To create a spatial index on the column of a table, you should always specify `INDEXTYPE is mdsys.spatial_index`. See Listing 14-13 or 14-15, or Chapter 8 for examples. If you do not specify this clause in the `CREATE INDEX` statement, Oracle will raise the ORA-02327 ("Cannot create index on expression with datatype ADT") error.

Do Not Move, Import, or Replicate MDRT Tables

The `MDRT_<>$` tables (and the associated `MDRS_<>$` sequences) are used in storing information for spatial indexes. You should never operate on these tables as regular Oracle tables. This means

- *You should not move the* `MDRT` *tables from one tablespace to another.* If you do, the corresponding spatial index becomes unusable and all *spatial operators on the indexed table fail.* The only way to recover from this situation is to drop and re-create the spatial index. To avoid all these problems, make sure your DBA understands this restriction and does not move the `MDRT` tables around to perform some optimizations. You can specify the tablespace in which the `MDRT` table needs to be stored using the `tablespace` parameter during spatial index creation. Refer to Chapter 8 for more details.
- *You should not drop or alter the* `MDRT` *tables or the* `MDRS` *sequences.* You can drop them, however, if they are *not associated* with any spatial index (this should not happen under normal circumstances). You can identify all `MDRT` tables that are associated with the user's spatial indexes by inspecting the `USER_SDO_INDEX_METADATA` view:

  ```
  SQL> SELECT sdo_index_name, sdo_index_table, sdo_rtree_seq_name
  FROM USER_SDO_GEOM_METADATA;
  ```

- *You should not export the* `MDRT` *tables explicitly.* When you import a table, say `customers`, that has a spatial index, the appropriate spatial index information is also exported. During import, the spatial index (and the associated `MDRT` tables) will be re-created. You do not have to export or import any of the `MDRT` tables (or the `MDRS` sequences).
- *You should not replicate the* `MDRT` *tables to a replicated database.* If you want to replicate a user table, say `customers`, all you will have to replicate is that `customers` table. You will need to explicitly create the spatial index on the replicated instance.

Network Metadata

If you intend to define a network over existing structures, or manually create the network, you should explicitly populate the `USER_SDO_NETWORK_METADATA` view. Listing 10-10 shows an example. If, however, you use the `CREATE_SDO_NETWORK` function, as in Listing 10-1, to create the network, you do not need to populate the metadata.

Map Metadata

To create maps, you need to populate the `USER_SDO_MAPS`, `USER_SDO_THEMES`, and `USER_SDO_STYLES` dictionary views. Note that some of the columns (e.g., `DEFINITION`) in these views store information using XML. You need to be careful in populating/updating these columns. See Chapter 11 for details.

Common Errors

In this section, we list some common errors that you may encounter while location-enabling your application (starting with some of the frequently encountered errors). We also suggest the corrective actions for each error. Note that this list is not exhaustive. For other errors not listed here, you should refer to *Oracle Spatial User's Guide* and Oracle Technical Support for assistance.

ORA-13226: interface not supported without a spatial index

This error happens when you are using a spatial operator that cannot be evaluated without the use of the spatial index. This could happen if either there is no index on the column that you are using or the optimizer does not choose the index-based evaluation. Listing 8-1 shows an example of this error.

Action: If there is no spatial index on the columns in the spatial operator, create an index. Otherwise, if the optimizer is not choosing the spatial index, then you should specify explicit hints such as `INDEX` or `ORDERED` to ensure that the spatial index is used. Refer to the hints section in Chapter 8 for more details.

ORA-13203: failed to read USER_SDO_GEOM_METADATA view

This error occurs if the table you are trying to index does not have any metadata in the `USER_SDO_GEOM_METADATA` view. See Listing 8-2 for an example.

Action: Insert a row corresponding to the spatial layer (`table_name`, `column_name`) in this view. Listing 8-4 shows an example.

ORA-13365: layer SRID does not match geometry SRID

This error implies that the `SRID` in a geometry column in a table does not match the `SRID` value in the corresponding layer in the `USER_SDO_GEOM_METADATA` view. For instance, if the layer corresponds to the location column in the `customers` table, you can inspect these values using the SQL in Listing 14-27. Note that the `SRID` must be set to the same value in the `location` columns of all rows in the `customers` table.

Listing 14-27. *Determining the* `SRID` *Value in the Location (Geometry) Columns of a Table*

```
SQL> SELECT a.location.sdo_srid FROM customers a WHERE ROWNUM=1;
```

This gives the `SRID` stored in the location column of the `customers` table. You should compare it with the `SRID` for the layer (in the `USER_SDO_GEOM_METADATA` view), as shown in Listing 14-28.

Listing 14-28. *Determining the* `SRID` *Value for a Spatial Layer (Specified by* `table_name`, `column_name`*)*

```
SQL> SELECT srid FROM USER_SDO_GEOM_METADATA
WHERE  table_name='CUSTOMERS' AND column_name='LOCATION';
```

Action: Modify the SRIDs (in the geometries and the USER_SDO_GEOM_METADATA view) to be the same value. This error occurs mostly during the creation or rebuilding of an index. You might have to drop the index before re-trying the create-index/rebuild-index operation (after changing the SRID values).

ORA-13223: duplicate entry for <table_name, column_name> in SDO_GEOM_METADATA

This error indicates that the insertion of a new row for a specified <table_name, column_name> pair into the USER_SDO_GEOM_METADATA view failed. There is already a row that exists for the <table_name, column_name> pair in this view.

Action: Delete the rows in USER_SDO_GEOM_METADATA for <table_name, column_name> before inserting new values.

ORA-13249, ORA-02289: cannot drop sequence/table

This error occurs when you are trying to drop a spatial index. If the associated tables/ sequences do not exist, the DROP INDEX statement raises these errors (ORA-13249 and ORA-02289).

Action: Append FORCE to the DROP INDEX statement, as in the following example in which the customers_sidx is dropped:

```
SQL> DROP INDEX customers_sidx  FORCE;
```

ORA-13249: multiple entries in sdo_index_metadata table

This error occurs when you are trying to create a spatial index and there is leftover metadata from a failed DROP INDEX statement.

Action: You will have to explicitly clean up the metadata entries for the specified index in the SDO_INDEX_METADATA_TABLE table in the MDSYS schema, as shown in the following example:

```
SQL> connect mdsys/<mdsys-password>
SQL> DELETE FROM SDO_INDEX_METADATA_TABLE
WHERE sdo_index_owner = 'SPATIAL' AND sdo_index_name='CUSTOMERS_SIDX';
```

ORA-13207: incorrect use of the <operator-name> operator

This error occurs when the specified operator is used incorrectly. In most cases, this will happen when the SDO_RELATE, SDO_NN or SDO_WITHIN_DISTANCE operators are used on a three- or four-dimensional index (created by specifying SDO_INDX_DIMS in the parameter clause of the CREATE INDEX statement; see Chapter 8 for details).

Action: You can use only the SDO_FILTER operator (and not others, such as SDO_RELATE) if the SDO_INDX_DIMS parameter is set to a value greater than 2 (the default value) during index creation.

ORA-13000: dimension number is out of range

This error occurs when you are operating with geometries that have the SDO_GTYPE value (in an SDO_GEOMETRY object) to be <8. This might be from prior versions of Oracle Spatial where the SDO_GTYPE contained only the type (T) information. Starting with Oracle 9*i*, the SDO_GTYPE in an SDO_GEOMETRY is of the D00T, where D indicates the dimensionality and T is the type. Refer to Chapter 4 for more details.

Action: Modify your data to reflect this change. Alternatively, use the SDO_MIGRATE.TO_CURRENT function to let Oracle Spatial make the change. This function also corrects the orientation of polygon geometries.

ORA-00939: too many arguments for function

This error may occur while inserting an SDO_GEOMETRY with more than 1,000 ordinates in the SDO_ORDINATES array. For instance, it is likely to be raised by the following SQL statement:

```
SQL> INSERT INTO sales_regions VALUES
(
  1000,
  SDO_GEOMETRY
  (
    2004, - A multipoint geometry
    8307,
    NULL,
    SDO_ELEM_INFO_ARRAY(1, 1, 1100),  -- this geometry has 1100 points
    SDO_ORDINATE_ARRAY  -- store the ordinates
    (
      1,1, 1,1, 1,1, 1,1, 1,1 , -- repeat this line 99  times
      ......
      1,1, 1,1, 1,1, 1,1, 1,1
    )
  )
);
ERROR at line 5:
ORA-00939: too many arguments for function
```

Action: This is a SQL-level restriction. You can avoid this error by creating a PL/SQL variable (called geom in the following code) that holds this geometry and then binding this variable to the "insert" SQL statement:

```
SQL>
DECLARE
  geom SDO_GEOMETRY; -- PL/SQL variable to store the geometry with >999 ordinates
BEGIN
  -- construct the geometry here
  geom :=
    SDO_GEOMETRY
    (
```

```
        2004, 8307, NULL,
        SDO_ELEM_INFO_ARRAY(1, 1, 1100),
        SDO_ORDINATE_ARRAY
        (
          1,1, 1,1, 1,1, 1,1, 1,1 , -- repeat this line 99  times
          --
          1,1, 1,1, 1,1, 1,1, 1,1
        )
      );

    -- store the geometry in the sales_regions table using dynamic SQL
    EXECUTE IMMEDIATE
       'INSERT INTO sales_regions VALUES (1000, :gm )' USING geom;
END;
/
  PL/SQL procedure successfully completed.
```

ORA-13030: invalid dimensionality for the SDO_GEOMETRY, or ORA-13364: layer dimensionality does not match geometry dimensions

One of these errors may occur in a query if the dimensionality of the spatial index (layer) is greater than the dimensionality of the query window specified in a spatial operator. For instance, if you have a two-dimensional query that is coded on the threed table, which has three-dimensional geometries (and is indexed as three-dimensional), then these errors could occur.

```
SQL>
-- Create the threed table and a 3D index
CREATE TABLE threed (id  NUMBER, geom SDO_GEOMETRY);
INSERT INTO threed VALUES (1,
 SDO_GEOMETRY (3001, NULL, SDO_POINT_TYPE (1,1,1), NULL, NULL));
insert into user_sdo_geom_metadata values ('THREED', 'GEOM',
  mdsys.sdo_dim_array (
    mdsys.sdo_dim_element ('x', 1, 100, .0000005),
    mdsys.sdo_dim_element ('y', 1, 100, .0000005),
    mdsys.sdo_dim_element ('z', 1, 200, .0000005)), null);
CREATE INDEX threed_sidx ON threed(geom) INDEXTYPE IS MDSYS.SPATIAL_INDEX
PARAMETERS ('sdo_indx_dims=3');

-- Perform the query with 2D query window
SELECT b.id FROM threed b
  WHERE SDO_FILTER
  (
    b.geom,         -- 3-dimensional data (indexed as 3D, i.e., sdo_indx_dims=3)
    SDO_GEOMETRY    -- 2-dimensional query window
    (
```

```
      2003, NULL, NULL,
      SDO_ELEM_INFO_ARRAY(1, 1003, 3),
      SDO_ORDINATE_ARRAY(1,1, 3,3)
    )
  )='TRUE';
ERROR at line 1:
ORA-13030: Invalid dimension for the SDO_GEOMETRY object
```

You can verify the dimensionality of the index by examining the attribute `sdo_indx_dims` in the `USER_SDO_INDEX_METADATA` view. You can also determine the dimensionality of the query geometry by inspecting the `SDO_GTYPE` attribute of the geometry.

Even if the spatial index dimensionality is not greater than the query dimensionality, the ORA-13364 error may occur if

- The table data has more than two dimensions.
- The spatial index on this table is two-dimensional.
- The query dimensionality is not the same as the data dimensionality.

Action: These errors can be resolved by changing the query geometry to match the dimensionality of the data. For instance, you can change the query window as follows:

```
SQL> SELECT b.id FROM threed b
  WHERE SDO_FILTER
  (
    b.geom,          -- 3-dimensional data (indexed as 3-d, i.e., sdo_indx_dims=3)
    SDO_GEOMETRY     -- 2-dimensional query window
    (
      3003, NULL, NULL,
      SDO_ELEM_INFO_ARRAY(1, 1003, 3),
      SDO_ORDINATE_ARRAY(1,1,1,  3,3, 3)
    )
  )='TRUE';
```

Summary

In this chapter, we provided several tips to model spatial data; to tune the performance of spatial operators, functions, and updates; and to manage temporal or historical spatial data using table partitioning. We also covered several common pitfalls and errors, and described corrective actions for these errors. This information should come in handy when you incorporate spatial analysis and visualization into your business application.

With this chapter, we come to the end of the book. We hope the information in these chapters helped you in location-enabling your application. In the following appendixes, we give a brief overview of some specialized functionality, such as GeoRaster and Linear Referencing, which cater mainly to GIS and transportation applications.

APPENDIX A

Additional Spatial Analysis Functions

In Chapters 8 and 9 we described how to perform proximity analysis using the SDO_GEOMETRY data in Oracle tables. We described a variety of functions and index-based operators to perform proximity-based spatial analysis.

In this appendix, we describe more advanced functions to cater to specific business analysis. We consider the business application that is discussed throughout this book. Say, for example, that we want to start three new stores. Where are the best locations to start them? The advanced functions we discuss in this appendix enable the following types of analyses to aid in site selection:

- *Tiling-based analysis*: One approach is to examine population. Population statistics can be obtained using demographic datasets such as zip codes, census block groups, and so on. You can tile the possible set of locations and identify the tiles that have the greatest populations. In general, tiling-based analysis groups data into areas called *tiles* and computes aggregates for specified attributes (e.g., income, age, spending patterns, etc.) inside the tiles.

- *Neighborhood analysis*: Another approach is to identify a candidate set of locations (by some other criterion, such as proximity to a highway). Then, we can choose among these candidate sets by estimating the population in the neighborhood of each location.

- *Clustering analysis*: Yet another approach to identify the best places to start new businesses is to analyze the customer locations that are not covered by existing stores. You can arrange the set of customer locations into groups, or clusters. The centers of these clusters may be good choices for locating new businesses.

The SDO_SAM package in Oracle Spatial includes functions to facilitate the kinds of spatial analyses just described. In this appendix, we give an overview of how to use these functions. You can find a detailed discussion in *Oracle Spatial User's Guide*.

Tiling-Based Analysis

First, we will look at how to identify regions/tiles that satisfy a business criterion. For the business application discussed in this book, we describe how to divide the two-dimensional coordinate space in which all locations are partitioned into small regions called *tiles*. We then describe functions to estimate population statistics for each tile using demographic data stored in other tables.

TILED_BINS

Tiling is the process of dividing a two-dimensional space into smaller regions. Figure A-1 shows an example. If the tiling level is specified as 1, then the range in each dimension is bisected once. In Figure A-1, the x-dimension is bisected once and the y-dimension is bisected once. This produces tiles at tiling level 1. The boundaries of these tiles are shown by a thick border. At level 2, each level 1 tile is bisected once along the x- and y-dimensions again providing a total of 16 equal-sized tiles. This process is repeated until we obtain tiles of appropriate sizes (or at a specified tiling level).

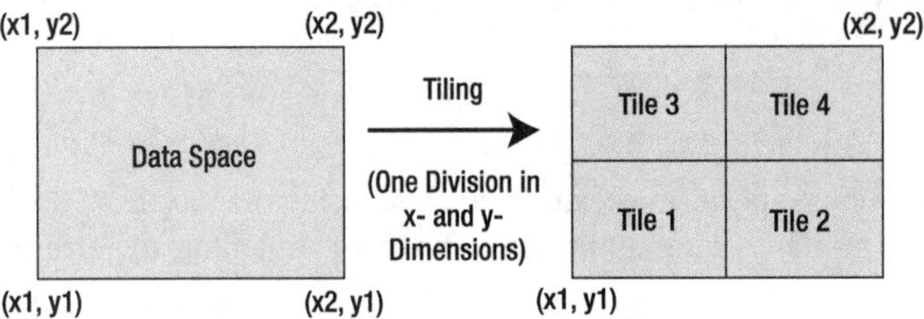

Figure A-1. *Tiling a two-dimensional space at level 1 by bisecting the range in x- and y-dimensions to yield four tiles*

How is tiling useful in business analysis? Tiling helps in dividing the entire two-dimensional space (over which the businesses and potential sites are located) into smaller regions. You can then analyze these regions and identify whether or not they are appropriate for the business task at hand.

The TILED_BINS function has the following syntax:

```
TILED_BINS
(
  lower_bound_in_dimension_1    NUMBER,
  upper_bound_in_dimension_1    NUMBER,
  lower_bound_in_dimension_2    NUMBER,
  upper_bound_in_dimension_2    NUMBER,
  tiling_level                  NUMBER,
  srid                          NUMBER DEFAULT NULL
)
RETURNS Table of SDO_REGION
```

where the SDO_REGION type has the following structure:

```
SQL> DESCRIBE SDO_REGION;
ID                                 NUMBER
GEOMETRY                           SDO_GEOMETRY
```

If the tiling_level is set to 1, the function returns four tiles (one bisection of x- and y-dimensions, causing four disjoint regions). In general, for tiling level *k*, the function returns 4^k tiles. Each tile is returned as an SDO_REGION data type. This type includes the ID and the

Geometry corresponding to the tile. The srid argument, if specified, indicates the spatial reference (coordinate) system for the returned geometries. Listing A-1 shows an example of this function. Note that the return type is a table, which means we should use the "table" casting operation as shown.

Listing A-1. *Tiling a Two-Dimensional Space*

```
SQL> SELECT * FROM TABLE
(SDO_SAM.TILED_BINS(-77.1027, -76.943996, 38.820813, 38.95911,1, 8307));
```

TILED_AGGREGATES

The next function that we will look at is TILED_AGGREGATES. This function implicitly computes the tiles using the dimension bounds for a specified table in USER_SDO_GEOM_METADATA. For each computed tile, the function returns the aggregated estimate for a user-specified column such as population. This estimate is derived from a specified *demographic* or *theme* table, and it uses proportion of overlap to calculate the aggregate value.

For instance, the table zip5_dc in Listing A-2 stores the zip code name, the zip code boundary (as an SDO_GEOMETRY object), and the population for each zip code in the county of the District of Columbia in the United States. (Note that the population values in this table are for illustrative purposes only and may not match current real-world values.)

Listing A-2. *Zip Code Table Used to Get Demographic Information*

```
SQL> desc zip5_dc;
 Name                            Null?    Type
 ------------------------------- -------- ----------------------------
 STATE_ABRV                               VARCHAR2(2)
 FILE_NAME                                VARCHAR2(8)
 AREA                                     NUMBER
 PERIMETER                                NUMBER
 ZCTA                                     VARCHAR2(5)
 NAME                                     VARCHAR2(90)
 LSAD                                     VARCHAR2(2)
 LSAD_TRANS                               VARCHAR2(50)
 GEOM                                     SDO_GEOMETRY
 POPULATION                               NUMBER
```

A variety of such theme tables store demographic information at different levels. The U.S. Census blocks, block groups, tracts, counties, and states are some examples. Such demographic data can be easily combined with application data to perform spatial analysis for business applications. For instance, we can use the zip code regions in the zip5_dc table to derive population estimates for an arbitrary tile or region (ref_geometry).

Only 20% of the zip code region from zip5_dc (demographic) table intersects, as shown in Figure A-2. The aggregate for ref_geometry is 20% of the aggregate associated with the zip code.

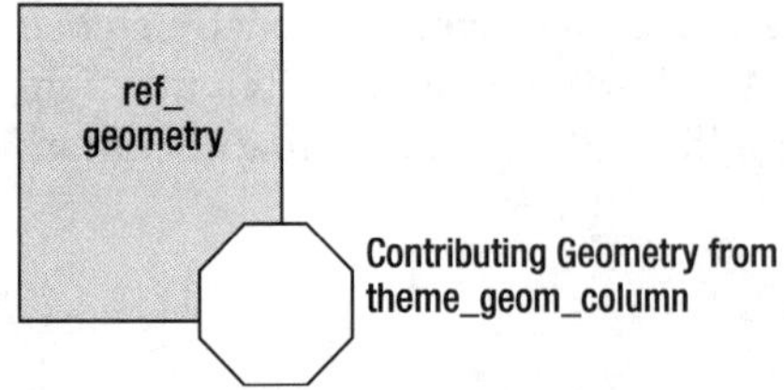

Figure A-2. *Estimating the aggregate for* `ref_geometry` *(tile or region)*

What if you have multiple zip codes intersecting the tile (or region)? You can specify how to combine the aggregate contributions from each of the intersecting zip codes. For instance, if 20% of zip code A intersects with the tile, and 30% of zip code B intersects with the tile, and these need to be *summed* up, then the resulting population estimate (aggregate) for the tile is as follows:

```
sum(0.2*(population of zip code A), 0.3*(population of zip code B))
```

The TILED_AGGREGATES function computes these estimates using a specified theme (demographic) table. It has the following signature:

```
Tiled_Aggregates
(
  theme_table                 VARCHAR2,
  theme_geom_column           VARCHAR2,
  aggregate_type              VARCHAR2,
  aggregate_column            VARCHAR2,
  tiling_level                NUMBER,
  tiling_domain               SDO_DIM_ARRAY DEFAULT NULL
)
RETURNS Table of MDSYS.SDO_REGAGGR
```

where the SDO_REGAGGR type has the following structure:

```
SQL> DESCRIBE SDO_REGAGGR;
Name                          Type
----------------------------  ----------------------------
REGION_ID                     VARCHAR2(24)
GEOMETRY                      SDO_GEOMETRY
AGGREGATE_VALUE               NUMBER
```

This function returns a table of SDO_REGAGGR objects. REGION_ID corresponds to `tile_id`. GEOMETRY corresponds to the geometry of the corresponding tile. AGGREGATE_VALUE contains the aggregate value for the tile—for instance, the sum of the population or the number of customers.

The function takes the following arguments:

- theme_table and theme_geom_column specify the name of the theme table and the geometry column. For instance, these arguments could be zip5_dc and geom (the geometric boundary of the zip code).
- aggregate_type specifies how to combine multiple contributions from intersecting zip codes. This could be any of the SQL aggregates such as SUM, COUNT, MIN, and MAX.
- aggregate_column specifies which demographic attribute needs to be estimated. In our example application, this can be POPULATION.
- tiling_level specifies the tiling level to construct the tiles.
- bounds specifies the tiling domain for the tiles. If this argument is not specified, then the tiling domain is set to the bounds for the spatial layer corresponding to <theme_table, theme_geom_column> in the USER_SDO_GEOM_METADATA view.

■ **Caution** AVG and other aggregates are not supported. These aggregates need to be computed using the SUM and COUNT aggregates. For instance, if the AVG income needs to be computed, then it can be computed as sum(total_income_per_tile)/sum(total_population_per_tile). total_income_per_tile and total_population_per_tile can be estimated with the TILED_AGGREGATES function using the total_income and total_population columns of the zip code tables (these two columns need to be explicitly materialized).

Listing A-3 shows an example of the TILED_AGGREGATES function. Note that by selecting only those tiles that have aggregate_value (population) > 30,000, we are identifying the most populated tiles from the set of tiles.

Listing A-3. *Searching for Regions (Tiles) That Have a Population Greater Than 30,000*

```
SQL> SELECT REGION_ID, AGGREGATE_VALUE, GEOMETRY FROM TABLE
(
  SDO_SAM.TILED_AGGREGATES
  ('ZIP5_DC', 'GEOM','SUM', 'POPULATION', 2)
  ) a
WHERE a.aggregate_value > 30000;
```

Note that the query returns tiles (regions) along with the population. In our site selection analysis, we can make these tiles (regions) the starting points for further analysis. In general, we can use the TILED_AGGREGATES function to determine candidate regions based on a selection criterion (e.g., a high population).

We can visualize these tiles using Oracle MapViewer. For instance, we can use the jview.jsp file in the mapviewr/demo directory for this purpose. Specify select geom from ZIP5_DC as query1 and the SQL in Listing A-3 as query2.

Figure A-3 shows the zip codes in dark gray and tile regions that have a population of more than 30,000 are shown in lighter gray boxes. You can further refine this analysis by identifying smaller tiles (i.e., tiles at level 3 or 4). Additionally, you can superimpose locations of roads and other businesses to aid in the site selection process.

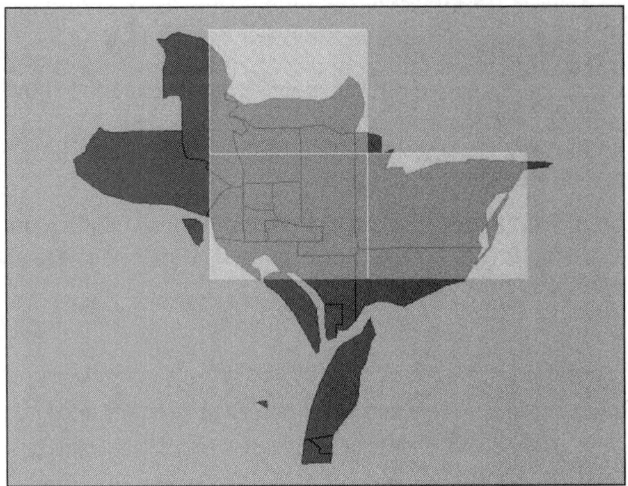

Figure A-3. *Displaying zip code boundaries and tiles that have population of more than 30,000*

Neighborhood Analysis

Instead of using tiles to compute estimates, can we compute the population for arbitrary sales regions? This might be useful if we already chose a set of candidate sites through other selection criteria. We can examine the population in the neighborhood of each such site (or location) by constructing a (quarter-mile) buffer around the location. The `AGGREGATES_FOR_GEOMETRY` function allows us to compute the estimates for an arbitrary geometry.

AGGREGATES_FOR_GEOMETRY

This function computes the estimated aggregate value from a theme table for a specified region: `ref_geometry` (as opposed to precomputed tiles in `TILED_AGGREGATES`). It uses the information in `theme_table` to compute this estimate. This function has the following signature:

```
AGGREGATES_FOR_GEOMETRY
(
  theme_table                VARCHAR2,
  theme_geom_column          VARCHAR2,
  aggregate_type             VARCHAR2,
  aggregate_column           VARCHAR2,
  ref_geometry               SDO_GEOMETRY,
  dist_spec                  VARCHAR2 DEFAULT NULL
)
RETURNS NUMBER
```

The function's arguments are as follows:

- theme_table and theme_geom_column specify the name of the theme table and the geometry column. For instance, these arguments could be zip5_dc and geom (the geometric boundary of the zip code). The demographic information at a fine or coarse level is stored in these tables.
- aggregate_type specifies how to combine multiple contributions from intersecting zip codes. This could be any of the SQL aggregates such as SUM, COUNT, MIN, and MAX.
- aggregate_column specifies which demographic attribute needs to be estimated. In our example application, this can be POPULATION.
- ref_geometry specifies the reference geometry for which the demographic information needs to be computed.
- dist_spec specifies additional parameters for ref_geometry. This can be one of the following:
  - *NULL*: In this case, the ref_geometry is compared with the geometries in theme_table. As in Figure A-1, the aggregate for the ref_geometry is computed by taking the area of intersection (of the theme geometries with the ref_geometry) into account.
  - *A string of the form* distance= <val> unit=<distance_unit>*:* In this case, the ref_geometry is expanded (buffered) by the specified distance and the aggregate is computed.
  - *A string of the form* sdo_num_res=<N>*:* In this case, the nearest N geometries (from theme_table) to the ref_geometry are considered. The aggregates of each neighbor are equally weighted, as the neighbors may or may not intersect with the ref_geometry. For instance, if N=2, and zip code A and zip code B are the neighbors of the ref_geometry, then the aggregate for the ref_geometry is sum(population of A and population B). The aggregate_type is sum and the aggregate_column is population in this example.

■ **Caution** AVG and other aggregates are not supported. These aggregates need to be computed using SUM and COUNT aggregates. For instance, if the AVG income needs to be computed, then it can be computed as sum(total_income_per_ref_geometry)/sum(total_population_per_ref_geometry). total_income_per_ref_geometry and total_population_per_ref_geometry can be estimated with the AGGREGATES_FOR_GEOMETRY function using the total_income and total_population columns of the zip code tables (these two columns need to be explicitly materialized: total_income=income*population).

Listing A-4 shows an example of the AGGREGATES_FOR_GEOMETRY function. In this example, we compute the population for sales region 1 (id=1) in the sales_regions table. Note that the sales_regions table is a quarter-mile buffered region on an existing store location. Likewise, we can perform the same population analysis on other regions that correspond to potential new store locations.

Listing A-4. *Estimating the Population in Sales Region 1 Using the Demographic Information in the* zip5_dc *Table*

```
SQL> SELECT SDO_SAM.AGGREGATES_FOR_GEOMETRY
('ZIP5_DC', 'GEOM', 'SUM', 'POPULATION', a.geom) population
FROM sales_regions a WHERE a.id=1;
```

AGGREGATES_FOR_LAYER

Instead of analyzing sales regions one by one, we may want to compute the population for all sales regions in the sales_regions table. The AGGREGATES_FOR_LAYER function performs this operation.

This function computes the aggregates for a set of geometries in a specified ref_table (instead of a specific geometry). This function has the following signature:

```
AGGREGATES_FOR_LAYER
(
  theme_table                  VARCHAR2,
  theme_geom_column            VARCHAR2,
  aggregate_type               VARCHAR2,
  aggregate_column             VARCHAR2,
  ref_table                    VARCHAR2,
  ref_geom_col                 SDO_GEOMETRY,
  dist_spec                    VARCHAR2
)
RETURNS Table of SDO_REGAGGR
```

where SDO_REGAGGR type has the following structure:

```
SQL> DESCRIBE SDO_REGAGGR;
Name                           Type
----------------------------- -----------------------------
 REGION_ID                     VARCHAR2(24)
 GEOMETRY                      SDO_GEOMETRY
 AGGREGATE_VALUE               NUMBER
```

Note that the function arguments are mostly same as in AGGREGATES_FOR_GEOMETRY. The only difference is that instead of taking in a single ref_geometry as in AGGREGATES_FOR_GEOMETRY, the AGGREGATES_FOR_LAYER function takes a table of a such geometries. These are specified using the ref_table and ref_geom_col arguments. This function returns a table of SDO_REGAGGR objects, where each object contains the aggregate computed using the ref_geometry in a row of the ref_table. The SDO_REGAGGR object stores the ROWID in the region_id attribute, the ref_geometry in the geometry attribute, and the computed aggregate in the aggregate_value attribute.

Listing A-5 shows how to obtain the population for all sales regions in the `sales_regions` table.

Listing A-5. *Estimating the Population for All Rows in the* `sales_regions` *Table Using Demographic Information in the* `zip5_dc` *Table*

```
SQL> SELECT b.id, aggregate_value population FROM TABLE
(
  SDO_SAM.AGGREGATES_FOR_LAYER
  ('ZIP5_DC', 'GEOM','SUM', 'POPULATION', 'SALES_REGIONS', 'GEOM')
  ) a, sales_regions b
WHERE b.rowid = a.region_id;
```

Note that the `population` attribute is not part of the `sales_regions` table. It is derived from the demographic table. These functions allow us to easily incorporate external demographic information into business analysis.

Clustering Analysis

Another approach for site selection is to examine where the potential customers are. If we want to start three new stores to cater to these new customers, then we can group or cluster the customers into three groups. In the following sections, we will look at how to perform clustering of customer locations.

SPATIAL_CLUSTERS

This function computes the clusters for a set of geometries in a specified table. Additional analysis can be performed to identify the cluster center or for visualization using Oracle MapViewer. This function has the following signature:

```
SPATIAL_CLUSTERS
(
  geometry_table                VARCHAR2,
  geometry_column               VARCHAR2,
  max_clusters                  NUMBER
)
RETURNS Table of MDSYS.SDO_REGION
```

where the `SDO_REGION` type has the following structure:

```
SQL> DESCRIBE SDO_REGION;
Name                            Type
--------                        ---------
ID                              NUMBER
GEOMETRY                        SDO_GEOMETRY
```

The arguments to this function are as follows:

- `geom_table` specifies the name of the table storing the geometries.
- `geom_column` specifies the name of the `SDO_GEOMETRY` column. This column needs to have a spatial index. The geometries in this column are clustered and returned.
- `max_clusters` specifies the maximum number of clusters to be returned.

This function computes the clusters based on the geometry columns of the specified geometry table. It returns each cluster as a geometry in the `SDO_REGION` type. The `ID` value is set to a number from 0 to `max_clusters` – 1. The function returns a table of such `SDO_REGION` objects. Listing A-6 shows how to cluster the customer locations in the `customers` table.

Listing A-6. *Finding Three Clusters for Customer Locations*

```
SQL> SELECT ID, GEOMETRY FROM TABLE
(SDO_SAM.SPATIAL_CLUSTERS('CUSTOMERS', 'LOCATION', 3));
```

You can visualize the customer locations and the three clusters using Oracle MapViewer. Use `jview.jsp` in the demo directory of MapViewer, and specify `select location from customers` in query1 and the SQL in Listing A-6 for query2. Figure A-4 shows the customer locations (points with an *x*) in dark gray and the clusters (rectangular regions) in lighter gray.

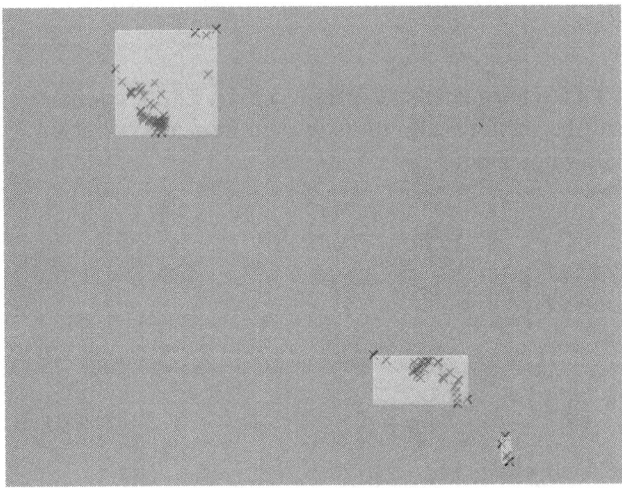

Figure A-4. *Displaying the customer regions and three clusters for Listing A-6*

Once the clusters are identified, we can determine their centers using the `SDO_GEOM.SDO_CENTROID` function. This will give candidate locations for starting new stores to cater to the three groups of customers.

Refining the Candidates for Site Selection

The spatial analyses functions (discussed in previous sections) enable users to identify regions (tiles or clusters) that satisfy a specific business criterion. For instance, the business criterion could be `population>30000` in the tiling analysis. Once the candidate set of regions is identified, we can refine the set further using visual or other analysis techniques. For instance, we can refine the candidate set by visualizing these regions using Oracle MapViewer. As part of this visualization, we can overlay other appropriate data, such as roads and other business locations. Such combination of spatial analysis functions with other techniques including visual refinement can serve as an efficient and effective mechanism for site selection in business applications.

Geometry Simplification for Speeding Up Analysis

Most site-location analysis involves analyzing demographic data associated with county, zip code, tract, or blockgroup regions. The boundaries of these entities are stored as complex shapes involving thousands of vertices. Spatial analysis using geometries with very large number of vertices tends to be slow and may not be acceptable in an interactive system that requires fast responses. To alleviate these performance issues, we have a simple solution: simplify each geometric shape in your demographic dataset (also known as *generalization* in GIS parlance). Oracle Spatial provides two functions for this purpose: the `SIMPLIFY` function in the `SDO_UTIL` package and the `SIMPLIFY_GEOMETRY` function in the `SDO_SAM` package (the latter is a wrapper around the former and hides complex usage).

Listing A-7 shows an example of how to use the `SIMPLIFY_GEOMETRY` function in the `SDO_SAM` package. The function takes as arguments a geometry and a tolerance, and returns a simplified geometry (or the original geometry if the geometry cannot be simplified after certain number of iterations).

Listing A-7. *Simplifying the Geometry for New Hampshire*

```
SQL> SELECT SDO_SAM.SIMPLIFY_GEOMETRY(a.geom, 0.5)
FROM us_states a WHERE a.state_abrv='NH';
```

It is recommended that you simplify your demographic datasets using these functions before proceeding with analysis functions described in this appendix. Doing so may speed up spatial analysis functions such as `SDO_RELATE` and `TILED_AGGREGATES`. Note that the simplification may lead to changes in results and can only be applied if the application can tolerate small deviations in analysis results.

Summary

Spatial analysis functions in Oracle estimate attribute values for a region or a neighborhood. In addition, the functionality can cluster geometry objects into a specified number of clusters. These analysis functions can be combined with the visualization capability in Oracle MapViewer to aid in site-selection applications. In warehouse applications, spatial analysis functions can be used to materialize the influence of neighborhood in warehouse data and to mine for spatial patterns in the data.

APPENDIX B

Linear Referencing

In all the chapters of this book, we use coordinates to locate spatial objects on the surface of the earth. Coordinates locate objects in a two-dimensional space, for example, longitude and latitude. As you've seen in Chapter 4, a large number of different coordinate systems can be used in this way. They are all defined as *spatial reference systems*.

Spatial coordinates are not the only way to locate objects. Some objects are better identified by their position along a linear feature: their location can be described by a *measure* value (such as travel distance) with respect to some known point on the feature (such as its start point). This type of location referencing using a measure value (instead of the latitude/longitude values) is called a *Linear Referencing System* (*LRS*).

Let's say that the delivery truck for your business breaks down on a particular segment of a highway. How do you report its location to other agencies? One method is to mention the actual geographic coordinates, say –76 degrees longitude and 45 degrees latitude, obtained from a GPS receiver. An alternate method that is more frequently used in transportation applications is by specifying that the truck is "12 meters (measure) from Exit 5 (a reference point on the highway) going north on the highway." In short, this method specifies a reference point on a linear feature and the measure of the location from the reference point. This approach of specifying linear measures is widely used in transportation and utility (electric cables, gas pipelines, etc.) industries.

In this appendix, we will describe the functionality of the *Linear Referencing* component of Oracle Spatial. This functionality, available in the `SDO_LRS` package, allows you to associate *measures* with a linear feature stored in an `SDO_GEOMETRY` object. We will refer to such geometries as *linear referenced* or *LRS* geometries. In addition, Oracle allows you to perform the following operations on LRS geometries:

- *Project* a two-dimensional point onto a linear feature and identify the corresponding measure along the linear feature. This functionality is useful to determine the closest mile post on a highway when a car breaks down. For example, the popular OnStar positioning system uses such an approach to convert the geographical coordinates of the car into the nearest mile post on the highway and inform the appropriate road service.[1]

1. The OnStar system, developed by General Motors Corporation, combines an on-board GPS and cellular phone and allows a driver to be located and get assistance at the press of a button.

- *Locate* a point using the measure value and identify the corresponding two-dimensional coordinates. You can use this functionality to identify the coordinates of stop signs and other objects that are specified using measures along a linear feature.
- *Clip* a linear feature by specified start and end measure values. This function allows you, for example, to obtain specific sections of a road that will be closed to traffic.

In the next section, we will describe concepts of linear referencing and how it is used in applications. Then, we will show you how to create LRS geometries and perform *projection, location,* or *clipping* types of operations.

Concepts and Definitions

First, let's describe some basic concepts using the geometry in Figure B-1. The figure shows a line string from "start" to "end." Such line strings could typically represent highways, flight paths, gas pipelines, electric cables, and so on.

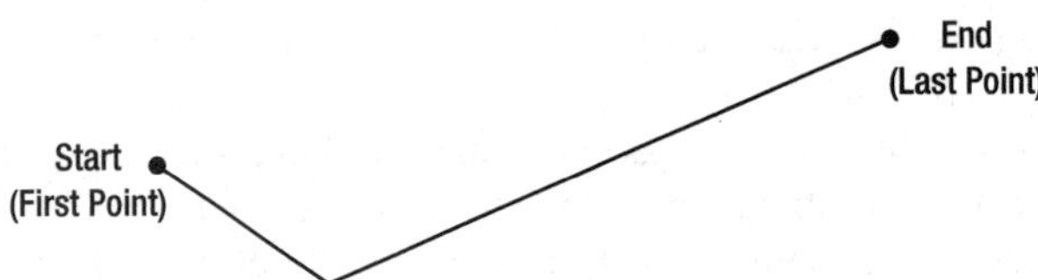

Figure B-1. *Linear feature with start (first) and end (last) points*

Measure

The *measure* of a point along a geometric segment is the linear distance to the point measured from the start point (for increasing values) or end point (for decreasing values) of the geometric segment. In Figure B-1, the start point may be associated with a measure value of 0 (or any other value). Likewise, other points of the line string may be associated with measure values.

Linear Referenced Segments

A *linear referenced segment* is a linear geometry with measures. It is usually a line string, but could also be a multiline string or even the boundary of a polygon. For all the following examples, we only consider the most common case of simple line strings. In Figure B-1, if you associate measure information with the end points, the line string is a linear referenced, or LRS, geometry.

The measures may be increasing or decreasing along a linear feature, and they can start at any value.

Direction

The *direction* of a geometric segment is indicated from the start point of the geometric segment to the end point. The direction is determined by *the order of the vertices (from start point to end point) in the geometry definition.*

Shape Points

Shape points are those points of the line string that are assigned measure information. The start and end point of a line string must always have measure information. Intermediate points may or may not have measures.

Points that do not have any set measure will be populated by linear interpolation between the points with measures. Figure B-2 illustrates how missing measures are populated. We only specified measures of 0 and 100 for the start and end points respectively, and the measure for an intermediate point is internally assigned as 25.

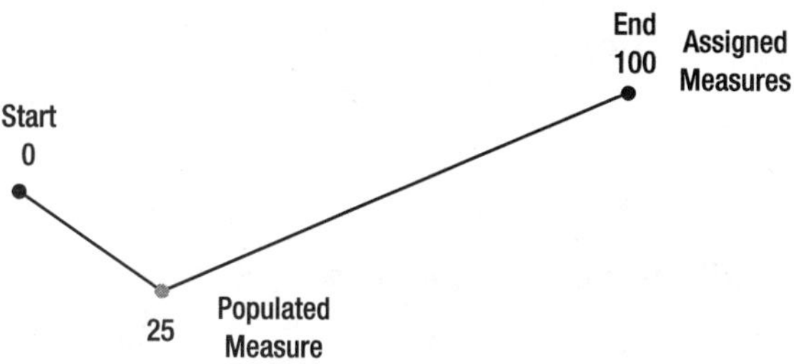

Figure B-2. *Populating measures for intermediate points*

Offset

The *offset* of a point along a geometric segment is the perpendicular distance between the point and the geometric segment. Figure B-3 shows an example. Offsets are positive if the points are on the left side along the segment direction and negative if they are on the right side. Points are on a geometric segment if their offsets to the segment are zero.

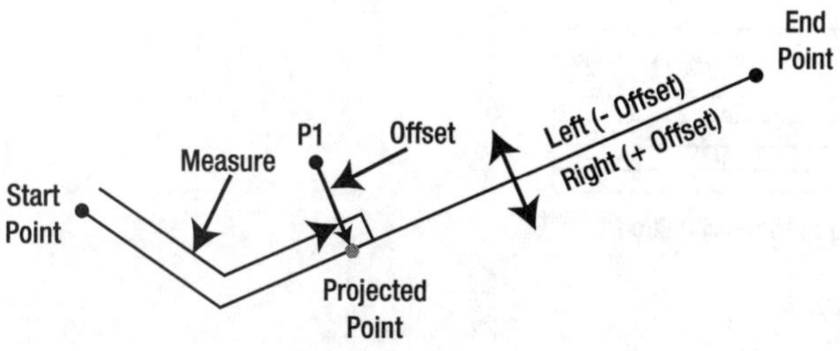

Figure B-3. *Offset of a point*

Typical Application

Linear referencing is widely used in transportation networks (flight paths, highways, etc.), and utility networks (gas pipelines, etc.). Linear referencing is most useful to *position* objects or information such as accidents, traffic conditions, road conditions, road equipment (traffic lights, road signs, etc.) with reference to a linear feature. This is illustrated in Figure B-4.

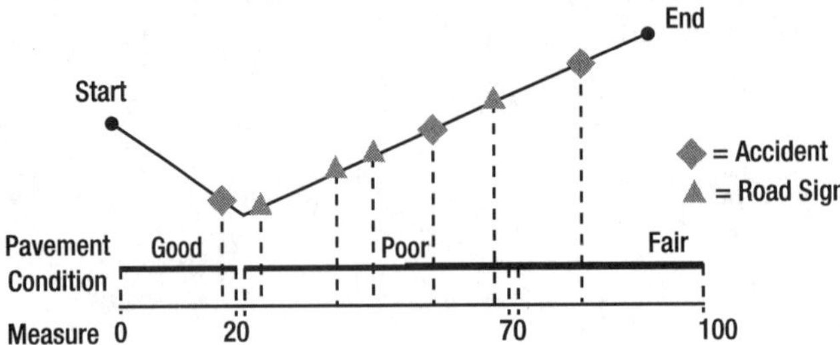

Figure B-4. *Accidents, road signs, and road conditions modeled using a linear feature*

An LRS application uses tables like the ones shown in Figure B-5: one table (`roads`) contains the actual LRS geometries. The other tables (`accidents`, `road signs`, and `pavement condition`) only contain references to the `roads` table together with their measure information.

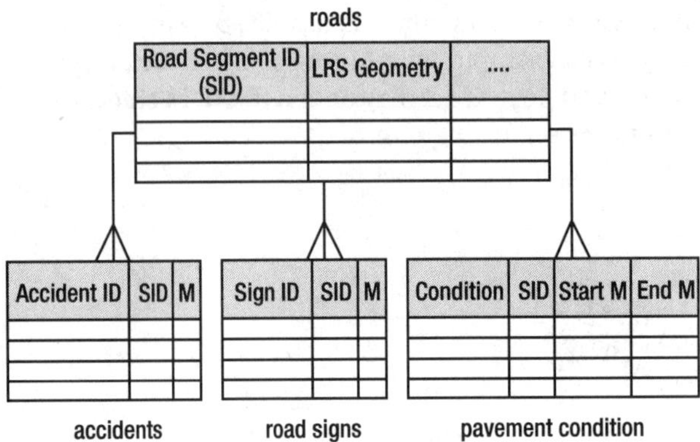

Figure B-5. *Tables in an LRS application*

To reference locations along a line, the line must first be registered with measure information: each point that describes the line has the usual *x* and *y* coordinates, but also a *measure* that represents the distance from the start of the line.

For example, the linear referenced geometry in Figure B-6 is registered with measure information (start measure = 0 and end measure = 100).

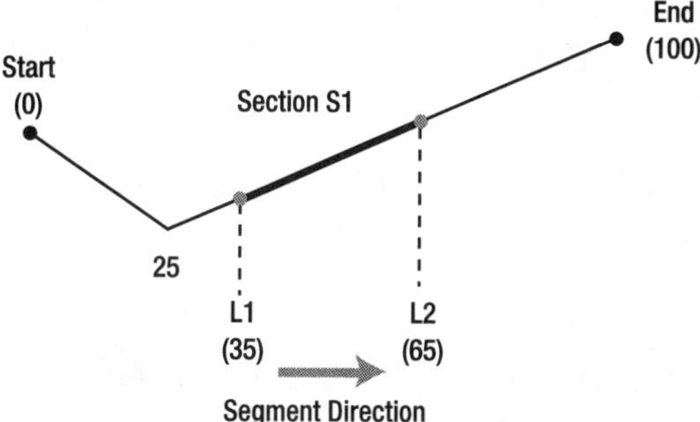

Figure B-6. *A linear referenced segment with dynamic segmentation*

Locations on this geometry can be described in terms of their measures on the geometry; for example, location L1 is at measure 35, and location L2 is at measure 65. Use this technique to represent *point events* such as accidents or road signs.

Sections are represented by specifying a start and end measure. In Figure B-6, section S1 is represented as having a start measure of 35 and end measure of 65 on the geometry. Use this technique to represent *line events* such as road works or road condition.

You can now materialize locations and sections as new geometries using specific functions. The ability to generate points or line segments dynamically from measure information is called *dynamic segmentation*.

■ **Note** The measures on a line segment do not have to start at zero. For example, roads are typically modeled as multiple road segments, whereby each segment is a stretch of road between intersections. The end measure of one road segment is then usually carried on as the first measure of the next segment in sequence.

Measures do not have to represent distances: they can represent anything as long as all measures on a line segment are all increasing or decreasing. For example, they could represent the elapsed time on the route of a boat. This then allows you to find out where the boat was at a certain date and time.

Creating Linear Referenced Geometries

The easiest way to populate measures in a linear feature is by using the CONVERT_TO_LRS_GEOM function. This function takes as arguments an SDO_GEOMETRY object representing a linear feature, and two numbers representing the measure values to be associated with the first and the last vertices of the linear feature. The measure values for all intermediate vertices are linearly interpolated.

```
SQL> UPDATE road_segments SET geom =
SDO_LRS.CONVERT_TO_LRS_GEOM
(
  geom,
  0,    -- start measure value
  100  -- end measure value
);
```

Alternately, you can explicitly construct LRS geometries as follows: linear referenced geometries are stored in the SDO_GEOMETRY object just like regular lines. However, there are two exceptions: (1) the SDO_GTYPE of an LRS geometry has additional information to indicate the measure dimension, and (2) each point in the LRS geometry uses three ordinates (instead of two in the regular one): an x value, a y value, and an m value—the measure. First let's look at the changes for SDO_GTYPE in LRS geometries.

SDO_GTYPE in LRS Geometries

The geometry type attribute (SDO_GTYPE) described in Chapter 4 changes from D00T to DM0T. The second digit m specifies the position of the measure dimension. For instance, if this attribute is set to 3302, it means the following:

3 = Each point in the geometry uses three ordinates (x, y, m).

3 = The third ordinate is the measure.

0 = Not used.

2 = This is a simple line string.

Constructing LRS Geometries

For example, the following SQL shows how to insert a (non-LRS) line segment into a database table:

```
INSERT INTO road_segments (id, geom) VALUES
(
  65328,
  SDO_GEOMETRY
  (
```

```
    2002,      -- SDO_GTYPE for regular geometries is of type DOOT (see chapter 4)
    8307, null,
    SDO_ELEM_INFO (1,2,1),
    SDO_ORDINATES
    (
      x1,y1,
      x2,y2,
      x3,y3,
      x4,y4,
      x5,y5,
      x6,y6,
      x7,y7,
      x8,y8,
      x9,y9
     )
    )
  );
```

The same line segment with measures on shape points is inserted as follows.

```
INSERT INTO road_segments (id, geom) VALUES
(
  65328,
  SDO_GEOMETRY
  (
    3302,  -- SDO_GTYPE for LRS geometries is DMOT where M is the measure position
    8307, null,
    SDO_ELEM_INFO (1,2,1),
    SDO_ORDINATES
    (
     x1,y1, 20,  --  third number (in all following rows) is measure value
     x2,y2, null,
     x3,y3, null,
     x4,y4, 50,
     x5,y5, null,
     x6,y6, null,
     x7,y7,  100,
     x8,y8, null,
     x9,y9, 160
    )
  );
```

Note that some shape points have no explicit measure set: the measures are passed as NULL.

Metadata

The spatial metadata for a linear referenced layer must describe three dimensions: the *x*, the *y*, and the *measure*. For example, the SQL would look like the following:

```
INSERT INTO USER_SDO_GEOM_METADATA
  (TABLE_NAME, COLUMN_NAME, DIMINFO, SRID)
VALUES
(
  'ROAD_SEGMENTS',
  'GEOM',
  SDO_DIM_ARRAY
  (
    SDO_DIM_ELEMENT ('X', -180, 180, 1),
    SDO_DIM_ELEMENT ('Y', -90, 90, 1),
    SDO_DIM_ELEMENT ('M', 0, 1000, 1)
  ),
  8307
);
```

Spatial Indexes and Spatial Operators on LRS Geometries

Note that in the preceding example, the USER_SDO_GEOM_METADATA view specified three dimensions (i.e., three SDO_DIM_ELEMENTs in the DIMINFO attribute), one for the *x*, *y*, and *m* (measure) dimensions for the spatial layer corresponding to <road_segments, geom.>. In order to create a spatial index on the preceding spatial layer, use the same CREATE INDEX statement that we have seen in Chapter 8. The following code shows the SQL:

```
SQL> CREATE INDEX roads_seg_sidx ON road_segments(geom)
INDEXTYPE IS MDSYS.SPATIAL_INDEX;
```

You can then use the spatial operators such as SDO_NN, SDO_WITHIN_DISTANCE, or SDO_RELATE on the geom column of the road_segments table. This column contains LRS geometries (i.e., geometries populated with measure values) but the operators use only the *x* and *y* dimensions of the LRS geometries.

Dynamic Segmentation Operations

At the beginning of the appendix, you saw the principles of linear referencing and the main dynamic segmentation operations: *clip*, *locate*, and *project*. Let's now examine how Oracle performs those operations.

Clip a Segment

This is the main dynamic segmentation function. Given a start and end measure, it extracts the section of a line between those two measures. Figure B-7 illustrates this process of extracting that part of the line between measures M1 and M2.

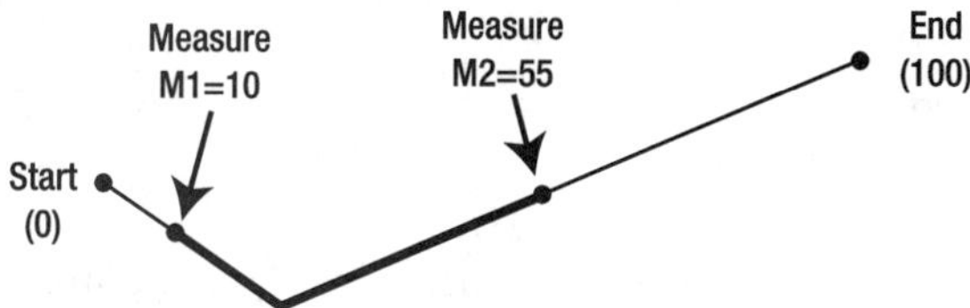

Figure B-7. *Clipping a line segment*

The following code shows how to use the CLIP_GEOM_SEGMENT function to perform this operation. This function takes an LRS geometry as the first argument, and start and end measures (to use in clipping) as the second and third arguments.

```
SQL> SELECT SDO_LRS.CLIP_GEOM_SEGMENT
(
  geom,
  5,    -- measure value for the start of dynamic segment
  15    -- measure value for the end of dynamic segment
) new_lrs_geom
FROM road_segments;
```

Examples of Uses

- Extract the section of a street that will be closed to traffic due to road repairs.
- Extract the route that a boat followed on a certain day. The line is the route followed by the boat, and measures represent time fixes. The start and end measures are the timestamp at the start and end of the day.

Locate a Point

Locating a point is similar to clipping, except it extracts a single point from the line. Given a measure, it returns the point located on a line at that measure. It can also position the point away from the line at a chosen offset. A positive offset locates the point on the left side of the line. A negative offset is on the right side of the line. Notion of left (right) implies left (right) of the geometry as you traverse from the start to the end of the geometry.

Figure B-8 shows how point P1 is located along a linear referenced segment from a measure and offset.

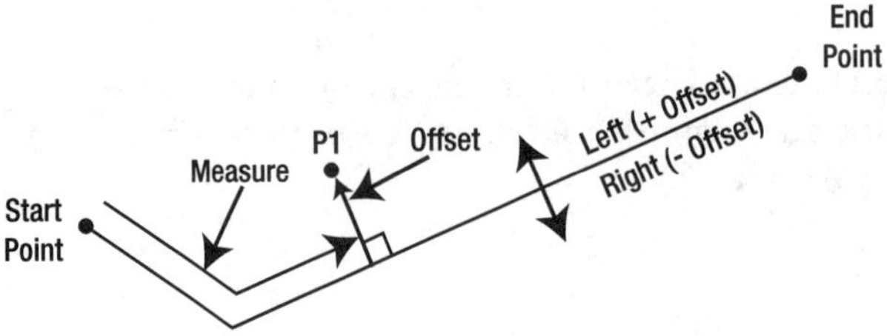

Figure B-8. *Locating a point on an LRS geometry*

The following code shows how to use the LOCATE_PT function to perform this operation. This function takes an LRS geometry as the first argument and a measure value as the second argument.

```
SQL> SELECT SDO_LRS.LOCATE_PT
(
  geom,
  5   -- measure value for the point to be located
) point_2d
  FROM road_segments;
```

Examples of Uses

- Locate a stop sign along a street. The measure indicates how far down the street the sign is located. The offset indicates how far on the left or right the sign is located.
- Find where a boat was on a certain date and time. The line is the route followed by the boat, with measures that represent time fixes. The measure of the point to locate is the timestamp to find.

Project a Point

This is the reverse of the locate operation: given a point and a line, it returns the measure of that point on the line. The point does not have to be on the line: the projection of a point on a line segment is the point on the segment that is on the perpendicular from the point and the geometric segment. This is illustrated in Figure B-9.

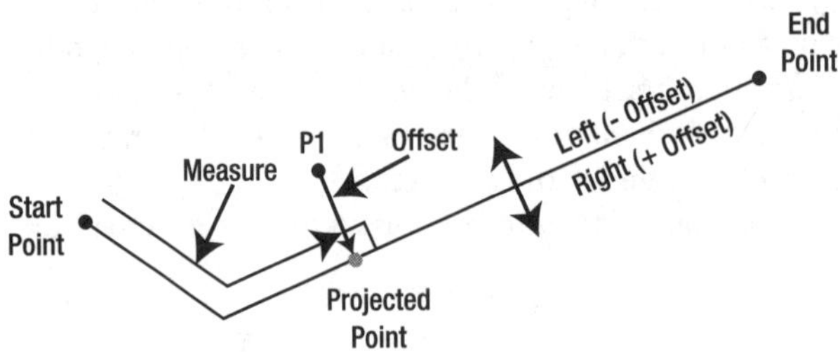

Figure B-9. *Projecting a point onto an LRS geometry*

The following code shows how to use the PROJECT_PT function to perform this operation. This function takes an LRS geometry as the first argument and a *reference point* (i.e., the point to be projected) as the third argument.

```
SQL> SELECT SDO_LRS.PROJECT_PT
(
  geom,
  SDO_GEOMETRY(2003, 8307, SDO_POINT(-76, 45, NULL), NULL, NULL)   -- ref. point
) projected_pt
FROM road_segments;
```

The preceding SQL statement returns the point on the LRS geometry where the reference point is projected. You can combine the preceding code with the GET_MEASURE function to obtain the measure value for the projected point as follows:

```
SQL> SELECT SDO_LRS.GET_MEASURE
(
  SDO_LRS.PROJECT_PT
  (
    geom,
    SDO_GEOMETRY(2003, 8307, SDO_POINT(-76, 45, NULL), NULL, NULL)   -- ref point
  ) -- projected_pt
)
FROM road_segments;
```

Examples of Uses

- A car breaks down while traveling on a highway. The current location of the car (collected by the on-board GPS) is sent to a service center. A "projection" query returns the position of the car as a distance along the highway. The offset indicates the side of the road.

Validation of LRS Segments

Oracle provides several functions to determine whether an LRS geometry or measure value for a given segment is valid, whether the measure value is valid for a given segment using the functions VALID_GEOM_SEGMENT, VALID_MEASURE, and VALID_LRS_PT. Alternately, you can directly invoke VALIDATE_GEOMETRY_WITH_CONTEXT, described in Chapter 5, to validate an LRS geometry. The latter function invokes the corresponding LRS-specific validation functions internally.

Dynamic Segmentation on 3D Geometries

The dynamic segmentation operations can also operate on three-dimensional lines, i.e., on lines with points defined by *x*, *y*, and *z* coordinates: they use the *z* values to compute measures, or in other words, they consider the slope of the lines.

These operations are particularly useful for working with lines where slope is important, such as water or gas pipes.

The 3D LRS operations are implemented using the same functions and procedures as listed previously, except that the function names end with the `_3D` suffix. For example, function `CLIP_GEOM_SEGMENT_3D` clips a line in 3D.

The lines must be defined as 3D geometries with measures: each point contains *x*, *y*, and *z* coordinates followed by a *measure*.

Other Operations

There are a number of other operations on LRS geometries. These include concatenation, splitting, and offsetting.

Concatenate

Given two lines with measures, this returns a single line with measures. The second line may be in a different direction, and measures do not have to be continuous with those of the first line. The resulting line has measures adjusted from the two input lines.

Split

This splits a line into two lines at a chosen measure.

Offset

Same as the clip operation, but the resulting clipped line is shifted at a chosen offset (left or right from the input line).

Summary

In this appendix, we described how to associate measures with a linear feature stored in an `SDO_GEOMETRY` object. You can refer to locations on a linear feature using these measure values. This type of referencing, called *linear referencing*, is popular in the transportation and utility industries.

The Linear Referencing component in Oracle provides a powerful set of functionality to store, manage, and operate on linear referenced geometries. In this appendix, we presented a brief overview of this functionality, including how to convert from standard two-dimensional coordinates/geometries to linear referenced geometries and vice-versa.

APPENDIX C

Topology Data Model in Oracle

In the preceding chapters, we described how to store and perform analysis on SDO_GEOMETRY data inside an Oracle database. In most cases, these geometries represent different *spatial features* such as roads, rivers, land parcels, city boundaries, property boundaries, and business locations. These features can be stored as columns in one or more tables in Oracle. For instance, an application may store land parcels and rivers, that share edges, as different features in different tables. Figure C-1 shows an example of this. Figure C-2 shows an example of what happens if a shared edge e is updated.

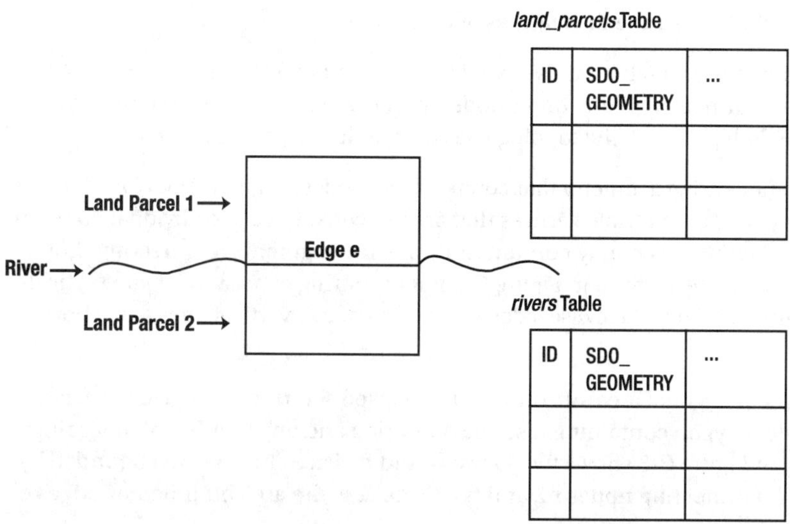

Figure C-1. *Spatial features of different types are stored in one or more tables as* SDO_GEOMETRY *objects. Features can share boundaries.*

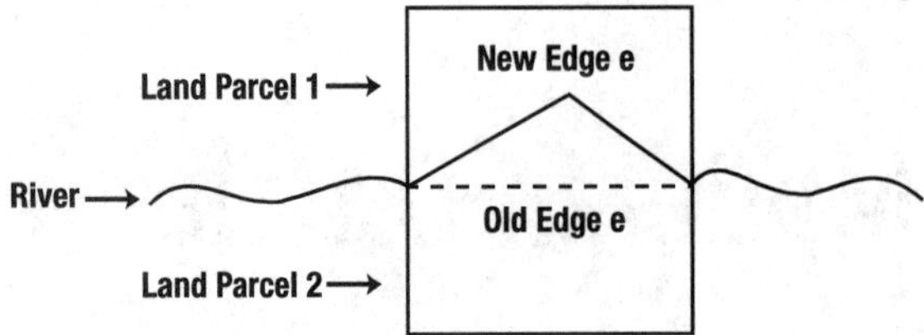

Figure C-2. *Updating edge e as the river changes course. Geometries for Land Parcel 1, Land Parcel 2, and River need to be updated in the* `land_parcels` *and the* `rivers` *tables.*

In this appendix, we describe an alternate model, the *Topology Data Model*, for effective management of shared geometry features.

Topology Data Model

How can you effectively share and manage boundaries between multiple features? You can accomplish this using Oracle's Topology Data Model. The Topology Data Model stores the individual features using three topological primitive elements: *nodes, edges,* and *faces*. These elements, described next, are internally stored as `SDO_GEOMETRY` objects. Figure C-3 shows the topological elements that constitute the features of Figure C-1.

- *Node*: This is a point geometry that is shared by one or more features. A node can be an island (i.e., not connected to any other node), or it can be connected to one or more edges (nodes). In Figure C-3, the topology has four nodes: n1, n2, n3, and n4.
- *Edge*: This is a line-string geometry that connects two nodes in a topology. Note that this line string may contain multiple vertices that are not considered as individual nodes in the topology. That means it may contain multiple line segments (connecting those vertices). For instance, edge e3 in Figure C-3 is a line string consisting of two vertical lines and a horizontal line. Likewise, edge e4 consists of two vertical lines and a horizontal line.
- *Face*: This is the polygonal area surrounded by a closed set (ring) of edges. The face is always a single polygon containing just one outer ring and any number of inner rings. The topology of Figure C-3 shows two faces: f1 and f2. Face f1 is the area bounded by edge e and e4 (connecting nodes n2 and n3). Face f2 is the area bounded by edges e and e3.

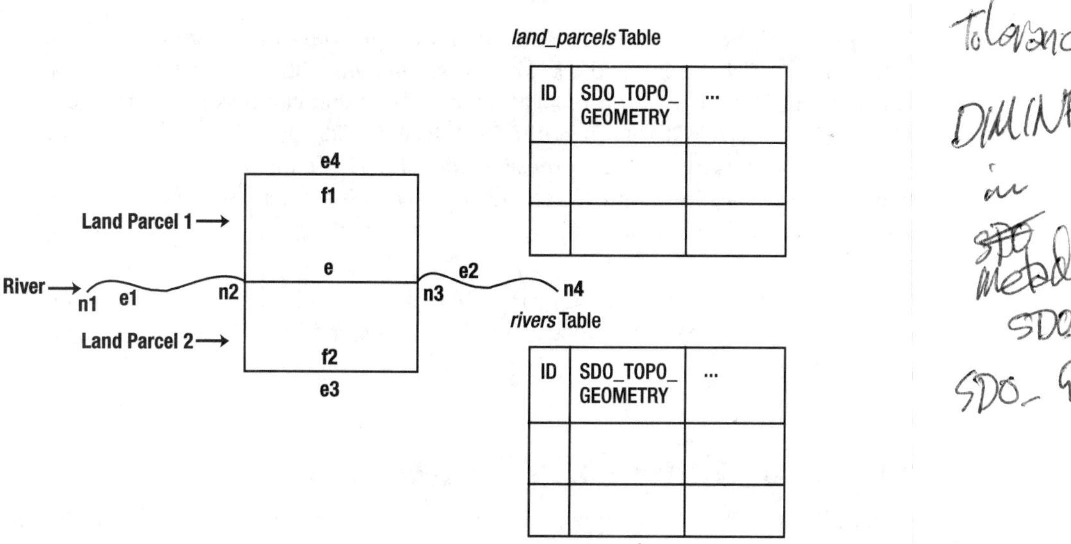

Figure C-3. *Representing features using the Topology Data Model. Each feature is represented using an* `SDO_TOPO_GEOMETRY` *object consisting of underlying topological elements such as nodes, edges, and faces.*

Note that the features in the corresponding feature tables are not stored as `SDO_GEOMETRY` objects. Instead, they are stored as `SDO_TOPO_GEOMETRY` objects, which we will describe later in this appendix. These objects specify a list of underlying topological elements to construct the feature. For instance, the "River" feature in Figure C-3 is specified as a list of edges (e1, e, and e2). The "Land Parcel 1" feature is represented using the face f1, and the "Land Parcel 2" feature is represented using the face f2.

Benefits of the Topology Data Model

What are the advantages of representing spatial features using the Topology Data Model as opposed to storing them using simple `SDO_GEOMETRY` data? The benefits include the following:

- *No redundant storage of data*: For instance, edge e in Figure C-3, which is shared among multiple features, is stored just once. All features that include edge e just store (direct or indirect) references to the edge via the `SDO_TOPO_GEOMETRY`.
- *Data consistency*: Updating a topological element *implicitly defines* updates to all features that share the element. For instance, if edge e is modified (the associated geometry is updated), the Land Parcel and River features that share edge e are implicitly updated. This avoids possible data inconsistencies due to multiple updates at feature layers.

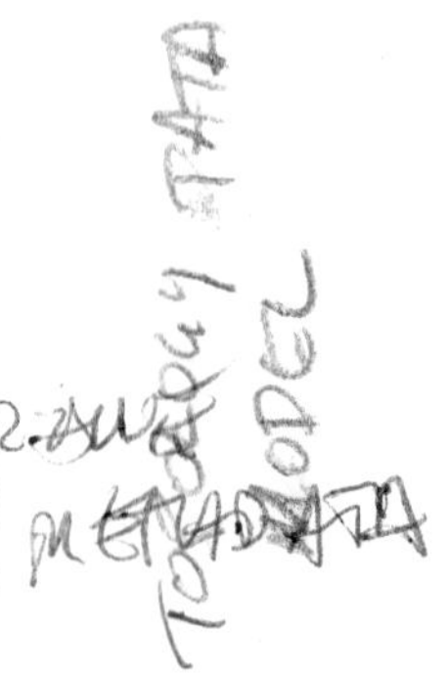

ɔpological relationships: Since the topology is precomputed, identification of all es that satisfy a specified *topological relationship* with a query feature is easy ficient. The types of topological relationships that can be specified include ANYINTERACT, OVERLAPBDYDISJOINT, OVERLAPBDYINTERSECT, CONTAINS, INSIDE, COVERS, DBY, and EQUALS. We discuss these relationships in detail in Chapter 8. Note that gical relationships are preserved even if the coordinate space is stretched or twisted. ce relationships are not topological relationships.

of these benefits, the Topology Data Model is widely used in GIS applications for nent, where the primary focus is on data consistency, nonredundant storage, and ıeries.

a Topology Data Model in Oracle

allows users to share, update, and manage information between multiple feature layers using an associated topology. Figure C-4 shows the schematic for storing a topology constructed from two feature layers, `land_parcels` and `rivers`. As shown in Figure C-3, the features are decomposed into the constituent topological primitive elements, such as nodes, edges, and faces. The node elements are stored in the `<topology-name>_NODE$` table, simply referred to as the `NODE$` table. Likewise, the edge elements are stored in the corresponding `EDGE$` table, and the face elements are stored in the corresponding `FACE$` table. The `RELATION$` table associates the constituent primitive elements for an `SDO_TOPO_GEOMETRY` in a feature layer. Oracle also refers to the `SDO_TOPO_GEOMETRY` as a *topology geometry*.

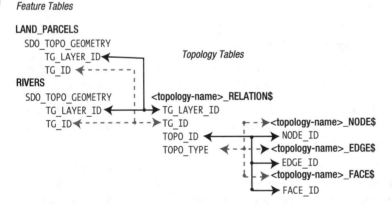

Feature Tables

LAND_PARCELS
SDO_TOPO_GEOMETRY
TG_LAYER_ID
TG_ID
RIVERS
SDO_TOPO_GEOMETRY
TG_LAYER_ID
TG_ID

Topology Tables

<topology-name>_RELATION$
TG_LAYER_ID
TG_ID
TOPO_ID
TOPO_TYPE

<topology-name>_NODE$
NODE_ID
<topology-name>_EDGE$
EDGE_ID
<topology-name>_FACE$
FACE_ID

Figure C-4. *Associating a topology with two feature layers,* `land_parcels` *and* `rivers`

The topology model consists of the following tables:

- `NODE$` table: This table stores all the node elements in the topology. This table has the following fields:
  - `NODE_ID`: This is a unique ID for the node.
  - `EDGE_ID`: This is the ID for the edge that is associated with this node (if any).
  - `FACE_ID`: This is the ID for the face containing this node if the node is an island node.
  - `GEOMETRY`: This is a point-type `SDO_GEOMETRY` to represent the location of the node.
- `EDGE$` table: This table stores all the edge elements in the topology. Edges have direction. As a result, they have a `start_node` and an `end_node`. This table has the following fields:
  - `EDGE_ID`: This is a unique ID for the edge.
  - `START_NODE_ID` and `END_NODE_ID`: These are the IDs of the starting and ending nodes of the edge.
  - `NEXT_LEFT_EDGE_ID`, `PREV_LEFT_EDGE_ID`, `NEXT_RIGHT_EDGE_ID`, and `PREV_RIGHT_EDGE_ID`: These are the IDs of the next and the previous left/right edges.
  - `LEFT_FACE_ID` and `RIGHT_FACE_ID`: These are the IDs of the left and right faces.
  - `GEOMETRY`: This is a line string type `SDO_GEOMETRY` that represents the shape and location of the edge. Note that for the edge, only the first and last vertices correspond to nodes in the topology. All other vertices do not have a corresponding node.
- `FACE$` table: This table stores all the face elements in the topology. Faces can also store one or more *island* nodes and *island* edges. These *island* nodes and *island* edges are not on the boundary of the face but are inside the face. This table has the following fields:
  - `FACE_ID`: This is a unique ID for the face.
  - `BOUNDARY_EDGE_ID`: This is the ID of an edge on the boundary of the face. All other edges can be traced from this edge (by following the next and previous edge pointers for this edge).
  - `ISLAND_EDGE_LIST` and `ISLAND_NODE_LIST`: These are lists of IDs for the island edges and the island nodes.
  - `MBR_GEOMETRY`: This is a minimum bounding rectangle that encloses the face. Note that the geometry of the face is not explicitly stored here. The geometry is traced by constructing the boundary using the `BOUNDARY_EDGE_ID`.

- RELATION$ table: This table stores the topological primitive elements for each feature in an associated feature table. Note that the feature objects are stored using the SDO_TOPO_GEOMETRY object, which is also referred to as the *topology geometry* (TG) object. Spatial automatically generates an ID for each such TG object, called TG_ID. Each feature layer is referenced using a number called TG_LAYER_ID. This table has the following fields:
  - TG_LAYER_ID: This is the ID of the feature layer.
  - TG_ID: This is the ID of the feature object in the preceding feature layer.
  - TOPO_TYPE: This is the type of the topological element: 1 for NODE, 2 for EDGE, and 3 for FACE.
  - TOPO_ID: This is the ID of the topological element associated with the feature object.

The following are other attributes of the topology:

- For each feature object in a feature table that is associated with the topology, the RELATION$ table stores *N* rows if there are *N* associated topological elements. For instance, the Rivers feature in Figure C-3 has four nodes and three edges, so it will have seven rows in the RELATION$ table.
- The feature tables store the feature using the SDO_TOPO_GEOMETRY data type. Like the SDO_GEOMETRY data type, SDO_TOPO_GEOMETRY also captures the shape and location of a feature. But unlike SDO_GEOMETRY, SDO_TOPO_GEOMETRY does not store the coordinates explicitly. Instead, it stores only references to topological elements from which the shape can be derived. This data type has the following structure:
  - TG_TYPE: The type of topology (i.e., feature) geometry. 1 indicates a point or multipoint, 2 indicates a line or multiline, 3 indicates a polygon or multipolygon, and 4 indicates a heterogeneous collection.
  - TG_ID: A unique ID generated by Spatial for this feature.
  - TG_LAYER_ID: A unique ID assigned by Spatial for this feature layer. This ID is assigned when the layer is associated with the topology.
  - TOPOLOGY_ID: A unique ID of the current topology. This ID is assigned by Spatial when the topology is created.

Figure C-5 shows the association between feature tables and topology tables. Given a feature ID (TG_ID) along with the feature table (TG_LAYER_ID), you can identify the topological elements that constitute this feature. The shape of this feature can be derived from these elements. The SDO_TOPO_GEOMETRY has a method to return the shape as an SDO_GEOMETRY object.

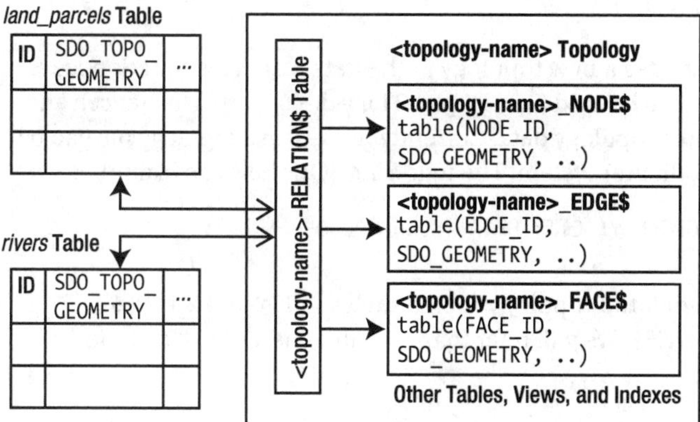

Figure C-5. *Association between feature tables and topology tables*

Given this background on how topology is stored in Oracle, next we will examine how to create a topology, associate feature tables with the topology, populate the tables, and query the topology.

Operating on a Topology in Oracle

Oracle Spatial provides the following functionality to operate on the Topology Data Model:

- Creating a new topology in the database. This includes creation of new tables for the storage of topological primitive elements (nodes, edges, and faces) associated with a topology.
- Associating feature layers (tables) with a topology.
- Inserting new features into feature tables using the topological elements already in the topology.
- Updating the underlying topological elements.
- Querying features for topological relationships.
- Other functions to drop a topology, drop the association of a feature table with a topology, and so on.

Oracle Spatial provides both PL/SQL and Java APIs for the preceding operations. In this appendix, we will discuss only the PL/SQL functions. The `SDO_TOPO` package includes these functions, each of which we will describe in brief. For a detailed discussion, please consult *Oracle Spatial User's Guide*.

Creating a Topology

The CREATE_TOPOLOGY procedure creates a new topology in the database. This function takes a name for the topology, the tolerance to be used (see Chapter 3 for a discussion of tolerance), and the Spatial Reference ID (SRID) for the topology data. Currently, all data in a topology have to be in the same spatial reference (coordinate) system. The following SQL shows an example:

```
SQL> EXECUTE SDO_TOPO.CREATE_TOPOLOGY('CITY_DATA', 0.00000005, NULL);
```

This function creates the associated topology tables such as CITY_DATA_NODE$, CITY_DATA_EDGE$, and CITY_DATA_FACE$. We will refer to these tables as NODE$, EDGE$, and FACE$ when there is no ambiguity.

Populating a Topology

Note that the user has to populate the topology—that is, the related tables such as NODE$, EDGE$, and FACE$. You can bulk load the data into these tables using Oracle utilities such as SQL*Loader, Import/Export, and Data Pump. You can easily construct the topological element data for the example in Figure C-1 and load the data into these tables. We leave this as an exercise for the reader.

Associating a Feature Layer with a Topology

Once the topology is populated (i.e., the topological element information is filled in), you can create a feature layer as follows:

```
SQL> CREATE TABLE land_parcels
(
  parcel_name     VARCHAR2(30) PRIMARY KEY,
  feature         SDO_TOPO_GEOMETRY
);
```

You can then associate this feature layer with a topology using the ADD_TOPO_GEOMETRY_LAYER function in the SDO_TOPO package. This function takes the topology name as the first argument, the feature table name and the column name as the second and third arguments, and the type of the features (whether they are points, lines, or polygons) as the fourth argument. The following SQL shows how to add the land_parcels feature layer, which has just polygon data, to the city_data topology:

```
SQL>
DECLARE
BEGIN
SDO_TOPO.ADD_TOPO_GEOMETRY_LAYER
('CITY_DATA' 'LAND_PARCELS', 'FEATURE', 'POLYGON');
END;
```

Inserting, Updating, and Populating Feature Layers

You insert into the feature layers using the SDO_TOPO_GEOMETRY constructor. This constructor uses the ID and types of topological primitive elements such as nodes, edges, and faces stored in the NODE$, EDGE$, and FACE$ tables, respectively. The following SQL shows an example:

```
SQL> INSERT INTO land_parcels VALUES
(
  'P1',
  SDO_TOPO_GEOMETRY -- construct using topology elements(no explicit geometry)
  (
    'CITY_DATA',  -- topology_name
    3,            -- topo_geometry_type for polygon (or multipolygon)
    1,            -- feature layer (TG_LAYER) ID representing 'Land Parcels',
    SDO_TOPO_OBJECT_ARRAY -- Array of 2 topo objects (two faces)
    (
      SDO_TOPO_OBJECT  -- Constructor for the object
      (
        3,        -- element ID (i.e., FACE_ID) from the associated topology
        3         -- element TYPE is 3 (i.e., a FACE)
      ),
      SDO_TOPO_OBJECT -- Constructor for topo object
      (
        6,        -- element ID (i.e., FACE_ID) from the associated topology
        3         -- element type is 3 (i.e., a FACE)
      )
    )
  )
);
```

The feature is a multipolygon composed of two faces, one with ID 3 and another with ID 6. These two face elements that constitute the feature are specified using the SDO_TOPO_OBJECT_ARRAY in the preceding SDO_TOPO_GEOMETRY constructor. This method will populate the RELATION$ table appropriately, and insert a row in the land_parcels table with the TG_ID and TG_LAYER_ID filled appropriately (Spatial generated) in the SDO_TOPO_GEOMETRY column.

Updating features in a feature table can be processed by invoking the constructor method to generate the SDO_TOPO_GEOMETRY object.

Updating Topological Elements

As we mentioned earlier, the Topology Data Model is ideal to propagate updates on the underlying topology elements to the feature layers. For instance, if you update the geometry of edge *e* (with an EDGE_ID of 10, for instance) from *g* to *g1*, then this will be reflected in all features that contain edge *e*.

Oracle Spatial provides a variety of functions such as ADD_NODE, ADD_EDGE, and SPLIT_EDGE to add, update, or delete topological primitive elements. We refer you to *Oracle Spatial User's Guide* for details.

Querying for Topological Relationships

Oracle Spatial provides allows a number of operators to query the features tables. These include the SDO_FILTER and SDO_RELATE operators that we discussed in Chapter 8. The SDO_RELATE operator specifies the desired topological relationship as a third parameter. If the desired relationship is ANYINTERACT (i.e., any type of interaction other than being disjoint; see Chapter 8 for more details), then the SDO_ANYINTERACT operator can also be used. The following SQL shows an example of how to retrieve all Land Parcel features (features from the land_parcels table) that interact with River features:

```
SQL> SELECT a.parcel_name FROM land_parcels a, rivers b
WHERE SDO_ANYINTERACT (a.feature, b.feature) = 'TRUE';
```

Note that both the first and second arguments are SDO_TOPO_GEOMETRY objects. In some cases, the query window (the second argument to the SDO_ANYINTERACT operator in the preceding SQL) need not be a feature geometry that is part of the topology. Instead, it can be a query window represented using an SDO_GEOMETRY object. To support such queries, all the operators also allow the second (i.e., the query) argument to be an SDO_GEOMETRY object. The following SQL shows an example of how to retrieve all Land Parcel features (features from the land_parcels table) that interact with a specified SDO_GEOMETRY query window:

```
SQL> SELECT a.parcel_name FROM land_parcels a
WHERE SDO_ANYINTERACT
(
  a.feature,
  SDO_GEOMETRY
  (
    2003,NULL, NULL,
    SDO_ELEM_INFO_ARRAY(1,1003,3)
    SDO_ORDINATE_ARRAY(14,20,15,22)
  )
) = 'TRUE';
```

Both queries use the topological information to identify the features that satisfy the query criterion. Since the topological information is precomputed and already stored persistently in the database, such queries will be answered efficiently.

Hierarchical Feature Model

The Oracle Topology Data Model supports a hierarchical feature model. This means if we consider the Land Parcel and River features as Level-0 features that are derived/constructed from the topological primitive elements (nodes, edges, and faces), we can construct Level-1 features using these Level-0 features. We can accomplish this by specifying Level-0 feature IDs (TGIDs) in the SDO_TOPO_GEOMETRY constructors (for the Level-1 features). In general, Level-*N* features can be derived from Level-(*N* – 1) features.

This hierarchical modeling of data is very useful in several applications. For instance, we can model the U.S. Census Bureau data hierarchically as follows:

- The Census *blocks* are Level-0 features constructed using the faces in a topological representation.
- The Census *blockgroups* are Level-1 features derived from the Census *blocks*.
- The Census *tracts* are Level-2 features derived from the *blockgroups*.
- The Census *counties* are Level-3 features derived from the *tracts*.

This hierarchy can be extended to multiple levels until we have the United States as a Level-7 feature derived from a list of regions.

You can construct similar examples for other countries. For instance, you could use data from the Ordnance Survey to construct such a hierarchy for Great Britain.

Summary

Oracle Spatial provides the Topology Data Model to store feature layers that share boundaries. This topology model is very effective in maintaining data consistency, in reducing or eliminating storage redundancy, and in identifying topological relationships. Updates to underlying topology model can be reflected in the feature layers without any explicit updates to the feature tables. Since topological relationships are precomputed, features interacting with a query feature can be answered very efficiently. Distance queries such as nearest-neighbor queries, though, cannot be answered efficiently using this model. Spatial also provides validation routines to detect inconsistencies in the data. This functionality is widely used in land management and other GIS applications.

APPENDIX D

■ ■ ■

Storing Raster Data in Oracle

Real-world spatial features can be represented in either a *vector* or *raster* model. In a vector model, each spatial feature (a river, a road, a shop location, etc.) is represented as an object with geometric features (the shape and location) and a set of attributes. In Chapter 4, we discussed the SDO_GEOMETRY data type to store such vector spatial data. To represent the complexity of a city, for instance, you may need myriad points, lines, and polygons. A raster model, on the other hand, associates collections of *pixels* or *cells* to spatial entities, by making a discrete approximation of spatial features into grid cells. Each cell takes on a single value. You can consider a raster object as a two-dimensional array or grid of regularly spaced *cells*. Some common examples of raster objects include satellite images, aerial photos, and digital elevation models.

A road in a vector model corresponds to a line object described by road attributes (e.g., the road type, the road size, the pavement type, the last maintenance date, etc.). The same road in a raster model would be a collection of grid cells sharing the same value specific to that road. Vector and raster models are, in theory, equivalent: it is always possible to extract a vector model from a raster one and vice versa. In practice, they have different uses and varying abilities to represent real-world spatial objects. Vector models are the most commonly used and are appropriate whenever you want to identify and describe spatial objects with their relationships. With vectors, it is easy to find overlaps between objects, create buffers around objects, calculate the distance between objects, and so on. Although the same operations can also be performed on the basis of a raster model, the raster model (and raster analysis) has the following differences:

- *Raster data* is typically used to model *spatially continuous* data such as elevations or environmental data—for instance, to display a digital elevation of land or to model the diffusion of a pollutant from a chemical spill. At present, the bulk of raster data corresponds to satellite images, aerial pictures, digital terrain/elevation models, gridded data, and medical images. Most of the rest is vector data.

- *Raster analysis* consists of spatial processing on a grid or a two-dimensional array/grid of cells. Typically the analysis includes map/matrix algebra operations such as overlay, addition, and subtraction of multiple rasters, or neighborhood/clustering analysis functions on individual rasters.

To illustrate the difference between the raster and vector models, let's consider an example. In Figure D-1, (a) shows a small section of an urban area as seen from an aircraft, whereas (b) and (c) show the corresponding vector and raster representations (simplified here for convenience). As you can see, both models are capable of representing the same picture. In a vector model, objects are easy to identify and are modeled using points, lines, and other geometric shapes. In a raster model, the spatial patterns are more visible, and the objects are models using different colored cells or pixels.

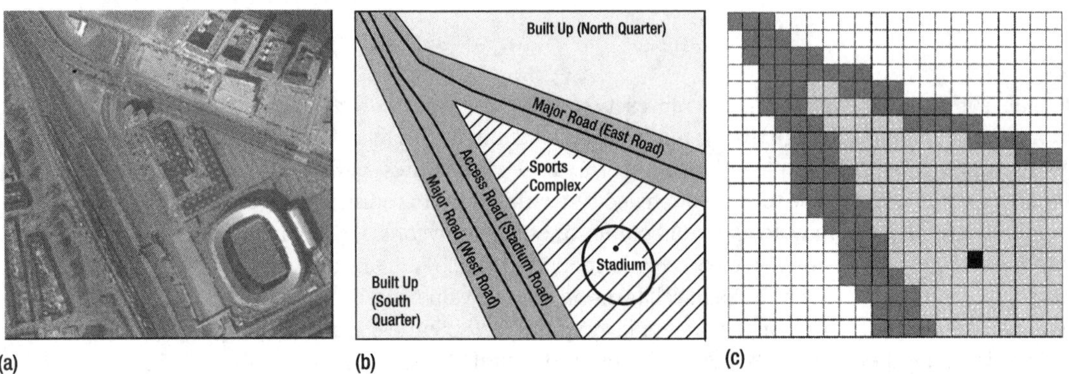

Figure D-1. *(a) is an aerial photograph of a small section of an urban area. (b) is a vector representation and (c) is a raster representation of the spatial objects in the picture shown in Figure D-1(b).*

In this book, we primarily focus on how to store, analyze, and visualize spatial data in the vector model. The SDO_GEOMETRY (see Chapter 4 for more information) provides an easy mechanism to store spatial data in the vector format. The spatial indexes and geometry functions (see Chapters 8 and 9 for more information) provide an appropriate mechanism to search/analyze these vector data, and Oracle MapViewer (see Chapter 11 for more information) enables visualization of vector data. Typically in a business application, you will store the locations of businesses and customers as vector data. However, as shown in Figure D-1, you may also want to store and visualize aerial photographs of your businesses and other entities in addition to the vector data.

In this appendix, we describe how to work with "raster" spatial data in Oracle. Specifically, we examine the GeoRaster component in Oracle, which stores raster data using the SDO_GEORASTER data type and provides preliminary analysis functions (such as generating pyramids and subsetting). We then describe how to visualize the stored raster data using Oracle MapViewer. Note that GeoRaster only enables the storage and visualization of raster data (and very basic analysis). Once you store the raster data in Oracle, you can use a variety of third-party tools to perform more comprehensive analysis operations, such as map algebra, that are typical on raster data.

SDO_GEORASTER Data Type

Oracle Spatial provides the SDO_GEORASTER data type to store spatial data in raster format. Conceptually, an SDO_GEORASTER object is an *N*-dimensional matrix of *cells*. The dimensions include a row dimension, a column dimension, and other optional dimensions. These optional dimensions can contain a *band* dimension to represent multiband or hyperspectral images, and/or a temporal dimension.

For most raster data, such as an RGB image, there will be a row, a column, and a band (or color) dimension. Each cell in an RGB image is addressed by (row, column, band) and specifies an intensity value for the corresponding pixel (row, column) in the specified color/band, as shown in Figure D-2.

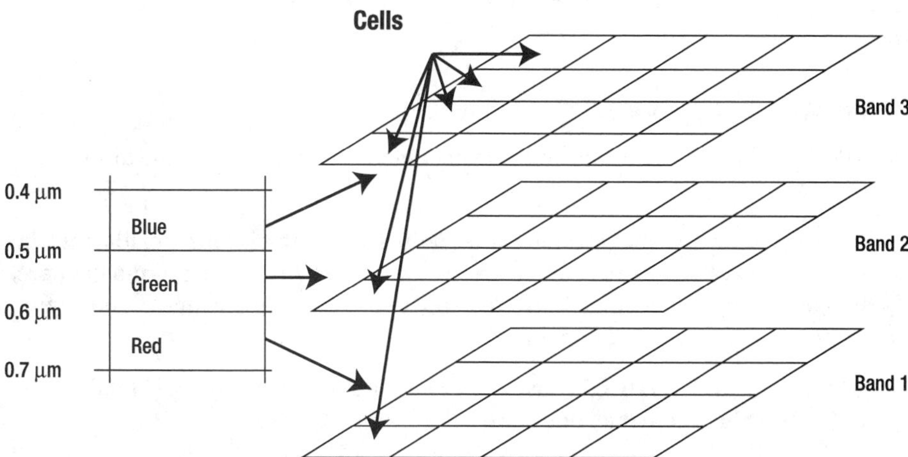

Figure D-2. *Bands in an RGB image*

The cell values in a GeoRaster object are stored in a *raster data table*, which we will explain later. In addition to the raster information, the SDO_GEORASTER could also capture information about which region on the earth's surface is represented by this raster object. This makes the raster object georeferenced.

The SQL in Listing D-1 shows how to add an SDO_GEORASTER column to the branches table. The idea is to store the aerial photograph for each branch (along with its location).

Listing D-1. *Altering the* branches *Table to Add the* georaster *Column*

```
ALTER TABLE branches ADD ( georaster    SDO_GEORASTER);
```

Next, we will look at the structure of the SDO_GEORASTER type, as shown in Listing D-2. Typically, a GeoRaster object can be very large. In the following subsections, we will describe how to specify different storage options. If you just want a general idea of how to store raster objects, you can skip to the section titled "Populating SDO_GEORASTER Columns."

Listing D-2. *Structure of* SDO_GEORASTER

```
SQL> DESC SDO_GEORASTER;
 Name                                      Null?     Type
 ----------------------------------------- --------  ----------------------
 RASTERTYPE                                          NUMBER
 SPATIALEXTENT                                       MDSYS.SDO_GEOMETRY
 RASTERDATATABLE                                     VARCHAR2(32)
 RASTERID                                            NUMBER
 METADATA                                            SYS.XMLTYPE
```

The following list describes each attribute's purpose:

- RASTERTYPE: This specifies the type of the raster object. It is a number of the form [d][b][t]01.
    - [d] is the number of spatial dimensions. If the spatial dimensions include x, y, z in the model space that correspond to row, column, depth in the cell-coordinate space, then this number is set to 3. Currently only two spatial dimensions (x and y) are supported (i.e., d should be set to 2).
    - [b] is either 0 or 1. It is 0 if the raster object has a single band, and it is 1 if the raster object has more than one band.
    - [t] specifies whether or not there is a temporal dimension. Currently it is set to 0 (not used).
- SPATIALEXTENT: This is an SDO_GEOMETRY object storing the minimum bounding rectangle (MBR) of the raster object on the earth's surface. This spatial extent is represented in a *model coordinate system* to model the earth's surface.
- RASTERDATATABLE: This is the name of the table that stores the cell information for the raster object. The two-dimensional row-column matrix of cells is referred to as the *cell coordinate system.*
- RASTERID: Combined with the RASTERDATATABLE, this is a unique identifier for the raster object.
- METADATA: This is an XML object that stores information regarding the raster object. For instance, it stores information on how to convert from the model coordinate system (e.g., the spatial extent) to the cell coordinate system.

Storage for SDO_GEORASTER Data

Each SDO_GEORASTER object may be subdivided into multiple blocks, and the cell values in each block are stored as a binary large object (BLOB) in the raster data table. Figure D-3 shows how SDO_GEORASTER objects are internally stored using the raster data table. You could also have additional tables such as the Value-Attribute Table (VAT) to store a meaning/interpretation for each cell value. For instance, the value of 1 for a cell value in the red band indicates a light red color, and value of 3 indicates a dark red color.

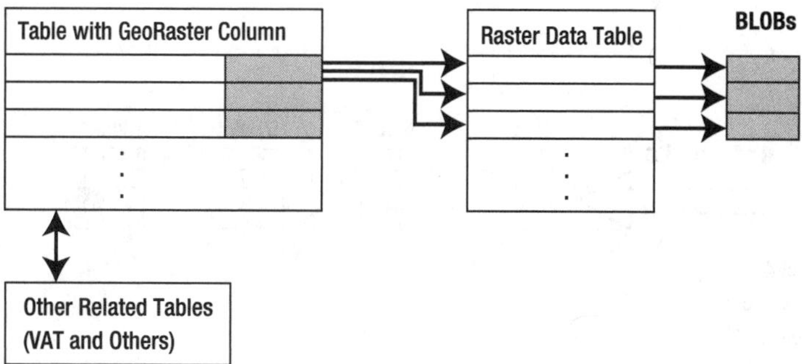

Figure D-3. *Storing* SDO_GEORASTER *objects in an Oracle table. Each* SDO_GEORASTER *object is internally stored using the BLOBs in the raster data table.*

Raster Data Table

The cell information for a raster object is stored in a raster data table associated with the GeoRaster object. Next, we will look at the raster data table. The raster data table is a table of the SDO_RASTER data type. This table splits a raster object into blocks and stores the two-dimensional matrix of cell values (indexed by rows and columns) for each block as a RASTERBLOCK object. This table needs to be created explicitly by the user. The table will be associated with a GeoRaster object using the SDO_GEOR.INIT procedure, which we describe later. Listing D-3 shows how to create the raster data table.

Listing D-3. *Creating the Raster Data Table*

```
CREATE TABLE branches_rdt OF SDO_RASTER
(
  PRIMARY KEY
  (
    RASTERID, PYRAMIDLEVEL, BANDBLOCKNUMBER,
    ROWBLOCKNUMBER, COLUMNBLOCKNUMBER
  )
)
LOB(RASTERBLOCK) STORE AS (NOCACHE NOLOGGING);
```

The RASTERID attribute corresponds to the unique identifier for the raster object. We will explain other fields of the SDO_RASTER data type as we proceed in this section. The raster object is divided into smaller pieces called *blocks*. The cell values in each block are stored in the RASTERBLOCK.

Blocking

A raster object could consist of a large number of cells. In such cases, it may be worthwhile to divide the object into smaller pieces (blocks). The cell values in each block are stored together as a single RASTERBLOCK (BLOB) object. Figure D-4 shows an example for a single-band raster object.

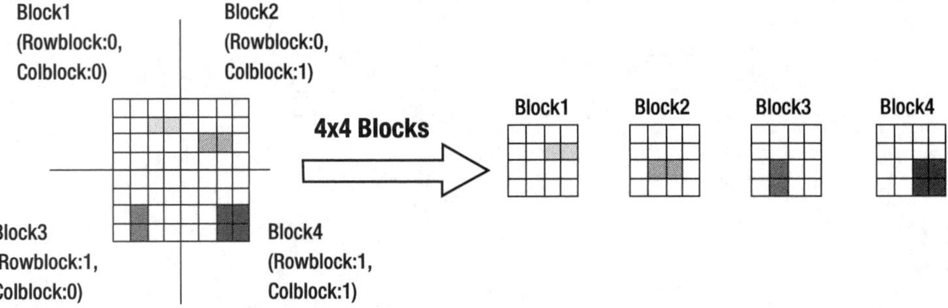

Figure D-4. *Blocking to store a 16×16 raster object using 4×4 blocks*

Note that each block is uniquely addressed by the `rowblocknumber` and `columnblocknumber` (and `bandblocknumber`, if it exists) fields.

Interleaving

What if you have multiple bands, as in Figure D-2? Let's name the cell values (by the band number for simplicity) as shown in Figure D-5. In what order do you store the cell values for each band? This is specified by *interleaving* of bands.

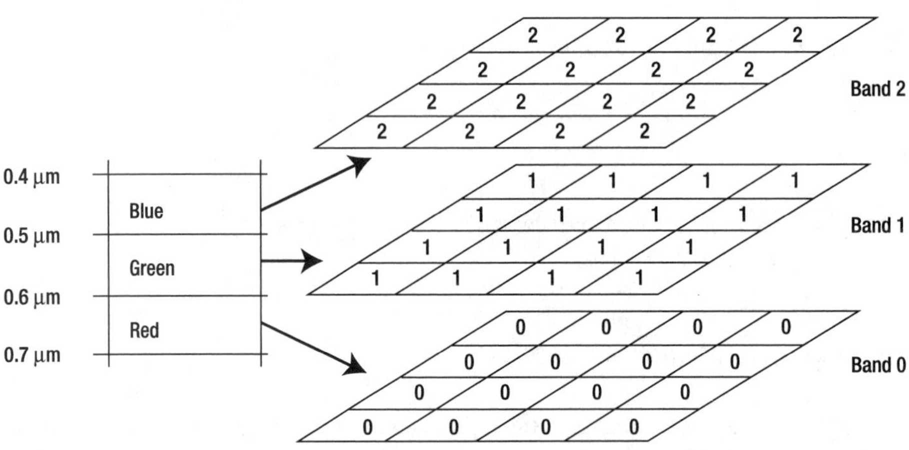

Figure D-5. *An RGB image (three-band raster object)*

You can store (cell values for) each band in sequence (i.e., one after another). This interleaving is referred to as *Band Sequential* (BSQ). Figure D-6 shows the storage of cell values for this interleaving.

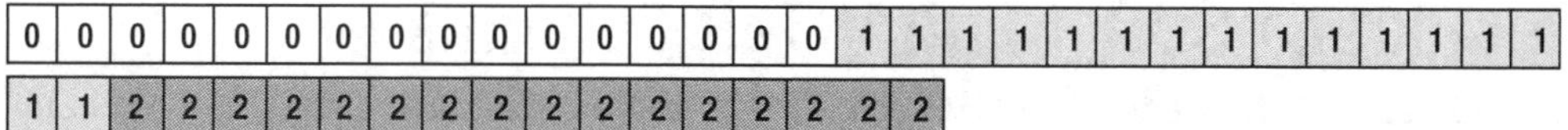

Figure D-6. *Band Sequential interleaving for the RGB image in Figure D-5*

Alternatively, you can alternate the rows (lines) of each band. This means you store the row (i.e., all four cells of the row) of band 0, then the row of band 1, and then the row of band 2. This interleaving is called *Band Interleaved by Line* (BIL). Figure D-7 shows the BIL interleaved storage of cell values for Figure D-5.

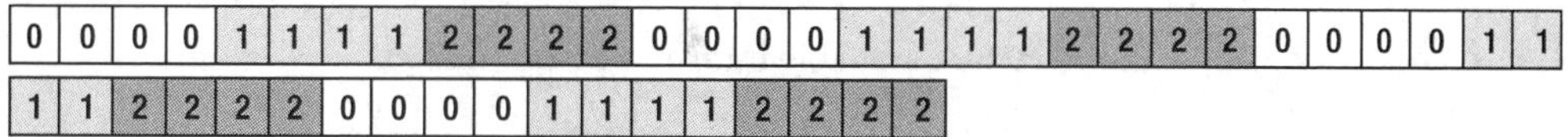

Figure D-7. *Band Interleaved by Line interleaving for the RGB image in Figure D-5*

A third alternative is to store each cell of each band one after another. This interleaving is called *Band Interleaved by Pixel* (BIP). Figure D-8 shows the BIP interleaved storage of cell values for Figure D-5.

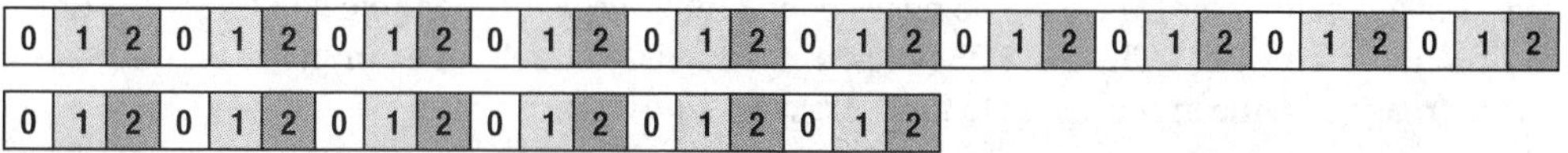

Figure D-8. *Band Interleaved by Pixel interleaving for the RGB image in Figure D-5*

Which of these interleaving options should you use? It depends on the application. For instance, if the application expects to retrieve one band at a time, you would achieve optimal performance with BSQ interleaving.

Metadata in SDO_GEORASTER Data

The last attribute of the SDO_GEORASTER is an XMLType to store the metadata associated with a GeoRaster object. This metadata can include information regarding the blocking, interleaving, and so on. The metadata may also include parameters to convert from the model coordinate system to the cell coordinate system of the GeoRaster object. We refer you to Oracle Spatial GeoRaster documentation for a list of attributes that you can specify in the metadata field of SDO_GEORASTER.

Populating SDO_GEORASTER Columns

How do you populate the SDO_GEORASTER columns? As we described earlier, you create a column of the SDO_GEORASTER type and a raster data table to contain the cell data for the raster objects. You also need to create a trigger on the table containing the SDO_GEORASTER column so that any updates, inserts, or deletes to this column are internally propagated to the raster data table. Listing D-4 shows how to create this trigger.

Listing D-4. *Creating a Trigger to Populate the Raster Data Table*

```
SQL> call SDO_GEOR_UTL.createDMLTrigger('BRANCHES','GEORASTER');
```

Now you can initialize a GeoRaster object in the branches table as shown in Listing D-5. Note that the SDO_GEOR.INIT function takes the raster data table name, branches_rdt, and returns a SDO_GEORASTER object with the raster data table information populated.

Listing D-5. *Initializing the* georaster *Column in the* branches *Table*

```
SQL> UPDATE branches SET georaster = SDO_GEOR.INIT('BRANCHES_RDT'); WHERE id=1
```

Once you initialize the GeoRaster object, you can upload images from TIFF or other standard image formats into (or out of) the GeoRaster object using the SDO_GEOR.IMPORTFROM (or the SDO_GEOR.EXPORTTO) procedure. This procedure invokes internal adaptors to read from/write to different image formats such as TIFF, GeoTIFF, JPEG, GIF, PNG, BMP, or ESRI world file.

The SDO_GEOR.IMPORTFROM procedure takes a GeoRaster object, the blocksize parameters, the type, and location of the image file being uploaded into the GeoRaster object (along with some additional parameters). The PL/SQL block in Listing D-6 shows an example of loading the r1.tif image into the branches table for georaster id=1.

Listing D-6. *Populating the Georaster Column with a TIFF Image*

```
DECLARE
  g SDO_GEORASTER;
BEGIN

  -- Select the georaster column
  SELECT georaster INTO g FROM branches WHERE id = 1 FOR UPDATE;

  -- Import into the georaster object
  SDO_GEOR.IMPORTFROM
  (
    g,  'blocksize=(512,512)', 'TIFF', 'file',
    '/usr/rasters/r1.tif'  -- specify the name and location of the image file
  );

  -- update the column
  UPDATE branches SET georaster = g WHERE id = 1;
END;
/
```

Before performing the preceding import procedure, you may want to ensure that the "spatial" schema and the MDSYS schema both have "read" permission to read the specified file into the database. You can grant this permission using the DBMS_JAVA.GRANT_PERMISSION procedure as shown in Listing D-7. The first parameter specifies the schema name, the second parameter specifies the permission type, the third parameter specifies the file name, and the fourth parameter specifies the permission action.

Listing D-7. *Granting Permissions to Import Data into a GeoRaster Column*

```
SQL> CONNECT system/manager  -- Replace with password for system
-- Grant permission to user 'spatial'
SQL> CALL DBMS_JAVA.GRANT_PERMISSION( 'SPATIAL', 'SYS:java.io.FilePermission',
'/usr/rasters/r1.tif', 'read');
-- Grant permission to the MDSYS schema
SQL> CALL DBMS_JAVA.GRANT_PERMISSION( 'MDSYS', 'SYS:java.io.FilePermission',
'/usr/rasters/r1.tif', 'read');
SQL> connect spatial/spatial; -- connect back as spatial
```

Manipulating Raster Objects

Once raster objects are stored in the SDO_GEORASTER columns of a table, Oracle Spatial allows you to perform a number of operations on each of these objects. These operations include the following:

- Generating pyramids, an operation that allows you to generate raster objects of different resolutions
- Subsetting, which involves clipping the GeoRaster by band or a specified region
- Georeferencing, which involves identifying a portion of an image by specifying the coordinates in the model coordinate system
- Changing the interleaving or blocking for a raster object
- Copying a raster object to another
- Generating the spatial extent of an image or a subset returned
- Creating a mosaic of all of the GeoRaster data in a column of type SDO_GEORASTER

We will briefly discuss some of these operations in this section. You can find a full reference for all the operations in the Oracle Spatial documentation.

Generating Pyramids

In some cases, the raster objects are too large and have a high resolution. How do you reduce the size? By reducing the resolution by specifying a pyramid level. Figure D-9 shows an example of low-resolution objects created at different pyramid levels from the original raw object.

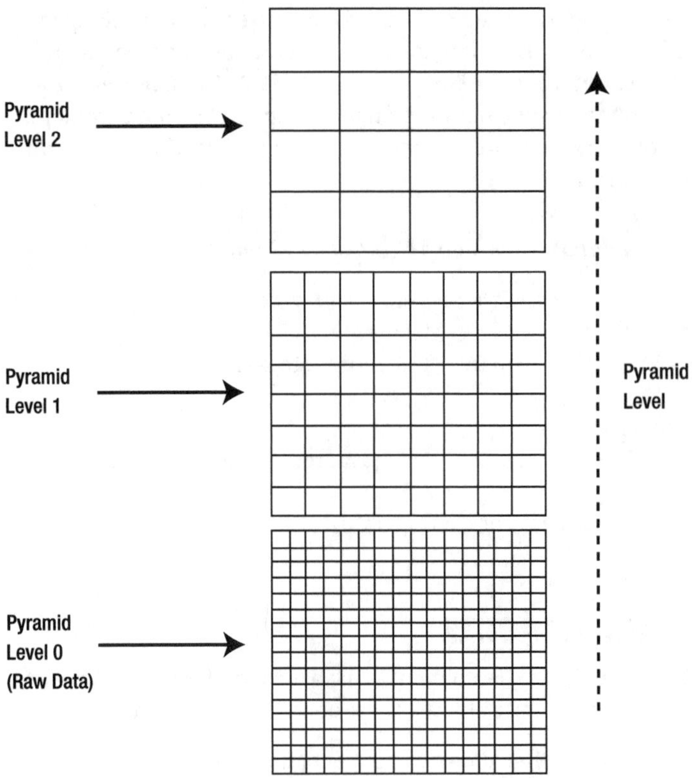

Figure D-9. *Generating raster objects at different resolutions. The higher the pyramid level, the lower the resolution (and the smaller the storage requirement of the object).*

You can generate pyramids for a raster object using the `SDO_GEOR.GENERATEPYRAMID` procedure. The SQL in Listing D-8 shows an example for generating pyramids for four levels. Note that the second parameter, `'rlevel=4'`, specifies the number of pyramid levels to generate. You can specify other parameters such as `'resampling=NN'` to use a specific algorithm such as nearest-neighbor to create the pyramids.

Listing D-8. *Generating Pyramids for a GeoRaster Object in the* `branches` *Table*

```
DECLARE
  geor sdo_georaster;
BEGIN
  SELECT georaster INTO geor FROM branches WHERE id = 1 FOR UPDATE;

  -- Generate four levels of pyramids
  SDO_GEOR.GENERATEPYRAMID(geor, 'rlevel=4');

  UPDATE branches SET georaster = geor WHERE id = 1;
END;
/
```

Subsetting

Another important operation is subsetting. Here, you can clip the GeoRaster data by band and/or regions. For instance, you can select only the raw data (pyramid level 0) corresponding to band 0 for the specified window (in cell space), as shown in Listing D-9.

Listing D-9. *Subsetting a GeoRaster Object*

```
DECLARE
  g SDO_GEORASTER;
  b BLOB;
BEGIN
  SELECT georaster INTO g FROM branches WHERE id = 1;
  DBMS_LOB.CREATETEMPORARY(b, true);
  SDO_GEOR.GETRASTERSUBSET
  (
    georaster => g,
    pyramidlevel => 0,
    window => sdo_number_array(0,0,699,899),
    bandnumbers => '0',
    rasterBlob => b
  );
END;
/
```

The subset of blocks is returned as BLOB.

Georeferencing

Georeferencing associates real-world (referred to as *model space*) coordinates with a GeoRaster object. For georeferenced raster objects, Oracle Spatial enables you to specify real-world coordinates and convert them into cell coordinates in a GeoRaster object. Figure D-10 shows an example of a GeoRaster object covering a region that contains a national park and a restaurant. The national park will be represented by a subset of pixels in the cell coordinate system of the GeoRaster object. The restaurant will be represented by a single pixel in the GeoRaster object.

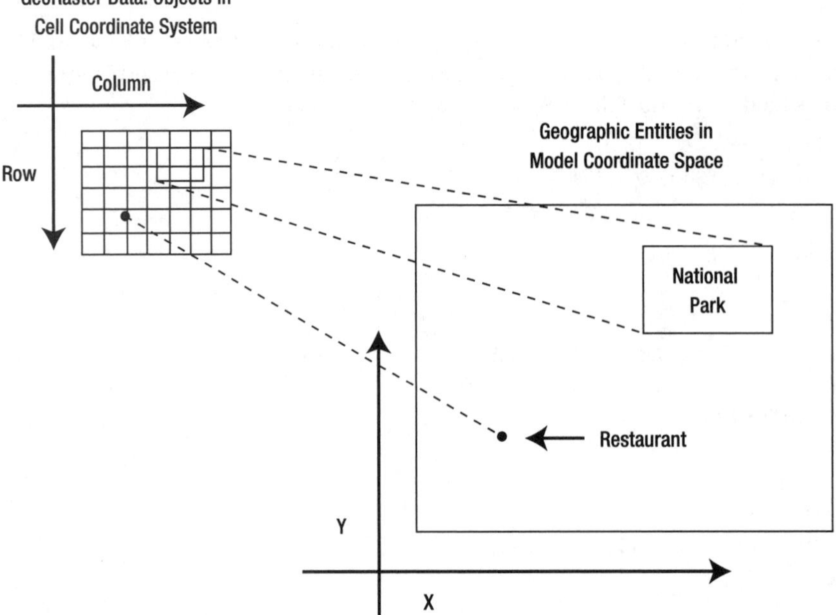

Figure D-10. *Georeferencing is the process of relating objects in model coordinate system (x, y space) to the objects in cell coordinate system. Oracle supports such model-to-cell space transformations for georeferenced raster objects.*

So, if x, y are the real-world (model space) coordinates, then you can identify the row, column of the GeoRaster object that corresponds to these coordinates using the following transformation:

```
row = a + b * x + c * y
col = d + e * x + f * y
```

The parameters *a, b, c, d, e,* and *f* are transformation coefficients and are stored in the metadata associated with the GeoRaster object. Note that determining the right values for these parameters is part of georeferencing. Such georeferencing is not supported by Oracle. Instead, Oracle supports the transformations between model space and cell space for georeferenced GeoRaster objects. Oracle provides the `SDO_GEOR.GEOREFERENCE` function to associate this transformation (including coefficients *a, b, c, d, e,* and *f*) with a GeoRaster object. Listing D-10 shows the example SQL.

Listing D-10. *Georeferencing a GeoRaster Object*

```
DECLARE
  g SDO_GEORASTER;
  b BLOB;
```

```
BEGIN
  SELECT georaster INTO g FROM branches WHERE id = 1;
  SDO_GEOR.GEOREFERENCE
  (
    georaster => g,
    srid => 8307,
    modelcoordinatelocation => 0,  -- 0 for center of the picture
    xCoefficients => sdo_number_array(30, 0, 410000.0),   -- values for a, b, and c
    yCoefficients => sdo_number_array(0, -30, 3759000.0) -- values for d, e, and f
  );
  UPDATE branches SET georaster = g WHERE id = 1;
 END;
 /
```

Oracle Spatial provides a variety of other manipulations, such as changing the formats of the GeoRaster objects. Oracle Spatial also provides additional functionality for viewing and loading GeoRaster objects. We refer you to *Oracle Spatial User's Guide* for a full discussion of these topics.

Visualizing Raster Data in Oracle MapViewer

Once you store raster data in Oracle, you can visualize the data using Oracle MapViewer version 10.1.2.[1] To visualize GeoRaster data, MapViewer uses the "GeoRaster" themes. Before you can use MapViewer with the GeoRaster themes, you must perform the following actions with the GeoRaster data:

1. Georeference the GeoRaster data to establish a relationship between cell coordinates of the GeoRaster data and the real-world ground coordinates (or some other local coordinates). See Listing D-10 for an example.

2. Generate or define the spatial extent (footprint) associated with the raster data. You can do this by using the GENERATESPATIALEXTENT function as shown in the SQL in Listing D-11.

   Listing D-11. *Generating and Populating the Spatial Extent of the* georaster *Column*

   ```
   DECLARE
     extent SDO_GEOMETRY;
   BEGIN
     SELECT SDO_GEOR.GENERATESPATIALEXTENT(a.georaster) INTO extent
            FROM branches a WHERE a.id=1 FOR UPDATE;
     UPDATE branches a SET a.georaster.spatialextent = extent WHERE a.id=1;
     COMMIT;
   END;
   /
   ```

3. Insert a row into the USER_SDO_GEOM_METADATA view that specifies the name of the GeoRaster table and the SPATIALEXTENT attribute of the GeoRaster column (i.e., the column of type SDO_GEORASTER). The SQL in Listing D-12 shows an example.

1. This is not possible in MapViewer version 9.0.4.

Listing D-12. *Populating the Metadata for the Spatial Extent of the* `georaster` *Column*

```
INSERT INTO USER_SDO_GEOM_METADATA VALUES
( 'branches',
  'georaster.spatialextent',
  SDO_DIM_ARRAY
  (
    SDO_DIM_ELEMENT('X', -180, 180, 0.5),
    SDO_DIM_ELEMENT('Y', -90, 90, 5)
  ),
  8307   -- SRID
);
```

4. Create a spatial index on the spatial extent of the GeoRaster table. The SQL in Listing D-13 shows an example.

Listing D-13. *Creating an Index on the Spatial Extent of the* `georaster` *Column*

```
CREATE INDEX geor_idx ON branches(georaster.spatialextent)
INDEXTYPE IS MDSYS.SPATIAL_INDEX;
```

5. Optionally, generate pyramid levels that represent the raster image or data at different sizes and degrees of resolution. See Listing D-8 for an example.

To support visualization of GeoRaster data, MapViewer defines a new type of theme called the `GEORASTER` theme (see Listing D-14). This theme can have elements to specify the name of the raster data table.

Listing D-14. *Creating a Predefined Theme for the* `georaster` *Column in the* `branches` *Table*

```
INSERT INTO user_sdo_themes  VALUES
(
   'BRANCHES_Images',  -- Theme name
   'Tiff Image',       -- Description
   'BRANCHES',         -- Base table name
   'GEORASTER',        -- Column name storing georaster object in table
   '<?xml version="1.0" standalone="yes"?>
    <styling_rules theme_type="georaster" raster_table="BRANCHES_RDT"
                   raster_id="1" >
    </styling_rules>'  --  Theme style definition
);
```

You can use this predefined theme in the definition of a map. Alternatively, you can create a *dynamic* theme using the `JDBC_GEORASTER_QUERY` element as shown in Listing D-15.

Listing D-15. *Creating a Dynamic Theme for GeoRaster Objects*

```
<theme name="georaster_theme" >
  <jdbc_georaster_query
    georaster_table="branches"
```

```
    georaster_column="georaster"
    jdbc_srid="8307"
    datasource="mvdemo"
    asis="false"> SELECT georaster FROM branches WHERE id =1
  </jdbc_georaster_query>
</theme>
```

Once you incorporate either the predefined themes or the dynamic themes in a client request for a map, you can view the raster data at different pyramid levels as you zoom in and out using MapViewer. MapViewer automatically determines which pyramid level to use; you don't have to do anything special.

Summary

Oracle Spatial provides a new data type and storage mechanism called `SDO_GEORASTER` for storing spatial objects in a raster (image/grid) format. Oracle Spatial provides a number of adapters to import and export data into this `SDO_GEORASTER` format from external image and raster formats. Once the object is in an `SDO_GEORASTER` column, you can visualize this data using Oracle MapViewer.

In short, Oracle GeoRaster type provides efficient storage and retrieval of a variety of raster data, including aerial photos, digital terrain/elevation models, gridded data, and medical images inside the Oracle database server.

Index

B

H

I

J

M

O

P

T

U

V